BULGARIA 1878–1918
A HISTORY

D1454011

RICHARD J. CRAMPTON

EAST EUROPEAN MONOGRAPHS, BOULDER
DISTRIBUTED BY COLUMBIA UNIVERSITY PRESS,
NEW YORK

1983

EAST EUROPEAN MONOGRAPHS, NO. CXXXVIII

Richard J. Crampton is Senior Lecturer in History
at The University of Kent at Canterbury

Copyright © 1983 by Richard J. Crampton
Library of Congress Card Catalog Number 83-80483
ISBN 0-88033-029-5

Printed in the United States of America

For Celia

CONTENTS

v

PREFACE

It requires a degree of presumption to attempt a history of another nation but the history of Bulgaria has been surprisingly neglected by historians in the west. Despite a small number of excellent monographs from North America there has been no general history of Bulgaria. That being so the purpose of this book is a simple one: to provide an essentially narrative history. I have attempted little in the way of interpretation, though the short 'Summary and Conclusions' does proffer some ideas for discussion.

The period covered spans that between the foundation of the modern Bulgarian state in 1878 to the end of the First World War, a period in which the Bulgarians had to face the problems, familiar to all emergent nations irrespective of geography, of building a nation state, and more specifically of trying to fuse nation and state when the state's borders did not coincide with ethnic divisions. This period is also one in which the Balkans were at the centre of world affairs. The history of Bulgaria is therefore an integral part of that drift to the calamity of 1914–18 so it is hoped that the story described here will be of interest not only to students of Balkan history but also to those who wish to widen their understanding of Europe in the days before and during the First World War.

All writers on Balkan affairs are faced with the difficulties caused by the multiplicity of proper names. In general, when they are available, I have used westernised and familiar forms such as Constantinople, Adrianople, and Smyrna, though their modern equivalents are given the first time they are used, as in Constantinople (Istanbul). When no familiar western equivalent is available the Slav rather than the Turkish form is used, though here again both versions are given when the name is first introduced, as in Skopje (Üsküb).

The use of the Julian calendar in Orthodox states before the First World War makes for some confusion, for the Julian version is twelve days behind the Gregorian in the nineteenth century and thirteen days in the twentieth. Despite the cumbersome result I have given both dates.

As this is intended to be an introductory history for the non-specialist I have given footnotes only for the direct quotations used. A list of sources is given for each section of the book and for each chapter.

ACKNOWLEDGEMENTS

Generous grants from two institutions have made this work possible. A donation from the Nuffield Foundation's Small Grants Scheme enabled me to spend some months in Vienna whilst a bursary from the British Academy helped to finance a stay in Sofia. To both these institutions I am greatly indebted. It would be churlish to omit from this list of those who have helped me both the British Council and the Bulgarian Academy of Sciences whose generosity made possible other visits to Sofia. The Tsentŭr za Bŭlgaristika and the Institute of History, both constituent parts of the Bulgarian Academy of Sciences, have continually provided support and help by sending me books and journals.

I have made great demands on librarians and wish to express my gratitude to those of the Kiril i Metodi Bibliotek, Sofia, the Haus- Hof- und Staatsarchiv and the National Bibliotek in Vienna, and in Britain: the Public Record Office, the Foreign Office Library, the British Library, the libraries of the London School of Slavonic and East European Studies, London University and Cambridge University, and last but by no means least to the Library of the University of Kent at Canterbury, and especially to Miss Enid Dixon and her colleagues in the inter-library loan section.

The University of Kent at Canterbury has been most generous in its provision of study leave and secretarial assistance. For the latter I am most particularly indebted to Mrs Mollie Roots and her staff. Their patience and efficiency has earned my admiration as well as my gratitude, and to Miss Mary Thomas I give especial thanks for her painstaking work with the bibliography.

I would like to thank Professor Stephen Fischer-Galaţi for his encouragement in the final stages of this work. My father very kindly agreed to help in the reading of the proofs and I am enormously grateful to him for his careful and persistent efforts in this task.

Finally my greatest and most intangible debt is to my wife. All others mentioned here have combined to make this work possible. She has made it worthwhile.

Canterbury, September 1982.

MAPS

BULGARIA: Mountains and Rivers

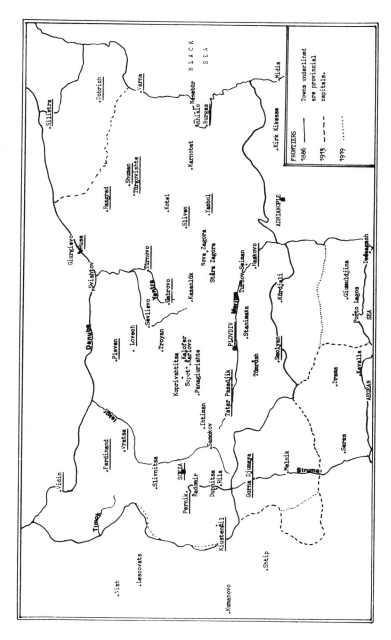

BULGARIA: MAIN TOWNS

A NOTE ON TRANSLITERATION

Transliteration is not a subject on which I would wish to go to the academic stake and at times I have felt great sympathy with T E Lawrence who announced that he was going to use as many different systems of transliteration as possible in *The Seven Pillars of Wisdom* as he saw this as the only effective form of protest against the inadequacies of them all. I do not however have his courage and have tried to adhere to the system set out below.

а - a
б - b
в - v
г - g (always hard)
д - d
е - e
ж - zh (but дж has been transliterated 'dj')
з - z
и - i
й - y
к - k
л - l
м - m
н - n

о - o
п - p
р - r
с - s
т - t
у - u
ф - f
х - h (but 'kh' in Russian words)
ц - ts
ч - ch
ш - sh
щ - sht (but 'shch' in Russian words)
ь - u
ю - iu
я - ya

The Russian ы has been rendered into 'y'. The hard sign has not been transliterated.

In the transliteration of plurals I have moved slightly closer to T E Lawrence, giving some in their directly transliterated form, e.g. *esnafi,* and others in a slightly anglicised form, e.g. *chifliks*. In doing so I have not been entirely guided by whim and caprice; those two admirable qualities have been modified by considerations of euphony.

THE BULGARIANS BEFORE
THE LIBERATION OF 1878

In the mid-thirteenth century the Second Bulgarian Empire dominated the Balkan peninsula. By the end of the following century factional divisions between Bulgarian feudal landlords had gravely weakened the cohesion of the Empire which therefore collapsed before the invading Ottoman armies in the 1390s. The Bulgarians, most of whom lived in the quadrilateral contained by the Danube, the Aegean coast of Thrace, the Black Sea and the valley of the Vardar in the west, now entered upon five hundred years of Ottoman domination. Bulgarian institutions at anything above the village or communal level were dismantled and the separate Bulgarian Church was merged into the Orthodox Patriarchate in Constantinople (Istanbul), although a small, semi-independent Bulgarian Church did survive at Ohrid until 1767.

The conquerors also assumed virtual ownership of the land, though legal ownership was vested in Allah's representative on earth, the Sultan. The function of the new tenurial system imposed by the Turks was to provide the Ottoman army with cavalry troops, the *spahi* or landlord being required to provide a number of men proportionate to the amount of land held. He was maintained economically by his tenants, or *rayahs*. For the Bulgarian peasant the new system offered greater security than the old Bulgarian Empire had been able to provide and exceptional privileges were enjoyed by peasants living on *vakŭf* land, that is land whose income had been permanently entailed for the upkeep of a religious or charitable institution. Such privileges were the right of all tenants, Christian or Moslem who lived on *vakŭf* land, but in general the Christian subjects of the Sultan had to endure a number

1

of disabilities; they usually paid more taxes than Moslems, they were not given legal equality with Moslems, they could not carry arms, their clothes could not be as colourful as those of Moslems nor could their churches be as high as mosques. The new rulers made few attempts to enforce conversion to Islam and relatively few Bulgarians were attracted to the new ruling faith by the legal privileges its adherents enjoyed. Those who did convert, the pomaks, retained their native language, dress and customs, and were to be found primarily in the Rhodope mountains.

The Ottoman system at its height did much to protect the *rayah* but by the seventeenth century the system was in decline and at the end of the eighteenth had all but collapsed. Central government had been weakening for decades and this had allowed a number of local adventurers and free-booters to establish personal ascendancy over separate regions. These local *ayani* employed armed retainers and having established their authority frequently imposed new and far more arduous tenancies on the peasantry under their control. During the last two decades of the eighteenth and first decades of the nineteenth centuries the Balkan peninsula dissolved into virtual anarchy, a period known in Bulgarian as the *kurdjaliistvo* after the armed bands or *kŭrdjalii* who plagued the area at this time. In many regions thousands of peasants fled from the countryside either to local towns or more probably to the hills or forests; some even fled beyond the Danube to Moldavia, Wallachia or southern Russia. In the mountainous areas of the south-west and north-west of the Bulgarian lands however the *ayani*, or *gospodari* as they were known in the north-west, established stricter control and this was a control which, because of the terrain, was less affected than other areas by the reassertion of central government authority after 1810. The problems of the north- and south-west were not solved until after the Liberation.

In the 1820s the fortunes of the Bulgarians improved. Despite the revolt in Greece the Sultan's authority was to a large extent re-established in most of the remainder of European Turkey and his suppression of the Janissaries and the creation of a regular army not only increased his political power but also promoted the well-being of many Bulgarian communities, for in later years the cloth and mutton to supply the new army came from Bulgarian suppliers. Other merchants and manufacturers took advantage of the large markets of Adrianople (Edirne) and Constantinople. By the second quarter of the nineteenth century sizeable Bulgarian mercantile communities had been established in these cities as well as in Braila, Bucharest, Odessa and Smyrna (Izmir). Within the Bulgarian lands smaller towns had also experienced a gradual growth in prosperity, one which was often to be signified by the appearance of a clock tower, a covered *charshiya* or market place, a new building for a monastery or, in later years, a school or reading room.

The production of the goods on which this new and still relative prosperity was founded was concentrated in the *zanayati*, or workshop-based craft trades, with only a handful of factories being set up in Bulgaria before 1878. The *zanayati* were organised into guilds (*esnafi*) which regulated production, controlled relationships within the guild and, especially in later years, played a vital role in financing education and cultural development.

Whilst the urban centres grew in wealth the rural peasantry enjoyed a frugal but for the most part stable life. Upheaval had accompanied the Russian armies which moved into the Balkans during the Russo-Turkish War of 1828-9 but thereafter the legal abolition of the old system of land tenures in the 1830s and various legal reforms in later years, together with a chronic shortage of labour in the plains, meant that the Bulgarian peasant was saved from outrageous exploitation, and by the mid-1870s had become to all intents and purposes the individual proprietor of his land, though his legal right to his property was not entirely clear. Furthermore, most peasant households could survive on their land without having to employ wage-labourers or sell their own labour. Even on the few large-scale, commercially-oriented estates (the *chifliks*) the bulk of outside labour came not from permanent local wage-earners but from the gangs of harvesters who, by ancient tradition, descended each year into the plains from the mountains of Macedonia and central Bulgaria. The fact that the majority of Bulgarian peasants had the use if not the undisputed legal ownership of their land explains the distinct lack of social content in the programmes eventually produced by the Bulgarian nationalists. Only in the north- and south-west were there intolerable social conditions for the mass of the peasantry, a fact attested by the frequency of revolt in those areas from the late 1830s to the early 1850s. In the 1850s and 1860s there was also some disquiet in the region along the northern slopes of the Balkan range for here the Turks settled Circassians and Tatars displaced by Russian expansion.

Within most peasant communities there were some divisions but these were ones of wealth rather than class. Most villages had a few elders one or more of whom would be responsible for liason between the community and the nearest Ottoman officials and might be made responsible for the collection of taxes within the community. These elders, or *chorbadjii*—the name means providers of soup—later became the bogey-men of radical propaganda, but they performed an essential function with no more nor no less wickedness than similar groups in other societies.

The relative well-being which most Bulgarians enjoyed from the beginning of the second quarter of the nineteenth century was an essential prerequisite for the cultural revival which came to dominate Bulgarian affairs in the next half century.

Though the Ottoman conquest dismantled the highest institutions of Bulgarian culture, the Bulgarian Church and state, that culture was not destroyed. A sense of separate Bulgarian identity, though it was seldom articulated in political terms, was kept alive in the peasant customs of the villages and the Bulgarian districts of the towns. The *haidutsi* of the mountains also helped preserve such an identity for though in most cases they were nothing more than bandits, they were also Christians who attacked Moslems and the representatives of Ottoman power. Of much greater importance were the monasteries. It was here that the heritage of Bulgaria's past was preserved, above all in their libraries, and it was here too that that past was rediscovered. Also, in placid times pilgrims gathered to exchange views and experiences and to learn that communities in many parts of the Balkans shared their culture and their problems. The monks who went each year to recruit or to collect taxes on monastic properties also helped to keep isolated communities in touch with other Bulgarian groups and with developing Bulgarian cultural organisations.

With the expansion of trading and manufacture the *esnafi* also began to play an important role in promoting Bulgarian culture. Many members of the *esnafi* were in constant commercial contact with the peasant and town-dweller whose aspirations they came to know and perhaps to mould. By the 1840s the *esnafi* were beginning to engage in the financing and promotion of Bulgarian cultural development, but in many urban centres Greek influences were still strong and it was not until the 1850s that differences over the financing of educational and religious institutions forced the powerful *aba* guild (*aba* is a coarse cloth) of Plovdiv (Philipopolis) to divide into separate Bulgarian and Greek organisations.

The communal councils also helped preserve and then during the national revival to promote Bulgarian culture. After the Ottoman conquest the new regime required some villages to perform specific functions in return for which they enjoyed certain privileges. The functions required varied from the defending of passes to the provision of falcons or horses for imperial use, or, as in the case of the village of Dedovo, the supplying each day of two barrels of water from the village spring to the nearby city of Plovdiv. Most specialised villages were purely Bulgarian and they were given the right to organise by themselves the fulfilment of their duties. Thus did virtually autonomous Bulgarian communities survive. In the towns the councils had appeared as adjuncts to the church and though they too acquired extensive powers in local administration, especially immediately after the *kŭrdjaliistvo*, here Greek influences were stronger and not till the 1850s was there a consistent attempt within the urban communal councils to assert their specifically Bulgarian as opposed to their generally Christian character. Once that process of assertion had begun however the communal councils, and above all that of the Bulgarians in Constantinople, provided invaluable service in supporting education and in the campaign to secure an independent Bulgarian Church. Like the specialised villages the urban communal councils also provided the Bulgarians with some experience in administration and limited self-government.

The efforts to promote education and even more so the struggle to create a Bulgarian Church in which the *esnafi* and communal councils played important roles were the central themes of the Bulgarian national revival of the second and third quarters of the nineteenth century. The first proponent of that national revival was a monk, Paiisi Hilendarski, the latter part of the name reflecting his membership of the monastery of Hilendar. In the mid-eighteenth century in the rich library of his monastery Paiisi learned much of the old Bulgarian Church and Empire and from his researches he emerged with both a strengthened pride in the history of his people and a concern at its present neglect. His passions he poured into *A Slavonic-Bulgarian History of the Peoples, Tsars and Saints, and of all their Deeds and of the Bulgarian Way of Life*. The book, written in a modified form of Old Church Slavonic, was intended by Paiisi to warn his fellow Bulgarians against the danger of Hellenisation and he urged them to 'keep close to your heart your race and your Bulgarian homeland'. There were good reasons, he said, to be proud of such a homeland because

Of all the Slav peoples the most glorious were the Bulgarians; they were the first who called themselves kings, the first to have a Patriarch, the first to adopt the Christian faith, and they it was who conquered the largest amount of territory. Thus, of all the Slav peoples they were the strongest and the most honoured, and the first Slav saints cast their radiance from among the Bulgarian people and through the Bulgarian language.

Along with praise of the Bulgarian went scorn for the Greek and his culture.

But, they say, the Greeks are wiser and more cultured, while the Bulgarians are simple and foolish and have no refined words. That is why, they say, we had better join the Greeks. But . . . there are many peoples wiser and more glorious than the Greeks. Does any Greek abandon his language and teaching and his people as you, madman, abandon yours . . .? Bulgarians, do not deceive yourself, know your nation and language and study in your own tongue.

Paiisi soon found followers. Sofroni Vrachenski (i.e. of Vratsa) had met Paiisi in Kotel in 1764-5 and was so impressed by the *History* that he had it copied and placed in his church where it was protected by a notice which would not be out of place in many a late twentieth century library:

May he who appropriates or steals this book be anathematised and cursed by the Lord God of Sabaoth and by the twelve apostles, by the Holy fathers and the four evangelists. May hail, iron and stone fall on him and may he perish for ever.

Many other copies of Paiisi's work must have been made as over forty manuscript versions still survive, all of them dating from before 1845 when the first printed edition appeared in Budapest.

Despite its popularity Paiisi's book did not have much effect because of the political and social turmoil which afflicted the Bulgarian lands at the end of the eighteenth century. With the return of relative stability others began to advocate the same policy, more particularly in the movement for Bulgarian-based education and, most important of all, in the struggle to defend Bulgarian interests within the Orthodox Church. The latter was necessary because of advancing Greek power. During the eighteenth century the Phanariots assumed an ever more influential position within those parts of the Ottoman administration which still operated effectively and, at the same time, the Orthodox Church fell more and more under the spell of Hellenist ideas which were spreading into the Balkans from the Aegean islands and from Venice. For the Bulgarians the advance of Hellenism within the Church meant the closure of the Bulgarian Church in Ohrid in 1767 and the more frequent appointment of Greek bishops or priests in predominantly Bulgarian areas. At times even confession had to be said through an interpreter. The struggle against ecclesiastical Hellenism was to end with the creation of an independent Bulgarian Church, the first Bulgarian institution in modern history.

Before that was to be achieved, however, much had to be done to develop the still largely dormant sense of Bulgarian national identity, in Paiisi's phrase to 'know your nation and language and study in your own tongue'.

After the *kŭrdjaliistvo* serious but sporadic efforts were made to promote education in Bulgarian. In 1824 Neofit Bozveli, a monk and pupil of Sofroni Vrachenski, had had some success in introducing Slav liturgical training in the seminary at Svishtov but lasting success in the campaign to further education in Bulgarian did not come until 1834 when Vasil Aprilov established in Gabrovo a Bell-Lancaster school teaching in the vernacular. The school's first teacher was a monk, Neofit Rilski. The new school and others which followed it met with fierce opposition from the Greek hierarchy. This opposition however did not represent a conscious attack upon nascent Bulgarian cultural consciousness because the Greek bishops were equally opposed to the teaching of modern Greek. Nor were those who promoted education in Bulgarian necessarily anti-Greek, for both Aprilov and Neofit Rilski believed that Bulgarian should be taught in addition to rather than in place of liturgical Greek, and both these early enlighteners remained faithful to the Greek Patriarchate.

The early Bulgarian schools were frustrated by a lack of suitable teaching manuals. In 1824 in Brasov Petur Beron had published his *Riben Bukvar* (Fish ABC), so called because of the motif on its back cover. Beron's book, like others after it, was based on Greek models and, being as much a small encyclopaedia as a grammar, was far from ideal for use in schools. In the 1830s grammars were produced by both Neofit Rilski and Neofit Bozveli but neither enjoyed wide currency. In 1844 Ivan Bogorov published a grammar which did find fairly widespread acceptance and did much finally to ensure that the literary form would be based on the spoken language, though it was to be a further two decades before it was generally agreed which dialect should serve as the model for standard written Bulgarian. Aprilov and the early publicists had however saved their nation from the inconveniences of a Bulgarian *katharevoussa*.

The spread of vernacular education was systematic rather than rapid. Five years after the opening of Aprilov's Gabrovo enterprise there were thirteen additional schools and by the 1850s most sizeable communities had a school teaching in Bulgarian. A number of secondary schools were also established and in Pleven in 1860 a girls' school was founded. By 1878 there were some two thousand schools in the Bulgarian lands, most of them financed by local *esnafi* or communal councils and offering free education to all Bulgarian children. By the Liberation literacy rates in Bulgarian communities were as high as in Britain or France, though very few Bulgarian children had more than primary schooling.

The spread of literacy and education was hampered in the early years by the lack of printing facilities. Some Bulgarian books had been produced in central Europe at the beginning of the century but it was to be almost five decades before presses were available within the Ottoman Empire, and even then the first were not to be found in the Bulgarian lands. In 1840 a Greek in Smyrna had begun printing with Slav type imported from the U.S.A. at the request of the British and Foreign Bible Society, and in the same year a Bulgarian press was also set up in Salonika (Thessaloniki). These produced mainly religious books, including the first vernacular Bulgarian bibles, but it was also on the Smyrna press that Konstantin Fotinov in 1844 began printing his *Liuboslovie* (Love of Words), the first Bulgarian periodical, though it lasted for no more than two years. By the late 1840s the Bulgarian community in Constantinople had its own press and on it Ivan Bogorov produced the first Bulgarian periodical which had more than an ephemeral existence; his *Tsarigradski Vestnik* (Constantinople Gazette) appeared first in 1848 and continued publication until 1861.

An important feature of Bulgaria's educational movement and national renaissance was the *chitalishte*. The standard English translation of 'reading room' does not justly describe this peculiarly Bulgarian institution which provided not merely a place to read books or newspapers but also a venue for lectures, meetings, plays and other forms of entertainment. In later years they occasionally provided excellent cover for secret meetings of revolutionary conspirators. The first *chitalishte* was set up in Svishtov in 1856 and from there they spread rapidly to most Bulgarian communities, there being a total of 186 by 1878. Ivan Vazov, the national poet, described them as 'Bulgaria's ministry of national education'.

Some credit for the development of the educational movement in Bulgaria must also be given to the various learned societies. As early as 1823 Vasil Nenovich in Brašov had set up the Philological Society to promote the use of Bulgarian as a literary medium and to stimulate the publication of books in Bulgarian, but it was not until 1856 that a successful institution was established, this being the Society for Bulgarian Literature. The Society was founded in Constantinople and published the bi-weekly *Bŭlgarski Knizhitsi* (Bulgarian Literature) which lasted from 1857 to 1862, having as many as six hundred subscribers at its peak. The most lasting success, however, was to be enjoyed by the Bulgarian Literary Society established in Braila in 1869, for this was to provide the embryo from which emerged the Bulgarian Academy of Sciences.

The spread of education and literacy produced a new phenomenon in Bulgarian society: the Bulgarian intelligentsia, of which the main representatives were the teachers and priests. Priests there had long been but the teachers were a product of the national reawakening. The most able students within the schools, particularly those in the larger towns, were frequently sent abroad for higher education, the costs being met usually by a local merchant, *esnaf* or communal council; in 1867, for example, Plovdiv could boast five students in Paris, four in Vienna, seven in Russia, two in Britain, and forty in Constantinople. Not all these educational émigrés returned but a sizeable proportion of those who did became teachers or otherwise engaged themselves in the enlightenment of the peasantry: often there was little alternative to a teaching career. The strength of the peasant-intelligentsia alliance and its importance as a politically creative force can easily be exaggerated. The intelligentsia numbered only between two and three thousand and not all teachers had taken up their posts through a sense of mission. Nevertheless it was to the intelligentsia that the peasants looked for guidance when faced with political or religious questions, and it was thus the relationship between peasant and *intelligent* which formed the bed-rock of the movement for an independent Bulgarian Church. Likewise many peasants again looked to the intelligentsia in the confused days of the mid-1870s when established political order in the Balkans was destroyed. In return the political activists who attempted to raise the nation in revolt in the early 1870s and who played a vital role in fashioning the new Bulgarian state, derived a number of ideas from the supposedly egalitarian and democratic structure of the Bulgarian village and its communal council.

Like intelligentsias elsewhere that of the Bulgarians was to some degree divided. Many of the young teachers returning from abroad found their ideas to be in conflict with the leaders of the local communal councils which employed them. Dissatisfaction arose too from disputes over salaries and from the restricted, parochial life which teaching in a small village entailed. Thus as the intelligentsia developed in the 1850s and 1860s distinct radical, or 'Young', and moderate, or 'Old', factions appeared, though this division was by no means watertight and individual leaders could be 'Old' on one issue and 'Young' on another, and, like all men, their opinions and attitudes changed with time. In general it could be said that as far as the leaders were concerned the 'Young' were to be found more often in Bulgarian communities outside the Ottoman Empire and the 'Old' in communities within it, though the dominant Constantinople community was by no means lacking in radical members.

*   *   *

The division between 'Young' and 'Old' was also apparent in the later stages of the movement for greater recognition of Bulgarian identity within the Orthodox Church. The movement had begun with instinctive and isolated outbursts against two factors which had affected Bulgarian communities since the mid-eighteenth century. The first was the advance of Hellenist influence within the Church, against which Paiisi's angered voice had been raised, the second was the increasing venality of the clergy. The Church had always enjoyed the right to levy taxes for its own upkeep but in the second half of the eighteenth century the practice of selling ecclesiastical office also developed significantly. The Patriarch secured his position by bribing the appropriate Porte officials and members of the Church hierarchy, recouping the costs from those whom he appointed or promoted when in office. This process percolated down the ecclesiastical structure until the final burden rested on the peasant. By the 1820s many Bulgarian peasants were paying to the Church twice what they were required to pay to the state. This inevitably caused anger and prompted the demand for redress whilst the fact that Hellenist influences were gaining ground within the Church helped to point that anger towards the

Greeks. As early as 1784 a Serb, Gerasim Zelić, had argued the need for Bulgarian as opposed to Greek clergy. In 1820 the inhabitants of Vratsa translated argument into action and refused to pay dues to their Greek bishop, Metodi, who was notorious for his avarice even in the competitive world of the Greek episcopate. The Vratsa protest did not succeed and those who led it, most of them local merchants, were given long sentences of exile by the Ottoman authorities. A similar protest against the Greek bishop of Skopje (Üsküb) in 1825 also failed. By the late 1830s some Bulgarian clerics were receiving further training in Russia whilst inside Bulgaria there was a strong movement to secure the appointment of Neofit Bozveli to the recently vacated see of Tŭrnovo, but though Bozveli's canditature was supported by the Porte it was blocked by the Patriarch. The demand for Bulgarian bishops however could not be suppressed. The Nish rebels of 1841, though their main complaints were social, asked for the appointment of 'bishops who at least can understand our language'. By the late 1840s there had been protests against Greek bishops in Ruse (Rustchuk) Ohrid, Seres, Lovech, Sofia, Samokov, Vidin, Tŭrnovo, Leskovats, Svishtov, Vratsa, Tryavna and Plovdiv (Philipopolis). By now these protests were not against corrupt Greek bishops but against Greek bishops in general.

The most notable success of the Bulgarian movement in the 1840s was the setting up of a separate Bulgarian church in the Phanar district of Constantinople. For some years the city's Bulgarian community, led by a number of wealthy merchants and supported by the Bulgarian *esnafi*, had been demanding a church of their own where they could worship in their own language. In 1848 the Porte agreed and the foundation of a Bulgarian church was laid; the church, dedicated to St Stefan, was consecrated in October of the following year. The land on which the church stood had been donated by a local Bulgarian who was also an Ottoman official, but the church itself was to be the property of the Bulgarian nation, whilst its administration was to be entrusted to a twenty-man governing council which may be considered the first officially-recognised Bulgarian organisation to appear during the national renaissance. In matters of doctrine and ecclesiastical justice however the new church was to remain subject to the Patriarchate.

The new church showed Bulgarians everywhere that their desire for greater national self-assertion within the Orthodox Church need not be expressed solely in attacks upon a Greek episcopate but could also be articulated in the setting up of separate religious institutions. This was a message which gained widespread approval, a circular letter of 1851 from the Bulgarian community in Bucharest ending with the pregnant phrase, 'Without a national Church there is no salvation'.

The foundation of St. Stefan's also meant that the centre of the Bulgarian movement was now firmly fixed in Constantinople where it was best placed to capitalise upon favourable political developments within the Empire. One such development was the series of reforms enacted by the Ottoman government in the 1830s and 1840s. These had been necessary to adapt the legal structure of the Empire to the abolition of feudalism and one consequence of the movement towards reform by the Porte had been reforming pressure from that quarter on other institutions within the Ottoman state, including the Patriarchate which was expected to allow lay elements greater influence in the government of the Church. With the increasing cultural awareness of the Bulgarians such a reform in the Church would inevitably mean a greater say for the Bulgarians in ecclesiastical affairs, and this the Patriarch would not contemplate. Bulgarian frustration therefore accummulated, the more so after the Protestants and the Armenian Catholics had been recognised as separate *milleti* or religious communities in the 1850s.

In the mid-1850s further stimulus to the movement for greater Bulgarian autonomy within the Orthodox Church was provided by the Crimean War. Russian defeats weakened the arguments of those who had looked to that power for an eventual settlement of the divisions between Greek and Bulgarian, for now clearly Russian influence in the Near East had been limited: the Bulgarians were being forced into greater self-reliance. The decline in Russian influence also helped the Bulgarian Church movement in that Russia, though supporting the call for the appointment of Bulgarian bishops, had always and would always do all she could to prevent a division in the Orthodox Church within the Ottoman Empire, not least because the Tsar's already tenuous treaty rights to protect his co-religionists in the area applied to 'Orthodox' Christians, not to those of a Bulgarian or a Greek Church. The Crimean War also ushered in another round of reform by the Porte and once again the Patriarchate was expected to follow suit. This time it did so. Mixed councils of lay and clerical members were created but when the new system failed to give the Bulgarians the increase in power they had come to expect they were pushed yet farther along the path towards ecclesiastical separatism. In 1856 the Sultan was presented with a petition asking for a separate Church and this petition claimed to represent the six and a half million Bulgarians living in his Empire. In the same year the Bulgarian communal council in Constantinople circulated a letter to all sizeable Bulgarian communities asking them to send elected delegates to the capital to join in petitioning for an independent Church. These delegates, when they assembled, constituted the first remotely representative body in modern Bulgarian history, and amongst them were many figures prominent in the national revival and in the political life of the nation after 1878.

The call for a separate Bulgarian Church was not however universally accepted in Bulgarian circles. The bishops of Vratsa and Lovech, who were among the four Bulgarian bishops nominated by the Patriarch, resisted any idea of separation from the Greek Church, as did Neofit Rilski, now abbot of the great Rila monastery. The separatists nevertheless had increasingly powerful arguments on their side. In October 1859 a conference to discuss Church reform was opened under the presidency of the Patriarch; the Bulgarian delegates demanded the restoration of the Ohrid and Tŭrnovo Patriarchates but these demands were blocked by the conference's solid Greek majority. The legal path towards greater recognition of Bulgarian claims within the existing framework of Church, it seemed, would lead nowhere. As that path closed an alternative opened. Roman Catholic propaganda amongst the Bulgarians had been increasing in the 1850s and the Uniate Church was prepared to offer the Slavs the use of their own language and liturgy in return for little more than the recognition of the Pope as head of the Church. The Uniates, who from 1851 to 1861 had a powerful supporter in Dragan Tsankov, an able Bulgarian in the Ottoman civil service, could also argue that after the Crimean War sponsorship by the Catholic powers would be more advantageous than that by Russia, and already some Orthodox communities in Macedonia had accepted papal terms. There was a growing body of opinion within Bulgarian communities elsewhere, Constantinople included, that the Bulgarians should do the same if they did not receive some major concession from the Greek hierarchy.

The Uniate threat did much to bring about the final breach between the Bulgarians and the Patriarchate in 1860. Ilarion Makriopolski, the priest in charge of St Stefan's in Constantinople, with the full backing of the governing council of his church and of the city's Bulgarian *esnafi*, decided that on Easter Sunday 3/15 April, he would omit from the liturgy the customary prayers for the Patriarch. Instead he would pray for all Orthodox bishops and for the Sultan. The significance of this was threefold; Ilarion was altering the order of service without the permission of the Patriarch; the prayer for all bishops deposed the Patriarch from his singular status within the Orthodox Church; and, most importantly, the prayer for the Sultan implied that the Bulgarians, by praying for him directly rather than through the medium of the Patriarchate, were announcing their existence as a separate religious group within the Empire.

The reaction of the Bulgarians to the events of Easter Sunday 1860 was swift. Thirty-three towns petitioned the Sultan expressing their solidarity with Ilarion, as did 734 merchants who were gathered at the Uzundjovo fair. A number of bishops associated themselves with the new Church, and included among these was Gideon of Sofia who, though Greek, dared not offend his Bulgarian flock. The events of Easter Sunday encouraged Bulgarian communities in other ways. During the 1860s many Bulgarians refused to pay taxes to the Greek Church whilst the towns of Lovech, Samokov, Shumen, Preslav and Vidin all refused Bulgarian bishops who had been appointed by the Patriarch. By 1866 only ten of the ninety villages in the Varna diocese were loyal to the Greek Church, though the city itself remained Patriarchist; in Macedonia Skopje remained loyal to the Patriarchate only because a Bulgarian bishop had been appointed in 1865, though two years later Veles broke with the Greek Church. In fact between 1860 and 1869 there were few dioceses in Bulgaria, Macedonia and Thrace which had not in one way or another declared themselves for the Bulgarian as opposed to the Greek Church, though only Plovdiv had a representative permanently at the Bulgarian Church in Constantinople from the virtual declaration of ecclesiastical independence in 1860 to official recognition of that independence a decade later.

After 1860 the main preoccupation of the Bulgarian national movement, as it may now legitimately be called, was to secure recognition of the new Bulgarian Church. Official recognition of the Church meant official recognition of the Bulgarians as a separate religious group or *millet*. In the Ottoman Empire each *millet* had extensive rights in cultural and intra-communal legal affairs, but for the Ottoman mind it was of little importance whether a *millet* was ethnically homogeneous, for cultural identity in the Ottoman framework was consequent upon religious affiliation. The Bulgarians wished to reverse that order and make religious affiliation a consequence of national allegiance. This had enormous political implications, especially for the Greeks whose dominance in the Orthodox Church would be shattered by the general

application of this principle. The Patriarchate was therefore implaca-
bly opposed to the official recognition of a separate Bulgarian Church.
The Porte, too, was not over-anxious to grant recognition because the
dispute kept a wedge between two powerful Christian subject peoples
and because it caused the Russians embarrassment. The Russians, for
their part, would have liked the Patriarchate to make enough concessions to retrieve the loyalty of the Bulgarians, but were also desperate
to prevent a fracture in the Orthodox Church within the Ottoman
Empire.

Throughout the 1860s a series of meetings and councils thrashed
around the issue but no real progress was made until 1867 when Patriarch Gregory VI offered the Bulgarians an autonomous church within
the Patriarchate. The Bulgarian religious community would be headed
by an Exarch, an ecclesiastical rank mid-way between Metropolitan
and Patriarch, but was to be confined to the area between the Balkan
mountains and the Danube. These geographic restrictions ruined any
chance that the scheme would be accepted but the offer was important
because 'for the first time the Patriarch had recognised the right of the
Bulgarians to their own separate Church'.[1]

By 1867 the pressures on the Porte and the other parties to the
dispute were growing. The Russians, under the able direction of their
ambassador in Constantinople, Ignatiev, were pressing for a compromise. The Porte meanwhile was alarmed at the first signs of an armed
political nationalist movement amongst the Bulgarians. It was also
concerned that the air of general European instability following the
Austro-Prussian War was reaching down into the Balkans with stirrings of irredentism in Serbia, Montenegro and Rumania, passions
from which Prince Michael Obrenović of Serbia was attempting to
fashion a Balkan alliance. Above all, however, the Porte feared the
Cretan insurrexion of 1866 which reawakened Turkish fears of Greek
territorial aspirations and strained Greek-Ottoman relations to such a
degree that there was a natural instinct for the Porte to support the
Bulgarians. It was this more than any other factor which finally persuaded the Porte to move towards recognition of the Bulgarian
Church, whilst Russia's reluctant acceptance of this move was secured
by her own worsening relations with Athens and by her fear of Uniat-
ism. In February 1870 the Sultan issued a *firman*, or declaration of
intent, to recognise a separate Bulgarian Church headed by an Exarch.

Though a huge national gain the *firman* of 1870 was not entirely
satisfactory for the Bulgarians. The Exarchate was required still to

mention the Patriarch in its liturgy, to allow the Patriarch control in the procuring of Holy Oil, and to defer to him in matters of doctrine. Much more important were the territorial limitations of the new Bulgarian Church. In 1869 Gavril Krŭstevich, a Bulgarian in the Ottoman service, had submitted to the Porte a plan for the settlement of the church dispute and this plan had formed the basis of the *firman* issued in the following year. In the original proposal the Bulgarians were to have twenty-five of the existing Orthodox dioceses, the Greeks forty-one and the remaining eight were to be divided. By 1870 the Bulgarian share had been whittled down to fifteen, namely Ruse, Silistra, Shumen, Tŭrnovo, Sofia, Vratsa, Lovech, Vidin, Nish, Pirot, Kiustendil, Samokov, Veles, Varna and Plovdiv. The cities of Varna, Plovdiv (the Virgin Mary quarter excepted), Anhialo (Pomorie), Mesembriya (Nesebŭr) and Stanimaka (Asenovgrad), together with a number of villages and monasteries, were to be excluded from the Exarchate. The territorial provisions of the 1870 *firman* disappointed the Bulgarians for their Church was all but confined to the north of the Balkan range. Some comfort, however, was derived from the provision that if it could be proved that at least two thirds of the Orthodox Christians within any Patriarchist see wished to join the Bulgarian Church then that see would be included in the Exarchate. In later years such majorities were proved in a number of sees, though the promised transfer did not always take place and this provision, as Patriarch Gregory VI predicted, was to provide 'an apple of eternal discord' between Greek and Bulgarian.[2]

* * *

The Bulgarian Church had been created primarily by the Bulgarian people and its intelligentsia. It was not a movement for national liberation, and no force with its centre in the Ottoman capital could pretend to serious secessionist aspirations. It did, however, have profound political implications, a fact recognized by Gregory VI who, when making his proposal for an autonomous Bulgarian Church in 1867, had said, 'With my own hands I have built a bridge to the political independence of the Bulgarians'.[3]

The movement for political independence, however, was always weaker than the Church movement. Political activists were few in number and not very influential except in some of the larger communities. Their effectiveness was decreased by continual disagreements on methods and objectives, disagreements which can, with more convenience than accuracy, be summarised as a split between the 'Young' and 'Old' factions. This is not to detract from the dedication and courage of the activists, particularly those who risked and not infrequently lost their lives in a cause which to them was sacred, for those who did take the risks and made the sacrifices provided their contemporaries and later generations with inspiration and with the martyrs necessary to a modern nationalist movement.

Bulgarians had taken part in a number of movements against Ottoman rule, including the Serbian and Greek insurrections and the Russo-Turkish Wars of 1806–12 and 1828–9, but had not emerged from those experiences with a burning desire to liberate their homeland. In the mid-1830s some merchants and craftsmen lent support to a half-cock rebellion in the Tŭrnovo region but it was betrayed and those involved executed or exiled. In the late 1830s and early 1840s there was a series of uprisings but these were spontaneous outbursts of social discontent in the north- and south-west rather than national efforts to change the political structure. Even after the Crimean War Bulgarians were concentrating overwhelmingly on cultural and religious issues rather than political ones. At this time, however, the first plan for the achievement of Bulgarian political liberation had been produced by Ivan Kishelski, a Bulgarian who had fought with the Russian army, and though Kishelski's programme itself had little immediate effect its ideas were to be taken up by later activists. In the 1850s and early 1860s there were a number of external stimuli to the development of political nationalism. To the north the two Rumanian provinces of Moldavia and Wallachia had united, in Serbia Prince Michael Obrenović had declared himself hereditary ruler, and above all there had been the example of Italy. In 1862 a number of nationalist Serbs had attempted to drive the Ottoman garrison out of Belgrade and taking part in that action had been a small Bulgarian legion under the command of Georgi Rakovski.

Rakovski had been active in émigré nationalist circles for some years and in forming the Bulgarian legion he implemented the ideas preached in his own journal, *Dunavski Lebed* (Danubian Swan). Rakovski favoured the creation of a Balkan republican federation, though Greece was not to be included. He believed that Ottoman power would be destroyed only by the armed action of its subject peoples and for this reason he urged that small armed units, *cheti* (bands), should be sent into Bulgaria to harrass the local administrators and to raise national consciousness. During the 1860s this view gradually gained wider currency in exile circles, not least because the Church struggle seemed to have ended in stalemate. In the mid-1860s the advocates of political, that is revolutionary, action were again encouraged by events outside the Bulgarian lands. The Rumanians, despite Russian and Turkish opposition, removed their Prince, the Poles rose against their Russian masters, and most important of all was the Cretan rebellion of 1866, which put the Bulgarians' two chief adversaries at each others' throats. By 1866 Rakovski had established a somewhat amorphous Bulgarian Secret Central Committee in Bucharest, whither he had moved in 1862. In 1866 his organisation was ready to equip its first *cheti* and in that year and early in 1867 they crossed the Danube under the leadership of Panayot Hitov and Filip Totiu. The bands achieved nothing in Bulgaria and were soon destroyed or dispersed. A similar fate awaited those sent in the following year under the command of Hadji Dimitŭr Ashenov and Stefan Karadja, though the incursions, particularly those in 1868, did help move the Porte towards eventual recognition of the Bulgarian Church.

By 1868 Rakovski was dead, a victim of tuberculosis. Leadership of the revolutionary movement passed to the Bulgarian Revolutionary Central Committee based also in Bucharest. The BRCC was dominated by the triumvir of Liuben Karavelov, Vasil Levski and Hristo Botev. Karavelov was the chief ideologist of the new organisation, publishing his views in newspapers such as *Nezavisimost* (Independence), and *Svoboda* (Freedom). Like Rakovski, Karavelov was a federalist, willing even to accept a Bulgaro-Turkish compromise similar to that between Austria and Hungary, but also believing that Bulgaria's complete liberation and a Balkan federation could only come about as the result of a general Balkan uprising. His political inclinations were radical and he admired the *narodnik* ideas then so powerful in Russia, a fact which gave him cause to be suspicious of Tsarism. Levski too was influenced by the *narodniki* for his first contribution was to stress the need for a mass peasant rising but only after careful preparation, for which 'apostles' would have to be sent into the villages. His second contribution was his heroic death. In 1872 Levski was in Bulgaria carefully building up a revolutionary organisation when his second in command was arrested for robbery. In order to prove his status as a political protester rather than a common criminal the second in command betrayed the organisation and its architect. Levski was hanged in Sofia in 1873. He was to remain one of the great, if not the greatest of Bulgarian national martyrs. The third of the trio, Botev, was the only one of the three to hold socialist views, though his real contribution to the national movement at this stage was his poetry rather than his political ideology.

With the death of Levski in February 1873 the BRCC and its embryonic organisation within Bulgaria all but collapsed. The failures of the early *cheti* and then the disaster of Levski's betrayal forced Karavelov and Botev to see more clearly the need for reliance on foreign help, in the first instance from other Balkan states. In 1875 a new Bulgarian Revolutionary Central Committee was founded in the Rumanian town of Giurgiu on the Danube. By then a serious rising was under way in Bosnia and this seemed to provide the Bulgarian extremists with an opportunity they could scarcely miss. The new BRCC therefore set about preparing for a further revolt to be led this time by Georgi Benkovski. Bulgaria was divided into four revolutionary districts with headquarters at Vratsa, Sliven, Tŭrnovo and Plovdiv, and in each district apostles began once more to preach the gospel of revolt. By the spring of 1876, with Bosnia still in turmoil and Serbia on the verge of war with Turkey, a number of local revolutionary committees had been formed and from 10/22 to 13/25 April representatives from fifty-eight such bodies met at Oborishte in the woods between Panagiurishte and Koprivshtitsa. The Oborishte assembly elected a special commission which after three days of discussion decided upon a simultaneous rising in all four revolutionary districts on 13/25 May, though in the event the revolt broke out prematurely in Koprivshtitsa on 20 April/2 May.

The April uprising, if judged by its immediate accomplishments, was a disaster. There was little popular response. In the Sliven revolutionary district the rebels could muster, at the end, no more than sixty men. Around Tŭrnovo action was confined to a few isolated monasteries and villages. In Vratsa there was no popular rising at all, though it was here that Botev earned immortality. He and two hundred followers commandeered an Austrian steamer on the Danube and landed in northern Bulgaria; having advanced twenty kilometres inland Botev and his followers were slaughtered by Ottoman irregulars, or *bashibazouks*. The *bashibazouks*, most of them Bulgarian Moslems, also played a fateful role in the fourth revolutionary district, that centred upon Plovdiv. Here Benkovski had succeeded in drawing a number of villages into the struggle. His flying column, however, was no match for the *bashibazouks* who were being used because the main body of the regular Ottoman army was being deployed to meet the growing danger of war with Serbia. In southern Bulgaria these Ottoman irregulars wreaked a fearful revenge on a number of Bulgarian villages, most particularly Bratsigovo, Perushititsa and Batak. In the latter some five thousand Bulgarian Christians, most of them women and children, perished.

The rising had finished. It had not broken Ottoman authority in the Bulgarian lands but it had sharpened the national confrontation immeasurably; indeed in most areas it had created the confrontation. Yet apart from the two and a half thousand who fought with the Serbs in the Serbo-Turkish War there were few Bulgarians who were in any position yet to do anything constructive with their newly-roused national passions. Their fate and that of their nation now rested with European diplomacy for in addition to sharpening the national confrontation in Bulgaria the April rising and the atrocities which it provoked had made the Bulgarian problem one of international concern. Reports of the Batak massacres had aroused a storm of indignation in many European nations. In Russia, naturally, Orthodox and Panslav opinion had been outraged. By December the ambassadors of the great powers in Constantinople had begun meeting to work out a scheme of reforms whereby the subjects of the Sultan were to be saved from further tribulation and the powers were to be spared the fears of a war over the Eastern Question.

The deliberations of the Constantinople ambassadorial conference produced an admirable scheme of reform for the Ottoman Empire but could not persuade the Sultan that there should be European inspection of its application. The Russians were insistent that the application of the reforms be guaranteed in this way and with the Sultan remaining obdurate the Tsar declared war in April 1877. The Russian army, with its right wing protected by the Rumanians, crossed the Danube in June. Its progress thereafter was not as rapid as had been expected despite help from the newly-formed local Bulgarian *opŭlchenie* (militia). An advanced detachment under General Gurko did manage to free Tŭrnovo and force its way through the Balkan mountains only to be turned back at Stara Zagora by a large Ottoman force recently arrived victorious from the Serbo-Turkish War. Gurko dug in in the Shipka pass where, with the help of local Bulgarians, they withstood fearsome assaults. The main body of the army was in the meantime bogged down in the seige of Pleven to the north of the central mountains. For five months the Ottoman garrison held out but once it had

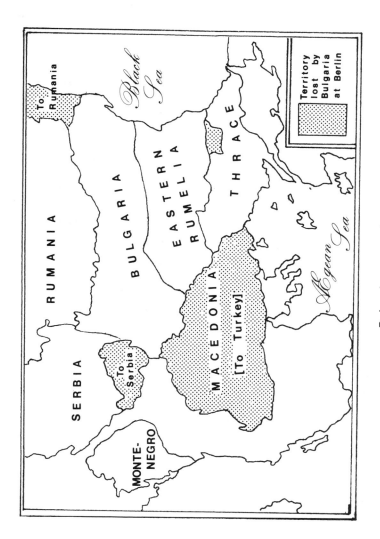

Bulgaria according
to the treaties of San Stefano and Berlin

capitulated, in December 1877, the Russian army could move rapidly forward. In January 1878 Sofia was taken and thereafter the Russians pressed speedily south-eastwards until the Turks signed a truce at Adrianople later in the same month. On 19 February/3 March the Turks signed a peace treaty at the village of San Stefano on the outskirts of Constantinople.

The treaty of San Stefano created a Bulgaria whose geographic extent was enormous. The northern limits were to be formed by the Danube, though the northern Dobrudja was to be included in Rumania. In the west the Bulgarian border was to follow the river Timok from its junction with the Danube southwards to a point somewhat north of a line drawn from Pirot to Nish; it then ran south and west towards the river Drin thus leaving in Bulgarian hands all of the Vardar valley, Skopje included. After following the southward line of the Drin the frontier struck westward to touch the Aegean coast near Salonika and then join it permanently at the gulf of Rendina, thus including in the new state Ohrid, Bitolja (Monastir), Kastoria, Seres and the mouth of the Vardar, though Salonika itself was to remain an Ottoman possession. The Bulgarian border left the Aegean coastline to follow the river Despata to the heights of the Rhodope mountains along which it marched eastward towards the Black Sea, swooping southwards to include Lule Burgas in Bulgaria but leaving Adrianople to the Turks. San Stefano Bulgaria gave the new nation almost all it could ask in territorial terms and was to remain for generations after 1878 the national ideal of the Bulgarian people. It was far too much, however, for the politicians of London and Vienna who saw in it a vast wedge of Russian influence in the Balkans. Furious diplomatic activity resulted in the calling of an international congress in Berlin where the frontiers of the new state were drastically trimmed. The new Principality was to be confined to the area between the Danube and the Balkan mountains. To the south of this range was to be a new creation, Eastern Rumelia, an autonomous province of the Ottoman Empire whose southern limits were to follow the San Stefano line across the Rhodopes and then to continue eastwards to the Black Sea without the generous southward diversion of the previous line. The whole of Macedonia was to be returned to Ottoman rule with a promise of reforms in its administration, whilst in the north-west a narrow but valuable strip of territory, including the towns of Pirot and Vranya, was to be handed to Serbia. The Exarchist sees of Nish, Pirot and Veles had been lost to Bulgaria and the total land area of the Principality reduced from the 172,000 square kilometres of San Stefano Bulgaria to the 64,500 square kilometres of the Berlin variant.

The status of the Principality as defined in Berlin was no different from that decided upon at San Stefano. Bulgaria was to be an autonomous Principality with a Christian ruler and a national militia, but it was still to pay tribute to the Sultan and acknowledge his suzerainty. The Berlin agreement also followed its predecessor in decreeing that the Prince of the new autonomous unit was to be elected by the Bulgarians subject to the confirmation of the Porte and the great powers; members of the dynasties reigning in the great powers were ineligible for election. Other stipulations concerning the internal organisation of the new Principality were copies almost without alteration from the San Stefano settlement. Before the election of a Prince an Assembly of Notables must meet at Tŭrnovo to draw up a constitution which was to guarantee freedom of worship to all faiths and was to avoid all forms of discrimination on the grounds of religion. Whilst the constitution was being defined Bulgaria was to be ruled by a Russian Provisional Administration acting in consultation with the Porte and consular representatives of the other signatory powers. The new Principality was to be bound by the international obligations of the Ottoman Empire with regard to tariffs and railways. The former meant a significant limitation on the freedom of the new state and the latter was to cause considerable difficulties by involving it in obligations to purchase the Ruse to Varna line and to construct the Bulgarian section of the international trunk route from Vienna to Constantinople. Furthermore, in the new Principality those foreigners who in the Ottoman Empire enjoyed the protection of the Capitulations were to continue to enjoy the same rights. The new Bulgarian government was also obliged to pay not only an annual tribute to the Sultan, at a rate to be fixed by the powers, but also a proportionate share of the Ottoman Public Debt, with the great powers again fixing the sum involved. The Ottoman army was to leave Bulgarian soil but the new state was to be required, at its own expense, to demolish all fortifications on its territory and was forbidden to build new ones. Finally, the property rights of all Moslems and others who chose to reside outside the Principality whilst retaining land within it, were to be protected, and a joint Bulgarian-Turkish commission was to be established to settle the questions of Ottoman state and *vakŭf* properties.

The treaty of Berlin declared that Eastern Rumelia was to be under the direct political and military authority of the Sultan. The Sultan was to be allowed to erect and man fortresses along the Rumelian-Bulgarian border though he was not permitted to place in those fortresses either *bashibazouks* or Circassians, nor were Ottoman troops in transit through the region to be billeted on the local population. The maintenance of internal order was to be entrusted to a locally-recruited gendarmerie whose composition was to reflect the interests and relative strengths of all ethnic groups in the locality. Officers of the gendarmerie were to be appointed by the Sultan. If there were a serious internal or external threat to the stability and security of Eastern Rumelia the Sultan had the right, after informing the signatory powers, to move troops into the area for its own protection (Article 16). The Governor General of Eastern Rumelia was to be nominated by the Porte and confirmed by the great powers; he was to serve for five years. His powers were to be defined by a European commission which would determine the nature of the province's judicial, financial and general administrative machinery. Like Bulgaria to its north, Rumelia was to be bound by the international obligations contracted by the Imperial Ottoman government, and once again this had major implications in questions of trade and railways. The Capitulations were also to remain in force in Rumelia.

The combined strength of the Russian forces of occupation in both Bulgaria and Rumelia was not to be greater than 50,000 and was to be paid for by the host areas. These forces were not to stay longer than nine months after the signature of the treaty.

The treaty of Berlin, which also regulated the status of other areas in the Balkans, was signed on 1/13 July 1878. The history of the modern Bulgarian state had begun.

Part I
The Price of Stability, 1878–1896

". . . whence comes this restraint?
From too much liberty . . ."

Measure for Measure, Act I, scene ii.

"Les constitutions, commes les femmes jolies, ne demandent qu'à être violées."

Prince Dondukov-Korsakov

Chapter 1

CONSTITUTION MAKING AND
CONSTITUTION BREAKING, 1878–81

As the Russian army drove the Turks out of Bulgaria a pre-planned administration was established in the conquered territory. At the head of this was the Imperial Russian Commissioner, Prince Cherkassy who, having solved by dying the difficulties his abrasive personality was causing, was replaced by Prince Dondukov-Korsakov. The Commissioner was assisted by a small bureaucracy in Sofia, which was soon to be designated the capital of the new state, with the rest of the country being divided into five provinces each of which had a governor and each of which was subdivided into districts and, at the lowest level, village communes. Communes, districts and provinces all had elected councils, though the franchise was restricted and indirect. The judicial system was based on elected village courts with an apparatus of higher and appelate courts for districts and provinces.

The personnel running the new central and provincial administrations were at the outset predominantly Russian with the Tsarist authorities intending a gradual transfer to Bulgarians during the two years which the treaty of San Stefano had allotted for the Russian occupation of the country. The treaty of Berlin cut this period to nine months from the signature of the treaty by which time all Russian personnel, military and civilian, were to leave Bulgaria and the Bulgarians were to devise for themselves a constitution and find a Prince.

These terms were, with some difficulty, respected. By the beginning of 1879 Russian civilian administrators had almost all been withdrawn and native Bulgarians had taken over the running of the Provisional Administration, though Dondukov-Korsakov remained as head of the executive until the Prince had been elected and brought safely to Bulgaria. The task of drawing up a constitution for the new state was in accordance with Article 4 of the treaty of Berlin entrusted to an Assembly of Notables. This met in the medieval Bulgarian capital, Turnovo, on 10/22 February 1879. There were approximately two hundred and thirty delegates, the exact number being obscure because a handful of them never actually attended the assembly. The majority, in all one hundred and seventeen members, attended *ex officio* and these included thirteen Bulgarian bishops, one mufti, a rabbi and some hundred and five representatives of the legal or administrative apparatus. Many of these *ex officio* members were popular and prominent local figures who would have been returned if the elected element had been larger. There were in fact eighty-nine elected members, one for every 10,000 of the adult male population. There were also five members nominated by monasteries or other institutions, and nineteen members chosen by Dondukov-Korsakov, half of these being Turks but others being figures of national importance who had not found entrance to the Assembly in any other way. There were sixteen non-Bulgarians, most of them Turks but including also some Greeks and Jews. The largest occupational group was that of teachers who numbered sixty, but there were also fifty-three who were actively engaged in trade or the craft industries; no more than a dozen at the maximum came from the small villages which were still the quintissential Bulgarian community. The Tŭrnovo Assembly of Notables, or Constituent Assembly, included representatives not only from the Bulgarian Principality as defined at Berlin but also from Rumelia, from the Bulgarian mercantile communities in Vienna, Braila and Odessa, from Bulgarian settlements in Bessarabia, and, despite Russian opposition, from the now alienated territories of Macedonia, Thrace, the Dobrudja and Nish.

The inclusion of the latter was another reminder to the powers that the Bulgarians had not yet accepted the dismemberment of the large Bulgaria established at San Stefano. The Bulgarians had also, often with the encouragement of Russian officers, rapidly formed an armed militia whose organisation and skill impressed foreign observers. Less successful was the attempt to raise a rebellion in the Kresna and Razlog (Mehomia) areas of eastern Macedonia. The rising was not well-prepared and liaison between the rebels and their supporters in Bulgaria was weak. The only result of the episode was to encourage the Turks to provoke unrest in the Moslem areas of the Rhodope mountains and to put the western powers even more on their guard as to Bulgarian intentions. The Bulgarians themselves were not yet clear as to what these intentions were but as the delegates arrived in Tŭrnovo it became obvious that there was a large body of opinion which favoured a boycott of the Constituent Assembly: better unity under the Turkish yoke than a splintering of the nation argued the extremists. Had the Bulgarians rejected the treaty of Berlin in this way the Russians would have been faced with international complications which, in their exhausted state, they could not afford, and Dondukov-Korsakov was therefore ordered to open the Assembly before the representatives disappeared. Even so, before they settled down to a discussion of the constitutional questions those delegates insisted upon debating the great issue of national unity and how the divided people should respond to the Berlin *Diktat*.

The extremists, led by Dragan Tsankov, Petko Slaveikov and Petko Karavelov, urged that the Tŭrnovo Assembly be disbanded; others argued that it should be postponed whilst a deputation pleaded the Bulgarian case in the European capitals. The most moderate line was that put forward by a small group led by Dimitŭr Grekov, Marko Balabanov, Grigor Nachovich and Konstantin Stoilov, all of whom pleaded that to offend the powers would only make matters worse and the best course in these bleak circumstances was to carry on with the Assembly whilst at the same time addressing a petition to the powers. Their cold realism was supported by the powers' representatives, including the Russian. The Assembly decided after a few days debate to establish a commission of all factions to consider and report upon the question of national unity. That report was delivered to the Assembly on 27 February/11 March and until 6/18 March the debate raged with great intensity. The commission had recommended acceptance of the moderate policy but if the members of the commission had been captured by the sense of political reality, the extremists had not, and they refused to accept the recommendation. It was an emotional week the highpoint of which was a dignified speech by the head of the Bulgarian Church, the Exarch Antim, whose peroration reduced the Assembly to unashamed tears:

> Thus saith the Lord; refrain thy voice from weeping and thine eyes from tears: for thy work shall be rewarded, said the Lord; and they shall come again from the land of the enemy.

And there is hope in thine end, saith the Lord, that thy children shall
come again into their own border.

(Jeremiah 31, 16-17)

The Exarch's speech provided the catharsis through which national
emotion was discharged; thereafter realism prevailed and on the 6/18
March the 'irreconcilables' forced the last vote on the question of
national unity and were once again defeated. As a concession to the
extremist view it was agreed to establish a new commission to draft a
petition to the powers but this was of little use for the Bulgarians were
given to understand by the Russians that it was not within the Assembly's competence to address missives to foreign governments, though
there would be no impediment to sending private messages to the
consuls in Tŭrnovo, all of whom did later receive copies of the projected petition. Having discharged its understandable emotions on the
national issue the Assembly could now set about its proper business of
defining a constitution for Bulgaria.

The constitutional debate was focused upon proposals drawn up by
Dondukov-Korsakov and submitted for preliminary perusal to a
commission of the Assembly, the commission making its own recom-
mendations to the Assembly on 21 March/2 April when the real debate
began. The most important feature of the debate was the emergence of
two distinct political attitudes which later crystallised into the Conservative and Liberal factions. The division had to a large extent
been foreshadowed in differences of attitude towards the nationalist
struggle before 1878 with those taking up a Conservative position at
Tŭrnovo being those who had held moderate or 'Old' opinions before
the Liberation. The hallmark of the Conservative was the belief that
political responsibility should be the prerogative of an educated or
administratively-experienced élite. The mass of the peasantry, they
believed, was still immature, conditioned by five hundred years of
Ottoman domination to distrust authority and thus prone more to
destruction than creation. The Conservatives alloted an important role
to foreign influence in Bulgarian affairs, Todor Ikonomov characteris-
ing both this feeling and the distrust of the native peasantry when, in
1885, he expressed the fear that Bulgarian soldiers would not have
sufficient respect for native officers and would desert at the first sign of
danger. Many, but not all Conservatives, came from wealthy mercantile backgrounds though economic issues were not at stake in the discussions of 1879.

Whilst the Conservatives patronised or, at worst, mistrusted the peasant, the Liberals idolised and to some extent idealised him. The Liberals were those who before 1878 had advocated mass action rather than secret diplomacy as the only method of securing national liberation and they covered a wide spectrum of political opinion from Karavelov, the student of Bagehot and Mill, to Stefan Stambulov who had been translating Chernyshevski when the 1876 rebellion broke out. The Liberals rejected the paternalism of the Conservatives and pressed hard for full political equality which, they argued, was only natural for a people which was blessedly free of major social divisions. Nor would they accept that the peasant lacked political experience for they regarded the village communal council as the repository of all that was best in the evolution of the nation; when, in August 1879 the new Prince dissolved the municipal council of Sofia the furious Liberals declared that not even the Turks had done such a thing and that the system of local elected self-government 'has saved our faith, our nation and our language'.[1]

The division between the two factions was most clearly expressed during the debate on whether the constitution should include a Senate. The Conservative case was put most energetically by Ikonomov. His argument began with the standard defence of the bicameral system, namely that a second chamber acts as a check upon the caprice and enthusiasm of the elected assembly. He then went on to present the Senate as a form of constitutional buffer, contending that without it the Assembly would inevitably press upon the Prince unwise measures which if accepted would harm the interests of the state and which if rejected would provoke equally debilitating constitutional conflict. Constitutional weakness would mean an enfeebled state and one which therefore would never be able to achieve the agreed national aim of the reunification of all Bulgarians. Therefore, said Ikonomov, the General Will could only be represented in a Senate. The Liberals would have none of this. Karavelov, buttressing his argument with reference to political theorists and practitioners from Plato to John Morley, stressed Bulgaria's social homogeneity and urged that this lack of division meant that the national interest would be effectively represented in a single chamber and to create a second house would only precipitate dangerous and unnecessary fissures within the nation. Slaveikov's arguments were similar but presented in a more picturesque and vernacular form. He too stressed the great uniformity of Bulgarian society and insisted that the popular will was determined that Liberation had not been brought about simply to hand the Bulgarian masses from the tyranny of the Turks to the domination of the *chorbadjii*. The Liberals may have overestimated the extent to which the Bulgarian villages were socially homogeneous and the purity of peasant democracy, but their political argument scored; in the popular mind the Conservatives, with their wealthy backgrounds and moderate political pedigrees, were inevitably associated with the *chorbadjii*. In an Assembly intoxicated with the notion of popular sovereignty Slaveikov's thrust went home. Liberal victory was assured though the final stages of the senate debate were attended by scenes of violence which ill-suited the sophistication of the content of the debate and which served as an unfortunate augury for Bulgarian party politics.

The Liberals' supremacy in the Tŭrnovo Assembly, so clearly shown in the debate on the Senate, was apparent in other sections of the constitution. The new state, the treaty of Berlin had decided, was to be an hereditary monarchy with the succession based on male primogeniture and the Constituent Assembly went on to define further the nature of the new executive. The Prince was to be appointed 'By the Grace of God and the Will of the People', was to be Commander in Chief of the armed forces, and was to represent the Principality in its relations with foreign states, though he was still a vassal of the Sultan. The Prince enjoyed the right of ministerial appointment and dismissal and chose which of his ministers was to act as Chairman of the Cabinet or Council of Ministers, the body through which the Prince's executive functions were exercised. The Prince also had the power to convene, adjourn and prorogue the legislature but this power was restricted by the constitutional enactment that only two months might elapse between prorogation and reassembly or between dissolution and new elections, and in the event of fresh elections being held the new Assembly had to meet within four months of the preceding dissolution; any emergency ordinances issued when the Assembly was not in session had to receive *post facto* approval in the legislature and the levying of taxes by emergency decree was specifically forbidden. The Prince had to give his consent to all legislation and could exercise the prerogative of mercy except in the case of ministers condemned for violation of the constitution; the right of amnesty was to be exercised jointly with the legislature. The Liberals made their suspicion of executive power felt at a number of points. They reduced the civil list from the million francs suggested by Dondukov to 600,000 francs, they insisted that the Prince should not have the right to create orders or bestow titles and decorations except those awarded for bravery in battle, and they threw out Dondukov's proposal that the Church be allowed to make grants of land to the Prince.

The legislature was to be unicameral but there were to be two types of assembly, a Grand National Sŭbranie (Assembly) and an Ordinary National Sŭbranie, a cumbersome arrangement copied from the Serbian constitution. The Grand National Assembly was to meet irregularly and was to consist of Church dignitaries, representatives of the judiciary and local government, and twice as many elected members as would sit in the Ordinary National Assembly. The Grand National Assembly was to be called to elect regents, to choose a new Prince, to sanction the loss or acquisition of territory or to change the constitution, a two thirds majority being necessary in the latter case. The Ordinary National Assembly was to be summoned every year in October, after the harvest had been gathered. Its members were to be elected for three years in the proportion of one representative for every 10,000 adult citizens. The franchise was to include every sane male over twenty-one, and every literate elector over thirty was eligible for election. These rules were also to apply for elections to councils in the provinces and districts into which the country was divided. The Sŭbranie was to sanction all legislation including the annual budget and had the right to amend bills initiated by the executive. It was to verify the accounts of the individual ministries, to question the ministers and if necessary to set up commissions to inquire into the conduct of the administration. Individual members of the Assembly were to be paid an attendance fee and expenses, and it was this which led the Liberals to restrict the length of the regular Sŭbranie session to the two months, 15/27 October to 15/27 December. It was also parsimony, combined with a suspicion of the executive, which led them to confine the number of ministries to six, those for the Interior, Justice, Education, Finance, War and finally Foreign and Religious Affairs, a combination which indicated the importance of the Church in areas containing large Bulgarian populations but still under foreign rule.

Political power and responsibility were vested jointly in the executive and the legislature. Executive authority lay with the Prince but was to be exercised through the Cabinet or Council of Ministers which had to be chosen from members of the Sŭbranie. Legislation could be initiated by the executive or the legislature but had to be approved by both, Article 153 of the constitution enshrining this doctrine of joint responsibility:

Ministers are responsible to the Prince and to the National Assembly collectively for whatever measures they take in common, and individually for the administration of the departments entrusted to them.

The constitution promised a number of individual freedoms. The Bulgarian citizen was guaranteed the inviolability of his person, his property, and his correspondence; there were to be no arbitrary arrests, nor any religious discrimination. Freedom of movement was to be unlimited, that of expression was guaranteed by the interdiction of any limitation upon the press, though publications for use in the Exarchate's religious and educational institutions had to be spiritually innocuous; freedom of association was limited to the extent that it was not to endanger the security of the state, this qualification being insisted upon by the Russians who were nervous of 'nihilist' conspiracies. In return for these freedoms the Bulgarian citizen was required to obey the law, pay taxes, send his young children to school and his young men to the army for two years' national service.

An important part of the constitution was that which regulated the relationship between Church and State. In this ever sensitive area the Liberation created some problems. It was easily decided that Orthodoxy should be the official religion which must be professed by all but the first of the Princes, but after that the difficulties began. The Church had been the first institutional expression of Bulgarian nationhood and it was through the Church after the treaty of Berlin that the Bulgarians remained in communion with their fellow nationals everywhere. Yet at the same time Orthodox canon law generally abided by the principle of 'One Church, One State'. If that were now to be applied the Exarch would have to leave his seat in Constantinople and establish himself in the Principality. This the Russians would have welcomed because it would, they believed, have made it easier to end the schism between the Exarchate and the Patriarchate. On the other hand the Bulgarians had much to fear from such a change. If the Exarch left Constantinople what would happen to the Exarchist Church in Macedonia and Thrace, or even Rumelia? In Sofia the Exarch would have little influence over the Porte and the Exarchist flock in the Ottoman Empire, which still outnumbered that in the Principality, would be in grave danger of falling once more under the domination of the Patriarch; in that eventuality the cause of Bulgarian unification would receive an insuperable setback. In the face of this feeling Dondukov's argument that an Exarch in the Turkish capital would always be subject to overbearing Turkish influence carried no weight. Article 39 of the constitution declared that the Church in the Principality was to be 'an inseparable part' of the Bulgarian Exarchate and the highest body of that Church, the Holy Synod, was to have its seat in Sofia. The Exarch, however, was to remain in Constantinople. As the Exarch Yosif wrote later, 'Dondukov wanted the Exarch to be in Sofia, near the Prince . . . but I told him that we understood our own interests better'.[2] Religious salt was not to be rubbed into the political wounds inflicted in Berlin.

Many contemporaries wondered that Imperial Russia could preside over the granting of so liberal a constitution. Yet Russia could not leave the Bulgarians with a political structure less free than that of its neighbours, especially the Rumelians whose separate existence was the work of Russia's opponents. St Petersburg recognised that if Bulgaria were noticeably less free than Rumelia then union, when it came, could take the form of the absorption of Bulgaria into Rumelia, that is the disappearance of Russia's creation and the enlargement of that of her opponents. Nor were the Russians blind to the fact that because the treaty of Berlin had decided that the Prince was to be neither a Russian nor a Bulgarian it would be no bad thing to hedge his power and balance his influence by that of Russophile popular opinion. At the same time it is easy to exaggerate the democratic nature of the Tŭrnovo constitution. The people had not been declared sovereign, there was no provision for the independence of the judiciary, nor was there a specific statement that the constitution could not be suspended. The obstacles it attempted to place in the way of electoral corruption were totally inadequate and the misconduct of elections together with systematic malversion of state funds soon became glaring contrasts to the theoretical rulings of the constitution. The most serious flaw in the constitution, however, was the lack of any machinery to ensure it was obeyed and thus too much depended on the integrity of those who were to implement it, primarily the Prince, the members of the government and the Sŭbranie deputies.

When the constitutional debates had been concluded it became an immediate priority to find a Prince. The choice fell upon Prince Alexander of Battenberg, whose name was first put forward by the Russians. Alexander had many advantages. The Bulgarians rejoiced in the fact that he had served with the Russian army in the war of 1877–8, and his youth—he was only twenty-two—served to increase his attraction. The Tsar had been doubtful about the candidature but had been won

over by his wife, an aunt of Alexander's. The Austrians welcomed him
for he was the son of an Austrian general and Bismarck would not
object to anyone on whom Vienna and St Petersburg were agreed. The
French were happy because they imagined Alexander and his family to
be anti-Prussian, and the diplomatic circle was finally squared because
Alexander was acceptable not only to the Tsar but also to Queen
Victoria to whom he was related and by whom he was much liked. On
17/29 April Bulgaria's first Grand National Sŭbranie assembled in
Tŭrnovo and five days later voted unanimously to offer the throne to
the young Hessian. It remained to convince only Alexander himself.
This was not easy. He thought the Bulgarian constitution 'absolutely
ridiculous' and these opinions were confirmed by constitutional lawyers in Darmstadt.[3] Assurances from the Tsar, however, that he would
never leave Alexander without support in Bulgaria finally won over the
young Prince who by the end of June, after a tour of the European
capitals, presented himself to his new suzerain in Constantinople. It
was not a happy meeting for Alexander offended the Sultan by wearing Bulgarian national costume with a *kalpak* or fur cap rather than
the fez expected of all good vassals.

From Constantinople Alexander went by way of an unusually turbu-
lent Black Sea to Varna, setting foot in his new country on 24 June/6
July. From varna he travelled to Tŭrnovo where he was to take
power from the Imperial Russian Commissioner. As an augury of
Alexander's future relations with the liberating power his meeting with
Dondukov was not encouraging for the two disliked one another
immediately and intensely. The populace, it seemed, sided with
Dondukov rather than Alexander for when, two days later, the Prince
set out for Sofia there were few to see him off whereas on the same day
huge crowds bid Dondukov an emotional farewell. Yet this was natural. Dondukov was the last remaining link with the Russian administration which had replaced Ottoman rule; he was an established hero
whereas Alexander had yet to make his reputation. Alexander's spirits
revived, however, as he progressed towards his new capital for he
sensed a steady increase in the warmth of his reception; in Sofia itself
the festivities to celebrate his arrival lasted a full seven days.

When the celebrating had subsided Alexander and the Bulgarians set
about implementing the political system devised at Tŭrnovo. Within a
few months it was clear that this would not be an easy business and
Bulgarian politics rapidly took the form of a non-too-decorous quad-
rille danced by four separate political factors.

At the centre of the dance was the Prince. His major political strength was his right to appoint ministers, his chief weakness his inability to exercise this right with tact and moderation, and Bulgarian politics were to suffer considerably from his unshifting conviction that all who did not subscribe to the principles and practices of Bismarckian conservatism were dangerous subversives. Alexander was held in considerable awe by the populace but he did little to invest this political capital. He spent most of his time in the company of leading Conservatives such as Stoilov and Burmov, and had no social dealings with popular leaders on the Liberal side. What was even more damaging in popular eyes was Alexander's obvious inability to cooperate with influential Russians in Sofia.

The Russians were very much a part of Bulgarian politics and their major strength was the popular respect they enjoyed. In more concrete terms the Russians had great influence over the new Bulgarian army for most of the officers and all the senior officers in that body were Russian. So too was the Minister of War. This meant that any policy, be it in the direction of national reunification or a drastic revision of the constitution, adventurous enough to need the support of the army was therefore at the mercy of a Russian, for though the Minister of War was technically in the Bulgarian service he could never forget his duty to his own sovereign in St Petersburg. The weakness of the Russian position in Bulgaria was that one Russian did not always pursue the same goal as another. The Russian foreign service in the nineteenth century was notoriously susceptible to individual initiative by its functionaries and this was seen in Bulgaria; Bulgaria also witnessed clear distinctions of policy between Russia's military and diplomatic representatives in the country, particularly in the early months after Alexander of Battenberg's arrival when the Russian diplomatic agent, Davydov, supported the Prince in his designs against the constitution whilst the Minister of War, Parensov, strenuously resisted those designs.

The Conservatives were the weakest of the four political forces. Their paternalist attitudes made them natural allies of the Prince whose confidence many of the Conservatives enjoyed. They also had considerable wealth at their disposal and this enabled them to maintain a rightist press, represented first by *Vitosha* (1879–80) and *Bŭlgarski Glas* (Voice of Bulgaria) which began where *Vitosha* left off and appeared for four years under the editorship of Grekov, Stoilov and Ikonomov. Like other newspapers they appeared twice or thrice weekly but, again typically, did not exercise much political influence, the Austrian agent thinking in May 1880 that it was not worthwhile buying control of a Bulgarian newspaper. The wealth of the Conservatives could not make good their chief deficiency, their lack of popular support. This had been underlined at Tŭrnovo when they were branded with the mark of *chorbadjii* and was not lessened by their western image, for unlike most educated Liberals whose schooling had been received in Russia, a number of leading Conservatives had western training. The Conservatives suffered also from a number of personality clashes, particularly that between Ikonomov and Nachovich, and from their inability to compete with the Liberals in the hurly-burly of Sŭbranie politics.

Where the Conservatives were weak the Liberals were strong for they enjoyed widespread popular support, as both the Constituent and the Grand National Assemblies in Tŭrnovo had shown. The Liberals were also better organised than their Conservative opponents, particularly in Tŭrnovo which the young Stambulov had turned into a personal political fiefdom. The Liberals were also much helped by the Conservative determination to resist popular sovereignty for this united what might otherwise have been a much divided group. On the left of the Liberal Party stood men such as Zahary Stoyanov, Nikola Suknarov and Stefan Stambulov whose advanced views owed a good deal to the revolutionary hero Hristo Botev and not a little to the Russian Populists. They were also in touch with Socialists in other Balkan states and some socialist ideas were present in papers such as Suknarov's *Nezavisimost* (Independence) published in Sofia and provincial papers such as *Bratstvo* (Fraternity) in Ruse and *Rabotnik* (Worker) in Varna. The most powerful faction was that in the centre of the Party headed by Petko Karavelov and Petko Slaveikov, both of whom in word if not always in deed stood by the classical liberal doctrines of political liberty and civil rights. Petko Karavelov, brother of Liuben, soon earned his own political spurs; after a somewhat chequered education he gained a certificate of law from Moscow University and went on to serve as deputy governor of Vidin in the Russian Provisional Administration. Armed thus with legal qualifications and administrative experience and uncompromised by association with any political faction before the Liberation, Karavelov rapidly established a dominant influence over the Constituent Assembly. Slaveikov lacked the intellectual breadth of Karavelov but performed the invaluable service of presenting ideas in a picturesque form easily understood by the Bulgarian peasant. The third and most moderate wing within the Liberals was that led by Dragan Tsankov who was more willing than other Liberal leaders to compromise with the moderate Conservatives. Tsankov had served the Bulgarian cause for so long that all Liberals paid him deference and recognised him as the titular leader of the Party. Tsankov's many years in the Ottoman civil service had made him wise in the ways of politicans but it had not taught him consistency and even his most obvious political characteristic, his ardent Russophilia, was liable to variations of intensity.

In addition to these four main forces Bulgarian politics in the immediate post-Liberation period were also affected by factors such as the Church and, of course, international developments. For the first two years after the formulation of the constitution, however, the chief struggle was an internal one: that between the Prince and the Conservatives on one side and the Liberals on the other. The Russians attempted to preserve their neutrality but their failure to join with the Prince and their refusal to consent to his plans for a change in the constitution meant that their neutrality was to the benefit of the Liberals.

In July 1879 Alexander was faced with the need to appoint his first Cabinet. His preference, despite the strongly pro-Liberal national opinion revealed in the Constituent and Grand National Assemblies, was for a Conservative administration. The Russians pressed him to try for a coalition and this he did. Much to his relief personal animosities made this impossible and a purely Conservative ministry was formed with Todor Burmov being nominated Chairman of the Council of Ministers or Minister President. Grekov and Nachovich were also included in the ministry; the Minister of War was the Russian Colonel Parensov.

The administration occupied itself with several tasks including a number of alterations to the governmental machine established by the Russians. It also tackled the very difficult problem of what to do with returning Moslem refugees who found their property had been seized by Bulgarians, a problem which will be discussed in detail in a subsequent chapter. A further difficulty was that of brigandage. The mountainous areas of the Balkans had always provided shelter for bandits and after the departure of Russian troops in 1879, particularly in the hills between the river Yantra and the coast, a number of Moslem bands were organised with the express purpose of settling accounts with the local Christians. The most serious incident was in June when the town of Omurtag (Osman Pazar) had come under siege for two hours and one of Burmov's first acts, therefore, was to place the Varna province and parts of the Ruse and Tŭrnovo districts under martial law. These measures were not entirely successful for in the autumn peasants in some areas were still too frightened to go out into the fields.

The population and the Liberals accepted the need for measures against brigands but the government came into sharp conflict with the Liberals on a number of constitutional issues. For the Liberals the constitution was of paramount importance. The national liberation movement had been frustrated in its efforts to achieve a united Bulgaria, but it had left Bulgarians in the principality with political freedom. The constitution was the guarantee of that freedom and was therefore also the guardian of the achievements of the national liberation movement. For the Liberals the constitution was sacrosanct and to defile it even in the most insignificant way a sin equal almost to treason. Alexander Battenberg held other opinions. He regarded the constitution in general as 'an act of negligence or ignorance on the part of the Russians' and the Sŭbranie in particular he saw as 'a dangerous plaything in the hands of a young people'.[4] The Conservatives shared the Prince's view.

Their sensitivity on the constitutional issues made the Liberals react to the slightest infringement of the new holy writ. Thus when the Prince wanted to use the title *visochestvo* (Highness) rather than the *svetlost* (Serenity or Excellency) prescribed by the Tŭrnovo constitution, there were fierce protests by the Liberals and, significantly, by Parensov who only reluctantly agreed that documents in his ministry should use the lower title if written in Bulgarian and ascend to the higher one if in French. This was far from being the *opéra bouffe* it might appear for Parensov's stance showed the Liberals they could count on some Russian support. A second and more serious clash came about when the Prince issued the decree allowing himself the right to nominate half the members of city councils. The Liberals were also suspicious, and here they enjoyed unequivocal Russian support, that the Prince was trying to increase German influence in the Principality at the cost of Russian. The new national army was at the centre of this controversy. Alexander wished to introduce German methods of drill and training and, more seriously, German officers. Parensov resisted. German officers could be employed, he argued, only with the consent of the Sŭbranie and this would never be given, and if it were, he asked, how were German officers to cope with the language problem? After much discussion Alexander was allowed in 1880 to import two German officers for his personal staff; he had asked for over five hundred.

Liberal anger at these moves was expressed in a number of ways, one of the most effective being a popular song. More conventional methods included attacks on the ministry in newspapers such as Stambulov's *Tselokupna Bŭlgariya* (Undivided Bulgaria) and in *Nezavisimost*. There were also a series of protest meetings beginning with one in Tŭrnovo, and many of these attracted large crowds. Popular anger at government policies was increased by economic distress. The recent increase in the salt tax had been unpopular; the rouble, still the main unit of currency, was worth less in Bulgaria than in Rumania, which gave rise to speculation and cash shortages in the northern areas of the Principality; the war had disrupted the traditional pattern of trade which relied very much on the Ottoman market and, most important of all, the country was suffering from a prolonged drought which threatened to ruin the harvest.

The government could do nothing to improve the weather but it could act to contain discontent. The ministers were conscious that many government employees, especially at the local level, were actively engaged in the Liberal campaign and it therefore purged the bureaucracy of its opponents, the most prominent victim being Petko Slaveikov who, after the Constituent Assembly, had been made prefect of Tŭrnovo province. The purge set an irresistible precedent.

Alexander would have liked to go much further and postpone the Sŭbranie elections due to be held at the end of September. This, however, would be so major a breach of the constitution that it could not be effected without Russian consent. Davydov supported the Prince but Parensov did not and his view prevailed. Russian objections were understandable. So early a repudiation of the constitution which she had done so much to devise would be a severe dent in Russia's prestige abroad. More seriously, if the Prince's action were contested and the Russian-officered Bulgarian army employed to suppress civil disorder Russia's hard won influence in the new state would be destroyed. Besides Russia had no wish to increase Alexander's and the Conservatives' power, for they were too pro-German. Finally Alexander was dissuaded from his *coup d'état* by his moderate-minded *aide-de-camp,* Colonel Shepelev.

The elections therefore went ahead with troops being stationed in a number of towns. In each constituency an electoral bureau was established to organise the voting and both Parties realised immediately that control of this body was the key to electoral success for it could be used to falsify returns, exclude opponents, or otherwise secure the desired outcome. In later years such methods were to determine the results but in 1879 Liberal opinion was so strong that it could not be suppressed. In the first ordinary Sŭbranie, therefore, the government of Burmov could count on the votes of only about thirty of the one hundred and seventy members.

The dispute between the Liberals and the executive found immediate expression in the Assembly. Liberal complaints that the Prince wore his *kalpak* during the speech from the throne met with a patronising lecture on how parliamentary affairs were conducted 'in Europe'; the Prince also clung to the title 'Highness'. More serious was the Liberal complaint that the speech from the throne, though containing fulsome praise and thanks for Russia, did not mention Alexander II which, said the Liberals, was an insult to the Tsar Liberator. The government soon launched a counter-attack by trying to have Stambulov excluded from the Assembly on the grounds that he was too young. The government lost and the Liberal extremist was much increased in prestige. The government then annulled the elections in the town of Svishtov where, it was claimed, there had been irregularities; fresh elections would be held when the government saw fit. The latter point roused the Liberals to fury for if the executive were allowed to decide the date of by-elections it could mean the postponement *sine die* of any contest which the Liberals would undoubtedly win. The Liberals were now determined to secure the appointment of a ministry with which they could cooperate and they were in a strong position to do so because with the Russians having vetoed a change in the constitution the government must soon come to the Sŭbranie with its budget proposals; were these to be rejected the government would collapse. In fact there was no need to wait for the budget proposals. The Sŭbranie voted for the exclusion of the Conservative members from the Assembly and then passed a vote of censure on the government. Burmov and his colleagues resigned.

Again acting upon Russian advice Alexander sought for a second time to engineer a coalition and this time Karavelov showed signs of interest, being willing to accept as the price of office the Prince's conditions that some restrictions be placed upon the freedom of the press,

that the title 'Highness' be recognised, and that future speeches from
the throne need not include thanks to both Russia and its ruler. These
conditions, however, were too much for the Liberals in the Sŭbranie
who were organised by Stambulov. Even the Russians now had to
accept that the attempted coalition would not come about and with
their consent the Sŭbranie was dissolved on 24 November/6 December.
The following day a new ministry under the Metropolitan Kliment was
appointed. It was predominantly Conservative.

Kliment took office reluctantly, agreeing to serve as a caretaker
Minister President until the elections had been held. His government
therefore did little to initiate new legislation, and though it was responsible for setting up a model agricultural school near Ruse, it generally
contented itself with continuing the previous administration's work in
the suppression of brigandage and the rationalisation of the administration. It also took steps to alleviate food shortages, purchasing 100,000
francs worth of grain and selling it cheaply to those in need, and at the
same time setting up a welfare organisation to help destitute refugees
from Macedonia. Kliment's personal dislike of party politics was
reflected in decrees stating that officials could be dismissed for professional reasons only and insisting that the government should not exercise pressure on voters during a general election. This was crying in the
wind.

In the meantime Liberal attacks on the ministry continued and the
number of Liberal votes cast in the elections of January and February
1880 was greater than in 1879, though, as in the first elections, a second
polling day was necessary in many constituencies because the victorious candidates had not received the twenty-five percent of the possible
vote which the electoral law made the condition for a valid return.
Alexander would have liked to avoid the elections and, after they had
been held, to delay calling the Sŭbranie, for without a change in the
constitution it would inevitably mean the end of the Conservative
ministry. The Prince therefore used the celebrations for the twenty-
fifth anniversary of the Tsar's accession as a pretext to visit St Petersburg where he pleaded for Russian consent to a change in the
Bulgarian constitution. Alexander II would not agree. He pointed out
that such a step would damage Bulgarian and Russian prestige and it
would be unfair to make a change before the Liberals had been given a
chance to govern; if after they had been given such a chance they still
made life impossible for the Prince then the Tsar would reconsider his
decision. Alexander II then announced he was recalling Davydov

which, said Nachovich, was 'the heaviest blow' the Conservatives had suffered.[5] The blow was softened when, after much pressure, the Tsar agreed to recall Parensov too. His replacement as Minister of War was General Ehrenroth who was to prove far more valuable to the Conservatives than Davydov had ever been.

Given the Tsar's refusal to agree to a change in the constitution Alexander was bound by constitutional law to call the Sŭbranie within two months of the elections. Thus the Second Ordinary National Assembly was opened on 22 March/3 April 1880. On the previous day Kliment had resigned.

Alexander now had to offer power to the Liberals and a ministry was formed by Tsankov who became Minister President and Minister for Foreign Affairs. Karavelov was made Minister of Finance and these two, with Ehrenroth, were the dominant figures, the others being somewhat colourless moderate Liberals. Slaveikov, who had hoped to become Minister of Education, was made President of the Sŭbranie.

For the first time Bulgaria now had a ministry which enjoyed the confidence of the Sŭbranie and a large amount of constructive and reforming legislation was therefore prepared, Alexander's speech from the throne mentioning fourteen major items. Most of these dealt with the administration of justice, the organisation of the educational system, and the regulation of the nation's finances. In the latter domain Karaelov's word went unchallenged and his legislation included the introduction of a new and specifically Bulgarian coinage based on the *lev**, equal to the French franc and divided into one hundred *stotinki.**** Karavelov held to nineteenth-century notions of state financing and therefore pared government expenditure wherever he could, cutting the salaries of army officers, civil servants, and bishops and ending various state subsidies such as that to the Model Agricultural School, though military and bureaucratic salaries were soon to rise again. Karavelov also did what he could to reform the tax system, though he sensibly refused to end the Ottoman practice of having a multiplicity of small taxes. Karavelov knew this was inefficient and irrational but he also knew that people pay most readily those taxes with which they are familiar, and for this reason he did not carry out the Liberal promise to substitute a land tax for the tithe, though the

---

*Lev, plural leva, means lion, that being the national emblem.
**Stotinki means hundredths.

latter was now to be paid in cash rather than kind. Overall there was a slight reduction in taxes but despite this, and notwithstanding the familiarity of the levies, there was some popular resistance to tax collection, perhaps because some peasants had taken seriously Liberal promises that once in office they would abolish or greatly reduce the burden. In some instances the authorities were forced to execute the recalcitrant.

Whilst his colleagues were designing the administrative structure of the state Ehrenroth tackled the old problem of brigandage, thrown into particularly sharp focus by the murder in June of the wife of the great Slav hero, General Skobolev, who was travelling through Bulgaria without her husband. A battle near the village of Belibe (Bulair) in April/May had already persuaded the Sŭbranie to grant the Minister of War emergency powers and these he used to good effect. The army was concentrated in the disturbed areas, the local Turks were disarmed and the army, having required each community to form an armed detachment, made it responsible for the maintenance of order within its own boundaries. Failure meant condign punishment. These measures, together with the end of encouragement from Constantinople, meant that the problem of brigandage subsided.

Neither this success nor the spate of reformist legislation meant that the conflict between the Liberals and the Prince had ended. The Liberals, it is true, had made some concessions. They had followed the Tsar and accepted the use of the title 'Highness' for the Prince, and the parsimonious Karavelov had even agreed to spend state funds on making Alexander's residence, the old Turkish *konak*, more worthy of the name 'palace'. Yet the Prince was still wary and convinced that the Liberals were little more than nihilists. Nor had the Liberals lost their fear of the executive. Soon after they took office the Prince had asked for the recall of his Russian *aide-de-camp*, the moderately pro-Liberal, Colonel Shepelev, and this Tsankov saw as a trick to compromise the new ministry in the eyes of its more extreme supporters in the Sŭbranie.

An even more important conflict arose over the sacred issue of national reunification. This goal had not been forgotten during the constitutional wranglings of the previous months and hopes had been rekindled by Gladstone's return to office in Britain. In April the Prince's private secretary, the Conservative Stoilov, together with three members of the Sŭbranie, visited Plovdiv. There it was agreed with local enthusiasts to establish a central committee for the achievement

of a unified Bulgarian state, and both sides accepted the need for both
Bulgaria and Rumelia to coordinate their policies and institutions
wherever possible. In a secret session the Sŭbranie agreed to subsidise
the Rumelians to the tune of 8,000 leva. On 10/22 May nationalist
groups in Rumelia met secretly in Sliven with Stambulov and another
Sŭbranie deputy, Zhivkov; Bulgaria's help was promised as long as
local action was correctly timed, that is that it did not embarrass
Russia. At the same time Panaretov, who had been educated at Robert
College in Constantinople, was sent to make soundings in London.
Knowledge of what was afoot was soon made public and provoked a
series of warnings from the powers that the *status quo* must be preserved. Alexander was not entirely cowed. A bold attempt to further
union would certainly strengthen him at home and so before he left for
St Petersburg to attend the funeral of his aunt, the Empress Maria
Alexandrovna, he suggested to the Cabinet that the army be mobolised
and the union with Rumelia declared and, if necessary, defended.
Alexander has often been accused of political naivety and incompetence, but this was an astute move. Had the Liberal ministers accepted
the plan they would have fallen foul of the Tsar who wanted no disturbance of the peace. This would transform the political climate in Bulgaria for the Liberals deprived of Russian support could never defend
their constitution against a Prince engaged actively in the sacred work
of reunification. If, on the other hand, the Liberals demurred, Alexander could taunt them with the accusation that they valued the good-
will of the Tsar more highly than national unity. Tsankov solved the
dilemma by revealing all to the Russians and Alexander was rebuked
by the Tsar for his adventurism. For the Prince it showed that Tsankov
held no more allegiance to him than he did to the Tsar who was, after
all, a foreign sovereign. Alexander determined upon Tsankov's fall.

The removal of Tsankov would also solve another problem which
greatly worried Alexander and the Conservatives, that of the Liberals'
Militia Bill. This aimed to provide Bulgaria with a militia similar to
that in Rumelia and was part of the programme to create parallel
institutions, but it was also used by the Liberals as a means to create an
alternative to the armed force which the executive had at its disposal.
Thus in the proposed militia not only would all officers be elected
by those over whom they held command but the supreme command
would rest with a six-man central committee appointed by the
Subranie. The Bill produced both the longest debate the Subranie had
yet experienced and the most intense clash between the Liberals and

the Prince's camp. The Liberals saw the proposed citizens' army as a defence against the coup which they believed Alexander was planning to effect through the army. Alexander for his part saw in the militia confirmation of his worst fears as to Liberal intentions; the proposed force would, he said, be 'ideal for a revolutionary army',[6] whilst Ehrenroth drew an analogy with the Paris Commune. Luckily for the Conservatives the Liberals squabbled amongst themselves over procedural issues with the result that an entirely new bill had to be submitted to the Sŭbranie and this contained a reasonable compromise for though officers were still to be elected command of the whole militia was to be vested in the ministerial council thus preserving Alexander's constitutional position as head of the armed forces.

Before the compromise on the Militia Bill had been found the Liberals had alarmed the Conservatives in other ways. The Sŭbranie had adopted the common parliamentary procedure of verifying all election results and this the extremists used to exclude as many of their opponents as they could, even though their arguments were often dubious and were not similarly applied to the government benches.

The Conservatives were also concerned at Tsankov's attack upon the higher dignitaries of the Church. The first clash came when Tsankov, bending to pressure from the western powers, ordered the annulment of all baptisms of Moslem children and all marriages of Moslem women to Christian men carried out during the recent war. Such an annulment, said the Exarch, was illegal. Tsankov was undeterred and soon angered the religious hierarchy, already displeased by the reductions in their stipends, by enacting regulations concerning the Church's temporal affairs. Ecclesiastical protestations that this too was illegal were swept aside and then Tsankov intensified the conflict by announcing a radical reorganisation of the Church's administration under which the number of bishops would be drastically reduced and the influence of the lower clergy increased. This, said the Minister President, would remove the alien, hierarchical structure which the Greeks had imposed upon a democratic, Slav Church. By the time Tsankov's plans reached the Sŭbranie in the autumn he had been anathematised and had accumulated a powerful set of enemies, most notably the Russian Holy Synod and the Bulgarian bishops. Their combined weight was too much for Tsankov and when the Bill came back to the Sŭbranie from the final drafting committee it had been shorn of all its contentious clauses.

Tsankov was making enemies abroad as well as at home. All the diplomatic representatives in Sofia were offended by his brusque methods and by his over-sensitivity to any sign of Bulgaria's vassal status, a sensitivity which led him to make complaints to the Austrians that one of their vessels on the Danube had not respected the Bulgarian flag and that a number of their consuls were still wearing the fez. With the French there was a long argument over the Cabinet's desire to dismiss a French financial advisor whose salary of 40,000 leva per annum offended Karavelov and his colleagues, not least because their own income was only 12,000 leva. Britain complained at the number of Russian officers with the Bulgarian army, at the failure to dismantle fortifications in the Principality, and at the Bulgarian government's refusal to purchase the British-owned Ruse to Varna railway. This purchase and the destruction of the forts had been written into the treaty of Berlin. The treaty also required the Bulgarian government to construct that part of the Vienna to Constantinople railway which ran through its territory. This was an item of very serious disagreement with Austria. The Bulgarians could not yet afford to build railways and they therefore stalled on this issue, exploiting some ambiguity about the route which the line was to take. The Bulgarians in fact were pressing that the line should follow the original *tracé* from Sofia via Kumanovo and Skopje to Nish, whereas the latest proposal foresaw a line linking Sofia and Nish via Tsaribrod and Pirot. It was a most important issue because the original route would have linked Bulgaria with the main towns of northern Macedonia and the railway question was therefore linked to the national one. This the Austrians knew for they were not anxious to see Bulgaria expand into Macedonia; the Ballhausplatz might not have been seriously considering 'running down to Salonika' but it did not want Bulgaria expanding in that direction, particularly if such expansion were to the detriment of Serbian ambitions, for Serbia was at this time a client state of Austria. Tsankov was thus much mistrusted in Vienna which, correspondingly, welcomed Alexander's plans to be rid of his Minister President.

The most important and startling development under Tsankov, however, was not the coolness between the Liberals and the Austrians, for that had always existed, but a weakening in the alignment of the Russians with the Liberals.

There had been signs of this even before Tsankov took office. On the day on which Alexander had arrived in St Petersburg in February 1880 the terrorist threat to the Tsar has been underlined by the explosion of

matic success, the assassination of Alexander II on 1/13 March 1881.
This transformed the political situation in Bulgaria as well as Russia.

The Liberals immediately denounced the murder of the Tsar Liberator, with *Nezavisimost* praising his memory and cursing his assassins in
unequivocal terms. Yet despite such clear statements rumours, much
encouraged by unscrupulous Conservatives, were soon current that the
Liberals condoned such acts of political violence, and a letter published in the Varna socialist paper, *Rabotnik*, was taken as confirmation of these allegations. The letter, signed 'an educated worker',
bemoaned the assassination but also hoped that it might produce
reform in Russia, and this was interpreted as welcoming the *attentat* as
a beneficial act. Such wild exaggeration fitted in well with the mood of
near hysteria in Conservative circles where a law and order lobby had
already appeared following an alarming rise in crime in Sofia, much of
it the result of the gun-toting frontier atmosphere which then prevailed
in the capital. Ehrenroth put himself at the head of this lobby and
when the Prince returned from the funeral in St Petersburg the Minister of War told him that if determined efforts were not made to save
the country from anarchy he would resign and resume his commission
in the Russian army.

Alexander needed no encouragement. In Russia he had been well
received by the new Tsar, Alexander III, and the reactionary atmosphere in St Petersburg meant that though he received no express official approval for a coup the Prince did not meet with discouragement.
Berlin, meanwhile, was neutral and Vienna positively encouraging and
the Prince therefore determined upon action. After consultation with
all the diplomatic agents with the exception of Kumani's successor,
Khitrovo, he issued a proclamation on 27 April/9 May announcing the
dismissal of the Karavelov government and the formation of a new
ministry under General Ehrenroth who in addition to being Minister
President was also to be Minister for Foreign Affairs and Minister of
the Interior. Alexander declared that this action had been forced on
him as the only way to preserve stability; he was not, he said, acting in
defiance of the constitution but in its defence for he was exercising his
power to dismiss a ministry and at the same time he gave notice that a
Grand National Assembly would be summoned to which he would
submit proposals for constitutional change. If these were not accepted
he would abdicate.

Acceptance of the coup depended on both the Russians and the
Liberals. The Russian representatives in Sofia, Khitrovo, Lyshin and

Ehrenroth, all favoured Alexander's action as did most leading figures in St Petersburg. The only doubting voice was that of the Russian War Ministry which argued that to allow Alexander to assume personal power would be to hand Bulgaria over to German influence but this argument the Foreign Ministry turned around by insisting that since Germany and Austria had approved of the coup it would be the denial of Russian consent which would consolidate Teutonic influence in Sofia. Furthermore, if Russia opposed Alexander's action when the Bulgarian population showed no signs of doing so the other powers would interpret this as Russian interference in Bulgaria.

Russian approval was not as yet made public and the Liberals, caught unawares by the coup, interpreted St Petersburg's silence as disapproval of Alexander's action, and from this the Liberals arrived at the conviction that Russia would stop the Prince before he went much further. They therefore did little beyond sending telegrams of protest to Gladstone, Gambetta and Mazzini. The Liberals were reassured by the pronouncement of 27 April/9 May which had promised that elections would be held for a Grand National Sŭbranie and so it was assumed that the Assembly would be allowed an open and free debate and, given a reasonably free election, the Liberals could be confident of dominating it.

Liberal confidence was soon to be shattered. In the first place Khitrovo made it clear that Russia did in fact approve of the change of government and that the Liberals were expected to be conciliatory and moderate. This provoked one of the most famous outbursts in modern Bulgarian history. Tsankov issued an open letter to Khitrovo in which he stated that the gratitude of a liberated people towards its liberator was enduring but that did not mean that the former must sacrifice its liberty; the letter concluded, '. . . this and similar points will force Russia and the Bulgarians, as the Serbs have already been forced, to recall the words with which an ancient sage addressed a bee, "I want neither your honey nor your sting" '.[7] Khitrovo's message, however, remained unchanged and the Liberals realised that they were on their own in the struggle against the Prince.

They were soon made to realise also that this struggle was not of the type they had initially imagined. On 11/23 May Alexander made known his proposals for constitutional change. He was to be given full powers for seven years during which he was to introduce a new executive body, the State Council; the Sŭbranie was to be reduced to seventy members elected on an indirect franchise, civil liberties were to be circumscribed and government was to become the prerogative of an educated few. After this seven years the Grand National Sŭbranie was to be reconvened to study any changes that might be necessary in the new system. The proposals were very similar to those put to the Constituent Assembly by the Conservatives and were based on the notion of a paternalist oligarchy rather than the royalist absolutism which Ehrenroth would have preferred. For the Liberals this was a shock for the Grand National Assembly was clearly not going to be allowed a free debate; it was to be asked rather to rubber stamp a plan handed down by the executive.

Despite this blow the Liberals stuck to their policy of trying to make the best of the election. They studiously avoided any provocative appeals and attacked their Conservative opponents rather than the Prince, for to depart from this path might provide Alexander with an excuse to impose martial law.

Yet the Liberal policy, though noble, was hopeless, for the government did not intend to play the electoral game by the same rules. On 1/13 May the country had been divided into five administrative regions each of which was placed under the control of an 'extraordinary commissioner' who had complete control over the army, police and civil administration within his region. Military tribunals were set up, the civil courts being insecure because when in office the Liberals had filled them with politically reliable officials, and the new tribunals were empowered to hand out one of only two sentences, two months' imprisonment or death. Each commissioner had a number of sub-commissioners who were to cleanse the bureaucracy of pro-Liberal elements and to prepare the region for the election. Constituencies were given the right to elect their deputy by 'collective declaration' but where voting took place a Russian officer was to be posted at each polling point 'to prevent fraud' and 'to aid illiterates'. There was also frequent use by the pro-government agencies of *shaiki* or groups of thugs armed with sticks who attacked opposition meetings, speakers, and offices, including that of *Nezavisimost*. At the same time the government could count on the support of the clergy, certainly at the higher levels. Metropolitan Mileti of Sofia had organised the first demonstrations of support for the sacking of Karavelov and when the Exarch visited the country shortly after the coup this was taken as a sign of the Church's approbation.

These were severe blows to the Liberals but perhaps less severe than that suffered when the Tsar gave public support to the Prince. This was in no small measure the Liberals' own fault for their constant assertions that the Tsar did not approve of what Alexander had done forced the Russian ruler publicly to announce that he did approve and that the Bulgarian people should not listen to those agitators who were trying to sow discord between the Prince and his people. To make sure the message was understood in the provinces the Tsar allowed Khitrovo to accompany the Prince on an election tour; a few weeks later the Tsar accorded Alexander a further token of approval when he granted him the Order of Alexander Nevski.

The elections were held on 14/26 June and 21 June/3 July. On the day before the first vote the Liberals had issued an electoral appeal which finally broke with their legalistic approach for it declared that the coup had dissolved the people's legal obligation to obey the Prince. This achieved little beyond the arrest, against Ehrenroth's advice, of those Liberals who had signed it, and the confirmation by an appeal court that the 1865 Ottoman press law which the government had used to justify these arrests was still in force.

On election day the government made sure that sufficient force was available to contain any unrest, though the polls in Kiustendil and Kutlovitsa had to be postponed because of disturbances. Things went reasonably well in Samokov, noted the Minister of Education, the Czech scholar Jiriček, because there 'only three people were badly beaten'.[8] It was an apt summary of the way in which the elections had been conducted. The results were never in doubt. In fact only two constituencies, Gabrovo and Tŭrnovo, returned Liberal deputies; the two from Gabrovo were stopped *en route* to the Assembly and replaced by others whilst the Tŭrnovo quartet of Slaveikov, Tsankov, Karavelov and Sarafov, reached Svishtov where the assembly convened, but were subjected to such threats and harassment that they left the town and on the day of the Assembly. In Svishtov itself the government was to take no chances when the Grand National Assembly opened on 1/13 July. The town was packed with three companies of infantry, two cavalry squadrons and an artillery batallion. They were hardly necessary for the Assembly sat for no more than an hour and obediently passed the constitutional changes proposed by the Prince.

In the two years since the opening of the First Ordinary Sŭbranie much had apparently changed in Bulgarian politics, and most notable of the changes had been the decline of Liberal influence. This was to a large extent the result of differences of opinion with the Russians and this was in itself a contributory factor in the decline of Liberal popularity at home. The Bulgarian peasant remained deeply devoted to the Russians and would not support those with whom the Tsar quarrelled. As Tsankov once remarked if the Tsar stuck a *kalpak* on a pole and told the Bulgarians to elect it as their Prince they would do so, and the events of 1881 seemed to back his case, much to the discomfiture of the Liberals who had to ask themselves if in the long run their democratic aspirations and principles could ever allow them to cooperate with the reactionary politicians who dominated Russia after the assassination of Alexander II. Strained relations with Russia were not the only cause of the peasants' indifference to the Liberals in the summer of 1881. A journalist touring the country during the election campaign reported a crowd in Radomir denouncing priests, officials and teachers for bringing nothing but increased taxes. This was not an isolated incident for in a number of areas the peasants had become painfully conscious of the disparities between the promises made by the Liberal intelligentsia and the policies they had followed once in office. For many peasants their old allies in the intelligentsia were irredeemably compromised for they had joined the small and rapacious clique which was beginning to take control of politics and the nation.

Power in 1881 seemed to lie with the Conservatives and the Prince who had shown considerable skill in the timing and staging of their coup, particularly in the way in which they had reassured external opinion. These advantages were to be squandered with amazing rapidity.

THE FAILURE OF ALEXANDER'S PERSONAL REGIME AND THE RESTORATION OF THE CONSTITUTION, 1881–3

The Prince's bold actions in May and June 1881 had been intended to provide Bulgaria with stable government in which conservative ideas and Conservative politicians predominated. No such stability appeared and the switching of alliances between the various political factions in the country intensified rather than declined whilst neither the Conservatives nor any other group emerged much strengthened from the experience of the so-called *pŭlnomoshtiya.**

After the Svishtov Grand National Assembly Ehrenroth returned to Russia. He was not replaced as Minister President though the Tsar nominated Colonel Krylov his successor as Minister of War, and General Remlingen to replace him as Minister of the Interior. Most of the other members of the Cabinet were unconnected with Bulgarian party politics but despite this the Conservatives exercised a dominant influence, particularly through the Minister for Foreign Affairs, Vŭlkovich. As Alexander had intended, Bulgaria was now to be ruled by a coalition of Russians and the Conservative-Princely axis.

After the formation of the Cabinet the first task of the government was to define the powers of the State Council which was to dominate the new executive. A commission under Marin Drinov, a Bulgarian who had earned high repute as a scholar in Russia, decided that the State Council should give advice on the drafting of legislation and

---

*A difficult word to translate. It is a compound whose compound parts mean 'full power'. The nearest English equivalent is perhaps, 'authoritarian rule'.

ministerial decrees, exercise considerable powers over finance, mediate in cases of differences of opinion within the bureaucracy, review complaints of administrative malpractice, and act as a watchdog warning the Prince when a breach of constitutional law seemed likely. It was less easy to decide on the composition of the new body. The commission finally recommended that only four of the twelve permanent members should be appointed by the Prince with the remainder being elected, albeit on a restricted franchise. Elections for the eight members were carried out in November but the composition of the State Council was still in some doubt and a number of problems were solved by the decision to admit a bishop elected by his peers, and Cabinet ministers whose departmental interests were under consideration.

The discussion on the powers and composition of the State Council and the conduct of the elections for its eight permanent elected members had shown that the new Russian ministers, and especially Remlingen, aimed at the gradual reintegration of the Liberals into the political life of the nation, believing that only thus could permanent stability be achieved. The Liberal response to this was unsure and foreshadowed later divisions in the Party. Tsankov like others who had remained in the Principality after the May 1881 coup was prepared to cooperate with the new rulers in the hope that they could be persuaded to restore the Tŭrnovo constitution and parliamentary rule. Karavelov, Slaveikov and the others who had fled to Rumelia shared this objective but could not endorse Tsankov's methods. The exiles wanted swifter and more certain means, Slaveikov declaring in the picturesque language of which he was the master, that 'You cannot dig wells with needles'.[1] For the exiles popular action on a wide scale was, as yet, the only acceptable means of securing a return to constitutional rule.

The prospect of a realignment of Liberals with the Russians naturally worried the Conservatives. They regarded it as largely responsible for the increasing political difficulties which faced the government by the end of 1881. There was, by this time, still no agreement as to who should be made President of the State Council and in addition there were alarming signs of growing discontent; troops had to be sent into Gabrovo to arrest dissident teachers and officials whilst at Christmas a Sofia mob ejected the pro-Conservative Mileti from his cathedral. The Conservative press criticised Remlingen for the lack of internal order and the minister replied in the official journal, *Dŭrzhaven Vestnik* (Official Gazette). After a short but intense press battle the Minister of the Interior closed down the chief Conservative paper, *Bŭlgarski Glas* but this was too much for the Prince who sacked Remlingen on 31 December/12 January 1882. Nachovich took over the Ministry of the Interior and the Conservative hold on both the Council of Ministers and the State Council was strengthened. The Russians, who were not ready for a complete break with the Prince, accepted the dismissal of Remlingen, and their diplomatic agent, Khritrovo, was ordered not to meddle in Bulgarian party politics.

The breach between the Conservatives and the Russians had been some time in the making. The railway question had again been a point of contention. Shortly after the coup the Russians had pressed for the simultaneous construction of both the international and the Sofia-Danube lines. At this stage the Bulgarians dared not refuse outright but had insisted that the international line, because of the treaty of Berlin, had to take priority and if the other line were to be built at the same time then the Russians would have to provide the money for it. This had been an attempt to postpone the decision for Conservative preferences were for a contract to be decided by auction with construction work being entrusted to a consortium including leading Bulgarian financiers. In the months after the coup the largest native consortium was still that led by Hadjienov, who now had French backing, and this group continued to contest the claims of the Ginsburg group which had long sought the contract to build the Danube-Sofia line. The Conservative Cabinet refused to commit itself insisting with much justice that as railways were so costly and as they were of great importance to the nation as a whole, no decision could be made without the consent of the Sŭbranie. This did not deter Khitrovo. He accepted the Conservative demand that simultaneous development could take place only if the Russians would provide the money for the Sofia-Danube line and believed he had found the means of doing this. Under the treaty of Berlin it had been agreed that Bulgaria should pay for part of the expenses Russia had incurred in the post-war occupation of Bulgaria and in September 1881 the Russians at last computed the total Occupation Debt at twenty-eight million francs. Khitrovo suggested that this be reinvested in Bulgaria to finance the Sofia-Danube railway. The Tsar refused. He objected to the notion of subsidising railway development in Bulgaria and he feared complications with Austria, who wanted agreement on the international line, and with Britain who was still waiting for the Bulgarians to lay out money to purchase the Ruse-Varna line.

The stalemate on the railway issue and then the dismissal of Rem-lingen seemed to indicate that the Russians in Bulgaria were in a weak position. This encouraged the Liberals. Early in December 1881 there had been discussions between some leading Liberals in Bulgaria and the moderate Conservative Ikonomov but these had come to nothing. Early in 1882 Tsankov, spurred on by a challenge to his authority from the Party's more extreme elements which wanted immediate and force-ful action to restore the constitution, issued a circular calling for an intensified campaign against the present system but insisting that the campaign be confined to legal means. The party rank and file responded enthusiastically and there was a surge of attacks upon the government in the newspapers, in public meetings and in petitions. The government replied by clamping down even on the legal methods of agitation. Meetings were banned, restrictions placed upon the press, leading Liberal activists in a number of provincial towns detained and finally, on 6/18 February, the ageing Tsankov was snatched from his bed and rushed to house-arrest in the Conservative strong-hold of Vratsa. This merely intensified the discontent. In Sofia there were strikes by teachers and officials and the whole Principality was swept by a wave of protest meetings and demonstrations which continued throughout March and into April.

The administration could contain the unrest but it was under con-tinuous pressure and could not govern permanently in this fashion. The Conservatives and the Prince needed an ally but as the contacts between Ikonomov and the more moderate Liberals had produced nothing there remained only the Russians.

An accommodation with the Russians would not be easily achieved. There was tension over the railway question and the dismissal of Rem-lingen. There were additional disagreements in the very sensitive area of the army. Russian officers serving in the Bulgarian army naturally tended to align with their fellow countrymen when the Bulgarians and Russians were at odds, and one such officer had given grave personal offence to the Prince.* Alexander, fearing the involvement of the army in political agitation had issued an order forbidding officers to take

---

*A Colonel Timmler had refused to toast the Prince and when Alexander demanded his expulsion the Colonel added impudence to insult by remarking that such treat-ment would be a great recommendation in Russia. He was right. The Tsar agreed to Alexander's demand that the officer be suspended for a year but before the year was out Timmler had been appointed assistant to the Chief of the Russian General Staff.

any part in politics and political demonstrations. This order Krylov had refused to implement and the Prince had therefore dismissed him. By convention the Bulgarian Minister of War was to be a Russian so Alexander, with backing from his Conservative allies, turned to St Petersburg for both a new Minister of War and a new Minister of the Interior.

Despite the difficulties between Sofia and St Petersburg the turn to Russia made political sense. From 1879 to 1881 Alexander had found that he could scarcely tolerate Liberal Cabinets but the experience of 1881 to 1882 indicated that the nation would not acquiesce in rule by the Conservative oligarchy. That oligarchy was therefore to be adulterated by the admission of Russians to important posts which would also show the nation that the Tsar approved of the present arrangements, a significant consideration when those arrangements were under heavy attack from the Liberals. The cynical observer might also have noted that if the new ministers did not improve matters then the blame could be placed on their shoulders rather than on those of Alexander and the Bulgarian supporters of the 1881 coup.

Alexander set out for St Petersburg on 15/29 April and the visit began well with the Tsar agreeing to the Prince's request that Khitrovo be recalled. Alexander III, however, could not be persuaded to allow Ehrenroth to return to Bulgaria and it was eventually decided that the vacant posts in Sofia should be filled by Generals Sobolev and Kaulbars, both of whom were young—they were both thirty-eight—both of whom had fought in the war of 1877–8, and both of whom had served in the Russian Provisional Administration.

This was the beginning of a disastrous year and a half for Bulgaria in general and for Prince Alexander in particular. Neither Sobolev nor Kaulbars had clear ideas about how Bulgaria's political problems could best be settled. Sobolev, who as Minister President and Minister of the Interior was to be more involved in domestic politics than Kaulbars who became Minister for War, was by sentiment an absolutist who disliked all parliaments, however weak, and who saw political parties as alien, western institutions ill-suited to a Slav people. On the other hand he was anxious to see political stability in Bulgaria and was willing to operate within the parliamentary and party framework if that were the best means of securing stability. He did not, of course, lose sight of the need to ensure that a stable regime in Sofia was also pro-Russian. This meant that as Minister President he was quite prepared to cooperate with the Prince's domestic political enemies if by so doing he could achieve the objectives of stability and good relations between Sofia and St Petersburg. The Prince could do little to prevent this for he had become the prisoner of his own system. His 1881 constitution had been intended to increase the power of the executive and although this had happened Alexander had been unable to secure personal control over that executive. He had also signally failed to realise the potential power of the State Council an instrument which, if used to the full, could have limited the power of his ministers. Alexander was eventually to conclude that if the new system were inadequate to his needs he might do better by returning to the old.

Initially, however, it seemed that the new administration would be a happy alliance of Russians and Conservatives. The latter were given the cabinet posts not filled by the Generals and in the State Council a number of hard-line Conservatives were given places whilst the moderate Ikonomov was nudged out. The Generals did not object to the increased measures of internal repression which the Conservatives had used to make sure that peace and order prevailed when the new ministers arrived in Bulgaria. The Conservatives were encouraged when Sobolev agreed to the restrictive electoral law outlined in 1881. This reduced the Sŭbranie to fifty-six members all of whom were to be elected on an indirect franchise confined to those with certain property and educational qualifications. The Prince was now to enjoy the privilege of nominating the Assembly's President and Alexander confidently expected that the new Assembly would vote with military obedience.

The returns to the III Ordinary National Assembly in the autumn of 1882 did not in fact show a clean sweep by the Conservatives, even though Tsankov had instructed his followers to boycott the elections. The few Liberals who were elected, however, resigned their seats in protest against the new franchise and thus the Conservative victory, which was already secure, was made absolute. The new Assembly consisted primarily of wealthy merchants, craftsmen and intelligentsia and, despite the influence Sobolev had exerted at the polls, was of a surprisingly independent frame of mind. Indeed it seemed as if the Conservatives were so emboldened by their electoral triumph that they had decided to shake themselves free of dependence on the Generals.

The deputies resented the heavy-handed efforts made by the Generals to bribe them, efforts which went even to the insulting expedient of putting sweets in the members' desks. A more substantive issue was that of the Dragoon Corps. The Dragoons were a mounted police force formed after the 1881 coup as part of the general increase in the machinery of control and, being proficient in their work, they were soon much disliked. As the Dragoons had been organised by Remlingen and were officered by Russians the Conservatives were able to direct popular anger over the Dragoons at the Russians, the Sŭbranie finally demanding the disbandment of the new force. Sobolev suggested that it be absorbed into the regular army as a new cavalry division, an idea which the Prince, ever keen to increase the size of his army, warmly endorsed. The Conservatives were not to be moved and both the Sŭbranie and the State Council resisted any solution but the disbandment of the force.

To the bitterness aroused by the debate on the Dragoon Corps was to be added continuing disagreement on the railway question. The Third Sŭbranie as one of its first acts had brought about the dismissal of a very young Russian whom Sobolev had nominated as Director of Railways in Bulgaria. Following this Nachovich, alarmed at Sobolev's close association with Ginsburg, presented to the Sŭbranie a bill which granted to a Conservative-backed consortium the right to carry out a survey for a line from the Danube to Sofia and thence on to the Macedonian border. This only redoubled Sobolev's energy and his inventiveness. Despite the Tsar's previous refusal to subsidise Bulgarian railway construction he suggested that if it were the lack of cash which was preventing the building of the line from Sofia to the Danube this could be remedied by Russia giving a secret undertaking to leading members of the Sŭbranie that she would lend Bulgaria the money to purchase the Ruse-Varna line and the money originally earmarked for this purpose could be put towards the Danube-Sofia railway. Once again the Tsar showed no interest.

As his differences with the Conservatives increased Sobolev looked around for an opportunity to weaken his opponents, and such an opportunity soon appeared in the form of that worldly cleric, Metropolitan Mileti of Sofia. Mileti had been an enthusiastic Russophile in 1877 and had joined the Russians in the war. This had worried the Exarch who feared that the Ottoman authorities might take reprisals against clerics still in their jurisdiction and for his alleged irresponsibility Mileti had been sentenced to a period of exile in Vratsa, though in the general euphoria of the Liberation his transgressions were forgotten and he was soon appointed Metropolitan of Sofia. Mileti was a Conservative and had organised the rejoicings over the 1881 coup but two years later when he found his Russophilia and his conservatism at odds it was the former which prevailed. He backed Sobolev in his dispute with the Conservatives and the latter persuaded the ecclesiastical authorities to reimpose his sentence of exile. Sobolev decided to contest the Metropolitan's expulsion, the more so as his successor was to be Grigori of Ruse a Conservative of such extreme hue that in 1877 he had insisted his flock offer prayers for their lawful sovereign, the Sultan. The Church, however, was a determined defender of its own powers and though the rigours of Mileti's sentence were reduced the sentence itself was not revoked. Sobolev turned this humiliation against Stoilov whom, as Minister for Foreign and Religious Affairs, he held responsible for the reimposition of Mileti's exile. Sobolev and Kaulbars informed the Prince they would resign if Stoilov stayed in office and Alexander, forced to choose between a Bulgarian minister and the two Russians, had to sacrifice the former. Alexander was to attend the Coronation of the Tsar in May and could not offend him by dismissing his Russian aides only nine months after begging for them. Stoilov resigned on 3/15 March and Nachovich and Grekov went with him.

The departure of the leading Conservatives left the administration so much under the dominance of the Russian Generals that Alexander and many of his Conservative supporters began to feel that Sobolev and Kaulbars now represented a real threat to the independence of Bulgaria. Evidence for these fears they found in the railway schemes, in the promotion of Russo-Bulgarian trade when there was almost nothing these two primary producers could profitably exchange, in the recent increase in scholarships offered to Bulgarians for study in Russia, and in the currency of ideas such as those presented by the bilingual journal *Balkan* which urged all Slavs to adopt Russian as their literary language. The Prince even feared for the loyalty of the army and after the Dragoon affair had been settled he issued a decree, strenuously but vainly resisted by Kaulbars and Sobolev, reinforcing the Prince's right to supreme command of the armed forces and leaving with the Minister of War responsibility merely for economic and administrative affairs within the army.

This blow to Russian influence was followed by another when it was announced in April 1883 that Bulgaria was to sign a convention *à quatre* with Austria, Serbia and Turkey for the completion of the international line from Vienna to Constantinople, the contract for the building of the Bulgarian section going to the Austrian Baron Hirsch with whom a number of leading Conservatives in Sofia still had close ties. This the Russians reluctantly accepted, insisting only that Hirsch renounce that clause of the treaty of Berlin which allowed the constructor also to operate the Bulgarian section of the line.

The railway convention marked the parting of the ways for the Generals and the Prince, and Sobolev turned openly to the Liberals to whom he gave official support in the local elections held in April 1883. There had been intermittent contact between Sobolev and the Liberals ever since the Generals arrived in Bulgaria. Sobolev had arranged for the release of Tsankov in the summer of 1882 and at the same time had allowed the Liberals to publish a new paper, *Svetlina* (Light). In 1883 he permitted them to publish another journal, *Sŭsnanie* (Consciousness) which was to prove both more influential and longer-lived than the already defunct *Svetlina*. The restoration of close relations between their Party and the Russians pleased many of the rank and file Liberals in the Principality for they had always been Russophile, but the new alliance was not welcomed by all, more especially by those in exile in Plovdiv. Sobolev, the doubters knew, was no constitutionalist, and his cooperation with the Liberals in Bulgaria was intended to weaken the Conservatives rather than to bring about the restoration of the Tŭrnovo constitution.

For his part the Prince was hoping that the Tsar could be persuaded to recall the Generals and reappoint Ehrenroth, and this Alexander hoped to achieve when he visited Moscow for the Tsar's Coronation in May 1883. For the Prince the visit was an unalleviated disaster. His own behaviour was very much to blame for in Constantinople he spoke indiscreetly of his discontent with Russian policy in Bulgaria and his words were rapidly relayed to Russia; in Russia itself he churlishly refused an Imperial decoration because it was not the one which he coveted; and he behaved with absurd tactlessness in holding a banquet during the Tsar's pre-Coronation retreat. The Russians were also concerned at Alexander's reported intention to marry a German princess. Alexander needed to found a dynasty to make his throne more secure but the Russians, as he knew full well, would resist his having a Hohenzollern princess as his consort for that might increase German influence in the Balkans. Whilst the Prince was blotting almost every page of his copybook Sobolev, who had arrived in Russia before Alexander, was poisoning all minds against him. To the Tsar he insisted that there was a powerful body of opinion in Bulgaria which wanted good relations with Russia and to substantiate his point he produced a delegation from the recently elected Sofia Municipal Council; the delegates were Liberals to a man and obliged their patron by immediately petitioning the Tsar for the deposition of the Prince. For this the Tsar was not prepared but he did accept Sobolev's view that the 1881 system had to be dismantled and agreed that the best strategy was to seek its gradual redefinition in cooperation with the local Liberals.

The Prince did not return to Bulgaria until July by which time much had happened. Most alarming for Alexander had been Kaulbars' attempt to strengthen the Generals' control of the army and the civil administration by dismissing over a hundred and thirty pro-Battenberg officers and magistrates, though he had no constitutional right to do this. Alexander conferred with leading Conservatives at Ischl but rejected their suggestion that he issue a proclamation threatening never to return to Bulgaria if the Generals did not resign. Instead he returned to Sofia determined to do battle there. He persuaded the State Council to enumerate and publicise the misdeeds of the Generals, called for elections in sixteen vacant constituencies to be held in August and for an extraordinary session of the Sŭbranie to meet in September. He also appointed Stoilov as Bulgaria's first diplomatic representative to Russia, wanting the Tsar to learn of Bulgarian affairs from a source other than Sobolev, Kaulbars or the Russian diplomatic agency. The Tsar replied that he would not receive Stoilov until the new Russian diplomatic agent in Bulgaria, Ionin, had reached Sofia.

Alexander therefore turned to his old enemies the Liberals. Ikonomov made his way to Vratsa where he rapidly came to an agreement with Tsankov. A Grand National Assembly elected on whichever franchise the Prince preferred would be called to revise the constitution and return the country to parliamentary rule; the Liberals would be satisfied with the latter and the Conservatives would still have the chance to alter the 1879 constitution if they gained sufficient power in the Assembly. This agreement did not offer the Liberals much but Tsankov had now come to fear the Generals so much that he felt their continuation in office afforded less chance of a return to parliamentary rule than did an alliance with the Conservatives. In Sofia and much of the rest of the country, however, it was the *Sŭsnanie* Liberals rather than the Tsankovists who dominated the Party and the *Sŭsnanievtsi* opposed any deal with the Conservatives; instead they urged the return of Sobolev to Bulgaria for they believed he rather than the Prince and the Conservatives would restore the 1879 constitution. In this they were correct for when he came back to Sofia early in August Sobolev was considering issuing instructions for a return to the Tŭrnovo system.

The return of Sobolev and the almost simultaneous arrival of Ionin put new urgency into Ikonomov's search for an agreement with Tsankov. At last, on 8/20 August, an acceptable formula was found, and this was approved by the Liberal Party Central Bureau on the same day. The agreement provided for the calling as soon as possible of a Grand National Assembly to revise the constitution, that revision to be devised by a mixed commission or a coalition Cabinet according to the Prince's convenience but whichever method were chosen there had to be equal party representation; the franchise for the election of the Grand National Assembly was to be that which the Prince preferred but there must be a guarantee of no government interference at the polls. After acceptance of these terms by the Party's Central Bureau the Liberals submitted them on the following day to a party assembly in Sofia. Tsankov was given a rough ride. Acceptance of the 8/20 August pact was only secured by Stambulov's sophistic insistence that the agreement was with the Prince and not the Conservatives and by Karavelov's asking whether there was any alternative method of achieving the Party's aim of restoring constitutional rule.

The Prince was told of the compact on the following day, 10/22 August, and it seemed that the Liberals were now committed to cooperation with their old rivals. Then Ionin intervened. He presented to the Prince a string of demands from the Tsar, including the calling of a special session of the Sŭbranie which should decide on the railway question and the Occupation Debt, pass the budget and appoint a commission to work out constitutional changes. The Prince refused and Ionin therefore turned to the Liberals. He offered them a joint campaign for the restoration of the 1879 constitution; Sobolev had never gone as far as this and it was an unbeatable offer for it gave the Liberals their maximum programme for nothing. On 17/29 August Tsankov informed the Conservatives that the 8/20 August compact was dead. Alexander appeared beaten and on 25 August/6 September he made arrangements for the recall of the Sŭbranie and for the appointment of a commission to review the constitution. Ionin and Sobolev celebrated what they thought was their victory.

Yet on occasions Alexander had courage and great political skill. August-September 1883 was such an occasion for the Prince now capitalised upon an error or misunderstanding committed by his opponents. On 30 August/9 September rumours swept through Sofia that the Prince was about to be deposed. Some historians have accused the Russians and Kaulbars in particular of hatching the plot whilst present-day Bulgarian writers try to play down Russian involvement, though admitting that there may have been a vague Liberal conspiracy. The truth is probably that there was no serious plot by anyone but in a city so tense and in a political situation so volatile all contingencies were discussed by all sides. Such discussions could easily be exaggerated into rumour. Whatever the reality of the threat to the Prince an officer who spoke of the plot was immediately placed in custody and this led to a demonstration in front of the Prince's residence by pro-Battenberg officers. This greatly encouraged the Prince for, plot or no plot, it showed that his enemies could not depend absolutely on the army. Tsankov was also affected by the events of 30 August/9 September for they reawoke his fears of the Generals' intentions. He therefore went to the Prince and persuaded him that the dangers presented by the Generals could be avoided only if Alexander were prepared to offer the Liberals the same price for their support as the Russians were offering, that is immediate restoration of the 1879 constitution. Should he offer this, Alexander was persuaded, the Liberals could well vote acceptance of the railway agreement with Austria, something which Alexander needed desperately if he were to relieve pressure from the Russian railway lobby and avoid embarrassment in the Ballhausplatz which was beginning to suspect that he was unable to implement the *à quatre* convention signed in April. Such an agreement would also keep the Conservatives securely by his side.

Alexander now acted with great speed and skill. The Sŭbranie, he decided, would be recalled, as the Conservatives had always wished, and it would then restore the 1879 constitution as the Liberals wanted, at the same time satisfying Tsankov's wish that the constitution be restored before the Generals left office, thus ensuring their power was destroyed not merely transferred. The Sŭbranie met accordingly on 4/16 September, the Generals still believing that it would deal only with those issues designated by the Tsar: railways and the Occupation Debt. It did deal with the railway question, but only to approve the convention *à quatre* without making any mention of the Danube-Sofia scheme. After the first session the Conservative leaders met with their Liberal counterparts who, of course, were not members of the Assembly, and together it was agreed to ask the Prince to transform this emergency session of the Sŭbranie into a regular legislative session. This was in effect a request for an immediate return to the 1879 constitution for the Sŭbranie under the 1881 arrangements had no legislative powers. On 6/18 September the request for the transformation of the

Sŭbranie's status was included in the Assembly's reply to the royal address and it was accepted by the Prince that evening. The Generals had been outmanoeuvred. The Liberals had been given their maximum programme without the intercession of Sobolev and Kaulbars and there was nothing these two could do to dislodge the Liberals from the latter's new association with the Prince and the Conservatives. On 7/19 September the Generals resigned and a new government was formed with Tsankov as Minister President and Minister of the Interior; the other Cabinet members were Balabanov, Nachovich, Ikonomov, Molov, Stoilov and Grekov. There was no Russian but nor as yet was there a Minister of War.

Not all Liberals rejoiced at this turn of events. Though the Sŭbranie was once again a law-making body this would not prevent it from making future constitutional changes, indeed the composition of the Cabinet and the fact that there was now a legislative Sŭbranie elected on the 1882 franchise made such changes probable. Nothing had been said on the fate of the State Council or on legislation enacted since May 1881, and a number of Liberals also regretted the dramatic break with Russia. Tsankov hastened to assure the Party of the advantages of the changes, noting that the prime concern was to secure a return to Subranie rule, that there had been a large number of amnesties for political prisoners and that the restrictions on the press and the right of assembly had been relaxed. Liberal suspicions, however, were not entirely allayed and were rekindled later in the month. It was then announced that although it had completed the two tasks allotted to it, namely the sanctioning of the railway convention and of the payment of the Occupation Debt, the existing Sŭbranie was not to be dissolved; despite the fact that it had been elected on the 1882 franchise it was to be prolonged into November. In the meantime all Liberals joined in fêting the departing Generals who were made freemen of the city of Sofia; despite the recent difficulties many Liberals still saw the Russians as their main political ally and all Liberals remained deeply conscious of the political debt Bulgaria owed to Russia.

The departure of the Generals marked the end of two and a half years of constitutional experiment from which none of the main political forces in Bulgaria profited. Alexander's efforts to find supporters who would be loyal and yet not attempt to secure political supremacy for themselves had failed. The 1881 political system had collapsed thus damaging the Conservatives whose political ideals it had embodied; the over-bearing behaviour of the Generals had made some Bulgarians aware that too close an association with the liberating power had its dangers, and in later years Russophobe propaganda feasted on the conduct of Sobolev and Kaulbars; on the other hand no Bulgarian wanted the virtual breach with Russia which Alexander's policies had produced and for this, as for the failure of his domestic experiments, the Prince paid with a loss of prestige. The Liberals, eclipsed at the beginning of the period, were at its close again at the centre of affairs but the Party's cohesion had been sorely tested and a united Liberal Party survived the turmoil of August and September 1883 in name alone. Bulgaria itself lost respect in the world and seemed more unstable than in the years 1879–81 when at least the constitution had survived. Finally, and most damaging of all, the vast majority of the population, the apolitical peasantry, saw little in these events beyond the fact that Prince and politician had again angered the Tsar and this served only to deepen that popular indifference to national affairs which had been seen in the apathetic response to the coup of 1881.

Chapter 3

CONSTITUTIONAL SETTLEMENT AND THE REVIVAL OF THE NATIONAL QUESTION, 1883–5

The Tsankov-Nachovich coalition was to be a stop-gap administration but it was also one of reconciliation and made possible the relative peace which characterised Bulgarian politics in the years 1883 to 1885. The Prince and the Conservatives could accept the new Cabinet because it offered them the prospect of constitutional change, albeit by constitutional means. It was more difficult to establish good relations with the Russians. The Russians, it was true, had proved accommodating in agreeing to the railway settlement, expressing the conviction that the trunk line would help Bulgaria by tying it more closely to Rumelia, but they were, it was inevitably felt, much affected by the humiliation of Sobolev and Kaulbars. The bad personal relations between the Prince and Ionin and the Prince and the Tsar made matters no easier. The Liberals' attitude to the Russians was, in general, clear. They believed that the historic ties between the two peoples gave the Russians the right to dominate Bulgarian foreign policy, and they even opposed the appointment of a Bulgarian diplomatic representative in St Petersburg on the grounds that the relations between the two states should be so close as to make such formalities otiose. Unfortunately for the Liberals the main issue dividing Sofia and St Petersburg late in 1883 was one in which the boundary between internal and external affairs could not easily be drawn. That question was the role of the Russians in the control of the Bulgarian army.

For the Russians the Bulgarian army was important because in any forward move by the Russians in the Balkans it would form a valuable advanceguard, and if Russia did not wish to advance in that area then she would be concerned to ensure that the Bulgarian army did not fall under hostile influence. The army itself was illegal. The treaty of Berlin had stipulated that Bulgaria should have only a militia but soon after the Liberation the Russians had begun to fashion a new regular fighting force in the Principality, brushing aside objections with the assertion that it was necessary to maintain order. Russian influence over this force had been perpetuated through the two hundred and fifty to three hundred Russian officers and over two thousand 'young Russian commanders' on secondment to the Bulgarian forces—and as yet no Bulgarian held a rank higher than that of captain—and through the convention that a Russian officer should serve as Minister of War in Sofia. In Bulgaria Russian domination of the army had been accepted because the Liberals thought it Russia's right and because the Conservatives feared that the peasant conscripts would not obey Bulgarian officers. The events of 1883, however, and particularly the rumoured coup of 30 August/9 September, had determined the Prince on action to protect himself from hostile officers. The Conservatives agreed and on 19 September/1 October pushed through the Sŭbranie a bill which divided the War Ministry, making the Prince's control over the officer corps absolute and confining the War Minister to administrative duties; this was a restatement of the 1882 enactment the legality of which was now in doubt because of the return to the 1879 constitution. The Tsar resisted and pressed that the division of the War Ministry be left until a special envoy arrived in Sofia to discuss the issue. To this the Prince agreed and the envoy duly appeared in the person of the Russian military attaché in Vienna, N. Kaulbars, a brother to but a much more accomplished diplomatist than the former Minister of War. Kaulbars arrived at a time of great tension for the Tsar had recalled two prominent pro-Battenbergists and the Prince had replied by dismissing all Russian officers from his personal suite and recalling thirty-six Bulgarian cadets training in Russia, but the envoy's skill soon made possible a twelve-point agreement the main provisions of which were that Russian officers serving in Bulgaria were not to take part in any political activity, were not to be in Bulgaria for longer than three years, were to be subject to the Bulgarian military code and were to be responsible to the Bulgarian Ministry of War; only in those questions 'affecting them in their position as Russian officers' were they to be responsible to the Tsar.[1] The Prince was to appoint the Minister of War but the choice was to be sanctioned by the Tsar. In February 1884 Prince Kantakuzin was nominated for the post.

The bitterness aroused during the contest over the Ministry of War was increased by continued Russian opposition to the Prince's plans to marry a German princess, plans which were very much in his mind in 1884 and 1885. Some relaxation of tension followed the recall of Ionin in March 1884 but his successor, Koyander, despite his own conservative inclinations, followed the Tsar's instructions that Russian interests in Bulgaria were best represented by the Liberals whose unity and strength were to be promoted.

This was no easy task. The Left Liberals were still dubious about the constitutional intentions of Tsankov. They were also concerned at the tension with Russia; and they were dissatisfied with the route laid down for the international line, Karavelov wanting the Kumanovo and Skopje *tracé* rather than that via Tsaribrod. The major issue of debate within Liberal ranks was still, however, that of the constitution. A meeting of representatives of local party bureaux in October in Ruse and a full congress in Sofia in the following month saw intense discussions on the constitutional question with Stambulov working hard to preserve unity and find compromises. Great pressure was put upon Tsankov to declare against any change in the Tŭrnovo system but this he refused to do, insisting that he could not go back on the promises he had made to Nachovich and the Prince; he was committed to allowing the possibility of constitutional change by constitutional means. Finally the Party Congress decided that Tsankov and the Liberal Cabinet members could vote for constitutional change because such changes would be thrown out by the Grand National Sŭbranie when it was elected on the 1879 franchise. In the meantime the moderates who had aligned themselves with Tsankov had come to believe that some constitutional change might be necessary in order to preserve law and order in the country.

When the Liberal Party Congress met in November the legal position was that possible constitutional changes would be studied by a commission under the Conservatives Grekov and Stoilov and, it had also been decided, the present small Sŭbranie would continue until 15/27 December after which it and all relics of the 1881 system would finally be demolished, though the sitting did not end until 31 December/12 January. Its preoccupation in December had been the report published by the Grekov-Stoilov commission. The changes suggested were very much in line with Conservative thinking. The franchise was to be subject to a series of property and educational qualifications, the Sŭbranie was to be smaller and to sit for longer, and there was to be a second chamber with a large appointed element. These proposals were to be submitted to a Grand National Assembly in three years' time until when the Tŭrnovo constitution would remain in operation. The left Liberals were aghast, for this was no better than the hated 1881 system. Worse still in their eyes was the way in which the Bill was forced through the Sŭbranie on 5/17 December. The deputies had not been given the statutory notice of the debate which was held *in camera* to prevent popular demonstrations and two leading Liberals who had returned to the Sŭbranie after the agreement to restore the 1879 system and who now spoke against the Bill were ejected from the chamber. This, said Karavelov in his new paper, *Tŭrnovska Konstitutsiya* (Turnvovo Constitution), was 'a second coup'.[2]

The Bill was never put into effect for it was repealed by a Karavelov government in 1884, but it did serve to drive a huge wedge into the ranks of the Liberal Party. The *Sŭsnanievtsi* and the left in general were enraged at what they saw as Tsankov's apostasy and even many moderates who had clung to the leader in the belief that party unity was the first consideration now abandoned him. The three Liberal members of the Cabinet, Tsankov, Molov and Balabanov, were condemned by the Liberal Central Office as traitors to the Party and a series of meetings throughout the country endorsed that decision. Condemnation came too from Karavelov and Slaveikov both of whom were still based in Plovdiv, from Stambulov and Metropolitan Kliment in the Liberal bastion of Tŭrnovo, and from the two ejected Sŭbranie deputies, Suknarov and Velchev, who resigned their seats in protest.

The Bill of 5/17 December gave the Conservatives all they wanted and in accordance with a previous agreement with Tsankov they now resigned from the government and left the Minister President to construct a new Cabinet which with the exception of Ikonomov was moderate Liberal to a man. Tsankov also set about shoring up support for his regime. Any opposition activists who had survived previous purges of the administration were now removed and all civil servants ordered to avoid political activity directed against the government; all telegrams addressed to the Prince were routed via the Minister President on the grounds that the Prince could do nothing without consulting his ministers.

With the resignation of the Conservatives, the political stage was left to the contending factions of the Liberal Party. By the beginning of 1884 Karavelov had assumed leadership of the anti-Tsankov group, having set up the rudiments of a separate party apparatus, and launched a propaganda campaign with the slogan 'Neither a people without a Prince, nor a Prince without a people; neither a Prince without power, nor a people without rights'.[3] In February Liberal unity was just maintained in a Party Congress but this was a truce not a peace.

By January 1884 the Karavelists were concentrating on the call for elections, the date of which should already have been announced. At the same time the Karavelist leadership told its followers not to recognise laws passed before the full restoration of the Tŭrnovo system on 31 December/12 January, which meant, of course, the rejection of the constitutional changes enacted on 5/17 December. In reply the moderates were arguing for a postponement of the elections so that the government could prove to the doubting Liberals that the Tŭrnovo system had been completely restored, that relations with Russia were improving, and that Tsankov was not the unmitigated rogue which his opponents claimed him to be. Tsankov himself toured the country and then, convinced he had enough support to win, called for elections on 27 May/8 June.

Tsankov had misjudged the mood of the Liberals. Large and frequently unruly meetings all over the country showed the superiority of the Karavelists over the moderates. Karavelov had also mended his fences with the Prince whom he had assured that the extreme Liberals had no intention of declaring a republic or changing their ruler; 'There is no dynastic question in Bulgaria' he had told Alexander.[4]

In the Party itself Tsankov's handling of the constitutional issue had created many opponents and his position was made worse by his conduct during the debate on the Ruse to Varna railway question. This line had been the only one in existence at the Liberation. Its construction had been allowed by an Imperial Ottoman *firman* of 1861 and work began six years later. The intention of the original British company had been to cut out the long haul up the final, north-east running stretch of the Danube and so shorten the journey from central Europe to Constantinople by at least sixty-eight hours. However, the deepening of the river and improved port facilities at places such as Galats and Braila had allowed larger vessels to come further up stream and this together with the later announcement of the projected Vienna to Constantinople trunk line combined to wreck the prospects of the Ruse to Varna railway. Many shares were sold to the Ottoman government in 1869. In the treaty of Berlin the interests of the remaining British shareholders had been protected by a clause which called for the purchase of the line by the Bulgarian government. With the return of relative constitutional stability in 1883 the British began to exercise pressure for the fulfilment of this clause. The Bulgarians were told that unless they were ready to join in purposeful talks the matter would be referred to a conference of ambassadors in Constantinople at which Bulgaria would not be represented and from which she would have to take orders. Two Bulgarian delegates were therefore sent to London authorised to offer forty million francs for the line. It was not enough. By February 1884 the price had been forced up to fifty millions, minus one and a half million which the Bulgarians would have to spend making the line workable. These terms the Tsankov government accepted. The opposition, both Conservative and Liberal, were furious. Few believed the line was of any economic value to Bulgaria and all agreed that the price was outrageous, *Tŭrnovska Konstitutsiya* dubbing it 'day-light robbery';[5] the real value of the line, said the paper, was eighteen million francs. When it finally met to discuss the question the Sŭbranie threw out the plan.

His attitude towards constitutional reform and his willingness to pay too high a price for the Ruse—Varna railway were the chief causes of Tsankov's defeat by the 28.2% of the electorate who bothered to vote in the elections of May/June 1884, elections which were relatively free from the intimidation and corruption which had been apparent in previous polls. The Assembly was to meet in Tŭrnovo rather than Sofia and after the voting Tsankov still hoped to be able to win to his side enough deputies to guarantee the continuation of his ministry. He failed. When they arrived in Tŭrnovo the deputies held meetings at which the great majority rallied round a call for the repeal of the 5/17 December law; not even the conciliatory Stambulov could hold them to the government and Tsankov therefore resigned.

On 29 June/11 July Karavelov was appointed Minister President. He also took charge of the Ministry of Finance whilst the Ministry of the Interior was given to Slaveikov, despite his age and impaired health. The remainder of the Cabinet, the Minister of War excepted, came from the ranks of the left Liberals.

The split in the Liberal Party which had for long been apparent was now formalised and institutionalised. Tsankov established a completely separate party machine and took over the newspaper *Sredets* (Centre) which had been supporting him since its inauguration in

March. The Tsankovist 'Liberals' were now to be distinguished from the Karavelist 'Democrats'.

One of the first acts of the new Democratic government was to repeal the law of 5/17 December 1883. Karavelov also tackled the railway question to which he provided a long-needed definitive solution. The *à quatre* agreement had decided upon the Tsaribrod *tracé* for the international line and it had also been agreed that Baron Hirsch was to be responsible for financing the construction of the line but was not to exercise the option of controlling the line when completed. What the Sŭbranie had yet to decide was who should exploit the line when it was ready for use. The Assembly had already decreed that the total cost must not exceed seventeen million francs and had laid down rules governing the way in which the money should be paid. Karavelov now went much further. He insisted that institutions of such economic and strategic importance as railways must be owned and run by the state alone and in December 1884 his Railway Act placed the control of the trunk line in government hands and decreed that in future the government alone would have the power to construct railways, all of which would be state property. The nationalised Bulgarian State Railways (BDZh) had been created. This the Conservatives disliked, Stoilov arguing that the state would not build lines as cheaply as experienced European companies and that state ownership of completed lines was unwise as the country did not possess sufficient trained personnel to run them.

Conservative objections made little impression and Karavelov went on from this victory to deal in similar manner with the question of the bank. The National Bank set up by Dondukov-Korsakov had been the object of many foreign speculators who wished to turn it into a public joint-stock concern. In 1883 Nachovich had agreed in principle that this should be done. In 1884 pressure was still being exercised in this direction, the chief protagonist now being the Austrian financier, Schlesinger, who demanded implementation of Nachovich's agreement in principle. Karavelov refused. With the full backing of the leading traders and merchants of Sofia he put before a compliant Sŭbranie a bill which firmly declared the Bulgarian National Bank to be a state institution in which private investment would not be allowed.

In addition to these two major acts Karavelov's government passed a number of routine measures for the regulation of stamp duties, customs levies and other sources of government income. These occasioned little public comment but on other issues the Cabinet found itself facing mounting popular discontent. The craft-based manufacturing guilds, already suffering from cheap foreign imports, protested bitterly against a new tax on professions, and there was widespread resentment at the very high salaries being paid to civil servants, a legacy of the immediate post-Liberation days when high remuneration had been necessary to attract men to the newly-created bureaucracy. Few outside that bureaucracy believed the high salaries were still justified and this feeling was particularly strong in the provinces where resentment at centralised power and the capital's new western-oriented *mores* were already being felt.

The Cabinet was also embarrassed by its more extreme supporters. Slaveikov, whose health had not been able to bear the strain of office, had been replaced by Suknarov, an unsavory ruffian who filled the posts at his disposal with like personages. One of these, the mayor of Sofia, discomfited his political masters by announcing the government had organised bands of *shaikadjii* (thugs) to terrorise its political opponents. Suknarov refused to sack the mayor so Karavelov had to step in and remove both the offending official and his ministerial patron. The opposition reaped a rich propaganda harvest, and there were murmurs of discontent in the Democratic Party.

Karavelov could however overcome such discontent by posing as the defender of the constitution who had repealed the 5/17 December Act, and he could also present himself as the guardian of national integrity. It was the Bregovo issue which enabled him to do this. This problem centred upon a strip of territory along the Byala Timok river near Bregovo which had been ceded to Bulgaria in 1878 despite the fact that it was the personal property of the Obrenović family. By 1884 the issue had been complicated by the fact that Serbian political emigrés had taken refuge in the area and King Milan was now demanding their removal as well as the return of his property to Serbia. Alexander, who had had private talks with Milan, would willingly have complied with both demands but territorial questions could not be settled by princely fiat. This the Serbs refused to recognise and in protest withdrew their representative from Sofia. Still Karavelov stood firm, receiving support from his own Party, from the Tsankovists and from the Russian diplomatic agent who let it be known that Alexander could not dispose personally of territory won by the effusion of Russian blood; for a while Karavelov could enlist the nationalist passions of the pre-Liberation days and the constitutional enthusiasms of 1879.

The concern over Bregovo fuelled and was itself fuelled by that revival of the national question which was apparent in Bulgarian politics from the middle of 1884 onwards. The question of course had never died but it had been submerged by the overbearing concentration on constitutional problems. Settlement of those problems therefore allowed the national one to rise nearer to the surface.

There were two main strands to the national question, Rumelia and Macedonia. With Rumelia already having its own political institutions and with those institutions firmly dominated by the Bulgarians of the region there was little doubt but that Rumelia would one day join with Bulgaria; the problem was to choose the opportune moment for the merger. With Macedonia the issue was more complex. No-one in Bulgaria doubted that the Macedonian Slavs were Bulgarians, but the Serbs and the Greeks were by no means ready to admit that this was so. The ruling Turks were not particularly concerned whether the Christian inhabitants of Macedonia saw themselves as Bulgarians, Greeks, Serbs or even Macedonians, but they were determined that they should remain obedient subjects of the Sultan.* The task for the Bulgarians was first of all to make sure that the Christians of Macedonia regarded themselves as Bulgarians and secondly to work for the liberation of the region from Ottoman rule, the assumption being that it would then unite with the Principality and with Rumelia to recreate the Bulgaria of San Stefano. There was much to be said for concentration on the Macedonian rather than the Rumelian aspect of the national problem. If union between Bulgaria and Rumelia were brought about the powers and the Balkan states would thereupon determine to resist any further Bulgarian expansion lest the balance of power in the Balkans be totally destroyed. If, on the other hand, the more difficult problem of Macedonia were to be solved first there would be no force which could prevent the union of the two existing Bulgarian states, the Principality and Rumelia.

---

*As an Englishman, educated for some time in Ireland, and married to a southern Irish Protestant of moderate nationalist views, I know better than to attempt to champion any one side in the multi-faceted Macedonian problem. I shall try to relate what happened and to report what Bulgarians, rightly or wrongly, felt about Macedonia. I have used terms such as 'Macedonian', 'Macedo-Bulgarian', 'Bulgaro-Macedonian', etc. with an eye as much on style as on terminological exactitude in the secure knowledge that such exactitude is a chimera, and that, even if it were not, scientific precision could never overcome the passions of those committed to—or more forcibly against—any of the various parties to the Macedonian dispute.

If international considerations suggested a concentration on Macedonia rather than Rumelia so too did domestic ones. Since the Liberation large numbers of Macedonian refugees had settled in Bulgaria and many Macedonian associations had been founded, though few had been lasting or effective. Late in 1884 there were signs of greater coherence and the Macedonians threatened for the first time to exercise considerable political influence. The reasons for this were the subsiding of the constitutional squabbles in Bulgaria and the increasing difficulties facing the Bulgarian faction in Macedonia itself. For years the Exarchate had been vainly attempting to secure jurisdiction over the bishoprics which had been promised to it in 1870 but which had been withheld since the outbreak of the Russo-Turkish War.* In addition to this the Exarch was also having to combat continuing Russian moves to end the Orthodox schism within the Ottoman Empire. The Bulgarians bitterly resented any attempt either to separate the Bulgarian Church in Bulgaria from that in the Ottoman Empire or to unite any part of the Bulgarian Church with the Greek. As the Exarch's position seemed to weaken, so propaganda from the Serbian and Greek lobbies in Macedonia intensified. This itself meant a decline in political stability in the area which in turn led to increased measures of coercion by the Ottoman authorities. The Bulgarian public were disturbed by these developments and by the failure of their own government's diplomatic campaign to bring political reform to Macedonia. In the Sŭbranie there were angry scenes when in answer to a deputy's question on what was being done a government spokesman replied that there was nothing more that could be done but care for the refugees. In November and December there were large meetings in Sofia and elsewhere to protest at alleged Turkish mistreatment of the Christians in Macedonia.

These meetings had been organised by the Macedonian exiles. A new society, *Makedonski Glas* (Voice of Macedonia), which published a newspaper of the same title, was formed to campaign for the implementation of Articles 23 and 62 of the treaty of Berlin by which the signatory powers pledged themselves to see that reforms were introduced into the Ottoman Empire. Other new Macedonian associations were established, including that in Plovdiv under Zahary Stoyanov, a veteran of the national liberation struggle who was soon to publish a

---

*See above p. 16 and below, pp. 135–7, for further details of this complicated problem.

famous autobiographical account of those years, and that in Ruse led by a young friend of Alexander Battenberg, Captain Panitsa, who was to make his own dramatic invasion into the headlines in 1890.

By the spring of 1885 the Macedonians' propaganda in Bulgaria had sharpened noticeably. *Makedonski Glas* declared that the only hope for the territory lay in action by the 'terrorised local inhabitants', and that only 'forceful and desperate' deeds would make the European powers alive to their responsibilities to enforce all clauses of the treaty of Berlin.[6] There was action as well as words. In April 1885 a band of fifteen to twenty armed men crossed into Macedonia and in May a much larger incursion took place when a Russian, Kalmykov, led between sixty and seventy men into Turkish Macedonia, the band having previously helped itself to weapons from the Kiustendil armoury with the obvious complicity of the local soldiers and gendarmerie. The Kalmykov band, like another which had been raised in Ruse and which crossed into Macedonia in June, was soon destroyed by the Turks but the incidents embarrassed Karavelov greatly. He had previously been president of one of the Macedonian organisations but was now anxious to stress that he and his ministers had no connection with the agitation and though approving of its objectives could not endorse the violent means adopted. To prove his sincerity Karavelov ordered all known Macedonian activists to be removed from border areas and many families, not a few of them innocent, were bundled ruthlessly into the Bulgarian interior. Karavelov's enemies claimed he had betrayed the Kalmykov band in the hope of securing concessions from the Porte to the Exarchate, concessions which would deflate the Macedonian balloon in Bulgaria and thereby weaken the Macedonians who were rapidly constituting a potentially disruptive group on the left of the Democratic Party.

The revival of the national question could not but affect the disposition of political forces within Bulgaria. The Russians, increasingly preoccupied with central Asia, wanted only stability in the Balkans and Karavelov, to judge from his reaction to the Macedonian developments, would clearly cooperate in this regard; the Tsankovist faction of the old Liberal Party would be every bit as compliant for they stood with their leader in arguing that Bulgaria's foreign policy must be dovetailed with that of Russia. The Conservatives for their part were unlikely to be any more troublesome for they had withdrawn from the scene, their domestic political ambitions having been achieved and then dashed by the enactment and then the repeal of the law of 5/17

December 1883. What then of the Prince? He appeared greatly weaker than in 1879. He had to face the sullen hostility of the Russians; the Liberals, given Russian backing, had little need of him; and his main supporters, the Conservatives, had retired from the fray and with them had gone any hope of a permanent change in the constitution. His only hope of establishing greater personal control lay in exploiting the growing nationalist movement, but this was a dangerous card and one which could be played only for the highest stakes as the Prince was ultimately to learn. Yet this was the card which he now chose to play, albeit with due circumspection. He instructed his private secretary, Golovin, to establish indirect contact with the Macedonian and Rumelian nationalist leaders. The Prince's hopes for a controlled and cautious game were to be disappointed. By the time Golovin had established his contacts events were moving far more rapidly than Alexander could have envisaged and far from his controlling the nationalist movement the latter, in Rumelia at least, was moving under its own momentum and in a direction and at a pace of its own choosing.

The Prince who had set out to control or use to his own advantage events in Rumelia now became their prisoner and ultimately their victim, but before that can be described some account must be given of the political evolution of Rumelia itself.

Chapter 4

UNION WITH RUMELIA AND
WAR WITH SERBIA, 1885

The treaty of Berlin had decreed that Eastern Rumelia was to be an autonomous region of the Ottoman Empire under 'the direct military and political authority of His Imperial Majesty the Sultan'. The region was to be administered from Plovdiv by a Christian Governor General whose five-year appointment was to be made by the Sultan and approved by the signatory powers. Internal order was to be maintained by a locally-recruited gendarmerie and militia whose officers were to be appointed, with due regard for local circumstances, by the Sultan. The details of the new province's constitution were to be decided by an international body, the Eastern Rumelian Commission, which arrived in Plovdiv in October 1878 when the province separated from the Principality to the north.

The Commission immediately became the recipient of a flood of petitions expressing the fears of the Rumeliote Bulgarians. These fears were concentrated on those provisions of the Berlin settlement which allowed the Sultan to garrison the forts along the border with Bulgaria and which permitted the Governor General to call in Ottoman troops should the local militia prove incapable of preserving order. The most poignant of these addresses was that signed by 'the eight hundred and sixty-four widows of Karlovo', a small town on the Balkan foothills which had suffered grievously during the fighting and recriminations of 1876–8, and like the other petitions its chief request was a guarantee that the Sultan's soldiers should never again be allowed into Rumelia. These petitions were backed by demonstrations in a number of towns and by a two-man mission to the capitals of Europe pleading the dangers of any re-entry of Turkish troops. One of the two delegates, Ivan Evlogi Geshov, continued the campaign in his newspaper *Maritsa* published in Plovdiv. Rumelian warnings that the reappearance of Ottoman soldiers in the province would produce chaos were not hollow. As soon as the main provisions of the Berlin settlement had become known the organisation of resistance had begun with the formation under Russian guidance of 'gymnastic societies' in which Rumelians were drilled and given weapon-training. By October 1878 all Bulgarian communities in Rumelia had their own gymnastic society and the total strength of the societies was about forty thousand with the largest, *Orel* (Eagle), numbering some fifteen thousand. The societies gave great cohesion to the local Bulgarians and served as a powerful warning to those who took seriously the possibility that Turkish soldiers might return to southern Bulgaria.

This warning was soon taken into account. Early in 1879 the powers let it be known that they accepted the argument that the return of Ottoman troops could well produce horrors worse than those in 1876 and that therefore with the exception of the Governor General no Ottoman official, civilian or military, would serve in Rumelia. Further balm was provided by the Tsar. When Russian troops left Rumelia in April 1879 he issued a proclamation to the Rumelians who were promised that the civil administration they were now to experience would guarantee them a better and more secure life than any they had known before and this being so the Tsar appealed to those whom his army had liberated not to endanger their own well-being by threatening their newly-found peace.

With these statements the Rumelian Bulgarians were content and their worst fears disappeared. They could now concentrate on the constitutional settlement which the Eastern Rumelian Commission was defining. The Governor General was to exercise his executive authority through six ministries, or Directorates, those of Internal Affairs; Public Instruction; Justice; Public Works, Agriculture and Trade; Finance; and the Militia and Gendarmerie. The legislature was to be unicameral and was to be formed by the Regional Assembly consisting of thirty-six members elected indirectly with a small property qualification for the franchise, plus ten members nominated by the Governor General and ten members who were to hold seats *ex officio*. The Sultan had the right to veto legislation but it was generally, though incorrectly, assumed that this right would not be exercised. The Regional Assembly was to elect from its own number a ten-man Standing Committee which was to perform many of the functions of the Senate or State Council which the Conservatives in the Principality would have liked to create. The Organic Statute which promulgated details of the new constitution also guaranteed all Rumelians, irrespective of race or creed, full civil liberties.

As in Bulgaria so in Rumelia the definition of the constitution created the need to find someone to fill the executive post. The choice fell upon Aleko Bogoridi Pasha, a Bulgarian by birth but a Greek by education. He had served with distinction in the Ottoman public service but was acceptable to the Bulgarians because he had endowed the land for St Stefan's church in Constantinople. He set out for his new post in May 1879 and immediately faced the problem of how to dress in public. This was of great importance. Acting on orders from the Sultan he entered Rumelia wearing Ottoman uniform complete with fez, but so hostile was the reception he received at the first station inside the province that by the time the train reached Plovdiv he had changed and now sported a *kalpak;* the Plovdiv crowd, forewarned by telegraph to expect a fez, was delighted. This was not the trivial incident it might at first appear for the Governor General's adoption of their national headgear was a symbolic declaration to the Bulgarians that they would not be returned to their former servitude, that autonomy was not a cynical device to restore unimpaired Ottoman sovereignty.

Now reassured that their autonomy would be real the Bulgarians in Rumelia set about securing domination within the political machinery of the province. The presumed obstacles to this domination were the resident Turks and Greeks. Figures compiled by the Russian Provisional Administration showed that of the province's 815,000 inhabitants 70%, or 573,000 were Bulgarian, 21.4% (175,000) were Turkish and 5.2% (42,500) were Greek, the remainder being Gypsies, Armenians, Jews and others. The potential power of the Turkish element lay in their previous ruling position and the backing they could expect from the Sultan and his supporters in Europe. The Turkish question was also complicated because many Turks who had previously played an influential role in southern Bulgaria and who had fled before the Russian army in 1877–8 were now returning to their former homes no doubt expecting also a restoration of their former influence in local affairs. The Turks were supported by the other large minority group, the Greeks. The Greeks did not accept the statistics provided by the Russians, though no-one could doubt the overall numerical superiority of the Bulgarians. Greek influence, however, was not based on numbers. The Greeks had at least as much administrative experience and influence as their Turkish allies and in addition to this they exercised strong cultural sway in the cities of Rumelia, especially Plovdiv. Greek wealth and power was based primarily on the successful commercial bourgeoisie which had long dominated grain purchasing and exporting in the region. From this source had come much of the money which established and maintained the superb Greek schools in Rumelia and other parts of the Empire, schools in which many successful Bulgarian families had formerly educated their children, one example being Aleko Pasha himself. Together with this powerful native element the Greeks combined the influence in Constantinople which the Patriarch and the heirs of the Phanariot Greeks could exercise. The Greeks were formidable opponents and opposition between them and the Bulgarians was sharpened by the concurrent competition for influence over the Orthodox Christians in Macedonia. The presumed strength of their opponents forced upon the Rumeliote Bulgarians a fruitful unity, cohesion and discipline.

The great powers whose representatives had designed the Organic Statute had forseen the problem of the minority races and had taken steps to protect them. In local government the two regions and twelve districts of the Turkish system were replaced by six provinces and twenty-eight cantons in the hope that these smaller units would better represent minority interests; the religious leaders of all the main communities were among the ten *ex offico* members of the Regional Assembly; and the Greek, Bulgarian and Turkish languages were to be equal in all public debates and publications. The powers also hoped that all groups would be represented in the Standing Committee of the Assembly and to achieve this objective they arranged for that committee to be elected by proportional representation to ensure the election of at least four non-Bulgarians. One prominent Bulgarian, Ivan Salabashev, had other ideas. He also had a doctorate in mathematics from Prague and thus armed he showed his fellow Bulgarians how they could elect more than six members, even staging a mock poll to convince the doubters in the ranks. He succeeded and proved that even in Rumelian politics knowledge was power for all but two of the ten chosen were Bulgarian. This was but one sign that the Bulgarians were going to secure complete political domination in Rumelia without serious opposition from the Turks and Greeks. A further indication was Aleko Pasha's nomination of Bulgarian prefects in all six provinces and the appointment, without complaint from the other groups, of Bulgarians to many posts in the administration. Bulgarian political supremacy was finally and irrevocably established in the elections to the Regional Assembly in October 1879 for of the thirty-six elected deputies thirty-one were Bulgarian. The speech from the Governor General was delivered in Greek, Turkish and somewhat halting Bulgarian. The reply to the address was in Bulgarian only. Bulgarian political ascendancy had been established and it was not contested either within Rumelia or by any of the powers.

In the year or so after the election of the first Regional Assembly the politics of Rumelia were dominated by a small group of wealthy Bulgarians led by the cousins Ivan Evlogi Geshov and Ivan Evstratiev Geshov. The Geshovists formed themselves into the Nationalist Party, published their views in the newspapers *Maritsa* and *Naroden Glas* (Voice of the Nation), and secured their influence by filling the administrative machine with loyal placemen. Nationalist policies amounted to little more than the protection of Bulgarian political supremacy in Rumelia, support for Russian policy in the Near East, and the inevitable affirmation of and dedication to the notion of full national liberation and reunification. An opposition party also emerged. This was the Rumelian Liberal Party, known colloquially as the *kazionite* ('office seekers' would be a free but accurate translation) and again it was almost entirely a Bulgarian party. There were few real policy differences with the Nationalists and support for the *kazionite* tended to arise principally from personal factors. This did not make for a strong Liberal Party in Rumelia and lack of affective leadership was a further weakness. The Rumelian Liberals also lacked funds and a party press.

Party politics in Rumelia were much enlivened by the arrival of the Liberal refugees fleeing from the coup in the Principality in 1881. Leadership was now available in profusion and the powerful *Nezavisimost* was soon being published in Plovdiv. For the first time there were real policy differences between the two Parties. The Liberals began to demand changes in the internal structure of Rumelia and these were certainly needed for the administrative machine was very much the product of a committee with separate parts being based upon different European models. This had been done to save time and to prevent any one power securing overbearing influence in the region and thus the judicial system was copied from that of Austria, the financial from Italy, the educational from Germany and so on. This did not make for administrative clarity or efficiency. The Liberals also

pressed for a more rigourously independent attitude towards the Porte
and they were not prepared to accept the Nationalists' claim that Bulgarians should support Russian policy in the Balkans, for men such as
Karavelov, Slaveikov and Zahari Stoyanov had turned away from
Russia after the latter had backed Battenberg's coup in Sofia. The
enlivening effect of the new Liberal leaders was immediately felt and
was seen in the elections of October 1881, when half the elected members of the Assembly had to seek re-election; the Liberals won every
seat contested. In the Standing Committee chosen after the elections
the Liberals had half the seats.

Initially the Liberals received the backing of Aleko Pasha. This was
partly because the Governor General needed an alternative to the
Nationalists, but primarily because he had fallen out with the Russians. From the very beginning of his governor generalship there had
been personality difficulties with the Russians, his wife having quarrelled publicly with the Russian consul over the order of precedence in
a religious service, but there were also more serious issues at stake and
ones closely paralleling those dividing Alexander Battenberg from the
Russians in Bulgaria. The Russians were anxious that the Rumelian
militia should be under their influence or at the worst that it should not
fall under the dominance of potentially competing powers such as
Britain, Austria or Germany, and thus many Russian officers were
serving in the Rumelian militia and gendarmerie. Aleko, on the other
hand, was anxious to preserve his independence and prevent the domination of any power over his armed forces, and in pursuit of this
balance he appointed a number of non-Russian officers and placed a
Briton, a Frenchman and a German in the three highest gendarmerie
and militia posts, resolutely resisting Russian pressure to dismiss them
and appoint a Russian Chief of Staff. He also declined to purchase
25,000 Russian rifles with appropriate quantities of ammunition. All
this was intensely annoying to the Russians, but relations between
them and Aleko were strained beyond repair in 1883 when the Governor General refused to sanction plans for a Russian war memorial at
Shipka. This was a fearful insult. The money had been raised in Russia, the plans had been drawn up by a Russian architect, and no-one,
not even the Sultan, had objected. Aleko, however, insisted that with
walls so thick the proposed building was more like a fortress than a
war memorial and the treaty of Berlin forbad the construction of fortresses in Rumelia.

Aleko was never forgiven by the Russians, and when his term of office expired in 1884 they vetoed his re-election. His successor was Gavril Krŭstevich Pasha, a Bulgarian from Kotel who had been on the moderate side in the struggles of the 1860s and who in serving as Aleko's secretary and deputy had established close links with the Geshovist Nationalist Party. By the terms of the Organic Statute a change in Governor General brought about a general election for all seats in the Regional Assembly. Since 1883, when the second half of the elected seats had been recontested, the Liberals had held an absolute majority, but since those partial elections the Liberals had earned an unenviable reputation for corruption in office and of their leaders had returned to the Principality following the restoration of the constitution there. These facts the Nationalists used to their advantage in the election of 1884 in which they were victorious. But playing on Liberal weakness had not been the Geshovists' only electoral tactic. They also gave much greater emphasis to the call for the liberation and reunification of all Bulgarians, even changing the name of the Party from Nationalist to Unionist and taunting their opponents for being nationalists and unionists in word alone. The Liberals replied by branding the Geshovists pseudo-unionists'.*

There was a good deal of substance in the Liberal jibe, for the Unionists' invocation of the national cause derived primarily from considerations of internal policy. This was nothing new, for both sides in Rumelia had played the nationalist card when they believed it would help them. It had always been a safe one to play because external factors could be relied upon to prevent any dramatic developments; in the years immediately following the Liberation it had been British and Austrian interference which had made any steps towards further liberation and unification impossible, but in 1884 the Rumelian Unionists could rely on Russia to preserve the *status quo* for, fully occupied in central Asia, she did not want any complications in the Balkans. Furthermore, it was widely known that the Russians would not be happy to see Rumelia absorbed into Bulgaria if this meant an extension of Battenberg's power and an increase in his prestige, yet these would indubitably be the consequences of unification, for the Rumelian Unionists did not contemplate the deposition of Prince Alexander.

---

*This is a polite rendition of the original Bulgarian, *lŭzhecŭedinisti,* which more literally translated would be 'lying unionist'.

The national issue was to remain one for exploitation by local politicians for another year, but in 1885 the swelling tide of nationalist feeling both north and south of the Balkans was to sweep the politicians before it; the exploiters were to become the exploited.

Since the Berlin settlement the goal of national reunification had never been forgotten, but the circumstances in which it had to be pursued had fluctuated and factors promoting or retarding the cause had come and gone with some rapidity. In 1878–9 Bulgarian politicians in both states had done all they could to prevent the division of 1878 becoming entrenched. In the Principality the literary alphabet was based on that already in use south of the Balkans, the school organisations of both areas were similar, and the press of both states circulated freely in both Bulgaria and Rumelia. The Bulgarian Foreign Ministry also decided that all dealings with the administration in Plovdiv should be in Bulgarian rather than French or Russian, the languages used in communication with foreign states, whilst politicians in the south asked those in Sofia for advice and even documentation on affairs in Bulgaria so that Rumelian institutions could be similar and Rumelian policies, where necessary, aligned with the interests of Bulgaria. The Sofia Military Academy trained officers for both the Bulgarian army and the Rumelian militia and the Rumelians, despite Turkish protests, used the same national anthem as the Bulgarians, and refused to wear the fez or raise the Turkish flag.

The Rumelians clearly looked to Sofia and identified completely with Bulgaria as their nation-state. The Turks did little to deflect that gaze or to encourage closer association with Constantinople. The Porte used its right of veto over Rumelian legislation often to the great disadvantage of the province. Constantinople blocked laws concerning the press and the first stages of the educational system, in the latter instance because it was proposed to include gymnastics in the curriculum of elementary schools and the Ottoman authorities associated that activity with the formation of the Rumelian militia. The Porte also frustrated the raising of a loan which Plovdiv needed to help restore the devastated agriculture of the region, and a veto was placed on Rumelian plans to build a railway from Yambol to the port of Burgas, a line which would have released Rumelian merchants from their dependence on the rapacious Oriental Railway Company and would also have freed their goods from Ottoman customs levies. Similarly, plans to establish a Rumelian bank came to nothing because of opposition in Constantinople. In instances such as these the Ottoman veto seriously affected the development of Rumelia, but in others the Porte's opposition was less important and often ignored. Budgets which the Sultan's government had refused to sanction were nevertheless implemented, and when the Porte refused to approve the appointment of a number of Directors in Plovdiv the latter took up their posts notwithstanding. In this fashion Turkish sovereignty in Rumelia was gradually eroded, but the exercise of the veto in areas such as banking and railway development showed that that sovereignty still existed and that Rumelia was not as free as the Principality.

There were other ways in which the Principality appeared more attractive. Rumelia was over-administered. This was in large measure due to the powers' imposition of the complicated system of local government designed to protect minority interests, but the system was expensive, requiring as many as thirty officials to carry out tasks previously entrusted to a handful of gendarmes. The land tax in Rumelia was also unpopular. This was calculated according to the tithe values of the ten years before the war when wheat prices were higher and it was also applied to all land held, not merely to that worked, an important consideration in an agricultural regimen that included much fallow land. In Bulgaria the tithe in cash was based on the three post-war years and, being a tithe, was levied only on what was produced, not on land held. The Rumelians felt themselves over-governed and over-taxed. They were also unhappy with their official currency, the Turkish pound, which the authorities valued at one hundred groschen but which fetched one hundred and thirty groschen in the market, meaning that all who received their salaries from the administration were overpaid by a third, whilst all taxpayers were over-taxed to the same degree. In the year or so after the end of the war the villages of Rumelia were in a desperate state, for they had suffered much more heavily than those in the north. In these months it had been supplies of seed and animals from the Principality which had saved many peasants and townsmen in the south, and once again therefore the national bond was reaffirmed. In some areas of Rumelia the distress was more prolonged. Along the southern foothills of the Balkan mountains lay the towns which had grown in wealth and influence earlier in the century when they had become centres of manufacturing, chiefly in textiles. Their wool came primarily from the mountain flocks to the north and their finished products were sold chiefly to the south in the Ottoman Empire. After 1878 the markets were less accessible and the source of raw materials separated by a new and unnatural frontier; in Kotel property prices dived by over fifty percent in five years, Sliven's export trade, formerly with Rumania, fell by 75% from 1872 to 1879, and in other towns the decline was no less dramatic. For such communities hope seemed to lie—incorrectly as it turned out—in the abolition of the border between north and south Bulgaria.

Yet if the desirability of union were for the most part obvious, the means to achieving it were not. In the earliest years after the Liberation the Austro-British veto would have been applied and, given its need to remain on good terms with the Austrians and Germans, Russia would not sanction union either. This killed the possibility of union for the northern Liberals, who held to their notion that Russia should be the guiding force in the determination of Bulgarian foreign policy, and the initiatives towards union in the early years came from the southerners and the Conservatives in the north. The Prince and the Conservatives did not believe that much could come of such initiatives yet they were not above putting them to domestic political uses, but when the coup of 1881 suspended the Tŭrnovo constitution it was the Conservatives rather than the Liberals who had put the question of unification into cold storage. In Rumelia there had been little conflict between executive and legislature, largely because the latter had established very early its right to dismiss Directors and other members of the executive machine. Even before the coup the Rumelians had doubts as to the wisdom of coming closer to a system which in two years had seen seven Cabinets and two Sŭbranies dissolved, but after the suspension of the constitution it was absolutely clear that Rumelia could not allow itself to be absorbed by the Principality. This opinion, of course, the Liberal exiles encouraged, so successfully indeed that there was discussion of a possible union between Rumelia and Macedonia, and to combat such ideas and to attempt to repair his prestige in the south Alexander secretly financed the Rumeliote newspaper *Sŭedinenie* (Union) which began publication in December 1882. It was to no purpose; Rumelian leaders of both Parties would not contemplate union without the restoration of constitutional rule in the Principality.

Relations between Sofia and Plovdiv were further complicated by the issue of tariffs. The first Bulgarian administrations had exempted all exports from Rumelia and Macedonia from customs levies, but in 1880 Karavelov, after unsuccessful attempts to negotiate a reciprocal agreement with Rumelia, imposed tariffs on imports from that province. In the following year there were agreements to exempt various commodities, but this was of little use, for the chief exports of both sides were still subject to tariffs. There the matter remained until union in 1885, though in the previous year Karavelov had agreed with the Rumelians to make more satisfactory arrangements for each other's primary exports, but the Porte refused to allow Plovdiv to implement the agreement. The Rumelians had also been offended by Sofia's unwillingness to grant a loan to the Plovdiv administration, the money being needed to help the agricultural savings banks in the south, though in May 1884 after some eighteen months of negotiations the Bulgarian government at last sanctioned a loan of 60,000 leva on terms better than those being offered elsewhere.

From 1879 to 1885 union had been desired by all Bulgarians, but it had been impossible to achieve both for international and internal Bulgarian and Rumelian reasons. In 1884 and 1885 this changed as internal conditions, particularly in Rumelia, altered and because in the last resort the Prince and the Bulgarians were prepared to stand against the international factors before which they had previously given way.

In 1884, as we have seen in the preceding chapter, the Macedonian question became more pressing. This naturally had an effect in Rumelia, just as it did in Bulgaria. In the spring of 1884 the new Russian consul in Plovdiv, Sorokin, electrified the Rumelian Bulgarians by declaring at a banquet that Macedonia was a Russian question which would be settled by Russia; furthermore, to the statement that the Bulgarians were confident that Russia, having liberated them, would soon reunite them, he responded with the pronouncement that though there were two Bulgarias their reunification was only a matter of time. This was heady stuff, but it was meant as much for internal as external consumption, the Russians being anxious to discredit Aleko Pasha and prevent any Rumelian movement for his reappointment, and after his departure there were no more such statements from the Tsar's consul. Yet national passions were being stirred by others. In 1884 Zahari Stoyanov published his classic *Zapiski po bŭlgarskite Vŭstaniya* (Notes on the Bulgarian Risings), which in describing past triumphs provided an inspiration for future strivings. Many chose to believe that the nobility of the nationalist cause as portrayed in Stoyanov's book contrasted sharply with the cynical fashion in which the contemporary Rumelian politicians were exploiting the national question for their own short-term objectives, and disillusion with the existing political system in Rumelia gave great impetus to the nationalist agitation, as too did the growing movement in the north.

Agitation increased during 1884, but there was little organisation to accompany it. This did not appear until early 1885 with the setting up of committees in Ruse, Varna, Sofia and Plovdiv, the latter being headed by Stoyanov and calling itself the Bulgarian Secret Central Revolutionary Committee. As yet both the public agitation and the emergent organisation were directed towards the maximalist nationalist objective of liberation for Macedonia and Thrace and the union of these territories and Rumelia with Bulgaria. This remained the case until the summer of 1885 when Stoyanov reorganised his committee, switching its objective from liberation to the limited programme of the unification of Bulgaria and Rumelia, and renaming it the Committee for Union. The reason for this switch was simple: action in Macedonia had failed. The Bulgarian diplomatic offensive had come to nothing and the action programme launched by Kalmykov and the Macedonian exiles had been equally unsuccessful; indeed, by the summer of 1885 adventurism was being suppressed both in Bulgaria and in Rumelia. But if the prospect of effective action on behalf of the Macedonians was declining, nationalist agitation was increasing. In March 1885 a meeting of the Plovdiv guilds called to discuss general questions had ended by passing a resolution calling on the powers to do something about unification, and similar resolutions came from meetings of guildsmen in other Rumelian towns and in Sofia. On 24 April/6 May the annual St George's Day parade with which the Greeks of Plovdiv celebrated their national saint was disrupted by crowds of angry Bulgarians; on 19/31 May the Bulgarians noisily celebrated the anniversary of Botev's historic crossing of the Danube despite a prohibition from the authorities. At the end of May Stoyanov who was as yet still committed to the maximalist programme, published the first edition of a new journal, *Borba* (Struggle), which having denounced Rumelia as an officials' paradise called for the liberation of Macedonia and the re-creation of San Stefano Bulgaria. On 17/29 July the mass movement reached its apogee with an emotional meeting at Buzludja in the Stara Planina where in 1868 Hadji Dimitŭr Ashenov and twenty-five comrades had died heroic deaths in an encounter with Turkish troops; at this revered spot Hadji Dimitŭr's mother called upon an already emotional crowd not merely to honour but to emulate her son. Given so much public enthusiasm and so clear an indication that action in Macedonia would be fruitless, the leaders of the Rumelian movement inevitably concentrated their efforts on union with Bulgaria.

The reorganisation and redefinition of aims was carried out on 25 July/6 August at a meeting in Stoyanov's house. The new Committee for Union was to be under Stoyanov's chairmanship but included also two important representatives from north of the border, Captain Panitsa and Dimitŭr Rizov. The aim of the new committee was defined as 'The union of northern and southern Bulgaria under the sceptre of Alexander Battenberg'. The new Committee abandoned the idea of a mass rising previously favoured by leaders such as Stoyanov, and the tactic now was to recruit supporters amongst the officers of the militia, this being done on the assumption that a mass rising could be prolonged and costly whereas a military coup, for which the prospects were good given the number of Bulgarian-trained officers, would, if all went well, be bloodless and quick, speed being of the essence as the organisers had to gamble that once the union had been effected no power would wish to contest a *fait accompli*. The conspirators were soon to have important successes in the recruitment of Majors Nikolaev and Nikolov, commanders respectively of the militia and of the 2nd (Plovdiv) Regiment, both key posts. In the meantime, the leaders encouraged public agitation with meetings, demonstrations and articles in the press.

At the 25 July/6 August meeting it had been agreed that the coup, backed by popular demonstrations, should be carried out on 16/28 September, when the harvest would be complete and when the Bulgarian army would still be mobilised following its autumn manoeuvres, the backing of this force being necessary if the Turks contested the coup. This information was passed to Sofia, though not in absolutely explicit form. The Prince was at that time in Europe and was not much disturbed by the rumours of impending upheavals in Rumelia for there had been such rumours in the past, and he therefore informed those whom he met that he could guarantee the maintenance of the *status quo* in Bulgaria and Rumelia, one of those whom he reassured being the Russian Foreign Minister, Giers, who met Alexander at Franzensbad in Bohemia at the end of August. This was a fatal though not a deliberate error.

Shortly after the Franzensbad meeting events in Rumelia went beyond the control even of the conspirators. On 3/15 September the enthusiasm of leading unionists in Panagiurishte could be restrained no longer and the town, which had been one of the first to raise the flag of revolt in 1876, declared against the Rumelian settlement and for union with Battenberg's Bulgaria. Kotel followed suit and there was a danger that revolutionary energies would be dissipated in a series of unco-ordinated and premature risings, a danger increased on 4/16 September when the previously supine government in Plovdiv showed a momentary flicker of resolution and arrested a number of leading conspirators including Stoyanov and Panitsa. On the same day the village of Golyamo Konare (Sŭedinenie) near Plovdiv had joined those in revolt and the government, flushed with one success, set out to achieve another. This was its undoing. In command of the detachment sent to Golyamo Konare was Major Nikolov. Nikolov joined the rebels and two days later, on 6/18 September, returned to Plovdiv to depose Gavril Krŭstevich. The Governor General thought of resisting and requesting assistance from the Sultan, but he decided against it, admit-ting he could not expose his fellow countrymen to the danger of war with Turkey for, he said, 'I too am a Bulgarian'. Nikolov and his helpers met no resistance and did not even bother to detain those senior militia or gendarmerie officers who had not been party to the conspiracy. A provisional government was formed and a telegram sent to Prince Alexander informing him of the deposition of Gavril and asking him to accept the union of the province with the Principality. Only the tragic and accidental death of Nikolov marred the rejoicings of the Bulgarians in Rumelia.

North of the Balkans joy was not quite so unconfined. The govern-ment in Sofia, though it had given public support to the agitation in Rumelia, was much embarrassed, not least because of the Prince's recent reassurances to European diplomacy. The chief concern was the reaction of Russia. Their adventure in central Asia had now brought the Russians into sharp conflict with Britain thus making their tenuous ties with Austria, ties easily loosened by disturbances in the Balkans, all the more important; also with its encroachments in central Asia St Petersburg was anxious not to offend Moslem opinion any more deeply. To be added to this was the Tsar's distaste for any possible increase in Alexander Battenberg's power and prestige. Since 1883 St Petersburg had been firmly of the opinion that the union of Bulgaria and Rumelia would be 'detrimental to Russian policy', and this was well known in Sofia. Karavelov's first reaction to the union was there-fore equivocal; Bulgaria, he said, must put its own finances in order before it could assume responsibility for the Eastern Rumelian tribute. But the issues of 1885 were not to be decided by considerations as trivial as this and the man of the hour proved to be not the Minister President but the President of the Sŭbranie, Stambulov. He met Alexander in Tŭrnovo, where the Prince hurried from his summer palace near Varna. Stambulov told the Prince that the union was an accomplished fact which no man could undo and therefore the Prince could take one of two paths, either over the Balkans to Plovdiv or north to the Danube and back to Darmstadt. He also pointed out that any attempt to reject the union would mean not only the end of his political life in Bulgaria but a national revolt which could cause much more disturbance of the Balkan *status quo* than acceptance of the union. The Prince was persuaded. On 8/20 September he telegraphed to Plovdiv his acceptance of the union and, having ordered troops to the Turkish-Rumelian border and called an emergency session of the Sŭbranie, he set out across the Balkans. The following day he arrived to an ecstatic welcome in Plovdiv.

In Plovdiv the Prince set up a caretaker government, announced the imminent abolition of the tariff barrier between north and south, imposed martial law less to deal with internal unrest than to ensure firm government and relative stability in the event of a Turkish invasion, and, again to meet a possible invasion, manned the southern border with regular and volunteer units. Meanwhile, on 10/22 September in Sofia, the Sŭbranie had met in extraordinary session and approved the union by acclamation though some doubting voices, among them Tsankov's, were raised because the deed had been done without the consent of the Tsar. The Assembly then voted an extraordinary credit of ten million leva to cover the cost of mobilisation and, if the worst should happen, war.

The threat of war preoccupied the Prince and his advisers. Alexander therefore did all he could to placate the Sultan, reassuring him that no diminution of his sovereignty had resulted from events in Rumelia and making a particular point of visiting the chief mosque in Plovdiv to ask that a prayer be said for Abdul Hamid. Yet the danger of action by Turkey persisted and it made it all the more important for Bulgaria to be sure of friends elsewhere, primarily in St Petersburg. As soon as he had decided to go to Plovdiv Alexander had sent a telegram to the Tsar expressing the hope that in their adventure he and the Bulgarian people would have the support of the Russian government. The Tsar was visiting relatives in Copenhagen and for two days no reply came during which time the Panslav press in Moscow gave every reason to hope that Russia would bless the union. Disillusion came swiftly and brutally. Despite the opposition of his Foreign Office and in the face of Panslav opinion the Tsar not only pronounced against

the union but underlined his displeasure by ordering the immediate
recall of all Russian officers serving with the Bulgarian army and the
Rumelian militia. The Tsar felt, particularly after the reassurances at
Franzensbad, that he had been duped, though Alexander's knowledge
had been inexact and had the Russian foreign service been better organised the real nature of events would have been reported to the Tsar,
for they were clearly known by Russian officials in Plovdiv. For the
Bulgarians the blow was devastating. Deputations were sent to plead
with the Russian diplomatic agent, Koyander, and the Sŭbranie and
the still extant Regional Assembly both sent delegates to the Tsar
himself. He was unmoved. Publicly he chided the Bulgarians for their
ingratitude, insisting that Russia, after spending so much blood for
Bulgaria, had the right to be consulted before the Principality made
such important decisions. The Prince did not help matters by remarking that if the Russian officers were the sort who deserted their post at
the first sign of danger then Bulgaria should wish them good riddance,
an insult which caused the Tsar to strike Battenberg's name from the
Russian army list.

Bulgaria was in desperate need of friends. The other power most
concerned in Balkan affairs, Austria-Hungary, did not offer much
hope of support for she had to protect the interests of Serbia, then her
client in the region. Britain alone of the powers was keen to resist a
restoration of the *status quo* and this primarily to counter Russia. In
the Balkans itself Rumania, like Britain, welcomed the union because
Russia disliked it, but the Greeks became very belligerent and mobilised until they were warned off by the powers.

The real danger however came from Serbia. King Milan had always
said that he would demand compensation for Bulgarian expansion, but
the problem for him was where to find it. Bosnia and Herzegovina
were closed by Austrian occupation and northern Macedonia, Old
Serbia as the Serbs called it, would mean incurring Austrian displeasure and crossing swords again with the Turks, an experience which
the Serbs were not keen to repeat after the embarrassments of 1876.
Bulgaria, on the other hand, seemed to offer easy pickings. The country was suffering from political schizophrenia, torn between joy at the
union and distress at Russian hostility. It had few effective friends
abroad, its forces were concentrated on the southern border with no
complete railway to rush them northwards, and the command structure of the army had been devastated by the withdrawal of the Russian
officers. By mid-October Milan had decided to set out on his 'stroll to

Sofia'. He massed his army at Nish and on 1/13 November declared war, moving his troops forward on the following day.

The Bulgarians had been able to take only the minimum defensive measures. The Minister of War, Nikiforov—because of the withdrawal of the Russians the first Bulgarian to hold this post—ordered the arming of the Vidin fortress and arranged for surveys to be made of the areas along the Serbian border for no maps were then available. There seemed little to stop the two Serbian armies, one of which made for Vidin and the other and larger of which headed straight for Sofia. In the capital the foreign residents began to show signs of panic and on 5/17 November Alexander ordered the removal of the state treasury to Pleven and placed his own private archives in the hands of the German diplomatic agency. On the same day fighting began at Slivnitsa, a pass affording direct access to Sofia; the Greek consul was reportedly preparing to fête a victorious Milan. The conquering Milan did not appear. The Bulgarians had dug in at Slivnitsa because it was an excellent defensive position and because reinforcements had begun to arrive from the south. For three days the fighting raged but on 7/19 November the Serbs, thanks in no small measure to an adventurous but unauthorised attack from the Bulgarian right flank by a Captain Benderev, had begun to retreat. Milan's stroll to Sofia was soon turned into a headlong flight towards Belgrade. By 11-12/23-24 November the Bulgarians were on Serbian territory and when Pirot fell two days later there was nothing to prevent them from taking Nish, for the Second Serbian Army, having failed to carry the siege of Vidin, had also been defeated. After fifteen days of fighting the Serbian army had collapsed and Milan was offering to abdicate. He was saved by his diplomatic protector, Austria, who ordered the Bulgarians to halt lest they wished to fight Austrian troops too.

The Bulgarians had achieved a quite remarkable victory. The Serbian army, it was true, was not at its best, being unused to its new and improved rifles for which not enough ammunition was available; the artillery too was poor. Serbian tactics were also at fault in the narrow defiles around Slivnitsa but none of these factors could detract from the Bulgarians' achievement, and that achievement was the nation's as well as the army's. The main body of the army had moved itself from one end of the country to the other with little help from modern technology for not only was the railway incomplete but on that part of it which was working there were only five locomotives. Yet despite this the army, poorly clad and shod, covered between forty and sixty kilometres a day and not a single deserter was posted. There was no organised commissariat so on its march the army was fed by the local population who in many cases spontaneously set up feeding stations and rest points. Volunteers came from Bulgarian communities outside Bulgaria and full cooperation was given by all the non-Bulgarian ethnic groups in the country with the exception of the Greeks.

The war saved the nation and proved most dramatically Bulgarian capacity to organise and to fight without the help of foreign advisers. The argument once put forward by the opponents of Bulgarian independence that the Bulgarian nation was not sufficiently mature to be trusted with self-government would be heard no more; all Europe, wrote Jiriček at the time, looked upon Bulgaria in a new light.

Yet however dramatic her victory Bulgaria was to be allowed little profit from it. After Austria's intervention the powers insisted upon negotiations which led to the signing on 19 February/2 March 1886 of the treaty of Bucharest by which the *status quo ante* between Bulgaria and Serbia was restored. Not even the union was to be given international sanction. The powers in late 1885, despite British objections, had been determined to restore the division between northern and southern Bulgaria but by the end of the year it was clear that this was possible only at the cost of war and a greater disturbance of the *status quo* than that represented by the union. The powers therefore took up a British proposal by which Alexander Battenberg was to be made Governor General of Rumelia. This would undo the union in name only and could be effected with a few minor alterations of the Organic Statute and the treaty of Berlin. The Sultan, who had never wanted to take extreme measures, was quickly persuaded of the virtues of this scheme and in January 1886 had come to a four-point agreement with the Bulgarians: Alexander was to be nominated Governor General of Rumelia for five years; the Rumelian administration was to be absorbed into the Bulgarian and the militia was to be integrated into the Bulgarian army; there was to be a defensive alliance between Turkey and Bulgaria; and Bulgaria was to cede to Turkey the Pomak areas of Kŭrdjali and Tŭmrŭsh and to guarantee payment of the Rumelian debt. The Russians objected. They insisted on the scrapping of the defensive treaty as this could mean that one day Bulgarians might have to take up arms to fight alongside the Turks against the Russians; the Bulgarians were happy to give way on this point. A more contentious issue was the Russian demand that Alexander's name should not be mentioned in the treaty which should state only that the

Prince of Bulgaria was to be the Governor General of Rumelia; they also demanded that all the Berlin powers and not the Sultan alone should give quinquennial approval to the appointment of the Governor General. The implications were obvious; the Russians were leaving the door open for the removal of Alexander. The Prince attempted to resist this change but he had no support and gave way after his own delegate in the discussions in Constantinople, Tsanov, accepted the Russian proposals. In April 1886 the Constantinople agreement made the Prince of Bulgaria Governor General of Eastern Rumelia for five years; the defensive treaty was not mentioned but Bulgaria's obligation to cede Kŭrdjali and Tŭmrŭsh and to pay the Rumelian debt remained.

Alexander was soon to be made uncomfortably aware that whatever part he had played in winning the war he was likely to be the major casualty of the peace.

FROM ELATION TO DESPAIR:
THE POLITICAL CRISIS OF 1886

The war of 1885 had brought short-term unity but its legacy to Bulgaria was one of divisions many of them sharpened by the disagreement with Russia. The Prince did what he could to win back Russian confidence, giving fulsome praise to the Russian officers who had trained his army and without whom, he said, the victory of 1885 would not have been possible. He also ordered that at all official victory celebrations the Russian flag was to be flown alongside that of Bulgaria and the Russian national hymn was to be played as well as the Bulgarian. He even wrote in his own hand to the Tsar requesting his support and asking to be allowed to come to St Petersburg to discuss Bulgaria's and his own position.

Alexander III was immovable. Russian policy was now firmly toeing the line the Russian Foreign Ministry had long wanted but which the Tsar had not initially accepted, that of 'Union without Prince Battenberg'. The Bulgarians were to be made to understand that they would have Russian consent to the union, and it would be a complete union not the personal solution which emerged in the spring of 1886, only if they jettisoned their Prince. This attitude was implied in Russia's refusal to allow mention of Alexander by name in the Constantinople settlement, and it was seen too in Bulgaria's internal affairs where Russian officials encouraged all anti-Battenberg manoeuvres. Even during the war itself the Russians had done all they could to discredit the Prince, with the former Minister of War, Kantakuzin, letting it be known at the height of the battle of Slivnitsa that all was lost and that Russia would intervene as soon as the Prince had been persuaded to

abdicate, a *canard* which forced Alexander to hurry back to his capital
in the middle of the fighting. After the war the Russians complained
bitterly when the Bulgarian authorities refused to allow a group of
pro-Russian Rumelian Liberals who believed they could engineer a
reconciliation between Bulgaria and Russia to telegraph directly to the
Tsar, the Russian consul in Plovdiv declaring that by this act Alexander had pronounced himself an enemy of Russia.

In some quarters the Russian message that Bulgaria's political
troubles would end only when Battenberg took the road to Darmstadt
was being received and understood; the Foreign Minister, Tsanov, for
example, returned from the dismal negotiations in Bucharest convinced that abdication was the only solution. Yet though Alexander
faced many problems and had many critics there were few who would
yet openly advocate his removal. Russia therefore had patiently to
support the various opposition factions and hope that their increasing
strength would eventually bring about such internal tension that the
Prince would leave of his own volition or would at last be persuaded
to go by his exasperated subjects.

The opposition groups were numerous. The Tsankovists could
clearly be counted amongst them for Tsankov still adhered to the belief
that Bulgaria's foreign policy should be subjected to Russia's and that
the union had therefore been a blunder. They were joined by others
who were deeply disturbed by the incomplete nature of the final settlement. They resented Alexander's acceptance of the personal union
for that made him, as Governor General of Rumelia, a Turkish official
nominated by the Sultan; in rowdy meetings it was crudely suggested
that Alexander should take to wearing the fez, whilst press articles
raged that the Prince had degraded himself to a status as low as that of
the Prince of Egypt. More thoughtful and civilised critics, the Conservative Ikonomov among them, were worried that in acting against
Russia's wishes for the limited objective of union with Rumelia Bulgaria had sacrificed any hope of achieving full liberation and reunification within the San Stefano borders, an objective which could only be
achieved, it was believed, with Russian help. This was a substantial
argument for not only had union made Russia hostile but it had also
put other states, large and small, on their guard against further Bulgarian expansion, one result of this being an increase in Serbian and
Greek propaganda amongst the Macedonian Christians. Bulgaria,
Ikonomov and his ilk were saying, had seized the sprat but lost the
mackerel.

There was also widespread dissatisfaction amongst the political activists of Rumelia. They had considerable regional pride. They felt with justice that Rumelian society was more cultured and sophisticated than that of the Principality and Plovdiv was still more refined than Sofia. The Rumelians soon came to resent the fact that the Karavelov administration treated their territory merely as an additional province of the Principality, being offended when it was announced that alterations to the Rumelian Organic Statute would be decided upon by a commission of Bulgarian and Turkish but not Rumelian officials which was to meet in Sofia not Plovdiv. More offensive was the government's reluctance to pay Rumelian officials or even militiamen who had fought in the war because the Bulgarian budget had made no provision for such expenditure. The Rumelians had to take the cash out of the vaults of a Plovdiv bank and distribute it themselves. When a united Súbranie first met in the summer of 1886 a number of Rumelians complained that the political system of the Principality had never been sanctioned by the Rumelian people and that what had happened in 1885 was not the union of two consenting parties but the conquest of one by the other; it had been rape rather than seduction. A further cause for discontent south of the Balkans was Karavelov's paring of the administrative machine. This was much needed but those deprived of their livelihood were embittered and many peasants were also puzzled; they had always assumed the only justification for taxation was the over-large bureaucracy and they expected the contraction of the latter to be followed by a diminution in the former, an improbable consequence at any time. The Rumelians, like the Bulgarians in the old Principality, were also much beset by doubts about the nature of the 1886 settlement and both the Unionist Party and a section of the Rumelian Liberals were agonised by the break with Russia and worried that the links with Turkey remained.

In both Bulgaria and Rumelia economic distress added to political malaise. The government had been forced to requisition animals and grain during the war and there was a shortage of seed in the following spring. Also the government had not yet been able to honour all its requisitioning debts and although there were moves to put these against taxes and tax arrears this was of little benefit to the peasant for taxes had in the meantime risen. There was particular distress in the tobacco-growing areas around Kiustendil because here mobilisation had taken place before the completion of the harvest and in 1886 the entire country suffered particularly badly from that bane of the Balkan farmer's life, hail.

By May 1886 when the elections for the first united Sŭbranie were held the government was being assailed from all sides. There were also tensions within the Cabinet. In the spring a Russian officer who had served in the Rumelian militia, Nabokov, attempted to raise a rebellion near Burgas. He failed hopelessly and was arrested but the Russian diplomatic agency insisted that, in accordance with the Capitulations, he be handed over for trial by Russian law in the Russian consular court. In the vain hope of improving relations with Russia Karavelov complied immediately but he did so without consulting his tough-minded Minister of Justice, Vasil Radoslavov, who submitted his resignation, which however the Prince refused to accept. This was wise for Karavelov and his beleaguered government had need of Radoslavov. He had already shown his resolution in December 1885 by imposing Bulgarian law in Rumelia and in the election campaign he now exercised government pressure to such a degree that he earned himself the nick-name, *shopadjiya* (bully). The election results were interesting for government pressure had its usual effect in the north which returned mostly pliant members, but the Rumelian deputies were by no means so amenable. For the first time an administration in Sofia had been informed of what was henceforth to be a constant factor in Bulgarian politics: that no government could afford to neglect the powerful south-Bulgarian lobby.

It was clearly going to be a stormy session and in an initial attempt to weaken what was potentially the most damaging attack the Prince announced the end of the personal union; Rumelia was to be fully integrated into the Principality though obviously he could not guarantee foreign and above all Russian approval for such a step. This move deflected rather than disarmed the attack which during the debate on the address was concentrated on the government's alienation of the Kŭrdjali and Tŭmrŭsh areas. The alienation or acquisition of territory, the opposition insisted, was unconstitutional without the consent of a Grand National Assembly and these particular areas offered the Turkish army a useful route into Macedonia should it ever need to suppress disturbances there. The government's reply was the reasonable one that the area had never been brought under the control of any central administration, was completely Moslem and in comparison with the gains from the union its loss was insignificant. The government also argued that whatever the shortcomings of the 1886 settlement it was the best that could have been achieved given the danger of simultaneous invasion from Turkey and Serbia. To those who insisted that Macedonia too should have been grasped, Stambulov, the President of the Sŭbranie, replied that in the face of so fundamental a disruption of the Berlin settlement the powers would not have remained inactive, Austria-Hungary would have 'run down to Salonika', and Bulgaria itself might have been destroyed. After this argument opposition deputies attacked other aspects of government policy wanting to know why martial law and press controls had been maintained so long after the end of the war and why civilians, Karavelov included, had accepted decorations and orders from the Prince when the constitution specifically banned them for anything but bravery in the field.

In the end the government managed to carry the vote on the address but once this had been accomplished it faced an even more difficult task, that of persuading the Subranie to agree to the purchase for forty-four and a half million francs of the Ruse-Varna railway shares in British ownership. This produced one of the most stormy debates yet seen in the House with some of the strongest opposition coming from those who two years previously had been prepared to pay even more. In the middle of the debate on 8/20 July Radoslavov crossed the floor to join the opposition which included not only the Tsankovists but also the Rumelians who had no desire to purchase the line at all for it could not benefit their part of the country and they found it hard to accept that a government which had refused to pay the Rumelian militiamen would part with so much for a dilapidated railway. The debate produced extraordinary scenes. The onlookers made as much noise as the deputies and when the galleries were cleared the public burst into the chamber itself; mayhem prevailed until a hastily summoned detachment of troops forced the mob out at bayonet-point. By this time Karavelov was in a state of nervous collapse and the government was saved by Stambulov who rushed through a third reading of the Bill and forced a vote by a show of hands. This, he declared, demonstrated the chamber's approval but most neutral observers present believed the majority had been against the government.

Karavelov had secured a technical victory but had suffered a massive moral defeat. For the government's opponents and the Russians who supported them the Ruse-Varna debate was a considerable propaganda coup. It was widely assumed the purchase of the railway was the price the government was paying for British support during the union crisis but, the opposition asked, could Bulgaria afford such a price; would it not be much easier to buy back Russian protection? For that a much lower price was being demanded, merely the abdication of the German Prince of Slav Bulgaria.

The disorders in the Sŭbranie during the Ruse-Varna debate were symptomatic of a general decline in the authority of the government and the Prince. Violence erupted in the streets of many towns and the Russophile press did much to encourage it, now openly calling for Alexander's removal and going to any lengths to defame him, even accusing him of homosexual relations with some of his officers. Against this background of increasing civil disorder grew the military conspiracy which was to precipitate the final crisis of August 1886.

The army had long been politicised. The more senior officers, especially after the promotion blockage had been broken by the departure of the Russians, tended to be pro-Russian. They had been trained in Russia and in the early days of their service in Bulgaria had been angered by the Prince's patronising and suspicious attitude towards them; he had, for example, ordered their Russian superiors to make sure the Bulgarians dressed properly, and in 1881 he had vetted all officers, even those training in Russia, for their political reliability. The younger officers were less happy with Russian domination and supported Alexander for his stance against the Generals in 1883, and these officers, whose careers had begun after the Liberation, were not as burdened with gratitude to the Russians as the older ones who had fought in the war of 1877–8. Relations between Alexander and the senior officers had not improved during the war of 1885 when there had been sharp disagreements over tactics, the Prince even reprimanding Benderev for the unauthorised attack which did so much to turn the battle at Slivnitsa. Tension had also built up during and after the war over the issue of promotions. Rumelian officers had to be given a share of the higher ranks and thus some Bulgarian officers did not rise as rapidly or as far as they had hoped, and there were also suspicions of political bias and personal favouritism in some promotions; incredulously Benderev was not promoted at all.

By May 1886 a small number of influential officers had come together in a vague conspiracy. The originator of the plot was Major Radko Dimitriev who, with the help of the Russian military attaché in Sofia, soon recruited Benderev and the Commander of the Military Academy, Gruev. With the support of a number of Russian agents the conspirators spread rumours that the Serbs were about to invade again. This caused the loyal 1st (Sofia) Regiment, the one usually entrusted with guarding the palace, to be sent towards the frontier, leaving guard duties in the hands of the 2nd (Struma) Regiment, one of the chief centres of the conspiracy. By mid-July most members of the Cabinet were aware of what was afoot though most of them argued that if the Prince were to be deposed this must be done by the civil rather than the military arm of the state, a view which Benderev rejected on the grounds that Alexander would never accept defeat unless he was shown that his beloved army had turned against him. Karavelov realised the significance of the troop movements but since the Ruse-Varna debate he had sunk into a dejected apathy and could not now find the resolution either to cooperate with or to denounce the conspirators. When, on 8/20 August he was asked to give his approval he merely requested three days to think the matter over, as did Stambulov. Both were anxious to see what would come of the meeting at Gastein of the Emperors of Austria, Germany and Russia for if the *Dreikaiserbund* were not renewed then Russia, freed of the fear of offending her allies, could be more active in the Balkans.

The Prince in the meantime did not take the rumours of a coup seriously. There had been many such rumours before and he saw the movement of the Sofia Regiment as a defensive measure against a possible Serbian incursion. Of the conspirators he regarded Gruev as reliable and Dimitriev and Benderev as unimportant. Alexander was also disinclined to take the plot seriously because he had always said that if the Bulgarians wished him to leave they had only to say so. He would not use force, he said, to remain where he was not wanted.

He did not resist therefore on the night of 8/20 to 9/21 August when troops from the Struma Regiment with the help, albeit mostly unwitting, of cadets from the Military Academy entered the palace and ordered Alexander to sign a deed of abdication. After some days of confusion and discomfort he arrived at the Danubian town of Reni on th Rumanian-Russian border. He was then dispatched in comfort to Lemberg, the first stage of an intended journey to Darmstadt.

The *putsch* itself had been well-organised and efficiently executed but the conspirators had thought comparatively little beyond the deposition itself. They realised their first task was to establish a government which would enjoy the confidence of the Russians and the support of the majority of the population at home. To this end a Cabinet was formed under the Russophile Metropolitan Kliment and the Russians promised to support this administration with funds, to protect it from external enemies, and not to interfere in Bulgaria's internal affairs. Yet there had been, of course, massive interference in that the coup had received Russian backing and encouragement. For many Bulgarians this was worse than the many sins of Battenberg. Universal approval of the enforced abdication was not forthcoming. By 10/22 August Stambulov had put himself at the head of opposition to the coup and he was soon joined by Mutkurov who commanded the Plovdiv garrison. Two days later garrisons in Sliven, Varna, Stara Zagora, Chirpan, Nova Zagora, Svishtov, Kotel, Gabrovo and Tŭrnovo had joined Stambulov who was acting with enormous determination and skill. He had solid military backing and, of almost equal importance, he knew through contacts with the Bulgarian legation in Bucharest, with which he was in telegraphic contact, that the Prince was still alive and was willing to return to Bulgaria. He was also soon to learn that the other powers were willing to take steps to oppose Russia if she intervened to prevent Battenberg's return. This knowledge gave Stambulov a tremendous political advantage over the putschists. Stambulov and the Battenbergists concentrated loyal forces around Sofia and it seemed that civil war could break out at any moment. The conspirators, who had not expected opposition, rapidly lost heart and after Karavelov had failed to form a government to replace that of Kliment, Stambulov himself formed a caretaker regime,* being able to do so because he could reassure his followers that he could bring back the Prince.

Having formed his administration Stambulov urged Alexander to return to Bulgaria. This he did, arriving in Ruse to a tumultuous welcome on 17/29 August. He was met by the caretaker government, by local dignitaries, and by the local consuls, all of whom, including Shatokhin from Russia, were in full dress uniform. This Alexander took as a sign that Russia did not object to his return, an impression which was seemingly confirmed by Russia's not having given public approval to the events of 9/21 August, by her considerate treatment of the Prince during his brief stop in Russia, and by the fact that the Tsar

---

*What Stambulov formed was a *namestnichestvo* for which no accurate translation exists. In this context it most specifically did not mean regency, Stambulov's whole attitude being based on the claim that Article 19 of the constitution provided for a regency only when the Prince had died or abdicated without an heir apparent. In 1886, he said, this was not the case for the abdication, having been exacted under duress, was not valid. The situation was therefore no different from any other occasion on which the Prince was out of the country leaving one or more of his ministers *in loco principis.*

was sending a close friend of Battenberg's, Prince Dolgorukov, to Bulgaria to study local conditions. It seemed that Alexander III had forgiven all and to secure absolute confirmation of this the Prince telegraphed to the Tsar:

> I thank Your Majesty for the attitude taken by Your representative in Ruse. His very presence at my reception showed me that the Imperial Government cannot sanction the revolutionary action taken against my person. . . . I should be happy to give Your Majesty the final proof of the unchanging devotion which I feel for Your Majesty's illustrious person. As Russia gave me my crown, I am prepared to give it back into the hands of its Sovereign.

The Prince was acting under a tragic misunderstanding. Shatokhin had been present at the reception only because the confusion of the preceding days had delayed instructions that he was not to have anything to do with Battenberg should the latter return to Bulgaria. For the Tsar, therefore, the Prince's telegram was a godsend offering him what he had long given up as unattainable: the chance to remove Battenberg without international complications or even real opposition inside Bulgaria. After publishing the Prince's telegram he let it be known that he did not approve of Alexander's return; he was sure, he told the Prince, that in these circumstances 'you will understand what devolves upon you'. Alexander did. It was now impossible for him to remain in Bulgaria and he did so only long enough to appoint a regency and to allow this to assume power peacefully. Stambulov and Mutkurov were obvious candidates for the three-man body but the third member was more difficult to find, the choice falling finally upon Karavelov whom Stambulov thought would be less troublesome inside the tent than outside. After taking leave of his politicians and the foreign representatives Alexander left Bulgaria for the last time on 26 August/7 September.

In Bulgaria he had been faced with enormous difficulties many of which, despite his prejudices and obstinacy, he had overcome with a skill and dexterity amazing in one so young. The remainder of his short life was not unclouded. His plans to marry into the German royal family remained under Bismarck's interdict and the German Emperor refused him a commission in a German regiment. He therefore joined the Austrian army and after taking the title Count Hartenau married an opera singer with whom he had fallen hopelessly in love. Their bliss was shortlived for in December 1893 Alexander died aged only thirty-six. Since his departure he had been remembered with affection by the Bulgarian nation and by many of his politicians. When Stoilov, his former secretary, was in Vienna negotiating to find his successor, he wrote daily to Alexander and the possibility of his return to Sofia was never totally abandoned. After his death his body was brought to his former capital for burial.*

---

*It is still there in a small church opposite the zoological gardens on Boulevard Marshal Tolbukhin. The church and the small cemetery are closed and notices inform the public that their preservation is 'the patriotic duty of every citizen'.

Chapter 6

THE INTERREGNUM AND THE ELECTION
OF FERDINAND, 1886–7

With the departure of the Prince Bulgaria was left in the hands of the three regents, Stambulov, Mutkurov and Karavelov, administering through a Cabinet under the minister presidency of Radoslavov which contained all the major political factions with the exception of the extreme Russophiles. The prime objective of the regency was to call a Grand National Assembly which would then elect a new Prince and, as quickly as possible, restore the country to regular constitutional government. In this they were opposed by the Russians and their supporters. The Russophile cause was now headed by General Nikolai Kaulbars who in 1884 had helped patch up the agreement on the Russians serving in the Bulgarian army. He was now in Bulgaria as the Tsar's special commissioner with a brief to study the situation and to assist the Bulgarians in putting an end to the present crisis.

Kaulbars immediately adopted a hectoring tone with the regency which he said was unconstitutional as none of the three regents had fulfilled the strict requirements for their office. This claim could be settled only by constitutional lawyers but to politicians fell the responsibility of having to decide whether to grant or refuse Kaulbars' three main demands: the lifting of the state of siege imposed in August, the release of all those arrested after the events of that month, and the postponement of the elections for the Grand National Assembly announced for the end of September. If these demands were refused, Kaulbars said, Russia would regard the Grand National Assembly and anything it might decide as invalid for the elections had not received the consent of the Porte which strict constitutional law demanded.

Stambulov did lift the state of siege but he would not release those arrested for fear of interfering with the judicial process and he insisted that he must hold the elections if he were not to be in breach of the constitutional law governing the maximum time allowed between Assemblies. Stambulov in later years was not always to show complete reverence towards the judicial process and constitutional law and his major consideration even in 1886 was not legality but the need to return the country to a regular political life in the shortest possible time; delay, he knew, could only increase the likelihood of serious internal disturbance.

Kaulbars was forced to accept that the elections would take place, though he did not drop his insistence that they were invalid, making this point to the regents again on the very day of polling. Having accepted that the voting would take place Kaulbars concentrated on trying to secure the return of acceptable candidates. He addressed a twelve-point programme to Russian consuls in Bulgaria and the latter were ordered to present these to the electorate as arguments for voting against the government, and he also appeared at public meetings both in Sofia and during a pre-election tour of the provinces. He had little success and it was now that he earned for himself the unenviable nickname of 'general Sofiasco', for his interventions at public meetings were ineffective and in many cases resented.

The elections were held on 28 September/10 October and resulted in a massive government victory. In Sofia only twenty-seven voters supported Karavelov and of the five hundred and twenty-two delegates only fifty-two were not definitely committed to the government. This victory was helped by the government's use of force; martial law had been reimposed on the day before polling and on 28 September/10 October *shaikadjii* had been in evidence in many towns, with deaths reported in Kutlovitza and Dupnitsa (Stanke Dimitrov). Yet the use of thugs alone could not explain the government's victory. The August plot had been far from popular and its perpetrators the object of a good deal of anger; the officers and men of the Struma Regiment who had deserted after the collapse of the coup, for example, had been refused food and shelter even by the peasants of their native region. In addition to distate for the events of August the electorate was disturbed by the Russophiles' failure to give clear answers to two questions: on what conditions would Russia recognise the union of 1885, and who was the Russian candidate for the Bulgarian throne? It was the issues at stake rather than the manner in which the election was conducted which ensured the government's success.

Kaulbars nevertheless immediately denounced the elections as determined by the *shaikadjii*. He complained of the way in which the government had treated the voters and he complained too of the maltreatment of Russian subjects. His complaints were given dramatic emphasis on 12/24 October when it was announced in St Petersburg that two Russian warships were to be sent to Varna to protect Russian lives and property. Five days later Kaulbars delivered his strongest note yet on the mishandling of Russian subjects and so strong was the tone of this note that the Bulgarian Foreign Minister, Nachovich, concluded that Kaulbars did not really want an agreement but wished rather to provoke the Bulgarians into extreme measures which would then serve as a justification for the landing of Russian troops at Varna. There was in fact no danger of a landing because the Tsar had forbidden the engagement of Russian troops in Bulgaria but this could not be know in the Principality. Stambulov, more resolute than most of his colleagues, believed that if the worst came to the worst Bulgaria could withstand a Russian incursion for up to ten months, but he was anxious to ease tension so as to prevent any complications in the convening of the Grand National Assembly. On 17/29 October therefore as a further concession to the Russians those officers arrested after the August *putsch* were released.

This concession did not stem the pressure from the Russian diplomatic agency but it bought enough time to allow the Grand National Assembly to open in Tŭrnovo on 19/31 October, four days later than originally planned. Tension, however, remained high. Stambulov attempted to relieve it by coming to an agreement with Tsankov to form a coalition administration. Tsankov inclined towards acceptance but his followers hoped that if they waited a little until it was Kaulbars rather than Stambulov who was distributing the Cabinet posts they would have all rather than a few of them. Stambulov therefore reported the negotiations and their outcome to the Assembly to the great discredit of Tsankov and his supporters. Stambulov's prestige was correspondingly enhanced.

At the same time as bolstering his already considerable authority within the Assembly Stambulov was able to record another important success. With Russian ships off the coast there was always a danger of an internal rising by the Russophiles. The anarchy and chaos which would follow could easily force the Tsar to change his mind and allow

Russian troops to land to protect Russian lives. The regency therefore felt itself in great danger when a rebellion broke out in three southern Bulgarian garrisons, Perushtitsa, Burgas and Sliven. The risings, whose organiser was Radko Dimitriev, were poorly co-ordinated and those in Perushtitsa and Sliven were soon contained, having encountered little popular support. This was also the case in Burgas where Nabokov was again at the head of the rebels, this time hoping for assistance from a Russian ship. A vessel did eventually appear but by then Nabokov had been captured; he was once again to use the Capitulations to escape punishment but this time his captor, Captain Panitsa, refused to hand him over to the Russian consul until a Bulgarian military tribunal had tried him and found him guilty. The risings were ineffectual but important. Without the politicians of Bulgaria knowing it Russia's direct intervention had always been unlikely; after the southern Bulgarian risings it was seen to be unlikely.

If Russian sailors did not land on Bulgarian soil Stambulov and his supporters nevertheless could not escape from the suspicion that there had been complicity between Kaulbars and the rebels. The government lamented that the Russians accused it of being unable to maintain order and then howled with rage when it took steps to prevent or contain disorder. Russian complaints were particularly loud over the alleged mistreatment of Russian subjects. Despite his recent successes Stambulov needed desperately to secure the election of another Prince if the country were to return to a normal political life.

The preference of most delegates would have been the restoration of Alexander Battenberg but this, Stambulov persuaded them, was impossible. The choice fell upon Prince Waldemar of Denmark who was favourably regarded by all the powers and who was believed to be the Tsar's favourite candidate. This was not so for Alexander III vetoed Waldemar's acceptance of the crown.

This was a setback for Stambulov and Karavelov chose this moment to cut away from the regency. He had long been out of sympathy with Stambulov, Mutkurov, and the Cabinet and in one meeting had even tried to belabour the Minister President with a stick. Karavelov, in fact, had come to believe that the only salvation for Bulgaria was abject acceptance of whatever terms Russia might choose to dictate and with such opinions there was clearly no place for him in Stambulov's team. This the Grand National Assembly accepted with equanimity for Karavelov had little political standing left. It was more concerned with the problem of the succession and, having nominated Zhivkov, a staunch defender of the Bulgarian Macedonians, to replace Karavelov, it appointed a three-man delegation to tour the European capitals and discuss the question of who should follow Alexander Battenberg.

The quiet departure of Karavelov and the continuing search for a new Prince represented defeats for Kaulbars in that the Bulgarians were undeterred by his insistence that the Assembly was illegal and its enactments invalid. Kaulbars now accepted defeat and decided to leave the country. Two days after the nomination of Zhivkov he protested over an incident in which the *kavass* of the Russian consulate in Plovdiv had been manhandled and arrested by the police. The authorities replied that the *kavass* had been drunk and out after curfew, but Kaulbars was not looking for explanations and declared that he would leave Bulgaria within forty-eight hours unless senior officers of the Plovdiv police together with all those responsible for this insult to Russia were dismissed and amends made by a public saluting of the Russian flag. When no satisfaction was given Kaulbars broke all relations with the regency and left Bulgaria with his staff on 8/20 November. Diplomatic relations between Bulgaria and its liberator were severed. They were not to be restored for almost a decade.

Alexander III and the Russians now hoped that the regency would collapse under the emotional strains generated by the breach with Russia. Stambulov, therefore, had to show that Bulgaria was capable of existing independently of Russia as well as Turkey. This meant primarily preserving order long enough to persuade a foreign Prince to accept the Bulgarian throne. Yet the preservation of order was itself in the long term dependent upon finding a Prince; Stambulov and Bulgaria were in danger of being trapped in a vortex which would suck them down to anarchy and chaos.

An attempt was again made to break free from this danger by coming to an agreement with the Russophiles in Bulgaria. Stambulov offered the Tsankovists a share in an all-party coalition but the two extremes could not agree on which parties should be included in such a coalition let alone how the posts should be distributed. Tsankov finally wrecked the negotiations by making a series of impossible demands which were reducible to one, that political power in Bulgaria pass either directly or through the medium of Tsankov into Russian hands, a condition which not even Kaulbars at his most zealous would have dared to make. Obviously Stambulov would not accept such terms and Tsankov, now in exile in Constantinople, settled down to systematic opposition and support for all anti-Stambulovist movements, his own

programme being set out in an appeal from the Ottoman capital in
February.

If the danger was not to be escaped by agreement with the Russophiles then it had to be contained by imposing the most rigid control
on internal affairs, for only thus could Bulgaria show a potential
Prince that the country was governable. The mass of the peasant population were by now exhausted by politics and bemused by the break
with Russia but, as the lack of response to the southern Bulgarian
revolt showed, it was not prepared to take to arms against the regency.
Stambulov, though he had little to fear from the masses, could not be
entirely sure of the reliability of the whole officer corps. Shortly before
the departure of Kaulbars a minor conspiracy had been discovered, but
neither its leader, Panov, a personal friend of Stambulov, nor his
associates were important or influential, all being of junior rank.
Meanwhile leading Russophile officers, Gruev, Benderev, Dimitriev,
and Encheevich, the leader of the Sliven rising, were in Bucharest
anxiously waiting for a sign that the nation and/or its army had had
enough of Stambulov and his regency. This sign they thought they saw
in an incident on 7/19 December when the commander of the Tŭrnovo
garrison refused to move his men to Svishtov to contain rioting in the
town. The exiles immediately set to work to organise a full scale rising
in north eastern Bulgaria, their chief agent in the country being Captain Uzunov who after becoming a war hero through his defence of
Vidin in 1885 had then opposed the coup of August 1886 but had
turned against the regency because of its harsh treatment of political
detainees. His chief co-conspirator within the Principality was Captain
Krŭstev of the Silistra garrison. The plan evolved by Uzunov, Krŭstev
and the exiles was that a military rising take place in Silistra on 10/22
March to be followed by others in Ruse and the other garrisons of the
north east. By mid-February the government was aware of the plot
and began to take steps to frustrate it. Krustev, of his own initiative,
acted immediately and on 16/28 February took control of Silistra
whither came Dimitriev and some of the other conspirators to establish a provisional government. This they hoped soon to transfer to
Shumen, the country's largest garrison which it was assumed would
declare for the rebels as Ruse and Varna had already done. But the
Shumen garrison remained loyal to the regency as did other units
moved into the north east to suppress the revolt. The suppression was
quickly but brutally carried out. Uzunov and eight other conspirators
who had not managed to escape were executed, Panov amongst them,

and despite some misgivings on the part of Stambulov himself a virtual reign of terror was imposed upon the disaffected areas with some regiments having one man in twenty, chosen by lot, executed by their comrades. Civilians, too, were exposed to much ferocity, the most notorious case being Ruse whose new prefect, Mantov, was so energetic in his persecution of the rebels that the French consul left the city in protest and even the pro-Stambulovist Austrians were moved to suggest a slackening of Mantov's ardour.

A prominent victim of the repression which followed the Silistra rising was Karavelov against whom nothing could be proved but who was suspected of complicity in the plot for he was now, for the first time since 1881, in open collaboration with Tsankov. Karavelov was mistreated in prison by his old personal enemy, Panitsa, and Stambulov had to submit to some uncomfortable reports in the foreign press much of it organised by Karavelov's wife, a formidable figure in Bulgarian political intrigues. The severity with which the north eastern rising was suppressed was however forced on Stambulov who had to show that the existing political system in the country could defeat the plots hatched by its opponents, for if it could not no foreign Prince would consider taking the vacant Bulgarian throne.

Nor did the containment of the revolt mean that the dangers were exhausted and the need to find a Prince therefore less urgent. Violence begets violence and if a military conspiracy had failed Stambulov's enemies could easily turn to other methods of precipitating disorder. That they might be doing so was hinted at a few days after the end of the rebellion when Russophiles in Bucharest made an unsuccessful attempt upon the life of the chancellor of the Bulgarian diplomatic agency in the city. Similar fears were raised in April when a bomb exploded in front of the home of one of Stambulov's most ardent supporters, Major Popov. Shortly afterwards the police announced they had uncovered a wide-ranging plot by Tsankovists who had given up the idea of military conspiracies and were planning now to destabilise the government by random acts of terrorism against individuals.

The April bomb had not in fact been the work of the Tsankovists but of their most extreme opponents, the Battenbergists. Affection for the young Prince Alexander had never faded and with the continuing impasse in the search for a new Prince his return was seen by some as a possibility. The departure of Kaulbars made restoration less difficult for the previous argument that such a move would so anger the Tsar that he might break completely with Bulgaria was no longer applicable.

Shortly after Kaulbar's departure came the first anniversary of the battle of Slivnitsa and the telegrams Alexander had exchanged with many civilians and military bodies had been published in the Bulgarian press thus reminding Bulgarians simultaneously of Alexander and of their recent triumphs together. By December *Nezavisimost,* once one of Battenberg's severest critics, had decided that his return was the solution to the nation's present problems. The Battenbergist cause had even more powerful backing in the form of the 'Patriotic Associations'. These had appeared during the crisis of 1886 in Ruse and had rapidly spread to all towns, uniting the more dedicated of Russophobes behind the slogan, 'Bulgaria for itself, free and independent'. By the spring of 1887 the Battenbergist movement was gathering strength rapidly and in March the Minister President, Radoslavov, and the War Minister, Nikolaev, declared publicly in favour of restoration. Stambulov was convinced that this could provoke Russian intervention and he pressed the former Prince to disavow any intention of returning to Bulgaria but Alexander's statement when it came was equivocal.

Stambulov was by now in desperate need of an alternative candidate. After the veto of Prince Waldemar the Russians had put forward the name of Prince Mingreli. This was an insult to the Bulgarians and not even Tsankov could bring himself to approve of it in public. Mingreli was a Circassian whose father had sold his independence to the Russians; the son was now squandering the proceeds as a *boulevardier* in Paris. Stambulov said he would not even make a good stable-boy. By the beginning of 1887 the Russians had begun to drop Mingreli's name and Stambulov had turned to the Sultan. He proposed a form of Bulgarian-Turkish compromise similar to that engineered between Austria and Hungary in 1867. The plan was for the Sultan to assume the title Prince of Bulgaria and for Bulgaria itself to become an autonomous Principality but including Macedonia and Thrace as well as the post-1885 unified Bulgaria. The Sultan liked the idea and it was much discussed in Bulgarian political circles but it fell victim to the Tsar's veto. Stambulov then looked northwards and asked King Carol of Rumania if he would contemplate some form of personal union which could become the first step in the formation of a Balkan confederation capable of fending off all foreign interference in the peninsula. King Carol declined.

During its visit to the European capitals in the winter the Grand National Assembly's three-man delegation had been told in Vienna that Prince Ferdinand of Saxe-Coburg-Gotha might be interested in the Bulgarian throne. It was said that Ferdinand had the support of the Austrian Emperor and it was known that he was on good terms with Kaulbars and Lobanov, the Russian ambassador in Vienna; Ferdinand also maintained he enjoyed good personal relations with the Tsar though the latter had in fact taken a particular dislike to him during the Coronation in Moscow in 1883. Futhermore it was known that, whatever his feelings for the person concerned, the Tsar would not accept any candidate produced by the three-man delegation because that delegation had been appointed by and was working on behalf of the Grand National Assembly which the Russians insisted was illegal. Yet by late spring 1887 Stambulov knew that he had begged so long that he had no privilege of choice. Ferdinand was the only candidate in sight and even he would make no definite decision, pleading the need to secure Russian approval. By early summer Stambulov decided to force a decision. He arranged elections for another Grand National Assembly in Türnovo and a dependable majority was secured. The regents now pressed Ferdinand to accept the throne or renounce it publicly. He accepted and on 7/19 July the duly-primed Assembly in Türnovo elected him Prince. There was enormous relief in Bulgaria, a relief not impaired by the resignation of the avowedly Battenbergist Minister President, for Stoilov was immediately put in charge of a caretaker ministry. On 14/26 August 1887 Ferdinand appeared before the Grand National Assembly and took his oath of allegiance as Prince of Bulgaria. He was to remain Bulgaria's ruler for thirty-one years.

Ferdinand's was a complex character containing many incongruities, and it was the latter which perhaps accounted for his indeciveness and for his constant preference for intrigue and conspiracy as opposed to open and uncomplicated confrontation. The first of these incongruities arose from his despising of the martial and equestrian enthusiasms which were generally expected of those who aspired to wear a crown. There was certainly no doubting Ferdinand's aspiration in this respect and it was one powerfully endorsed by his mother, Princess Clementine, a daughter of King Louis Phillippe. When he did become Prince his distaste for and incompetence in equestrian affairs, in part the consequence of a delicate childhood, made him the butt of numerous jokes and sometimes provoked unflattering comparisons with the attitudes and accomplishments of his predecessor. But if Ferdinand did not love horses and military parades he was fascinated by science and technology. Ferdinand's scientific expertise had been established by his work on botany and lepidoptera and his technological interests were

seen above all in his passion for railways which he often indulged by
taking control on the footplate. These interests Ferdinand pursued in
public as well as private and Bulgaria benefited from them in various
ways, be it from the Prince's promotion of afforestation, from his stock-
ing of the streams in the Rhodopes with trout, or from his persuading his mother to donate four million francs of her own money for the
construction of railways in Bulgaria. Yet here too there was an internal
personality conflict for alongside this scientific rationalism there
existed a strong strain of irrational superstition. Ferdinand would
never sign documents on the thirteenth of the month, be it in the Julian
or the Gregorian calendar, nor would he allow the number to be
spoken in his presence, and he would never set off on a journey on a
Friday. There was perhaps a further conflict in that he was suspected
by many of homosexual tendencies and he certainly overcompensated
his lack of strength in the martial arts by adopting an extremely effem-
inate bearing. The final incongruity was that this scion of one of
Europe's most influential aristocratic families, this lover of all that was
comfortable and civilised, should take office in one of Europe's newest
and, at that time, most backward and most disturbed nations.

Chapter 7

THE CONSOLIDATION OF THE
NEW REGIME, 1887–90

The contrast between Ferdinand's refined upbringing and his new political environment was most strongly expressed by the comparison between the Prince and Stambulov. This 'rough-hewn genius' as the great *Times* correspondent, James Bourchier, described him was born near Tŭrnovo in 1854, the son of an inn-keeper. Stambulov was apprenticed to a master tailor in Tŭrnovo but soon forsook this for a school run by the noted nationalist and educationalist Dr. Shishmanov who had recently returned from Paris. Stambulov immediately marked himself out as an exceptional pupil and though the school was closed by the Turkish authorities his education continued privately, still with Shishmanov, until he was awarded a scholarship endowed by the Tsarina to the theological seminary in Odessa. Before leaving Tŭrnovo, however, Stambulov had come into contact with radical thinkers and once in Odessa he turned to the Populists rather than the scriptures with the result that he was expelled from the seminary and from Russia. He went next to Bucharest where he established contact with Liuben Karavelov's Revolutionary Central Committee and when he returned to Bulgaria shortly afterwards it was as an organising agent of that committee. Stambulov's enormous energy and intelligence, combined with his dedication, guile and resourcefulness rapidly made him, despite his slender years, a prominent figure in the more extreme branch of the revolutionary movement.

Relations between Ferdinand and Stambulov were never good and were to end in bitter enmity, but initially the two were in absolute dependence on one another. Stambulov had to have Ferdinand

125

because he, Stambulov, was a kingmaker without an alternative king and Ferdinand as the new and insecure 'king' could not dispense with the kingmaker.

Ferdinand learned of his own dependence soon after he had taken the oath of allegiance when he made an unsuccessful attempt to construct a Cabinet without Stambulov. After his role in recent events Stambulov could not be excluded and was made both Minister President and Minister of the Interior in a Stambulovist-Conservative coalition, the Conservatives being represented by Stoilov, the Minister of Justice, and Nachovich who became Minister for Foreign Affairs. Elections held early in September provided the new ministry with reliable but not entirely docile support in the Sŭbranie.

The formation of a government and the holding of elections showed that Bulgaria's internal political machinery had returned to normal but the international status of Ferdinand was still anomalous. Russia continued to refuse to recognise him as the legitimate ruler and no other power was willing to recognise him until Russia did so. The Berlin treaty's insistence that any Prince had to have the approval of the signatory powers therefore remained unfulfilled. About this Stambulov and Ferdinand could do nothing. They simply had to continue in the direction upon which they had set out, that of returning the country to its normal domestic life and consolidating their own position within that normalised framework; they had to prove themselves the *de facto* rulers of a stabilised and orderly state if they were to have any hope that they would receive *de jure* recognition.

Security was their major preoccupation and Stambulov, as Minister of the Interior, kept a tight control over the police and the judicial machine. The regime's principal opponent, Russia, had in 1886 formulated the principle that there could be no direct Russian intervention in Bulgaria save with the consent of all the other powers and this Britain and Austria would never give. In the second half of 1887, however, the Russians initiated a diplomatic campaign to try and bring about Turkish intervention, the intention being that the Sultan, as suzerain of Bulgaria, should send in his troops who would remove Ferdinand and Stambulov before establishing a new regency under Ehrenroth. The Sultan, like others, was appalled at such cynicism.

There was then no danger of Russian or Turkish intervention but Russia's continuing insistence that Ferdinand's election had been illegal was dangerous for the government in Sofia in that it enabled the Tsarist regime to argue that any action taken to depose Ferdinand was not revolutionary but merely an attempt to restore legality. Internal subversion, then, would receive no opposition from Russia, rather the reverse for in October 1887 Khitrovo had reappeared on the scene and from the Russian legation in Bucharest was encouraging dissident Bulgarians to look to him for help and guidance. Late in 1887 there was an attempt by a number of Russians, Montenegrins and dissident Bulgarians to unseat Ferdinand, a band of some forty armed desperadoes crossing into southern Bulgaria from Turkey. Predictably the band was led by Nabokov but his previous failures seemed to have taught him little. His intention had been to spark off a local rising, capture Burgas and from this base unite the nation against Ferdinand and Stambulov. But as in his previous incursions and as in the Silistra rising the population showed no interest and the Bulgarian authorities, forewarned of the attack, soon tracked down Nabokov, killing him and most of his band; it was not a difficult exercise as most of them were wearing Russian army uniforms. Documents on Nabokov clearly implicated Russian officials in Bucharest, Khitrovo included.

The Nabokov incident was a severe defeat for Russia, showing once again that the Bulgarian people would not respond to this type of incursion. The Russians therefore changed their tactics issuing a statement on 11/23 February 1888 announcing once again that in future Russia would not intervene in Bulgarian affairs but would continue to regard the present regime as illegal. The worst of dangers for Ferdinand and Stambulov had passed but there could be little relaxation for St Petersburg was still hoping to show that independent Bulgaria could not survive without the blessing of the liberator, that, in other words, the new regime would be toppled by internal discontent.

There seemed every likelihood in 1888 that Russia's expectations would be fulfilled. Shortly after his arrival Ferdinand seemed to have offended every important political group in the country. The intelligentsia were disturbed by the Waldapfel scandal. Waldapfel was an Austrian journalist who was demanding payment of monies which, he said, had been promised him for his support of Ferdinand's candidature. Waldapfel's case was dismissed by a Budapest court but the affair rumbled on in the European press much to the embarrassment of the regime in Sofia. On arrival in Bulgaria Ferdinand had also made the mistake of parading his Catholicism before his new people. All Bulgarians were shocked by this and Ferdinand rapidly abandoned any public show of his faith, but his initial behaviour entrenched the opposition of the Church whose hierarchy included strongly Russophile elements. The Church was powerful but not as powerful as the army and the disagreements between the administration and a large part of the officer corps early in 1888 were the most serious of all the internal dangers facing Ferdinand and Stambulov. In February Major Popov, a friend of the Prince and commander of the prestigious 1st (Sofia) Regiment, had been arrested for malversion of the regiment's funds. He was sentenced under a tough new disciplinary code to five years hard labour. The officer corps immediately divided into pro- and anti-Popov factions and some politicians, primarily Radoslavov, became involved in the dispute hoping that they could ease Stambulov—though not Ferdinand—out of office. The Minister of War, Mutkurov, insisted that the disciplinary code be respected, his motive being to ensure that officers be deterred in future from contesting the disciplinary machine or colluding with opposition politicians. Stambulov had hoped that the affair might not become politicised and had done all he could to keep out of it but eventually he had to intervene and managed to secure acceptance of a compromise whereby the Cabinet confirmed the sentence but recommended clemency. A further measure of the difficulties facing the regime early in the year was that Tsankov put out feelers to Stambulov in January that they should co-operate and bring about the deposition of Ferdinand in return for a guarantee from the Russians that they would recognise a new regency including both Stambulov and Tsankov. Stambulov refused.

From outside Bulgaria there were other threats in addition to Tsankov. In the face of Russian schemes to promote Ottoman intervention and in the hope of securing recognition from the suzerain power Ferdinand had done all he could to placate the Sultan, telegraphing an effusive declaration of loyalty as soon as he arrived in Sofia and even announcing that Bulgaria would resume payment of the Rumelian tribute which had been left unpaid since 1885. But these gestures could not counter-balance Russian pressure on the Porte, pressure which intensified rather than slackened early in 1888. In March the Sultan bowed to Russian demands and declared for the first time that Ferdinand's election had been illegal, a severe blow for Stambulov who was still hoping that the Sultan could be persuaded to recognise Ferdinand and that other powers would then follow suit.

By the summer of 1888 Stambulov was in need of a success to bolster his and Ferdinand's sagging morale and prestige. In May 1888 a railway between Nish and Salonika had been completed thus offering the Serbs a direct route into Macedonia. Immediately there had been demands in Bulgaria that the Principality must seek compensation, preferably in the form of a rail link from Sofia to Kumanovo. Some form of success in Macedonia would please all Bulgarians and therefore Stambulov used his party and government newspaper, *Svoboda* to launch a campaign for reforms in Macedonia in accordance with Article 23 of the treaty of Berlin; Ferdinand talked grandly of rasing Macedonia to a man if reforms were not granted. The campaign achieved nothing. It had been conceived under the mistaken impression that Britain, Austria and Italy would support it, and when the Subranie met in October it formed another item in the lengthening list of government failures.

Stambulov who rather than Ferdinand dominated Bulgarian politics at this stage was in no real danger from the Assembly which, after the debate on the rather dismal address, went on to pass a number of important bills, including one allowing the return to Bulgaria of a small number of those officers implicated in the 1886 plot, and another providing for a fifty per cent expansion of the standing army, a measure which would both increase the national defence capabilities and, it was hoped, decrease the likelihood of political discontent in the army by greatly increasing the chances of promotion.

To increase the army placed an extra burden on the state's finances. Bulgaria in 1888 was already in sore need of financial help from abroad but was having little success in finding it. The Conservatives in the Assembly attacked Bulgaria's financial negotiator in London, Slanski, a brother of the Minister of Finance, who, they said was incompetent and had been appointed mainly to placate the southern Bulgarians who were themselves adding to the government's discomfort by grumbling at Sofia's refusal to do anything to contest the power of the Oriental Railway Company in southern Bulgaria. The financial issue placed a heavy strain on relations between the Stambulovist and Conservative members of the Cabinet and when Stambulov altered two clauses of Stoilov's Penal Bill the latter resigned. Nachovich, who had likewise been angered by interference with his plans for a land tax, went too. The Conservatives' successors were both Stambulovists and this gave the Cabinet a homogeneity not previously experienced, but Stoilov and Nachovich were men of ability well respected in Britain and Austria and their departure did nothing to strengthen the government, although Nachovich did agree to serve as diplomatic agent in Vienna.

Not till the very end of 1888 could Stambulov offer the Prince and
the country any real alleviation in the continuing pattern of disappointment, but success when it came was significant as well as sweet. It came
in two forms. The first was Britain's agreement in November to provide Bulgaria with a loan of 46.7 million francs. The loan was to enable
the Bulgarians to implement the 1886 agreement to purchase the Ruse-
Varna railway. Bulgaria gained little financial benefit from the loan
but at last the financial ice had been broken and soon afterwards the
Deutsche Bank lent ten million francs to the Bulgarian National Bank.
In 1889 more loans were to follow, the most important being the thirty
million francs offered, despite Russian opposition, by the Länderbankverein of Vienna. The second success achieved by Stambulov late
in 1888 was the signature of a tariff agreement with Britain. The treaty
of Berlin had obliged Bulgaria to impose the Ottoman customs regime,
namely that of eight per cent *ad valorem,* and these were not to be
changed until 1890 except with the consent of all signatory powers. In
December 1887, however, the Sŭbranie had encouraged the government to take advantage of Article 8 of the treaty of Berlin which
allowed the Bulgarians to conclude temporary tariff agreements with
foreign states and in Sofia there was a strong desire to enter into
discussions with the European powers for it would advance the
government's competence into an area from which the Berlin treaty
had excluded it and so represent a step away from the limited independence which that treaty had imposed on Bulgaria; after August
1887 such negotiations would be even more important for they would
imply recognition of the Bulgarian regime by the government with
which it was negotiating. By November 1888 Britain was not only
engaged in such negotiations but an agreement had been reached and
in January 1889 was signed.* Once again the British precedent was
rapidly followed and by the autumn of 1889 Germany, Austria, Italy,
France, Switzerland, and Belgium had concluded similar agreements.
For the Bulgarians the tariff agreements, like the first loan, offered no
financial or economic benefits for the new levies were little higher than
the old and did nothing to stem the imports of foreign-made factory
goods which were devastating home manufacturing; nor did the new
tariffs significantly increase governmental revenues. Political profit
however was thought more important than financial gain as a number

---

*Details of these agreements will be found in chapter 11.

of European states had for the first time dealt with Bulgaria as if it was a fully independent state.

Trade agreements and loans helped to create the more stable political atmosphere which was apparent in Bulgaria in 1889. This greater stability did enable Ferdinand, for the first time since his arrival, to leave Bulgaria, and persuaded Stambulov to allow, again for the first time, the Sŭbranie to discuss the question of Russo-Bulgarian relations. Yet in 1889 the government still faced problems. In January the Tsar received Tsankov and the latter was quick to advertise this mark of Imperial approval. In March King Milan abdicated and the regency appointed had a distinct pro-Russian bias. This created the fear in Sofia that Serbia might become a base for subversive operations by Bulgarian exiles and Tsankov was soon established in Belgrade. The political changes in Serbia also meant that for the first time for a number of years the Russians had a secure foothold in the Balkans. Thus there was now no urgency for the Russians to restore relations with Bulgaria and in that situation there was nothing the Bulgarians could have done to placate the Russians beyond surrendering to their every demand.

1889 also saw the beginning of a conspiracy which was to serve as the great dividing line in the story of the consolidation of Ferdinand's and Stambulov's regime. In the summer of that year a military revolutionary committee was set up in Sofia. The parties to the conspiracy included Tsankov, still in exile, and Karavelov who, however, soon dropped out. The leading figure was Captain Panitsa. A Macedonian by birth Panitsa was a man of mercurial personality who had fought for liberation before 1878, had been prominent, as we have seen, in nationalist agitation over Rumelia and Macedonia between 1878 and 1885, and had fought with great distinction in the Macedonian Volunteer Brigade in the war of 1885. Panitsa also become a personal friend of Prince Alexander who stood godfather to Panitsa's son. In the turmoil of 1886 Panitsa co-operated with Stambulov but as a dedicated Battenbergist he could not tolerate Ferdinand. Somewhat paradoxically he feared also that there could be no hope for the liberation of Macedonia without Russian co-operation and there could be no hope of Russian co-operation as long as Ferdinand remained in Bulgaria; Ferdinand, Panitsa therefore concluded, had to go. Panitsa's nationalist pedigree, his passionate devotion to the Macedonian cause, and his personal popularity enabled him to recruit followers easily. The conspirators decided to arrest or eliminate Ferdinand and his chief supporters at a Court ball to be held on 21 January/2 February 1890. So wide a conspiracy, however, could not remain secret, the more so as Panitsa's expansive personality led to numerous indiscretions. The police knew what was intended, Panitsa's valet was one of their chief informants, and on the night before the ball the conspirators were rounded up and interned. The ball went ahead but in a tense atmosphere as many of the male guests were carrying revolvers.

At first Stambulov, anxious to avoid the embarrassments of a politico-military trial such as that of Major Popov, was prepared to play down the incident but as investigations revealed the extent of the conspiracy this became impossible. Predictably many disgruntled Macedonians were involved but far more serious was the report that the plot also embraced three quarters of the Sofia garrison, some of whom had been on the losing side in 1886 and had only just returned from exile. The plot also had extensive foreign connections. Panitsa's papers included letters linking the conspirators with Khitrovo in Bucharest and with other Russian diplomats. Stambulov could not prevent some leaks to the press but he forbade full publication knowing that it would dispel the few remaining hopes of reconciliation between Ferdinand and St Petersburg. At the same time Stambulov insisted on condign punishment for Panitsa and those Bulgarians convicted with him. Stambulov rightly regarded the Panitsa plot as the most serious of all the threats he and Ferdinand had so far faced for it had brought together all the discontented elements in Bulgaria, had managed to link them with the Prince's chief external enemy, and, given a less volatile leader, could well have succeeded. It was a very different affair from the cavortings of Nabokov. Stambulov was therefore determined that despite the defence plea that the conspirators had acted from the respectable patriotic motive of wishing to further the Macedonian cause, the guilty must be severely punished. Ferdinand was less resolute. He feared that the execution of Panitsa and his accomplices might swell rather than abate Macedonian extremism, would divide the officer corps and would consolidate Battenbergist sentiment into hard political feelings. Stambulov, however, was adamant and threatened to resign if Panitsa were not executed. In June therefore Panitsa was tied to a tree in front of the assembled Sofia garrison and shot by a firing squad drawn from Macedonian companies.

After the execution of Panitsa there were reports of dissatisfaction in some garrisons but despite the personal popularity of Panitsa once again there was no mass response. Indeed after the arrests the palace in

Sofia was inundated with protestations of loyalty. Most of these had been concocted by local officials whose posts depended upon their political reliability but this was not always the case; Vratsa, once a Conservative stronghold converted to Russophilia by Tsankov's dignified behaviour during his exile, begged Ferdinand to visit the town. When he did so, to unveil a memorial to the national hero Botev, he was enthusiastically received and for the first time prayers were said for him in an Exarchist church.

The plotters had aimed to secure the removal of Ferdinand and concessions for the Bulgarian cause in Macedonia. The former Stambulov could on no account contemplate but he could try to secure the latter. This would disarm any Macedonians who might wish to emulate Panitsa. It could also help ease relations between Ferdinand and his one large remaining internal adversary, the Bulgarian Church, and if brought about in the correct fashion concessions in Macedonia might also improve relations between Bulgaria and Turkey and possibly make recognition by the Sultan more likely. The key to the problem was ecclesiastical.

Relations between Stambulov and the higher clergy had never been good. His early extremism was still alive in his mistrust of the ecclesiastical hierarchy which he, like Tsankov, regarded as a foreign accretion on the democratic, Slav church. The bishops themselves feared Stambulov's radicalism and their fears were justified in 1886 and early 1887 when the regency refused to allow a synod to meet, adjusted the stipends of the clergy, and, of course, fell foul of the Russians. Matters were much worse after the arrival of Ferdinand. Kliment of Tŭrnovo, the Principality's senior and most Russophile bishop, refused to celebrate a *Te Deum* for the new ruler and when he did officiate at a service to mark his entry into Sofia there were no prayers for Ferdinand who was bluntly reminded of the need not to underestimate Bulgaria's debt to Russia. Stambulov hit back by trying to engineer the deposition of the Exarch who had approved of this insult to Ferdinand, and the Minister President also suspended payment to the Exarchate of the annual subventions for the support of Exarchist churches and schools outside the Principality, chiefly in Macedonia. He also took action against Kliment of Tŭrnovo. The ex-Minister President was now the nominated deputy of the Exarch in Bulgaria and as such was the head of the synod; he was also in receipt of 50,000 leva from the Russians. Stambulov ordered him out of Sofia but Kliment remained until a mob had threatened his life and the Exarch had ordered him to return to his flock in Tŭrnovo. In the spring of 1888 Kliment refused to welcome Ferdinand in Tŭrnovo during the latter's tour of the provinces. For this Kliment was suspended by the Ministry of Foreign and Religious Affairs.

The Exarch had by now come to believe that some accommodation with the government was essential but Stambulov would not compromise until there were clear signs that the Church, and particularly its bishops inside Bulgaria, were prepared to recognise Ferdinand in some way. In January 1888 Stambulov therefore pushed through the Cabinet a scheme under which new prayer books were to be printed on state presses and distributed to every church in the country; the new text would include prayers for Ferdinand in place of those for the Tsar which the existing version contained. The plan was never put into operation but it showed Stambulov's determination to bring the bishops into line. The bishops themselves showed no sign of being willing to accept the new government and when Stambulov at last allowed the synod to convene their recalcitrance was proved anew. The synod met in Sofia in January 1889 and began badly for the government whose two supporters amongst the hierarchy were both unable to attend; the synod therefore consisted solely of the three Russophiles, Kliment of Tŭrnovo, Simeon of Varna and Konstantin of Vratsa, and marked a new low in Church-State relations in Bulgaria. The bishops complained bitterly at what they called the government's persecution of the Church, and Ferdinand was attacked for asking them to offer requiem masses for the two German Emperors who had died in 1888, for profaning Orthodox churches by hearing the Catholic mass before attending state religious functions, and for a series of minor sins including the wish to build a villa in or near the grounds of the famous Orthodox convent of Kalofer. Such intense criticism Stambulov could not tolerate and, declaring that there had been irregularities in the election of at least two of the three bishops, closed the synod. The bishops resisted and both sides appealed to the Exarch but in the end Stambulov ordered gendarmes to escort the bishops back to their dioceses.

The bishops found little support amongst the opposition parties or the masses and this was one of the reasons which made the Church ready for a truce, something which the Exarch had wanted for months. In February 1889 therefore all bishops in the Principality, Konstantin of Vratsa excepted, celebrated the Prince's birthday and even the allegedly offended nuns of Kalofer sent a protestation of loyalty. As a further conciliatory gesture the Exarch suggested that the next synod should be held in Ruse. Yet Stambulov was still not prepared to give way for there was no indication that the Church was yet willing to accept Ferdinand as the legitimate ruler.

It was the Panitsa plot which made Stambulov more amenable for there was now a premium on pulling the nation together to prevent another wideranging conspiracy. The Exarch was by now desperate for a settlement with the government in Sofia. Ever since 1885 the position of the Exarchate in Macedonia had been becoming more difficult. The union of Bulgaria and Rumelia put the Greeks and Turks on their guard against further Bulgarian expansionism and this meant official Ottoman support for the Greek rather than the Bulgarian Church in Macedonia. Russia too supported the Patriarchate. After the political changes in Belgrade in 1888–9 the Russians also began to back the growing Serbian propaganda campaign in northern Macedonia. The Exarch could do little in reply for the suspension of the Bulgarian government subsidies had deprived him of the cash he needed to promote rival Bulgarian-language schools and publications. Even more distressing for the Exarchate was its total failure to secure from the Porte any movement towards the implementation of the already-acknowledged claim of the Bulgarian Church to a number of bishoprics in Macedonia. This was a complicated issue. When the Exarchate had been established in 1870 the only Macedonian diocese it had been given was Veles, though it was hoped plebiscites in other dioceses would lead to their transfer from the Patriarchate to the Exarchate. In 1873 the requisite majorities had been secured in the Skopje, Ohrid, Bitolya and Kukush sees but the Turks then suspended the voting for fear it would create too strong a Bulgarian element in Macedonia. Little was then done until 1877 when, in a reaction to the Russian invasion of his empire the Sultan suspended the Exarchist bishop of Veles and withheld the already long-delayed *berats* or letters of investiture for the dioceses which had voted for transfer in 1873. These suspensions greatly disturbed the religious life of the Bulgarians in Macedonia* and

---

*The religious life of the Bulgarian villages in Macedonia was organised by elected communal councils acting with the local priest. After the foundation of the Exarchate a large number of communities collected funds to build new churches and as many of these were not finished until after 1878–9 they had to remain unconsecrated. In such cases Bulgaians had either to attend services in the Greek church or to hold separate ones in the local Bulgarian school or another building. There was also a difficulty after 1878–9

it became the prime object of Exarchist diplomacy to secure *berats* for Veles and the other bishoprics. In 1883 the Porte had promised to issue them for Skopje and Ohrid, dioceses of great strategic importance for they were the centres of northern and western Macedonia respectively, whilst Ohrid was also of enormous historic significance as the centre of that small part of the first national church which until 1767 had survived the Ottoman conquest. Yet the Turkish promises of 1883, like so many before and after that date, remained unfulfilled, and by 1890 a despairing Exarch Yosif was willing to accept help from almost any quarter. In April of that year, therefore, he responded to discreet and unofficial overtures from Sofia whence it was suggested that the Bulgarian government might be prepared to help the Exarch in his Macedonian troubles if in return Yosif would make some acknowledgement, even by way of a private letter, of the existence of Prince Ferdinand. No definite agreement was concluded but with the Exarch desperate for help and the government anxious in the face of Panitsa's criticisms to do something to help the Bulgarians in Macedonia, the door towards a reconciliation between State and Church was slowly opening. Whether it would open fully would depend on whether Stambulov could extract concessions from the Porte; Bulgaria's *Kulturkampf* had been subsumed into the problem of Bulgarian-Turkish relations.

Bulgaria under Stambulov had few friends in the Balkans. The Bregovo dispute had been settled in 1887 but with the advent of the pro-Russian regency in Belgrade relations with Serbia were once more tense with divisions over Macedonia, over Serbian willingness to shelter Bulgarian exiles, and over railway policies; when the Serbian Minister President, Pašić, attempted to negotiate a division of Macedonia, Stambulov not only declined but even reported the Serbian initiative to Constantinople. The Greeks too were hostile. Macedonia was the

---

in providing the villages with new priests for with no Exarchist bishops in Macedonia ordination could not take place locally; ordinands had therefore to travel to Constantinople or Bulgaria and in a number of cases local communities could not afford the cost of sending their prospective priest on such a journey even if the local authorities had given them permission to do so. In a number of villages therefore the inhabitants, even if they had voted to joint the Exarchate, could receive the sacraments in none but the Greek church and some communities in their frustration turned to the Uniate idea rather than return to the Patriarchate. The lack of local bishops also affected the Macedo-Bulgarians in their relations with the civil authorities. The administrative framework of the Otto-

main bone of contention and with the continuing competition between
the Patriarchate and the Exarchate there was little prospect of cooperation between the two governments as Stambulov found in April 1890
when he offered to support Greek claims over Crete if Athens would
give full diplomatic recognition to the Bulgarian representative there.
Turkey was therefore a friend in need. But the relationship between
Bulgaria and Turkey, Stambulov believed, went much deeper than
mere considerations of the balance of power in the Balkans. The two
states were in symbiotic interdependence. Stambulov needed to keep
the Turks in Macedonia for if they departed or even if their hold on the
region became visibly weaker there would be strong pressure on the
Bulgarian government to intervene; if the government resisted such
pressure it could easily be swept away, yet if it gave way and intervened
the Greeks and Serbs, with Russian support, would also become
involved and Bulgaria would be out-balanced. In either event, therefore, Ferdinand and Stambulov would be defeated and removed from
the political scene. This the Turks could not afford, for whatever
regime followed that of Ferdinand and Stambulov would be forced, by
popular will, to adopt a more aggressive attitude over Macedonia and
this regime would also now enjoy Russian backing; under those circumstances the Porte would inevitably be forced to make far-reaching
concessions over Macedonia and those concessions would be of a
type dictated by Russia and a hostile Bulgaria. If on the other hand
the Porte were to grant concessions to Ferdinand's regime those concessions need not be so far-reaching but they would disarm the
Macedonian lobby in Bulgaria and thus strengthen the pro-Turkish
Stambulovist regime in Sofia. These arguments dovetailed with Stambulov's long-term strategy for Macedonia, which, he was determined,
should one day all come to Bulgaria. As yet, however, the Bulgarian
army was nowhere near strong enough to attempt unilateral action,
nor did Stambulov believe that a Balkan alliance could wrest the

---

man Empire provided for the representation of the various communities only through
their religious institutions. Thus the local vilayet councils contained nominees of all local
religious leaders which meant that after 1878–9 the Bulgarians lost whatever voice they
previously had in the vilayet councils. Equally distressing in areas which had voted
Exarchist but which had not yet received *berats* was the fact that the local church's
property and funds, including its schools and its cemetries, remained in Patriarchist
hands and were used therefore for the benefit of the local Patriarchist community, even if
it were a tiny minority.

region from Ottoman control, besides which an alliance would also mean having to share the spoils and this Stambulov was determined to avoid. The only way Bulgaria could secure her full Macedonian inheritance was, he insisted, by patiently building up Bulgarian cultural dominance, more particularly through the creation of a strong Bulgarian urban, property-owning element. For this strategy to succeed Ottoman political power in Macedonia had to be preserved but concessions had to be made to allow the more rapid economic and cultural development of the Bulgarian element. With this strategy the Exarch was in complete agreement.

It was these long-term strategic objectives in Macedonia as well as the post-Panitsa need to bolster his regime within Bulgaria which prompted Stambulov to approach the Porte with a request for concessions. As soon as the Panitsa trial began Stambulov had approached the Turks pointing out the common dangers for Bulgaria and Turkey of Ferdinand's unrecognised status and suggesting recognition and concessions in Macedonia. When nothing came of this soft approach he sent a much tougher note on 4/16 June 1890 threatening that if these requests were not granted Bulgaria would declare full independence, discontinue payment of the Rumelian tribute and suspend the three Patriarchist bishops in the Principality, this latter threat being a manoeuvre to warn off the Patriarch who was already voicing loud opposition to any concessions to the Exarchists in Macedonia. Stambulov was now helped by external factors, most notably by Germany whose support of Bulgaria was one of the first indications of a post-Bismarckian willingness to operate separately from Russia in the eastern Balkans. Within two weeks the Porte had given way. There was no chance of recognition because Russian opposition to that would have been too intense but the Turks did agree to send a representative to Sofia, nominally to supervise the fate of the *vakŭfs,* and, more dramatically, *berats* were promised for the Skopje, Ohrid and Bitolya dioceses. The Exarch was also given the right to establish official contact with the Bulgarian communities in the Adrianople vilayet and, under certain conditions, to publish a Bulgarian newspaper in Constantinople.

These concessions were a triumph for Stambulov and a turning point in his career. He had proved that despite intense Russian hostility a regime could not only survive but could win from the Porte concessions more striking than those secured by any Bulgarian government since 1878. Relations with the Church improved immediately. In July a synod, held at Ruse as the Exarch had suggested, agreed that prayers for Ferdinand should become part of the liturgy in Bulgaria, and at a second synod, this time in Sofia in November, almost all difficulties between Church and State were removed, so much so that Ferdinand could receive four of the bishops in his palace. In August the government had also agreed to provide three million leva a year for Exarchist schools in Macedonia.

With the reconciliation between the government and the Church there was little opposition left within Bulgaria. All the Parties in Bulgaria, including the Tsankovists, had now accepted Ferdinand as leader, even if some exiled party leaders still dissented. The opposition Parties were in fact concentrating upon attacking not the objectives of the Stambulovists but their methods. These Parties, however, had little impact; most of them were generals without armies and they exhibited a chronic inability to combine in the face of their common enemy. Even the south Bulgarian lobby was relatively quiescent. This was principally because the government had built a railway to the port of Burgas. This did not enable all Rumelian merchants to escape from the Oriental Railway Company for the new line was connected not to the BDZh system but to the ORC's Tŭrnovo-Seimen (Maritsa) to Yambol branch. Nevertheless the Yambol to Burgas line was the first constructed in Bulgaria according to the needs of Bulgarians rather than foreign investors or merchants, and it had been built quickly and cheaply with the use of army conscripts as manual labourers. Stambulov was also helped by the fact that the 1889 and 1890 harvests were good ensuring social contentment, and even Bulgaria's hard hit industries were showing signs of recovery. The state treasury, too, was in healthy shape with the budget of 1890 looking forward to a surplus of some five and a quarter million leva, thanks in no small degree to the loan from Vienna.

Stambulov's enormously increased political security and power were reflected in the elections held in the autumn of 1890. Governmental influence was as usual brought into play in support of the Stambulovist candidates but there was little need for this. The popularity of the government was to be measured not so much in the size of its majority in the new Sŭbranie, for that was due in part to the use of government influence, but in the relative absence of physical violence during the polls themselves; there had been no need to coerce the electorate.

1890 was Stambulov's *annus mirabilis.* The granting of the *berats,* the reconciliation with the Church and the easy election victory showed that the 1887 regime was firmly consolidated in Bulgaria.

There was every reason to hope that after the concessions of the summer the Turks might be persuaded to go further and recognise Ferdinand as the legitimate sovereign, the more so if Germany continued to distance herself from Russia in Balkan affairs. If recognition could be secured then the political situation in Bulgaria would be normalised for the first time since the *putsch* of August 1886.

For Stambulov, however, there were dangers in this increased internal stability. Ferdinand was now accepted by all except a few extremists in exile and being relatively safe on his throne he could begin to think of ruling without Stambulov whilst the latter, as in 1887, was still a kingmaker without an alternative king.

Stambulov was also to some extent threatened by the methods he had been forced to employ. His Macedonian strategy demanded more patience than many Macedonians and their supporters in Bulgaria could muster. Yet if further concessions were to be won from the Porte then the latter must not feel itself threatened by Macedonian extremists in Bulgaria. Rigid control of the Macedonian lobby in Bulgaria had therefore to be imposed and this was not always popular. No Minister President after Stambulov treated the Macedonians in Bulgaria in so tough and uncompromising a fashion, perhaps because Stambulov eventually paid for this with his own life, but also no Minister President after Stambulov secured for the Exarchate so many important concessions from the Porte.

It was not only against the Macedonians that these tough policies were used, for all opposition Parties felt the force of Stambulov's repressive machinery. The press was controlled, an administrative order being used to circumvent the constitutional guarantee of free speech and to impose preventive censorship. Police spies were everywhere, the mail was censored and the newly introduced telephone service was restricted to government employees only. The police had wide powers to arrest and detain on suspicion; in 1887 the police budget was two-thirds greater than in the preceding year and in subsequent budgets it continued to rise until in 1893 it stood at 4.23 million leva, some 133% above the 1886 level. If the police or *shaikadjii* did not ensure order then the army could always be used, and units were frequently billeted on villages which had offended the authorities in some way, usually by refusing to pay taxes. The election machine was almost completely under government domination with local officials filling in spurious pro-government ballot slips, destroying opposition votes or physically excluding known opposition supporters. To do this the pro-government faction had to secure control of the electoral bureau which was responsible for conducting the poll and which was to consist of the first voters to arrive at the polling point. If the government party failed to do this then there were other more desperate measures; in Pleven in 1887 when anti-government activists established control over the electoral bureau the police promptly arrested them *en bloc*, whilst in other constituencies the authorites declared they could not guarantee order if the elections took place, in which case voting would be postponed giving the government faction time to ensure its victory, this device being used again in 1887, to prevent the election of Radoslavov in Lovech. Once the Sŭbranie met there was a further chance to exclude the unwelcome, for the Assembly always had to validate the elections and opposition candidates were not infrequently ejected at this stage. The Sŭbranie too was subject to a good deal of control and any contentious business was invariably left until the very end of a session when there would be little time for discussion.

Stambulov's supporters could argue with much justice that these unpleasant methods had been forced on the regime. Had it not been for the unending subversion by Russian-sponsored Nabokovs and Panitsas the government could have relaxed its grip but as long as the duly elected Prince and government were not recognised and therefore exposed to conspiracies and subversion tight control was necessary. This argument most thinking Bulgarians had accepted between 1887 and 1890 but thereafter they were less convinced. Moreover, they were increasingly prone to ask whether recognition was ever going to be achieved. If they decided it would not then Stambulov and Ferdinand would have no political future in Bulgaria and, as the Russians were hoping, the regime would be toppled by internal dissatisfaction. The consolidation achieved by 1890 was therefore an internal consolidation and external recognition remained as necessary yet as distant as it had always been.

Chapter 8

THE DECLINE AND FALL OF STAMBULOV, 1891–4

The successes in Macedonia which had followed from the Panitsa plot did much to consolidate the regime of Stambulov and Ferdinand but they could not protect it from renewed outbreaks of terrorism. On 15/27 March 1891 Stambulov was taking his customary walk back to his home after dining in a restaurant with his Minister of Finance, Belchev. Contrary to his usual practice Stambulov walked on the inside rather than the outside of the pavement and this departure from habit saved his life, for the assassins who had determined to kill the Minister President gunned down Belchev instead. Stambulov and Ferdinand had known for some time that a plot was being hatched and it was not long before they had clear proof that Belchev's assassins had been acting to avenge Panitsa. The government also had documents incriminating the Russian legation in Bucharest and even hinting at the passive involvement of figues as elevated in the Russian hierarchy as Pobedonostsev, the Procurator of the Holy Synod and adviser to the Tsar. These documents purported to show that the Russian government approved of such plots and that after the murder of Stambulov, and of perhaps Ferdinand too, St Petersburg would declare that it could not tolerate anarchy in Bulgaria and would send a commissioner to restore order; the latter would bring with him a large number of Russian officers and a Russian Minister of War who would between them take control of the Bulgarian army. If international pressure threatened this Russian venture then a Grand National Sŭbranie would be convened but would be so prepared that it would petition the Tsar to make Bulgaria a Russian protectorate until the Tsar himself thought the Bulgarians ready for a new Prince.

The authenticity of these documents, which Stambulov eventually published in book form, is open to doubt but Stambulov and Ferdinand believed them to be genuine and acted accordingly.[1] After the Panitsa plot an extensive secret police network had been established in Bulgaria but after the Belchev murder there came a virtual rule of terror. Those arrested included the Macedonians directly concerned with the assassination, including Dimitŭr Rizov and the brothers Tiufekdjiev, and also some three hundred Russophiles, Karavelov amongst them. All those detained were subjected to harsh treatment in prison. The machinery of repression was never entirely relaxed and a number of observers who knew the Minister President believed that he had been somewhat unbalanced mentally by the events of 15/27 March 1891.

Repression soon provoked the menace of counter violence with scores of Bulgarian officials from Ferdinand and Stambulov downwards receiving threats against their life. One of them was the able and much respected Vŭlkovich, the Bulgarian representative in Constantinople and one of Stambulov's most important agents and advisors. He received his letter of warning on 13/25 February 1892 and was brutally attacked in the street that very day. Within twenty-four hours he was dead.

The murder of Vŭlkovich showed the frustrating impasse in which Stambulov and Ferdinand found themselves. The population as a whole had accepted the new regime, the country was enjoying a period of economic advance which was soon to be shown off to the world in the first Plovdiv International Exhibition held in the summer, yet despite these advances there could be no security against attempts to destabilise the country and, the government was convinced, these attempts had the implicit backing of Russia. Only if Ferdinand could secure recognition would such support be withdrawn and the nation's leadership made safe from the gunmen.

Stambulov was still convinced, as he had been since Ferdinand arrived in Bulgaria, that the key to recognition lay in Constantinople and that once the suzerain had been persuaded to accept Ferdinand other powers, and eventually Russia itself, would do likewise, for three of them, Austria, Britain and Italy, had almost done so when they admitted that Ferdinand's election had been legal; the three powers, however, still refused to see his assumption of power as legal. In 1891 the Turkish commissioner in Sofia for the first time asked for an interview with Ferdinand and in 1892 Stambulov was hoping to arrange for a visit to Constantinople by himself or the Prince, a fact which made the murder of Vŭlkovich an even more severe blow. Stambulov now tried once again to show the symbiosis of Turkey and Bulgaria and just as he approached the Porte after the Panitsa plot, stressing the vulnerability of Bulgaria's unrecognised ruler, so now after the killing of Vŭlkovich he made another formal attempt to secure recognition from Constantinople, a note being presented to the Ottoman government on 31 March/ 12 April. Much of the note dealt with the murder of Vŭlkovich and catalogued the part which Russian officials and their supporters had played in it; Bulgarians involved in the plot, it was alleged, had been provided with Russian passports and this had enabled the Russians to insist on the release of those arrested by the Ottoman police. With such skulduggery was contrasted Bulgaria's own good behaviour for the Principality had scrupulously fulfilled all its international obligations, even those to Russia. The Bulgarian note therefore expressed the hope that the Bulgarians would meet with the cooperation of Turkey in their attempt to secure the arrest of those guilty of the recent murder but more importantly the note suggested that further incidents of this sort would most easily be avoided if the Porte gave formal recognition to Ferdinand.

The Sultan was not prepared to risk Russian anger by recognising Ferdinand and Stambulov's note achieved nothing. As a consolation prize Stambulov was allowed to visit Constantinople and was accorded an audience with the Sultan. Meanwhile the Prince had visited Britain where he was received privately by Queen Victoria and lionised in the fashionable salons, but the political implications of these developments were ominous for the regime and particularly so for Stambulov. The Minister President had achieved internal order and control; he could enhance or maintain his own political standing only by external success, that is recognition for Ferdinand, and the lesson of the March/ April note seemed to be that this goal was unattainable in the existing conditions.

There was one way in which conditions might be changed. Since 1890 Stambulov and Ferdinand had been considering the possibility of the Prince's marriage. The Belchev and Vŭlkovich murders made this a matter of great urgency. For the Prince to acquire a bride would increase his prestige and the birth of an heir would make the regime far more stable, for then if Ferdinand were killed the way would not be open for the immediate nomination of a Russian-backed Prince, indeed assassination would serve little purpose for it would simply pass authority to a regency appointed by the late Prince's advisers none of whom, in such circumstances, would be very favourable towards Russia. Early in 1892 it seemed that a possible bride had been found in Princess Marie Louise of Bourbon-Parma. The main difficulty was that her intensely devout Roman Catholic family would not permit the marriage without guarantees that any children would be brought up in the Roman faith, though this was impossible under Article 38 of the constitution which required all Bulgarian Princes except the first to profess the Orthodox creed. In the extreme dangers of 1887 the Bulgarians had been prepared to regard Ferdinand as still being the first Prince but to make an exception of any of his heirs was a much more difficult undertaking. Yet this is what Stambulov insisted had to be done.

Stambulov believed that an amendment to Article 38 would have been necessary even if Marie Louise had not been waiting in the wings. If the article remained in its original form no Roman Catholic or Protestant would consider marriage to Ferdinand, and that being the case the only possible bride would have been an Orthodox one; in practice that meant a Montenegrin or a Russian prince, for there were no other appropriate Orthodox candidates. With the present government in power in Sofia the Russians would not permit either one of their own or one of the Montenegrin princesses to come to Bulgaria, yet there was no possibility of the present administration changing for that would produce the sort of instability which would frighten away all brides, Orthodox and non-Orthodox. Stambulov and his government therefore had to stay if a bride were to be enticed to Bulgaria and that meant that only a Catholic or a Protestant could be considered. Article 38 therefore had to be changed. For Stambulov a non-Orthodox princess and heir would have the additional advantage of being a further bulwark against Russian influence in Bulgaria. Ferdinand was less resolute. After his initial gaffe in parading his own faith he was careful not to offend popular religious feelings, and he knew that the proposed change would be disliked; he knew too that it would be greeted with enormous resentment in Russia and would provide the Russians with yet another stick with which to beat him. Ferdinand seriously considered issuing a declaration stating to the nation that the proposed change in the constitution, though made for his benefit, had been made against his better judgement, but a compromise was eventually produced by the Minister for Foreign Affairs. He suggested that the present proposal, which left all future Princes free to adhere to whatever form of Christianity they might prefer, should be scrapped and instead the original form of Article 38 be left untouched but that the exemptions from the requirement to profess the Orthodox faith should be extended to include the first Prince and his heir.

Stambulov faced enormous opposition. The Russians knew full well the political implications of the change in Article 38 and of Ferdinand's possible marriage to a non-Orthodox bride. So great did Russian censure become at one point that Stambulov warned foreign diplomatists in Sofia that the country had to reckon with the possibility of a Russian invasion and he even asked the British representative if, in such an eventuality, the Royal Navy would allow the Russian fleet uncontested freedom of movement in the Black Sea. At the same time the Rumanian representative was asked whether his government would allow the Russian army right of passage through Rumanian territory; Bucharest at least gave a comforting answer.

Opposition to the proposed change in Article 38 came also from the Church hierarchy. Relations between the government and the Church had been poor since the previous year when Stambulov had ordered the police to search the home of bishop Methodius, the Exarch's personal representative in Sofia, and had then refused the bishop a passport when he wished to travel to make a direct complaint to the Exarch. Stambulov, however, would not allow clerical opposition to stand in his way and the proposed amendment to Article 38, together with a number of changes in the composition of the Sŭbranie, was submitted to the Assembly; after a two-week debate all the proposed constitutional changes were passed by a vote of two hundred and forty-five in favour to thirteen against.

Soon after the closure of the Sŭbranie session Ferdinand set out for Europe where it was announced on 3/15 February 1893 that he had become betrothed to Princess Marie Louise. The wedding took place in Italy in April. In the following month a Grand National Assembly ratified all the constitutional amendments. This was a severe blow to St Petersburg. The Russians had still hoped that clerical influence, bolstered and encouraged by the Exarch and by the Russian embassy in Constantinople, might mobilise popular indignation and secure the return of a sufficiently large number of anti-government deputies to defeat the scheme. In fact there was little popular indignation, rather the reverse for congratulatory letters and telegrams poured in for Ferdinand, the most welcome being that from the Exarch himself. At home of the bishops only Kliment remained unreconciled and when he denounced the Prince in a sermon in March his enraged congregation drove him from his church, declared him deposed and locked him up in a nearby monastery; he was later brought before a civil court despite protests from the Exarch but with public opinion so clearly with the government on this issue the Exarch was not going to play Becket to Ferdinand's Henry II.

The marriage was in the first place a political contract but both parties to it performed their duty with admirable diligence and punctuality for nine months later, on 18/30 January 1894, Princess Marie Louise gave birth to a son, the first heir to a reigning Bulgarian monarch for over five hundred years. The national rejoicing was great and it was intensified when it was learnt that the heir was to bear the name Boris; this was Ferdinand's decision for no Cabinet minister had dared to suggest the name of a Bulgarian king who had once assailed the walls of mighty Constantinople itself. There could have been no more popular choice of name.

In July 1893 Stambulov crowned his recent successes with yet another victory at the polls. The new Sŭbranie was smaller than its predecessors, that of 1881 excepted, for the constitutional changes recently enacted had reduced the number of deputies, Stambulov hoping thereby to ensure the return of better qualified representatives. At the same time the quorum for the Assembly had been decreased from a half to a third to prevent a minority group paralysing the House by mass abstentions; the deputies were to be better educated but equally obedient. They were to sit for five rather than three years.

Government influence was again exercised during the election and a dependable majority secured, but there was less resort to naked terror than there had been in some previous polls, especially that of 1887. Yet if the nation did not have to be coerced with a rigour seen in earlier years and even though the Sŭbranie was dependable, Stambulov's political position had begun to weaken.

In the first place there was growing but as yet uncoordinated and largely unarticulated social tension. This was in part the result of natural causes for since 1892 the volume of harvests had been in decline and, to make matters worse for Bulgaria, world grain prices were falling. Despite these factors the administration had to find more and more money as loan obligations, development projects, and above all increased military spending were forcing up government expenditure. Extra sources of revenue were not easy to find. The Capitulations forbade the taxing of foreign subjects who formed a significant proportion of the new commercial element; native traders and producers were not faring well with the impact of cheap factory-made goods from Europe; and the political strength of the new civil service made it almost immune from increased taxation. There remained the great mass of the population and it was on them that Stambulov placed the extra burden, confidently declaring, 'The peasant can still pay'. In 1892 the government therefore reverted to a tithe in cash because the fall in grain prices had devalued a levy in kind. For many peasants this was a crushing blow. The problem of indebtedness* was beginning to assume major proportions in many areas and few peasants in these areas could find the extra cash which the revised tithe demanded of them. Their resentment at their own declining position was intensified when they saw that other sections of society, above all the despised civil servants, were not asked to shoulder similar new burdens. There were a number of sporadic outbursts of peasant anger but these the Stambulovist police could easily contain. Less easy to control was the alienation of many of the younger intelligentsia who were distressed by the growing social problems in the countryside and by the suppression of political freedom. Anti-government and even revolutionary views became entrenched in the educational system and though Ferdinand complained bitterly at the government's failure to combat such ideas Stambulov hubristicly laughed them off as youthful exuberance and extremism. The truth was that the nation was facing economic and social problems which had not been experienced by any government since the Liberation and which were but imperfectly comprehended by Stambulov and his ministers.

Whilst the peasantry and the younger intelligentsia were being alienated Stambulov and his ministers gratuitously made enemies of the country's Greek population by passing a law stating that all Christian children, irrespective of denomination, must be taught in Bulgarian in elementary schools. This provoked a major conflict between the government and the Greeks for the latter naturally saw the law as a threat to their cultural identity and were offended by the fact that their children should be denied the education in their own language which the children of Turks and Jews could still enjoy. Finally the Cabinet decided that though the law was to remain on the statute book it was

---

*See below, pp. 208–9 for a discussion of this problem.

not to apply to the 60,000 or so Greeks in Bulgaria. The Greeks, then, had been angered to no purpose whatever.

The foreign powers meanwhile were disturbed when Stambulov expelled the French journalist, Chadourne. It was true that Chadourne had not displayed great sensitivity in his dealings with and his writings on Bulgarian politicians but the authorities had clearly breached the Capitulations by expelling him, and this the governments of even those powers well disposed to Stambulov found embarrassing.

The Macedonians and Stambulov had been on bad terms ever since the Kresna-Razlog rising of 1878–9 when the latter had acted as a liaison officer between rebels in the field and the organising committees in Bulgaria. Enmity deepened after the breach with Russia and the execution of Panitsa, nor could Macedonians ever reconcile themselves to Stambulov's policy of cooperation with Turkey; even the concessions granted to the Exarchate in 1890 did not impress many younger Macedonians for they had begun to question the desirability of associating their cause with that of the Bulgarian Church, and some of them had even begun to think in terms of autonomy for Macedonia. Stambulov allowed the Macedonians little public expression and as soon as their propaganda threatened to complicate relations with Turkey he would intervene, as he did in closing down the newspaper *Makedoniya* in 1893. The Macedonians remained potential allies of any anti-Stambulovist faction which could itself tolerate the political extremism which was associated with the Macedonian issue.

That the influence of the Macedonian lobby in the army was considerable had been shown by the extent of the Panitsa plot. Immediately after the execution of Panitsa, which had shocked many officers, there had been considerable military reorganisation with some units being broken up and their officers distributed amongst other, more reliable regiments. More repostings and reorganisations had come in 1891. The most trenchant of Russophile officers had of course left in 1886–7 but some sympathy for the liberating power remained and this was sharpened in 1892 when it was announced that henceforth all officers must learn French or German and that senior officers would be expected to know both. This had been Ferdinand's decision but much of the blame was laid at Stambulov's door; it was entirely his decision in 1893, however, that the payment of billeting allowances to junior officers had to be suspended as part of a cut-back in government expenditure. In his earlier years in office Stambulov's hold over the army had been strengthened by the close relationship between himself and his Minister of War, Mutkurov, who had also become Stambulov's brother-in-law. Mutkurov had resigned in February 1891 because of ill-health—he was to die in March—and Stambulov had wanted to take over this vital post himself. This Ferdinand would not allow and insisted that General Savov be made Minister of War. Savov had been trained in Russia and was not to be numbered among the inveterate Russophobes, a fact which enabled him to keep the Russophiles within the army under control. This was to keep Stambulov safe from any threat from the army, but when Savov was removed from office it was the prelude to the fall of Stambulov himself.

In the summer of 1893 Stambulov was concerned less with a threat from the Macedonians or the army than with a recrudescence of organised political opposition within the constitutional framework. In the elections in July Stambulov and his National Liberal Party had campaigned on their success in bringing about the royal wedding; they won not because of this but because they were able to exercise the usual decree of influence over the polls. Opposing Stambulov was a new coalition of former ministers and their political dependents. Tonchev, leader of one faction of southern Liberals, had joined with Radoslavov, head of a northern Liberal group, and Nachovich who had returned to the government after the murder of Belchev but left again in November 1891 deeply resenting attacks upon him in a government newspaper. Thereafter Nachovich nursed a vehement hatred of Stambulov and was not unconnected with his eventual murder. The new coalition grouped around the newspaper which it founded, *Svobodno Slovo* (Free Speech). Its policy was based on acceptance of Ferdinand as Prince but rejection of Stambulov and his methods. They agreed with the Minister President on the need for international recognition of the Prince but insisted that this could not be achieved with Stambulov still at the helm, for he and with him the Prince would always be subject to attack from one of the many groups he had cudgelled into silence. This view was given depressing credence late in 1893 when the police uncovered a particularly unsavory plot by which two political refugees, the Ivanov brothers, had returned to Bulgaria with the intention of assassinating the Minister President during the interment of Alexander Battenberg's remains.

The death of Alexander Battenberg strengthened the new opposition coalition. Alexander's former secretary, Stoilov, had always been able to rally Battenbergist sympathisers and had also established contact with a number of moderate Russophiles who were anxious to see an accommodation, though on reasonable terms, with Russia. With the death of Alexander, Stoilov's group could not be suspected of wanting to remove Ferdinand and bring back the first Prince and Stoilov with his moderate Russophile and Conservative allies could cooperate with *Svobodno Slovo.*

What had brought the *Svobodno Slovo* and the Stoilov groups together was a common detestation of Stambulov's tough political methods. Clearly the Minister President would have been better off had he allowed a relaxation of political control for this would no doubt have meant that the various opposition factions would have spent more time attacking each other than in confronting the government, but the murder of Belchev so frightened Stambulov that he would not take this course. By the time the most rigid of controls were relaxed, in 1892, the experience of the *Stambulovshtina** had been so scored into opposition politicians' psyches that they were determined to remove the Minister President lest he reimpose the strictest of controls. Ironically by late 1893 when he saw the need to repress the new paper Stambulov dared not do so for, as he admitted to the Austrian representative in Sofia, he did not know when he himself might have need of a free press.

By the end of 1893 Stambulov was, then, conscious of his own weakening position. Much had changed since the early years of Ferdinand's reign when the balance of power between Prince and Minister President had been very clearly to the advantage of the latter. Stambulov was so confident of his strength in those years that he had treated Ferdinand with scant respect. The strict Court ceremonial upon which Ferdinand insisted and which contrasted markedly with the relaxed atmosphere prevailing in the days of Alexander Battenberg was ridiculed by Stambulov; when the Prince suggested purchasing a coronation robe Stambulov advised instead investment in a bullet-proof vest; when the Prince grumbled at the numerous complaints which he had received of electoral malpractices in 1890 Stambulov brusquely told Ferdinand that such complaints were always heard after elections in Bulgaria and had been particularly loud after the voting for the Grand National Assembly which had nominated him as Prince in 1887. Stambulov even accused the Prince of contributing to Mut-

---

*Added to a personal noun the suffix *shtina* in Bulgarian means the events, attitudes, atmosphere etc. associated with that person.

kurov's death by keeping the Minister of War standing for long periods despite his heart ailment. So dominant was Stambulov in the Bulgarian political scene before 1893 that when a possible resolution of the conflict with Russia was discussed it was discussesd in terms of the sacrifice of Ferdinand not of Stambulov. Pašić had put forward a solution along these lines during his discussions with Stambulov in 1889 and it had been proffered from the Russian side by Prince Dolgorukov, the publicist Tatishchev and the ambassador in Constantinople, Nelidov.

These indignities were endured but never forgotten by the sensitive Ferdinand. At the same time the Prince knew that Stambulov's tough methods, particularly after the murder of Belchev in 1891, were creating widespread dissatisfaction and when the palace was inundated with complaints at the four executions which followed the murder of Vŭlkovich the Prince thought seriously of engineering the dismissal of Stambulov. But Ferdinand did not yet feel himself strong enough to do this, for there was no alternative Minister President and he could not yet risk the dangers of an election against Stambulov.

In 1893 Ferdinand's position seemed from some angles worse than ever. The closer ties between Russia and France meant Paris would never recognise him; London now had a Liberal government which would be less anti-Russian than that of Lord Salisbury, and Austria was unlikely to complicate its relations with a major power for the sake of Bulgaria. There seemed, then, even less chance than before of recognition. This did not perturb Stambulov. He argued that recognition was irrelevant; Ferdinand was firmly established in Bulgaria and tolerated by most European powers and should therefore content himself with this until such time as the Russians were prepared to become more amenable. This was a misjudgement of Ferdinand's character. He wanted to establish himself in Bulgaria less to exercise power internally than to use his position there as a base from which to cut a figure on the grand diplomatic stage, and it was this which compelled him to seek and long for recognition. In fact in 1893 Ferdinand's prospects were better than a glance at the international scene would indicate.

His marriage had been popular and if the population in general did not like the alteration to Article 38 of the constitution then they blamed that on Stambulov; Ferdinand had secured the prize but Stambulov had paid for the ticket. The announcement of the Princess's pregnancy and the eventual birth of the heir to the throne gave the Saxe-Coburg dynasty a permanence it had not previously enjoyed, as

Stambulov and Ferdinand had intended it should, but the very fact that Ferdinand had become more secure made Stambulov expendable; those who, like Stoilov's moderate Conservative group, thought of reconciliation with Russia knew that it would have to be at the cost of Stambulov, not, as before 1893 at the cost of Ferdinand. Recognition was now all that Ferdinand wanted and recognition was now clearly beyond Stambulov's grasp; there was therefore every reason to drop him.

Ferdinand was further encouraged in this direction by a series of renewed disagreements with Stambulov. The Prince was enraged when he learnt that Stambulov had, without consultation, approached the Rumanians for an alliance which could only be directed against Russia, and that he had also requested further Macedonian concessions from the Porte, launching a series of stage-managed meetings to give backing to this initiative. Marie Louise, the Court and many leading Sofiotes were also appalled by Stambulov's brutal insistence on the exercise of his constitutional right to be present when the wife of the Prince gave birth. After the birth there were further disagreements because Stambulov resisted making Boris Prince of Tŭrnovo, a title which he wished to reserve for Krum Asen, the son of Alexander Battenberg. This both offended and alarmed Ferdinand for it could mean that the king-maker had at last found an alternative king. Ferdinand was eventually to have his way in this question.

The Prince had every reason to wish to be rid of Stambulov. He also now had in the *Svobodno Slovo*-Stoilov group an alternative government. Early in 1894 *Svobodno Slovo* launched a new campaign against the government. As before Stambulov and his colleagues were blamed for all the evils which Bulgaria was having to endure but now those with grievances were urged to make complaint not to the government but directly to the Prince. This cleverly played on the growing mistrust between palace and government, giving Ferdinand much ammunition to use against the Minister President, and showing him the growing strength of opposition to the regime. In the opening months of 1894 there was much cause for complaint. Supplementary elections were due to be held in a number of constituencies and the obvious growth of opposition power produced an escalation of government violence. There were ugly scenes in Razgrad and in the village of Sadina in the Popovo district where a score or more villagers were killed. In retaliation Stambulov billeted two companies of soldiers there for two months but this provoked angry meetings in the provincial capital,

Shumen, and in a number of other towns whilst the students of Sofia High School soon to become the University, added this to the long list of grievances about which they were increasingly vocal. In March the Prince toured the provinces and saw for himself how real was popular anger and resentment; Richard von Mach wrote, '. . . we are coming to a turning point and the reason for this is to be found in the way Stambulov exercises power'.[2]

Though he was convinced of the popular desire for a change, and though he had an alternative government to hand, Ferdinand needed one more asset before he would make his dramatic move: assured control of the army. This could be achieved by securing the appointment of a completely pliant Minister of War. Whilst Ferdinand was touring the provinces the opposition press published rumours that Stambulov had had an affair with Savov's wife. Savov challenged the Minister President to a duel and seconds were appointed. The duel never took place for no evidence could be produced of this liaison which Stambulov categorically denied. If no shots were exchanged it was however clear that the two men could not remain together in the Cabinet and Stambulov demanded the dismissal of Savov. Ferdinand agreed to this but he would not accept Stambulov's candidate, Lt. Col. Marinov, as successor. In his place Ferdinand installed General Racho Petrov who was as yet entirely the Prince's man, and who was already Chief of the General Staff; the combination of this post with that of Minister of War meant that Petrov had greater authority over the army than his predecessors in both offices. His appointment added enormously to Ferdinand's political power, and it was clear that the army would not be able to deal with this Prince as they had with Alexander Battenberg in 1886.

A symbolic measure of the change in the balance of power between Ferdinand and Stambulov can be seen in the fact that on the very day on which Savov left office Stambulov secured a major diplomatic triumph over Macedonia. For some time the Turks had been acting against Bulgarian teachers in Macedonia, many of whom had been arrested and their schools closed. Stambulov made fierce complaint to Constantinople, and the Porte, sensing the danger to its friend in Sofia, and mindful of the symbiosis which he had always preached, gave way. A recent order for the closure of more Bulgarian schools in Macedonia was rescinded, the Exarchate was allowed to establish a seminary in Constantinople, and the Exarch himself was to be allowed to have an official residence in the centre of the Ottoman capital, but most important of all the Exarch was to be given *berats* for the sees of Nevrokop and Veles.

These were massive concessions but they could do nothing to retrieve Stambulov's political position. As soon as he had secured the appointment of Petrov Ferdinand scurried off to Vienna where he was to have secret talks with the Russian ambassador, Lobanov; before leaving he arranged that the new War Minister need not have documents countersigned by other *namestnitsi** thus giving Petrov the power to move or not move troops as he thought fit and so depriving Stambulov of access to armed support.

The final break between Ferdinand and Stambulov came quickly and arose from the publication of various telegrams in the Bulgarian press. The opposition had compromised Stambulov by printing a number of doctored letters and protocols and Stambulov, in self-defence, published the complete and innocuous versions in his own paper, *Svoboda* (Freedom). One of these letters, it referred to the Savov affair, was from Ferdinand but as it was an official rather than a private communication Stambulov had had no reason to regard it as confidential. Ferdinand, then in Vienna, thought otherwise and telegraphed his anger in splenetic terms to his political secretary, Stanciov. Part of this telegram was published, clearly with the connivance of Stanciov, in *Svobodno Slovo,* and Stambulov therefore submitted his resignation; when Ferdinand returned to Sofia on 16/28 May the Minister President was not with the other members of the Cabinet who met the Prince at the station. Within a few days Stambulov's resignation had been accepted and a new administration formed under the chairmanship of Stoilov.

Stambulov had fallen because he had fulfilled his function. He had brought Ferdinand to the throne, established him upon it, seen him married and blessed with an heir, and all the time had provided a government which was firm and loyal and which until the last months had general if passive popular support. Yet he had not achieved the final goal, recognition for Ferdinand. Without this the internal situation in Bulgaria could not improve, indeed it seemed after the Belchev murder and again in the early months of 1894 to become worse as terror was let loose upon the population. Stambulov's dictatorial methods could be tolerated when they were achieving something, as in

---

*Ministers to whom the Prince entrusted executive powers whilst he was abroad.

1887 and even in 1891 when they were defending the state against serious internal disruption, but after 1892 there was no such danger. By 1893 Ferdinand was securely installed and if he was not popular then he was accepted as the only alternative to anarchy or foreign domination. Only a real chance of securing recognition could have justified Stambulov's continued use of rough methods and there was no possibility of recognition whilst the fiercely anti-Russian Minister President remained in office. By 1894 Stambulov had become an anachronism.

The last days of Stambulov's period in office had seen frequent anti-government demonstrations in the streets of Sofia, something inconceivable a year before. Violence which in fact was to accompany him to and even beyond the grave. In June 1894 the Prince at last brought himself to publish a letter of thanks to Stambulov and this persuaded the former Minister President to call at the palace and express his gratitude to Ferdinand. On his way home Stambulov was made the subject of a hostile demonstration by students from the High School. Thereafter he was subject to constant vilification in the official press and attacked in numerous demonstrations. Stambulov replied with vigorous articles in his own paper. In 1895 he complained of illness and requested permission to travel abroad for medical treatment a request which, much to Ferdinand's chagrin, was turned down because of pending legal action over Stambulov's misuse of power. In mid-July Stambulov launched a vituperative attack on Ferdinand which was widely printed in central Europe and which even contained intimations of homosexuality on the part of the Prince. The government papers replied in kind, one article declaring that the homes of Stambulov and his newspaper colleagues should be attacked, another that such people deserved to have 'the flesh torn from their bones'. The day after this article appeared Stambulov was viciously attacked in the street; the flesh was indeed torn from his bones and his hands had to be amputated. Within a few days he died. When he was at the very point of death a barrel organ began playing Viennese waltzes under his window, the man insisting that he had been paid to play at precisely that spot; when a wreath arrived from the Prince Stambulov's widow refused to receive it; instead she showed its bearer her husband's hands which she kept preserved in a jar. The grotesque incidents continued. When the funeral cortège moved off it was found that one of the wheels on the gun-carriage had been loosened and when it stopped for a few words of commemoration at the point where the original attack on

Stambulov had taken place a mob attacked it. Even at the graveside there was trouble; swearwords were shouted into Madame Stambulova's face and the mourners had not left the grave before it had been desecrated. A year later a memorial tablet erected over the tomb was demolished by a bomb.

Events such as these brought little credit to Bulgaria and it was widely believed that Ferdinand was implicated in or at least had foreknowledge of the murder and its repulsive sequels. Yet this is unlikely. As a recent biographer of Ferdinand points out, 'There is not a single bit of evidence to suggest that Ferdinand instigated or connived at the murder'.[3] Moreover Ferdinand's whole character, his revulsion at the thought of bloodshed and his unwillingness to resort to bold decisive actions suggests that he was not involved. Ferdinand benefited to some extent for the death of Stambulov removed one complication in Bulgaria's relations with Russia but it was not, as will be seen in the following section, the major one. Had Stambulov lived recognition would still have been possible. In fact Stambulov was the victim of a vengeance killing by the Macedonians. Before his death he had predicted that he would be murdered and that Tiufekdjiev would be one of his assassins. He was right for Tiufekdjiev was among those later convicted of but lightly punished for the assassination; Tiufekdjiev's brother had died under torture in a Stambulovist jail.

*   *   *

In the early years Stambulov had been forced by the ever-present threat of subversion, civil strife and anarchy to use dictatorial methods, and these had saved Bulgaria's independence for under Stambulov the nation had learnt that it could survive even as an international pariah. But Stambulov's continued use of these methods when the justification for them was no longer apparent inflicted terrible damage on the nation's political institutions and upon its political psyche. The ideals of the Tŭrnovo constitution had been completely discredited and would never now be realised; the mass of the nation could not believe that its politicians were operating for the common as opposed to their own best interests; when the peasantry did become politically active it would not look to the established parties for redress of its many grievances.

Not all the blame for this can be laid on Stambulov's shoulders. He certainly used police and military force more and for longer than previous Minister Presidents but he introduced no new method of electoral and political management; rather he entrenched existing malpractices. By the mid-1880s the rigging of polls was routine. The vital tactic was control of the electoral bureaux which in each constituency supervised the voting, for those exercising such control could exclude opponents, manufacture votes for their own faction, destroy opposition votes etc. If these methods failed to keep out a candidate unwelcome to the government, or if the wrong party captured the electoral bureau, the ruling faction could expel the deputy for alleged malpractice when the Sŭbranie reviewed the elections after the completion of the debate on the address from the throne.

Stambulov also continued rather than introduced the combination of party-political trafficking in office and the client system which percolated down through the administrative machine and which was known in Bulgaria as *partisanstvo*. The roots of this ugly phenomenon were to be found in the early post-Liberation days when the new state was in desperate need of administrative personnel whom it recruited primarily by offering high salaries. These attractive salaries soon satisfied the initial demand for civil servants but they also created amongst most educated men the expectation that such rewards were theirs by right, and many such men refused to take any form of employment other than high- or middle-ranking civil service posts. This meant that by the mid-1880s the supply of qualified men for these posts was far greater than the demand and thus there was created what Geshov, writing in the prestigious *Periodicheski Spisanie* (Periodic Review) in 1886, called a 'civil-service proletariat'. This discontented but potentially powerful group was attractive to the opposition parties who glibly promised that once in office they would give employment to such men. Thus party cadres at national and provincial level came to consist primarily of would-be civil servants who expected administrative posts when their Party came to power. When a Party was included in a ministry, therefore, it had to provide its leading supporters with jobs and the first task of a new ministry was to sack large numbers of government personnel including all regional prefects and sub-prefects, most mayors and appointed town and village officials, and even policemen, all of whom, of course, had been given their posts by the out-going administration. Once the new men were installed their first priority was to ensure victory for the new government in the elections which were always held to provide that new government with a dependable Sŭbranie and obedient local councils. To secure this the recently installed placemen turned to the local *prominenti* who controlled blocks of votes. Such local figures were frequently merchants or money-lenders whose local economic power enabled them to determine how their clients voted. This power was seldom exercised in the constant favour of one Party or faction, for the local bosses were not party men but rather electoral mercenaries who sold their votes to the group offering the highest price. With so much patronage at their disposal it was almost invariably the newly-appointed local officials who could offer the best reward for a block of votes, this reward coming in the form of a government contract, a bribe, or a minor office from which the local mercenary could dispense his own patronage at a lower level.

Electoral malpractice and *partisanstvo* had existed before Stambulov. His unremitting exploitation of them and of armed force however meant that they could never be erradicated and Bulgaria's political system would remain almost the sole property of a small minority of self-seeking politicians. The lack of real content and substance in party conflict meant that in later years most separate Parties were little more than claques calling for and expecting reward from one particular leader.

Chapter 9

RECOGNITION BY RUSSIA AND THE ACHIEVEMENT
OF STABILITY, 1894–6

Recognition by Russia, given up by Stambulov as unnecessary, was eventually to be achieved in February 1896, and was made possible by a combination of internal and external factors, the former being Stoilov's need to secure internal support and the national desire for reconciliation, the latter being changes in the personnel directing Russian policy and, more importantly, a general international concern at the stability of the Ottoman Empire.

Stoilov had become Minister President in May 1894 and had concocted a Cabinet consisting mainly of Conservatives like himself, southern Unionists led by Nachovich, and the Liberal factions of Radoslavov and Tonchev. Stoilov came from a wealthy family and had been educated at Robert College in Constantinople before going to Germany and Paris to study law. He was considered the best orator in Bulgaria and was distinguished by a widespread reputation for personal honesty; an equally unusual trait for a Bulgarian statesman was his genuine religious conviction. If his faith was strong his political position immediately after taking power was not. The country was tense and though there were popular demonstrations against Stambulov a backlash by his supporters could not be ruled out. The Prince was not yet convinced that Stoilov would be anything more than a stopgap, telling Grekov before the ministry was formed, 'J'appellerai Stoilov, mais je lui dirai que c'est comme pis-aller, et que je n'ai pas confiance en lui'.[1] Once in office, therefore, Stoilov had to concentrate upon finding political support sufficient to keep him there. In June he announced the formation of a new party, the Nationalist Party, which consisted essentially of the leading northern Conservatives and of the southern Unionist faction headed by Nachovich and Geshov. The slogan of the new Party and that of the new administration was to be 'Freedom and Legality, Order and Recognition'. Having formed his new Party, which was to guarantee electoral support, Stoilov dissolved the Sŭbranie with its Stambulovist majority and called a general election for September. Before the election he instituted a widespread purge of the administration, but what was surprising in Stoilov's application of the rules of *partisanstvo* was the rigour with which his new broom swept clean. All but three of the country's twenty-four prefects were sacked immediately, five hundred mayors and communal heads were replaced in a month as were seventy out of the eighty-four rural magistrates and police inspectors. The purge continued less intensely for over a year and by the end of 1895 almost the entire personnel of the civil service and the police apparatus had been changed. Nor was the process, especially in the early days, always peaceful. The new authorities, many of whom had felt the heavy hand of the old, frequently used violence and there were a number of deaths.

Violence was seen, too, at the elections in September. Nationalist Party enthusiasts even campaigned in some constituencies against other supporters of the coalition, and in Sliven, for example, government *shaikadjii* beat up Radoslavists. Opponents of the regime fared worse and the usual methods of influence were employed to exclude a number of them; thus the famous satirical writer Aleko Konstantinov failed to win the Svishtov poll, despite a clear popular preference for him. The exiled Tsankov was, on the other hand, returned despite considerable government pressure on the electorate; Tsankov's election was then declared void and the seat offered to the southern Liberal, Tonchev, who declined it when news of how the voting had been arranged became public. The government secured a sound but not a convincing majority. The new Assembly was to consist of forty-six Nationalists, twenty-six Conservatives together with the remaining southern Unionists, thirty-seven Radoslavists, forty followers of Tsankov, all of whom were prepared to accept Ferdinand as their legitimate Prince, plus an irreconcilable opposition of four Socialists and eight supporters of the imprisoned Karavelov. Of Stambulovists there were none, both because of the 'purification' of the administration and because the former premier had denounced the dissolution of the Seventh National Assembly as unconstitutional and the consequent elections as thereby invalid; he told his followers to boycott the poll.

Stoilov now needed to consolidate behind the government a sizeable majority in the Sŭbranie, but personal squabbles between the Unionist supporters of the National Party and the Radoslavists made this difficult. Like the Radoslavists, Tonchev's southern Liberals were concerned at the way government influence had been used in the election and Tonchev resigned, claiming that such conduct could not be reconciled with Stoilov's professed programme of 'Freedom and Legality'. Tonchev's moralising carried little conviction; he had waited twenty days before making his declaration and then it was generally assumed he was acting out of pique, having lost contests at Samokov and in Sofia, and then being put in the embarrassing position of being offered the cooked result in Tsankov's constituency. Radoslavov, like Tonchev, had not been returned to the Sŭbranie but stayed in the Cabinet, primarily because he could not find any other group willing to form a coalition with him. Radoslavov and his party colleagues, however, soon fell out with the southern Unionists and in addition to these personal conflicts there was a deep difference between the two factions over attitudes towards Russia.

Stoilov could not continue with a divided Cabinet and a Sŭbranie which, it was soon apparent, was not subject to governmental control. Most of the allegedly pro-government deputies had, it seemed, proclaimed their allegiance only to secure the backing of the governmental machine during the election. Stoilov therefore resigned and insisted that he would continue in office only on condition that any Party entering the governmental coalition must accept his terms. For a few days Radoslavov, as eager as ever for office, attempted to stitch together a coalition, but he made little progress and Stoilov was soon reappointed to head a Nationalist Party government which had support in the Assembly from the Conservatives, the Unionist faction from Rumelia, and the Tsankovists.

That the Tsankovists were prepared to support the new administration was possible because there had been a significant change in official attitudes towards Russia. After the fall of Stambulov, Russophile politics had revived, and even the extremists of the Karavelov faction who were now almost alone in calling for the removal of Ferdinand to make reconciliation possible, were allowed to publish a newspaper, *Zname* (Banner), and to contest seats in local and general elections. Amongst the less extreme, though no less passionate advocates of Russophilia, Metropolitan Kliment, who had been released from detention by the Prince shortly before the fall of Stambulov, made public peace with Ferdinand, and the Tsankovists, though their leader remained in exile, also accepted the Prince. They were partly helped by Stoilov's attitude. As soon as he had taken office he had assured the Turks and the Austrians that there would be no change of direction in Bulgaria's foreign policy, but it was not long before he was telling the *Frankfurter Zeitung*'s correspondent in Sofia that he was not prepared to provoke the Russians in the way Stambulov had done; 'It is not in our character', he said, 'to provoke Russia. If Germany and Austria and the other great powers are well disposed towards Russia why should we, a small state, play the role of the dog which barks at her?'.[2] From Russia itself the initial response to the change of government was cool, but by the summer of 1894 there were signs of a thaw. The Tsankovist press had declared that Ferdinand had established 'deep roots' in the hearts of all Bulgarians and was to be seen as 'the guarantor of national freedom and independence'.[3] Even more important were growing fears in St Petersburg, as in other European capitals, that the Ottoman Empire was on the point of collapse, the growing disturbances in Armenia being the origin of such fears. The Tsar still ruled out any compromise with 'the Coburg', but both his Foreign Minister, Giers, and Nelidov, the ambassador in Constantinople, knew that if the Ottoman humpty-dumpty were to fall then Russia, for the sake of her political influence in the Balkans, would have to be reconciled with Bulgaria. Such thoughts Nelidov confessed to the Exarch who relayed them to Bulgarian politicians. The latter, however, did nothing, hoping that the Russians would take the first steps, for if it were Bulgaria who took the initiative then the Russians would drive a hard bargain.

For the moment nothing could be done by either side. The Russians would make no move because they were not satisfied that Stoilov with an unruly Sŭbranie and a divided Cabinet was yet securely in power, and because by early autumn the Tsar was seriously ill. Stoilov, too, was restrained by his own lack of security and by the illness of Alexander III; obviously, in view of the latter there could be no debate in the Sŭbranie on Bulgaria's relations with Russia, and so crucial an issue was the health of the Tsar that the Minister President demanded two telegrams per day from the Bulgarian legation in Vienna giving the latest information on this question.

The Tsar died on 20 October/1 November. Ferdinand immediately ordered requiem services to be held in all churches in Bulgaria, put the army into mourning for eight days, and telegraphed condolences to

Nicholas II in his own name and in that of the Bulgarian people. Stoilov meanwhile sent a telegam to Giers. On 24 October/5 November Stoilov made a major speech to the Sŭbranie on foreign affairs. He began by a routine statement of Bulgaria's priorities: first, good relations with the suzerain power, secondly, good relations with neighbouring states, and thirdly, good relations with the powers. Bulgaria, he said, was prepared to do all it could to secure good relations with Russia but there were limits to the concessions she could make. She could not, as some Russophiles had said, allow Russia possession or even use of Burgas and Varna, she could not accept Russian officers again into the Bulgarian army, and, of course, she could not consider any change of Prince. The sensational passages of the speech came when Stoilov spoke of the Tsar's death, for not only did he have to report that Ferdinand had telegraphed to Nicholas II, but also that the new Tsar had replied, thanking the Prince 'for the words which you have sent to me in the name of the Bulgarian people'. Stoilov's peroration was a rousing call to delete the words 'Russophile' and 'Russophobe' from the Bulgarian political vocabulary, and the Sŭbranie voted massively its confidence in the government's foreign policy.[4]

The Tsar's telegram to Ferdinand was not, as some Bulgarians hoped, tantamount to recognition, but it was a sign that at last the ice had been broken. The government attempted immediately to continue the process of thaw and on the day on which Stoilov made his speech asked St Petersburg for clarification as to the exact significance of Nicholas's telegram and whether a delegation from Bulgaria would be allowed to take part in Alexander III's funeral procession. No clear answer was received to the first question but that to the second was all too plain; a delegation would not be welcome.

It was to be almost a month before the Bulgarians were given further indication of Russian attitudes. On 26 November/8 December Nelidov passed through Bulgaria *en route* to his post in Constantinople. Vŭlkovich, who like his assassinated namesake had spent some years in the Ottoman capital and knew Nelidov, joined the train in Sofia and for the three hours which it took to reach Ihtiman had a private and unofficial conversation with the ambassador. From this it became clear that the Russians would insist on the Bulgarians taking the initiative; that they would also insist that any delegation to Russia must come from the Sŭbranie, the representative of the Bulgarian nation, and not from Ferdinand or the government appointed by him, for both of these were still regarded as illegal by the Russian authorities; that only when such a delegation visited Russia, perhaps to lay a wreath on the grave of the late Tsar and to ask his successor for forgiveness, would Russia's terms for recognition be made known officially, but it was already made clear that one of those terms would be that Prince Boris be received into the Orthodox faith.

It would be some time before negotiations were in sight, but late in 1894 the Bulgarian government took a number of steps to improve the atmosphere in which those talks would take place when eventually they did begin; Stoilov was, in effect, showing his good intentions to Russia. The first of these measures was the Cabinet reconstruction which eliminated Radoslavov, since 1886 an advocate of good relations with Austria rather than Russia. In December the government enacted the Amnesty Law. This relaxed a number of strictures imposed upon the Russophiles by Stambulov, and it enabled Tsankov to return to Bulgaria and Karavelov to be released from prison. The law did not, however, apply to the army officers who had fled from the country after taking part in the *putsch* of 1886 or one of the risings that followed it. Whilst measures against the Russophiles were being relaxed, those against the Stambulovists were tightened. In December it was decided to set up a commission to inquire into the activities of the recent ministry; a year later the commission was to present the Assembly with a seven-hundred-page catalogue of the misdemeanours of Stambulov and his associates. In December 1894 Stoilov also reimposed controls on the press, and though these were not as thorough as in the first half of the *Stambulovshtina* they were directed almost solely against the Stambulovists, and represented only one of a series of measures taken by the government to circumscribe the activities of the former Minister President and his colleagues. Stoilov's gestures towards Russia were helped by clumsy retaliatory action by the Austrians. They had disliked recent legislation which made it possible for the Bulgarian authorities, notwithstanding the Capitulations, to tax foreign businessmen and manufacturers in Bulgaria, many of whom were Austrian subjects. Austrian protests, however, were delayed until December when the gestures of conciliation to Russia had begun and when Radoslavov had not only left the Cabinet but also announced his willingness to form a new administration. Austria's protests looked too much like an interference with Stoilov's attempts to improve relations with Russia and were widely resented.

The first half of 1895 was to see but slow progress towards Stoilov's and Ferdinand's desired reconciliation with St Petersburg. The year

began with an encouraging development for Bulgaria when the death
of Giers brought Lobanov back to St Petersburg as Foreign Minister.
He had been on good terms with Ferdinand and was known to believe
that Russo-Bulgarian relations had been poisoned primarily by the
ill-advised behaviour of some Russian officials and officers in Bulgaria.
Yet Lobanov's arrival at the Russian Foreign Ministry made little
difference to Russo-Bulgarian relations. By the spring the Russians
were concerned at the growing agitation by the Macedonians in Macedonia and Bulgaria which was forcing the government in Sofia into an
increasingly difficult position vis-à-vis the Porte. On the other hand,
the Russians' own anxieties as to the viability of Turkey meant that
they were not keen to see the thaw with Sofia cease, and they accordingly let it be known that they would now receive a delegation from the
Sŭbranie. The Bulgarians had never wanted to take the initiative, but
they had little choice if they were to appear serious in their professions
of a desire for better relations with Russia, and serious they were, not
least because they were desperate for support in their demands for
reform in Macedonia. The government therefore agreed in May that
the Sŭbranie should send a delegation to place a golden cross on the
grave of Alexander III. There were still delays for foreign bishops
could not travel in Russia without the permission of the Holy Synod
and this could be secured only through the intervention of the Exarch,
and even when this had been granted it was decided that the clerical
part of the delegation should be headed by Kliment rather than Grigori
of Ruse, the former being much more acceptable in Russia. Kliment
was, in fact, to act as head of the delegation amongst whose other
members were the poet Ivan Vazov, Geshov and the President of the
Sŭbranie, Todor Todorov. The delegation left Bulgaria in June.

It had no power to negotiate but was to inform the Russians of
Bulgaria's position and find out what Russian thoughts were. The
Bulgarian position was essentially that described by Stoilov in his
speech in October/November; the Bulgarians regarded the dynastic
question as settled and would mention it only to request recognition of
Ferdinand in accordance with the treaty of Berlin; the Bulgarians
would not accept Russian consular representation in their country
before recognition. On the question of the faith of Prince Boris the
Russians were to be told that conversion was a possibility but if it
happened it would be because it was in Bulgaria's rather than any other
country's best interests, and the final decision had to rest with the boy's
father. The Russians were to be disabused of the opinion, sometimes

voiced in the Panslavist press, that Bulgaria's foreign policy was determined by Russia's opponents, but nor were the Russians to be left in any doubt that the old Liberal notion of Bulgaria's foreign policy being an extension of Russia's was no longer acceptable in Sofia. The delegates, in fact, had few chances to exchange opinions. Early in the visit they had welcomed a statement from two senior Russian army officers that the Bulgarian army had proved at Slivnitsa that it did not need foreign advisers, but soon after this the visit was engulfed in sentimentality. Kliment grovelled, telling his hosts, despite his instructions, that Bulgaria would do virtually whatever Russia asked to secure recognition. In return, Pobedonostsev declared that 'The souls of the two people are united in the possession of a common Orthodox faith'. Ferdinand was spoken of only once by the Russians when the Tsar asked, without waiting for a reply, 'Comment va votre Prince?' Todorov alone managed to have some serious discussions. A senior Foreign Ministry official had let the delegation know that it was the Tsar's especial wish that Boris should be received into the Orthodox Church and Todorov, after consulting with Sofia, went on a few days later to ask Lobanov what conditions Russia would make for recognition and whether the conversion of the Prince of Tŭrnovo alone would be sufficient. Lobanov, despite his general sympathy for Bulgaria, merely burst out laughing and the subject was not raised again.[5]

In the other European capitals the visit of the Sŭbranie delegation was not welcomed, primarily because it coincided with the murder of Stambulov and his funeral. For the Bulgarian government it had brought no direct advance but it had not marked a regression. The Russian terms, it seemed, would be little different from those stated by Nelidov to Vŭlkovich, and the conversion of Boris was without any doubt going to be the major issue.

The delegations returned from Russia in July, and in August there were no further developments. The Russians were still concerned at the state of Bulgaro-Turkish relations over Macedonia, and they were also disturbed by signs of increasing political instability within Bulgaria itself. Whilst Stoilov preached 'Freedom and Legality', his prefects and sub-prefects wielded power in a very unsophisticated and primitive fashion, and Stoilov could not exercise over them the control which had been at the command of Stambulov; Bulgaria, noted one observer, was now suffering not from one dictator but from many. At the same time the government came under fire from Russophiles such as Kliment, who claimed it was unwilling to make the reasonable concessions which the Russians were demanding for recognition. On the other side, and equally critical, were the Radoslavists and Tonchevists, who claimed that the policy of seeking *rapprochement* had failed, that the Subranie delegation had proved the validity of the old Stambulovist maxim that 'A Russophile ministry as the Russians understand it is impossible without Russian bayonets in Bulgaria'. The scent of office was now strong in Radoslavov's ever-receptive nostrils and it grew stronger when Tsankov embarrassed his followers a few weeks later by admitting in an open letter that he wanted the relationship between Bulgaria and Russia to be similar to that between Britain and Egypt. Such statements only confirmed the Russophobes' worst suspicions.

This was all deeply depressing for Stoilov and for Ferdinand. The latter had even begun to think in terms of a possible military coup. Few doubted that this was feasible, for the Prince enjoyed the confidence of his senior officers, many of whom were concerned at the possible return of those who had fled in 1886 and 1887 and who might, once back in Bulgaria, compete for promotions and for political influence. In the summer a new journal, *Voenen List* (Soldiers' Bulletin), appeared, directed at the officer corps and openly calling for a military take-over and the purging of all corrupt civilian politicians. Ferdinand did not take to such extremes. He did, however, pay numerous visits to his even more numerous relatives, discussing with all of them the problem of recognition, and above all the issue of his son's religious allegiance. He also enlisted the diplomatic aid of Russia's ally, France, to whom he offered an alliance if she could bring about a reconciliation between Sofia and St Petersburg.

The French initiative sank on the rock of conversion. On this issue Ferdinand had been concentrating with increasing intensity. To the Pope he sent one of his most able young diplomatists, his former political secretary, Dmitri Stanciov, but Leo XIII was adamant that abdication was preferable to the spiritual murder of the young Prince. Yet political pressures forced Ferdinand in the other direction. The King of Rumania had already allowed his heir to be baptised into Orthodoxy and although as a Protestant he did not have the Pope to contend with, it was inevitably asked in Bulgaria why their Prince did not have the courage of his neighbour. Ferdinand knew that a third non-Orthodox ruler would be dangerous for Bulgaria's internal solidarity, and that the conversion of the Prince would also deprive the few remaining anti-dynasts of their most powerful argument. Nachovich proposed a scheme whereby Ferdinand should declare that Boris would only come to the throne as an Orthodox, an arrangement which would have obviated the need for any immediate change and would have left the real decision to Boris himself, providing there was no regency. Stoilov did not rule out this idea but he would do nothing to put direct pressure on Ferdinand, insisting still that the decision had to be the Prince's alone. Stoilov feared that any pressure might be counter-productive and he guessed that, if left alone, Ferdinand's sense of political reality would convince him of the need for conversion. So determined was the Minister President to leave this question to Ferdinand that he forbad the Holy Synod in Sofia to discuss the issue lest the Prince regard this as a form of pressure on him.

When Ferdinand opened the Sŭbranie in the middle of October, he praised the delegation which had been to St Petersburg but said nothing on the question of conversion. In its reply to the address the Assembly asked specifically that the Prince of Tŭrnovo be received into the Orthodox faith. The pressure had begun and soon even Stoilov was to join it, conniving with some government deputies who once more requested conversion, this time by using a parliamentary question. The reason for Stoilov's change of mind was that at the end of October the Exarch had been informed that Lobanov was still convinced that conversion would help the Bulgarians and might even secure for them all they wanted. The explanation both for Lobanov's approach and for Stoilov's rapid response to it lay in the political situation within Turkey itself. From its two major diplomatic posts, Constantinople and Vienna, the Bulgarian government heard constant rumours that the Armenian outrages would bring within a few months either war or the partition of the Empire. If partition were to come the Bulgarians, having offended Austria by their pro-Russian attitudes, would be absolutely dependent on Russia if they were to secure a decent share of the spoils in European Turkey. The Russians for their part were now anxious to have Bulgarian support in the Near East because Nelidov had at last persuaded his government to draw up plans for a seizure of the Straits in the increasingly likely event of a Turkish collapse; then Russia would need all the friends she could muster in the Balkans.

In the face of this pressure Ferdinand made his first major concession. In replying to the concocted parliamentary question he let it be known on 31 October/11 November that he would implement the deputies' request when he had overcome the many difficulties involved. This was far from the unambiguous commitment the Subranie had hoped for, and there was a good deal of suspicion of Ferdinand's intentions. This was fuelled by rumours that a priest from the Capucin mission in Sofia who frequented the palace had reported that Ferdinand had sworn not to implement his promise over Boris; suspicions as to Ferdinand's good intentions were increased also by the very recent birth and immediate and secret Catholic baptism of Ferdinand and Marie Louise's second son, Kyril; like most political secrets in Sofia, this was general knowledge within a few days.

Stoilov now added yet more pressure on Ferdinand, telling him that if he did not make a clear-cut commitment over Boris the government would resign at the end of the Sŭbranie session in January; if Stoilov went the only factions willing to form a government would be the Radoslavists and others who were not in favour of *rapprochement* with Russia, but there was serious doubt as to whether the nation, believing reconciliation to be around the corner, would peaceably accept such a reverse. Ferdinand seemed to be faced with a decision between the conversion of Boris and probable anarchy within the Principality.

Ferdinand's was a conscience not frequently troubled, but it was now genuinely disturbed. Once more he visited his and his wife's relatives and once more he pleaded his case to the Pope, but with similar results. In January Ferdinand was back in Sofia in so depressed a state of mind that he spoke of abdication. Stoilov rejoined that that would mean anarchy for Bulgaria, and that the Prince had to make personal sacrifices for the sake of his adopted nation. Yet Ferdinand had political as well as spiritual doubts. Ever since Lobanov's intimations via the Exarch he had seen that if he were to defy the Pope together with his own and his wife's relatives he had to be sure that this sacrifice would secure all he wanted; the Russians, for their part, could not give such a guarantee until they were convinced that Ferdinand had the political will to carry through his decision in the face of such opposition. Ferdinand, then, had to take the gamble.

By the second half of January that sense of political reality on which Stoilov had counted brought Ferdinand to a decision. On 22 January/3 February he announced that Prince Boris would be received into the Orthodox Church on 2/14 February. The Tsar was asked to stand as godfather to the convert, and to this Nicholas II gladly agreed. The ceremony was performed by the Exarch in the presence of the Tsar's personal representative, Golemishchev-Kutuzov, and Tcharykov, a counsellor in the Russian embassy in Berlin who was to be Russia's diplomatic representative in Sofia when Ferdinand had been officially recognised and relations restored. Recognition came on 19 February/2 March—the anniversary of San Stefano—when a special envoy from the Sultan presented Ferdinand with a *firman* officially recognising him as Prince of Bulgaria and Governor-General of Rumelia. Amid a national rejoicing as yet untainted by this reminder that Constantinople had not yet accepted the union of 1885, other powers soon followed Turkey in recognising Ferdinand as the legal monarch. Ferdinand celebrated his triumph with a mawkish speech to the Sŭbranie and then with a long tour, spending almost three weeks in Constantinople before visiting St Petersburg, Berlin, Paris, Coburg, Munich and eventually Moscow for the Coronation of Nicholas II. Vienna was conspicuously absent from the itinerary for the Emperor was disgusted at the conversion of Prince Boris. The Pope meanwhile had anathematised Ferdinand and Marie Louise had slipped quietly away to stay with her affronted family.

*   *   *

Recognition and the restoration of official relations between Bulgaria and Russia did not resolve all the issues disputed between the two states as a subsequent chapter will show, but developments between 1894 and 1896 did greatly increase Ferdinand's internal political power. The politicians controlled the political machine through *partisanstvo,* which could ensure a dependable support once in office. It was Ferdinand, however, who would decide when a Party was to come to or leave office. This was made possible by his domination over two vital ministries, those of War and Foreign Affairs. He had secured control over the former in an effort to dominate the army and the officer corps, and so prevent a second 1886. His domination of the Foreign Ministry he based on his own personal diplomatic experience and his many family ties with the crowned heads of Europe. Control over the two ministries enabled him to precipitate a ministerial crisis at will; he had merely to order his own nominees to resign, for no Cabinet could survive without these two ministers. In addition to this Ferdinand was helped by the fact that by 1896 the political Parties were far more fragmented than they had been earlier and thus he could play off one faction against the others in a way which would have been impossible for Alexander Battenberg. Ferdinand also had by the mid-1890s great knowledge of internal affairs and considerable mastery over many individual politicians whose every peccadillo he knew; his secret archive was reputed to be the envy of every secret police chief in Europe, and this sinister science he had learnt, he said, from the master practitioner, Stambulov. The Prince was ably assisted by his personal secretary, Dobrović, an illusive figure who in the coming years exercised great influence.

From 1896 onwards Ferdinand charted the general direction in which Bulgaria was to move. He, to a large extent, decided its foreign policy and he determined the make-up of its successive governments even if he did not regulate every detail of domestic policy.

The contest between the legislature and the executive for supremacy which had begun immediately after the drawing up of the Tŭrnovo constitution had finally been decided by patience and guile in favour of the executive; the era of Ferdinand's 'personal regime' had begun.

Chapter 10

THE SOCIAL IMPACT OF THE LIBERATION
I. RURAL

The most important social consequence of the Liberation was to entrench the small, peasant proprietor as the characteristic figure of the Bulgarian countryside. This can be attributed to two main causes; the fact that before the Liberation most Bulgarian peasants were already masters of their own property, and the emigration of Moslem landholders during and after the war of 1877–8.

During the war of 1877–8 many Moslems, including large and small landowners, left the Bulgarian lands. Though many returned after the signing of the treaty of Berlin they were soon to find the atmosphere of the liberated lands uncongenial and large numbers emigrated once again to the more familiar cultural and political atmosphere of the Ottoman Empire. The decline in the Turkish-speaking population of Bulgaria in the period 1880–1910 is set out in table 1. The figures given in this table are for mother-tongue and do not therefore give an absolutely accurate picture of Moslem emigration for a large number of the Moslem refugees were Tatars and Circassians who left before the first census was taken, as did many Turkish Moslems. Furthermore there were a number of Bulgarian-speaking Moslems who remained in the Principality, though their total number changed little during these years, rising from about twenty thousand in 1880 in northern Bulgaria to 21,143 or 0.6% of all Bulgarians in Bulgaria in 1910.

Despite their obvious shortcomings the figures given in table 1 do show a weakening of the Turkish-speaking population which was without exception Moslem. The emigration of the Moslems was to have profound social effects in post-Liberation Bulgaria. It was to

Table 1. Population of Bulgaria by Mother Tongue, 1880–1910

Mother Tongue	1880/1		1887		1892		1900		1905		1910	
Bulgarian	1,909,067	67.84%	2,326,250	74.60%	2,505,326	75.67%	2,887,860	77.13%	3,205,019	79.41%	3,523,311	81.23%
Turkish	701,984	24.95%	607,331	19.48%	569,728	17.21%	539,656	14.41%	497,820	12.35%	504,560	11.63%
Greek	42,659	1.52%	58,326	1.87%	58,518	1.77%	70,887	1.89%	69,761	1.73%	50,866	1.17%
Gypsy			50,291	1.61%	52,132	1.57%	89,549	2.39%	94,649	2.35%	121,573	2.80%
Jewish			23,541	0.75%	27,531	0.83%	32,573	0.87%	36,455	0.90%	38,554	0.89%
Others	160,158	5.69%	52,636	1.69%	97,478	2.95%	123,758	3.31%	131,942	3.26%	98,649	2.28%
Total	2,813,868	100.00%	3,118,375	100.00%	3,310,713	100.00%	3,744,283	100.00%	4,035,646	100.00%	4,337,513	100.00%

i. The figures for 1880/1 are a combination of the Rumelian census of 1880 and that taken in the Principality in 1881. The figures for Greek-speakers in this column applies to Rumelia only.

ii. Figures given for 'Jewish' speakers are a combination of all Jewish dialects and languages. This category was used in the censuses and measures ethnicity rather than language.

provide large areas of land for the Christian Bulgarian peasants who frequently over-borrowed to purchase available property; it was to enable the small, self-sufficient, peasant proprietor to remain the predominant figure in the country even in a time of increasingly rapid population growth; by focusing attention on the question of property rights the emigration was to clear away many of the legal obscurities surrounding land ownership in the latter years of Ottoman rule; it was to destroy most of the *chifliks* and thereby retard the development of commercialised agriculture; and it was to do away with the vexatious tenures of the north- and south-west.

The transfer of land from Moslem to Christian ownership which was the most important effect of Moslem emigration was a complex process. Such transfers had taken place before 1878 and in the Tatar Pazardjik district, for example, where Christian landowners had been unknown in 1840, some two thousand plots had been bought by them between 1872 and 1875. In 1877 and in the following years the process of transfer took place on an immensely greater scale, both here and elsewhere.

With the outbreak of war some Moslems sold their property, mostly to wealthy local Christians. Other Moslems rented their lands, usually to dependable local Bulgarians, on the understanding that it would be handed back if and when the owners returned. Most departing Moslems, however, simply abandoned their land and fled, the rate of emigration increasing considerably after the fall of Pleven had made it clear that the Russians were to win the War. As the Moslems fled many Bulgarians left the hills and forests where they had recently been living in partial hiding and inevitably they seized some of the land now made vacant. The incidence of seizure varied regionally. In the north-east the Moslems were numerous and, feeling safety in numbers, few of them had left and those remaining were therefore strong enough to discourage seizures by Christians. In the north- and south-west on the other hand almost all Moslems had fled and their lands were immediately taken over by the local Christians who often divided up the large estates found in these areas. In the remainder of northern Bulgaria transfers, often under the cloak of renting, took place in approximately one third of the communities. In the Tŭrnovo province, for example, there were seventy-seven Turkish or mixed Turkish-Bulgarian villages of which twenty-four (31.1%) were seized by Bulgarians, twenty-two (28.5%) were later repossessed by returning Moslem refugees, and another twenty-two remained unaffected; the fate of the remaining

nine is unknown. In the south there was much more tension and violence. Here the incidence of *chifliks* had been higher but more importantly it was also in the south that most Moslem revenge for the rising
of 1876 had been exacted. Here there was no polite fiction about
renting and there were cases of peasants not only seizing land but also
destroying buildings. Yet even here the incidence of violent expropriation can be exaggerated for in the Plovdiv province in the spring of
1878 the Russians found that despite the intensity of the agrarian
movement six of the nineteen vacant Turkish *chifliks* had not been
affected.

In the vast majority of cases it was local Christians who seized the
vacant land, but some Moslem peasants also did so. Others who took
part in the seizures were Christians from other parts of Bulgaria where
there had been little Moslem emigration, and also Bulgarian refugees
from areas which were still under Ottoman control, primarily Macedonia and western Thrace. In later months the publication of the terms
of the treaty of Berlin naturally intensified the flow of refugees from
these areas and they were reported by the prefect of Burgas province as
helping themselves to émigré land 'in a most arbitrary fashion'.[1]

In Burgas and the rest of Rumelia the treaty of Berlin intensified the
land struggle by making the Christians more determined to seize sufficient land before Ottoman sovereignty was restored. It also encouraged the former Moslem owners to return. With these problems the
Russian Provisional Administration had to contend.

The Provisional Administration did not have the power, even if it
had had the will, to prevent so popular a movement as the seizure of
vacant Moslem land, but nor could the Administration allow this
movement to go completely unchecked for this would give the Turks
and the British the excuse to interfere in the internal affairs of the
liberated territories. Given these dangers the Russians handled the
agrarian problem with considerable skill. In the summer of 1877 Bulgarian refugees from Macedonia, Thrace and unliberated Rumelia had
been allowed to harvest the crops left by Moslems émigrés and in September all Bulgarians, the incoming refugees and the indigenous, were
allowed to sow vacant Moslem land, though it was insisted that this
did not in any way signify a transfer of ownership. With the mass
exodus of Moslems after San Stefano the Provisional Administration
had little choice but to allow the Bulgarians to work the vacant land,
most of which was given not to individuals but to communal councils
with rent, set at half the value of the harvest, to be paid to the legal

owner should he return and to the Provisional Administration if he did not. In many cases councils simply refused to pay this rent, believing that the land in any case belonged to the local Christian community, and the Russians were not over-zealous in collecting such monies. At the same time, however, careful steps were taken to record the land being cultivated by Bulgarians, presumably in the expectation that this would pave the way for the eventual legal transfer of the property. The Russian Provisional Administration also settled some twenty thousand Christian refugees on vacant land.

With the end of the Russian Provisional Administration the agrarian question became the responsibility of the new governments in Sofia and Plovdiv. There were some categories of land which presented no real difficulties. The state lands of the Ottoman Empire, including large areas of forest, became in the Principality the property of the Bulgarian government, whilst those in Rumelia, though remaining technically the property of the Sultan, were placed at the disposal of the authorities in Plovdiv. The same was true of the lands of the Tatars and Circassians. With the advance of the Russian armies in 1877 these settlers fled and most of the villages which at the end of the war were completely depopulated were former Tatar and Circassian communities; they also formed a large proportion of the villages in which seizures took place, the local Christians feeling particularly strongly that such lands were in any case theirs by right. In the early 1880's legislation was passed in Bulgaria, where most of the Tatars and Circassians had been settled, giving the land of absentee owners back to those from whom it had been taken in the 1850's and 1860's and who, in many cases, had already repossessed it. Such legislation was uncontroversial because few Tatars or Circassians had dared to return to their former homes and not even Britain was prepared to wage a diplomatic battle for their property rights.

There was no such easy solution to the problem of the returning Turkish landowner. As early as January 1878 a few had begun to return to Bulgaria but when the treaty of Berlin guaranteed Turkish property rights and restored southern Bulgaria to the Sultan's sovereignty many émigrés interpreted this as a virtual return to the *status quo ante* south of the Balkan mountains and the trickle of returning Turks became a flood. Of the 150,000 Moslems who had fled during the war, over half, 80,000, had returned by September 1878.

This caused enormous problems. There was the political difficulty that some of the returning Turks had been implicated in the massacres of 1876. There was also the problem of housing the returnees. In September local authorities ordered that any houses taken over by Bulgarians were to be restored to their former owners on the latter's demand, whilst other returning Turks were given Tatar or Circassian land. For the administration of these measures the Russian Provisional Administration had to pay, the Porte making no response to Russian suggestions that Turkey pay two million roubles a month towards the upkeep of the former exiles.

These problems were insignificant compared to those raised when the returning Turks demanded the restitution of their lost lands.

In July the Russian Provisional Administration had come to an agreement with the Porte by which Turkish refugees were allowed to return under military escort, if necessary, and were to have their lands back on condition that they surrendered all their weapons. In the following month it was decreed that those returning would not be immune from prosecution for excesses committed during and after the 1876 rising and anyone against whom such charges were substantiated would be deprived of his lands; this decree did more than anything else to discourage the return of even more Moslems and from the date of its enactment, 21 July/2 August 1878, the flow of returning refugees began gradually to diminish. There were, however, many claims still to be dealt with and in November 1878 mixed Turkish and Bulgarian commissions were established in all provinces to examine these claims. The decisions were to be made in accordance with rules drawn up by the Russian embassy in Constantinople in consultation with the Porte, and under them Bulgarians could secure the legal right to a piece of land if they could produce the authentic title-deeds, *tapii,* and thereby prove that the land at dispute had originally been taken from them forcibly or fraudulently.

After the departure of the Russians in the Spring of 1879 the administration in Plovdiv took a relatively tough line against attempts to sequestrate land from the Turks, for if the latter should raise the cry of discrimination the Sultan, with British backing, might invoke those clauses of the treaty of Berlin which allowed him to put Ottoman troops back into Rumelia in the event of civil disturbance there. Such disturbances would also discredit the local Bulgarian leaders and so frustrate their efforts to establish political supremacy over the Turks and Greeks within the province. All Rumelian officials were therefore ordered to enforce court decisions returning land to the Turks— approximately half of the courts had recorded such decisions—and to report every fifteen days on the action they had taken to enforce those decisions. The government also threatened peasants that if they refused to comply with the courts they would be denied the right to bear arms or to belong to gymnastic societies; in some cases coercion had to be used to enforce the law, as when the inhabitants of Shipka were forcibly ejected from the Turkish village of Sheinovo which they had occupied. Other actions were less emotive and in 1880 the position of the Bulgarians in Rumelia improved when the Plovdiv government introduced new methods for authenticating claims, allowing local courts to issue new title deeds if they were satisfied that existing documentation proved ownership, or if local communal councils had issued certificates attesting ownership. Most local councils were dominated by Bulgarians and decided in favour of their co-nationals far more often than did the mixed commissions with whom the prerogative of adjudication had previously rested. In many instances, too, Bulgarians refused to relinquish land they had seized and as late as 1884 there were still Turkish landlords demanding the implementation of court orders restoring their property.

The Bulgarians in Rumelia were also helped from 1880 onwards because the Turks began to drift once more into exile. This was very much the result of disappointed hopes for a full restoration of Turkish power south of the Balkan range. By 1880 the Bulgarians had established political ascendancy in the province and to this many Turks, and particularly the richer and previously more influential ones, could not adapt. The Turks had seldom actively persecuted the Christians, that had been the intermittent pastime of Tatar, Circassian and Pomak, but the Turks had never allowed the Christians social or legal equality. Now they were forced to concede their superiority and for many Turks this was too much to bear and they gratefully accepted offers of land from the Sultan and returned to the more familiar atmosphere of the Ottoman Empire. The Turks were also encouraged to emigrate by regulations against the cultivation of rice, a crop which the Rumelians prohibited because the paddy-fields in the Maritsa Valley were a dangerous breeding ground for malarial mosquitoes; rice was nevertheless a staple crop for the Turks and in its prohibition many of them saw yet another sign of unacceptable Christian domination. An even more important impulse to Turkish emigration was the Rumelian land tax of 1882. By Moslem law all land was owned by God but after the abolition of feudalism in the 1830's use of that land conferred temporary wardship upon the user, and thus the tithe which had been the main levy on land until 1882 conformed to traditional Moslem codes of thought and practice. The land tax did not. Furthermore the land tax applied to all land in a man's possession not, as under the tithe, merely to that part which had been cultivated. This hit the Turks hard for they customarily left a large proportion, in many cases as much as a half, of their land fallow. Taxation now fell on the fallow land too but production and earnings could not be increased by the same proportion and as a result many of the remaining Turkish owners of large estates left Rumelia, as the government in Plovdiv had intended they should. Significantly 1882 was the peak year for the sale of larger Turkish properties in Rumelia, though the sale of such properties continued steadily throughout the first half of the 1880's. From the Liberation to the summer of 1880 only six large Turkish *chifliks* in Rumelia had been sold but the five years before union saw the sale of about a hundred; in the Stara Zagora district there had been about a hundred *chifkliks* before the war but by 1884 their number had fallen to forty-six and two years later, after the union, there were but four, three of which were owned by Bulgarians. That most of the larger Turkish owners and many smaller ones left the Bulgarian lands was undoubtedly an important factor in the easy attainment of Bulgarian supremacy in Rumelia during the early 1880s.

In Bulgaria as in Rumelia the chaos of war had allowed a number of seizures to go unrecorded meaning that the new occupiers were to be left in untroubled possession of their land. The Constituent Assembly had considered a proposal to legalise such transfers but no action had been taken as Karavelov had easily persuaded the Assembly that it was pointless to legislate about so widespread a phenomenon. The Bulgarians in the Principality could afford such a bold stance as there was little danger of direct Turkish intervention over the land question. A great deal of land was also sold by former Turkish owners to Christians through the established legal machinery. This continued long after the Liberation for there was a constant stream of emigration by Moslems from Bulgaria and by the early 1890s so many Turks had left the former Turkish stronghold of north-eastern Bulgaria that the government in Sofia began to fear that the area would be seriously under-populated; in 1891 the Minister of Finance reported to the Sŭbranie that there were 26,315 vacant plots in the country, many of them in the north-east and most of them under twenty dekars in extent. There was talk of settling these areas with immigrants from Slovakia, Italy or the ghettoes of Russian Poland, and Stambulov even spoke of bringing back the Circassians.

As in Rumelia so in the Principality the government took into its own possession the former state lands and forests, and the property of the Tatars and Circassians, much of the arable land being rented or sold to local communities. Some of it was also given away and some had been put aside for official use, such as the two thousand *uvrats** placed at the disposal of the Model Agricultural School established in Sadovo near Ruse. In Bulgaria the government also took possession of Turkish land which had been vacant for three years, this being done in accordance with Ottoman law, and a number of returning Turkish refugees who demanded restitution of or compensation for their lands were denied both on the grounds that they had without duress left their property unworked for three years. Contested cases which had originally been decided by the mixed commissions set up under the Russian Provisional Administration were after May 1880 to be submitted, as in Rumelia, to local courts and devolution of responsibility inevitably meant diversity of practice with some courts issuing certificates on very slight evidence and others demanding much more rigorous proof. Initially the Liberal administrations in Sofia attempted to differentiate between the land of poor Turks and that which had not been worked by its owner, but this proved too difficult and in October 1880 it was decided that all émigré land should be treated equally. The three-year rule was therefore applied to all vacant land with a deadline for repossession fixed at 1/13 November 1882, though this was soon extended to 1/13 January 1885. In 1891 the danger of depopulation forced the Stambulov government to give the absentees a further period of grace ending on 1/13 July 1893, though there was also in this law a provision allowing the government to sell rather than rent out unoccupied plots under thirty *diuniuma*** in extent.

The Sofia administration faced serious difficulties over returning Turkish émigrés in only one area, the south-west where the proportion of Turkish landowners had been higher than elsewhere in the Bulgarian lands and where the estates had been larger, many of them being worked by share-croppers or by tenants paying the *kesim* or fixed rent in kind. During the war most of the Moslem owners of large estates

---

*An *uvrat* was 1,600 square meters or 1.6 dekars.

**A *diunium* was 0.919 dekars.

had fled and the local Christians had seized and often partitioned the land. After the war the former owners returned demanding restitution or compensation. The government was in some difficulty because most of the land transfers in the south-west had been illegal and the problem was compounded by the almost total lack of documentary evidence of ownership, many of the Turkish owners having acquired their land during the anarchic days of the *kŭrdjaliistvo*, often simply seizing and destroying the *tapii* (title deeds) of the peasants and imposing new and more onerous tenancies upon them. If the land had been paid for the Turks' local political power had often been used to drive the price down to a risible level. In many cases therefore the returning Turks in 1879 did not have the original title-deeds or if they did they were unwilling to produce them as they would reveal purchase prices so low that the resulting compensation would be minimal, and though Turks who returned to most other parts of Bulgaria and Rumelia were furnished by the Ottoman authorities with tax records supporting their claims, such documents were not given to the Turks who went back to the south-west. In 1879 a crop failure in the Kiustendil and Izvora districts threw local problems into particularly sharp relief and the Sŭbranie therefore sent a delegation to study the land question in the south-west. The result of these enquiries was an attempt to tackle the problems raised by the former large estates in both the south- and the north-west of the country. The Law for the Improvement of the Condition of the Agrarian Population of the *Gospodar* and *Chiflik* Lands, passed late in 1880, decreed that the government would buy all vacant *chiflik* and *gospodar* land and over a million leva was set aside to compensate the former owners. The peasants were to buy the land from the central government with their redemption payments being spaced out over fifteen years.

This left a number of important issues unsettled and also created new problems. The share-croppers and those previously subjected to the *kesim* were bitterly disappointed for they had not been exempted from the payment of redemption dues and were left therefore to pay for land which they believed had been taken from them illegally a few generations ago. It was also now clear that if a peasant could prove his land to have been state, Tatar or Circassian property, rather than *gospodar* or *chiflik* land, he would not have to pay redemption dues, and well into the twentieth century such pleas were being heard by the courts. If the status of the land was unclear its value was also unknown and had to be assessed if compensation were to be paid and redemption dues fixed. The government made extensive enquiries into both the status and value of a great deal of land but the results of these investigations were lost in a fire which destroyed the Sŭbranie building in 1882. Many Turks had in the meantime decided to wait no longer and had sold their land privately on the open market, but there remained numerous cases where transfer had not taken place legally and where titles were still in dispute. In 1885 the government decided to cut the Gordian knot. It arranged to buy all land previously worked by share-croppers, the latter being required to redeem their debt to the government over ten years. The poorest and most exploited peasants, those who had paid the *kesim,* were to be given their land free. At the same time the question of ownership was much simplified by the decision that any peasant who had worked a piece of land for ten unbroken years was its rightful owner. This did not, of course, exempt the peasant in question from redemption dues and these, particularly in the agrarian crisis of the late 1890s could be burdensome, so much so that in 1896 the repayment period was extended by twenty years. In 1905 the Bulgarian Agricultural Bank cancelled a large number of redemption debts and two years later a number of villages successfully declared that they would no longer pay, though not all communities were so resolute and by the beginning of the First World War a large number of Bulgarian villages were still paying off their debts to the government or the Agricultural Bank.

The absence of accurate statistical data makes it impossible to calculate how much land was transferred in Bulgaria and Rumelia in the period from the war to the mid-1890s. Clearly the extent of illegal seizures can never be known, though the very scale of legal transfers suggests that the extent of illegal expropriation can easily be overestimated. In Rumelia the courts made over to Bulgarians some 100,000 *uvrats* in the second half of 1878 alone and in the period from the spring of 1879 to the beginning of 1883 the value of Christian purchases of Moslem land was almost fourteen and a half million leva involving at least one million dekars of land. Statistics for the Principality are less accurate but the most reliable estimates would suggest that the land transferred in both Bulgaria and Rumelia by 1888 was not less than four and a half million dekars, or a quarter of the total arable area, at a total cost of sixty and a half million leva, or thirteen and a half leva per dekar. By the end of the century continued Turkish and some Greek emigration together with the impoverishment of some Bulgarian peasants had brought the total of land transferred to about

Table 2.   Distribution of land by category of owner, 1897.

Category of owner	Area in Hectacres	%age of Total land	%age of Usable land
Private	3,977,670	41.28	53.65
Provincial authorities	441	under 0.01	0.01
Village communes	2,291,156	23.78	30.91
State	1,015,903	10.54	13.70
Religious and educational institutions	128,366	1.33	1.73
National and Agricultural Banks	211	under 0.01	under 0.01
Total	7,413,747	76.94	100.00

Some 902,600 hectacres (88.85%) of the state land and 1,583,093 hectacres (69.1%) of communal land was moorland or woodland, which, particularly in the case of village land, was frequently used for communal grazing.

seven million dekars. The vast majority of this land went from Moslem to Christian ownership so that from 1876 to 1885 the proportion of land in Rumelia in Turkish hands fell from around fifty per cent to twenty-eight per cent, and of this latter figure half again, or fourteen per cent of the total land worked, was held by Moslem small peasants with total holdings of no more than a hundred *uvrats*. The proportion of Moslem owners in northern Bulgaria was by the early 1890s even lower.

Land transferred from Moslems was acquired by local authorities and religious institutions as well as by the state and private individuals. The first reliable register of agricultural land in Bulgaria in 1897 revealed that of the country's 9,634,550 hectacres, the 7,413,747 hectacres classified as usable land was distributed as shown in Table 2.

During the land transfers large holdings had been amassed by a few individuals including Mr. Brophy, the British consul in Varna, Prince Alexander, Stambulov, who bought up the deserted village of Tuzluka, and the wealthy Neichev brothers who purchased over three thousand hectacres of arable, pasture and woodland in and around Karnobat.

Table 3.   Distribution of land holdings, by size of holding. 1897.

Size of holding	No. of holdings	%age of total holdings	Area of land in hectacres	%age of total area
Very small	363,646	45.48	265,653	6.68
Small	334,384	41.82	1,681,119	42.27
Medium	92,509	11.57	1,409,890	35.44
Large	9,049	1.13	620,896	15.61
Total:	799,588	100.00	3,977,558	100.00

Yet few of these large holdings were worked as commercial units, most of them being subdivided and rented, and the large landowner was very much the exception, for the vast majority of those who acquired land in the 1870s and thereafter were small peasant proprietors. Bulgaria became even more the land of the small and medium peasant.

Table 3 gives the distribution of land by size of holding based on the figures for 1897 and using the following categories for the size of holdings: very small—those below twenty dekars in extent and insufficient to support the average peasant household; small—from twenty to one hundred dekars, and large enough to support the average peasant family; middle—from one hundred to three hundred dekars and large enough to provide surplus for the market and perhaps to need the occasional employment of labour from outside the family; large—over three hundred dekars, needing full-time wage labour to work, and if not subdivided and rented, clearly capable of capitalisation and commercialisation.

From the foregoing figures it would appear that 45.48% of the holdings, being less than twenty dekars, were not large enough to support the average family, but it did not follow that each of those small holdings was all that an individual family possessed. The 1897 census was based on village tax returns and therefore each plot of land in that village was returned as a separate entity, yet very often a small plot in one village was the property of a family in another community, and, conversely, an individual peasant family might well have small plots in a number of villages. A plot held in a village other than that in which the family resided was known as *parakende* land. A great deal of

parakende land had come into the possession of a family as a gift from
a bride's family and it was often kept separate so that it might revert to
the bride should she be widowed. Also if one particular locality were
especially suited to the cultivation of one specialised crop it was often
divided into plots which were owned by peasants from a number of
surrounding villages. This was often the case with vineyards, which
have specific requirements of climate and soil and where crops adequate for individual, domestic needs can be raised on relatively small
plots. In 1897 a sixth of all vineyards in Bulgaria were on *parakende*
land.

Other *parakende* plots belonged to peasants who had moved into
towns but wished to retain some land on which to grow vines, vegetables etc., whilst others were the property of larger landowners who
preferred to rent their *parakende* land. Full statistics for *parakende*
land in 1897 are not available but figures from 1908, when the pattern
of land distribution was little changed, indicate that a very large proportion of the smaller plots came into this category; in 1908 *parakende*
plots made up 49.96% of the holdings under twenty dekars and 60.92%
of plots under five dekars.

In addition to their *parakende* land peasants also had access to
common land for grazing, and this could mean as much as an extra ten
or fifteen dekars per household. The role of *parakende* and common
land was vital for in many cases it made the difference between self-
sufficiency and being forced into reliance on partial wage earning.

The phenomenon of *parakende* land makes it difficult to establish
the average size of holdings in each category but an approximation
would suggest that the very small averaged 15 dekars, the small
58 dekars, the medium 150 dekars and the large 1,100 dekars. Most
families had enough land for their own needs and no more than two
per cent of the population at the end of the nineteenth century, when
conditions in the countryside were particularly bad, had been forced
into full-time wage-labouring. Even many of this two per cent were not
true agricultural protetarians for they were men who owned one or
more small plots which were insufficient for subsistence and which the
owner therefore hired out to other peasants, thus becoming both a
wage-earner and a renter of the means of production. Other peasants
who owned only small plots also hired themselves out as seasonal
labourers some of whom, as will be seen later, migrated considerable
distances at harvest time. Yet neither the seasonal labourer nor the

full-time agricultural worker could dent Bulgaria's image as the land of the small, independent peasant farmer.

By the mid-1890s twenty-three per cent of the nation's grain crop was being exported. Most of the exports were produced by the small, independent peasants who sold their surplus produce to local merchants who then organised its transportation to the export ports. Large commercialised farms were not numerous enough—there were only thirty-five in 1900—to play any significant part in national production and in the export trade.

In view of the large amount of land which had changed hands between the Liberation and the mid-1890s this conspicuous absence of capitalised and commercially-oriented agriculture demands explanation.

There were some legislative impediments to the acquisition of large estates. Tsankov's government in 1880 forbad the selling of land in plots of over twenty-five *uvrats,* about fifteen dekars, and the same law, reinforced in 1885, insisted that no-one buy more than one hundred *uvrats,* approximately ninety dekars, though this was not a serious obstacle as the law was seldom enforced.

The political divorce from Turkey and the consequent separation from the large markets in Adrianople and Constantinople did something to discourage commercial farming but a much more important factor was the lack of labour. The redistribution of property during and after 1877 meant that nearly all those who had previously been wage labourers had acquired land of their own and were no longer willing to work for others. In the two decades after the Liberation the population increased steadily—the net annual reproduction rate by the 1890s was 1.82—but this did not mean there was a surplus on the land for as the population increased so did the land available for use. Continued Turkish emigration provided some of the extra land but if this were not available village pastures and state or communal forests could be cleared and put under the plough. In the Stara Zagora province of Eastern Rumelia the area of land in use increased by ten per cent between 1880 and 1884, mainly as a result of the clearance of forests, whilst in Bulgaria as a whole the area of private land worked increased from just over three million hectacres in 1889 to 3.977 million hectacres in 1897. The clearing of state and communal forests was illegal but so widespread was the practice that, despite a number of attempts, effective legislation to contain it was not enacted until 1907. Even with the restriction of forest clearance the supply of land did not dry up, for throughout the country there were sizeable tracts of unused land.

Another important impediment to the emergence of capitalised farming, especially in the immediate post-Liberation years, was the lack of draught animals. In the war the Turks had mobilised large numbers of horses, oxen and buffalo, and the fleeing refugees had taken many of those that remained. The Russian Provisional Administration did all it could to encourage the import of large draught animals but in the three years after the Liberation, when most of the land transfers were taking place, these animals remained in desperately short supply, a fact which not only acted as a disincentive to the setting up of new, commercially-oriented *chifliks* but also caused the break-up and sale of some of those which had survived the war.

The relatively low profits to be made from agriculture was a further and very important disincentive to capitalised farming. Backward methods meant low productivity and profitability was decreased yet further by the decline in the world price of Bulgaria's main export, grain. Between 1878 and 1895 the average price on the European exchanges for a hundred kilos of wheat fell by over fifty per cent from 25.95 to 10.95 gold leva. Nor were there as yet any obvious alternative crops. There was no industry in Bulgaria to absorb industrial crops and the manufacturers of the rest of Europe exacted standards far in excess of those which the Bulgarian farmer could achieve; with the notable exception of the rose-oil produced in the Valley of the Roses near Kazanluk, there were few cash crops to encourage capitalisation in agriculture. Karavelov once spoke of the need to develop the commercial production of wine and tobacco, for world prices in these commodities were rising, but this was impossible because of the devastations of phylloxera and because tobacco is a notoriously vulnerable and fickle plant. Animal husbandry was also incapable of commercial development. Foreign veterinary regulations could ruin exports, as the Rumanians had learned in the 1880s, and the quality of Bulgarian animals was well below that which was acceptable in the markets of central and western Europe; in 1902 the average price per head for Bulgarian cattle was only 76 leva compared with 159 leva for Serbian and 198 leva for Rumanian animals. Even the hides of Bulgarian cattle were of such poor quality that Bulgarian leather-workers used imported raw-materials.

Further obstacles to the development of commercialised agriculture were the high cost of imported machines and fertilisers and the almost total ignorance of modern farming methods. The government made some attempts to encourage spending on agricultural implements but at the beginning of the 1890s total spending in this area was a mere 98,000 leva. There were also efforts to increase education with the setting up of the Model Agricultural School in Sadovo and other specialised institutions later in the 1880s. Ordinary schools were also encouraged to give more attention to vocational education but little came of these endeavours, the school masters taking little interest in agrarian affairs, and most graduates of the vocational institutes preferring a lucrative career in the civil service to one on the land.

For these reasons surplus land, rather than being farmed commercially, was sold or rented to peasants who used it primarily for subsistence and low-productivity farming.

Whilst surplus land did not attract capital, surplus capital had better outlets than agriculture. In the post-Liberation orgy of land sales many peasants had borrowed heavily to purchase land and as land prices and taxes increased in later years the peasants, whose income often declined because of the world fall in cereal prices, were forced into continued dependence on credit. With the state banking facilities and the cooperative credit movement little developed the private money-lender was left free to charge what he liked and before the turn of the century interest rates were seldom below twenty-five per cent and levels of up to two hundred per cent were recorded. Only in the non-productive and socially destructive business of usury were sizeable fortunes to be made and it was thus money-lending rather than agricultural improvement which absorbed available capital, to the detriment of the individual peasant and of agricultural development in general.

The main crops of this predominantly self-sufficient agriculture were cereals, chiefly wheat, rye, barley and oats, with the first two tending to displace the latter after the Liberation as the staple for grinding into flour. By 1897 the figures for the area of land devoted to various crops and for total agricultural production were as indicated in Table 4.

Most villages kept communal flocks but it was only along the foot-hills of the Balkan range that animal husbandry was a commercial undertaking. Here before the Liberation large flocks of sheep were raised and in 1878 Bulgaria had the highest number of sheep per head of population in Europe. Many of the sheep were driven by their Vlach shepherds from the Balkan hills to the mountains south and west of Sofia for summer grazing and thence to Constantinople. After 1878 the

Table 4.   Agricultural production by type of crop.

Crop	Area in hectacres	%age of total area	Total production in tonnes	% of total production
			Grain 2,113,809	29.04
			Straw 3,557,894	48.89
Cereals	1,811,890	74.08	5,671,703	77.93
Fodder crops	439,836	17.98	1,271,713	17.47
Vineyards	114,816	4.70	Grapes 153,525	2.11*
Kitchen gardens	12,710	0.52	86,172	1.18
Vegetables	27,739	1.13	41,808	0.58
Orchards	24,929	1.02	40,000	0.55
Roses	4,844	0.20	Flowers 8,920	0.12**
Industrial crops	8,771	0.36	3,564	0.05
Mulberries	178	0.01	461	0.01
Total	2,445,713	100.00	7,277,866	100.00

* Producing 750,638 hectolitres of must wine.
**   "   539,000 flasks of rose-oil.

traditional system of transhumance declined. Before 1885 the political
border between Bulgaria and Rumelia divided winter from summer
pasture and, more importantly, meant that the sheep tax was levied in
both areas. After 1885 the frontier between Turkey and the now unified Bulgaria meant that the Constantinople market was less accessible.
Transhumance was also inhibited by brigandage, particularly along the
Macedonian and Thracian borders, whilst further blows were delivered
by the development of the railways and then of refrigeration. At the
same time the transition from 'black' to 'green' fallow meant that peasants no longer needed the winter flocks to dung fallow land. Legislation also contributed to the decline of traditional transhumance. There
were attempts to protect the state and communal moorland on which
the flocks grazed and in some areas the land available to the flocks was
restricted because of the damage caused by the straying animals and
by their shepherds' improvident use of fires. Despite the decline in
traditional patterns of sheep-rearing, which was in any case reversed
for a while at the turn of the century, sheep remained of great importance and continued to be the chief source of milk in the country, the

native grey steppe-cattle providing insufficient milk-yields until scientific breeding began in the 1900s. Large herds of pigs, like those kept in Serbia, were unknown in Bulgaria though the number of pigs in the country increased rapidly after 1878. Goats, on the other hand, declined in number, mostly because of taxation. Horses had been kept by the Turks but were seldom reared by Bulgarians before 1878 and by 1897 the urgent need for cavalry mounts had forced the government to set up a state stud. Water-buffalo provided a large proportion of the draught animals, especially in the south. All peasant families kept poultry, usually selling birds and eggs for a source of cash income.

Following the Liberation the Bulgarians who had been driven into the hills and woods by the arrival of the Tatar and Circassians had been able to return to their original settlements and in later years moved to establish new communities near the railways, but despite these changes of location, which affected only a small minority of the population, most Bulgarian villages changed little as a result of the departure of the Turks. On the plains most villages were still concentrated settlements of between two and three thousand inhabitants and if, despite the various emigrations, the villages were still ethnically mixed, then each race would generally have its own *maxale,* or quarter. The mountain villages were not concentrated. They were basically groups of hamlets (*kolibi*) which could be up to a kilometre or more apart. Such communities were usually derived from one original extended family, each *koliba* being a settlement founded by a subgroup of the original household. Some mountain villages, however, were collections of a number of distinct families and their communities, like those in the plains, usually formed around a prominent topographical, economic or social feature, for example a ford, a cross-roads, a fort, a mill, a workshop, a *chiflik,* or a monastery.

Conditions in the villages varied considerably. In Rumelia Jiricħek noted that the Greeks, generally more commercially-minded than the Bulgarians and the Turks, had the prettiest villages. Many Greeks took advantage of the proximity of Adrianople and Constantinople and concentrated upon market gardening and the cultivation of vegetables and fruit. Vines, mulberries, hemp (for the coarse cloth used in everyday clothing), tobacco and garlic were also grown commercially, though there were very few large-scale, capitalised concerns. In the 1880s the growth of Sofia was to encourage market gardening—walnuts and plums were popular crops—in what was until then one of the most backward areas of Bulgaria, Jiricħek finding villages near the capital in a very primitive state with ill-kept roads and with taxation accounts, local and national, kept on tally sticks.

Though by the Liberation the old distinction between *mülk* (private) and *mirii* (communal) land had to a large extent disappeared most of the former *mirii* land used by the peasants was still in strips in the large fields which had once comprised the village's communal property.

The traditional Bulgarian system had been one based on two fields where a mixed grain crop alternated with a year of fallow, usually 'black' rather than 'green'. Before Liberation the traditional system was giving way to one based on three fields and although in 1878 the two-field system still predominanted in the mountains to the west and south-west of the capital and could still be found in the east, the more modern three-field system was everywhere predominant by the turn of the century. In the latter there was generally a field given over permanently to maize with the other two alternating between mixed grain and fallow on the traditional model. In some favoured areas there was a four-field system which was similar to the three-field variety except that on one field a second spring-wheat crop could be raised thus enabling a village to produce three grain crops in a season.

The working of land held privately but in the large fields was in many areas regulated less by the individual owner than by the communal council, a body elected by all male heads-of-household in the village. The council decided on the rotation of crops and when harvesting should take place, a vital event for the village had the right, as did each family within it, to graze animals on the stubble. Traditions such as these blurred the distinction between individual and communal property and prevented the more progressive farmers from raising a second hay crop, and they also meant that whatever the foreign observers might record, the peasant proprietor in Bulgaria was not the complete master of his strips at any time other than that between sowing and harvest. On the other hand the surviving spirit of communality could help the individual peasant for if his crop were late ripening other villagers would give help to ensure it was gathered before bad weather ruined it. The traditional, communal attitudes also provided a healthy climate for the agricultural co-operatives which developed rapidly in the early twentieth century.

The communal councils were also responsible for the areas of communal pasturage and forests on which grazed the village flocks, both individually and communally owned. The council employed shepherds and field-guards to protect village haystacks and each household was obliged to contribute in cash or kind to the payment of these village employees.

Traditional attitudes still prevailed in the social life of the villages where the communal spirit was much in evidence. Youths would gather in the evenings for singing, story-telling or other forms of mild merry-making, often combining this socialising with light tasks such as spinning or the shelling of maize or beans. On religious festivals the celebrations would be more formal with dancing and, if possible, feasting.

In most villages life was in general frugal but secure. The peasant could grow his own food and depended on the outside world for very little; a report from the British vice-consul in Ruse in 1885 described the methods used in that area for the construction of peasant houses in which the only bought-in items were roof-tiles, windows and window-frames and, perhaps, German nails, and in few cases would the total cash expended exceed £5. The average peasant diet was unexciting but wholesome for though meat was for most an occasional luxury there was an abundant supply of vegetables, eggs, and dairy produce. Cloth was spun and sometimes woven in the village, most every-day garments being made from coarse-spun wool. Furniture was primitive and Turkish rather than occidental, Jiriček recording that in villages near Sofia the homes had no furniture other than a few three-legged stools and a primitive table, the most valuable features being the floor-rugs on which the occupants slept, though western furniture spread from the towns to the villages in the 1890s. Jiriček also noted that the houses were ill-lit, ill-ventilated and damp. Families were not exceptionally large, the average number per household being between five and six, though in the mountains of the Sredna Gora and around Sofia, where the communal family proved more resistant to modern forces, the average was between six and seven.

Though the village was for most Bulgarians the centre of their social life by no means all remained forever in their villages. Before the Liberation many had become migrant labourers. Some went, either as individuals or in groups, on *pechalba* (literally, 'profit') to the larger towns of the Ottoman Empire, Rumania and central Europe. The labouring gang, or *taifa,* was also to be found after the Liberation and represents another survival of pre-Liberation collectivist traditions. Some *taifi* were recruited and worked in Bulgaria itself, especially to the south of the Balkans in the Stara Zagora, Burgas and Karnobat regions. Before the Liberation the *chiflik*-owners of these areas had made good the lack of local labour by employing gangs of harvesters from the mountains where there was a surplus of man-power. After the Liberation these gangs still existed but were fewer in number as many of those previously forced to go labouring had now secured enough land to free them from dependence on outside work. On the other hand the number of *chifliks* left to employ labour had declined even more than the number of labourers so that for the remaining gangs wage rates fell by as much as fifty per cent. There were better returns in the labour market outside Bulgaria which was one well known to Bulgarian *taifi* before the Liberation and in 1880 there were an estimated twelve thousand Bulgarians working outside the country in seasonal labour gangs. The most frequent destination for the migratory labourer was Rumania but others went to Austria-Hungary, Russia, Serbia and Turkey.

The size of a *taifa* varied from as few as ten or a dozen to around fifty or more, the larger ones usually being the gardeners who worked near large cities such as Bucharest. Many of these groups were organised on a guild basis with apprentices being paid a fixed sum but fully-fledged members receiving a share of the profits. For the gardening gangs the provision of capital was a major concern for they were abroad for the whole of the season from sowing to selling and needed cash not only for travel and maintenance but also for seed, animals, the renting of plots and stalls, the provision of water-wheels for irrigation and frequently for the employment of local wage-labour; in the late 1880s a *taifa* setting out from Sofia would need nearly nine hundred leva per man in capital. The harvesting gangs had less substantial needs and unlike the gardening *taifi*, which were all male, included entire families, indeed many of those setting out from the Stara Planina in the early 1890s consisted almost entirely of women and children led by a few men. These gangs often had their own bag-pipe player or even a group of singers who would console those who worked in the fields in heat so fearsome that each year it killed a number of women. The leader of a labouring gang was known variously as *taifadjiya, dragomanin* or, where a guild-like organisation pertained, a *maistor;* however named he usually received 150 or 300 per cent more than ordinary members. His powers were wide-ranging and he could discipline members by fining, flogging or even expelling them. In the gardening *taifi* the *prodavaya* (salesman or marketeer) was second only to the leader in importance. Both the *provadaya* and the *taifadjiya* had the heavy responsibilities of finding work and/or markets as well as maintaining order and harmony amongst their band; for these were needed a knowledge of foreign languages, and, even more difficult to acquire and retain, a reputation for honesty.

Cooperative working, as opposed to an established guild system, was to be found amongst other groups of migrant workmen. These included the shepherds of Panagiurishte, some cattle-drovers, the carters based on Gabrovo, the copper-smiths of northern Bulgaria, the *sapundjiya* or soap-makers who went from village to village selling soap or exchanging it for poultry, eggs or other local produce, the halva-makers who came mostly from Macedonia, and the potters of the Trŭn, Troyan, Pirot area who also used an almost incomprehensible secret language.

Cooperative working was also to be seen in a number of urban occupations, especialy those dominated by the Macedonians, for example baking and, above all, stone-masonry. Much of the construction work in Sofia after the Liberation was carried out by Macedonians, especially from Krushevo, Palanka and Dibra. Initially they came to Bulgaria in labouring gangs, organised on much the same pattern as the Bulgarian *taifi,* but the cooperative system was sorely tested by and frequently fell victim to the rampant individualism which held sway in the frontier atmosphere of Sofia in the 1880s. Nevertheless the gangs did not disappear altogether and a sixty-man gang from Palanka had worked as a unit on the construction of the Bulgarian section of the international trunk railway, whilst labouring gangs could still be found in Sofia in the closing years of the decade.

The most famous of all collective institutions in the Balkans was the communal, extended family household known generally as the zadruga, though this name was seldom used in Bulgaria itself where at least fifteen alternative terms were available to describe the phenomenon. Philip Mosely has recorded that no single definition could embrace all variations of the zadruga but that 'it may be considered, tentatively, as a household consisting of two or more biological or small families, closely related by blood or adoption, owning its means of production communally, producing and consuming the means of its livelihood jointly, and regulating the control of its property, labour and livelihood communally'.[2]

Each zadruga had its own organisation; in some, for example, the constituent nuclear families ate separately or even lived in separate buildings though continuing to work the land communally. In some zadrugas nuclear families were allowed to farm some individual, private strips as well as the common fields, such separate strips being usually the gift customarily given by the groom to his bride on the morning after the wedding-night. But despite these concessions to individual property the zadruga remained a communal institution; all earnings, whether from the communal land or from employment outside the zadruga had to be paid into the communal coffers to meet general communal expenses. Most zadrugas consisted of no more than two or three nuclear families with the total number for the household being between ten and twenty persons, though there are recorded examples of much larger zadrugas with as many as a hundred or even two hundred members.

The zadruga aimed at economic self-sufficiency. In the larger ones the availability of labour encouraged specialisation and the greater efficiency which this generated was vital in the early nineteenth century when many communities were pioneers, clearing forest and bringing land under the plough. It was common for some specialisations, ploughing and shepherding for example, to become hereditary, and the specialist enjoyed considerable autonomy in his or her work. In some cases zadrugas built their own mills for grinding flour and for fulling yarn. In later years some members found employment outside the community but continued to be members of it, paying their earnings into the communal fund. It was not unusual for priests to be in this category and in the mid-1880s Gueshov discovered near Pernik a large zadruga of forty-one members the head of which was a former director of the Sofia Agricultural Bank who, whilst working in the city, had continued as leader, arranging zadrugal affairs during his weekends at home, and paying his salary into communal funds.

In Bulgaria the head of a zadruga was known as *domakin, napredyak,* or one of at least sixteen other names. The head was usually the most able male but female heads, though unusual, were not unknown. The *domakin* was generally nominated by his predecessor or, as the eldest surviving brother, succeeded automatically, but in a few cases where this did not happen he was elected by the senior male members of the zadruga. The *domakin* was head of the zadrugal council, a body made up of the senior males; in some zadrugas an age qualification of thirty was necessary for membership of the council and if this did not apply it was unusual for unmarried men to be admitted to it. The council had to sanction major decisions such as the buying or selling of land, the secession of individual families or even the break-up of the zadruga. Apart from these areas, however, the *domakin* had extensive powers within and without the zadruga. He represented the community in all its important dealings with the outside world, being responsible for the payment of taxes, for the buying and selling of goods and for the legal representation of the zadruga. It was common for the *domakin* to take an active part in local affairs, perhaps standing for election as a member of a local council or as mayor, positions in which he was well-placed to further zadrugal interests. Inside the community he was the keeper of the zadrugal monies and he allotted work in the fields to the individual males. He would also decide if members, whether they were his own children or not, could marry and whether the marriage terms were acceptable. His, too, was the decision as to whether or not any member could go and work outside the community and those who did not leave remained under his disciplinary powers which included the right to order and even to carry out the beating of other men's wives and daughters. By the third quarter of the nineteenth century authoritarianism on this scale was in decline for it could all too easily drive people out of the community. Nevertheless in 1900 one investigator discovered a *domakin* who would not allow any other member of his zadruga to enter a tavern—at least not whilst he was there.

The zadrugas were male-dominated communities in some of which females had to eat at separate tables, yet the senior female, the *domakina* or *domachitsa,* was a person of considerable influence. In the majority of cases she was the wife of the *domakin* and to her was entrusted the running of the household itself. She allocated work, decided who should sleep where, for whom clothes should be made— the larger zadrugas might have their own tailor—and she supervised the care of the children and the sick. Religious affairs were usually her responsibility, though it was the *domakin* who read the prayers. The *domakina* also looked after the zadruga's domestic animals and would organise the selling of eggs, poultry and wool in the local markets, the money being used for the purchase of domestic necessities such as salt and for items of purely female consumption such as jewellery. Any surplus cash was paid into the communal fund.

The virtues of the zadruga were easily recognised. In the first place it had economic advantages. Its economies of scale, albeit not great, did mean that specialisation of labour could come about without any division of property. The zadruga was not usually dependent upon one or two men for its labour, as were many nuclear families, and in the late nineteenth and early twentieth centuries this gave the zadrugas the distinct advantage that they could send off two or three of their men to the army and still have enough males left to work the land. Some supporters of the zadruga argued that it was ideally suited to mechanisation for its arable land was not split into strips, but this argument did not take into account the disrupting effect a decrease in the need for labour would have on a collective community, nor did it recognise that many zadrugas were to be found in the mountain areas, a long way from markets and the railways, and where the terrain was not always suited to machinery.

Its supporters ascribed to the zadruga moral as well as economic advantages. Many believed that there was still good sense in the argument that the zadruga was wise to place authority in the hands of its most experienced and able member but at the same time to provide procedures for removing him if he should become unfit, a process which was not necessarily a feature of the nuclear-family. A zadruga would care for all its members, no matter what contribution they made to production within it. This meant that there was no differentiation of wealth in the community and it also meant that the zadruga performed a number of social welfare functions, doing away with the need for any form of 'poor law'. Moral obligations within the community were very strong; widows, the sick, the aged and orphans, even if they had been taken out of the community, were cared for and, said the zadruga's champions, the acceptance of these collective responsibilities taught individuals how to be good citizens, whilst the maintenance of material equality within the community did away with envy and the crimes which were its natural consequence. There were more tangible expressions of the zadruga's moral force. Credit institutions were quite happy to lend to a *domakin* because they knew that the traditions of the zadruga would ensure that the debt would be recognised by any later *domakin* and by other members of the zadruga.

The zadruga also had political advantages. Conservatives like Gueshov noted that it would not, except in exceptional circumstances, alienate its land and therefore it was an obstacle to the concentration of property into the hands of a few rich peasants and the consequent emergence of a landless agrarian proletariat. Whilst conservatives could prize the zadruga as a bulwark of the existing social order the left, especially those who held Populist opinions, could value it as an embryonic socialist organisation which already practised amongst its own members the principle of 'From each according to his ability to each according to his needs'.

The zadruga also had disadvantages. It inevitably bred tensions to have so many members of differing generations living in such proximity and in the more remote areas in-breeding could become a problem. There was, too, the danger of the *domakin* becoming too powerful and, as the critics of the zadruga were keen to point out, at a time when modernization and mechanisation were needed it was not necessarily the oldest or most experienced man who was the best leader of an agrarian community. The zadruga, continued its critics, was also dangerous in that it indulged the idle and stifled the energetic who all too easily came to believe that most of their efforts would be expended merely to maintain the lazy. The clash between the individual and the communal spirit clearly posed great problems for the zadruga.

The zadruga had once been the predominant social unit in the countryside but by the middle of the nineteenth century it was generally held to be in decline and by the Liberation was confined in the main to the mountainous areas of the north-west, the Sredna Gora and the Rhodopes, though in the latter, especially amongst the Moslems, the extended families were patriarchal rather than communal in organisation. In a patriarchal household property belonged solely to the patriarchal head, an arrangement which conformed to Moslem cultural traditions and which differentiated it from the zadruga where property was communal. The number of zadrugas in 1878 was probably a few hundred, though quite a high proportion seem to have had more than twenty-five members. According to the census of 1900 the number of zadrugas had fallen to two hundred and seven, though the statistics are not entirely reliable and it is probable that many of the smaller zadrugas were not recorded as such for the same census showed nearly thirty thousand families with between ten and twenty members. By 1910 there were still one hundred and ninety-six households with more than twenty-five members but here again there were many more families with between ten and twenty members. Even in 1938 the Bulgarian zadruga was far from dead, and Mosely discovered communities fifty, seventy and, in one instance, eighty-three strong.

Despite the resilience of some zadrugas, however, the institution was under considerable pressure. After the Liberation it conflicted in many ways with the new ideas current in the country. Many zadrugas had been established to clear unused land or as defensive settlements but with the land brought under the plough or with the Tatar, Circassian or Turk no longer a threat, the original function of the zadruga had disappeared. Furthermore, at its height the self-sufficient, defence-oriented zadruga had fostered introspection but after 1878 the new social and political atmosphere encouraged extroversion. Education had spread during the national revival but after 1878 primary education became a legal necessity, for girls as well as boys, whilst secondary education also expanded; from an early age the children of the zadruga were forced to go outside their native community and inevitably their horizons widened. Even more important in this respect was the introduction of conscription which took the young males away from the zadruga at one of the most impressionable and formulative periods in their lives. Many who returned felt baulked and restricted by the unchanging traditions of the communal household. This was particularly the case with young men who had been given responsibility and recognition outside their zadruga, usually as army officers, or who had travelled far from their homes, some even emigrating for a few years to North America. Naturally those in these categories were the more able and adventurous and the individualism which their experiences had encouraged could not coexist with the fortress mentality bred in the traditional zadruga.

The rise of individualism was, of course, part and parcel of the advance of the money economy in Bulgaria. A casualty of this advance was in many instances the self-sufficiency for which the zadrugas had originally striven. From the mid-nineteenth century onwards, and especially after 1878, many of the items previously produced within the community were readily and cheaply available in local markets, often as a result of foreign imports. At the same time, certainly up to the mid-1890s, land was also plentiful in supply and, initially at least, relatively low in price. The combination of these factors meant that the setting up of an individual, nuclear-familial household was a viable and often attractive alternative to living in a zadruga.

In some cases the manufacturing processes originally established within the zadruga became its major source of revenue and its major preoccupation. This could be dangerous. Contemporaries noted that as the volume of cash revenue increased members became increasingly anxious lest they receive less than their due share of the spoils. Contemporaries also claimed that an increase in cash revenue led to greater peculation by the *domakin*. If this took place then individual members of the household would also be tempted into activities alien to the traditions of the community, even if it were only the private selling of cheese or another community product. The moral strength of the zadruga was often sufficient to overcome the dangers posed by the renting of its productive processes and expertise, but it could seldom survive if the majority of its members became wage-earners outside the community. For one or two members to work outside the community and pay their wages into the common fund had not been unknown but for all or the majority to do so was unmanageable. With individual work being given individual recompense the consciousness of disparities between effort and reward were heightened and the collective spirit dissipated. The same effect could be produced by poverty and here there was the additional danger that respect for the *domakin* could be destroyed by his failure to secure a decent living for all his members. Proletarianisation or poverty was thus far more likely to wreck a zadruga than prosperity.

It was a common assumption amongst members of zadrugas that many of the problems facing the collective households were caused by their womenfolk. According to a Croat proverb, 'Two cats at one mouse, two dogs at one bone and two women in one house can never be at peace', and most Balkan peasants were happy to accept these traditional prejudices and condemn the women, especially those without children and those daughters-in-law whose education had made them reluctant to accept traditional customs and authority within the zadruga. These prejudices were almost entirely misplaced. Wayne Vucinich recalls Serbian proverbs such as, 'Mending and suffering hold the house together' or 'A house does not rest on the land but on a woman' which clearly indicate other attitudes to the distaff side. Close contemporary observers in late nineteenth-century Bulgaria also perceived this truth. One described the sisters-in-law, so denigrated by others, as fortresses of the zadrugal spirit, and Jiriček records that in the area around Trun, where the men went working abroad for long periods, the survival of the zadruga was entirely the achievement of its female members.

Throughout the Balkans it was generally believed that the zadruga survived better where female inheritance of land was not allowed, for land in the hands of married daughters or of widows would leave the original family for that of the husband or father. In Croatia and elsewhere this fact was recognised in the legal system but the law-makers of Bulgaria, being western-trained, had little knowledge of and less concern for the zadrugal system and its specific needs, and thus the Bulgarian Inheritance Law of 1889 allowed daughters to inherit land, albeit only half the amount inherited by sons. By 1896 revision of the law was necessary to limit the parcellisation of land in non-zadrugal holdings and henceforth in bequests involving plots of under one and a half hectacres women could inherit only moveable property and cash. The revised legislation did something to ease the strain on the zadrugas as did the fact that in a number of cases women in zadrugas failed to exercise their right to inherit either because they did not know of it or, as was definitely the case in some instances, because they believed that to do so would harm the zadruga. Nevertheless, female inheritance did speed up the dissolution of a number of zadrugas.

Other factors also undermined the stability of the zadruga. The regulations concerning conscription exempted youths from households where there was no male head or where he was over fifty and this led a number of widows and older men with children to secede from their zadrugas so that their sons might escape national service. In later years, and especially after the First World War, legislation to enforce village planning hit the zadrugas for streets had to be straightened and boundary walls built. Whereas previously zadrugas had, if possible, extended their holdings in a haphazard fashion whenever the need arose, this organic growth of the community was much more difficult if such legislation were enforced. Much more important was the fact that from the early 1900s land, though not scarce by the standards of other countries, was less available and rapidly becoming more expensive. This made it more difficult for zadrugas to expand as their numbers grew and inevitably led to a greater incidence of splitting or of complete disbandment of zadrugas.

The general impression received by foreign observers who visited Bulgaria immediately after the Liberation was that in contrast with other predominantly peasant societies such as Russia or Ireland it was relatively prosperous. The soil was good and the Bulgarian peasant worked hard and thus the country had been able to feed the Russian army from 1877 to 1879 without inflicting serious harm on the local economy. Twenty years after the Liberation the picture was less encouraging.

Like all peasant economies Bulgaria's was subject to the caprice of the climate and hail storms could inflict severe damage on crops. As in other backward societies disease was rampant. There were outbreaks of cholera and the incidence of tuberculosis was high, mainly because of the consumption of unboiled milk and uncooked meat and because of the wearing of insufficiently cured animal skins. In 1883 the Rumelian administration relaxed its ban on the cultivation of rice, because its yields were two or three times that of other grains; this meant a considerable increase in cases of malaria and it was not until 1904 that a systematic campaign was instituted against this scourge. Matters were made much worse by the lack of health-awareness amongst the population for few peasant homes had running water and many provided shelter for animals as well as humans. Medical services for man and beast were totally inadequate. In 1878 Bulgaria and Rumelia had only seventy-four doctors, thirty-two pharmacists and four hospitals. The number of doctors increased in later years but few of them were prepared to work in rural areas and mortality remained high; in 1884 seventeen out of every thousand births were still-births and 43.89% of all deaths in that year were of children under five.

This was not new for conditions had been every bit as bad under the Ottoman regime, but what was new was the widening gap between conditions in the countryside and those in the towns which now were also different in that Bulgarian influence within them had grown at the cost of Greek and Turk. The peasant would therefore focus his resentment on his fellow Bulgarian in the towns.

If the state of the peasant's health was no worse after the Liberation the financial burden he had to bear was noticeably heavier. Government expenditure increased steadily from the twenty-nine million leva of the Principality in 1879 to 39.75 million in 1887 and 95.29 million in 1894. Government income could not keep pace with such an increase and loans from abroad had made good much of the deficit but nevertheless the government was anxious to maximise its revenue from internal sources.

In June 1880 Karavelov had told the Sŭbranie that he would maintain the large number of small taxes which had been the chief characteristic of Ottoman fiscal policy. Thus the government continued to raise small sums from stamp duties on all documents from passports to fishing licenses, from fines, from the state monopoly on tobacco, from excise duties on salt, beer and other items and from the limited import duties which the treaty of Berlin permitted; occasionally new levies were introduced such as the taxes on musicians, cafés and brothels in 1882 and the *octroi* levied on agricultural goods entering towns in December 1883. In 1885 urban taxation was substantially reformed. Because of the difficulties in assessing private income all non-agrarian occupations and professions were placed into one of four categories and a total annual tax obligation for each group fixed. A commission, to which tax-payers could elect representatives, then decided upon the distribution of the burden among individual members of the group, the result being a general levy of about three per cent of income.

The main source of internal revenue was not, however, the professional tax or the myriad of minor levies and dues remaining from Ottoman times, but the tithe. The tithe had many disadvantages. From the governmental point of view there was the obvious fact that it was unrewarding to rely heavily on a levy in kind when the main crop, cereals, had to be sold on an increasingly competitive international market at ever lower prices. Furthermore, the tax on production often meant that the peasant was reluctant to grow more than his own immediate family needs dictated, and it was difficult for the authorities to tax what the peasant consumed, particularly in the non-cereal crops such as vegetables and fruit. For the peasant the tithe meant that he could not harvest his crop until its tithe value had been assessed. This could lead to corruption but a more substantial complaint was that it led to delay for it was villages rather than individuals which were taxed and therefore no-one could cut his crop until the entire village's produce had been valued and individual contributions to the village tithe calculated. Not infrequently crops rotted in the fields while the calculations were made. Also most peasants were required to provide or to pay for the transportation of their tithe payment to the official point of collection which could be some distance from their homes.

The tithe had been the object of peasant complaint before the Liberation and after 1878 the Rumelian authorities had replaced it with a land tax. In the Principality the Tŭrnovo constitution had not made specific mention of the tithe but the protocols of the Constitutent Assembly record a decision that no tax in kind was to be levied in Bulgaria. In 1882 payments in cash at the equivalent of the tithe value were introduced but the costs of collection were high and this, together with a poor harvest, produced a drop of twelve per cent in real revenue from the tithe. The cash payments were also unfair to the peasants. Although the less productive areas were assessed at lower levels the cash-tithe was based on the returns from the tithe in kind at a time when grain prices were noticeably higher. The peasants simply could not accumulate enough cash to pay and by 1884 some six million leva remained uncollected. The political upheavals of the next few years prevented any major change but in 1888 Stambulov reverted to payments in kind. This did not please the peasant nor after 1891, when world grain prices again fell sharply, did it greatly benefit the government, as the graph in Table 5 illustrates. In 1892 cash payments were

Table 5. Tithes, land taxes and the price of grain, 1878–1900

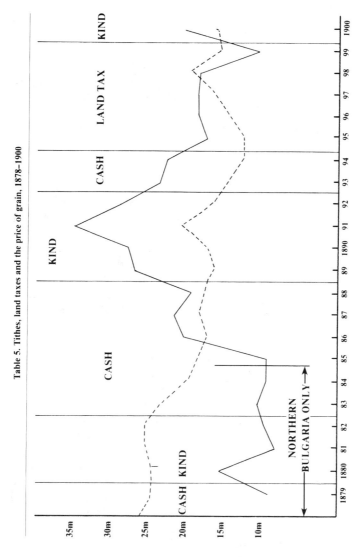

The unbroken line shows governmental income in millions of leva from whatever form of imposition on the land was in operation. The broken line shows world wheat prices in francs per kilogramme.

reintroduced this time based upon the average tithe returns for the previous four years minus fifteen per cent, but this failed to increase governmental income or to mollify mounting peasant discontent. In 1894 the modernising Stoilov administration scrapped the tithe altogether and replaced it with a land tax.

Whatever form taxation on the land assumed the peasant felt with a good deal of justice that it was unfair. A peasant with fifty dekars of land and between ten and twenty sheep would pay about an eighth of his income in tax, in absolute terms as much as a money-lender with an annual income of 100,000 leva. A study of the Varna area in 1890 revealed that peasants there paid an average of eighty-four leva per annum in tax, twenty times more than an official, six times more than a member of the free professions, and two and three quarter times more than a merchant. The burden on the peasant was not only unfair but increasing. If his tax outlay from 1879–83 is taken as an index of 100, the index for 1889–92 was 154, by which year the Bulgarian peasant was paying 12.5% of his income in tax, compared to the Belgian's 6.5% and the Englishman's 7.5%. The method of collection was at times as much a cause for complaint as the weight of the burden; under Karavelov a number of peasants were executed for non-payment of taxes whilst under the Stambulov government brutality was widespread and again there were killings both when tax-collectors called in troops or police to assist them, and when the land of defaulters was taken over by the authorities.

Taxation was not the only financial burden on the peasant; there was also the problem of indebtedness. Bulgarian peasants like those elsewhere had always borrowed for occasional needs such as weddings, with private lenders usually providing such credit. After the Liberation many peasants, however much or little land they already possessed, wished to take advantage of the low prices produced by the glut of sales during and after the war, but few of these anxious purchasers had capital and they therefore borrowed heavily. As the limited cooperative borrowing facilities which had been built up during the final years of Ottoman rule had been destroyed during the war the peasant was forced to borrow from the private usurer, and once possessed of his new property he frequently borrowed again to buy seeds, implements and draught animals. Interest rates were inevitably high for there was neither effective control nor competition. Many peasants also fell victim to *zelencharstvo* whereby a creditor would buy up a crop on the stalk—*zelen* means 'green'—and write off debts equivalent to the purchase price of the crop. That price, however, was set by the creditor himself and was frequently far below that for which he eventually sold the produce. Indeed the price was often so low that it forced the peasant to borrow yet again later in the year and thus intensified his dependence on the usurer; in some cases the peasant had to sell his land and either emigrate to the towns or rent his former property from the money-lender who now owned it.

There were few defences against the private money-lender. An act of 1880 intended to curb *zelencharstvo* had been virtually useless and an attempt to limit ordinary usury in the Varna and Silistra provinces in the early 1890s was no more successful. In these, as in so many other instances in Bulgaria, the real problem was that those responsible for the application of the law at the local level were the very people who stood to lose from its application, and nothing, therefore, was done. As an alternative source of credit the banking system in these years had little to offer. The Bulgarian National Bank had only five branches and three agencies outside Sofia in 1893, and commercial banks were non-existent outside the largest towns. The Agricultural Savings Banks, first established by the reforming Midhat Pasha in the 1860s, had suffered badly from the war and the Liberation; in many cases their records had been destroyed whilst many borrowers after 1878 refused to pay their interest or, if Moslem, had fled. The Agricultural Savings Banks recovered only gradually, amassing twenty-five million leva of capital by 1891 but this was totally inadequate to the national need for responsibly-administered credit, and it was not until the reorganisation of the Bank in 1894 that it could begin to reshape itself to meet the needs of the rural borrower. There was some discussion of the need to organise private credit cooperatives, and in 1890 the first agricultural cooperative society in Bulgaria was established at Mirkovo in the Pirdop district but it remained an isolated example and the real beginnings of cooperation in Bulgaria came too late to save the country from a severe agrarian crisis in the late 1890s.

Chapter 11

THE SOCIAL AND ECONOMIC
CONSEQUENCES OF THE LIBERATION
II. THE TOWNS, MANUFACTURING
INDUSTRIES AND COMMERCE

Between 1883 and 1893 the number of independent farmers in Bulgaria fell by 18.6% from 524,925 to 427,289. Few of these formerly independent farmers, however, took up permanent residence in the towns. By 1892 it was true that the proportion of urban dwellers in Bulgaria had risen to twenty percent but this merely reflected the beginning of the agrarian crisis which was to reach its peak at the end of the decade. After the early 1890s the proportion of urban dwellers to the total population fell slightly, registering 19.9% in 1900, 19.6% in 1905 and 19.1% in 1910; even in 1920 with the towns still swollen with refugees the percentage was not greatly different from 1880, 19.9% as opposed to 19.3%. In absolute numbers those living in towns totalled 543,000 in 1880 and 649,000 in 1892. In 1881 the number of settlements classified as towns was sixty-five of which five had fewer than 2,000 inhabitants, sixteen had between 2,000 and 5,000, twenty had from 5,000 to 10,000, nineteen had between 10,000 and 20,000, and five— Sofia, Plovdiv, Ruse Varna and Shumen—had over 20,000. By 1905 eight towns were in the largest category, the newcomers being Sliven, Stara Zagora and Pleven, eighteen had between 10,000 and 20,000, twenty-one from 5,000 to 10,000, and those under 5,000 numbered seventy-three, though this increase was primarily the result of an administrative redefinition of the term 'town'.

Only to a very limited extent can the growth of towns be attributed to the emergence of industry in Bulgaria. The war of 1877–8 had de-

stroyed most of what little mechanised industry was to be found in the
country and Bulgaria's only surviving factory at Liberation was the
former Ottoman state textile enterprise in Sliven. New foundations
came after the Liberation. By 1887 there were an estimated ninety-two
factories in the country; thirty-six steam or water mills, twenty-three
small tobacco processing plants, ten breweries, five distilleries, five
textile manufacturing enterprises, eight leather works, three soapmaking enterprises, and one each for dyeing and cement-making,
though few of these concerns employed more than a handful of
workers. More rapid expansion, especially in textiles, took place in the
early 1890s when some fifty-four new manufacturing concerns were
established. Once again, however, most of these were very short-lived
and almost all were very small indeed, qualifying for the title 'factory'
only because they used machinery and did not come under the jurisdiction of one of the established guilds. Almost all the larger and more
successful enterprises were foreign-owned and managed. In some
cases the state had been responsible for promoting industrial enterprises, the most notable example outside the state-owned railway system being the mining complex in Pernik where extraction began in
the second half of 1891 with production of 8,429 tons of coal. In 1900
the figure was 120,514 tons. The government also continued working
the lignite mines at Radomir, opened by the Turks in 1874 and until
the late 1880s these mines supplied Sofia's as yet modest needs. State
intervention was also seen in the brick-making industry, one of particular importance at a time of considerable urban construction and
reconstruction. The state also assumed responsibility for a failing
brewery in Pavlovo.

But industrial development is a feature of the second rather than the
first period of post-Liberation Bulgarian history, and such urbanisa-
tion as took place in this earlier stage was as much or more attributable
to the rise of the bureaucracy. This was particularly the case in Sofia.
In 1878 Sofia had been smaller than Plovdiv, Ruse, Varna and Shumen
and was chosen as capital not because of its size but because it was
relatively near Macedonia and stood at the crossroads of the Balkans'
north-west to south-east and north-east to south-west routes. Its size
grew rapidly thereafter, rising from 20,248 inhabitants in 1881 to
30,428 in 1888 and 82,621 in 1905, an increase of four hundred percent
in twenty-five years. A large section of the city's population were newcomers for whilst in 1881 55.6% were native born, in 1893 only 38.7%
could make this claim. By the early 1900s Sofia's population, as a

proportion of the national total, was little different from the ratio of capital to total in other European states.

During its expansion the capital naturally underwent considerable transformation. In the early 1880s most Sofiotes had a cow or two grazing on nearby meadows under the care of the cowherd whom most sections of the city employed. At the turn of the century few were left. At the Liberation the only effective form of street cleaning had been the packs of wild dogs which roamed the streets and which were still large enough in 1882 to kill three people. The dogs were put to the sword in 1884 but at the turn of the century wolves could still menace those who visited the Prince Boris gardens in the centre of the town during winter. By this time, however, the city had assumed a modern shape. The maze of crooked streets, small houses, and separate wards which had characterised the Ottoman city had gone to be replaced by one based largely upon the grid system with western-style housing and government buildings.

Similar transformations took place in other towns. The old Balkan town had consisted of a series of separate wards, *mahale,* grouped usually around a central market place. Each *mahala* had enjoyed considerable powers of local self-government and had almost always been religiously and ethnically homogeneous, and some in the larger cities had been both religiously and professionally homogeneous, consisting for example only of Christian tailors and their families. In Bulgaria these towns for the most part disappeared. The Law of the Communes in 1882 ended the autonomy of the *mahala* whose physical disappearance usually followed soon upon its legal demise. By 1885 thirty-six towns had begun extensive rebuilding, usually on the grid pattern. In the bigger towns the old ethnic and religious divisions were replaced by ones of wealth and by the mid-1880s both Plovdiv and Sofia had clearly discernible poor quarters. In Sofia a square metre of land in the wealthy quarter had cost one gold lev in 1880 but fetched between forty and fifty leva four years later.

Although Sofia's population, as a proportion of the national total, was little different from the ratio of capital to total in other European states, the proportion of civil servants within the capital was disproportionately high, both in comparison with other states and with the rest of Bulgaria. One in four of Sofia's working citizens was classified as a bureaucrat whilst in the rest of the country the figure was one in twelve. This bureaucracy was a new sociological feature in Bulgaria where previously administrators had been relatively few in number and only infrequently Bulgarian by race. At the end of the Russian Provisional Administration there were a mere 2,121 native Bulgarian administrators and clearly the new state could not manage with so few. Some were therefore recruited from the estimated hundred thousand Bulgarians who moved into the Principality after the Liberation, and many of the remaining gaps were filled by foreign experts. During the 1880s unification and such expansion of governmental functions as the creation of the state railway system increased the need for civil servants as did decisions in the early 1890s to centralise the administration of education and to make the state responsible for the payment of clerical stipends. By the turn of the century there were over twenty thousand civil service posts in the country, few of which were now filled by foreign experts. In the early years of the post-Liberation era the government attracted able men to its service by offering high salaries, a device which was justified on the grounds that it would prevent Ottoman-style corruption. In the first years this was indeed the case but later the bureaucracy became compromised both by its involvement in party politics and because the high salaries paid to civil servants stripped other professions, especially teaching, of their best personnel; when the Sŭbranie agreed to vote money for a new pedagogic institute to be built in Shumen in 1884 one of the most telling arguments in favour of the proposal was that it would redress the shortage of teachers caused by the expansion of the civil service. Vocational training establishments also found their work vitiated by the allure of the bureaucratic salary; fewer than half the graduates from the Industrial Training School at Knyazhevo and the Model Agricultural School at Sadovo actually used their training in the relevant occupation.

The new bureaucracy could not by 1900 be described as a new class as its ranks were still open to peasants' sons with sufficient intelligence and education, though to an ever increasing degree recruitment was from the towns. The new social group was much resented by the majority of the population for its expense, for its often sybaritic city lifestyle, for its frequent brutality in its dealings with the ordinary people, and for its compromising involvement with the worst features of Bulgarian party politics.

The reservoir from which Sofia and the other expanding towns took their new population included not only the villages but the depressed manufacturing towns which had expanded in the nineteenth century and had grown prosperous on traditional craft industries, particularly those producing textiles and metal goods. All such industries were based on the traditional craftworkshop (the *zanayat*) and were organised into guilds (*esnafi*) with the usual pattern of apprentices, journeymen and masters. Many of these towns, for example, Pirdop, Sopot, Karlovo, Kalover and Kazanlŭk, were to be found along the foothills of the Balkan range, but others were in the plains and river valleys of northern and southern Bulgaria. Their decline was often dramatic. In the Gabrovo area, for example, the total number of workshops fell from 937 in 1880 to 601 in 1902, and by 1902 some revival had actually taken place; in the lace-making industry the number of workshops had fallen from seventy in 1880 to twenty-three in 1893, and Gabrovo weathered the post-Liberation storm better than most other areas.

In some cases the decline had immediate and specific causes. In the north-west of Bulgaria Vidin declined initially because the new frontiers drawn at Berlin cut the town off from its natural hinterland which was now in Serbia. Similarly, as was seen in chapter 4, Kotel suffered because the new Bulgarian-Rumelian border cut across its established lines of economic communication. In most cases, however, the decline could be attributed to one or more of a number of factors which included the import of cheaper factory-produced goods, the loss of established markets and the changes in social habit and customs which followed the transition from Ottoman rule to a western-oriented European state.

A number of examples may be taken to illustrate these processes. Nail-making in Bulgaria virtually ceased after the Liberation because nails from factories in Austria and Germany could be sold for half the price of home-produced ones. Cheaper lighting oil from western Europe, Russia and Rumania meant ruin for most Bulgarian chandlers and whereas Sofia produced 100,000 *okas** of candles in 1875, by 1898 the figure was only a tenth of that whilst in Kazanlŭk the decline was even steeper, from 28,000 *okas* in 1875 to 1,000 *okas* in 1898. Textiles had been the dominant branch of the traditional manufacturing sector and they suffered enormously from the importation of European factory-produced cloth which was often also of better quality, as well as being cheaper than the home products. Textiles also suffered from a loss of traditional markets. The tariff barriers put up by Rumania and Serbia in the 1880s did some damage but far more injurious was the

---

*An *oka* was 1,225 grams.

loss of much of the Turkish market. Bulgarian craftsmen, especially around Plovdiv, had for long produced the *aba* (coarse cloth) and the *gaitan* (braid especially used for decorative piping) from which the uniforms of the Ottoman army were made, and on the basis of this trade, the *aba*-makers guild of Plovdiv had become one of the most influential in the city. After 1878 that market was lost and there was nothing to replace it. Samokov, which had once provided cloth for two Turkish army corps and which also suffered because of a fall in demand for its metal products, declined from being a major Balkan city to a small town. The loss of an established market also hit the leather-making workshops which survived in appreciable numbers only in Sliven and Haskovo, both of which had large Turkish populations who continued to wear leather belts and traditional rather than western footwear. There were a number of specifically local crafts which were also severely hit, one of which was shear-making. Shears had been much in demand amongst shepherds and flock-owners before the Liberation and so brisk had the trade been that the shear-makers were able to separate from the knife-makers and establish their own guild, but after 1878 the traditional pattern of sheep-rearing began to decline and with its decline the demand for shears disappeared.

For other trades the decisive blow was the departure of the Turks who had been their chief customers. This was particularly the case in those crafts engaged in the production of luxury goods such as gold- and silver-ware, but they were not the only ones to suffer because of Moslem emigration. Slipper-makers had been largely dependent on Moslems for sales and in liberated Bulgaria there was no likelihood that the Christians would adopt Moslem footwear.

The switch to western habits damaged many native craft producers. Western porcelain became popular and, being cheap, replaced the tradition copper for tableware in most homes, and a rapid increase in the use of the European bed meant a drastic fall in demand for the carpets and cushions on which most Bulgarians had previously slept. Even the new colours which were fashionable after the Liberation and which were easily available in imported cloth damaged the native craft industries because these colours could not easily be reproduced by traditional methods of dyeing. Conscription was indirectly a great foe of the old industries for it did much to spread the new western fashions and habits. Most barracks were in towns and it was here that young men from the country learnt to prefer boots to leggings, gas rather than tallow lamps, and to value the comfort and utility of western institutions such as the knife and fork, the table and chair and the bed.

The knife-makers suffered because of a change of habits and for other reasons. The traditional Bulgarian knife was a long, multipurpose instrument and the knife-makers could not adapt their machines and skills to produce a western style knife as cheap as that coming from the factories of Austria and Germany. The Bulgarian knife-maker also suffered because his product had been excluded from its established foreign markets by the Rumanian and Ottoman tariffs of the 1880s and at home the decline in demand was due not only to the arrival of the western knife but also to the suppression of brigandage which in some areas had previously made the carrying of the long traditional knife necessary for personal protection. Even more, however, was the decline in the demand for the traditional knife the result of the change to western styles of dress, for European trousers could not accommodate the heavy belt which was essential to the unembarrassed carrying of a traditional knife. Before the Liberation there had been hundreds of knife-making workshops in Gabrovo, Sliven, Plovdiv, Stanimaka, Karlovo, Kazanlŭk and elsewhere, but by the mid-1890s they survived in any number only in Gabrovo.

Some established crafts suffered from particular political developments as well as from the factors described above. The production of heavy-duty sacks had been an important activity in a number of towns but this suffered because the railways cut demand for the product, as did the cessation of rice-growing in Rumelia between 1879 and 1883, whilst the government's prohibition of free-roaming goat herds deprived many producers of their only source of cheap raw material; as goats now had to be penned and reared on bought-in food the price of sacks doubled. Only with the expansion of the tobacco industry in the mid-1890s did the demand for heavy-duty sacks revive.

A few trades were able, after the initial impact, to adapt to changed conditions. It did not take long for tailors in the cities to copy western styles. In the Gabrovo textile industry a number of owners moved over to factory production of high quality cloth on imported German or British machinery; between 1888 and 1893 in Gabrovo seven new textile mills were opened and ten new leather works, three of them joint stock companies.

Some master guildsmen tried to combine in an effort to survive, but this was seldom successful. The only hope for many communities was to turn to entirely new products. Beer, virtually unknown in Bulgaria before the Liberation, was soon manufactured in a number of towns, the first breweries being in Sofia and Ruse but by the mid-1890s there were twenty-nine in all. Distilleries, too, were often a useful alternative area of production. Samokov was one of a number of towns where match factories were established and the development of the tobacco-processing industry gave employment in Haskovo, Plovdiv and Dupnitsa. Other manufacturers found a livelihood and gave employment by producing western-style goods, for example in furniture, or by adding the finishing touches to factory-produced goods. Yet few of the truly depressed towns, with the exception of Gabrovo, could stand the impact of the post-Liberation changes.

The decline of the traditional industries and dislocation of established trading patterns meant the end of the periodic fairs which had once been the chief forum of exchange for the Balkan tradesmen, though that at Tŭrgovishte (Eski Djumaya) survived for a few years after the Liberation because the local Turkish population did not emigrate immediately.

The post-Liberation changes also meant a weakening of the guilds or *esnafi*. These institutions had not only controlled the manufacturing process concerned but had also played an extremely important part in the social life of the Bulgarian communities, and not an inconsiderable one in the national revival. They had endowed churches, monasteries, schools and reading rooms; they had provided scholarships for promising pupils to study abroad; they had often played a significant part in local government, collecting taxes and settling disputes between members of the Christian community; and of course they had cared for guild members and their families who had fallen upon hard times. After 1879 the judicial and administrative functions of the guilds were taken over by local and national governments as were many, but not all, of their educational activities, but the state had no welfare provisions for those whose livelihood was endangered. With the decline in traditional manufacturing after 1878 the guilds in many cases found that distress was too widespread and their own resources too depleted for them to be able to carry out their tasks in this sector. For the depressed traditional manufacturing towns of the 1880s and 1890s, therefore, there was little to do but protest and hope for governmental assistance.

The most famous protest was that at Sopot in March 1883 when women burnt bales of imported cloth and attacked the home of the importer, but such outbursts were rare and uncoordinated. The opposition press sometimes took up the cause of the depressed craft-workers. The Conservative *Maritsa* in October 1883 argued that many of the articles then being imported could be produced at home, and on another occasion the radical Liberal *Sŭedinenie* (Unification) described Tŭrnovo as declining day by day and insisted that there had been a ten-fold fall in the number of workshops functioning in Pirdop, Samokov, Etropole, Vidin, Silistra, Varna, Shumen and other towns. A number of prominent politicians accepted the need for government assistance, Geshov, for example, pressing the case for the state encouragement of industry. Some action did follow. The most important was the attempt to provide selected industries with guaranteed markets. In 1881 a law decreed that all messengers and civil servants must wear uniforms made from home-produced coarse cloth (*shiyak*) and braid and in December 1883 this ruling was extended to include the gendarmerie. In 1891 it was broadened once again and by now army uniforms too had to be made from home-produced cloth. Such legislation had only a marginal effect for in textiles the successful home manufacturers were already adopting modern techniques and they, rather than the old workshops, benefited most from such legislation.

The government was anxious to encourage home industry in other ways, most of which favoured those prepared to try new techniques rather than those who clung to the old. The Plovdiv Exhibition of 1892 was meant to encourage native producers but did not do so in every case for some foreign manufacturers saw how poor the local product was and immediately began an export offensive; such was the case with silk which after Plovdiv was subject to deadly competition from Austrian factories. The government also tried to encourage more efficient production through education. The Rumelian government in 1882 set up a school in a factory which had once supplied the Turkish army with cloth and here foreign teachers instructed young Bulgarians in modern methods of textile production. In the Principality the government set up the Model Agricultural School at Sadovo and followed this with the setting up of a manufacturing school at Knyazhevo near Sofia. The Knyazhevo school was well organised with departments for smithing, carpentry, ironwork and ceramics but despite an enrolment which increased from 53 pupils in 1883 to 117 in 1888 too few graduates went on to work in manufacturing industry; they could, as we have seen, earn more in the civil service. Other acts of government encouragement included the setting up of a special committee for industry within the Ministry of Education in 1887 and of a full Ministry of

Trade and Agriculture in 1892. Direct subsidies were also given.
Among the beneficiaries were an earthenware firm in Sofia which
received 10,000 leva in 1890, a metal smelting concern, also in the
capital, which was given the same sum in the following year, and the
Gabrovo lace-making firm, 'Uspeh' (Success), to which the government made a grant of 100,000 leva in 1889 after the firm's factory had
been burnt. Government monopolies were also used to encourage and
protect home industry. In Sofia one Stashevski was given a monopoly
in the early 1880s for the use of the heremetically-sealed cess carts
which greatly improved the quality of life in the capital; Angel Popov
of Tŭrnovo was given a ten year monopoly over the production and
sale of spaghetti and macaroni. Some concessions came with conditions attached and the Frenchman, Bergie, who opened a distillery in
Sofia in 1881 was obliged to use local unskilled labour and Bulgarian
raw materials. The government also assisted Bulgarian commerce by
providing 90% of the capital for the Bulgarian Steamship Navigation
Company, founded in 1893. As yet, however, government involvement
in the industrial sector was haphazard and more a response to individual cases and emergencies than a consistent, planned strategy. For that
Bulgaria had to wait for the Nationalist administration of the second
half of the 1890s.

Some sense of national strategy had been worked out in 1884 with
regard to railway development, the Railway Act of that year outlining
the network of lines which it believed the nation would need and
which, it insisted, the nation must own. The most important lines were
to be the international trunk line, a trans-Balkan line, and the lines
from the northern and southern plains to the ports of Varna and
Burgas. There was great need for an improvement in communications;
in the winter of 1888 Stambulov had found that the quickest route
from Tŭrnovo to Plovdiv was via the Black Sea and Constantinople.
Yet by the mid-1890s little of the national rail network had been completed. The international line had been opened to through traffic in
July 1888 and in 1890 Yambol had been joined to Burgas; soon after
this the capital was linked to the mining area around Pernik. These
lines served the nation in a variety of ways. The trunk line enabled
perishable products such as eggs to be sold in the distant markets of
central Europe, whilst the Yambol-Burgas railway made cheap salt
produced in Anhialo available in most other parts of Bulgaria; Sofia
benefited from the easy availability of Pernik coal, whilst in Rumelia it
was common practice for the local intelligentsia to meet the interna-

tional trains to learn the latest news from Europe. Despite these advantages, however, there were still many gaps in the national rail system, most noticeably that of a line across the Balkan mountains, and many of the lines in operation had been built with cheapness rather than function or quality in mind, with the result that curves were sharp and gradients steep and the monies saved in construction were lost in high operating costs. For a number of years waterways, and above all the Danube, continued to carry a large amount of traffic. The roads remained decrepit and little suited to anything but the pack-horse.

Bulgaria was, however, integrated into the world communications system, becoming a member of the International Postal Union soon after Liberation, but a full inter-village postal system was not introduced until the mid-1890s. Telephones were first used in the country in 1886, but it was not until 1892 that Sofia was linked to Plovdiv.

Whilst the basis of a communications network was being laid the outlines of a financial system were also emerging. The government had adopted the lev as the unit of national currency in 1880, the first coins being struck the following year. The introduction of the new currency did not mean the disappearance of those previously used. Turkish money circulated widely in the bazars, especially in southern Bulgaria, and throughout the country the Russian rouble was current until the end of the century. The lev was to be equal to the French franc and in the period up to 1912 the rate of exchange for the gold lev varied from 99 to 101.5 francs. An indication of the low level of economic development was the fact that up to the end of the nineteenth century no more than two million leva's worth of bank notes were in circulation in Bulgaria, and in 1893 the sum was as low as the equivalent of £50,000. Note issue was the sole prerogative of the Bulgarian National Bank (BNB). The Bank was required to keep bullion to the value of one quarter of the notes issued and it was in the BNB that the national gold reserves were deposited. The Bank also provided credit and other financial services to companies or official bodies; it did not accept deposits from or lend money to individuals. In its earliest years the BNB's activities had always been circumscribed by the political controversies which raged around it but Karavelov's Act of January 1885 ensured that it would be a nationally-owned institution safe from political intrigue. The Agricultural Savings Bank was the second most important native financial institution, but it made little impact until the second half of the 1890s.

Foreign banks played some part in the finances of Bulgaria in this early period. The first foreign bank to be established after the Liberation was Girdap and Co. in Ruse in 1881, but in Rumelia the International Commission had re-introduced the Ottoman Bank which had closed during the war. The Ottoman Bank was to remain the chief credit institution in southern Bulgaria until the Union when it was again closed. Better relations between Bulgaria and Turkey under Stambulov, however, brought about in 1889 a second re-opening of the Ottoman Bank in Plovdiv and there were soon branches in Sofia, Ruse and Burgas. The Ottoman Bank had extensive deposits of private credit and, because of its international experience and connections, more foreign currency than other banks and it played a considerable part in the financing of mercantile activity; by the mid-1890s it had lent up to fifteen million leva whilst the BNB's lending had reached no more than thirteen million leva. The Ottoman Bank finally closed its Bulgarian branches in 1899, partly because of deteriorating political relations between Sofia and Constantinople, but also because the Bank had lost heavily in Turkish and South African investments.

Of the other foreign banks the Anglo-Foreign Bank had become involved in the financing of Bulgarian exports soon after the Liberation but foreign banks did not become heavily involved in Bulgaria's commerce until the 1890s. In 1890 the French bank, Louis Dreyfus and Co., had established itself in the country and soon had branches in all important towns. By the mid-1890s this company, together with the firm of Alatini, another French concern, but with operations based in Salonika, had a near monopoly in the financing of southern Bulgarian grain exports. French influence was always stronger in the south than in the north of Bulgaria and in the latter during the 1890s Austrian capital made significant advances in the banking sector, the chief agents being M. Heller and Co., the Austro-Hungarian Export Co., and Naifeld and Co., the last named of which was to take second place to Dreyfus in the financing of Bulgaria's grain trade. Not until 1895 did Bulgarian capital succeed in establishing a private bank, the Bulgarian Central Bank in Ruse.

Foreign capital played a major role in the development of insurance in Bulgaria. This was a profitable business for the peasants were gradually becoming more insurance conscious and the plates of British, European and even American insurance companies were appearing on the houses of Bulgarian villagers in the 1890s. The first two large

Bulgarian insurance companies, 'Bŭlgariya' and 'Balkan', were both founded in the 1890s.

The Treaty of Berlin's insistence that the Capitulations remain in force in Bulgaria meant that the Principality had little freedom in its tariff policies. In fact, Bulgaria could set its own tariffs only for those states which did not enjoy the special benefits laid down by the Capitulations, viz. Rumania, Serbia and Turkey itself. In trading relations with the fourteen privileged states, states which accounted for four fifths of Bulgaria's external trade, Sofia could not impose a tariff higher than that of the 8% *ad valorem* which had been set as the maximum Ottoman tariff, though 0.5% could be imposed for harbour dues. This restriction was politically degrading and economically harmful, not least because the prices from which the *ad valorem* figures were derived were those current in the early 1860s when the system was introduced. Price movements since then meant that the 8% of the 1860s could be as little as 4% twenty to thirty years later, clearly no barrier to the penetration of foreign produce and no great source of state income. The Bulgarians struggled against this injustice for some years but made no progress until 1889 when Britain agreed to a general 8% *ad valorem* tariff on current prices, with spirits paying 10%. In addition, Bulgaria was to enjoy most-favoured-nation rights in Britain and benefited greatly from the opening up of the British market to Bulgarian mutton, poultry and eggs. The agreement, valid initially for two years, was ratified in January 1890 and similar treaties followed almost immediately with Germany, Austria, Italy and France. It was the first break with the tariff restrictions of the treaty of Berlin, but did not go far when compared with the breaches which were to be made by the Stoilov administration in the second half of the 1890s.

In an agrarian country such as Bulgaria trade was naturally to some extent dependent upon the quality of the harvest but in general trade expanded gradually with the pace of the increase sharpening noticeably towards the end of the period. Quinquennial figures were as follows:

Table 1.   Value of Foreign Trade, 1881–95. In millions of leva.

Quinquennium	Imports	Exports	Balance of Trade
1881–85	48.84	38.47	− 10.37
1886–90	70.56	62.40	− 8.16
1891–95	83.55	77.54	− 6.01

Table 2.   Trade by categories of commodity. In millions of leva.

A. IMPORTS

Type of commodity	1886–90	1891–95	%age change
Live animals	0.681	0.528	−22.45
Food and drink	12.962	15.370	+18.58
Raw materials and semimanufactured goods	7.488	8.508	+13.62
Manufactured goods	49.430	59.143	+19.65
Total	70.561	83.549	+18.41

B. EXPORTS

Live animals	6.183	6.122	− 0.99
Food and drink	48.193	64.176	+33.16
Raw materials and semimanufactured goods	0.541	0.431	−16.31
Manufactured goods	7.534	6.822	−11.67
Total	62.451	77.551	+24.18

The main export commodity was grain which averaged 57.16% of the value of all exports in the period 1879 to 1895 with many of the remaining exports being agricultural produce or goods derived almost directly from farming. In imports it was manufactured goods which predominated. Trade by categories is summarised in table 2.

In the five years 1891–5 Bulgaria's exports were worth an average of 77.551 million leva per annum. The largest single customer was the Ottoman Empire which accounted for 22.5 million leva or 29.01% of total exports per annum. The other important markets were France with 15.95 million leva (20.57%) per annum, Britain with 13.53 million leva per annum (17.45%) and Germany with an average of 12.85 million leva per annum (16.57%). Russia bought little from Bulgaria, an average of only 0.05 million leva's worth per annum or 0.06% of total exports. A rising star in the export sky was Belgium whose yearly average purchases were 2.15 million leva (2.77% of the total) but whereas she had bought only 0.702 million leva's worth of goods in 1891, in 1895 she bought 5.324 million leva's worth. Apart from the advance of Belgium the significant feature of the export pattern between 1891 and 1895 was the continued dominance of the established partners, Turkey and France, even if sales to the former were considerably lower as a proportion of total exports than they had been before the Liberation. Bulgaria's imports cost an average of 83.549 million leva per annum in these years. The chief source of imports was Austria-Hungary which provided an average of 30.3 million leva's worth, or 36.27% of the yearly total. Britain was second, supplying imports worth 17.9 million leva (21.42%) per year, Turkey was third with 10.37 million leva (12.41%), and Germany fourth with 9.22 million leva (11.04%). Russia contributed to Bulgarian imports goods worth an average of 4.05 million leva per annum or 4.85% of the yearly total; for France the figures were 3.6 million leva per year or 4.31% of the yearly total.

Part II
The Personal Regime, 1896–1912

"Corrupt are they, and become abominable in their wickedness; there is none that doeth good."

Psalm 53, verse 2

"For each age is a dream that is dying,
Or one that is coming to birth."

Arthur O'Shaughnessy, Ode

Chapter 12

MACEDONIA AND FOREIGN AFFAIRS, 1894-9

The restoration of relations with Russia did not resolve all the issues in dispute between Sofia and St Petersburg. Soon after recognition the Russians raised the question of the schism between the Patriarchate and the Exarchate, hoping still to bring the two Churches together again and to use the reunited body as the main vehicle for Tsarist influence in the Balkans. With conditions in Macedonia worsening there was little or no prospect for the achievement of this long-standing Russian objective, nor were the Bulgarians prepared to contemplate a renunciation or a weakening of their national Church, and the Russian proposals were therefore quietly dropped.

A more persistent problem was that of the fifty-two Bulgarian officers still in exile in Russia. Tcharykov raised this question as soon as he took up his new post as Russian diplomatic agent in Sofia and in April 1896 Ferdinand, anxious to maintain the momentum towards better relations with the Tsar, accepted three exiled officers back into the army, even though one of them had been involved in the 1886 plot. Yet Ferdinand had to tread carefully for the return of the exiles was resented by many officers who understandably questioned whether disloyalty on such a scale should ever be forgotten. Petrov, who had remained at the Ministry of War when Stambulov fell, agreed with these officers. When he was subjected to pressure to agree to the return of more officers he insisted that there were no vacancies and that most of the exiles had not spent sufficient time abroad to expiate their crimes; a few would be allowed back, he conceded, but they must return to the Bulgarian army at one rank below that held when they went into exile, no matter what further promotions they may have re-

ceived in Russia in the interim. Petrov was clearly defending the interests of the officers who had remained in Bulgaria and who had been
promoted to higher ranks, for these officers stood to lose by competition from the returning exiles, a number of whom had proved their
ability and courage in the war of 1885. Ferdinand was anxious to make
further concessions to the Russians but Stoilov joined with Petrov in
opposing them; only in December 1896 did the Minister President
agree to an amendment of the Amnesty Law of 1894 allowing all
political refugees the right to return to Bulgaria, but with the face-
saving formula that each one intending to take advantage of this
amendment must write personally to the Prince requesting his permission to return. A later statement dealt with the particular issue of the
army officers, making detailed arrangements for pension payments if
they returned but also making absolutely clear that such provisions
would not apply to any future deserters. Stoilov had felt strong enough
to make these concessions because in the autumn of 1896 he had
received a massive, if engineered, vote of support in the general elections. He had also been relieved of the objecting Petrov. Ferdinand
had taken offence because his Minister of War had not attended a state
dinner for Marie Louise and because the Emperor Franz Josef, who
since the conversion of Boris had been exceedingly cool towards the
Prince, had sent Petrov a signed miniature. Petrov had also allowed
one of the returning army officers, a Major Stoyanov, to be put on trial
for his part in the events of 1886, and this had greatly angered the
Russians and Ferdinand; Petrov was therefore sacked in November
1896. His successor, Ivanov, was much more pliant and in 1898 signed
an agreement with the Russian military attaché in Constantinople
which removed all obstacles to the return of the exiled officers with the
exception of Benderev and a handful of his closest accomplices. By the
middle of 1898 most officers eligible to return to Bulgaria had done so.

The return of the exiles was resented by some officers in Bulgaria but
welcomed by the majority of the population. Disappointment was all
but universal, however, at Russia's failure to give effective help to the
Bulgarians over Macedonia. With the fall of Stambulov the Macedonian lobby in Bulgaria could again become active. It was a very
considerable lobby for by this time the number of refugees in the
Principality was at least 200,000, most of whom had become townsmen
and were therefore more easily drawn into the active political life of the
nation. They had smouldered under the repression of Stambulov and
were now prepared to ignite the Macedonian movement once again.

They were bitter that whilst, they alleged, little had been done to further the interests of the Bulgarians in Macedonia, the Serbs and the Greeks had advanced their causes considerably. The government of Stoilov in 1894 did not have the political authority to hold down the Macedonians as Stambulov had done, nor did it have the will to do so. In the first place Stoilov needed the support of the Macedonians but in the second place the collaboration with Turkey which had been the corollary of Stambulov's internal repression was becoming less attractive as disorders in Armenia and the prospect of the dissolution of, or at least European intervention in Turkey increased; there was little point in seeking concessions from a regime which seemed about to disappear. The dissolution of Turkey would also mean that Bulgaria would have to counter Serbian and Greek efforts to win over the Macedonian Christians. Furthermore the example of the Armenians was taken by the Macedonians in Bulgaria to mean that revolutionary activity in Turkey could be effective, for the powers were already beginning to discuss the question of forcing reforms on the Sultan if his regime lasted long enough to carry them out.

Soon after the reports of disturbances in Armenia reached Europe the Austrians warned Sofia not to take advantage of these events by meddling in Macedonia. The warning was too late. The government of Stoilov had already released a number of imprisoned Macedonian activists, and had intimated secretly to them that the government would be willing to help the Macedonian cause with money, arms and men. Both Petrov and the Minister of Foreign Affairs, Nachovich, were in contact with leading Macedonians in Sofia and it was Nachovich who provided Stambulov's assassin, Tiufekdjiev, with a sinecure job with the Bulgarian State Railways. Towards the end of 1894 a number of Macedonian leaders, from within Bulgaria and elsewhere, gathered in Sofia and decided to reactivate the Macedonian agitation, calling for a union of all Macedonian associations, and setting up a Central Committee under Kitanchev. In March, to a backcloth of increasing public excitement, a congress convened which confirmed Kitanchev as President of the Central Committee. Kitanchev had the support of Karavelov and Tiufekdjiev but there was also a Stambulovist opposition group present at the congress.

Mounting public pressure at home, indications that the powers were genuinely concerned with reforms in Armenia, and hopes that recognition by Russia might be brought nearer by a conspicuous success in the Balkans, persuaded the Stoilov government to take up the Macedonian issue with the Turks in April 1895. The Porte had complained that the government in Sofia was doing nothing to contain the Macedonian wildmen and Stoilov now replied, in arguments similar to those employed by Stambulov, that such control could be imposed only if the Ottoman government did something to help the Exarchist cause in Macedonia; the Bulgarians demanded the concession of a rail link between Sofia and Kumanovo, *berats* for all dioceses with Bulgarian majorities, permission for the synod to meet in Constantinople, and complete freedom for the Exarchate to open and maintain schools and to build churches. In addition the Bulgarians wanted the application in Macedonia of all the reforms which the Porte had recently announced it was prepared to grant to Armenia. The Porte declined even to receive the Bulgarian note on the grounds that it came from a vassal of the Sultan and the Bulgarian representative was temporarily withdrawn from Constantinople.

The abortive spring diplomatic offensive was followed by more violent pressure. Guerrilla bands were forming in the mountains along the Macedonian border and though the government took a few face-saving measures, including the transfer of the most extreme activists in the army to garrisons some distance from the border and the strengthening of the frontier forces, there was secret connivance with the bands many of which crossed into Macedonia. Few of them had any success except that under the leadership of Boris Sarafov which occupied the town of Melnik for a few days. The government had permitted and secretly encouraged such exploits partly because the Macedonian lobby was becoming ever more powerful. The government was publicly embarrassed when four officers resigned their commissions and before their resignations had been confirmed crossed into Macedonia where two of them were killed; despite government orders officers in Bulgaria organised a service of remembrance, receiving widespread public approval for doing so. An even more important reason for the government's connivance at the raids of 1895 was Ferdinand's hope that such actions would show the febrile state of the Balkan peninsula and that his subsequent clamping down upon them would spotlight him as the guardian of peace and order and thus increase the likelihood that Russia would recognise him as Prince. It did not work out in this way for although general restraint was imposed after the Melnik raid the Russians interpreted this not so much as a sign of Ferdinand's authority as of his obedience to Russian orders, for Lobanov had told the Subranie deputation of 1895 that Bulgaria must on no account stir up trouble in Macedonia. Nevertheless the government had gained a good deal from the Melnik incident. The public greeted it joyfully and the involvement of a number of high ranking officers on 'temporary discharge' redounded to the government's credit in popular eyes. Also the powers had been forced to take notice once more of Macedonia. Though it was little remarked upon at the time the raid had also put the Sofia-based Macedonian movement, which the government could influence, into the forefront and had therefore kept the initiative away from an indigenous Macedonian organisation which was already beginning to question the strategy of the Sofia organisation and which was soon to be in fierce competition with it. In December 1895 the Sofia organisation convened the second Macedonian congress. The congress agreed to raise a 'Patriotic Loan' of 300,000 francs, to reduce the size of the central committee and to replace Kitanchev with Reserve General Nikolaev as President, and because of the emergence of possible rival organisations, to rename the central committee, 'The Supreme Macedonian Committee'.

1896 was a relatively quiet year in Macedonia. The government in Sofia no longer wanted friction with Turkey for in January it was moving towards the long-awaited reconciliation with Russia and immediately after recognition it did not wish to cloud its relations with the suzerain power; in February Stoilov had told the Austrian minister that relations with Turkey had never been so good and Ferdinand's visit to Constantinople a few weeks later was an obvious success. Without official backing the Supreme Committee was not in a position to launch any spectacular raids and attention was therefore focused on peaceful means of improving the Bulgarians' lot in Macedonia. Grekov advocated a gradualist solution based upon a reorganisation of the Exarchate. It was at that time impossible to fill any church post without the involvement of the Porte but any alteration to the existing arrangements could not be achieved without a meeting of all Exarchist bishops under the presidency of the Exarch himself. Such a meeting could not be held in Bulgaria for the Porte would allow neither the Exarch nor the Macedonian Exarchist bishops to go to a foreign country to discuss the administration of Ottoman territory. Unfortunately for the Bulgarians such a meeting could not be held in the only other obvious place, Constantinople, because the Russians, determined that the schism should not be emphasised, placed intense diplomatic pressure on the Porte not to allow a synod to take place in the Ottoman capital.

The government turned instead to the established diplomatic practice of requesting that the Turks impose the reforms they had promised
Macedonia and other areas in Articles 23 and 62 of the treaty of Berlin.
In May 1896 the Supreme Committee published a reform scheme
which it had drawn up at the prompting of the government. Stoilov's
Cabinet then used this as the basis for a twelve-point reform proposal
submitted to the Porte in April 1896. The proposal called for the
application of reforms in the vilayet of Adrianople and in a new
Macedonian administrative unit to be formed from the merging of the
existing vilayets of Salonika, Bitolya and Skopje. Further demands
were for equality between Christian and Moslem, greater local representation in a reformed administrative structure, a mixed gendarmerie,
reforms in taxation and education, improved communications, and an
inspectorate to supervise the working of the justice and finance
departments. The Porte agreed to these suggestions and confirmed its
reforming intentions in November 1896 when the concessions recently
granted to the Armenians were extended to all other communities in
the Empire. The call for reforms was not new, nor was the Sultan's
acceptance of them, but as usual nothing was done.

The Sultan had agreed to the reform proposals because he was under
great pressure from the powers over Armenia and because of mounting
tension in Crete. The Bulgarians attempted to capitalise on the latter
and looked for a joint initiative by the Balkan states to force a solution
to the problem of Macedonia. A Bulgarian legation was opened in
Athens and Stoilov suggested joint Graeco-Bulgarian pressure on the
Porte demanding the implementation of the promised reforms in
Macedonia. The Greeks refused and the Bulgarians therefore turned to
Serbia with much more significant results. On 19 February/2 March
1897—the anniversary of San Stefano—a secret Serbo-Bulgarian
treaty was signed. The two sides agreed to confine their actions in
Macedonia to cultural and ecclesiastical propaganda and to help each
other in this sector. They would take joint military action only if
Austria intervened in the region or if Turkish maladministration
became so grotesque as to make life intolerable for the Macedonian
population. The agreement was significant in two ways. The question
of reform for Macedonia had declined in importance but, much more
importantly, although there was no delimitation of spheres of interest,
the Bulgarians had for the first time accepted officially that the Serbs
would have a part in the settlement of Macedonia; the old Stambulo-

vist doctrine that Bulgaria must inherit all of Macedonia had it seemed been dropped.

The need to think in terms of possible military intervention had been created by the rapidly worsening relations between Greece and Turkey over the question of Crete. Some of the powers stepped into the dispute in the island itself but they could not prevent Greek incursions into mainland Turkey and these in April 1897 precipitated war between the two countries. Early in the year, as the crisis was developing, Stoilov took advantage of the Porte's supposed difficulties and, against a threat of mobilisation, demanded *berats* for the sees of Melnik, Kukush, Strumnitsa, Bitolja and Dibra; at the end of the war the Turks agreed to grant the first three and also to allow the Bulgarians to appoint commercial agents to the cities of Salonika, Skopje, Bitolja, Dedeagach (Alexandroupolis) and Adrianople. These were sizeable gains but were not commensurate with what Bulgaria had originally demanded. The reason for this was that the Turks had won a rapid and overwhelming military victory in the campaign against Greece. Also the Russians had refused any help to the Bulgarians. The Bulgarian agent in Constantinople had been told by the Russian ambassador there that Bulgaria 'had only recently been reconciled with Russia and had not yet done anything to inspire his government with confidence. Till Russia felt such confidence in Bulgaria she would insist on the latter keeping quiet'.[1]

Russian policy had in fact changed direction. Nelidov's plans for a seizure of the Straits had been put away for the prospect of an Ottoman collapse had been receding even before the war of 1897 caused it to it vanish for some years. Russian policy therefore turned once more to the Far East and as in the mid-1880s Russia now wanted stability in the Balkans. When the Austrian Emperor visited St Petersburg in April 1897 he and his Foreign Minister found an unexpected community of opinion on this issue and Russia and Austria therefore came to an unofficial agreement that the Balkans should be kept 'on ice' for as long as possible. For a successful policy in Macedonia any Balkan state had to have the backing of either Austria or Russia. Neither was now prepared to provide such backing and thus the possibility of serious territorial or even administrative changes in Turkish Europe, a possibility created by the disorders in Armenia in 1894, no longer existed; Sofia was forced back into the Stambulovist policy of attempting to secure concessions by cooperation with the Porte, but that also meant strict control over the Macedonian activists and the government's struggle to assert that control formed the next stage in the evolution of the Macedonian question in Bulgaria.

In the early months of 1897 Nikolaev had resigned as President of the Supreme Committee, Ferdinand insisting that the diplomatic initiatives over the *berats* must not be compromised by insurgent activity, and during the summer of 1897 there had once again been relatively few incursions into Macedonia from Bulgaria, and nothing had clouded the Prince's second visit to Constantinople that year in August. However, any hopes that the Sofia regime was in complete control of the Macedonian movement were dispelled in November 1897. In the village of Vinitsa a band organised in Bulgaria but now short of funds had robbed and killed a Turkish *bey* or landlord, and in the ensuing search the Ottoman authorities discovered a large quantity of arms, including over a thousand Mannlicher rifles with ammunition. Fierce repression followed and under torture the whereabouts of other arms caches were revealed. The Porte took this as confirmation of their repeated assertions that the Bulgarian government was responsible for organising a widespread subversive movement which would bring chaos to Macedonia and war to the Balkans. The important point was that although the band which raided Vinitsa had been formed in Bulgaria and had been connected with the Supreme Committee, the arms caches were not. They had been collected by a different group, formed first in 1893 and known by 1896 as 'The Bulgarian Macedonian-Adrianople Revolutionary Organisation', though the title was changed in 1902 to 'The Secret Macedonian-Adrianople Revolutionary Organisation', whilst in 1905 it adopted the title 'The Internal Macedonian Revolutionary Organisation', giving it the acronym by which it is best known to historians, IMRO.*

The Internal Organisation did not dissociate itself in any way from Bulgarian culture but it refused to commit itself to the Bulgarian state. Its objectives were Macedonian autonomy within a Balkan federation. The Supremacists also advocated autonomy but for them this was to be but the preliminary to the absorbtion of Macedonia into Bulgaria; that the Supremacists intended Macedonia to follow the same path as Rumelia was shown when they suggested both former Governor Generals of that province as possible *valis* for the united Macedonia which their 1896 reform scheme envisaged.

---

*For convenience I shall refer to it from the beginning as the Internal Organisation.

Differences between the two factions did not reach serious proportions until 1898. The Supremacists and the Sofia political establishment which backed them had been shocked by the extent of the Internalists' network as revealed after Vinitsa. In January 1898 the Supremacists began once more to organise bands and to prepare for further large-scale incursions such as that which took Melnik in 1895 and this, Stoilov told the Bulgarian commercial agents in Macedonia, was part of a deliberate attempt by the government to re-establish control over the Macedonian movement. It was an ill-chosen tactic. Since the Melnik raid the Internalists and their supporters in Bulgaria had been questioning the relationship between the movement and the government and such questioning led rapidly to the conclusion that Ferdinand and his Cabinet had been using Macedonia as a pawn in their struggle to win recognition from the powers and, once that had been achieved, to wrest further concessions from the Porte. As genuine autonomists they also questioned the advisability of outside forces fighting the Macedonian battle for that would commit Macedonia by implication to the Bulgarian state which backed those outside forces. The Internal Organisation with its Central Committee in Salonika wanted to achieve autonomy by a full-scale rising and if it were to bring this about it had to increase the national consciousness of the peasants. By 1896 the leaders of the Internal Organisation, Gotse Delchev and Damian Gruev, had organised their 'canals' of communication with Bulgaria and Delchev was in Sofia trying to persuade the Supremacists to suspend further incursions until the Macedonian peasantry had been properly roused and organised. The renewed activity of early 1898 showed that the government would not allow this and the Internal Organisation therefore ordered all its branches in Macedonia to organise their own *cheti* (bands) which were to fight against Turkish repression and for liberation, but they were to fight when the Central Committee in Salonika decided the time was ripe rather than when the ruling clique in Sofia might think it convenient. The determination of the Internal leaders to prepare for their own struggle had been increased by Russia's agreement with Austria to maintain the Balkan *status quo* for although Sofia might try to make tactical, political use of the Macedonian issue through the Supreme Committee it was unlikely, given the new Russian attitude, that the Bulgarian army would ever be committed against the Tsar's wishes to an all-out war of liberation for Macedonia: the Macedonians had been given time to prepare their *sara da fe*. Knowledge of the 1897 agreement between

Sofia and Belgrade also intensified autonomist feelings in Macedonia for this agreement was seen as an indication that the Bulgarian government was prepared to be a partner to the partition of Macedonia. The new armed units together with the extremely sophisticated organs of self-government which the Internal Organisation had developed since 1893 meant that by 1899 it had become a virtual state within the Ottoman state.

In addition to increasing its own organisation and power inside Macedonia the Central Committee in Salonika also decided to attempt a take-over of the Bulgarian organisations and eventually of the Supreme Committee itself. This proved relatively easy and by 1900 a new Supreme Committee had been elected under the presidency of Boris Sarafov, now committed to the Internal Organisation rather than the old, government-dominated Supreme Committee. For just over a year the two organisations functioned as one and a despairing government had no real authority over a movement which was becoming ever more powerful and disruptive both in Macedonia and in the Principality.

*   *   *

Recognition by the great powers of the legitimacy of Ferdinand's position as Prince enabled him and his government to develop relations with foreign states. The special relationship which most Bulgarians believed their nation had with Russia had yielded disappointing results. Russia had given no encouragement to Bulgarian claims in Macedonia and by the end of the 1890s was clearly thinking of an ultimate partition of the territory with the Serbs having supremacy west of the Vardar, for Russian consuls in that area were openly favouring Belgrade's propaganda. Pressure from St Petersburg on the question of the emigré officers and even more so Russian attitudes on religious issues, primarily on the need to end the schism, were far from welcome; in October 1897 even Karavelov's *Zname* had dropped its insistence that the Bulgarian cause in the Balkans could be advanced only with the help of Russia. Relations with Austria were no better. Austria had refused any help over Macedonia and felt considerable resentment at the conversion of Prince Boris. This did not prevent the Viennese banks providing Bulgaria with loans but political relations were seldom cordial and there had been real tension in 1897 over the abduction and alleged murder of Anna Szimon, a Hungarian girl who was the mistress of one of Ferdinand's aides, Stoilov complaining bitterly and publicly when the Austrians demanded that the suspect aide be handed over to their consular court in accordance with the Capitulations.

One result of the cool relations between Vienna and Sofia was that Ferdinand was not allowed to pay an official visit to the Austrian capital. He satisfied his diplomatic *Wanderlust* by journeys to other cities, including Constantinople which he visited twice, Bucharest and Cetinje. In Rumania his visit helped to smooth over difficulties arising both from competing Bulgarian and Rumanian claims to the Danubian island of Eshek Adassi, and from Bulgarian allegations that Bulgarians living in the Dobrudja were being discriminated against by Rumanian officials. There were few political issues to be discussed with the Prince of Montenegro other than that of Macedonia and Ferdinand and his host found no differences of opinion over this. The Prince did not visit Greece. To have done so before 1897 would have offended the Turks for little possible gain, and after the war the Greeks were concentrating on rebuilding their relations with the Porte, an operation which would not allow conspicuous cooperation with the Bulgarians. In 1898 the two states were in some disagreement following the takeover by Bulgarian officials of Greek churches in Kavalkii (Topolovgrad) and Stanimaka.

With Serbia relations were much more complicated. The treaty of 1897 was the product less of a willingness to cooperate than of mutual distrust for with the Turco-Greek dispute about to flame into war neither side was prepared to let the other steal a march. With the collapse of the Greek army and the reinvigoration of the Turks the old rivalry between Bulgaria and Serbia in Macedonia was renewed. In September a Bulgarian teacher was murdered in Salonika and swift revenge was taken upon a Serb. Stoilov maintained that such incidents could not impair the Bulgaro-Serb entente and were the work of the Porte which wished to set the two Balkan states at each others' throats, but there could be no pretence of friendliness or entente over the question of Firmilian, a Serbian priest who in 1897 had been nominated as administrator to the archbishopric of Skopje, the key centre of northern Macedonia. The nomination of Firmilian, which was as yet unconfirmed by the Sultan, was made possible only because Russia withdrew its objections to the candidature, another reason for Bulgarian disappointment with Russian policy. Fierce anti-Serb demonstrations in Skopje itself and an equally fiery campaign in the Bulgarian press had followed the nomination of Firmilian for everyone knew that whichever faction dominated Skopje would be supreme in northern Macedonia. The following year saw no improvement. In Skopje the Bulgarian commercial agent, Naumov, was mistreated by a Serbian mob and the diplomatic heat which this incident generated was so intense that King Alexander threatened to withdraw his representative from Sofia. There were other minor irritants such as the disruption of a Bulgarian church service in Kumanovo by angry Serbs, and incorrect reports in the Bulgarian press that King Alexander had spoken publicly of seeking revenge for Slivnitsa. In 1889, shortly after Stoilov left office, a major wrangle developed over the church in Kumanovo. This church had been in dispute for a number of years and for some time had been closed to prevent disorders. In 1897 the Porte decided that the existing church rightfully belonged to the Exarchate but that the Serbs, operating within the Patriarchate of Constantinople, should be allowed to build a new church some of the costs of which the Exarchists were to meet by way of compensation. This the Exarchists refused to do and they also claimed that the land on which the new church was to be built belonged to and was of historic importance for the Bulgarian Church. So violent did the clashes become that some deaths occurred until the Turks finally insisted on the building of the new church, a settlement which left Kumanovo, like so many towns in the area, divided into Bulgarian and Serbian camps. And even when the Kumanovo dispute had died down there remained the issue of Firmilian and the Skopje see, an issue which was not to be settled for three years.

Chapter 13

INTERNAL POLITICS, 1896–9

The recognition of Ferdinand by the powers undoubtedly strengthened the regime of Stoilov. In by-electons held in March 1896 his candidates secured easy if not unassisted victories in most contests. The real indication of the new power of the administration was not in the seats it won but in its attitude to the major one it lost; in Sofia a government supporter had fallen some two hundred votes behind Tsankov but now that a reconciliation with Russia had been reached Tsankov's main political demand had been met without his playing any part and the government did not even bother to invent electoral irregularities to remove him from the Sŭbranie as it had in 1894.

With the settlement of the major foreign policy issues outside Macedonia Stoilov was free to continue his efforts to modernise Bulgaria. This process had already begun with the Encouragement of Industry Act passed in 1894, details of which will be given in a later chapter. Yet if Stoilov were to make Bulgaria 'The Belgium of the Balkans', as he frequently said was his intention, then he had to do more than encourage home manufacturers, and a good deal of his energy was therefore channelled into questions such as the modernisation of the banking system, tariff reforms, the securing of foreign loans and the promotion of capital projects such as railways and harbours. The settlement of the dispute with Russia and the consequent recognition of Ferdinand normalised Bulgaria's foreign relations and made it easier for Bulgaria to seek these loans and to enact changes in its tariffs, but in promoting railway development Stoilov was to face insuperable problems.

The focal point of the problem was Rumelia. Local pride had been dented in 1896 when Ferdinand was recognised as Governor-General

of Eastern Rumelia as well as Prince of Bulgaria, a wording which
reaffirmed southern Bulgaria's separate and more subjugated legal
status; further trouble came in the summer of the same year when
Stoilov's Unionist allies threatened to vote against government candidates in the forthcoming Plovdiv municipal elections because the city's
prefect, a government appointee, had refused to allow local Unionists
complete control of official appointments in the region. The Rumelians
also disliked the commercial agreement with Austria. Their trading
links were with the Mediterranean rather than with the Danube, and
the new agreement would allow more Austrian goods into the south
without any compensating stimulation of southern exports. The more
serious grievance, however, concerned the Oriental Railway Company,
the ORC.

The first concession to build a rail link through Turkish Europe
towards Vienna had been granted to a Belgian firm in 1868 but this
company soon found itself in difficulties and the concession passed to
Baron Hirsch. His original plan had been merely to construct the line
but in 1869–70, with the whole scheme in danger of collapse, he formed
a second company which was to operate the line for ninety-nine years.
This second company, the Companie Générale pour l'Exploitation des
Chemins de Fer en Turquie d'Europe, known in English as the Oriental
Railway Company, had its headquarters first in Paris and after 1879 in
Vienna, and it ran the trains on all the lines in European Turkey. By
the mid-1870s Hirsch's lines ran from Constantinople through what
was to become Eastern Rumelia as far as Bellovo with branches to
Dedeagach on the Aegean and from Türnovo-Seimen as far as Yambol, though this branch was originally intended to go as far as Burgas
on the Black Sea. During the upheavals of the mid-1870s Hirsch negotiated new terms for the ORC whose lease was now cut to fifty years;
the new agreement also confirmed that responsibility for completing
the construction of the remaining lines in European Turkey lay with
the Ottoman government. In 1878 Articles 10 and 38 of the treaty of
Berlin transferred this responsibility to the governments of the territories through which the lines would be laid. By 1885 the Serbs had
brought the line to the Bulgarian border at Tsaribrod, and the Bulgarians had continued it thence to the Rumelian frontier at Vakarel. The
difficult forty-six kilometres from Vakarel to the railhead at Bellovo
remained uncompleted until 1888 the Bulgarians having decided after
the union of 1885, to assert their sovereignty in Rumelia by completing

the line. On 21 July/2 August 1888 the first through train from Vienna to Constantinople reached Sofia.

For the Bulgarians this was the beginning rather than the end of the difficulties. Bellovo where the ORC operating rights ceased was unsuitable for an exchange point and this led to numerous arguments and frequent disruptions of traffic until early in 1894 when representatives of Bulgaria, Turkey and the ORC agreed that Bulgarian operational control should be extended a further nine kilometres from Bellovo to Sarambei where the necessary exchange-sidings, locomotive turning-points and so on were available. Yet this did not alter the fact that though most people might accept that Rumelia was an integral part of the Bulgarian Principality the railways of that area, so vital for economic and strategic reasons, were not under the control of the Bulgarian government but of a foreign company which had no responsibilities to Bulgaria or the Bulgarians. The ORC in fact had a monopoly over long-distance bulk transport in southern Bulgaria for the only alternative, the river Maritsa, was slow, shallow and, after the construction of the ORC's own bridges, virtually unnavigable. The ORC's monopoly was exercised directly contrary to Bulgaria's interests. Services on its lines were poor, and the regulations vexatious, but the most intense local resentment was directed against the Company's pricing policies. These could be eccentric; timber, for example, paid 15½ cents per ton per kilometre when carried from Sarambei to Bellovo, but 33 cents per ton per kilometre when travelling in the opposite direction. The ORC charged only 12 cents per ton per kilometre on imported rice but 23 cents for rice intended for export, a fact which seriously damaged governmental efforts to promote rice as an export commodity when its large-scale cultivation began again in the 1890s. Most important of all, however, was the fact that the Company's rates were always higher than those of other railway administrations involved in the trunk line, including BDZh whose charges were kept at the same level as those of the Austrian and Serbian railways. The price differentials were most acutely felt in the carriage of alcoholic products, for which the ORC charged 20 cents per ton per kilometre as opposed to the 6 cents levied by the other administrations, and in grain which the ORC carried at 7½ cents per ton per kilometre rather than 3 cents which was the standard rate elsewhere on the trunk line. This was a cruel disadvantage for the southern Bulgarian grain farmer, the price of whose produce was being artificially increased just when world prices were falling. The ORC also discriminated in favour of the port of Dedeagach where it had the concession to levy harbour dues. Thus the Company intrigued against the Yambol to Burgas line built by Stambulov for this could take goods directly from the ORC system to a port where the Company did not have harbour concessions; the ORC claimed that Article 10 of the treaty of Berlin gave it the right to veto any new line planned in southern Bulgaria and when construction of the Yambol to Burgas line did go ahead the ORC attempted to frustrate it by delaying carriage of rails and other materials from Dedeagach.

Until 1885 the Plovdiv regime, though deeply resentful of the Company's behaviour, was too weak to grapple with an opponent which had such powerful backing in Europe, though the Rumelian regime did plan to build a metre-gauge line from its capital to Burgas, this line falling victim to the political upheavals of 1885–7. Under Stambulov the Bulgarian government, though prepared to build the Vakarel to Bellovo section and the Yambol to Burgas line, did not dare to antagonise European, particularly Austrian, financiers by interfering directly with the ORC's policies on the lines already in existence. Stoilov's economic objectives and the composition of his coalition party, however, forced him to adopt more determined attitudes. His bill to encourage Bulgarian manufacturers had included a provision that the raw materials for and the products of manufacturers in designated areas should be carried at preferential rates on the state railways. These preferential rates could not be forced on the ORC but that could only mean that the industrialists of the south would be discriminated against in the race for development. This was extremely dangerous for a Minister President whose government and Sŭbranie support was based upon alliance with the Unionists of southern Bulgaria.

The Rumelians in the Cabinet put the Minister President under great pressure. For Stoilov there were three possible solutions. He might nationalise the ORC lines on Bulgarian territory, but this drastic action he could not afford as it would so antagonise European financial interests that Bulgaria would be cut off from essential sources of capital. The second option was to purchase the ORC's operating rights. This too was impossible. In 1889 Hirsch had sold his shares in the ORC to a consortium dominated by the Deutsche Bank and the Wiener Bankverein and by the second half of the 1890s German politicians and financiers were thinking seriously of the railway to the Persian Gulf and of the eventual domination by Germany of the line from Berlin to Baghdad. The leading bank involved in this enterprise was the Deutsche Bank which would therefore not contemplate alienating an important section of the railways which joined central Europe with Constantinople. The only remaining alternative was for the Bulgarian government to build a new line to by-pass the ORC tracks. This was the origin of the ill-fated parallel line. The basic plan was to construct a line from Sarambei parallel to the ORC's as far as Plovdiv whence it would swing northwards through Chirpan and Stara Zagora to Nova Zagora; from there another new line would link it to the Yambol to Burgas line, thus joining that line and the port with the remainder of the BDZh network. In August 1896 a reluctant Stoilov accepted this third solution, hoping thereby to save his Cabinet.

In this aim he was to be disappointed. Nachovich, who was already unhappy in the Cabinet for personal reasons, thought the decision to build the parallel line insane and resigned. Petrov the Minister of War was also insecure, though for very different reasons, his disagreements being with the Prince over the émigré question and over their attitudes towards each others' wives. It seemed that Stoilov's present administration could not last. The Minister President therefore persuaded Ferdinand to dissolve the Sŭbranie and call new elections in the autumn, Stoilov arguing that the political situation in the country had been altered by the recognition of Ferdinand and that the electorate should be allowed to register its reaction to such a momentous event.

As soon as it was clear that his concessions to the Rumelians on the parallel railway were not going to preserve his government Stoilov attempted to escape from the commitment, asking the ORC on what terms it would be willing to sell its operating rights in Bulgaria. No acceptable answer was forthcoming and thus the parallel line remained on the government's programme and was confirmed by the Assembly in February 1897. At least it guaranteed the support of most of the Rumelian deputies in the new Assembly who together with eighty of his own supporters and thirteen Moslems gave the Minister President a comfortable majority.

Despite its comfortable majority, Stoilov's government never achieved the stability it desired, or which its majority indicated it could reasonably expect. Early in 1897 it was criticised for its failure to take sufficient advantage of the Cretan episode to secure wide-ranging concessions in Macedonia, and there were also rumours of too many concessions to the Serbs in the February agreement, the existence but not the precise content of which was general knowledge. Even the granting of the three *berats* in the spring did not still all critics and in April there were protest meetings in the capital. Students had been

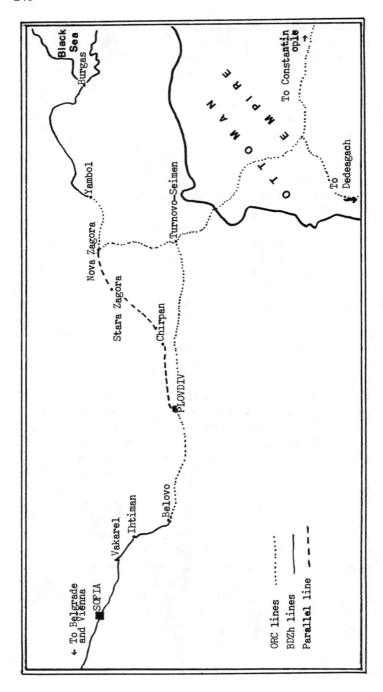

THE PARALLEL RAILWAY SCHEME

prominent in the meetings over Macedonia but in May Sofia had its first taste of university unrest when classes were boycotted and demonstrations staged following the murder of Aleko Konstantinov.

Later in the same year Stoilov found his Cabinet once more in danger of disintegration. The Minister of Finance, Geshov, had been made the executor of the large fortune bequeathed to the Bulgarian nation by Evlogi Georgiev, a participant in the cultural revival and a wealthy merchant resident in Bucharest. Geshov considered the administration of these funds incompatible with his government post and resigned. As a southerner Geshov had to be replaced by someone from the south but Stoilov's choice, Markov, the Bulgarian agent in Constantinople, was rejected as being too anti-Russian for he had acted as a prosecutor in the trial of those involved in the Ruse rising of 1887. In the end Stoilov had to move Todorov from the Ministry of Justice to that of Finance; he also added lustre to his administration by persuading the poet, Ivan Vazov, to become Minister of Education, but despite this success he could only complete his team by making the General Secretary of the Ministry of Justice the minister of that department. Both this appointment and that of Vazov showed that Stoilov could no longer persuade established politicians to join his ministry. The ship was not yet sinking but the rats were no longer willing to come aboard.

Encouraged by the difficulties Stoilov experienced in forming his Cabinet after the departure of Geshov the opposition became more active. The anniversary of the union of 1885 saw large demonstrations which ended with the laying of a wreath near the memorial chapel to Alexander Battenberg and with the sending of a telegram to his widow. More serious from the government's point of view was the fierce attack launched in the Sŭbranie when it met in October. The chief cause for complaint was the lack of success in foreign policy. The Prince, it was pointed out, had not been officially received in Vienna, relations with Russia were poor because of the émigré question, whilst the much-talked of entente with Serbia was a joke; even relations with Rumania were strained because of the Bucharest government's treatment of the Bulgarians in the Dobrudja. There were also awkward questions for Stoilov on Macedonia. These he could field because the *berats* granted earlier in the year were about to be implemented but later in the session the Assembly was disturbed by reports of increased repression following the Vinitsa incident. An additional cause for anxiety for Stoilov was the Prince's flirtation with the Stambulovists in the autumn of 1897. Ferdinand praised their dead leader as the man who had put him and kept him on his throne, and even admitted that had he been alive Stambulov would have been back at the helm, though Ferdinand did urge the Stambulovist Party to prove their ability and fitness to rule by controlling Petkov, the firebrand editor of their newspaper.

The early months of 1898 saw little improvement. Stoilov, never in robust health, was ill and spent a good deal of his time taking the cure at Karlsbad, where he was also in touch with representatives of various financial houses. Such contacts were secret and at home dissatisfaction mounted. In August Tsankov, though he had resigned the leadership of his Party, now known as the Progressive Liberals, invited opposition political chiefs to a conference. Radoslavov and even Nachovich sent representatives whilst Karavelov and Petkov attended personally. All agreed on the need to establish a common front against a regime which had promised free elections but which exercised, they said, tyranny over the land. Stoilov made some response to this, allowing some relaxation of government control, this time in the form of a bill intending to make electoral contests more open.

Such gestures had little effect because the basic problem affecting the country and exciting the opposition was not constitutional but financial. The *fons et origo malorum* was the parallel line.

The government had never imagined that internal sources of revenue could cover the costs of the new line; the other capital projects undertaken since 1894 would have ruled that out and whilst government expenditure grew its revenue had not increased as rapidly; in 1894, as part of the modernisation programme, a land tax had replaced the tithe and this had brought about a fall in income from the land whilst a fall in customs revenue followed from new tariff agreements and from those clauses of the Encouragement of Industry Bill which allowed manufacturers of sponsored items to import their raw materials free of duty. In 1896 the government had borrowed ten million francs from the Agricultural Savings Bank to begin work on the parallel line but this was by no means enough for the entire project. Early in 1897 Geshov, whilst he was still at the Ministry of Finance, had announced that the government would like to take out the remaining part of a loan granted in 1892, and was prepared to allocate the revenue from the parallel line and the other lines then under construction for the payment of interest on this second part of the loan. The banking consortium refused. This was partly because the Deutsche Bank was involved and was disturbed by the government's attempt to weaken the ORC, but also because the Bulgarian government had in 1896 suspended payments to the Ottoman Public Debt Administration. This had been done in retaliation against the Porte's failure to hand over monies due to Bulgaria under the Ruse-Varna railway agreement of 1887 but the Ottoman Public Debt Administration was a powerful body and it ensured that Bulgaria was denied access to the European money markets. Stoilov was forced therefore to swallow his pride and resume payments to the Debt Administration. This was seized upon by the opposition as a humiliation for Bulgaria.

Throughout 1898 Stoilov, in Karlsbad and back in Sofia, was searching for additional finance to meet the mounting costs of the parallel line. There was little capital available in Europe because of international tension, especially in South Africa, and because much of what was available was already being absorbed into the great Baghdad railway project. Nevertheless in December 1898 a Franco-Austro-German consortium agreed to lend the Bulgarian government 290 million francs. The first charge on the loan was to be the conversion of the existing 1888, 1889 and 1892 loans from six percent to five percent, and this was to absorb all but fifty-two million francs. The sensational part of the agreement, however, was that which stated that twenty-five million of this residue was to be spent on purchasing the ORC's operating rights in southern Bulgaria, together with its rolling-stock, locomotives and equipment. The remaining money was to finance other railways but these did not include the parallel line. The deal was not a good one for Bulgaria. The previous loans, before conversion to five percent, were to be paid back at nominal value although the government had received only the emission value, twelve and a half or fifteen percent below the nominal value, and only a small proportion of the loan-period had expired. The government also had to assume all the ORC's obligations towards Turkey, to retain present tariffs, and to keep existing staff for at least a year without changing their conditions of service. The line itself was to remain the property of the Turkish government and in addition to handing over twenty-five million francs to the ORC the Bulgarians would have to pay an annual rent to the Porte of at least 1,500 francs per kilometre. The only concession to the Stoilov regime was that the ORC agreed to pay 400,000 francs as compensation for the work already completed on the parallel line.

When the Sŭbranie had opened in the autumn of 1898 the government had been anxious to stress the health of the nation's finances. Agricultural production had risen and was worth four and a half million leva more than in the corresponding period in 1897; a comfortable

surplus on next year's budget was, as usual, forecast, and the national
debt at one hundred and seventy-five million leva was, said the
government, respectable for a state of four million people. Yet despite
these assertions of faith in the nation's financial well-being the Sŭbranie was in December faced with a proposed loan which belied all
such statements and which was deeply injurious to national prestige
and pride. Even the public was shocked; when the two-day debate
began on 7/19 December the galleries of the Sŭbranie were packed and
there were large crowds outside still hoping to find a place, a most
unusual occurrence in Bulgarian political life. The debate was predictably stormy and ended with a five-hour speech from Todorov who
tried to persuade the deputies that nationalisation of the ORC lines
had been impossible and that twenty-five million francs was not a high
price to pay for the operating rights. In the uproar that followed the
government insisted that the Bill had been given a majority, but, as in
the debate over the Ruse-Varna railway agreement in 1883, this was
disputed by many of those present.

The dubious passing of the Bill only increased opposition and public
dissatisfaction. A furious attack was launched against the Minister for
Trade and Agriculture, Velichkov, whose brief included railways. He
knew nothing of finance and in the face of embarrassing accusations of
corruption resigned. The allegations of corruption were then directed
at other members of the Cabinet and at the Court. Public meetings
were held throughout the country, some four hundred in all, and one in
Sofia attracted over eight hundred people, a large number for a political meeting which did not concern Macedonia. A Sŭbranie petition
against the proposed loan and the purchase of the ORC rights was
signed by over fifty deputies which meant that a number of government supporters had joined the opposition on this issue. In fact Stoilov
was almost bereft of support in the Assembly where he could count
only on ministers, placemen, holders of government contracts, and
Moslems; it was not an impressive or a morally convincing force.
Above all Stoilov's fate reflected national anger that a government
which had come to office dedicated to the modernisation of Bulgaria
and to the assertion of its independence had subjected it to humiliation.

Ferdinand decided that Stoilov could not survive. The Prince therefore delayed giving his consent to the unpopular loan agreement and
underlined his dissociation from the government by failing to appear
in person for the closing ceremony at the end of the Sŭbranie session;
Ferdinand feared that his appearing in public might spark off popular

demonstrations but his absence was also intended to mark his disapproval of the government's conduct. Stoilov retaliated by failing to attend the Prince's New Year's Day reception, a significant insult to a Prince who demanded punctilious observation of Court ritual. The final blow to the incapacitated Cabinet came when the Sultan, bending to German diplomatic pressure, refused to sanction the loan agreement by which the ORC and therefore the Deutsche Bank would have lost control over the southern Bulgarian railways. The parallel line and the humiliating loan agreement which it occasioned had been unnecessary. The government's strategy was totally discredited and Todorov the Minister of Finance resigned immediately. Stoilov wished to do the same but this gave rise to one final argument with the Prince who did not want the Cabinet to leave office whilst the Court was preoccupied with the illness of Princess Marie Louise. Stoilov, however, refused to be swayed and despite the Prince's insistence that ministers came and went when he decided not when they wished, the Minister President resigned on 13/25 January 1899.

* * *

Stoilov had set out to modernise Bulgaria but for two years his freedom of action had been restrained by the fact that he was shackled to the Stambulovist inheritance. To shake off this he needed to repair the breach with Russia and dismantle the domestic machinery of repression established by his predecessor. In the first case he clearly had some success with the final recognition of Ferdinand by the Tsar in 1896, and this had allowed Stoilov to go ahead with tariff and loan negotiations and the other external aspects of his modernisation programme. Yet the reconciliation with Russia had not been, as some Bulgarians had fondly hoped, the magic solution to Bulgaria's problems, and it did little for the sacred cause of Macedonia.

Stoilov, of course, had not been one of those who had had exaggerated expectations of what Russia could do for Bulgaria, but he did benefit from the reconciliation in that the intense Russophilia of previous years was now politically discredited. That, however, only increased the pressure on him to rid himself of that other part of the Stambulovist legacy, the domestic repression and terror which Stambulov had used. There was considerable relaxation in the Sŭbranie where the government was subjected to attacks which Stambulov would never have tolerated. Outside parliamentary politics there was more oppositional activity, particularly amongst those holding extreme opinions. Again the Stoilov regime was generally more tolerant than its predecessor. Socialist journals such as *Borba* (Struggle) in Plovdiv, *Progress* in Tatar Pazardjik and *Rabotnik* in Tŭrnovo and then Sofia, had appeared albeit irregularly in the last days of the *Stambulovshtina* and continued to do so afterwards, and four socialist deputies were elected to the Sŭbranie in 1894. By the end of Stoilov's premiership even anti-dynastic ideas were appearing in print and were gaining currency. In 1898 there were sharp attacks on Ferdinand and these were not always from republicans for some were accompanied by efforts to popularise the young Count Hartenau, the son of Alexander Battenberg. There were also more direct, republican attacks, one of which in November 1898 was published under the title 'An Appeal to the Bulgarian People' and accused the Prince of filling his pockets with eighty million francs from the state coffers. But though these excesses were permitted the government still exercised considerable control over elections to the Sŭbranie and to local government bodies. If Stambulov had denied the Bulgarians the heady wine of freedom Stoilov only whetted their appetites with half a glass. Other complaints centred on the conduct of local officials who were not restrained by the central government as they had been in the days of Stambulov. Stoilov pleaded ignorance, saying he could not be expected to know what was going on everywhere in Bulgaria, a remark which contrasted sharply with Stambulov's boast that a bee could not leave Varna without his knowing of it.

If the old problem of relations with Russia had been resolved and that of internal repression relieved new ones had appeared. From 1894 onwards the Macedonian movement had rapidly built up a head of steam which could not be kept long confined. The government knew that it could do little in Macedonia now Austrian or Russian backing was unobtainable, though the Turks, secure of German support, could increase their repressive measures against the Macedonian malcontents. In Bulgaria itself the Macedonians were demanding action but without European help this was impossible. In that problem lay great danger. The Stoilov government had also experienced the problems involved in sponsored modernisation for their contact with the European capital markets and financial interests over the parallel line and the ORC had shown that money could be obtained only with difficulty and at a price that was likely to cause political tension as well as economic strain. The years following recognition had also shown some of the dangers which flowed from the new power which the Prince was accumulating. For some Bulgarians his control of foreign policy, which was clearly asserted after recognition, had pushed the country too far down a dangerous pro-Russian slope, particularly in the way in which Bulgaria had reinstated army officers who had broken with their oaths and plotted against their Prince. In domestic politics the Prince had not yet chosen to use his latent power to destabilise a ministry but what had become quite clear by 1899 was that Bulgaria was in the depths of a financial crisis of great severity.

The financial crisis and the question of Macedonia were to dominate Bulgarian politics for the next four years.

Chapter 14

THE CRISIS OF 1899–1903
I. MONEY

To succeed Stoilov in January 1899 Ferdinand appointed Dimitŭr Grekov. He had played an important caretaking role during the transition from Stambulov to Stoilov and in February 1896 had become leader of the National Liberal or Stambulovist Party. This post he had relinquished in March 1897, ostensibly for family and business reasons, but in reality because he could not feel comfortable with Petkov, the editor of the party newspaper. Though nominally an independent Grekov remained close to the more restrained members of the National Liberal Party but they would not join in his government which consisted of three further independents, the Conservative Nachovich and three Liberals, Radoslavov, Peshev and Tonchev. The latter were the most powerful section of the Cabinet with Radoslavov as Minister of the Interior having control of patronage.

The new Cabinet's programme contained no surprises. As with most incoming governments it pledged itself to uphold and protect the constitution, to increase administrative efficiency and honesty, and to curb official spending. Again as with most incoming governments its first task was to organise support for itself. The Sŭbranie was dissolved and elections held in May. Both the Prince and the independent members of the Cabinet were sensitive to public pressure and demanded that there be less official interference with the voting than had occurred in the past and this insistence together with certain minor electoral reforms enacted by Stoilov did allow more freedom in the poll. This was seen most dramatically in the return of no less than fifty-two opposition deputies, a result also encouraged by the fact that the Tsankovists, the Unionists, and Stoilov's Nationalists had agreed not to oppose each other but to vote for an agreed anti-government candidate in most constituencies.

With a more open election the campaign was even more intense and personal than usual; it was also violent. Five people were killed and twenty wounded on the election days and voting had to be postponed in five constituencies because of the violence; so fierce were the Radoslavists during this campaign that they earned themselves the nickname, *Cherkezite* (Circassians). Once the Sŭbranie had come together the opposition replied in verbal kind. Governmental policy in Macedonia was attacked for having secured nothing but *Berati i Attentati* (*berats* and outrages) whereas many deputies were hoping for real reforms or even more dramatic action to save the Macedonians from Turkish repression. One Liberal, and therefore in theory a government supporter, attacked the Cabinet because it had come to power, he said, unconstitutionally in that it had been nominated by the Prince and not the Assembly, a nostalgic echo of the debates of the late 1870s and early 1880s. A Socialist deputy even complained that too much money had been spent on the funeral of Princess Marie Louise, who had died a few days after Stoilov's resignation.

The major attack on the Grekov government, however, was to come on the interrelated questions of the ORC and finance. Government negotiators had agreed terms with the ORC at a conference in Vienna in March. It was a total victory for the Company. The Company was to retain its operating rights in southern Bulgaria and the government undertook during the next twenty-five years not to begin work on any line which might compete with the Company's or which would run within forty kilometres of ORC track; this gave the Company complete domination over railway development in the area. For the same period the ORC was to rent that part of the parallel line already built and was also to rent other BDZh lines in southern Bulgaria, a clear contradiction of the Railway Act of 1884. The settlement also gave the Company exemption from Bulgarian stamp duty and other taxes both local and national; this liberty the Company interpreted as licence and did not even bother to pay full rent on the properties and land which it used but did not own. In the years up to the take-over of the ORC by the state in 1908 the Company's estimated income from southern Bulgaria was a tax-free 1,800,000 leva per annum. The Company also retained complete autonomy in pricing policies and it therefore continued to discriminate in favour of Dedeagach and by 1908 carriage rates on the branch to that port were seventy percent lower than on the line to Burgas. Even in wartime the ORC was not required to provide extra services or equipment for the state and could even claim compensation from the government for losses incurred as a result of war; and still the Company declined to recognise Bulgarian as an official language in its administration. Should the Bulgarian government fail to fulfil its side of the March 1899 agreement the Company could claim compensation from the revenues of BDZh and in extreme circumstances had the right to take over the running of lines in the north of the country. The only concessions granted to the Bulgarians were that the Company would in future abide by the Encouragement of Industry Act and charge lower rates for sponsored raw materials and products; its general rate was at the same time slightly reduced. The Company also agreed to set up a new administrative division centred upon Plovdiv in addition to its three existing traffic zones based on Constantinople, Adrianople and Salonika.

Two weeks after the signature of the railway treaty came a loan agreement by which a consortium of Viennese banks agreed to lend the Bulgarian government two hundred and sixty million francs at five percent with an emission value of 89.5%. Like the abortive loan of 1898 the new one was to convert the 1888, 1889 and 1892 loans to five percent, and the Bulgarians were obliged not to take out further loans from other banks for five years.

The opposition to these agreements was predictably intense. In *Ikonomicheski Pregled* (Economic Review) the respected, non-party Bobchev argued that the agreements because of the interference which foreign interests could now exercise in Bulgaria's internal affairs, marked '. . . the beginning of the end of the state as an independent entity'.[1] In June the Sŭbranie, after some delay, was asked to approve the agreements. It did so by seventy-seven votes to forty-nine but only after withering criticism of the government. M. Sarafov denounced the agreements by which national wealth was given away not to foreign governments but to a foreign company; Shipkov declared the nation had been reduced to an economic enslavement equal to that of Greece, Turkey or Egypt.

Grekov had few successes to put against this unavoidable humiliation. Early in the year he had made approaches unofficially to Russia to see whether there was any prospect of support there for an insurrection in Macedonia; there was not. In the face of this Grekov had to tell the nation that the Macedonian question could only be solved by the great powers and in the meantime the Bulgarians could best occupy themselves by securing good relations with the Porte in the hope that this might bring forth concessions. His sole consolations were the eventual settlement of the dispute over the church in Kumanovo and his successful blocking of a *berat* for Firmilian in Skopje.

The government was in an extremely weak position. The conversion loan had done little to help in the long run for more money was needed for capital projects, for the army and, in the not too distant future, for the servicing of the loan itself. The Cabinet was also divided. The coalition between the independents, the basically Stambulovist Grekov, and the Radoslavists had never worked, more especially as the Stambulovists and Radoslavists in the country and the Sŭbranie could not cooperate. The two factions had come to blows in Vratsa when trying to agree upon a joint candidate in the May election, and when preparations were being made for the supplementary elections in September the Stambulovist Party organisation told its provincial offices not to cooperate with the Liberals, their complaint being Radoslavov's return to government interference in the campaign. Radoslavov did in the end agree to back down and ordered Ministry of the Interior officials to give equal support to Radoslavist and Stambulovist candidates but it was too late and in the supplementary poll success went to one Stambulovist, one Tsankovist and thirty-one Radoslavists. At the beginning of October Grekov resigned after he had failed to rebuild his Cabinet and Ferdinand had refused to dissolve the recently-elected Assembly.

The new Minister President was Ivanchov who moved up from the Ministry of Education. He had no particular party affiliation but the continuation in office of Radoslavov and his Liberal colleagues gave the Cabinet support in the Assembly. The change of premier did nothing to ease the financial problems which had beset the state ever since Stoilov decided to build the parallel railway. The government needed a loan and whilst terms for a large one were still considered too harsh the administration agreed to borrow twenty-five million francs from a Franco-Viennese consortium and this went a considerable way to meet the immediate problem of a budget deficit of some 26,300,000 leva. There was a significant condition attached to the loan for as a guarantee of interest payments the government had to pledge the revenue from the banderolle, a tax on processed tobacco, for the years 1901 to 1904, and this was 'the first time that part of the national income had been specifically earmarked for the repayment of a loan.'[2]

The domination of the consortium by the Banque de Paris et des Pays Bas (Pariba) also delineated the beginning of the French dominance of Bulgarian finances which was to last almost a decade.

The small loan covered only immediate needs and the capital costs of railway and harbour developments, together with a desire to spend even more on the army, meant that a large loan had to be found. Capital was still scarce and the administration in Sofia had to be prepared to make concessions to foreign investors and their governments. Thus the Ivanchov Cabinet, knowing that Paris was the only possible source of money, agreed to drop charges pending against Gailloux, a French financier resident in Bulgaria, a sacrifice of national sovereignty which the Grekov government had refused to contemplate. Still there was no positive response from Paris and the Bulgarians therefore turned to France's ally, Russia. On the personal initiative of Ferdinand it was arranged that a Russian financial expert, Kobeko, should visit the Principality to inspect its books and assess its economic prospects.

Kobeko was not entirely dismissive but Russia was in no position to lend Bulgaria the sums which the latter needed. Paris remained the only source of capital available but before a serious attempt to raise a large loan could be undertaken the government in Sofia sought first to find further sources of internal revenue, for this would both improve the country's credit-worthiness and, it was hoped, do away with the humiliating need to commit specific revenues, such as the banderolle, to the service of a loan. This search for extra internal revenue precipitated the worst domestic crisis since the Liberation, for, unlike those of 1881–3 and 1886–7, it involved a large proportion of the population rather than the politically conscious minority, and on occasions it assumed the form of a struggle against the whole political system rather than simply one for the control of that system.

In looking for extra internal revenue there were a number of steps the government could take without antagonising the populace. No-one objected when Ferdinand agreed to forgo half his civil list for the year 1900, nor did anyone but those directly involved complain when it was announced that officers' and officials' pay would be reduced by seven percent in January 1900, with some of them receiving back-pay from September 1899 in the form of treasury bonds redeemable two years hence. Nor was there reaction against the decision to decrease the military budget by one and a half million leva in 1900, despite increases in spending on the army in Serbia and Rumania. The government's decision to allow the exchange of gold and silver coins so that the gold could be deposited in the state treasury also caused little popular comment. Yet these were small measures and a significant increase in revenue was necessary if the commitment to monopolies and the tying of specific revenues to loan servicing were to be avoided. The government could not hope to raise more money by increasing customs dues for this would infringe the treaty of Berlin and gainsay the provisions of the Encouragement of Industry Act of 1894; industry and commerce were not developed enough to be seen as sources of income, for they were recipients rather than providers of funds; as during the *Stambulovshtina* only the land remained.

Like most Bulgarian Cabinets that which sought electoral confirmation in 1899 had promised to reduce taxation. Few people took this seriously but what did shock the nation was a government announcement on 29 October/10 November that for the five years 1900 to 1904 the land tax introduced in 1894 would be replaced by a tithe in kind on arable land; vineyards and meadows would continue to pay the land tax. For the government a tax which was collected in kind and then sold for cash had obvious monetary attractions and these were enhanced early in 1900 when reports indicated that frost had delayed the winter sowing of wheat in Hungary and Rumania, thus incapacitating Bulgaria's competitors and increasing the price of wheat on the European exchanges. The government also argued that the tithe was a more equitable form of taxation in that payment varied directly with the quantity and quality of production rather than with the amount of land owned. This, the government continued, would allow the peasant to liberate himself from the money-lender and this, said official spokesmen, was why the money-lenders and their allies, 'Socialists, opposition politicians and other self-seeking riff-raff', were so prominent in the agitation against the tithe.

The government's arguments were grotesque and a travesty of the real state of the nation. By the late 1890s the Bulgarian countryside was heading for a major crisis, and so bad were conditions becoming that the phrase *ot tursko po losho* (things are worse than under the Turks) had wide popular currency. A series of bad harvests was one cause of the crisis. Taking 1912 as 100, the index of agricultural production was only 86 in 1897 and though 1898 was a good year with an index of 105 this only made good some of the previous year's damage, and it could not cushion the peasants against the tragedy of the following year, 1899, when spring and summer droughts drove the production-index down to 64. So severe was the crisis that the central administration of the Agricultural Savings Bank provided relief, most of it by distributing grain, to more than 60,000 families. In addition to the vagaries of the climate and the harvest the peasant had also to contend with the ravages of phylloxera and rinderpest.

Whilst these factors depressed peasants' incomes others forced up costs. The major problem was indebtedness. This had become widespread in the post-Liberation land sales and had been intensified by high interest rates, by the widespread practice of *zelencharstvo,* and by peasants borrowing to pay mounting taxes and redemption dues. By the late 1890s there was a 'morass of debt'.[3] In 1897 the Agricultural Savings Bank estimated the total at forty-five million leva and in November that year an alarmist article in *Bŭlgarski Pregled* (Bulgarian Review) warned of the dangers facing the nation's smaller producers, but by this stage little that was effective could be done. By 1901 301 villages were listed as being completely ruined by debt and in the hands of the usurers, whilst a further 470 were all but ruined. Individual examples show the extent of the tragedy. In Trustenik, a large rural community of which more will be heard in due course, 3,800 souls in 400 households worked 58,600 dekars of land but in 1899 owed in all 298,250 leva, 45,250 leva to the Agricultural Savings Bank, 43,000 leva to other banks, but 210,000 leva to private money lenders. In the previous year the Agricultural Savings Bank had cited the case of twenty-seven people in various villages who had borrowed 8,049 leva with average repayment periods of five to five and a half years, but at the end of that period the debt totalled 21,174 leva, 10,302 leva of which was still unpaid.

Taxation also had a role in forcing up peasants' costs. By 1897 average taxation per capita for the Bulgarian peasant was 29.52 leva per annum, compared with 15.31 leva in 1887; the average level per household by 1897 had reached 153.5 leva which, the Socialist deputy Gabrovski told the Sŭbranie, was six times higher than in Russia and four times greater than in France. The increase in the peasant tax burden was in large measure due to a change of fiscal strategy in the mid-1890s when the Nationalist government moved towards greater concentration upon indirect taxation. In 1894 forty-two million leva had been raised by direct taxation and twenty-two million by indirect; in 1895, with increases in the excise on thirty articles including petrol, sugar, matches, olive-oil, coffee, tea and dried fish, indirect taxation contributed thirty-five million leva as opposed to the thirty-six million leva raised by direct taxes. Since the Liberation the change had been dramatic for in 1879 the total tax revenue had been divided 81:19 between direct and indirect taxes; in 1900 the division was 63:37. For the peasant whose cash income was relatively low these taxes, many of them on necessities, were crippling. To add to the peasants' sense of woe the tax system was irrational and discriminated strongly against those on the land. In 1901 it was calculated that a man who derived an income of 5,400 leva per annum from property and capital would pay 180 leva per annum in taxes, yet if he turned his capital into sheep and paid the *beglik* or sheep tax at fifty stotinki per head his annual tax bill would be 2,700 leva. Similarly a man whose income of 5,400 leva per annum was derived from the exercise of one of the professions would pay taxes to the sum of 162 leva per year, yet if he were to possess land to the value of his annual professional income his contribution to the state treasury would then be 2,565 leva per annum.

Their disproportionate share of the tax burden intensified the peasants' already existing consciousness of the disparities between life in the countryside and in the towns, and this consciousness was a further cause of the alienation of the peasants from the state at the turn of the century. These disparities were glaring. The villages had only elementary schools and many of these were in buildings unfit for use. There were no night schools for adults, nor were there facilities such as crèches, kindergartens and baths which were available in a number of towns, and roads and postal services were poor. Public health services were virtually non-existent; in 1901 Bulgaria had 504 doctors and 102 pharmacies with only twelve of the former having rural practices whilst of the pharmacies only two were in non-urban communities and these were seasonal ones in the spa resorts of Vŭrshets and Hissar.

For some peasants the only escape from the impact of rising costs and declining income had been dispossession, many selling their land to the usurer and themselves becoming agricultural labourers, sharecroppers or perhaps migrants to the towns. Some of that dispossession which took place was temporary as peasants were able to redeem their lands in better times, whilst others sold off part of their property and, though becoming agricultural labourers or share-croppers, still retained some land. These factors, together with the continuing availability of Moslem émigrés' land, has inflated some statistics concerning permanent agricultural impoverishment and dispossession in Bulgaria.

What cannot be exaggerated is the deep anger felt in the countryside at the worsening conditions and it was this deep anger which fuelled the disorders of 1900 and which in the long-term nourished Bulgaria's most individual contribution to modern European history, the Bulgarian Agrarian National Union.

The spark which ignited the resentment of the peasants was the announcement of October 1899 on the tithe. For the last three years, when the harvests had with one exception been poor, the government had exacted a fixed sum by way of the land tax and now when an improvement was generally expected the authorities were switching to the flexible tithe which offered it more than the old fixed rates of the land tax. To the peasant it seemed that the politicians would impose whatever tax was likely to yield more for the state. The disadvantages of the tithe for the peasant have already been described and were felt just as much at the turn of the century as they had been in earlier years. There was further resentment because the delays which were inevitable in assessing the tithe meant that Bulgarian grain was late coming onto the market thus missing the higher prices which the early season usually offered and so frittering away an advantage southerly Bulgaria enjoyed over competitors such as Hungary and Rumania. Peasant incomes fell as a result. The tithe also reintroduced into the grain market the government officials who would be required to assess and collect the levy, and greater involvement of officialdom meant for the peasant yet more corruption and exploitation.

The reversion to the tithe was in stark contrast to the ideas of economic modernisation which Geshov and the Stoilov administration had been anxious to promote and which Grekov had not repudiated. It also provided ideal material for the emerging Agrarian movement. This movement, which will be discussed in some detail in a subsequent chapter, was the product of the decline in agrarian living conditions in the 1890s and of the failure of successive governments to address themselves to this question. The centre of the movement was in the northeast of the country and by 1899 it was organised enough to call a congress of interested bodies in Pleven. It also had an important mouthpiece in *Zemedelska Zashtita* (Agrarian Defence), a newspaper which began publication under the able editor Yanko Zabunov on 6/18 September 1899.

The emerging Agrarian movement naturally played a considerable part in the organising of peasant discontent over the tithe, though frequently that part was one of moderation rather than provocation. Peasant reaction went through three distinct phases. In the first, which lasted from the announcement of October 1899 until confirmation of the new arrangements by the Sŭbranie in January 1900, it concentrated upon legal opposition with meetings and pamphlets trying to persuade the members of the Assembly not to accept so unpopular a piece of legislation. Meetings took place in some 184 villages and forty towns, involving over 350,000 participants from over five hundred communities. These meetings voiced a number of demands but all of them united in the call for the disbandment of the tithe programme, many wanting a complete overhaul of the tax system and the introduction of a progressive income tax. Of the many pamphlets which attacked the government's policy the most famous and influential was *Must the Peasants Pay the Tithe?* by Dimitŭr Dragiev, a leading figure in the Agrarian movement. At the end of this first phase, in December 1899, the Agrarians held their first congress in Pleven. This established the Bulgarian Agrarian National Union (BANU) which committed itself to an evolutionary programme and dissociated itself from party politics, though its general call for an improvement in the lot of the peasants was accompanied by the specific demand for the abolition of the tithe. This greatly encouraged the movement against the levy. With the acceptance of the tithe by the Sŭbranie on 16/28 January 1900 the agitation switched to concentration on an attempt to persuade the Prince not to sanction the Bill. Again huge meetings took place, many of them with over 10,000 participants and one in Tŭrnovo attracting a crowd estimated at over 20,000; even allowing for partisan exaggeration the figures were incomparably larger than those for any meetings yet held in the Principality. From these meetings came delegations and petitions to Ferdinand until on 3/16 March he announced that he would receive no more and could not understand why there should be so much unreasonableness over an issue on which the Sŭbranie had already decided. With that the agitation moved into its third and most violent phase. Initially the peasants staged passive resistance, refusing all cooperation with the officials who had been required to make a preliminary inventory of property in the villages. BANU urged the peasants to stick to legal means and to demand the end of the tithe and then the dissolution of Ferdinand's personal government. The authorities soon provoked violence, the first clashes occurring in Varna on 5/18 March when police ejected people from hotels where they were lodging prior to a large protest meeting. On 20 April/3 May came the first serious confrontation. In Trŭstenik the authorities had attempted to depose the mayor who sympathised with the peasants but this the villagers had prevented. Two companies of troops were sent to the

village and twelve people died in the fighting which followed; significantly a number of troops had to be court-martialled for refusing to
fire on the crowd. Martial law was then declared in the Tŭrnovo,
Gorna Oryahovitsa and Svishtov districts and the government also
invoked Article 47 of the constitution—that which allowed emergency
action when the Sŭbranie was not in session—to tighten the press laws
and place other restrictions on personal liberty. On 19 May/1 June a
much more serious clash took place in the village of Daran Kulak in
the Bulgarian Dobrudja. Between a hundred and a hundred and fifty
people died and over eight hundred were wounded, including two
officers and a number of soldiers. BANU now attempted to channel
the discontent into public meetings to be held on 11/24 June and 29
June/12 July. These meetings were to demand the abolition of the tithe
and repeat the calls for the dismissal of the present ministers and the
formation of a provisional government of professors and judges which
would guarantee free elections; if these concessions were not forthcoming, BANU's Central Committee warned, 'the Agricultural Union is
ready to go to extremes in the struggle against a regime imposed from
above and for the achievement of popular sovereignty'.[4]

The meetings called for June and July were in fact meant to control
rather than propagate popular anger and they were less well attended
than many held earlier in the year. The high point of the agitation had
passed and the peasants were concentrating now upon the harvest
which, though not as disastrous as that of 1899, was still below expectations. The peasants had never had the strength to defeat the government, and their leaders were inexperienced and wisely cautious, not
wishing to endanger the existence of the Agrarian movement at the
moment of its birth. For their part the authorities had acted swiftly and
toughly and, given the loyalty of the army, would always be in a
position to defeat the peasants.

The agitation had nevertheless been a shock to the political establishment. The government publicly wrote it off as the work of professional trouble-makers, and insisted that the fact that the agitation was
strongest in those areas where the Agrarian movement was most developed, primarily the north-east, was proof of this contention. This
was untrue. There were also many meetings in the south and if they
were not as large or as vociferous as those in the north this was because
in the south there was much more unused land and the peasants there
did not suffer so much from the tithe as did those in the north where a
much higher proportion of the land was used. Stoilov wryly gave the

lie to the government argument when he noted that if the movement had been the product of agitators the authorities with their developed spy network would have known much more about it and would have been able to nip it in the bud.

The political results of the agitation were predictable. In the summer the Sŭbranie's opposition Parties came together after a conference attended by Stoilov, Grekov, Karavelov, and Danev, who had succeeded Tsankov as leader of the Progressive Liberals. The investigations into the causes of the disorders revealed discomforting if unsurprising evidence on the inadequacies of local officials, most of whom owed their positions to *partisanstvo*. Ferdinand emerged from the crisis even more unpopular than before. It concerned him little that his stock with the peasants had fallen but what was worrying for him was the appearance of discontent in the army. The officer corps was still disgruntled by the salary cuts and to this injury had been added the insult of having to perform police duties at a time when Macedonia seemed to be crying out for the implementation of the national ideal. To make matters worse the civilian authorities, having called in the army, now wanted to make it a scapegoat, for one result of the inquiry into the Trŭstenik rising had been the punishment of a number of soldiers, including the commanding officer of the Second Infantry Regiment, Colonel Georgiev; he was dismissed the service whilst most of the peasants detained during the emergency were released unpunished. The teachers too had been involved. To a large extent they were already alienated from the political system but when the politicians insisted that teachers take part in the assessment of the tithe alienation went much further. In future years they were to play an important part in the running of the Agrarian Union and of the cooperative socities. In the long-term however the effect on the Agrarian movement was the most important of all the results of the disturbance. The peasant had long ceased to have any respect for the Sŭbranie Parties and now he had an alternative to which he could turn. Stoilov, more perspicacious as an observer than a practitioner, saw this truth. The Parties in the Assembly, he said, had no longer any representative function or significance for the peasants whose real defender was BANU which, he admitted, was already the strongest political force in the land.

When the second BANU Congress was called for the end of 1900 the government showed its fear of the new movement by attempting to stop the congress from meeting. Seizing upon an outbreak of scarlet fever in Tŭrnovo quarantine regulations were imposed around Pleven where the congress was to convene, but most of the delegates simply decamped to Sofia; on 3/16 December the Congress opened with over four hundred delegates crowding into the inadequate café 'Odessa'.

The upheavals in north-east Bulgaria in 1900 gravely weakened the Cabinet. It had already lost an important member in March when Nachovich resigned, because he said, in public, he disapproved of the visit of Kobeko, though it was believed that privately he was concerned at some aspects of the secret collaboration between the government and the Macedonian insurgents. Ferdinand had been worried by the defection of Nachovich and by the unpopularity and apparent instability of the Ivanchov-Radoslavov administration, and his mind had turned to the possibility of a military government under General Petrov but such action could easily have provoked the nation beyond its endurance and shifted BANU from its cautious legalism. By the autumn with the disorders behind him Ferdinand again thought in terms of authoritarian rule with a Cabinet comprised mainly of professional diplomatists ruling through a State Council in place of the Sūbranie which would be dissolved. Yet Ferdinand lacked the decisiveness for such an act and he did not have to wait long before he had the means to compromise the Ivanchov-Radoslavov team. In the first place the Prince persuaded his nominee, the Minister of War, to demand an increase of fourteen million leva in the military budget, a demand which the government was bound to refuse in the existing financial climate. The Minister of War resigned. Also the Prince could use against the leaders of the Cabinet the fact that they had made personal fortunes from an order placed in Germany for railway wagons; the wagons were needed to transport the grain collected from the tithe but when they arrived they were defective and in many cases useless. On 5/18 December 1900 the government resigned.

The natural successor to Ivanchov appeared to be Radoslavov. His Party dominated the Assembly and he had earned a reputation for toughness in dealing with the peasant unrest. It was his ability to handle unrest which made him unacceptable in the palace, not because Ferdinand had tender feelings about the way in which the peasants and the Agrarians should be treated but because he feared Radoslavov might apply his repressive abilities to the Macedonians. In order to secure personal control over the way in which the Macedonian activists were handled Ferdinand insisted upon the appointment of his confidant, General Petrov, as Minister of the Interior. This made life difficult for an incoming administration for with Petrov in that office the new ministers would not have control over the patronage and would not be able to guarantee themselves a majority in an election. For this reason the Tsankovists refused to join the new government. Until January 1901, therefore, Ivanchov stayed on as Minister President but without the Radoslavists and with Petrov as Minister of the Interior. Petrov was not happy in his new post and wanted to stay there only to supervise fresh, and this time free elections. These took place in February 1901 after Petrov had ordered police officials not to interfere in the voting; the returns proved that real choice had been exercised for no party enjoyed a majority. The Stambulovist faction, long out of office, was the largest but the Democrats under Karavelov, the Progressive Liberals (Tsankovists) under Danev and Stoilov's Nationalists were not far behind. Despite its lack of experience at elections the Agrarian Union secured thirteen seats; the Socialists had three. This inconclusive result meant a coalition. Karavelov became Minister President and Minister of Finance and Danev Minister for Foreign Affairs. The Minister of War was Ferdinand's nominee, General Paprikov, through whom the Prince maintained his contacts with the Macedonians. The other seats in the Cabinet were divided between the Democrats and the Progressive Liberals.

Karavelov's decision to become Minister of Finance as well as head of the Cabinet indicated not only his personal interest in that area but also the fact that the search for a loan was still one of the government's major preoccupations. The nomination of Danev as Foreign Minister indicated that Bulgaria would now be pursuing a pro-Russian policy, but the apointment of Paprikov showed that it was Ferdinand who would determine relations with the Macedonian movement.

Karavelov's Cabinet achieved little beyond a major redrawing of Bulgaria's local government boundaries. This eliminated six regions and fourteen districts and no previous administration had dared to prune so drastically the amount of patronage available through local appointments. It was a welcome if ineffective tilt at the windmill of *partisanstvo*.

The major preoccupation was however with the question of a loan. By 1901 Bulgaria's foreign debts amounted to 205.5 million gold francs and the charges on these absorbed 24.6 million leva a year or thirty percent of the exchequer's revenue. The administration's position was made more difficult by the disappointing return on the tithe of 1900 which because of heavy rain in August had been worth only twenty-two million as opposed to the expected thirty million leva. The government was not daunted. It was sure it could achieve major savings by administrative pruning and to gain much needed support in the Sŭbranie bowed to pressure from the Nationalists to abolish the tithe agreeing at the same time not to introduce any new or to mortgage to foreign bankers any present or future monopoly. It was easy for the Cabinet to commit itself to so popular an act as the abolition of the tithe but it was more difficult to remain true to the declaration over monopolies.

Since December 1900 negotiations had been in hand with Pariba for a sizeable loan but the French bankers were insisting that they must have the revenue from the tobacco monopoly. Towards the end of its days in office the Radoslavov-Ivanchov Cabinet seemed willing to agree to this condition in return for a loan of eighty to a hundred million francs, but Karavelov and Danev were not prepared for such sacrifices. Danev characteristically turned to Russia for help. In St Petersburg, however, he found little encouragement and was told by Witte that Russia did not have the sums which the Bulgarians needed and even if she did, 'The fifty million loan which you desire would, for your ailing and ruined finances, be like a glass of champagne for a dying man; it would give him a strength which would last but a few minutes'.[5] All Danev received from Russia was a short-term loan of four million francs to cover immediate obligations, and even this was to cause considerable embarrassment later.

After the cool response from Russia negotiations with Pariba were taken up again. By September Karavelov was ready to sign an agreement by which Bulgaria would borrow one hundred and twenty-five million gold francs at five percent but in return had to concede as guarantees for the loan income from the banderolle and the *mururie,* taxes on processed and raw tobacco respectively; the government would also be obliged to introduce a monopoly over the manufacture and sale of tobacco products and would have to consult representatives of Pariba whenever any change in existing financial arrangements was contemplated. The government had no choice but to accept whatever terms the bank chose to dictate for the Russians would soon be pressing for repayment of the four million lent during the summer and this, together with other obligations, made a loan absolutely essential; St Petersburg had advised that the terms offered were the best that could be obtained and that Bulgaria should therefore accept them. Karavelov sourly admitted that he had expected better treatment from the Russians.

The loan proposal was submitted to the Sŭbranie in December and was rejected. The Nationalists refused to agree to the monopoly clauses and even a section of Karavelov's own Party defected, these 'Young Karavelists' later forming the Radical Democratic Party. Karavelov resigned in January 1902 leaving Danev to form an administration of Tsankovists and independents, with Ferdinand's man, Paprikov, still at the Ministry of War. In the spring of 1902 Danev made a historic journey to St Petersburg which will be discussed in the following chapter. Here it must be recorded that in the Russian capital he renegotiated the loan terms. Pariba was now to provide ninety-two million francs and the Russians a further fourteen million. As before the government in Sofia was required to pledge the revenue of the banderolle and the *mururie* and was still required to secure the consortium's consent to any change in the financial structure of Bulgaria. At the same time the French and the Russians let it be known that they did not want a forward policy in Macedonia. Danev accepted these terms and in late July 1902 was able to persuade the Sŭbranie to do likewise.

Danev had found a solution to the problem of finance. He was to be far less successful in his dealings with the other preoccupation facing Bulgarian governments in these years, Macedonia.

Chapter 15

THE CRISIS OF 1899–1903
II. MACEDONIA

Whilst it was in desperate need of financial help the Bulgarian government had also to deal with the problem of Macedonia which in the years 1900 to 1903 assumed its most intractable form. Ferdinand was anxious to cooperate with the Macedonian activists in order to control them; the Russians were adamant that the peace and stability of the Balkans should not be disturbed, and the Macedonians were insistent that action be taken to bring about an improvement in conditions in the area.

Ferdinand's attitude was determined by a number of considerations, one of which was fear for his own safety; men who had disposed of Stambulov would not shrink from killing a Prince who refused to act on their behalf. Europe profited from Ferdinand's entirely understandable fears, for if he were violently removed his successor would be forced into more extreme policies which would bring about the Balkan turmoil which all powers dreaded. If, however, Ferdinand remained and permitted moderate pressure upon the Turkish authorities the latter could well be persuaded to grant effective reforms to Macedonia, a development which, it could be argued, would bring peace and stability to the area. From Ferdinand's point of view this latter development would also have the political advantage of increasing his own political power and prestige both at home and abroad; such conspicuous success might even enable him to move forward to what had long been one of his ultimate objectives, the declaration of full independence for Bulgaria and the assumption of a full royal title for himself. If, on the other hand, the Internal Organisation were able to secure autonomy for Macedonia then Ferdinand could be in real danger. The new unit might eventually join with Bulgaria but in such a way that Bulgaria was absorbed into Macedonia rather than vice-versa; it would be Rumelia in reverse. Ferdinand had no illusions about his own popularity in Bulgaria and if an autonomous Macedonia had a more attractive leader his prospect would be poor. This was not an idle consideration. In 1903 there was much talk in St Petersburg of making Alexander Battenberg's son, Count Hartenau, Governor General of an autonomous Macedonia, whilst in Cetinje Alexander's brother, a son-in-law of the Prince of Montenegro, was the favoured candidate.

For Russia the primary concern was to secure stability in the Balkans. Her interests in the Far East determined her upon the maintenance of the 1897 agreement with Austria and all the Balkan governments were left in no doubt that they must not disturb the *status quo*. Russia was also anxious to promote better relations between Sofia and Belgrade and after the treaty of 1897 there was some progress in this direction with exchange-visits by town councillors and students in October 1901, and in the setting to work in June of the same year of the long-established but previously dormant border commission to regulate the Bregovo dispute. These positive developments, however, were completely overshadowed by the dispute over the Skopje archbishopric and in 1899 the Radoslavov-Ivanchov Cabinet told the Russians that Bulgaria would unhesitatingly provoke a full scale rising in Macedonia if Firmilian or any other Serb were confirmed as administrator of the archdiocese.

For the most part Bulgaria could not afford to take so defiant an attitude towards Russia. Sofia was still in desperate need of Russian help in the search for a loan and there was always the danger that if Bulgaria were flagrantly disobedient Russia would abandon her and rely solely upon Serbia for its *point d'appui* in the Balkans. From 1899 to the final Russian *démarche* in December 1902, therefore, Ferdinand and his ministers made a series of gestures to Russia whilst still continuing their efforts to control the Macedonian movement by clandestine cooperation with its leaders in Bulgaria.

Like Alexander Battenberg in 1885 Ferdinand had chosen to play an exceedingly dangerous game; in the first case this game ended with a grave defeat for the Prince but gains for the Bulgarian national cause. In the second case the gains and losses were reversed.

For Ferdinand, like Alexander before him, the critical factor was control of the forces he was preparing to enlist, and of this control he was never certain. In 1900 it was non-existent. During that year, as has been noted, the Internal Organisation had secured domination of the Supreme Committee under its new president, Boris Sarafov. The new Committee was extremely effective and its power was soon a source of great embarrassment to the regime. The latter did not object to the new Committee's streamlining of the Macedonian organisations or to the setting-up of a number of safe houses in Bulgaria, but it was discomforted by Sarafov's ability to raise money. The most spectacular deed in this connection was the kidnapping and ransom of an American missionary in Macedonia, Miss Stone, but much more galling for the government in Sofia was the Committee's ability to raise large sums of money inside Bulgaria, an ability which the government of 1900 had good cause to envy. Most of the cash raised in Bulgaria came from the Macedonian levy. Throughout the Principality the committees persuaded local citizens to purchase Macedonian bonds which were to be redeemable at Macedonia's liberation, for, the townspeople of Vidin were told, the rich must serve their brothers in Macedonia with gold, the poor by bearing arms. The amounts involved were not small, nor were the means used to persuade citizens to contribute always peaceful, and this added to the general social fragility of the country in 1900.

Even more worrying for the government were the new Committee's activities outside Bulgaria, above all the murder in Bucharest in August 1900 of Professor Michealeanu, a prominent Rumanian opponent of the Slav cause in Macedonia. The Sofia government immediately disclaimed any responsibility for the murder but, ironically, there were few observers who believed the government was not in command of the Macedonian activists. The Rumanians made vigorous protest, demanding immediate and effective steps to stop any further terrorist activity on their territory. This was difficult. Strong measures could easily provoke retaliation and information from Bucharest that the Macedonians were planning to kill King Carol magnified Ferdinand's fear that he himself would be another prime target. Furthermore, the government, already weakened by its confrontation with the peasants was reluctant now to grapple with a foe as powerful and well-organised as Sarafov's Committee, and both Prince and Cabinet had to ask themselves whether the army, unhappy at its role in the suppression of the peasants, would take part in the coercion of the Macedonians whose cause was extremely popular in the officer corps. When Karavelov became Minister President in March 1901 there was more willingness to act but it was not until heavy Russian pressure had been applied that Ferdinand's doubts could be overcome. Colonel Grabo, the chief of the Russian political secret police in the Balkans, let it be known that St Petersburg wanted an end to the Committee and its disruptive activities. 'Sarafov', the Bulgarians were instructed, 'must be made harmless'.[1] In April 1901 therefore officers serving in the Bulgarian army were forbidden membership of the Macedonian committees and a few days later Sarafov and others implicated in the Bucharest killing were arrested. They did not stay long in custody, the case against them being dismissed in June for lack of evidence, but the legal proceedings had made it impossible for Sarafov to stand again for the presidency of the Supreme Committee. Leadership of that organisation now passed to 'the Generals', a faction which had always opposed Sarafov and which wanted to revert to the original Supremacist programme of using a large scale incursion headed by Bulgarian officers to raise a revolt in Macedonia. The government had backed this faction and it was widely believed that the two new leaders of the Committee, Tsonchev and Mihailovski, were both creatures of Ferdinand.

Although Ferdinand now had some control over the Supreme Committee this was not absolute. The new leaders had soon offended the Russians by refusing to meet the Russian diplomatic agent in Sofia, Bakhmetiev, even though the latter had said that the meeting could be of benefit to Macedonia, and the Generals were soon engaged in preparing the incursion and the hoped-for rising which had long been the aim of their faction, but which could only anger Russia whose desire for stability in the Balkans was as strong as ever. These activities could disturb the Russophile Cabinet now in office and Ferdinand was in danger of having to choose between his links with the Macedonians and his Russophile Cabinet which was still essential if Russia were to help Bulgaria find a loan. For the moment the Prince was able to convince the Cabinet that he remained in control of the Macedonians who would not be allowed to endanger Bulgaria's relations with Russia.

The removal of Sarafov and the establishing of closer government controls over the Supreme Committee had however created other difficulties. It had redivided the Macedonian movement. The Internal Organization could no longer cooperate with the Supremacists and as soon as Sarafov had been deposed it intensified its propaganda. The Salonika Committee feared that the incursionist tactics of the Generals would provoke a premature rising which the Turks would suppress, destroying the Internal Organisation's structure in the process and thus leaving the ground clear for the Supremacists and Ferdinand. In March 1902 the Central Committee in Salonika sent a circular to all Macedonian organisations in the Principality. The circular began by noting that in recent months Supremacist *cheti,* recruited and armed with the connivance of the highest authorities in Sofia, had been crossing into Macedonia to canvass the idea of an armed uprising in the autumn. This, said the Internal Organisation, could trick the Macedonians into rising before they were strong enough thus bringing down upon themselves another Batak. In subsequent months the Internal Organisation's propaganda continued and it laid ever greater emphasis on the notion of autonomy. The Internalists repeated their original contention that they did not want cultural separation from Bulgaria, for in linguistic and religious terms the Macedonian Slav Christians were Bulgarian, but political separation was a necessity. If Turkish power diminished or disappeared Macedonia, said the Internal Organisation, would have to remain a political integer. This could be achieved only by autonomy, a solution which would also allow for a new system of local government on the Swiss model to protect the interests of the numerous ethnic groups; autonomy would also put an end to the rivalry between the neighbouring states, the more so if all were offered free port facilities at Salonika. This solution might even prove the starting point for a Balkan federation which many commentators believed to be the only permanent solution for the political problems of the peninsula. Not only did autonomy have distinct advantages it was the only real option available for Macedonia, said the Internalists, for the alternatives were partition by the Balkan states which was undesirable and in the long run unworkable, or total absorbtion into one of those states which the great powers would resist.

The Supremacists took no account of the Internalists' propaganda and by the spring of 1902 were sending yet more *comitadjii,** or committee-sponsored guerillas, into Macedonia until, in the words of one observer, 'absolute anarchy' prevailed in that unfortunate region.[2]

Inevitably Russia became concerned at this development, as was made clear to Danev when he visited the Russian capital in March 1902. Danev had accepted the provocation of unrest in Macedonia as a

---

*Commitadjii means 'committee-men'.

justifiable means to bring about reform in the Ottoman Empire but he was unwilling to do anything to which Russia took serious objection. Indeed, given Bulgaria's need for help in finding a loan he could not afford to do anything which ran counter to the wishes of the Tsar. The Russian price for help over the loan, and for a military convention which Danev also wanted, was high: Bulgaria had to accept Firmilian in Skopje and had to put an end to the activities of the *comitadjii*.

The first of these conditions was a national disaster for the Bulgarians. Danev at first dared not tell his Cabinet colleagues let alone the nation. When the government press began to argue that the importance of the Skopje archbishopric could be exaggerated the public knew what was to follow and was outraged; the Exarch, who managed to persuade the Porte to delay the *berat* for a further six weeks, disclaimed all responsibility. He knew that the whole of northern Macedonia had been delivered to Serbian influence.

There was little difficulty in implementing the second Russian condition. In April the sale of weapons in a number of Bulgarian towns was proscribed and known Macedonian sympathisers in the army were transferred from border areas. Some activists were even expelled from the country and civil servants were, like army officers, forbidden membership of the committees. In May weapons and ammunition were seized and two months later the Sŭbranie agreed to defray 60,000 leva to set up a new armed frontier gendarmerie. Finally in September Tsonchev was arrested on the frontier and he and other prominent *comitadjii* were taken into custody. Danev's conduct had been consistent. He believed that the justification for action in Macedonia was that it would force the Sultan to introduce reforms or, if he refused, it would bring about the intervention of the Berlin powers who would insist upon the full application of Article 23 with its promises of a restructuring of the Ottoman administration. If, however, it appeared to the Turks and to the world at large that the disorders in Macedonia were the result of Bulgarian interference rather than of deeply felt local grievances then the Sultan could block all requests for reform with the argument that the troubles were 'made in Bulgaria' and would disappear when the Bulgarian government put its house in order. The Supreme Committee indeed seemed to Danev now to be retarding rather than advancing the prospect of reform in European Turkey.

Late in May 1902 Danev went to St Petersburg again, this time in the company of Paprikov, Tsankov and Ferdinand himself. By now the Bulgarians had done enough to convince the Tsar of their good intent and the Russians gave help with the loan negotiations and settled the final details of the military convention. Russia agreed to help Bulgaria if the latter were attacked by Rumania assisted by Austria. The Russians, however, would undertake no commitment to help Bulgaria in a war with the Ottoman Empire. Russian military attachés were to return to Bulgaria, Ferdinand having refused them hitherto because of their record under Alexander Battenberg. The attachés were to have the right of access to Bulgaria's secret mobilisation plans and would therefore be in a position to prevent any independent military action by Bulgaria; Russian approval was to be sought when making appointments to senior posts within the Bulgarian General Staff, and Bulgaria was to place armaments orders in Russia. The convention would have greatly increased Russian influence in Sofia if it had ever been implemented but it was not. It was never submitted to the Sŭbranie as it had to be if it were to be fully binding on the Bulgarians and the Tsar refused to sign it on the grounds that as a vassal state Bulgaria was in no position to make such an agreement. It remained a vague and somewhat contentious issue. Rumours circulated in Bulgaria that Danev had agreed to cede Burgas and Varna to the Russians and this was even included in the text of the treaty published after the First World War in both Russia and Bulgaria. Yet that text was apocryphal. Indeed the actual text of the 1902 convention is impossible to determine; even the government which followed that of Danev was in ignorance of it, for after the Danev Cabinet had left office no copy of the convention could be found in the files of the Bulgarian Foreign Ministry.

The measures taken against the Macedonian committees in the spring of 1902 were sufficient to secure Russian good-will but were not enough to put an end to Macedonian activity. Nor were they intended to. Ferdinand, having landed the loan, was now trying to secure advantages in Macedonia too. There were two main reasons why he should do so. In the first place the situation in Macedonia was becoming yet more complicated for not only were the Supremacists competing with the Internalists and with Greek, Vlach and Serbian apologists, but Sarafov was now showing signs of setting up as yet another faction. The government could not afford to let any group but the Supremacists, to whom it was still giving secret encouragement, steal a march in Macedonia. At home the time was also ripe for action. In the early autumn national emotions would be stirred by the twenty-fifth anniversary of the battle of Shipka. The celebrations began on 25th

September/8th October, with the consecration of a memorial church near the village of Shipka, a ceremony attended by Ferdinand and leading Bulgarians together with the Grand Duke Nikolai Nikolaievich, the Russian Minister of War and twenty-one other generals, including Count Ignatiev, one of the great heroes of 1877–78. Despite some unseemly wrangles over finance and precedence, the festivities passed off well and the emotional outburst which the Supremacists had anticipated came when Ignatiev, having returned to Sofia, told a large crowd, 'Do not despair; hold to your national ideal, think of and work for it, and rest assured that you will achieve it'.[3] For the Supremacists this charging of the national emotions was important. So too was the fact that the Bulgarian army was in a state of advanced readiness as it was holding its autumn manoeuvres. Two days before the Shipka celebrations a Supremacist rising centred upon Gorna Djumaya (Blagoevgrad) in the Struma valley had begun.

The emotional waves radiating from Shipka and Sofia did not reach the Struma valley. Few local Christians joined the incoming *comitadjii* and by November the rising had been snuffed out. Due retribution was taken with thirty villages being sacked and their precious cattle sold off at derisory prices in the market place at Seres; thousands more refugees trudged wearily into Bulgaria. For the Supremacists and their supporters however the rising had not been a complete failure. They had shown themselves to be the chief activist force in Macedonia and if a large rising had not taken place Danev and those who thought like him could take solace from the fact that European diplomacy had been mobilised. In Constantinople the powerful German ambassador, Baron Marschall von Bieberstein, persuaded the Sultan that some reforms must be granted and that an inspector should be appointed to supervise their implementation. Austria and Russia too were galvanised by the Djumaya rising which caused them to produce a reform scheme which they proposed officially in the spring of 1903 and which differed little in content from that announced by the Sultan.

The Djumaya rising also had considerable effect upon the political situation in Sofia. In December 1902 the Tsar's Foreign Minister, Count Lamsdorff, arrived in the city. The original purpose of his journey to the Balkans had been to explain to the governments of Sofia and Belgrade the details of the forthcoming Austro-Russian reform scheme for Macedonia. Now in addition to this message he delivered in both capitals stern warnings that all links between the government and the Macedonian rebels must be cut. These orders were repeated by

Bakhmetiev in January and this time they could not be evaded. In February Danev ordered the dissolution of the Macedonian committees in Bulgaria and the arrest of prominent committee leaders. After a three-day debate the Sŭbranie accepted the order and a few days after this the details of the Austro-Russian reform scheme were made public.

The visit of Lamsdorff was the beginning of the end of the Danev government. The Russophile Cabinet was not prepared to resist orders so categorically handed down from St Petersburg. Ferdinand would have delayed a little longer had not the King of Serbia announced in January that he would not assist the activists in Macedonia; if Bulgaria did not do likewise Russian diplomatic support would be concentrated in Belgrade. Once the links with the committees had been cut there was, as far as Ferdinand was concerned, nothing more for the Danev Cabinet to do. It had secured the loan and Sŭbranie approval of it, and it had brought the great powers into the Macedonian question with promises of reforms for the suffering. On the other hand, it had angered the nation by giving way over Firmilian and it had, in the military convention with Russia, encroached too far into Ferdinand's preserve of foreign affairs. There had also been a series of disagreements between Ferdinand and his Cabinet on other issues.

When Sarafov had been arrested in 1901 his supporters had been quick to point out that Haliu, and others suspected of implication in the murder of Stambulov, were still at liberty in Sofia. Why, asked the Sarafovists, if these deeds went unpunished should the Macedonian patriots suffer for acts committed in a sacred cause? The government could not move against Sarafov and leave Stambulov's assassins free; Haliu was therefore put in the dock. From the trial it emerged that the present Minister of the Interior, Liudskyanov, had been party to the conspiracies which led to the murders of Belchev, Vŭlkovich and Stambulov. Liudskyanov did not contest the evidence and even admitted to having taken part in a plot on the life of the Prince himself but this at a time when the Prince was, he insisted, an enemy of Russia and therefore of Bulgaria. Times and attitudes had changed since the *Stambulovshtina* but it was hardly surprising that Ferdinand demanded Liudskyanov's resignation together with that of Konstantinov, a co-conspirator who was now Minister for Public Buildings and Works, and the Prince's determination to be rid of this unsavoury pair was in no way diminished by an attempt on his own life at Evksinograd, his palace near Varna. The Minister of Public Buildings did

resign but his successor, Popov, was scarcely more appetising, for this
extreme Russophile poet had once written letters in blood to Princess
Clementine demanding, as the price of her son's life, that the Prince
change to a pro-Russian policy. Liudskyanov, however, stuck to his
guns—literally. He refused to resign and lest any of his colleagues
doubt his determination he fired his revolver at the ceiling of the
Cabinet room. The Cabinet understandably decided upon a policy of
total solidarity and declared that they would all resign if Liudskyanov
were dismissed, whilst the government press defended his past on the
principle of *mors tyranni salus patriae.*

There were also disagreements over appointments to the all-
important positions of Minister of War and Chief of the General Staff.
These posts were now even more important if the clandestine links
between the government and the Supremacists were to be maintained
for it was through the army that the connection was usually made.
Ferdinand wished to make Savov Chief of Staff. This the Russians
disliked and advised the Tsankovists in the Cabinet to oppose the
nomination. In fury Ferdinand refused to open the Sŭbranie in the
autumn of 1902, the first time in the history of the Principality that an
Ordinary National Assembly had begun its session without the
appearance of the Prince at the opening ceremony. Lamsdorff's pre-
remptory orders intensified the conflict on this issue and relations
between Ferdinand and his Cabinet in this general area were soon
made yet more difficult by a disagreement over the Ministry of War.
The Tsankovists had decided to attack the Prince's influence by removing his nominee, Paprikov, from this post, an act which threatened the
basis of Ferdinand's political power in Bulgaria. In January 1903
Paprikov, following orders from the Prince, asked the Cabinet for an
extra ten million leva for military expenditure. The request was
rejected. At the same time the Russian press launched a vituperative
campaign against Paprikov, casting doubt upon his morals, his sobri-
ety, and his ability. The Tsankovists and their Russian patrons wanted
to replace Paprikov with Radko Dimitriev who had earned his Russophile spurs by being exiled during the *Stambulovshtina;* Danev argued
that one day the exiles had to be fully reintegrated into the Bulgarian
army and there was no better way of doing this than making one of
them Minister of War. Had this plan succeeded and had the military
convention with Russia then been fully ratified Ferdinand's personal
regime would have been undermined. Luckily for the Prince his officer
corps was still very suspicious of the former exiles and this enabled

Ferdinand to block Dimitriev's candidature. A compromise was eventually reached whereby Paprikov was removed but was replaced by Savov whilst Dimitriev was made Chief of Staff. In that position he did manage to reassure the officer corps that the exiles could be taken back fully and he was to play a major part in the Bulgarian victories of 1912.

Meanwhile, however, Ferdinand on the one hand and his ministers and their Russian supporters on the other were exchanging further insults. Ferdinand was reportedly furious that Lamsdorff had told Karavelov that Russia now bitterly regretted its action in bringing down Alexander Battenberg; in January Ferdinand incurred the wrath of Bakhmetiev who declared that at the New Year's Day reception he had not been given the preferential treatment which Russia's representative had the right to expect, whilst Ferdinand replied with another insult, informing Madame Karavelova that it was a pity relief work for the Macedonian refugees was in the hands of a foreigner—Madame Bakhmetieva, who was an American.

Kindereien such as these deepened the rift between Ferdinand and his Cabinet and after the suppression of the Macedonian committees in February the Prince merely had to wait for a suitable opportunity to ditch Danev. Whilst he did so Danev's position weakened yet further. The suppression of the committees in Bulgaria did not mean the ultimate death of the Supreme Committee but that organisation in the spring of 1903 was in a state of total disarray. This left the field open to its competitors. There was a series of outrages in Macedonia culminating in a number of coordinated bomb explosions in Salonika at the end of April. The perpetrators of these crimes were anarchists who were all either killed or arrested, the latter because one of their number who had planted a bomb in a ship was the only one of the passengers who did not reclaim his fare. Yet although these arrests were made no-one believed that the Bulgarians were unconnected with the crimes. In May eighteen Bulgarians died in reprisals in Bitolja and public opinion in Bulgaria was outraged. Danev was now in an impossible position. His credit at home, in dissolution since his capitulation over Firmilian, was entirely dissipated; he had lost the confidence of the Prince, and now he was deprived of the bed-rock of his political position, the good-will of Russia who did not believe that the latest outrages in Macedonia were totally beyond the control of the Sofia administration. Ironically for Danev his success against the Supreme Committee had released other forces which wrecked his own political standing.

It was clear that Ferdinand would have no difficulty in removing him. The occasion for doing so was trivial but characteristic of Bulgarian politicking under Ferdinand's personal regime. The Prince had ordered the Minister of Education, Aleksander Radev, not to allow Bulgarian academics to attend a socialist economic conference in Rome and Radev had refused to obey what he declared was an unconstitutional instruction. Danev took little notice of the incident even when Ferdinand declared he never wished to see Radev again. The Minister of Education, however, appeared with his Cabinet colleagues at a Te Deum to celebrate Prince Boris's birthday. When Radev entered the palace to sign the book of congratulations after the service Ferdinand's anger could not be contained and he declared loudly in front of the assembled guests, 'Je ne veux pas voir ce vagabond'.[4] When Danev submitted the joint resignation of the Tsankovist members of the Cabinet it was gratefully accepted.

The new Cabinet was headed by the non-party General Petrov. Its political complexion was Stambulovist with the National Liberal leader, Petkov, having the Ministry of the Interior with its control of police and patronage, and the Stambulovist General Savov remaining at the Ministry of War. There were two other Stambulovists in the government.

The Petrov Cabinet's first task was to reassure the Russians. Bakhmetiev was flattered by the new ministers and the Stambulovist press carried long articles asserting that the extreme Russophobia of the Party's founder was a thing of the past. The new government also wished to reassert the old Stambulovist policy of good relations with Turkey. The common frontier was therefore policed more rigorously and Nachovich was despatched to Constantinople to argue for reforms, for without some concessions beyond the Austro-Russian reform scheme the government would not be able to persuade domestic opinion that cooperation with Turkey was worthwhile. Nachovich succeeded only in securing the release of a number of Macedo-Bulgarians who had been arrested and were still awaiting trial.

In the first half of 1903 there was little prospect that the Stambulovist policy of cooperation with Turkey would be successful. If it were to succeed the government in Sofia had to be in control of the Macedonian movement and after the suppression of the Supreme Committee Petrov and Petkov were no more able to control the other Macedonian groups than Danev had been.

The Djumaya rising had fulfilled the worst fears of the Internal Organisation who saw its whole position in Macedonia threatened by such adventurism. It decided that it must act even though a number of leaders were worried that such action might be premature. The decision to stage a rebellion in the summer was taken in January and the suppression of the Supreme Committee and its temporary dislocation in the following month helped the Internalists by removing a major rival. Other developments appeared to confirm the wisdom of the decision to act in the summer. The Austro-Russian reform scheme contained provision for the inspection of the administrative changes and this held out the prospect of real reform for Macedonia. The Central Committee could well lose support if effective reforms were introduced and it was anxious to press for the whole loaf before the Macedonian peasants were bought off with half one.

In the spring the Central Committee's plans ran into serious difficulties. The removal of the Supreme Committee had been of help but the appearance of the anarchist danger replaced the old competitor with one equally dangerous. The effect was the same. After the Salonika bombings in April the Ottoman authorities understandably instituted tough measures which did not distinguish one revolutionary group from another—even the Bulgarian representative in Constantinople had his room searched. The measures taken in 1903 seriously damaged the structure of the Internal Organisation and a further serious blow fell in May when Gotse Delchev, its leading military strategist, was killed in a chance encounter with Turkish troops. The demoralised leaders had no choice but to go on. To wait until the Organisation had been rebuilt could mean that all revolutionary potential would be sapped by effective reforms or expropriated by a rival faction. There was still some hope left that the summer rising could achieve autonomy or at least force the powers to intervene themselves directly in Macedonia to put an end to the Moslem misgovernment and fanaticism which would be presented as the causes of the rebellion.

By the summer Macedonia had been divided into a number of military districts and arms caches had been accumulated, many weapons being purchased from the poorly-paid Turkish troops in the area. On 2/15 August, St Elijah's Day or in Slavonic, Ilinden, full scale rebellion broke out in the Bitolja vilayet. A few days later, on the Feast of the Transfiguration (Preobrazhenie in Slavonic) villages in part of the Adrianople vilayet joined the revolt and those in the Salonika vilayet followed soon thereafter. In the liberated areas a well-organised governmental structure was established and a republic was declared both at Krushevo in Macedonia and at Strandja in the Adrianople vilayet, but the rebels faced impossible odds. By late September the revolution was losing momentum as more and more Ottoman troops were poured into Europe. By early October the rebellion was doomed. By the end of the month it had collapsed.

As Macedonia had come nearer and nearer to open revolution, tension had increased in the Principality. In June Whit Sunday threatened to bring disorders to the capital because the Macedonians objected to Socialist plans to combine a protest over the pogroms in Russia with a pro-Macedonian rally. The police kept the two factions apart on that day but the Macedonians still resented the linking of their cause with that of the Jews and on a later occasion Macedonians and Socialists fought street battles on this issue. In July Ferdinand sped abroad. He had no wish to stay with the Macedonians threatening to go on the rampage, the more so because the King and Queen of Serbia had just been done brutally to death. Only the severe strictures of the European and Bulgarian press overcame his reluctance to return and he came back not to Sofia, which in any case he loathed, but to his palace at Evksinograd where he was guarded by an entire regiment of loyal troops and off which stood a yacht permanently at the ready for an enforced departure. In late July there were some border clashes between Bulgarian and Ottoman troops but tension in general declined as the harvest had to be taken in. With the news of the Ilinden/Preobrazhenski rising tension rose to a new pitch. There were calls for intervention by the Bulgarian army, calls which became louder during the later stages of the revolution when the rebels were appealing for help. In the first week of the rising popular excitement had been fuelled by the arrival of Russian warships in Turkish waters in the southern Black Sea, though in fact the vessels were there not to encourage the rebels but to urge the Turks to strong measures against those who had murdered the Russian consul in Bitolja a few days earlier. There was also popular anger with the Oriental Railway Company. The ORC had been the victim of a number of bomb attacks in 1903 and as soon as the revolt in Macedonia and Adrianople began it instituted thorough searches of all trains coming from Bulgaria lest they were carrying arms; this delayed Bulgarian perishable goods *en route* for the markets of Constantinople. The Macedonians in the Principality were naturally the most vociferous of those calling for Bulgarian intervention and they carried out a number of terrorist attacks aimed at forcing the government to act. The most notable of these was the placing of a bomb in the first class saloon of the Bulgarian ferry boat, the *S.S. Vaskapu:* twenty-seven people died in the explosion.

The government was not to be moved. Petkov told a crowd in Ruse that the war fever was being whipped up by opposition politicians and that it would be an untimely adventure if Bulgaria were to go to war. It was not, of course, in the Stambulovist tradition to quake before public opinion but the Minister President, who was not a party man, was worried. He told the Austrian representative in Sofia shortly after the *Vaskapu* outrage that, 'In a very short time the government will have to choose between war and revolution'.[5] But the government could not go to war even if it wanted to. Austria and Russia stood by their 1897 agreement that the *status quo* should not be changed; nor would the two powers tolerate Bulgarian intervention even if it were allegedly staged to bring about an improvement in the Ottoman administration of Macedonia, for that had been the objective of the Austro-Russian reform scheme of February. Even if the two great powers had not been there to veto Bulgarian intervention that intervention would still have been improbable. Unilateral action by Sofia could not be guaranteed to succeed; the Greek experience of 1897 could not be disregarded. And certainly no other Balkan state would act with Bulgaria. On 23rd September/6th October the Cabinet decided finally that the rebels of Macedonia and Adrianople must be left to their fate, notwithstanding recent threats from the Macedonians in the Principality to provoke 'unprecedented disorders' in Sofia if the Bulgarian army were not committed to the struggle.

* * *

Between 1899 and 1903 Ferdinand had consolidated his personal regime. At home he had made and broken a number of Cabinets but he had also seen off an attempt to wrest control of the War Ministry from his hands. His authority in the arena of foreign and military affairs had been confirmed by his dictation of Bulgarian policy over Macedonia. This policy, that of clandestine cooperation with the Supremacists once the Sarafovists had been removed, had involved grave dangers, but it is difficult to see what alternative Ferdinand could have adopted. Open espousal of the Macedonian revolutionary cause, despite what extreme opinion at home might desire, was impossible because of the Austro-Russian demand for stability in the Balkans and their probable veto on direct involvement by the Balkan states, individually or jointly. Yet for Ferdinand to stand aside completely would have left the initiative with the men of action. They would not have been stayed by fears of Austrian and Russian disapproval, as the Sarafovist Committee had shown. Cooperation with the activists would at least offer Ferdinand some hope of controlling them. Complete suppression of the activists would also have been a dubious alternative to the policy actually adopted. Before Lamsdorff's categoric instructions and before the announcement of the Austro-Russian reform scheme an attempt to put down the Macedonians in Bulgaria could well have failed; had it done so a pro-Macedonian regime would have come to power and the stability and peace upon which the Austrians and Russians were insisting would have been shattered, and Bulgaria would have incurred the wrath of both these great powers. As it was some control over the Macedonians in the Principality was exercised and Bulgaria, despite its internal problems, was able, with due concessions, to secure the large loan without which its finances would have collapsed.

The internal health of Bulgaria, however, was maintained only at the cost of Bulgarian interests in Macedonia. The capitulation over Firmilian was a severe blow which greatly strengthened Serbian propaganda in northern Macedonia. The suppression of the Sarafovist Supreme Committee reopened the breach between the Macedonians in the Principality and in Macedonia itself and competition between the two led to the half-cock revolt in Djumaya and the tragically ill-prepared and ill-fated Ilinden/Preobrazhenski rising. The Christians of the affected area, homeless and demoralised, had to choose between emigration or remaining to face cold, starvation and the wrath of the irregular Ottoman units who so often scavenged on the carcass of thwarted revolution. In the long run the Bulgarian cause in Macedonia suffered, because those Christians who remained behind were placed under immense pressure to abandon the Exarchate for the Greek or Serbian cause; many, for whom starvation and homelessness were the only alternatives, gave way whilst others sold out to Serbs, Greeks or Albanians and left Macedonia for Bulgaria or further afield. Even the one successful outcome of Ilinden, the Austro-Russian reform scheme pronounced at Mürzsteg in the autumn of 1903, did little to help the Bulgarian cause in Macedonia for, as will be seen in the following chapter, it greatly intensified Greek and Serbian activity in the region. The Bulgarian case in Macedonia, in fact, never recovered fully from the injuries inflicted by the appointment of Firmilian and by the failure of the Ilinden revolt.

Chapter 16

THE SECOND STAMBULOVIST GOVERNMENT 1903-8

The predominantly Stambulovist Cabinet formed in May 1903 was under the Minister Presidency of General Petrov who was not attached to any faction. The government did much to continue the policies of modernisation and industrial encouragement begun by Stoilov and Geshov* and to this end it borrowed heavily from Pariba, though neither of the two major loans taken out by this administration occasioned the internal protests which had been experienced in 1901. Internal protest between 1903 and 1908 was to come from new sources and to take new forms.

Upon taking office, however, the major concern of the Cabinet was not finance but Macedonia. The Minister of Justice, Genadiev, was a Macedonian and the chief spokesman for that cause in the government but he was not to be numbered amongst those who favoured an adventurist policy. Like his colleagues, and most importantly Petkov, the Minister of the Interior and Stambulovist Party boss, he believed that the ultimate settlement of the Macedonian problem would have to be effected by the Bulgarian army. But that instrument was not yet ready for its chosen task. When they came to office the Stambulovists alleged that their predecessors had neglected it and that the military stores were desperately short of arms, ammunition and uniforms; forty three million leva were to be spent on these items in the next few years. Petkov remained loyal to this policy and in 1907 declared,

---

*See below Chapter 20.

The whole of Bulgaria is preparing itself for Macedonia and once the psychological moment has come we shall have our army on which we can rely. To bring this to the highest degree of perfection and, at the same time, so to order our relations with the great powers that their sympathies will be with us . . . that is our task. . . . Until the historic moment has arrived, and it could still be a long way off, we must live in peace with Turkey and maintain the best possible relations with her; for this reason we have to oppose the formation of bands with all our energy.[1]

The need to maintain good relations with Turkey was another standard item of the Stambulovist party tradition and it was one which the Cabinet had had in mind ever since it came to office in May 1903. Little could be done to implement that part of the party programme until the dust of Ilinden had settled but in November 1903 Petrov told the Sŭbranie that his government would follow a 'constant and moderate' foreign policy. It had little choice for circumstances would not allow any but the traditional policy of cooperation with the Porte. After Ilinden Bulgaria had no support amongst the powers or its neighbours and had therefore to accept the solution dictated for Macedonia by Austria and Russia at Mürzsteg; to maximise the returns for Bulgaria from this solution demanded good relations with Turkey.

The Minister President was sceptical about the need for cooperation with the Turks but this policy was pushed hard by the Stambulovists and by Nachovich who in this respect was *plus stambulovist que les stambulovistes.* In November 1903 he had returned to the Ottoman capital but negotiations made relatively little headway until February 1904 when he was given full plenipotentiary powers by the Prince and ordered to reach an agreement with Turkey. When a text had been agreed the Minister President objected that it made no mention of reforms being carried out in the vilayet of Adrianople. Bulgaria, said Petrov, was justified in frustrating the passage of bands into Macedonia because that area had the promise of remedial action by the Mürzsteg reforms but the Adrianople vilayet had no such hope and the Bulgarians therefore had a right to go to the assistance of the oppressed Christians of the area. Nachovich knew that the Turks could never agree to Bulgaria's dictating what they should do in a region so close to Constantinople and Ferdinand decided in favour of his minister plenipotentiary. In March 1904 a Turco-Bulgarian treaty was signed. Bulgaria promised to do all it could to prevent bands crossing into Macedonia, to control anti-Turkish agitation in the Principality, and to punish those guilty of such actions and agitations. The Turks promised to apply the Mürzsteg reforms, to grant an amnesty to all those arrested except those convicted of acts of sabotage against railways and other public institutions, to help resettle the returning refugees in Macedonia, to end the extra controls placed on the movement of Bulgarian goods in 1903, and to grant equal rights for Christians and Moslems in the public service in European Turkey. Both parties agreed to take greater care in policing their common borders and there were further clauses regulating extraditions, posts and telegraphs, the exchange of commercial agents and future railway policies which were to be determined to the common advantage of both sides, this being seen in Sofia as an implicit promise of the coveted link to Kumanovo. For Bulgaria the agreement meant an end to the danger of a war with Turkey in which Bulgaria, like Greece in 1897, would fight alone. It also meant an end to the frustrations suffered by Bulgarian traders since the outbreak of the Ilinden-Preobrazhenski rebellion, the return of many refugees and the release of some four thousand political prisoners held in Turkish jails. Furthermore it conferred on the Principality, along with the great powers, the legal right to insist upon the strict execution of the promised reforms. It did not bring these reforms to the Adrianople vilayet, nor did the Turks make any concessions concerning the Bulgarian villages in Patriarchist areas of Macedonia, a subject of much concern to the Exarchate as in January 1904 the Porte had forbidden such villages to transfer from the Greek to the Bulgarian Church.

There were some difficulties over the application of the agreement. The Porte periodically complained that the Bulgarians were not doing enough to stop the incursion of guerrilla units into Macedonia and the Bulgarians in their turn fidgeted at the slowness with which prisoners were being released and at the constraints they were placed under after their return to Macedonia; many, for example, were forbidden to resume their teaching posts or found that their schools had been closed. Late in 1906 there was another war scare when the Turks became convinced that the Bulgarians were about to launch an invasion, using the Macedonian bands as precursors of the regular army. At that time it was true that some 'Macedonian chieftains', especially the former Supremacist, Karaiovov, exercised a good deal of influence over Petrov, but there was no real danger of war. The scare, indeed, was in no small measure the result of the fact that the Turks and the Bulgarians had easy access to each others' diplomatic secrets and various suggestions in secret correspondence were exaggerated. Despite the emergency of 1906 the treaty of 1904 was in general faithfully observed and gave both states additional security when serious developments in the Balkans could have come about, for with Russia preoccupied with and then humiliated by the Japanese, Austria might, some feared, make this her opportunity to advance towards the Aegean.

Another insurance against such action by Austria was agreement with Serbia. In March/April 1904 a series of agreements were signed between Belgrade and Sofia. An economic convention provided for mutual cooperation with its most important clauses providing for the free import of each others' products and the eventual conclusion of a customs union. There was also a treaty of alliance by which both powers condemned the fighting between Bulgarian and Serbian factions in Macedonia, approved the Mürzsteg scheme, agreed to provide reciprocal military aid in the event of any attack upon each others' territory, and agreed to united action against any unfriendly interference in Old Serbia or Macedonia; in the event of disagreement over the interpretation of the treaty both sides agreed to ask the Tsar for arbitration. In July 1905 a detailed tariff agreement had been drawn up and this was to be imposed in March 1906 when, it was hoped, both sides would have come to an agreement with Austria, upon whose consent to the alteration of her existing commercial treaties with both parties depended the viability of the Serbo-Bulgarian agreement. The Serbs were therefore furious when the Bulgarians laid the supposedly secret agreement before the Sŭbranie on the rather feeble grounds that the Bulgarian government wished to have the new agreement with Serbia ratified before the old one of 1897 expired on 1/14 January 1906. Early in 1906 the Austrians, who had in fact known of the treaty since 1904, took public umbrage and ordered the Serbs to drop the proposed customs union with Bulgaria. When Belgrade refused a ban was imposed on Serbian pig exports to Habsburg territories; pigs were Serbia's main export commodity and the 'Pig War' was intended to ruin the small state's economy. The Serbian economy however survived but Austria's action ruined any likelihood of Serbia and Bulgaria developing any closer relations. In 1906 increasing conflict between Serbs and Bulgarians in Macedonia drove more nails into the coffin of the 1904 treaty.

This increasing conflict in Macedonia arose partly from the Mürzsteg settlement. That settlement had done much to improve the quality
of Ottoman administration. Unfortunately it had also created new
problems. Article 3 of the reform scheme called for the redrawing of
Ottoman local government boundaries so as to produce units of a
more homogeneous ethnic character. To the Balkan nationalists this
seemed like preparing the ground for the more easy absorption of
those local units into the appropriate neighbouring nation-state; before
the internal boundaries were redrawn each Balkan Christian race inevitably tried to persuade as many communities as possible to join its
particular faction. After 1903 therefore the Macedonian problem was
characterised as much or even more by the conflict between separate
Christian factions as by the conflict between the subject peoples and
the Ottoman authorities. Even in 1904 Serbs and Bulgarians had
clashed and in 1905 there was an intensely bitter struggle in the Kumanovo region. In 1906 the focus of the conflict had moved to the northern part of the Skopje vilayet where by the end of that year the Serbs
had established their supremacy. By 1907 the Serbs had even created
some support in the south, in areas such as Resen, though this support
was usually obtained only after considerable expenditure of cash;
children, for example, were encouraged to attend Serb schools by the
free provision of food, books and even clothes.

Conflicts between Bulgarians and Greeks in Macedonia were even
more bitter. Since the war of 1897 the Greeks had cooperated with the
Turks, and the defeat of the Ilinden-Preobrazhenski rising was of enormous benefit to the Patriarchists. Even before the rising a new society
had been formed in Athens with government backing and in February
1904 a secret anti-Bulgarian committee was established to conduct the
Hellenist campaign in Macedonia; in September the first Greek band
appeared in central Macedonia. Bulgarian condemnation of Greek
actions was fierce for the Greeks were now following the very policy of
government-sponsored incursion which the Bulgarians had used in
1902–3 but which Russia had forced them to abandon. Furthermore
the Bulgarian population, enfeebled by the revolt of 1903, could offer
little resistance and many villages went over to the Patriarchate. Where
resistance was offered it could bring down dreadful retribution. In
November 1904 thirteen people were murdered in the village of Zele-
nitse during an Exarchist wedding feast; in February 1905 eighty Exarchists died at Greek hands in the village of Zagorichane where
hundreds of animals were also slaughtered and where the toll would

have been much greater if a detachment of Turkish troops had not happened upon the scene. In the towns Bulgarian traders were threatened and three Bulgarian inn-keepers were murdered in Salonika within a year, whilst in Kavalla in 1908 all Bulgarian employees in a tobacco-processing plant were dismissed to make way for Greeks.

Whilst the strength of the Serbian and Greek bands increased that of the Bulgarian and autonomist forces declined. The Internal Organisation's leadership and structure had suffered greatly as a result of the Ilinden tragedy, after which it was desperately short of cash and recruits; efforts to make good these deficits by force only compounded the problem. A further weakening factor was the constant and frequently violent rivalry between the Sarafovists, now independent in all but name, the Supremacists whose legal suppression had not meant their disappearance from the scene, and the Internal Organisation. In 1904 a Supremacist unit and supporters of Sarafov had come to blows near Kiustendil and similar incidents occurred throughout 1905. In that year the Internal Organisation renamed itself the Internal Macedonian Revolutionary Organisation (IMRO) but even IMRO was not entirely united for its right wing wished to move a little closer to the Bulgarian state and the Supremacists whilst the left, led by Gruev and Sandanski, wished to follow a purely autonomist line. In the Rila Congress of 1906 the left had its way when IMRO declared that it was the only true defender of Slav Macedonia and though Bulgarian help would be welcome it could only be accepted on IMRO's terms; any group attempting to involve itself in Macedonia on any other terms would be regarded as an enemy to be persecuted 'at any price and with every means'.[2] Tsonchev and his Supremacists were not interested in collaboration in these circumstances. By the end of 1907 IMRO's two wings were in more or less open conflict with each other as well as with the Supremacists. In 1906 Gruev's name had been added to the ever-lengthening list of leaders murdered in the fratricidal squabble, and in December of the following year Sarafov and Garvanov, who was a prominent figure on IMRO's right-wing, were victims of a spectacular killing in Sofia. A British observer remarked that 'the Macedonian organisation has never been more disunited than at present'.[3]

This internecine strife not only weakened the Supremacists and the autonomists vis-à-vis the Serbs and Greeks in Macedonia, but also harmed the Macedonian cause inside Bulgaria itself. In May 1906 the Austrian representative in Sofia could note that the committees which had dominated all political conversation a few years earlier were now seldom mentioned, that Macedonian newspapers such as *Reformi,* *Makedoniski Pregled* (Macedonian Review) and *Makedonsko Delo* (Macedonian Action) had ceased to appear, and that many *cheta* leaders had retired to private life in Sofia. In 1906–7 there was some recrudescence of Bulgarian activity inspired by Genadiev who wished to divert attention from more serious conflicts at home and to check Greek and Serbian activity. It was this renewal of Bulgarian activity which worried the Turks and which prompted the war scare of late 1906 but Genadiev's efforts had little reward. Throughout 1907 only three NCOs and thirty men deserted from the Bulgarian army to join the bands, a tiny fraction of those doing so in the first years of the decade. The Macedonian leaders were losing even more public respect because they were now to be seen in Sofia and other Bulgarian towns indulging themselves with the money subscribed by their supporters, a phenomenon unthinkable in earlier years. This disarray was apparent at IMRO's congress in Rila in 1908 when a new central committee decided to abandon the bands for a campaign of individual terrorism; in Adrianople meanwhile the struggle had been almost given up, the activists there being told to confine themselves to 'passive resistance'. By the summer of 1908 IMRO and the other groups were having to compete with a new force in Macedonia, units inspired by Turkish reformers who enjoyed much local support for their objective of regenerating the Ottoman administration and doing away with all factional disputes in Macedonia. These Young Turks were soon to take power and shortly before they did so an Austrian consul reported that the Bulgarian cause in Macedonia was now so depleted that its restoration to its former influence was 'amongst the most unlikely of eventualities'.[4] In the long run this observer was to be proved wrong but by 1908 Bulgaria's cause in Macedonia was in eclipse, and the shadows were being cast not only by Serbian and Greek activity in the region but also by sharp and protracted social conflicts within Bulgaria itself.

Petkov had earned a reputation for toughness by losing an arm in the struggle for Liberation and then by forcing through the modernisation of Sofia whose mayor he became after 1878. Under Stambulov's leadership he learnt well the art of electoral manipulation, an art which he applied with effect in the general election of October 1903 and in the local elections which followed shortly thereafter; of Bulgaria's 1,820 local communal councils only a dozen or so were in the hands of opposition parties. There followed other typically Stambulovist measures. Restrictions were placed upon the right of the press to criticise the head of state and there was a massive increase of 600,000 leva in expenditure on the police, with a further 200,000 leva put aside in a new 'secret fund'.

In the first year of the government's tenure there was little need for serious restrictive action. The harvest was exceptionally good and this proved to be the first of a series of excellent returns, a fact which meant a decline in the political strength of the Agrarian Union. After Ilinden the Macedonian question was also subsiding and the government was therefore left free to initiate a number of tax reforms which increasing expenditure on the army and the economy were making necessary. The Minister of Finance, Payakov, although bringing in a new and very unpopular excise duty on spirits, was not anxious to introduce extra taxation; budgetary increments, he said, would come from a more 'just' and efficient levying of existing taxes. The demand for progressive taxation put forward by the Socialists and other leftist groups he dismissed as unfair and unproductive as it would exclude some ten thousand people from income tax and place too great a burden on the remainder.

Despite the generally quiet nature of the internal political scene in 1904 there was some criticism of the government, not least for its attitude towards finance. Geshov, the architect of the original encouragement of industry programme, declared that the government was relying on taxes for too great a proportion of its revenue. Geshov's Nationalist Party colleague, Todorov, agreed and also warned against over-taxing the peasant; the people, he declared, must not be forced to sell their oxen to pay their taxes. The Stambulovists were being warned not to repeat the mistakes of the early 1880s. In a year of such a manifestly good harvest it was relatively easy for the government to slough off such criticism. Nor did it heed much the voices raised against its handling of the army. A Sŭbranie deputy, Mihailovski, thought that Bulgarian officers were over-paid, their relative salaries being higher than those of officers in the British army, and what was the use, he asked, of Bulgarian military attachés attached to diplomatic missions abroad? Todorov, too, could not accept the need for the fifty percent increase in military spending which had taken place since 1902. Government spending on the bureaucracy also received unfavourable attention. Geshov declared that government proposals for the promotion of industry and agriculture would increase the number of state functionaries at a time when Bulgaria was already over-burdened with them, having twelve officials per thousand of the population whilst

Austria-Hungary had only one and Rumania four. Meanwhile all parties inside the Sŭbranie and thousands of farmers complained bitterly against the new exise on spirits though none of the meetings of protest seriously threatened the authority of the government.

In 1905 the administration was subject to a series of attacks on the grounds of corruption and financial incompetence, a particular objective being Popov, the Minister of Agriculture and Trade, who took venality to excesses even in the permissive world of Bulgarian government. Popov was a particular favourite of the Prince who was himself the subject of considerable criticism in 1905 despite the press regulations of the preceding year. The particular complaint was Ferdinand's absenteeism which Danev's *Den* (Day) calculated at a total of four years and two hundred days by the end of 1904. In addition to this specific complaint there was continued criticism of Ferdinand's 'personal regime' one of these being Stefan Mihailovski's *Mysteries of the Bulgarian Palace,* for which the author was placed on trial. The desire to limit princely authority was one of the chief aims of the new Radical Democratic Party founded in July 1905.

For most Slav nations, and above all for the Bulgarians, 1905 was dominated by events in Russia. Bulgarians contributed generously to charities to help the Russian war effort and though the Russian government refused to accept cash it was grateful for the hospital unit which the Bulgarians provided out of funds raised in the Principality. Bulgarians also reacted to the political turmoil which hit Russia in 1905. In February the compositors of Sofia struck for higher wages, free Sundays and an eight-hour day. This was but one of a number of strikes and like most of the others it failed to have any real effect. In the University there was a more prolonged and a more successful struggle. Bulgarian students felt great sympathy with their colleagues in Russia. They were influenced by the same writers, principally Tolstoi, Lavrov, Plekhanov and Gorki, and their sense of social justice was sharpened by the fact that most of them came from relatively humble backgrounds, the wealthy preferring to send their children to established universities in central and western Europe. In January 1905, in view of events in Russia, the University authorities in Sofia had banned student political societies and political discussion in apolitical associations. The students protested so vigorously that in April the University was closed. It did not reopen until the autumn but when it did so the authorities made a number of concessions, relaxing attendance requirements and decreasing the frequency of examinations, and although political meetings within the University were still under interdict students were now to be free from university jurisdiction outside the University itself; the previous ban on student participation in political groups in the city and the country was thus removed.

In the summer of 1905 a usually passive section of the intelligentsia showed uncharacteristic disaffection when the First Congress of Bulgarian Jurists agreed to send a telegram of congratulations to the Prince and the Minister of Justice but the majority in favour of doing this was insultingly small, only eight in a total vote of one hundred and eighty-eight.

1905 also saw the first serious outbursts against the Greeks of the Principality. They had been little disturbed since Stambulov's ill-judged attempt to force teaching in Bulgarian on their elementary schools but resentment at the activities of Hellenist bands in Macedonia led to an increase in tension between the two communities. In May there were anti-Greek demonstrations and in the following month the government banned the import of Greek newspapers because of their inflammatory attacks on Bulgaria. In the summer tension declined but it was not far from the surface and could be brought out into the open by any incident, as happened in October in Plovdiv when a Bulgarian was accused of raping a Greek woman and Bulgarian officials broke the seal of the Greek consulate in the city during their inquiries into the case.

In the autumn of 1905 the Cabinet lost two of its members, Staikov the Minister of Justice who had been compromised by the Jurists' Congress and who had criticised the absolutist nature of both the government and the palace, and Popov who had by now been completely discredited by his inordinate appetite for *bakshish*. 1906 was to see a replay of some of the events of 1905 for once again there were outbursts against the Greeks but this time on a much wider scale. The head which rolled as a result was also more important than that of Staikov or Popov.

The flash-point for the disturbances of 1906 was the arrival in Varna of Neophytos, the newly-appointed Greek bishop, who was refused permission to land as he was not a Bulgarian subject. The government relented in his case but not in their general assertion that all bishops in Bulgaria, even Patriarchist ones, must be Bulgarian subjects. After Neophytos landed in the city however a Bulgarian mob invaded the Greek church which Bulgarian priests then consecrated and claimed for the Exarchate. The Greek hospital in Varna was the next acquisi-

tion of the mob and attacks on Greek institutions, especially churches
and schools, were soon being reported in many parts of the country.
Only in Sofia did the police remain in control of the outbursts. By the
middle of July it was clear that the movement was being orchestrated
by the Patriotic Associations which had been formed in the mid-1880s
and which had been so influential a lever of Stambulovist power at that
time; suspicions that the Patriotic Associations were once more acting
at the bidding of the government were widespread. The disturbances
became more violent as the summer wore on. In August a Socialist in
Varna was killed during a brawl with supporters of the local Patriotic
Association and it was in August too that the anti-Greek excesses
reached their climax. The venue was the town of Anhialo in the Burgas
province. Near the town was a large and wealthy Greek monastery and
though the local Greeks were prepared to hand over to the Exarchate
the schools and churches in the town they were determined to defend
the monastery, if necessary by force. When the expected attack on the
monastery came the Greeks did resist and though relatively few lives
were lost the town was all but destroyed and the Greeks subjected to
great maltreatment. Until Anhialo the anti-Greek outbursts had been
directed primarily at Greek institutions not individuals; at Anhialo the
movement assumed the form of a pogrom.

Until the Anhialo affair Petkov had been in Karsbad taking the cure
and control of the Ministry of the Interior had been left in the
obviously inadequate hands of Petrov. Petkov now rushed back to
Sofia. He immediately organised relief accommodation, mainly army
tents, for the homeless of Anhialo, dismissed the officials who had
been implicated in the disturbances, and arranged a cash grant of
300,000 leva for relief work, though when the Sŭbranie met and sanctioned this it was included in a general grant of 800,000 leva most of
which was to help the victims of Greek atrocities in Macedonia. Petkov
also instructed all regional prefects that damage to property and person had to be prevented and that if it did occur those responsible must
be found and severely punished, and in Plovdiv a number of anti-
Greek activists were interned. As a further act of contrition the Cabinet
expressed a willingness to return to the Patriarchate those of the
churches recently occupied which had been founded by Greek communities, hardly a generous gesture in that it left in Bulgarian hands
those churches, and they were the vast majority, founded before 1870.
By the middle of September the anti-Greek movement had subsided
and the almost desperate calls from the Patriotic Association for more

anti-Greek meetings went unheeded. Petkov's firm action was in part responsible but so too was the massive wave of Greek emigration which followed the outbursts; by the middle of September some communities had no Greeks left against whom they could protest.

The events of the summer discredited Petrov. He was also implicated in yet another financial scandal, this one dating from 1904 when he and the then War Minister, Savov, were said to have taken bribes from the Austrian arms manufacturers, Manfred Weiss and Co.. Petrov had also angered the Prince by straining relations with Russia, though it is difficult not to feel sympathy with Petrov in this case for he had refused to accept notes from the new Russian representative, Shteglov, on the grounds that they were written in Russian not French, the common diplomatic language. By the time the Sŭbranie met Ferdinand had decided to jettison Petrov. Petkov was therefore made Minister President and Petrov's position as Minister for Foreign Affairs was filled by Dmitri Stanciov, a sophisticated and able young diplomatist. In the first change observers saw a strengthening of the government, in the second Sofia gossips noted that the Prince had replaced the husband of his former with that of his current mistress.

The new government began by reassuring the more exuberant of its patriotic supporters. It was announced that Article 10 of the School Law would at last be applied to the Greek communities, thus requiring them to teach in Bulgarian in their primary schools. This caused some despair amongst the Greeks many of whom decided to send their children to schools in Adrianople or other accessible Ottoman towns whilst the more pessimistic of them left altogether, and by October 1907 over ten thousand Greeks had emigrated from Bulgaria, though many returned later.

At the end of 1906 Bulgaria encountered a new crisis and one very different from any it had previously experienced. This was the first serious outburst of urban unrest. It was produced by social tension and assumed some of the characteristics of a class confrontation. Bulgaria's small but growing proletariat and its living conditions are discussed elsewhere but it was of political significance that this new social group was predominantly young and was living in the dreadful conditions engendered by early industrialisation. There was also a pre-existing socialist intelligentsia to channel the inevitable discontent into political lines and by 1906 the socialist movement and the attendant trade unions were already established, though these were also split into two competing factions, the Broads who accepted limited cooperation with bourgeois parties and the Narrows who rejected such collaboration.* Between 1904 and 1906 conditions for the urban poor became worse as increases in taxation and prices outstripped wage increments and there were a number of strikes, some of them inspired in part by events in Russia, the plants affected including the state coal mines at Pernik, a large sugar refinery in Sofia and textile mills in Sliven. The government responded with special legislation to bolster the old guilds as an alternative to trade unions and by decreeing that if work was interrupted without the employer's consent he was entitled to compensation from the striking workers. This provoked a large demonstration when 1,500 protested outside the Sŭbranie building in December 1906.

This was a minor problem in comparison with the crisis which was emerging on the railways. In December some two thousand poorly paid civil servants had petitioned the Minister President for an increase in wages. His response was to fine all petitioners a sum equivalent to a quarter of their meagre monthly salary, and all senior administrators were warned that they would be held responsible for the loyalty of their subordinates and should therefore urge their discontented staff to resign; this was a veiled order to dismiss the dissidents. Among the poorly paid public servants were the railwaymen. They made ready to strike under the guidance of their unions which were associated with the Broad Socialists. Petkov did not flinch. On 13/26 December he declared that he was not worried by strike threats from the railwaymen for such a strike would be illegal and if it did take place he would send in the army to keep the trains moving. To give substance to his warning he rushed through the Sŭbranie an amendment to the Civil Service Law. Any government employee who, without the permission of his superiors, refused to work was liable to instant dismissal, and a vindictive second amendment stripped of their pension rights any government servants who resigned or were sacked before completing fifteen years of service. Public servants, said Petkov, were in a different category to employees in the private sector for on them depended the maintenance of the state machine and therefore of the nation's defences and well-being; no person entrusted with such responsibilities could be allowed the luxury of the right to strike. This was the last straw for the railwaymen. On the day that the new law passed the Sŭbranie, 21

---

*For the emergence of the socialist political parties and the trade unions see Chapter 18, and for the development of the proletariat and living conditions, see Chapter 20.

December/3 January, they struck. Immediately the Cabinet posted soldiers in Sofia station and put technical troops to work on the railways. A tolerable if not entirely predictable passenger service was maintained but two weeks after the strike began there was chaos in the freight yards. The distribution of essential supplies virtually broke down and in the large towns the shortage of fuel was made acute by an unusually severe winter. By late January firewood was unobtainable in Sofia and coal was in desperately short supply for though the miners were now back at work coal from Pernik had to be carried to the capital by cart. The government, in addition to putting the army's railway battalion to work, also called up all railwaymen of military age. Many of these were in technical units and were now forced by military discipline to break their own strike, though general obstructiveness and a dogged work-to-rule ensured that the back-log of freight was cleared only slowly. Petkov and the Cabinet were in some embarrassment. They asked foreign governments for the loan of footplate crews and talked of doubling the size of the military railway battalion and dividing it into two sections with one or the other always in service with the army. They also intended forcing railwaymen not of military age to sign a declaration avowing their willingness to serve with railway troops in the event of mobilisation.

The tensions of the rail strike were greatly exacerbated by the most violent outburst yet seen against the person of the Prince. On 25 December/7 January Ferdinand was to open the new National Theatre in the capital, an institution built allegedly for the nation and indubitably with the nation's money but, it was felt in radical circles, for the amusement chiefly of the rich and the Court coterie. Feelings had run particularly high in the University whose rector had even written on the subject in the opposition press. The students decided to refuse the invitation to send sixty of their number to the gala opening and to stage a demonstration of protest instead. Petkov did not anticipate anything more than the usual silent protest but when Ferdinand arrived at the theatre he was met by a large and vociferous crowd of students and striking railwaymen. Whistles were blown, insults shouted and lumps of ice thrown at the Prince and his party. It was the first time that Ferdinand had been directly and publicly reviled and he took it very much to heart.

So too did the Cabinet, to such an extent that one opposition deputy declared that it had lost its collective reason. The crowd in front of the theatre had been savagely dispersed and the Minister of Education, who was in any case ill, was quickly eased out of office, but these were trivialities compared with what was to come. On 6/19 January 1907 Petkov decreed a six month closure of the University and sacked all members of the teaching staff. On the following Sunday a demonstration by students was broken up by cavalry units armed *à la russe* with *nagaiki* (whips) and students and teachers who tried to enter the University on the following day were locked out by troops; the city had all the appearances of an armed camp with frequent military patrols and soldiers stationed at every police post. To ensure order the government then called up all students of military age whilst those unfit for service were returned to their homes under military escort; it was even rumoured that the entire University was to be transferred to Tŭrnovo where it would be less exposed to the influence of the radicals and Socialists who were so numerous in the capital.

The closure of the University and the sacking of its staff were illegal. The University Act of 1904 stated clearly that this could be done only with the consent of the Rector but Petkov claimed that he had acted justifiably under Article 47 of the constitution. He also argued that his actions had been necessary because to leave such events unpunished would lead to national 'demoralisation'; he told the Sŭbranie, 'I hold the demonstration to have been a grave crime and the punishment has to be correspondingly severe'.[5] To protect Ferdinand from further embarrassment Petkov also introduced yet more legislation to restrict the press, editors of daily papers now being required to possess, paradoxically in view of recent events, a university degree or sufficient wealth to pay a hundred leva per month in direct taxes. For his part Ferdinand insisted that the government now carry out what he had long been demanding, a cleansing of the nation's educational system. The government willingly obliged. Entrance requirements for the University were made more exacting and in future students were to sit examinations at least once a year rather than once every four or eight terms. In February the government introduced a new National School Law under which the responsibility of school committees for hiring teachers was to be diluted by making appointments subject to the approval of the Ministry of Education or one of its regional inspectors. At the same time teachers were barred from any political activity and from membership of any political organisation or trade union, through which regulation the government engineered the dismissal of scores of politically unreliable teachers. In March the Sŭbranie sanctioned an extraordinary grant of 300,000 leva to expand the police forces.

The reaction of the opposition Parties was predictable. They came together to form a united block, even the Broad Socialists joining with Radical Democrats, or Radicals, the Democrats, the Nationalists, and the Tsankovists. The united opposition called for large protest meetings and in the provinces these caused widespread disturbances. In Sofia a huge meeting of over ten thousand protesters passed off quietly after the government had wisely decided to drop its plan to hold a counter meeting on the same day; even so the atmosphere in the city was sufficiently tense for the chief of police to warn foreign representatives to keep well away from the district in which the meeting was to take place.

The theatre demonstration had been aimed specifically at the Prince and the opposition did not lose sight of this target. The anti-government newspapers, despite the increased restrictions placed upon them, attacked the Prince's personal regime with renewed gusto. The Tsankovist *Bŭlgariya* consistently argued that the source of the evils afflicting the nation was Ferdinand's personal power, and similar messages were to be read in the Radoslavist *Narodni Prava* (People's Rights), in the newly-established *Balkanska Tribuna* (Balkan Tribune), which was close to the Nationalist Party, and in the Democrats' *Pryaporets* (Standard) which defined Bulgaria's political status as 'constitutional absolutism'. The satirical *Bŭlgaran* conveyed the same message and ironically suggested that Petkov be appointed to the now vacant chair of constitutional law.

Yet the government was safe. It had a huge and obedient majority in the Sŭbranie and the popular movement against the restrictive legislation soon lost its impetus. Only Ferdinand could remove the Cabinet but now that all the major Sŭbranie Parties had joined an unholy alliance which included the Radical Democrats and the Socialists the Prince was unlikely to drop his present crew, the more so as early in February he was grief-stricken at the death of his mother. The Cabinet had been helped in the beginning of February by the settlement of the railway strike. Petkov had at last relented and allowed Untenberg, the Director of BDZh, to offer concessions to the strikers, and this conciliation was supported also by the Prince who had been disturbed by the violence of the government's handling of the stoppage. It was also welcomed by the commercial lobby, the influential wheat-exporters of Varna, for example, having starkly defined in a petition to Ferdinand the dangers facing the nation's trade. The railwaymen, somewhat demoralised by the sudden and natural death of one of their leaders, returned to work in return for promises of higher wages and no victimisation. In March the Sŭbranie voted a credit of 600,000 leva to cover the cost of increased wages.

The end of the strike was not the end of political violence. On 27 February/11 March Petkov was gunned down in the centre of Sofia. There were suspicions of a widespread anarchist plot to remove the entire Court and government and the Prince even suspected that the Nationalist leader, Geshov, for whom he had an almost pathological hatred, was involved. He was not and the killing of Petkov, like that of Stambulov, was an act of personal revenge.

Gudev, the President of the Sŭbranie, was made Minister President. His policies were little different from those of Petkov though the atmosphere in which they were carried out was slightly more relaxed. Genadiev was made leader of the Party and his power increased considerably, this, together with a collective wish to deflect attention from immediate domestic woes, accounting in part for the increase in Bulgarian activity in Macedonia at this time.

Gudev's government was noticeably weaker than that of Petkov. The separation of the Minister Presidency from the leadership of the Stambulovist Party weakened the former, and the government had no popular policies to offer the nation. Even the attempt to strike a more assertive pose in Macedonia back-fired for it provoked a collective note from the powers to which the government returned what was popularly regarded as a demeaningly abject reply.

If the Cabinet was weaker than that of Petkov there were still good reasons why Ferdinand should keep it in office. The Stambulovists were in command of the Sŭbranie and any significant change of government would necessitate a general election. This would be expensive, might allow too much criticism of the political establishment, and could set a dangerous precedent which would indicate that political assassination was a means of securing fresh elections or a change of government. Furthermore Ferdinand did not want the excitement and possible embarrassment of an election in the summer of 1907 when he was due to celebrate the twentieth anniversary of his accession, and it would be appropriate for the Stambulovists who had brought him to the country to manage the festivities. The celebrations were held without untoward incident in August and included the unveiling of Zocchi's equestrian statue of Tsar Alexander II which still graces the centre of Sofia. Nor was Ferdinand yet decided upon who should succeed the Stambulovists, his willingness to accept any of the major Parties being still impaired by their association with the hated Geshov in the united opposition block. Nor were the opposition themselves yet ready to take office. In 1907 for the first time since the Stambulovists formed their second ministry the harvest was poor and this made the drawing up of the budget for 1908 a difficult undertaking. The opposition Parties were happy to leave that task to the Stambulovists during the Subranie session which would begin in the autumn. The same applied to another possible task facing the government, that of negotiating a commercial agreement with Austria-Hungary, a delicate matter following the abortive Serbo-Bulgarian customs union.

There were other problems arising from the government's past policies which the opposition were equally happy to leave in Gudev's uncertain hands. There was the high rate of Greek emigration which discomforted the Cabinet. In July the government faced the threat of another rail strike, this time over the disciplinary sacking of three engine drivers; terrified lest the nation be paralysed on the eve of the anniversary celebrations the government quickly gave in to the railwaymen. The University caused further humiliation for Gudev and his government. Enrollment for the new year was to begin in October but students picketed the building; only 101 names were entered on the lists compared with 1,300 in the previous year. The position as regards the staff was even worse for the government's efforts to recruit alternative teachers had failed lamentably; few of the foreigners who accepted these posts were suitable and even more galling for the government was the refusal of many Bulgarian school teachers to take jobs in the University. Even the National Theatre provided more trouble. Early in October, when the University fiasco was unfolding, Velichkov, who had been Minister for Education for a time under Danev, created uproar during the performance of a satire on the Russian bureaucracy. Incensed by what he saw as an insult to Russia Velichkov leapt to his feet with loud denunciations of the government. His performance outshone that on the stage and he was carried triumphant from the auditorium.

Since the anniversary celebrations it was obvious that the days of the government were numbered and Ferdinand had begun soundings for an alternative, approaching first a number of non-political figures such as Chaprashikov, his representative in Vienna. He made little progress but was happy to follow his general tactic of letting an incumbent ministry discredit itself completely. This was easily achieved. National morale was already low as exceptionally high emigration figures, for

Bulgarians as well as Greeks, indicated. This was primarily the result of the poor harvest which produced widespread discontent in the countryside and left many peasants with insufficient fodder for the coming winter. This discontent was soon exploited politically. It was easy for opposition deputies, including the writer Todor Vlaikov, to contrast the preoccupations of the peasant with those of an administration which could spend 100,000 leva on the anniversary celebrations. The two hundred and eighty protest meetings which the peasants' distress provoked soon moved from immediate economic to general political grievances, a popular demand being that for the reinstatement of village teachers sacked for their political beliefs. In the towns measures against the radical left went on undiminished and intensified the alienation of the urban poor; in October for example the police smashed up a socialist club and recreation centre. While the police were unrestrained in their dealings with the Socialists great indulgence was shown towards the Macedonians and their crimes. The murderer of Sarafov and Garvanov escaped thanks to the collusion of local officials in Dupnitsa, and a few weeks before that Genadiev had stopped the police arresting Sandanski who was then in Sofia.

In the final months of its time in office the government was compromised not so much by its failures in dealing with the nation's problems as by its own gargantuan corruption. Examples of self-enrichment were routine in Bulgarian politics by the beginning of the twentieth century; what was exceptional about the ministry of 1903–8 was simply the scale of these corrupt operations. Even most of the extra credits voted for the police after the events of January 1907 ended in ministerial pockets and Gudev, who until coming to office had earned a pittance as a translator for the British diplomatic agency in Sofia, managed in his nine months as Minister President to amass hundreds of thousands of leva and to build a sumptuous house. He was not an exception and no official transaction from the conclusion of a large foreign loan to the installation of central heating in the royal palace could be carried through without massive bribery. The *ne plus ultra* of corruption came in November 1907. The Stambulovist ministers, as conscious as everyone that they would not much longer be in office, set out to ensure that they would have sufficient financial reserves for their coming period in the political wilderness. Orders for new official buildings, including a palace in Plovdiv, were placed at a total price of twenty million leva, but the real cost of the buildings was no more than six million leva. The remaining fourteen million leva was to be deposited with the Banque Privée de Lyons-Marseilles, an institution with which a near relation of Mme Stanchiova had close connections, and this booty was to be shared between the bank and the ministers.

The time had come for the Prince to make his long-expected move. After completing the arrangements for his betrothal to Princess Eleonora of Reuss-Köstritz he began in November/December serious negotiations with opposition leaders, deciding early in the new year that the Democrats were the appropriate successors. On 8/21 January 1908 the Stambulovists finally slunk heavy-pocketed from office and in a little over a week Malinov had formed his Cabinet. The grand corruption of the out-going ministers did not remain unpunished. They were eventually tried on forty separate counts with the indictment covering some seven hundred folio pages. A number of those indicted actually served time in prison. In 1908, however, the main focus of attention was upon events in European Turkey out of which was to come Bulgaria's declaration of complete independence.

Chapter 17

THE GOVERNMENT OF MALINOV AND
THE DECLARATION OF INDEPENDENCE, 1908–11

The Democratic Party which came to office early in 1908 had been led by Aleksandŭr Malinov since the death of Karavelov in 1903. Malinov had committed himself and his Party unequivocally to a struggle against Ferdinand's personal regime, frequently boasting that he would not take office from the Prince but only from a freely-elected Sŭbranie. When the second Stambulovist government was on the point of collapse, however, he concluded an address to Ferdinand with the assurance that the Democratic Party and the nation were 'With you, for you and always by you'. Two weeks later, and without an intervening general election, Malinov accepted office as Minister President. Whilst in power he was to enact a number of reforms for which his mainly intelligentsia-based party supporters had long compaigned but on the other hand he was also to supervise developments which considerably strengthened Ferdinand's power and prestige.

Malinov's Cabinet included Mushanov, who stood to the left of the Party and was given charge of education; the geographical niceties of Bulgarian politics were observed by including Salabashev, the southern mathematician who had stage-managed the elections to the Rumelian Regional Assembly in 1879, and Liapchev, a Macedonian of moderate disposition. The latter's moderation meant that he did not raise his voice against the extremely vigorous constraints which the new administration immediately placed on Macedonian activists, constraints so severe that Takev, who as Minister of the Interior was responsible for them, was sentenced to death by an IMRO court.

The tough line taken with the Macedonians was to prevent any souring of relations with Turkey, for the government hoped to secure the rail link to Kumanovo which had been the objective of so many previous administrations. The government also hoped that this or a similar diplomatic success would help it in the forthcoming elections but in the event of failure there were still the usual methods for securing victory at the polls. These were in fact employed and the elections of June 1908 saw a reversal of party fortunes astonishing even in Bulgarian parliamentary politics, though even ballot rigging could not keep out a sizeable Agrarian representation. The Democrats who had had three representatives in the out-going Assembly now had one hundred and sixty-eight, and the Stambulovists who had previously been so powerful were now without a single deputy. Of the opposition Parties there were two Tsankovists, including Danev, four Nationalists but not including Geshov, five Radoslavists and one undiagnosed 'wild man'. Most significant of all on the opposition benches was the appearance of twenty-four Agrarians under the leadership of Aleksandŭr Stamboliiski.

The most striking act of the Malinov Cabinet was the declaration of full independence in September 1908. The disadvantages of incomplete independence had always been felt. They had enabled Nabokov and others accused of criminal acts to escape Bulgarian justice because of the Capitulations; they had allowed foreign governments to complain at the expulsion of Chadourne and to oppose changes in tariffs or the imposition of Bulgarian taxes on foreign nationals. In the commercial agreements concluded in the 1900s the role of the Capitulations was played down with Russia promising to renounce them *si omnes,* and Austria giving her word that she would not apply them. By 1905 there was little force left in the old stipulations that foreign subjects could be tried by consular courts according to the law of their own country, and Payakov told the Sŭbranie that all commercial cases 'will be decided according to Bulgarian commercial law and by Bulgarian courts without the intervention of consular authority'.[1] Yet despite these improvements many of the indignities of the 1878 settlement remained. In the 1880s Bulgaria had been reminded of her vassal status on numerous occasions, as for example when the Turks attempted to establish a separate department of the Grande Porte to deal with the subject peoples, or when, in 1886, a Turkish commissioner had been present at the Bulgarian-Serbian peace negotiations, or when in 1891 the Turks had protested at the new Bulgarian coinage which depicted the head of

Ferdinand—vassals, said the Porte, did not have the right to appear in effigy. After recognition in 1896 Bulgaria hoped that such attitudes would die but they did not and Turkey protested vehemently when Bulgaria was admitted as an independent participant to the Hague Peace Conference in 1907. It was then that Ferdinand determined that he should take the next opportunity to declare full independence, though in the event he predictably found it easier to take a decision of general principle than to act when opportunity arose.

There had frequently been rumours that the Prince was about to declare full independence for Bulgaria, but it was the convulsions precipitated in the Near East by the Young Turk revolt of 1908 which provided the desired opportunity.

Initially the government in Sofia, like those elsewhere, did not know how to react to the military revolt in Macedonia which soon led to the overthrow of the old regime in Constantinople and to the restitution of the 1876 Ottoman constitution complete with its elected assembly. There were inevitably those in Bulgaria who wanted to take adantage of the confusion in Turkey to attack and seize Macedonia and Thrace but such boldness could not be countenanced officially. There was little official opposition, however, to those who wanted to promote the Bulgarian cultural cause in Macedonia, to which purpose money, printing presses and advisors were sent into the territory. At the same time Nachovich set up a new committee to promote closer cultural, economic and political relations with the Young Turks; Madjarov, a veteran of Rumelian politics, declared that 'A friendly Turkey could be worth far more to Bulgaria than territorial gains'.[2] Yet there were those who were thinking not of territorial gains but of retaining what they already held, for the most percipient of observers had already detected the Ottoman nationalism which was so strong a feature of Young Turk attitudes. Stoev, the Chief of the Sofia Press Bureau who had been to Turkey to discuss the legal status of Rumelia, warned Malinov and the government that the Young Turks would try to reassert their sovereignty over all Ottoman territory, Rumelia included.

Stoev was correct and the new attitudes embarrassed not only Bulgaria but also Austria-Hungary who since 1878 had administered the Ottoman territories of Bosnia and Herzegovina. If, as seemed likely, the new regime were to call for elections to an Ottoman parliament they would no doubt expect Rumelia, Bosnia and Herzegovina to be represented. This neither Bulgaria nor Austria-Hungary would want. The Austrians had told Sofia in 1907 that they would not object to a declaration of complete independence by Bulgaria and the Russians had also said they would have no objection provided Bulgaria did not act in collusion with Austria. With this in mind and in the face of the increasingly hard attitudes in Constantinople on the question of Ottoman sovereignty, Malinov hurried to central Europe to consult with Ferdinand who, having taken in the Bayreuth festival, was vacationing in the Carpathians. Here the Prince was persuaded that the present crisis should be used to make the declaration but that its exact timing would depend on what provocations the Young Turks offered.

There was not long to wait for the first of these, the so-called Geshov incident. Geshov was at that time serving as Bulgarian representative in Constantinople but was not invited to the annual dinner to honour the Sultan's birthday, the Young Turks having let it be known that he would be invited to another function with his equals, the valis of the Ottoman vilayets and other Ottoman officials. The Bulgarians were furious, the more so because whilst Geshov was being snubbed Ferdinand, now in Vienna for the celebration of the sixtieth anniversary of Franz Josef's accession, was treated as a full reigning monarch. The Bulgarians complained to the Porte that the other Balkan representatives in Constantinople had not been treated in the same way as Geshov, nor, they insisted, had exception been made of Bulgaria in previous official ceremonies. In this they were not quite correct for Geshov had not been invited to the funeral of the British ambassador who died in Constantinople in March 1908, and the Austrian ambassador had complained when Geshov was present with other ambassadors to congratulate the Sultan on the granting of a constitution. Nevertheless Geshov was recalled, the Turkish Imperial Commissioner left Sofia, the frontier was closed and even excursion trains were stopped. Yet the Geshov incident was not one which the Bulgarians could use to make their declaration. Had they done so they would have been the first to make a major breach in the Berlin settlement; furthermore, a number of Turks were considerably embarrassed by the Geshov incident, for which they privately apologised and which, they insisted, could never justify tension or worse between the two countries. Within a few days Geshov was invited to return with an assurance that he would not be subjected to further indignities.

The incident which was to provide the Bulgarians with the opportunity for which they had been waiting came hard on the heels of the Geshov affair. Early in September workers in the Constantinople depôt of the Oriental Railway Company had gone on strike for higher

wages and better conditions. The strike spread and threatened to affect
ORC lines in Bulgaria. The government in Constantinople attempted
to avert this by sending officers into southern Bulgaria to negotiate
with the local workers but the splendidly equipped train was held by
the Bulgarians at the first station inside the Principality. The pressures
and dangers were clear. The Turks could argue they were acting to
protect Bulgarian interests in preventing yet another railway strike in
that country, but at the same time the appearance of Turkish officers in
southern Bulgaria could be interpreted as a reassertion of Ottoman
authority in the area. The Bulgarians, for their part, could denounce a
situation in which a strike in a foreign country could paralyse vital
railway lines; the Bulgarians could also see the strike as yet another
stick with which to beat the hated ORC. The Company was not
unconscious of that feeling and after the failure of Ottoman attempts
to settle the strike in Bulgaria ORC officials asked BDZh to take over
responsibility for running the lines in southern Bulgaria until the end
of the strike. The government in Sofia did not hesitate and by 6/19
September all ORC lines in southern Bulgaria were in Bulgarian
hands, with BDZh rather than ORC tariffs being charged; the first
trains with Bulgarian locomotives and crews received a rapturous welcome from the local populace. The southern Bulgarians immediately
began to argue that the lines must never be returned to the ORC and
meetings and petitions were organized to press this view. Within a few
days the strike was over and Bulgaria now faced the crucial decision.
To hand back the lines to the Company would infuriate the southern
Bulgarians and would lead Turk and Bulgarian alike to think that the
government in Sofia accepted ORC and indirectly Ottoman authority
in erstwhile Eastern Rumelia. Not to hand back the lines would be to
break with the ORC, and thus would be a breach of the treaty of
Berlin. If one breach of that treaty had been made there was little sense
in stopping there and not going on to the other and greater breach, a
declaration of full independence for a united Bulgaria. Yet there were
dangers in this course. The Young Turks would naturally be angry, but
so too would the Germans, for the lines involved formed part of the
Berlin to Baghdad route. The other powers, too, would not be happy,
particularly Britain who did not want to see major changes in the
treaty of Berlin and who did not wish to see the Anglophile Young
Turks in difficulties. Yet opposition from these quarters could be
weathered if Austria gave its blessing. The Ballhausplatz could be
expected to deprecate the nationalisation of what was still nominally

an Austrian company but given Vienna's predicament over Bosnia and Herzegovina could it still speak convincingly of the sacrosanct nature of the treaty of Berlin? The indications were that it could not and therefore that Austria would not object to Bulgaria's taking strong action. With this reassurance Malinov was able to press Ferdinand, arguing that even if Bulgaria did concede over the railway the Turks would continue to reassert their claims upon southern Bulgaria, and he used the vehemence of Turkish complaints at the detention of their train as an indication of Young Turk implacability. Ferdinand gave way and the ORC lines in southern Bulgaria were nationalised.

It did not take long for Ferdinand, who was now in Vienna, to be persuaded by his Minister President that the second and larger break with the Berlin settlement would better follow sooner rather than later upon the first, his final doubts having been dispelled by the information that the Ballhausplatz had in any case already decided upon the annexation of Bosnia and Herzegovina in the near future. Malinov, who had been in the Austrian capital with Liapchev, hurried back to Sofia where a long Cabinet meeting was held on 16/29 September after which the entire ministry repaired to Ruse to await the arrival of the Prince. When he appeared they all went straight to Tŭrnovo where on 22 September/5 October in the Church of the Forty Martyrs full independence was proclaimed. Bosnia and Herzegovina were annexed the following day.

The Russians were disappointed by the close association of Bulgarian and Austrian action but their hostility was directed more towards the latter and for Bulgaria the immediate danger came from Turkey. The Turks, their newly-found national pride affronted by the Bulgarian declaration, boycotted Bulgarian goods; there were a series of incidents along the border, and the Turks demanded a rectification of the frontier in the ever-troubled Kŭrdzjali district. In response the Cabinet in Sofia, without waiting to ask the Prince, mobilised the Eighth Infantry Division in southern Bulgaria. With tension mounting between Vienna and St Petersburg the great powers could not afford local conflicts in the Balkans and they therefore informed both Bulgaria and Turkey that in the event of war between the two states the powers would permit no alteration to the territorial *status quo*. With that tension between Sofia and Constantinople began to subside and the governments, aided by the powers, began the search for a settlement.

In Bulgaria itself there was not universal rejoicing at the latest dramatic turn of events. In a passionate debate which lasted five days, the government was accused of treachery to the Slav cause by its collusion with Austria at the expense both of Russia and of Serbia who had her own designs upon Bosnia and Herzegovina. Malinov replied that the Russians had been happy to see Austria take the two provinces as long ago as 1877. He went on to reject the charge of collusion with Austria. In this he was technically right for the two countries had not pre-concerted their actions but these actions, by the very nature of the problems involved, became intertwined and interdependent. Government spokesmen also dealt effectively with those who complained that the eventual costs of the amortisation of the tribute and the taking over of the ORC lines were too high, but there were no soft answers to turn away the wrath of those who claimed that Ferdinand had acted too boldly in taking the title King.* Why, they asked, had it been necessary to do this as well as declare independence? Stamboliiski said bluntly that independence had been ruined by its association with the person of the Prince. The Macedonians, too, were displeased for the declaration of independence was seen by them as meaning that Bulgaria was satisfied with the existing territorial arrangements in the Balkans.

These criticisms did not prevent the Sŭbranie accepting the declaration of independence and the changes in Ferdinand's title, pending approval by a Grand National Assembly, but international recognition also had to be secured. By late 1908 the dispute between Bulgaria and Turkey, though still sharp, had devolved into one over money. The Turks were claiming compensation both for the loss of the Eastern Rumelian tribute, though this had not always been paid, and for the monies Bulgaria was supposed to pay to cover Eastern Rumelia's share of the Ottoman Public Debt. Both these payments, Sofia insisted, would cease. The Oriental Railway Company was also demanding compensation for the loss of its property in southern Bulgaria and for all these the Bulgarians were prepared to offer 52.5 million francs. This the Porte rejected as insufficient and after a good deal of international pressure the Bulgarians raised their bid to 82 million francs, 40 million as amortisation of the tribute and 42 million for the ORC, but this fell far short of the 125 million francs which the Turks were still demanding. Early in 1909 Russian intervention solved the problem. The essence of the Russian offer was that the Turks should write off the difference between the 82 million and the 125 million francs in which

---

*The Bulgarian word is 'Tsar' which I have translated as King rather than Emperor.

case Russia would forget the war indemnities owed to her by Turkey since 1877. At the same time Russia lent the 82 million francs to Bulgaria in the form of a loan from the Russian State Bank at the extremely generous rate of 4.25%. The settlement was an ingenious one and, unlike most international agreements, left most parties conscious of its advantages rather than its shortcomings. All powers welcomed the reduction of tension in the Near East, for this was a time when Russia and Austria were still in bitter dispute over Bosnia and Herzegovina; for Bulgaria it guaranteed international recognition of her independent status and it had the additional and not inconsiderable advantage that it transferred to the Turks the responsibility for meeting claims from the shareholders of the ORC; Turkey could no longer be embarrassed by claims from Russia for the payment of the 1877 war indemnity, and for Russia it meant a welcome reassertion of her influence in Sofia. An agreement was signed in Constantinople in April 1909 on the lines suggested by the Russians and soon thereafter the powers officially recognised Bulgaria's independence. In the following years Bulgarian diplomacy worked steadily and effectively for the removal of all signs of Bulgaria's vassal status; by 1912 the last of these had disappeared for by then all the powers had recognised the abolition of the Capitulations, and a Grand National Sŭbranie in Bulgaria had confirmed the constitutional changes brought about by the events of 1908.

Though the declaration of independence was Malinov's most notable action and remains the one for which his administration is chiefly remembered, it had also enacted a number of purely domestic reforms. In an election address in Varna in June 1908 Malinov had made a string of promises. His government would reverse the reactionary policies of the Stambulovists, increase democracy by instituting proportional representation in local elections, guarantee the constitutional freedoms of speech, assembly and association, reform education and the bureaucracy, lessen the government's dependence upon extraordinary budgets, make taxation more equitable, increase the strength of the army but nevertheless make military spending more appropriate to what the nation could afford, and would make government less obtrusive, particularly in the sphere of justice.

The surprising feature about Malinov's election promises was not their breadth, any party-leader in his position would have been the equal of that, but that Malinov actually tried to implement some of them. One of the new Cabinet's first acts was to dismantle the

Stambulovists' settlement of the University. All the foreign teachers whom the previous government had brought in were sacked and given two years' salary, the dismissed Bulgarians being then reinstated. This restored some prestige to the institution and enrolments rose from the dismal 206 of 1907–8, to 738 for 1908–9, 1,510 for 1909–10, and 2,116 two years later. In the summer of 1908, shortly after the elections, the tough Stambulovist press laws were relaxed. This was as far as the government wished to go in the immediate redressing of recent wrongs but the Party in the Subranie wanted revenge as well as rectification, demanding the prosecution of members of the last Cabinet. The Minister President was reluctant but it was another indication of Malinov's more relaxed attitude to power that he allowed the Cabinet to be overruled by the Assembly. The appropriate committees of enquiry were established and eventually it was decided to prosecute Petrov, Genadiev, Gudev, General Savov and Halachev for peculation.

The debates over the conduct of the Stambulovist ministers took up a good deal of parliamentary time but it did not prevent the Cabinet tackling other parts of its electoral programme. It abolished the tax on buildings and reduced the amount of government monopoly charged for salt. The electoral programme had promised the abolition of this monopoly but the government pleaded that it was legally bound to maintain it until 1911, albeit with lower prices, and by 1911 the government had in fact made all necessary arrangements for its abolition. An electoral promise to replace the excise on spirits with a tax on vineyards and plum-orchards (the Bulgarians drink plum brandy) was not implemented though the government assured the Assembly that the excise would henceforth be collected in a more civilised manner. The most ambitious plan in the realm of taxation was for the introduction of a progressive income tax to replace the professional tax. In fact the professional tax was in very mild form something of a progressive income tax for each type of profession—the free professions, commerce, industry and the handicrafts—was divided into ten classes according to presumed income and a total tax obligation was then imposed on each class by the guild of that profession. In 1908 it was made clear that the presumed income was very often not forthcoming and plans were therefore announced by which each individual was to pay tax in accordance with his personal income, with a sliding scale starting at two percent for incomes under 3,400 leva a year, and climbing to the not very dizzy height of eight percent on incomes of over 100,000 leva. In December 1910 so insecure did the impending changes make the tradesmen, hoteliers and workshop-owners of Sofia that they took to the streets in protest. The plans were shelved, not because of the protest action but because in the following year the Democratic Cabinet fell before it had time to legalise the final arrangements for the new system.

As with taxation so with the promised reforms of the political structure, some but not all of the promises were implemented. In 1908 proportional representation was introduced for village, town and provincial council elections and there were constant assertions that the system would be extended to include elections to the Sŭbranie, and arrangements were in fact made to experiment with it in the Tŭrnovo and Plovdiv provinces where factional fighting had been particularly intense. Malinov had also proclaimed a belief in referenda as the most democratic of procedures and had assured voters that these would be made part of Bulgarian political life. Accordingly in 1909 it was enacted that any decisions of a local council which involved granting contracts for construction works, taking out loans, the sale of communal lands or merging with another commune must be put to a referendum and if the communal council failed to do this then a petition from thirty percent of the electorate could automatically bring one about. Further democratic reforms were included in the constitutional changes put before the Grand National Sŭbranie in July 1911 and which had been prepared by the Malinov Cabinet. The King was no longer able to suspend civil rights in a time of national emergency; this prerogative was to be the Sŭbranie's. If the Assembly were not in session then the King could suspend civil rights but his action had to be sanctioned by an emergency session of the Sŭbranie within five days. The King was also deprived of his power to establish special courts, and further protection for the citizen was intended by the ruling that henceforth soldiers accused of criminal acts in a time of martial law had to be tried in civil not military courts.

Under Mushanov's Education Act of 1908 the role of the state in education was increased as the ministry was divided into departments for primary, middle and higher education and the whole system placed under the control of five chief inspectors appointed by the government. There were also changes in the ages at which children changed schools; vocational and technical schools were to be encouraged and Agricultural and Technical Faculties were to be opened at the University. These changes, though they did mean that the often corrupt local authorities had less say in education, also involved the appointment of an extra four thousand teachers and administrators and this extended government patronage.

An immediate result of the relaxation of the Stambulovist political controls was the release of an enormous amount of pentup opposition and frustration and the years 1908 to 1911 saw a continuous political and constitutional debate of an intensity unknown since the prolonged arguments of the 1880s. At the centre of the debate was the role and the personality of Ferdinand. Ferdinand had never known or even courted popularity. It was to be expected, therefore, that the relaxation of the press laws would bring forth new anti-dynastic journals such as *Patriot* which appeared in 1908 and *Chas* (Hour) which came out the following year. In the meantime established left-wing periodicals intensified their attacks on the King, and shortly after the deposition of Sultan Abdul Hamid in 1909, the socialist *Kambana* (Drum) likened Ferdinand to and recommended him for the same treatment as the deposed monarch. The Agrarians could use their newly-found parliamentary strength to make similar attacks and always pressed in budget debates for a dimunition of the civil list. One of the most cogent criticisms came from the Nationalist Party. A party conference in February 1910 ended with the publication of a long attack on Ferdinand's personal regime. The King, it said, ruled by offering ministers chances for unlimited self-enrichment and this rule by placemen was destroying the constitution and the party system; 'In fact', declared the Nationalists, 'for many years, and especially since 1903, we have seen at the helm 'People without Party or Parties without People', whilst the stronger parties are made to keep their distance'.[3] Parliament had become 'a lamentable instrument for personal rule, devoid of initiative or value'.[4] Budgets were meaningless as the state was financed mostly by extraordinary credits. Even the Grand National Sŭbranie had been ignored, the statement continued, for the changes of 1908 should have been confirmed by that body. Even worse was the devaluation of justice which followed from the constant but unpunished peculation and corruption of the ministers.

Closely associated with attacks on personal rule and the dynasty was criticism of the army. The army was expensive and did not always give value for money, for in 1909 it was revealed that much of the equipment recently received from France was faulty—324 pieces of artillery, for example, had defective gunsights. This provided the left, and particularly the Agrarians in the Sŭbranie, with much good propaganda material, whilst the right fretted that so powerful a machine was not being used, even as a threat, to extract concessions in Macedonia. Malinov's electoral pledge to maintain military strength but to restrict expenditure to what the nation could afford did not prevent him in 1909 from taking out a loan part of which was used for military purposes, but he did abolish the French naval mission which had completed its original task of establishing a small Bulgarian navy. The army's popular image meanwhile was not helped by two ugly incidents. In December 1908 an officer had thrashed a journalist who had accused him of maltreating a soldier and an angry crowd had forced the officer into a police station and demanded his arrest. In Ruse early in 1910 a much more serious clash took place. The trouble began with the elopement of a Christian boy and the daughter of one of the leaders of Ruse's influential Moslem community. The couple fled to a village where, after the girl had been baptized, they were married. They returned to their native city to find that the two religious communities had divided over their conduct and the Moslems had even sent delegations to Sofia to plead for the return of the girl to her offended community and faith. The government, anxious not to alienate Moslem opinion, ordered the police to return the girl to her father. Severe rioting prevented this. On the following day, 28 February/13 March the Christians celebrated their triumph in the streets of Ruse but the authorities then took alarm fearing these celebrations would be interpreted as demonstrations against the Turks, for strict instructions had recently arrived from Sofia insisting that no outbursts of anti-Turkish feeling take place lest this should cloud Ferdinand's forthcoming visit to Constantinople. The Ruse authorities therefore sent troops to break up the celebrations; fighting began and in a few minutes fifteen to twenty people had been killed and scores wounded.

There were furious protests at the incident and these were not confined to Ruse for all major towns in the country saw demonstrations against the atrocity. In these protests the role of the army as a mechanism for internal repression came in for especially severe condemnation. The government itself was much embarrassed. The incident had brought about that concentration on Christian-Moslem tension which the government had been anxious to avoid and this not only threw a shadow over Ferdinand's forthcoming visit to the Ottoman capital but also embarrassed the government's efforts to put an end to the Capitulations, for if the Bulgarian authorities behaved in this fashion could the powers afford to let their subjects be left to the workings of Bulgarian justice? The ugly incident in Ruse was the main reason for the demotion in September 1910 of Takev who, as Minister of the Interior, was responsible; in the reconstructed Cabinet he served as Minister of Communications. A Cabinet reshuffle could not however end discussion of the Ruse affair which was still the subject of Sŭbranie debate as late as 1914, and the chief object of censure was not the hapless Takev but the Prince and the army.

In 1911 the focus of political attention switched from Ruse to Tŭrnovo and to the Grand National Assembly which met there in the summer to enact a number of constitutional changes, including those implicit in the declaration of independence of 1908. Malinov and Ferdinand had originally believed that these latter changes need not be submitted to a Grand National Assembly but this the opposition had always contested. By 1911 Malinov had brought forward other proposed changes, including an increase in the number of ministries, but by the summer of that year he was no longer in office. His successor, Geshov, was quite happy to endorse changes in the number of ministries but at the same time he insisted that the Grand National Assembly must approve the 1908 changes. When the Assembly convened it contained a large government majority but also over fifty oppositionists, most of them Agrarians. The latter, under the leadership of Stamboliiski, argued that Ferdinand had no right to open the Assembly until that body had itself approved of his elevation from Prince to King, and thus when Ferdinand began to address the deputies Stamboliiski too rose to his feet and began to speak. There were simultaneous demonstrations by Agrarians and Socialists in the streets of Tŭrnovo. A cognate objection was made when Ferdinand closed the Assembly, though this time Stamboliiski and his colleagues were absent from their seats, having left instead a letter of protest at the illegality of the proceedings.

Given its large majority the government had no difficulty in persuading the Grand National Assembly to accept the change of Ferdinand's title from Prince to 'King of the Bulgarians', a wording which could be interpreted as including those of the nation still in *Bulgaria irredenta*. Because of fears of increased patronage the government faced some opposition when it proposed the abolition of the Ministry of Trade and Agriculture and the setting up of separate Ministries for Trade and for Agriculture and State Property; a new Ministry of Public Health was also formed. There were a series of other minor changes, including the reduction of the term of an ordinary Sŭbranie from five to four years and the increase in the length of annual sessions which would now be of four rather than two months duration. Article 38 was again changed, this time to state plainly that all Bulgarian monarchs with the sole exception of Ferdinand had to be of the Orthodox faith. The Sŭbranie also accepted the limitations of the King's prerogative to suspend civil rights. This came near to touching the real issues which were at stake in Tŭrnovo in 1911, those surrounding the King's personal power. The opposition disliked the new clause of the constitution which not only reasserted that Bulgaria was a monarchy where succession was to be by male primogeniture but also stated that the line was to be that descending from Ferdinand of Saxe-Coburg-Gotha. The debate on this clause and on a proposal, later dropped, to increase the civil list gave Stamboliiski and others a chance to air their republican views and this was done in unrestrained fashion. The fiercest battle, however, was over the proposed changes in Article 17 of the constitution. Under the 1879 constitution the Prince was to have the right to conclude treaties with neighbouring states. This was obsolete by 1908 when an independent state in the Balkans or elsewhere could not confine its foreign agreements to ones with its immediate neighbours. The government proposed that the new clause should read that 'The King represents the state in all its relations with foreign countries. The King negotiates and concludes all treaties with foreign states, the King ratifies those treaties and informs his ministers of them if the interests and the security of the country allow it.' The protagonists of the new wording argued that the old one was obsolete and that the new one would allow the secret negotiation of, for example, loan agreements without the often disastrous need to debate the proposed agreement in the Sŭbranie. They also pointed out that other constitutional states, even Britain, did not always reveal all about their agreements with other countries and in the contemporary world with its increasing tensions, particularly in the Balkans, a ruler must be able, for the security of the state itself, to conclude secret agreements and alliances. The opposition to this view was fierce and not confined to the Agrarians, Socialists and Radicals. For many so naked an accretion of royal power was quite unacceptable and confirmed latent fears about the nature and evolution of the personal regime of Ferdinand; some deputies openly declared he would sell the country to Austria or Russia. Nor could they accept the absolute need for alliances. Why, they asked, would a state need secret alliances if it were not bent upon some dangerous adventure which could end in war? So strong was opposition that after ten days of intense debate the proposed clause was thrown out and instead the power to negotiate treaties was vested in the government rather than the monarch. The full final text read:

> The King represents the State in all its relations with foreign countries. The government, in the name of the King, negotiates and concludes all treaties with foreign countries. The King ratifies these treaties. The ministers inform the Sŭbranie of treaties if the interests and the security of the State allow it. (Article 92 of the Constitution.)
>
> In all cases peace treaties and commercial treaties and any agreement which imposes financial charges upon the state or involves modifications of existing laws or affects the political and civil rights of Bulgarian citizens shall not be valid until they have been approved by the Sŭbranie.
>
> Under no circumstances may the secret clauses of a treaty invalidate its public ones.

The King had not received all he wanted but given his customary dominance over the Cabinet the Foreign Ministry and the diplomatic service, he now had formidable powers, for it was not difficult to invoke Article 92 to keep secret any agreement which he might persuade his ministers to conclude. Given the state of international and particularly inter-Balkan relations in 1911 this was a most significant development.

The changes voted by the Grand National Assembly had been largely drafted by the Malinov administration but were enacted by one headed by Geshov and Danev. The factors which brought about the change of government are to be found in external rather than internal affairs.

* * *

The European crisis of 1908 had increased tension in the Balkans and had marked the reactivation of Russia's Balkan policy after her disastrous Far Eastern preoccupations. It became clear soon after Russia's rebuff at the hands of Austria in 1908–9 that St Petersburg was anxious to promote an alliance of the Balkan states to contain supposed Austrian ambitions in the area. Bulgaria certainly had nothing to lose from better relations with her neighbours. Malinov persistently stressed his desire for closer friendship with Constantinople and efforts to secure the concession to build a railway from Kiustendil to link up with the Turkish system at Kumanovo continued unabated. Malinov was also frequent in his denunciation of the men of violence in Macedonia itself. By 1909 however it was becoming plain that the Young Turk policies of centralisation and Ottomanisation were not going to pacify Macedonia. By 1910 the *comitadjii* were again active. A more sinister development was the collapse of Ottoman authority in Albania for this raised the danger that Austria and Italy might intervene; if that happened there could be no expansion by the Balkan states into Albania and the competition for Macedonia and Thrace would become even more fierce. The disturbed state of Turkey-in-Europe precluded any real and lasting agreement between Sofia and Constantinople, and in 1910 the Bulgarian General Staff drew up its Plan A for war with Turkey.

Developments in Macedonia and Albania drove a wedge between the Turks on the one hand and the individual Balkan states on the other. That at least gave these states something in common and in 1910 there was a remarkable show of Balkan solidarity when representatives of all the Balkan ruling houses met amicably in Cetinje to celebrate the fiftieth anniversary of the accession of King Peter of Montenegro. But such festivities did not bring the separate states any closer together. That obviously could be done only by a conjunction of real political interests.

In the crisis of 1908–9 it had been Serbia who had felt most aggrieved. The Annexation, she maintained, had deprived her of her rightful inheritance in Bosnia and she had received nothing in compensation. From 1909 Serbia was therefore seeking redress and would need accomplices if this were to be secured. Serbia's patron, Russia, was not yet capable of military intervention in Serbia's behalf and so Bulgaria was the most obvious candidate for an alliance and both Belgrade and St Petersburg exercised considerable pressure to bring about a Serbo-Bulgarian agreement. In 1909, as the financial agreement with Turkey was being worked out, the Bulgarians offered Serbia free transit facilities on Bulgarian railways and talked again of a customs union. Later in the year Ferdinand visited Mount Kapaonik in Serbia to collect botanical specimens but he also visited the Serbian Crown Prince in Belgrade, and a few months after this he broke his journey through Serbia to talk with King Peter, and these were significant developments for Ferdinand was known to dislike the Serbian Court intensely. In 1910 when the Serbian monarch was *en route* to Constantinople he was given a flamboyant reception by Ferdinand in Plovdiv. Such meetings caused excited talk in the diplomatic legations but they led to little change in the cool relations between Bulgaria and Serbia. The Serbs, and especially the Minister President, Pašić, had been deeply resentful of Bulgarian action in 1908 for the Bulgarians had breached the Berlin settlement at the very moment when the Serbs, because of their long-term ambitions in Bosnia, were arguing for its preservation. When these passions had cooled the Serbs had good reason to seek an alliance with Bulgaria but the Bulgarians could see little advantage in one. It could easily provoke a counter grouping of Turkey, Greece and perhaps Rumania; and above all there was the problem of Macedonia. In 1910 the Serbs had been given the bishopric of Dibra which the Bulgarians regarded as rightfully an Exarchist see. Malinov himself was deeply suspicious of the Serbs and he again used the differences over Macedonia as a reason for refusing another Serbian approach late in 1910.

A further reason for Malinov's mistrust of closer association with Serbia was that state's ties with Russia. After the Bosnian crisis European polarisation became more apparent and the smaller states were under pressure to align themselves with one or other of the great power blocks. In 1910 Bulgaria did make an effort to come closer to Russia and the possibility of reactivating the 1902 military convention was raised. The talks failed because the Russians, though willing to accept a Bulgarian Salonika, would not agree to Bulgaria's taking Adrianople, nor would the Russians commit themselves either to a political agreement defining the objectives of the military convention or to what Bulgaria might get as a result of military cooperation. This was the only major departure from the *politique d'oscillation* which Ferdinand and Malinov followed between 1908 and 1911, a policy which meant wavering between Triple Entente and Triple Alliance seeking favours from both but making lasting commitments to neither. At first this policy was remarkably successful. Independence had been secured by making common if not preconcerted cause with Austria, but the problems it raised had been solved by Russian intervention. Ferdinand paid successful visits to both St Petersburg and Paris but in 1909 the long association between Bulgaria and the bankers of Paris was broken first by the Russian State Bank loan but more seriously by a one hundred million leva loan raised by a Viennese consortium.

Yet by 1911 the *politique d'oscillation* had become outdated. Continued and increasing unrest in Macedonia and Albania had meant that the collapse of Turkey-in-Europe appeared likely. The government in Sofia had to be prepared to stake Bulgaria's claim in Macedonia for if it did not then the Greeks or Serbs or Macedonian activists would outrun them, besides which an inactive policy would invite serious internal unrest. Bulgaria could no longer afford to stand alone and as Malinov was not the man to direct a foreign policy which sought alliances, particularly with the chief competitors in Macedonia, he was dropped in March 1911. After a few attempts to patch up a widely-based coalition an administration was formed from Geshov's Nationalist and Danev's Progressive parties. Ferdinand was known to loathe Geshov personally so the political reasons for accepting him had to be compelling and as one of the chief platforms of the Nationalist Party was better relations with Russia, it was widely assumed that the Cabinet would fall in with Russian wishes for some form of Serbo-Bulgarian alliance. It was also widely assumed, not least in St Petersburg, that such an alliance would have a defensive purpose, namely to contain Austrian ambitions in the Balkans. The general impression abroad, therefore, was that the new government would be pro-Russian and that it would be dedicated to the preservation of peace and the territorial *status quo* in the Balkans. In the first supposition foreign opinion was by and large correct. In the second it was widely misplaced. The change of Cabinet was a momentous one for it began a new era in the history of Bulgaria, an era which opened with great promise and which ended in seemingly irretrievable tragedy.

Chapter 18

THE FAILURE OF THE TŬRNOVO SYSTEM AND
THE ORIGINS OF MASS POLITICS; THE AGRARIANS AND
THE SOCIALISTS IN THE PERIOD BEFORE THE WARS

Bulgaria's constitution had been fashioned by intellectuals for peasants. It did not succeed in winning the confidence of those for whom it was designed. Although the Bulgarian peasants, unlike those in Rumania, had no local aristocracy to depress political interest and independence, they did not take the active part in national politics which the Liberals at Tŭrnovo had anticipated. The 1879 and 1880 elections saw no more than a third of the eligible population voting whilst in 1884 only thirty per cent voted and in Samokov not a single elector appeared on polling day. The *Stambulovshtina* further inhibited participation with a total of only 12,631 votes being cast in the election of 1893. By 1899 the total had risen to 28,461, but even this represented no more than half the total electorate and by then the system had produced its own devices to deprive the peasant voters of any real influence.

The peasants' general failure to involve themselves in politics had many causes. Peasant horizons were limited and, for the older generations at least, extended little beyond the limits of their native village. The peasant had little comprehension of party politics and their conflicting programmes, and he certainly could not understand why Bulgaria should find itself at odds with Russia and the Tsar. In the 1890s the programmes of modernisation and economic change preached by most parties and practised by Geshov and Stoilov were totally alien to most peasants. Even within the village there was little for which the peasant had to thank the system as increasing taxation, usury and declining world prices for grain were dragging him bewildered to the agrarian crisis of the late 1890s.

More fundamental in explaining the political apathy of the peasant was his gradual divorce from the intelligentsia. The combination of peasant and *intelligent*, especially the teacher and priest, had been the bedrock of the national renaissance but a gap between the two had always existed. Before 1878 that gap had been bridged by the common belief that life would improve once Liberation had been achieved. For the peasant the material conditions of life did not improve; for the *intelligent* they did. The intelligentsia provided the main source of recruitment for the rapidly expanding and well-paid bureaucracy and thus the peasant's old ally became his new oppressor. The problem was made worse by *partisanstvo*. The need to maintain party cadres by rewarding supporters with office meant that no government dared cut the number of civil servants or, except in the most exceptional of circumstances, the salaries paid to them; by 1900 there were over twenty thousand bureaucrats in the country, many of them in entirely dispensable posts. Furthermore, because educated men refused to consider anything below a middle-ranking post, preferring periodic unemployment to a lower one, the quality of the lowest officials, the ones with whom the peasant came into contact, was poor and fewer than one in five of the twenty thousand civil servants in post at the turn of the century had anything more than elementary education, leaving them no better qualified than most of the peasants whom they exploited. People therefore began 'to look upon the civil servant as an uninvited guest feeding off the state, one reminiscent of the Turkish *aga* or *kaimakam*',[1] and the official report into the disturbances of 1900 in north-east Bulgaria made it clear beyond doubt that the peasant had suffered much at the hands of semi-educated and corrupt local officials who owed their posts to *partisanstvo*.

Partisanstvo was not the only factor to bring the Bulgarian political system into disrepute. There was also massive electoral malpractice. From the earliest days politicians had resorted to irresponsible promises and often to open bribery and there had also been violence or the threat of violence. This had been used on a significant scale in the election to the Grand National Assembly of 1881 and did not disappear completely with the restoration of the Tŭrnovo system in 1883. Under Stambulov it became standard practice. Stambulov feared the nation's security was so endangered that he could allow neither the abolition of the constitution nor the freedom it promised, and therefore there was massive use of *shaikadjii* (thugs), police and even troops, particularly in the elections of 1886 and 1887. The Bulgarian parliamentary system never recovered from the straight-jacket into which Stambulov had forced it; after his fall there was in general less use of naked force but there was now no hope, as there had been before 1886, of evolution towards stable and responsible representative democracy.

At any general election a Bulgarian government, both before and after the *Stambulovshtina,* could count upon a number of seats, the so-called 'government dowry' which consisted mostly of constituencies with large Jewish and Moslem populations. The other seats necessary for a majority could always be secured by *partisanstvo,* an evil which seemed ineradicable after the abandonment of a law enacted by the Tsankovists in 1903 which had guaranteed security of tenure to civil servants. There were always constituencies which could not be controlled but should the number of opposition deputies be too large or their political complexion too radical some of them could always be removed when the Assembly reviewed the returns from each constituency and disqualified any member against whom complaints of irregularities could be substantiated.

By the early twentieth century elections in Bulgaria had become little more than corrupt operations to confirm in office a ministry recently chosen by the Prince. Elections often brought complete reversals of fortune for a Party, reversals inconceivable in a less tainted system; in 1894 the Stambulovists who had completely outnumbered the other parties in the previous Sŭbranie were unrepresented, and in October 1903 the same Party increased its membership from eight to over two hundred. Elections had long ceased to be, if they ever had been, mechanisms by which the popular will was revealed and implemented. They were rather instruments for the enforcement of the Prince's will.

By the mid-1900s Ferdinand's personal regime was firmly established. It was a carefully constructed system. Its ultimate foundation was the loyalty of the army's officer corps which Ferdinand had tied to his side by offering it high salaries, social prestige and great material comfort. If necessary Ferdinand would also interfere in party politics, the first instance of this being in the election of 1899 when the palace newspaper, *Balkanski Kurier* (Balkan Courier), endorsed the Radoslavists who had just come to office. Control of the vital Ministries of War and Foreign Affairs was another essential feature of the personal regime but that regime would have been almost impossible had not the two main political Parties of 1879 split into the seven separate factions which existed by the middle of the 1900s. The forces bringing about these divisions were disagreements over constitutional issues and over foreign affairs, and the tendency of the Rumelian party groups to operate individually; but by the end of the nineteenth century the constitutional issue had been settled, the union with Rumelia consolidated, and party differences over foreign affairs nullified by Ferdinand's assumption of complete control in this area after the fall of Stambulov. Parties were therefore little more than factional groups held together by personal relationships and the greed for office, and Ferdinand had no difficulty in playing one group off against the others. The party chiefs for their part seemed unable to cooperate long enough to resist Ferdinand's scheming. The personal regime was denounced with varying degrees of force and conviction by all parties but the lust for spoils bred by *partisanstvo* made them helpless connivers in that regime.

The objectives of the Liberal intelligentsia of 1879 had clearly not been realised. In peasant eyes the intelligentsia itself had been compromised by its close association with *partisanstvo* and the failure of the Tŭrnovo system. A section of the intelligentsia was also alienated from the political establishment. Dr Kiril Krŭstev, a respected scholar and commentator, wrote in 1898 that the very worst of all the evil effects of *partisanstvo* was that it deprived the intelligentsia of moral purpose and commitment. He grieved at the lack of response to the agrarian crisis at home and to recent catastrophes such as floods and increased political repression in Macedonia; the generation which had brought about the great national triumph of 1885 had, he feared, '. . . lost all faith, and part of it has sold its soul to the devil'. The devil was the material reward offered by *partisanstvo* and, Krŭstev continued gloomily, 'It would be difficult to find in any other nation anything like our anti-social intelligentsia'. Bulgaria, he concluded, was forfeiting the right to call itself a nation.[2]

Krŭstev's gloom was not isolated. Dimitŭr Rizov had written in 1893 that Bulgaria's intelligentsia had concerned itself with 'everything except that which is most important: the establishment of some form of political morality',[3] but such views were not entirely justified. A small but increasing segment of the intelligentsia had begun to address itself to the social and political problems of the nation but had rapidly concluded that the existing Parties would never provide solutions to them. The 'new intelligentsia' turned instead to new movements which aimed to enrol the masses in the political process, defend mass interests and give the masses power. In a peasant society with strong cultural and political links with Russia it would have been most surprising if Bulgaria had not borrowed a number of political ideas from the liberating power. Tolstoi's influence was felt in Bulgaria as elsewhere. In 1903 a journal, *Lev N. Tolstoi,* had been founded, though it did not last long, but in 1907 a few youths established a Tolstoian community in the Burgas province and its journal, printed on the village press, was described by the master himself as the only periodical depicting Tolstoian ideals in their pure form. Much more important and lasting was the influence of Populism. The nationalist poet and martyr, Hristo Botev, had been much influenced by Bakunin and Nechaev, and in the late 1880s Russian Populism was the main inspiration behind the phenomenon of *Siromahomilstvo* (Pauperophilia). This movement, started by Spiro Gulabchev, a Macedonian who had settled as a teacher in Tŭrnovo, had a cellular organisation similar to the revolutionary movement in Russia, and Gulabchev himself translated Chernyshevski into Bulgarian. Like the pure Populists in Russia *Siromahomilstvo's* adherents were interested more in social transformation than in political libration but they had little chance to develop their ideas as the movement was destroyed by the Stambulovist police.

Others who had not joined the *Siromahomilstvo* movement remained under the influence of the Russian Populists, particularly Mikhailovski and Lavrov. From these sources a number of Bulgarian writers developed the theme that Bulgaria's chief problem was the backwardness of its peasantry. If this problem could be overcome by educating the peasant to use more efficient methods then the nation would become more prosperous and with prosperity would come a greater sense of political maturity, and this was the only answer to the evils of *partisanstvo,* political corruption and the personal regime. Once again such writers were interested primarily in social change, not political reform which, like all true Populists, they regarded as irrelevant or even dangerous. It was out of such attitudes that the Agrarian movement in Bulgaria emerged and it was from such attitudes that this movement derived its initial but transitory reluctance to engage in politics.

The attempts to educate and improve the condition of the peasant began in the mid-1890s after the end of the *Stambulovshtina* and was much encouraged by the growing impoverishment experienced in many peasant communities. A number of new, and mostly ephemeral newspapers appeared, including the apolitical *Oralo* (Plough) edited by Yanko Zabunov, Director of the State Viticultural Institute in Pleven. In 1896 an attempt was made in the Varna area to organise peasants into an effective lobby, this attempt being inspired by the successful foundation in 1895 of a national teachers' union. In the meantime Zabunov in Pleven was collecting around himself a group of teachers from the Viticultural Institute and from the Model Agricultural School near Ruse and together they established another journal, *Zemedelets* (Farmer) under Zabunov's editorship. *Zemedelets* was mainly technical in content but it did carry some political material and called for the political organisation of the peasantry. The journal collapsed in 1898 through lack of funds but in the same year another activist and propagandist, Yordan Pekarev, succeeded in setting up sixty local peasant organisations in the Varna province, these local units being known as *druzhini* (battalions) like the local branches of the National Liberal Party. Pekarev and fifteen colleagues also set up the 'First Constituent Committee' of an Agrarian organisation and soon had a journal of their own, *Nova Borba* (New Struggle), renamed *Zemedelska Borba* (Agrarian Struggle) soon after it began publication, and declaring in its motto that 'The moral and material improvement of the peasants is the business of the peasants themselves'. Pekarev was conscripted in 1899 and his call for the return of peasant candidates at the local elections held in that year had little response.

The announcement of the return to a tithe in kind transformed the nascent peasant movement. Early in 1899 Tsanko Bakalov, better known under his pseudonym of Tserkovski, had published with the cooperation of the agrarian enthusiasts in the Tŭrnovo district an *Appeal to the Peasants of Bulgaria* calling upon them to set up a national union to fight for agricultural improvement. Tserkovski was a socialist who believed that the peasants' plight had now become so desperate that they had to have some form of organisation similar to a trade union or a benevolent society, but not a political party which would inevitably compete with the Socialists' own political organisation. In April 1899 a meeting in the Tŭrnovo district endorsed Tserkovski's *Appeal* and urged all peasant communities to send delegates to the First Agrarian Congress which was to meet in Pleven in December. In September 1899 the movement was strengthened by the foundation of yet another journal, *Zemedelska Zashtita* (Agrarian Defence), to replace the already defunct *Zemedelska Borba*. The new journal was published only three times per month but it had a circulation of two and a half thousand, was under the able editorship of

Zabunov, and was an ideal mouthpiece for peasant discontent when the reversion to a tithe in kind was announced. The impact of that announcement in October upon the Agrarian movement was immediate. In the three years up to October 1899 a maximum of one hundred and fifty local peasant associations had been founded; in the last three months of 1899 new associations were being set up at a rate of over thirty per month, though these groups were as yet by no means agreed on policy or similar in organisation. All, however, could unite in condemnation of the return to the tithe in kind.

That united detestation of the tithe in kind was seen when the Congress met in Pleven after Christmas, a time chosen because there was no work to do in the fields and because the teachers were on vacation. There were eight hundred and forty-five delegates from forty-five out of Bulgaria's seventy-one districts, though the majority of the delegates came from the north-east where the origins of the Agrarian movement were to be found. Most delegates were peasants though there were sizeable numbers of teachers, priests, and agricultural advisers. The Congress set up the Bulgarian Agrarian Union, elected an eight-man Central Governing Council which included Tserkovski, Zabunov, Pekarev and Dimitur Dragiev, and voted a series of 'temporary statutes' in which the objective of the Union was described as being 'to raise the intellectual and moral standing of the peasant and to improve agriculture in all its branches'. The Union was to help the peasant by encouraging the consolidation of separate strips into compact holdings, by taking steps to provide cheap credit, by finding markets for agricultural produce, by settling disputes between members of the Union, and by conducting a general propaganda campaign on behalf of the agricultural sector. Membership of the Union was to be open to peasants, teachers, priests and other persons whom the local organisation might think acceptable. The First Congress made a determined effort to keep the Union out of national politics and the party-political system. Indeed after condemnation of the tithe detestation of the existing Subranie Parties was probably the strongest feeling expressed in the Congress and so strong did this feeling run that even the name of the local organisation was changed to *druzhba* (friendly association) to dissociate the Agrarian Union from the structure of the existing Stambulovist Party. Dissociation from existing Parties was easy to achieve but it was almost impossible to take up an entirely apolitical stance. The constant denunciation of the tithe by speakers in the Congress and by the Union itself had clear political overtones, as

did dissociation from party politics, particularly when it was expressed
in terms such as those which described the existing parties as '. . . the
gangrene which will destroy beautiful Bulgaria'.[4]

The question of how far the Union should strike political attitudes
was to dominate discussion within the movement's leadership for the
next two years. The First Congress had urged support in forthcoming
local elections for candidates who specifically committed themselves to
the improvement of agrarian conditions and this had proved a successful tactic with one hundred and twenty local communal councils passing into the control of pro-Agrarians. During the Second Congress,
held in December 1900, the Union made some changes to its original
programme, placing more emphasis on agricultural education, calling
for greater legal security for the peasant property owner, including the
right to a minimum of land which was to be inalienable even in the case
of bankruptcy, for the reorganisation of the Agricultural Savings
Banks together with other measures to combat usury, and for the
introduction of a progressive income tax. The Second Congress also
elected a new Central Governing Council which now had sixteen
members and chose a three-man Permanent Council under the presidency of Zabunov. Once again the Union declared itself to be a
pressure group not a political party, yet there were again political
implications in demands such as those for a return to constitutional
rule, for respect for the law, and for a decrease in official salaries and
pensions. It also decided, and this was a significant movement towards
greater political involvement, that peasants should be urged to vote in
the forthcoming general election for specifically Agrarian candidates.
Despite this, however, its leadership still maintained that the Union
was not a political organisation, declaring, 'We do not seek power, we
shall form no ministry'.

The elections in February 1901 proved a considerable triumph for the
Union as twenty-three Agrarians were elected, including Zabunov and
Tserkovski, and five out of the eight seats in the Tŭrnovo and Ruse
districts were captured by them. These successes encouraged those
within the Agrarian movement who wished to give it a clear political
orientation. The depressing sequel to the electoral victories encouraged
them even more in this direction, for no sooner had the Sŭbranie met
than all but seven of the Agrarians defected to other Parties, a large
proportion of them having been seduced by offers of enrichment from
the established Parties. The political lobby within the Union was now
convinced that if the movement was to involve itself in politics it must

do so whole-heartedly, and his argument won over a number of leading Agrarians, including Zabunov, who had originally been sceptical of political activity. He now committed himself to the political faction which was led by Dragiev.

At the Third Congress of the Bulgarian Agrarian Union held in Sofia in October 1901 the political faction made further advances; Tserkovski and those who wished to keep the Union out of party politics were defeated and to mark the change the Union altered its title to The Bulgarian Agrarian National Union (BANU) to demonstrate its belief that it was now a movement dedicated to the regeneration of the whole nation and not just the agricultural part of it. The declared aim of the renamed movement was '. . . the improvement of agriculture in all its branches, and the moral, political and economic improvement of the peasantry and of the entire nation'. Zabunov was re-elected President of the Permanent Council and Dragiev was made Vice-President; Tserkovski was dropped.

At the Third Congress BANU's leaders announced the movement had over 35,000 members and nearly eight hundred local *druzhbi*. This was an exaggeration and a much more desperate picture was revealed in October 1902 when Dragiev told the Fourth Congress, in Shumen, that of the four hundred *druzhbi* created during the tithe struggle only forty at the most were still in existence, and the situation was even worse in 1903 when the Fifth Congress, at Stara Zagora, had only a handful of delegates who learned that almost all the local organisations had ceased to exist and that the party newspaper was in such financial difficulties that it could appear only irregularly. There had also been great electoral disappointment for in the poll of 1903 the Agrarians had not returned a single candidate. This was partly to be explained by the tough policing of the polls which was Stambulovist tradition but it had also to be attributed to weaknesses in the Agrarian movement itself. The split between the political and apolitical factions had cost the movement a number of experienced and able leaders at the local level and at the national level the majority of the founding fathers, including Zabunov, had by 1903 retired. Of these founding fathers only Dragiev remained and the future leader of the movement, Stamboliiski, had not yet made any impact. Also such local *druzhbi* as had survived were heavily penetrated by members of the established political Parties and thus the local BANU vote was placed at the disposal of one of those Parties.

The prospects for BANU seemed poor, the more so as the living conditions of the peasants were improving because of better harvests and the development of the cooperative movement which greatly weakened the private money-lender; the real income of the average peasant increased by forty-four per cent between 1901 and 1911. Yet the dismal prospects of 1903 and 1904 were soon dissolved and in the general election of 1908 the Agrarians captured twenty-three seats and secured over one hundred thousand votes, or eleven point two per cent of the total poll; they were by far the largest of the non-governmental Parties in the Sŭbranie elected that year, the next largest being the Radoslavists who had only five seats and forty-six thousand votes. In local elections held in the same year the Agrarians secured control of almost three hundred local councils. At the same time BANU could boast 1,123 local *druzhbi* and six thousand subscribers for the party newspaper whose financial worries were long forgotten. In the elections to the Grand National Sŭbranie in 1911 BANU returned fifty-three representatives.

There were a number of reasons for this remarkable recovery, the poor harvest of 1907 being not the least of them. It was also due to changes within BANU itself. At its low point in 1903 the Fifth Congress had worked out a new code regulating the nomination of candidates for general elections, the conduct of electoral campaigns and the responsibilities to be undertaken by elected deputies, and in the long run these new regulations prevented any repetition of the mass defections which followed the 1901 election. In the Sixth Congress, held in 1904, the party programme was redefined giving yet more emphasis to the political aspects of its struggle and disowning any electoral pacts with the established Parties in the Sŭbranie. In 1907 BANU headquarters were transferred from Stara Zagora, Dragiev's hometown, to Sofia and this increased its political effectiveness. BANU also increased its prestige by the day-to-day improvements its members brought to many villages. The Party set up a life insurance scheme for local *druzhbi,* BANU members were prominent in many of the cooperative societies which were established in the 1900s, and in 1908 BANU was instrumental in establishing the 'National Store', a nation-wide retail cooperative. A further reason for BANU's revival was the merger in 1902 of the official *Zemedelska Zashtita* with another paper to form the new party paper, *Zemedelsko Zname* (Agrarian Banner), a development which brought Aleksandŭr Stamboliiski, a member of the editorial board, into the leading circles of BANU. In 1906 Stamboliiski became editor and under his guidance the paper became a most effective mouthpiece for Agrarian ideals and propaganda.

By 1908 Stamboliiski had become the dominant figure within BANU. He had first heard Agrarian ideas preached when as a student in the State Viticultural Institute in Pleven, he had attended lectures by Zabunov. By the time he became editor of *Zemedelsko Zname* Stamboliiski had worked out more clearly than anyone else a programme and an ideology for the Agrarian movement. These ideas he published in the columns of the newspaper and in two major political tracts, *Political Parties or Estate Organisations,* published in 1909, and *The Principles of the Bulgarian Agrarian National Union,* published ten years later. That BANU had so powerful a publicist and so effective an ideologist was another reason for its revival after the depressing years 1903 to 1904.

Stamboliiski's objective was a society which could offer justice and equality for all. He believed these goals could not be achieved without private property which was 'the motive force for work and progress' and which would give men satisfaction and a sense of purpose and dignity. At the same time he insisted that there were two aspects of human nature, an individual and a communal; private ownership satisfied the needs of the individual aspects of human nature but as productive relationships became more complex a communal consciousness would develop as it became obvious that the well-being of one was dependent on the well-being of others. As communal consciousness developed private farming would shed its primitive, individualist form and become more communal, though ownership would remain private. With his belief in private ownership went a Jacobin-like hatred of excess. No-one must be allowed to own too much and no-one must be left with too little private property, for from such inequalities all injustices stemmed, and it was this aspect of his ideology which allowed him and BANU to campaign for the confiscation of excess property from individuals and institutions such as the state and the Church, the property so taken being used to establish a fund to provide the means of subsistence for those who did not have enough land. It also led BANU to argue for state assistance to cooperatives. Stamboliiski hated all deviations from the simple village life, and saw them as destructive of the potential for human improvement. He told a meeting of exiled Russian Social Revolutionaries in Prague in 1920:

The mystic cult of the 'proletariat' is the most dangerous illusion in the world. I want freedom for the workers, but I don't believe in their ability to govern. In the name of the 'proletariat', clever politicians will always run the show while the workers themselves continue for another twenty or thirty years to turn screws. With peasants it's different. Each peasant is an encyclopaedia in himself. He understands the life of animals and plants, knows a little astronomy, tills the land, breeds animals, builds and repairs his own wagon, and predicts the weather better than any meteorological station. In the peasant are the seeds of the fully developed human personality. He needs only organization and more knowledge.[5]

Just as he disliked and feared industrialisation as a break from the wise and fulfilling life of the peasant so Stamboliiski castigated other such deviations as represented by the apparatus of the modern state, in particular the bureaucracy, the military and above all the monarchy and the Court.

Stamboliiski's political ideology was founded on the notion that society was divided not into classes but into 'estates', though the Bulgarian word he used, *sŭsloviya,* can also mean 'professions'. An estate was a group of people whose engagement in the same occupation gave them common economic interests, even though they may be of a different social background, making it possible, for example, for a small peasant farmer to have the same economic interests as the large estate-owner. The principal estates in Bulgaria in 1909 were defined by Stamboliiski as the agrarian, the artisan, the wage-labourer, the entrepreneurial, the commercial and the bureaucratic. Of these estates the most important was the peasant because it guaranteed that man would not exploit man, that wealth would be distributed equally, and that separate individuals by engaging in a variety of occupations on their own property would achieve self-fulfilment and satisfaction. Stamboliiski recognised that the more highly developed an economy the more estates it would have and thus social relationships were to become more rather than less complex with economic advance. Stamboliiski did not believe that the advent of industrialisation must mean the end of the peasant; Bulgaria could have both, he argued, if the state was prepared to pay to keep the peasant in business, but this it could do only if it stopped spending up to a third of its budget on the army. This in turn would mean the abandonment of all aggressive intentions and BANU was thus an advocate of a peaceful foreign policy, hoping to see autonomy and an eventual Balkan confederation as the answer to the Macedonian question.

BANU argued consistently for a decrease in military expenditure, a diminution of royal power and expenses, a retrenchment of the bureaucracy, and a foreign policy based on peaceful cooperation with Bulgaria's neighbours. It did not advocate revolution, nor did it consider it practical to call for a republic, though this was the preferred form of government. Instead it told the peasants to be 'patient and loyal' so that BANU could build up by legal means a large representation in the Sŭbranie which would then be used to cleanse Bulgaria and to reconstruct it as a true peasant society and state.

In the meantime there were tactical objectives to be pursued and these included the election of all officials, full civil liberties, the repeal of recent anti-trade union legislation, the introduction of female suffrage, proportional representation, and a progressive income tax, an end to police terror and to monopolies on necessities such as salt and matches, the granting of full regional and district autonomy, and the redirection of money spent on the army to finance more agricultural education, mass insurance schemes and better public health facilities. There were also demands for the redistribution of Church property, a maximum limit to the size of land-holdings, a ban on private usury, a reform of the Agricultural Bank together with better financial guarantees and insurance for cooperatives.

These policies attracted peasants of all categories but naturally appealed to those with most to gain, the small peasants holding less than fifty dekars who in 1919 accounted for fifty-one per cent of BANU membership. Lower-middle peasants, those holding between fifty and a hundred dekars formed thirty-two per cent of the membership, the upper-middle peasant, those with from one to three hundred dekars, were fifteen per cent, whilst the rich peasants, those with over three hundred dekars and the property-less made up only one per cent each. The small peasant represented the majority of the peasant body and as the peasants still formed the vast majority of the population itself it was fitting that it was BANU that should step into the political vacuum created by the temporary collapse of the old political system at the end of the First World War.

BANU's right to the inheritance was not uncontested because by the end of the First World War there was also in Bulgaria a powerful socialist movement whose origins predated those of the Agrarians.

Socialist ideas had appeared in Bulgaria in the 1880s when Dimitŭr Blagoev, a Macedonian who had been expelled from Russia, secured a post with *Makedonski Glas* and in 1885 published his own journal,

Süremenen Pokazitel (Contemporary Observer). Blagoev's journal did not survive long but the socialist gospel was preached by others, including *Rositsa* (Little Rose) published in Gabrovo in 1886 by Evtim Dabev who was clearly influenced by Marx. In the 1880s there also appeared a Bulgarian translation of Engels, the translator being the Georgi Rakovski who later won fame with the Bolsheviks and the Third International.

The beginnings of an organised and long-lasting Socialist Party are to be found in the early 1890s. In 1889 Nikola Gabrovski had attended a meeting of the Second International which encouraged him in his conviction that the intelligentsia had a duty to lead the masses in the struggle for their political and social liberation. In 1891 he convened a meeting of like spirits in a meadow owned by him near Tǔrnovo and at this meeting it was decided to call another meeting in the following year, the venue being Buzludja in the Balkan mountains and the occasion being the annual gathering to celebrate an encounter between Ottoman troops and a group of nationalists during the struggle for national liberation, this gathering giving the necessary cover under which the Socialists could escape the notice of Stambulov's police. At Buzludja on 20 July/2 August 1892 it was decided to set up the Bulgarian Workers' Social Democratic Party, (BRSDP) to use Yanko Sakuzov's *Den* (Day) as the party newspaper, and to set up a socialist library. The Party's statutes were based on those of the French and Belgian Socialists but in 1893 were remoulded in the image of the German SDP's Erfurt Programme.

The early programmes of the BRSDP were much influenced by the fact that Bulgaria was a predominantly peasant society. The 1892 programme, for example, included a call for the abolition of the tithe together with many other measures to benefit the peasant, including the provision of state graneries, more agricultural savings banks, financial aid for cooperative ventures, and improved educational, transport and medical facilities in the countryside. There was already a section of the Party which questioned the theoretical validity and practical advisability of close association with the peasantry. In his influential *What is Socialism and is there the Ground for it amongst Us?*, published in 1891, Blagoev argued that the small peasant farmer was a dying species and that the future lay with large capitalised agriculture, with its concomitant proletarianisation of the small farmer and the rise of class conflict in the countryside; Blagoev wanted less to solve the present grievances of the small peasants than to enlist their sympathies, for they were 'tomorrow's proletariat'. The early 1890s, when Bulgaria was heading rapidly for the agrarian crisis of the second half of the decade, was one of the few times in Bulgarian history when such an argument could have the appearance of validity.

There were those in the movement who did not accept that the proletarianisation of the small peasantry was near. Some of this opposition was voiced in Sevlievo and Kazanlŭk where regional jealousies added to the differences of opinion on policy. The Bulgarian Social Democratic Union separated from the main body of the Party in 1893 and advocated essentially Economist views, calling for piecemeal reforms and improvements in conditions rather than concentrating upon the political struggle and the preparation of a proletarian revolution; the Bulgarian working class, said the BSDU, was not yet sufficiently developed to set up a separate political party and until it was the movement should concentrate on piecemeal improvements. The BSDU was re-united with the BRSDP at the Turnovo Congress in 1894 but the divisions remained and they foreshadowed the split which was to divide the Bulgarian socialist movement in 1903.

In 1893 the BRSDP had decided to send a delegate to the forthcoming meeting of the International in Zürich and also to contest the general election to be held that year. The Party secured only five hundred and thirty-one votes, as its organisation was weak and untried and it had to contend with Stambulovist police harassment. In the more relaxed but far from open election of 1894 the party won four seats in the Sŭbranie though, as noted above, one of the deputies was disqualified.

Yet though it now had a party programme, representatives in the National Assembly and a place in the Socialist International, the Bulgarian Workers' Social Democratic Party had few workers to lead. After the Encouragement of Industry Bill in 1894 the number of industrial enterprises enjoying state sponsorship and the number of workers employed in them rose as follows:

Year	Number of Enterprises	Number of workers
1900	103	4,716
1904	166	6,149
1907	206	7,646
1909	266	12,943

The number of workers in factories not in encouraged industries was about two thousand in 1900 and double that twelve years later, but the total of workers in factories was never more than a small percentage of the total population and even in 1910 only 5.1% of all Bulgarian manufacturing concerns employed more than ten workers. This was an advance on 1900 when only 1.8% had had more than ten employees but the growth in the size of industrial enterprises was very slow; whilst the number of enterprises increased by 258% in the years 1900 to 1912, the number of workers employed in them increased by 274%, a rise only slightly greater than the increase in the number of enterprises. And even in 1909 22% of workers in sponsored industries still held land in their native villages and did not have that absolute separation from the peasantry characteristic of the true proletarian.

More important than its size was the age-profile of the small, new, urban working class. Of those employed in factories, mines and workshops in 1900 48.2% were under twenty whilst on the land only 32.3% of those earning wages were under that age. As the proletariat or semi-proletariat expanded it took more young men from the countryside to such a degree that whilst in 1900 only 8% of agricultural wage earners were female, in 1909 the figure was 34.3%. The towns therefore consisted of young men who during the 1900s could reasonably be expected to marry and rear families, a fact reflected in the figures showing that in 1900 there were fifty-four economically inactive bodies to every hundred workers whilst there were seventy per hundred in 1910. These above all others were the ones who were the victims of an economy which saw wages rise by 58% between 1889 and 1912 when prices climbed by some 65%. More relevant still to the urban poor was the fact that the cost of living for a family of two adults and two children rose from 67.22 leva per month in 1901 to 86.47 leva per month in 1907. In the latter year the average monthly income of an industrial worker was 49.56 leva. For most workers, however, wages were simply not sufficient to keep their young families.

Conditions and hours of work were as bad as anywhere in the early stages of industrialisation. The industrial workers reacted in a variety of ways. In the early years twenty-nine major petitions signed by over twenty thousand workers were submitted to the various ministries or to the palace, the main demand being the introduction of legislation to improve working conditions. There were also a number of strikes. There had been strikes in the early 1880s amongst the weavers and spinners whose domestic work was being endangered by cheap,

imported factory-made cloth and isolated strikes continued in the
1880s and 1890s in the textile and other manufacturing industries.
Between 1878 and 1903 there were over two hundred recorded strikes
in Bulgaria and some, such as that of the Sofia tramway workers in
1901, had considerable disruptive effect, but few if any secured lasting
gains. They were all economic in origin and purpose—the only political strikes were the May Day demonstrations held every year after
1892—and the weakness of the workers was seen in the poor organisation of the strikes and in the ease and speed with which employers
reneged on any concessions they had been forced to grant.

The relative ineffectiveness of these strikes was a reflection of the
weakness of the trade union movement. The first major union formed
in Bulgaria had been that of textile workers in Sliven in 1893 but like
most of the two hundred and fourteen unions founded between 1893
and 1903 it had little success. With the exception of the Teachers'
Union founded in 1895 Bulgarian unions remained local not national
organisations, and even after 1903 when more unions emerged they
still had to face enormous problems. There was, certainly from 1903 to
1908, a hostile and ruthless administration; the employers were increasingly well organised, some of them forming cartels and most of them
able to exercise local political influence through the regional Chamber
of Commerce. Many unions found that their first objective was to
break the old guild-style regulations which many employers, with the
cooperation of politicians at a local and national level, had reimposed
or foisted on industries which did not need them. The unions, before
they could become effective, needed to fight such battles as that for the
conclusion of collective rather than individual wage agreements between an employer and his work force. The latter was a particularly
divisive practice and one much hated by the union activists. In 1905
the printers on a number of Sofia newspapers won the right to collective wage settlements but there were still seven strikes that year against
employers who had broken their agreement on this issue. Many unions
in the 1900s were also still trying to establish themselves as national
rather than regional institutions whilst others were trying to bring
together workers in related industries or in differing practices within a
single industry; there was, for example, no metal-workers' union
though there were separate organisations for cutters, smelters and
other trades within the metallurgical industry. The unions also had to
contend with relatively large numbers of seasonal workers who did not
regard themselves as true proletarians and who were reluctant to join

the ranks of organised labour. Lacking cash, experienced leadership and national organisations the unions frequently found themselves powerless to prevent damaging spontaneous strikes, such as that in the state mines in Pernik in 1907, and these damaging strikes perversely made the workers yet more dubious of the value of the unions. By 1907 total trade union membership was only 4,750, representing at most 65% of those employed in encouraged industries. Many union members were also to be found in the small workshops which still dominated even the encouraged industries, so that 'the unionised workers evidently formed only a fraction of all those employed in Bulgaria's few modern plants'.[6]

The most important reason for the relative weakness of Bulgarian trade unionism was that it, like all sections of the socialist movement, was affected by the split in that movement which took place in 1903. The BRSDP had grown in strength during the 1890s returning six deputies in the elections of 1897 and eight in 1901; in the latter poll the party vote topped twenty thousand, though some of the elected deputies were denied their seats after the vetting of the elections. Their popularity stemmed as much from their vigorous attacks upon corruption as from the socialist doctrine which they preached, and after 1903 the Socialists were left unrepresented in the Sŭbranie until 1912. This was in part the consequence of an alteration in the electoral law in 1903 which meant that henceforth constituencies returned only one deputy, meaning that the established Parties had a stranglehold on urban seats and that after the end of the Stambulovist government in 1908 the Agrarians were unassailable in the few rural constituencies not under the domination of one of those existing Parties. Yet the lack of socialist representation was even more the result of the split of 1903.

The issues which brought about the split, already debated between BRSDP and BSDU in the 1890s, were those of how far the Socialists should collaborate with the peasants, and to what extent they should join the established Parties in their attack upon political corruption and the personal regime. A section of the Party under the leadership of Sakuzov had long argued that political democracy was a necessary prerequisite for socialism and that the Party should therefore cooperate with the left-wing factions in the Sŭbranie to achieve the rule of law, Cabinets responsible to the Assembly and full parliamentary government. This group publicised its ideas in the journal *Obshto Delo* (General or 'Broad' Affairs) and became known as the 'Broad Socialists'. Their opponents, who became known as the 'Narrow Socialists', were led by Blagoev and their ideas were purveyed in *Novo Vreme* (New Age). These ideas were Marxist. The Narrows had no time for collaboration with the 'bourgeois' Parties and wanted to concentrate solely on the preparation of a full-scale socialist revolution, a policy which left no room for working with the Agrarians. Differences of opinion occurred on a number of vital issues. In 1902 Sakŭzov declared that he would confiscate only the large estates and would not touch the land of the small peasant proprietor, a statement which he made to rebut rumours put around by Danev that the Socialists would confiscate all property. Blagoev repudiated Sakŭzov's view and said that the Socialists would indeed confiscate all private property. In 1903 Sakŭzov joined with other Sŭbranie Parties in voting against the change in the Tsankovist law giving security of tenure to all civil servants, a move which Blagoev ridiculed, insisting that Socialists should concern themselves only with the interests of the proletariat. There were also disagreements on trade unions. Sakŭzov recognised the need for economic concessions and was prepared to allow the unions to concentrate on these, and thus he was willing to see membership of the unions open to all irrespective of party political loyalty. Blagoev wanted to keep the unions in close harmony with the Party to prevent them from degenerating into mere wage-increasing lobbies.

These differing interpretations were aired with considerable personal animosity in successive party congresses until the final split occurred in March 1903. The split came when the Narrows within the Sofia party organisation seceded and declared themselves the true Party and branded the Broads unfit to carry the name socialist. At a national Party Congress held in Ruse that summer the Narrows formally expelled the Broads who now set up a separate party apparatus. The Narrows kept to a purely working-class policy and continued to repudiate cooperation with any other radical Party, even the Agrarians. Sakŭzov scorned this. He saw Narrow policies as unrealistic and declared their claim to be a purely proletarian party risible as the only predominantly proletarian party organisation was that in Sofia which was Broad rather than Narrow. Sakŭzov also began publishing a new newspaper, *Rabotnicheska Borba* (Workers' Struggle) which soon had a circulation of over two thousand as opposed to the fifteen hundred of the Narrow *Rabotnicheski Vestnik* (Workers' Gazette). The Broads were predominant in Sofia, Tŭrnovo, Kazanlŭk, Haskovo, Chirpan, Yambol and Panagiurishte, and the Narrows in Ruse, Sliven, Plovdiv, Varna, Gabrovo, Samokov and Pleven.

After 1903 there were a number of attempts to repair the split. Sakŭzov was anxious lest the advent of a Stambulovist regime mean the suppression of all mass movements and he set up yet another new journal *Edinstvo* (Unity) to argue that a common defence against Stambulovism was necessary, but he found few disciples. In 1907, during the governmental clamp-down which followed the events of January, Sakŭzov approached the Narrows with offers of trade union unity but the offer was rejected. The Amsterdam meeting of the International in 1905, at which both Broads and Narrows were represented, called for an end to the schism, as did the meetings of the International in 1907 and 1913, and the Seventh International Trade Union Conference in Budapest in 1911. None of these appeals met with any response.

The split in fact deepened. In 1906 Sakŭzov published *Caesarism or Democracy* in which he codified his beliefs. At the same time he continued cooperating with radical parliamentary Parties, the more so as the Socialists were completely unrepresented in the Sŭbranie, but these tactics received a severe setback when Malinov's Democrats, one of the Parties with whom Sakuzov had been working, fawned upon and then accepted office from the Prince.

The Narrows were hardly more successful. Their insistence on absolute doctrinal purity alienated valuable support and further divided the socialist ranks. By 1905 some leading Narrows, primarily Georgi Bakalov and Nikola Harlakov, were fidgeting under Blagoev's stern rule, and arguing that rigid ideological conformity was appropriate to a party of intellectuals but would not be comprehensible to working-class supporters. Blagoev would not compromise and the two men and their faction were expelled from the Narrow Party whereupon they established their own Liberal Socialist group which attracted a number of hitherto unaffiliated workers, and the proportion of workers in the Liberal Socialist ranks was always higher than in the other two factions; in 1907 a quarter of all organised workers were attached to the Liberal Socialists and their trade union organisation, although these groups had only 18% of total socialist membership. In 1908 Blagoev expelled another faction, that headed by Sakanov and Tineva who wanted to act upon the Second International's order to restore unity in the Bulgarian Socialist movement. The two dissidents aligned themselves with yet another faction, the Progressive Socialists who had been expelled by Blagoev at the same time. The Progressives, like the Liberal Socialists, eventually joined the Broads.

Despite these defections and expulsions and despite the continued insistence on doctrinal purity the Narrows did increase both their membership and the percentage of workers in the Party. Membership doubled between 1903 and 1912, rising from 1,174 to 2,923 and even if the Central Committee remained exclusively of the intelligentsia the working-class element in the Party at large increased from forty-one to seventy-one percent. This was a powerful propaganda weapon against the Broads who in 1912, despite slight numerical superiority, had a smaller working-class contingent and a large petty-bourgeois, that is mainly handicraft-worker following.

Competition between the Broads and Narrows was intense, so much so that '. . . the struggle against the bourgeoisie had become almost secondary'.[7] The split affected all sectors of the Socialist movement. In July 1903 the trade unions controlled by the Narrows dissociated themselves from those under Broad domination and set up the General Workers' Trade Union Federation which with its membership of one and a half thousand was totally subjected to the political will of the Narrow Central Committee. In reply the Broads set up the Free Trades Union Federation. This led to sharp conflicts. The Narrows criticised Broad support for strikes for such non-political objectives as collective wage agreements, and the two factions disagreed over the shoemakers' strike in Sofia in 1906 when the Broads were content to accept an increase in piece-work rates whereas, said the Narrows, they should have pushed for the complete abolition of the piece-work system. The Narrows had taken the major directing role in the Pernik miners' strike of 1906—though not in the spontaneous stoppage of 1907—but they adopted an ambivalent attitude to the great rail strike of 1906–7, the railwaymen being solidly Broad in their allegiance. This left a legacy of bitterness which was not overcome until after the First World War.

There were less dramatic contests. Broad and Narrow fought each other for representation on the Labour Committees which by the Women and Children's Employment Act of 1905 were to be set up to supervise the working of the Act until a factory inspectorate had been established. All party activities including the setting up of cooperatives were after 1903 affected by the split; the bread-producing cooperative established in Plovdiv, for example, was purely a Narrow preserve, and all existing socialist organisations divided between the factions. These organisations included the important social clubs which performed for the deprived working-classes such important functions as providing reading-rooms, gymnastic and sports facilities, children's parties, and stalls selling snacks and cheap non-alcoholic drinks. In that institutions such as these were divided and therefore weakened by the split of 1903 that split did considerable harm to the immediate interests of the small Bulgarian proletariat.

* * *

By the eve of the Balkan Wars in 1912 the mass Parties were well established in Bulgaria. The socialist movement, though divided, was the strongest in the Balkans and the Agrarian movement was to make a unique contribution to the history of modern Europe. Both movements had declared emphatically against an aggressive foreign policy and both believed that a confederation was the best long-term solution to the problems of the Balkan peninsula. Yet despite their growing popular following both Parties found themselves unable to prevent a military solution to the Macedonian problem. What is more, the mass Parties could not dent mass popular enthusiasm for that solution.

Chapter 19

SOCIAL AND ECONOMIC DEVELOPMENTS
FROM THE MID-1890s to 1912
I. THE LAND

The figures in Table 1 show a total population growth in the Bulgarian state of 15.84% between 1900 and 1914. Despite the emigration between 1903 and 1908 of 80,000 Bulgarians, mainly to North and South America, the Bulgarian element as a proportion of the total population grew more rapidly than that of the other main component groups. This was in part the result of continued immigration of ethnic Bulgarians into the Principality, with large numbers arriving from Macedonia and Thrace in the politically disturbed years 1903 to 1908. By 1910 the total numbers of Bulgarian immigrants since the Liberation had reached 150,000, the main source being Macedonia, Thrace, Bessarabia and Rumania. The dominance of the Bulgarians was furthered by the decline of their chief rivals. Turkish emigration continued steadily after 1900 and accounts for the 6.5% decline in the total Turkish population of the Principality in the first decade of this century. A new development was the emigration of substantial numbers of Greeks who fled after the persecutions of 1905 and 1906; the Greek populace of Bulgaria fell by 14.65% between 1900 and 1901 and by 27.09% in the years 1905 to 1910. Of the smaller groups the increase in the gypsy population, 35.76%, was larger even than that of the Bulgarians and was to be explained almost entirely by natural increase. The relatively large growth in the Jewish population, 18.36%, was on the other hand primarily the result of immigration, for Bulgaria accepted large numbers of Jews who were fleeing persecution in Russia or Rumania. Similarly the number of Armenians in Bulgaria increased

Table 1.   The population of Bulgaria, 1900–1910.

Mother tongue	1900	% of total	1905	% of total	1910	% of total
Bulgarian	2,887,860	77.13%	3,205,019	79.41%	3,523,311	81.23%
Turkish	539,656	14.41%	497,820	12.35%	504,560	11.63%
Greek	70,887	1.89%	69,761	1.73%	50,866	1.17%
Gypsy	89,549	2.39%	94,649	2.35%	121,573	2.80%
Jewish	32,573	0.87%	36,455	0.90%	38,554	0.89%
Others	123,758	3.31%	131,942	3.26%	98,649	2.28%
Total	3,744,283	100.00%	4,035,646	100.00%	4,337,513	100.00%

by as much as 134.9% because the Principality offered a safe haven from the insecurities of the Ottoman Empire.

For the thirty years from 1881 the rate of growth of the population in Bulgaria had been 1.31 per hundred inhabitants with the rate in the north being higher than that in the south, 1.41 as opposed to 1.01. This reflected the greater rate of Moslem and then Greek emigration from the south and, to some extent, the fact that the south had suffered more severely than the north in the disorders of the 1870s and therefore had fewer young men and women to raise families. The main reason for the difference in growth rates, however, was the more rapid expansion of towns in the north, the most important example of this being Sofia which by 1910 contained 2.4% of the total population. In the south were to be found most of the towns which had suffered severely from the economic impact of the Liberation and which were to continue to decline in the early twentieth century; Koprivshtitsa, for example, lost 5.4% of its population between 1900 and 1905 and a further 13.21% between 1906 and 1910, whilst Kalofer shrank by 6.6% and 5.5% in the same years. Negative growth rates were also recorded in Omurtag, Gabrovo, Karlovo, Shumen, Sopot, Dryanovo, Tryavna and Kotel.

The contraction of some towns was balanced by the growth of others. By 1910 there were fifty-one towns with populations sixty percent higher than in 1892, and the total urban population at this later date (1910) was 829,500, an increase of 11.34% over the 745,000 registered as urban dwellers in 1900. What is most striking, however, is

Table 2.   Distribution of land holdings, by size of holding, 1908.

Size of holding	No. of holdings	%age of total holdings	Area of land in hectacres	%age of total area
Very small	424,898	45.52	321,568	6.95
Small	386,725	41.43	1,954,854	42.26
Medium	111,632	11.96	1,689,371	36.52
Large	10,119	1.09	659,994	14.27
Total	933,374	100.00	4,625,787	100.00

Table 3.   Changes in distribution of land holdings by size of holding, 1897–1908.

Size of holding	%age of total holdings in 1908, compared to 1897	% age of total area 1908 compared to 1897
Very small	+0.04	+0.27
Small	−0.39	−0.01
Medium	+0.39	+1.08
Large	−0.04	−1.34

the fact that the proportion of urban dwellers to the total population changed hardly at all during the period 1900 to 1910, moving downwards slightly from 19.9% to 19.1%. Indeed the urban population as a proportion to the whole was in 1910 little different from what it had been in 1880.

Whilst the proportion of people living on the land remained remarkably steady so too did the distribution of property. Tables 2 and 3 show that between the two major land surveys in pre-war Bulgaria the small and medium peasant continued to dominate the social landscape, accounting in 1908 for 98.91% of the rural population and working 85.73% of the utilised land.

Whilst the distribution of property remained stable the size of the average peasant holding declined slightly from 6.28 hectacres in 1897 to 6.20 hectacres in 1908. The average extent of the very small and small peasant holding increased slightly whilst that of holdings in the other categories declined. (Table 4)

Table 4.   Average extent of holding per category of holding, 1897 and 1908.

Category of holding	1897	1908	%age of change
Very small	7.3 dekars	7.6 dekars	+4.11
Small	50.3 "	50.6 "	+0.60
Medium	152.4 "	151.3 "	−0.72
Large	1592.9 "	1579.8 "	−0.82

From table 4 it is clear that little structural change had taken place in Bulgarian land holding between 1897 and 1908. However, despite the relative prosperity of the agrarian sector and notwithstanding the decline in the outrageous profits formerly made from usury, both of which will be discussed below, the land was still not attracting large amounts of capital. The area of land held in large holdings had actually declined as a percentage of the total and the number of such units had increased by only 1.11%, from 9,049 in 1897 to 10,109 in 1908. Few of these large units were worked singly and most were split up for renting, a procedure reflected in the fact that in holdings over three hundred hectacres *parakende* land was more prevalent than non-*parakende* or 'local' property. Of the large holdings worked as single units most were to be found either in the Dobrudja, where Rumanian landholding patterns had some influence, or near the export ports where well-organised Greek wheat merchants had encouraged commercialised agriculture. Of the thirty-six non-*parakende* holdings over five hundred hectacres recorded in 1908 sixteen were in the Balchik and six in the Burgas districts; the other fourteen were distributed throughout the country. There was in the early twentieth century a considerable increase in the number of people employed on the land, the figure rising from about 59,000 in 1900 to circa 160,000 in 1911. This, however, is a misleading statistic. Most of those recorded as agricultural workers were part-time and/or seasonal employees and many of them had land of their own and used occasional labour to supplement their income; in no way could such people be described as a rural proletariat.

The survival of the small and medium peasant was possible because despite the increase in population the supply of land could in general keep pace with rising demand. There was, particularly towards the end of the period under discussion, some land hunger, especially in areas of poor soil and low productivity, areas such as the Kula district where grain yields were only 397 kilogrammes per dekar in 1897 compared to the 1,861 kilogrammes per dekar in the most favoured region, Pirdop. The Agrarians were conscious of the actual or potential shortages of land and in their 1904 congress called for a maximum limit on the size of all holdings. In 1907, a year of uncharacteristically poor harvests, there were numerous petitions to the Sŭbranie calling for the free sale of state and communal property, and in the previous year Todor Vlaikov had suggested to the Assembly that the land of émigrés should be transferred free of charge to the landless and the needy. Increasing pressure on land also made *parakende* property more valuable and profitable but the need to use such land made the inefficiency of the *parakende* system more obvious and as a result there were some attempts to consolidate dispersed holdings. Monasteries, much of whose property had been acquired by inheritance and was therefore likely to be even more dispersed than usual, took the lead in this activity but by 1912 there were also examples of voluntary consolidation amongst peasants. This, however, was on a small scale and all too often led to interminable legal disputes.

Despite these examples serious land hunger, such as that experienced in some parts of Russia, was not found in Bulgaria, and in 1910 there were still some twelve thousand vacant plots in the country. The absence of land hunger in most areas can be explained by a number of factors.

One was the continued emigration of Turks, Greeks and Bulgarians. Another was occasional government action to help the peasant and to save his land; a number of peasants on the margin of viability were saved, for example, by legislation enacted by the Nationalist government in the late 1890s which guaranteed to each Bulgarian family a certain amount of property which was to be inalienable even against the claims of creditors, though this did not satisfy the Agrarians who later campaigned for larger areas to be made inalienable and for the extension of the legal guarantee to livestock and agricultural implements. To some extent the slight drift of population to the towns in some areas also eased pressure on the land. All these factors, however, were of relatively small importance and the absence of land hunger and the consequent survival of the small and medium peasantry is to be explained primarily by the expropriation of state and communal property, much of it forest, by the private owner. (See Table 5)

Table 5. Distribution of land by category of owner, 1908.

	Total area in hectacres	Percentage of total	Percentage change from 1897
Private	4,630,083	58.00	+16.72
Provincial authorities	1,275	0.02	+189.12
Village communes	2,417,488	30.28	+5.51
State	760,530	9.53	−25.14
Religious and educational institutions	144,089	1.81	+12.25
National and Agricultural Banks	28,985	0.36	+13,636.97
Total	7,982,450	100.00	+7.67

Table 5 shows that between 1897 and 1908 the area of land in use had increased by 7.67%; other figures show that whilst in 1904 there were 84.8 hectacres of arable land per hundred of the population, in 1912 there were 92 hectacres per hundred people. The large increase in the land held by the provincial and, to a lesser degree, the village authorities reflects the extension of public ownership over land which was formerly not categorised, whilst the great expansion of property in the hands of the two large public banks reflects reforms in the credit system which will be discussed below. That state land was the only one to decline in extent is evidence of the widespread practice of private owners taking state land into their own possession, a process much encouraged by the pre-Liberation convention, sanctioned by Ottoman law, that the working of land for three or more years conferred virtual ownership. That much of this land was forest is seen in the fact that whilst the area of woodland and forest in 1906 was just over three million hectacres, by 1912 it was only two and a half million hectacres.

The expropriation of public property had originally been illegal but no administration had been able to stop it. In 1899 therefore Nachovich proposed that the old restrictions should be removed and that state and commune lands should be sold or rented to individual farmers. Nachovich's scheme was an ambitious one which could have involved an area as large as Belgium and his objective was to increase national production rather than to pursue social justice, but the plan was ruined by the political and social crisis at the turn of the century. Further legislation did not come until 1904 when the Stambulovist ministry passed a bill allowing the division and sale of state lands, with clauses providing for preferential prices and loan conditions for the poorer peasants. The Agrarians denounced the Act because it divided saleable public land into equal plots rather than allotting larger shares to the landless or those with too little property, but in reality the Act had little effect because the legal difficulties involved in these, as in all land transactions in Bulgaria, caused delay, frustration and prohibitive expense. This caused a good deal of bitterness as those who had previously made illegal seizures of state property were left unpunished and in complete possession of their land. In some areas, for example around Tŭrnovo, such seizures had been so widespread that state property had virtually disappeared. In 1909, after an unusually lively debate, the Sŭbranie enacted a new law aimed at curtailing the alienation of communal fields and state property and even allowing for the re-acquisition by the public authorities of land illegally taken over by the private farmer, but cases of such repossession actually taking place were few and far between.

Between 1897 and 1912 the peasant proprietor of Bulgaria not only survived but prospered. If the index for national consumption be set at 100 for 1896 then it had risen to 110 even in the disastrous year of 1900 and by 1911 stood at 411. Increasing prosperity was reflected too in the rising price of land. In 1880 the average price per hectacre for all types of land had been 33.86 gold leva. During the crisis of the late 1890s it fell to 15 gold leva but by 1912 had risen steeply to 177.49 gold leva. And the figures for the distribution of property show that it was still the small and medium peasants who were buying the land.

There are a number of explanations for this peasant prosperity. In the first place the climate was kind and only in 1907 was there a poor harvest. Whilst the harvests were good world prices were rising and the London price for a hundred kilograms of grain increased from 15.05 francs in 1900 to 16.66 francs in 1905, and 23.35 francs in 1909, though it fell back to between 19 and 20 francs in the two subsequent years. Though the peasant benefited less than the grain merchant from these price movements he was nevertheless spared the cruel pressures which falling world prices had created during the 1890s. A further cause of the relative prosperity of the countryside in these years was the steady growth in the size of many towns and the improvement in the internal communications network which made these expanding markets more accessible. Efficiency also increased with the average yield per dekar rising from 65 kilograms in 1897 to 125 kilograms in 1912, though there were still very great local variations. Nevertheless an indication of improving efficiency was the fact that in 1897 36.8% of the cultivable land had been left fallow but only 21.3% was untilled in 1911. Imports of agricultural machinery were another testimony to the improving spirit. In the years 1886–90 these averaged only 199 tons per annum, but in period 1900 to 1905 they rose to 551 tons per annum and the average for 1906 to 1911 was 2,612 tons. The value of these imports, including spare parts, rose from 723,289 leva in 1899 to 3,780,149 leva in 1907, an increase of 422.63%. Equally revealing was the fact that whilst the number of wooden ploughs increased by 8.45% between 1900 and 1910 (from 387,346 to 420,084), the number of metal ploughs rose by 133.35% (from 48,959 to 114,246); the number of mechanical sowers, reapers and harvesters increased in the same period by 462.63% (from 15,831 to 87,488), though most of the latter, suitable for use only on large and commercialised farms, were to be found in the Dobrudja. By 1911 the total value of agricultural machinery in Bulgaria was 16,340,000 leva, seventy times greater than the figure for 1887.

Grain continued to dominate Bulgarian agrarian production. In 1911 the area of land devoted to the growing of cereals was greater both in absolute terms and as a proportion of the total land used (Table 6) and cereals were also slightly greater as a fraction of total agricultural production. (Table 7) Figures for the value of production are not available before 1903 but others for that year show that cereals accounted for 72.5% of total agricultural production. By 1911 the proportion had fallen to 69.1% with an average of 69.4% for the years 1906–10. That cereals could account for an increasing proportion of the volume of production but a declining share of its total value indicates that high returns were to be made from other crops.

Before the outbreak of the Balkan Wars there were some moves towards newer and more profitable crops and the figures for 1911, when compared to those for the average over the years 1906–11, indicate that this movement was intensifying at the end of the period under review. (See Table 8) The decline in the cultivation of grapes was the result of phylloxera and that of kitchen garden crops reflects the transfer of the production of crops such as potatoes and fruits to the more organised categories of vegetables or orchard produce. Table 8

Table 6. Areas of land devoted to various types of crop.

Crop	Area of land devoted to various crops, in hectares			Percentage of total land devoted to various crops		
	1897	average 1906–11	1911	1897	1906–11	1911
Cereals	1,811,890	2,366,871	2,523,738	74.08	76.09	75.90
Fodder crops	439,836	523,016	558,031	17.98	16.81	16.79
Vineyards	114,816	83,289	67,872	4.70	2.68	2.04
Kitchen gardens	12,710	10,142	11,314	0.52	0.32	0.34
Vegetables	27,739	62,562	76,083	1.13	2.01	2.29
Orchard fruits	24,929	33,517	35,971	1.02	1.08	1.08
Roses	4,844	7,469	7,666	0.20	0.24	0.23
Industrial crops	8,771	21,768	41,542	0.36	0.70	1.25
Mulberries	178	1,895	2,742	0.01	0.07	0.08
Total	2,445,713	3,110,529	3,324,959	100.00	100.00	100.00

Table 7. Division of agricultural production according to type of crop.

Crop	Crops produced in tons			Percentage of total production		
	1897	average 1906–11	1911	1897	average 1906–11	1911
Cereals, − grain	2,113,809	2,284,861	2,876,305			
− straw	3,557,894	3,070,418	3,701,872			
	5,671,703	5,355,279	6,578,177	77.93	78.62	78.95
Fodder crops	1,271,713	1,015,698	1,328,499	17.47	14.91	15.95
Grapes	153,525	184,431	104,632	2.11	2.71	1.26
Kitchen garden produce	86,172	60,984	71,132	1.18	0.90	0.85
Vegetables	41,808	53,813	75,677	0.58	0.79	0.91
Orchard fruits	40,000	76,667	60,000	0.55	1.13	0.72
Roses, flowers	8,920	11,774	9,324	0.12	0.17	0.11
Industrial crops	3,564	47,658	95,212	0.05	0.70	1.14
Mulberries	461	5,053	8,979	0.01	0.07	0.11
Total	7,277,866	6,811,357	8,331,632	100.00	100.00	100.00

Table 8. Indices of production, 1897 equals 100.

Crop		average 1906–11	1911
Cereals,	– grain	108.09	136.07
	– straw	86.30	104.05
		94.42	114.75
Fodder crops		79.87	104.47
Grapes		120.13	68.15
Kitchen garden produce		70.77	82.55
Vegetables		128.71	181.01
Orchard fruits		191.67	150.00
Roses, flowers		132.00	104.53
Industrial crops		1,337.20	2,671.49
Mulberries		1,096.13	1,947.50
Total		93.59	114.48

also shows that established crops such as wheat and roses increased at a much less rapid rate than new products such as mulberries or industrial crops, though, of course, the increase in these categories is exaggerated by the very low base from which they started. The development of the silk-worm was a deliberate government policy, Genadiev telling the Subranie in December 1904 that the government's agricultural advisers would be ordered to encourage the planting of mulberry bushes and the culture of silk-worms. By 1911 some 50,000 families were involved. Production of industrial crops, which included rapeseed, sesame, aniseed, tobacco, flax, hemp and sugar-beet, was expanding in response to Bulgaria's industrial growth, a phenomenon which will be discussed in the following chapter. Between 1897 and 1907 the area devoted to growing oil-bearing plants had increased by 91.56% from 87,712.3 dekars to 168,023 dekars; tobacco cultivation showed an even more rapid expansion of 902.71% from 1,218 dekars in 1897 to 12,213 dekars in 1911. There was also greater diversification in animal husbandry with a noticeable growth in the keeping of hens and other poultry for Bulgarian eggs were now being sold in the large markets of central Europe; by 1911 22.8% of the average peasant income was derived from livestock compared with 17.9% in 1892.

Whilst good harvests, higher prices, a larger internal market and greater diversification of crops increased peasant income the burden of taxation and interest payments did not increase as rapidly. If the years 1879–83 are taken as an index of 100 then the direct tax payments per capita were 154 for 1889–96, 86 for 1900, 50 for 1905 and only 28 for 1911. The total tax burden, however, rose gradually because of increases in indirect levies; the total tax payments per capita per annum were 32.38 leva in 1900, 42.30 leva in 1905 and 46.63 leva in 1911, though as a primary producer the peasant could escape the indirect taxes levied on a number of items, and for the most part peasant incomes kept well ahead of increases in taxation in these years. At the same time the exactions of the money lender diminished as the cooperative credit movement became organised.

Though the general well-being of the Bulgarian peasant increased in the early years of this century this did not mean that the countryside was without its problems. Bulgarian agriculture was at the mercy of the climate and of nature, and though in general the weather was kind in these years the country still suffered severely from hail storms. From 1900 to 1909 a yearly average of 300,000 dekars and 56,000 households suffered damage from this cause. A scheme for compulsory insurance

against hail had been introduced in 1895 but the five percent supplement on the land tax which was to finance the project was insufficient
to meet the claims made and a voluntary scheme introduced by the
Democratic government in 1910 was just as ineffective. A more persistent and harmful natural enemy was phylloxera. In 1897 there had
been 114,815 hectacres of vineyards but this had fallen to 72,500
hectacres ten years later when the plague was at its height. The
government did what it could to help by cutting the land tax on vineyards and by subsidising the planting of American strains of vine but
the latter demanded more care and expense than many Bulgarian
peasants were accustomed to giving to their vineyards and the situation
was still serious when the Wars came; in 1914, for example, the prefect
of the Varna reported that the vineyards in his province were all but
destroyed.

A serious but man-made problem facing Bulgarian agriculture was
the lack of a land register. The legislation of the 1880s and 1890s had
cleared away many of the obscurities of the pre-Liberation land
tenures, but the boundaries between separate individual properties and
the divisions between public and private land were still indistinct and
this problem was exacerbated by the fact that most private land was
still held in dispersed strips. The lack of legal precision made consolidation of strips into compact holdings difficult and expensive and lead
to frequent disputes, with lawyers charging high fees for their services.
The legal profession in fact prospered on the obscurity of property
ownership and it is little wonder that the lawyer, along with the
bureaucrat, the courtier and the professional soldier, figured promi-
nently in the demonology of the Agrarians. In 1909 the Malinov
government attempted to improve the situation by passing an act
defining more closely the boundaries between public and private property. In the same year the government also passed an act to establish a
land register. The minister responsible for the latter admitted that it
would take twenty years to compile the register but he hoped it would
put an end to the 'disputes and murders' which all too frequently arose
from disagreements over land ownership. The Agrarians, however,
suspected the Act was merely an attempt to augment the returns from
the land tax and to provide the government with yet more patronage;
the money, they argued, would be better spent on increasing agricultural production by draining marshes, improving roads, and promoting agricultural education. Whether the Agrarians' fears were justified

was not to be known for war broke out before any real progress had been made towards compiling the land register.

Other weaknesses in the agrarian structure included the continued over-dependence on grain. Despite the late moves towards industrial crops cereals still played too large a part in the national economy and completely dominated the export trade, accounting for 120,000,000 leva of the total 150,000,000 leva earned from exports in 1911. Some of the land growing wheat would have been more profitably employed producing fodder crops. Though the production of fodder crops had increased between 1897 and 1908 that increase was a modest one of just over four percent and the land devoted to them had declined as a percentage of usable land. So scarce had fodder become in some areas that in 1909 the Agrarians in the Sùbranie were demanding, unsuccessfully, that communal property be allowed to grow only fodder crops. The lack of fodder together with a depressing lack of veterinary supervision meant that Bulgarian cattle were of very low quality. The government in the mid-1900s made some attempts to increase milk-yields by crossing the local steppe-cattle with the central European Voralberg strain but this had little effect.

The development of Bulgarian industry had done something to stimulate the diversification of agricultural production which appears towards the end of this period. It also did something to further efficiency. There was much need for improvement, the national predicament being encapsulated in the case of the foreign-financed sugar refinery built in the late 1890s. The intention had been to use locally grown sugar-beet but only when the factory was under construction was it realised that the wooden ploughs used by most peasants in the area could not cut to the 30 centimetres depth required to produce sugar-beet. This and other similar problems were overcome and agricultural efficiency and technology progressed, but this progress did not affect more than a minority of the peasants. Despite the increase in the import and production of more advanced agricultural equipment by 1910 only eighteen percent of the holdings in the country were using metal ploughs and other machines were even rarer. Also, despite the general rise in productivity fallow still accounted for too much of the potentially productive land, a Sùbranie deputy calculating in 1912 that wheat production could be doubled if all available land were cultivated.

Further and more serious impediments to increased efficiency were the strip system and the attendant evil of parcellisation. The need to walk from strip to strip could increase the time taken to complete a task by anything from a quarter to a half, and more time was lost because animals had to be kept in the villages or on village pastures, a not inconsiderable factor when these pastures could be some distance from the arable land and when the draught animals involved were the slow-moving oxen or water-buffalo. Strips could only be worked and har-vested properly if all strips in a field grew the same crop, and thus the progressive farmer was often frustrated in his wish to produce the more profitable cash-crops rather than grain or one of the other routine items in the village rotation. The strips themselves were usually divided by a narrow furrow and though this was reasonably economical of space the boundaries were not always clear and disputes over them were frequent; such disputes were particularly numerous when *para-kende* plots were completely surrounded by land of owners from a completely different village.

The strip system became ever more inefficient because of divided inheritance and by the end of the first decade of this century parcellisa-tion was becoming one of the major problems in Bulgarian agriculture. Between 1897 and 1908 the area of land used increased by 16.4% and the number of holdings by 16.7%, yet the number of parcels of land rose by 23.7% with a much higher increment in the incidence of parcel-lisation in the local, i.e. non-*parakende* land, *parakende* generally being in plots already too small to permit further division. In the most extreme cases plots even of local land could be as small as three by three metres, and the case of a certain Dyado Latov of Chepnitsa whose 18 hectares were split into forty separate plots was in no way unique. Parcellisation affected all types of property and was especially prevalent in land owned by schools, banks and—despite the efforts of some monasteries to consolidate some or all of their land—religious institutions. All but the smallest holdings suffered. Parcellisation was proceeding very rapidly in the larger holdings, the number of strips in these properties rising by 18.9% between 1897 and 1908, a reflection of the fact that most owners in this category preferred to split their land and rent it rather than farm it as a unit. In the medium holdings the number of strips increased by 11.4% in the same period, and in the small by only 5.1%. In the very small category, where parcellisation was often all but impossible, the number of strips actually decreased by 5.1%. This latter category was also an exception to the general rule that between 1897 and 1908 the size of the average strip decreased. (See Table 9.)

Table 9. Average size of strip by category of property
in dekars, 1897 and 1908.

Category of holding	1897	1908
Very small	2.5	2.8
Small	3.7	3.5
Medium	6.7	6.0
Large	49.6	39.9

There were some attempts to deal with the problem of parcellisation. The Nationalist government's bill to guarantee each family a minimum of property had prevented the division of some holdings and the Stambulovist administration's attempt in 1906 to allow easier sale of public land also helped in that the more property a family had the greater would be the extent of each share when it was divided. Yet the latter bill was to a large extent thwarted by the legal complexities of land transfer and the only helpful item of legislation in this period came in 1906 in the form of an amendment to the Inheritance Law which reinforced the restrictions preventing female inheritance of very small plots. Some individual peasant proprietors followed the example of the monasteries and tried to consolidate their holdings. In the village of Madon in the Ferdinand district the Simeonov brothers, by purchase or exchange, converted their twenty strips into a compact holding of over sixty hectares. So profitable was the new estate that others in the village decided to follow this example, but action by so many owners caused intense legal difficulties and by 1919 there were some two hundred law suits pending in the village. Consolidation remained an exceptional undertaking and not till the Agrarian government of the early 1920s was energetic action taken to tackle the problem of parcellisation.

Many peasants were content to accept parcellisation as the price to be paid for the retention of the strip system and the tradition of divided inheritance. Consolidation was resisted on the grounds that if all the land were in one part of the village it could then all be destroyed by hail; strips might mean that at least some of a family's crop was spared.

The government made some efforts to overcome such traditionalism. The service provided by the agricultural advisers was constantly reviewed and frequently expanded, the 1903 budget allocating three hundred thousand leva for expenditure on this item. In the decade before the Balkan Wars the number of agricultural schools increased from seven to fourteen; in 1911 the Agricultural Faculty was opened in the University, and in September of that year an exhibition held in the Royal Stables in Sofia helped to spread the gospel of agricultural progress. The real stumbling block, however, was to be found in the poor quality of primary schools in the rural communities. Despite the national belief in the excellence of its educational tradition the Minister of Education had to tell the Sŭbranie in 1911 that of the nation's 3,417 elementary schools—3,183 of which were rural—1,043 (30.52%) had inadequate buildings and 1,208 (35.35%) no special buildings at all, so that of the nation's 384,428 elementary schoolchildren 220,000 or 57.23%, were in improvised or inadequate classrooms. Nor, as the Agrarians constantly pointed out, did the syllabus in the schools take sufficient account of the needs of a peasant society, for little if any time was given to practical education in farming techniques. The rural schools were further debilitated by massive epidemics which could close them for months, and the incidence of tuberculosis was alarmingly high, though this is not surprising for in 1911 Bulgaria had fewer doctors per head of the population than Turkey.

    In comparison with their efforts to promote industry, which will be the subject of the next chapter, Bulgarian governments between 1894 and 1912 did little to stimulate agricultural production. Stoilov admitted that part of his motivation in bringing in a land tax in 1894 had been to increase the area of land under the plough by forcing fallow land into production as had happened in Rumelia when the land tax replaced the tithe in the 1880s. Early in its period of office the second Stambulovist ministry introduced a supplementary land tax to be levied on fallow land and this, the Minister of Agriculture and Trade told the Sŭbranie in 1905, had been largely responsible for the recent rise in agricultural production. This was unlikely as the increase was much more the result of better weather and higher world prices, and in any case even if the supplementary tax had some effect it was not enough, as the figures quoted above for the amount of fallow land in 1908 and 1911 indicate. Other forms of encouragement for agriculture were somewhat more effective. The abolition of all tariffs on imported agricultural machinery helped the progressive farmer, particularly towards the end of this period. The planting of cotton, tobacco and mulberries and the keeping of bees were actively encouraged by government agricultural advisers and government surveyors helped the farmers of the Dobrudja by discovering and exploiting new sources of water. In 1906 Agricultural Councils were established in all provinces and districts, though these never achieved the importance and influence of the Chambers of Commerce in whose image they had been shaped. The Councils were not universally popular and the Agrarians denounced them as attempts to extend the government's patronage and the scope for *partisanstvo*, an objection which was also levelled at the creation in 1911 of a separate Ministry of Agriculture and State Property. The Agrarians' distrust of administrative expansion was to some extent justified by the failure of earlier schemes such as that of 1903 by which the country had been divided into health districts each of which, it was said, would be provided with at least one doctor. Two years later an equally well-intentioned and equally ineffective act provided for the setting up of a model veterinary service.

Far more effective in promoting and protecting the peasant farmers' interests in this period were the cooperative societies which flourished in the decade before the wars. Cooperative ideas had appeared in Bulgaria partly as an inheritance from Russian Populism but in the 1880s they were being turned to local use and being advanced as a defence against usury. Cooperative literature was being circulated and included Mikhailovski's *Asotsiatsi*, translated from the Russian in 1886 by Stefan Kostov, for many years secretary to the Holy Synod in Sofia. More influential was Kostov's own *Sŭdrezhestva v Evropa* (Cooperatives in Europe) published in 1888; by 1894 cooperative ideas were so well-known that in the Sŭbranie Geshov could refer to Reiffeisen credit cooperatives without needing to explain the term. The first agricultural credit cooperative was founded in Mirkovo in the Pirdop district in 1890 but it did not survive for long, and remained an isolated example until 1897. In that year N. Buchvarov, the Deputy Director of the Model Agricultural School near Ruse, joined with a priest and a teacher from the village of Shtrŭklevo to set up a Reiffeisen type credit cooperative in the village. This was followed by others in villages nearby and in the Sofia area but, once again, none survived. These pioneering, though ephemeral societies suffered from a lack of experienced and skilled leadership. There was also a lack of capital. The government attempted to help by arranging for thirty million leva to be lent to the Agricultural Savings Bank in 1896 to finance rural credit but because of the financial emergencies of the late 1890s little of that money found its way to its intended destination. In

1898 the Bank itself went some way to help cooperative ventures by agreeing to accept individual capital deposits. The Agricultural Savings Bank also encouraged its increasing number of provincial branches to help cooperatives and it was the director of one such branch, Iliya Stoyanov of Ruse, who was responsible for establishing the first credit cooperative under the auspices of the Bank itself in 1899. After the crisis of 1900 the Minister President, Ivanchov, sent Asen Ivanov, another official of the ASB, to study cooperatives abroad and under the latter's guidance the Bank set up a special department to advocate cooperation; most of the credit cooperatives which were established in later years were financed by this special department. The most important factor in promoting the development of the cooperative credit movement, however, was the relaxation of the laws of liability. The Commercial Code of 1897 classified credit cooperatives as joint stock institutions whose directors were each required to guarantee a tenth of the total capital. In 1898 pressure from the BNB and the ASB succeeded in relaxing this rule but directors remained responsible for up to three thousand leva of the capital, still a formidable barrier for the individual. Not until 1902 was the hurdle significantly lowered and then it came down to two hundred leva. Thereafter the expansion of credit cooperatives was easy and was rapid from 1904, when Bulgarian participation in the Sixth International Cooperative Alliance held in Budapest injected helpful information and ideas about the legal requirements and organisational needs of cooperatives. (See Table 10). In 1907 the Stambulovist government passed a Cooperatives Law which gave legal definition and thus greater security to cooperatives and set out how they were to be formed, constituted and administered. The same government encouraged the merger of various cooperatives, the first taking place in Ruse under the guidance of the Bulgarian Agricultural Bank, as the ASB became known after its extensive reorganisation in December 1903. In 1907 the Main Union of Bulgarian Agricultural Cooperatives was formed and within a few months almost all agrarian cooperative societies had affiliated to it.

Most of the cooperatives were credit institutions of the Reiffeisen variety, 721 of the 931 societies registered in 1910 coming within this definition, and most of these depended on the Agricultural Savings Bank or, after December 1903, the Bulgarian Agricultural Bank (BAB). The other forms of society were consumer cooperatives, the first of which had been set up by the Social Democrats in Plovdiv in 1899, and the biggest of which was *Bratski Trud* (Fraternal Labour), a

Table 10. Cooperatives in Bulgaria, 1899–1910.

Year	Number of Societies	Number of members
1899	4	236
1900	2	234
1901	2	140
1902	17	683
1903	17	739
1904	24	1447
1905	91	5458
1906	147	11224
1907	238	19422
1908	approx. 450	)
1909	604	)not available
1910	931	)

consumer cooperative established in Sofia in 1903 by civil servants, most of them employees of the two state banks. In the same year the first cooperative bank was founded, also in Sofia. Soon cooperative ventures were appearing in the working of the land, in the supplying of thorough-bred cattle and quality seeds, in the marketing of wine, dairy produce, silk worms, eggs and wool, and for the encouragement of better crop rotation and other forms of agrarian improvement. At its Tenth Congress BANU established *Naroden Magazin* (People's Store) through which cooperatives could market their produce.

Much of the early success of the cooperatives was the result of their dissociation from party politics, despite the fact that the Agricultural Savings Bank administration had once been riddled with *partisanstvo* appointments. The Cooperative Law of 1907 reflected popular opinion by making it illegal to use cooperative society funds for the support of any political party but in 1909 a significant body of opinion within the cooperative movement became restive because of the large number of members of the Main Union who were associated with the Radical Democratic Party. In 1909 the Main Union split, the dissenters forming the Central Union of Agricultural Cooperatives, a division which was deepened by disagreements over finance. The latter were themselves aggravated by growing financial strains within the cooperative movement. By 1911 cooperative institutions owed over eight million leva and their profits were declining to such a degree that many of them, according to the reports of bank inspectors, were heading for bankruptcy. The worst of the financial dangers were avoided in 1911 when the Central Cooperative Bank was established but the inauguration of the new bank, which was tighter with its credit than the BNB and BAB had been, did not repair the schism in the cooperative movement. There was considerable popular pressure for an end to this schism. In September 1913 the Main Union and the Central Union agreed to mend their differences and in February of the following year a reunification congress was held in Sofia from which emerged the General Union of Bulgarian Agricultural Cooperatives, whose standing committee included Stamboliiski.

The popular pressure for reunification had been an impressive proof of how deep-rooted and important the cooperatives had become in the Bulgarian countryside. Though they did not affect all villages they included in their ranks more individuals than did the Agrarian Union, and the cooperatives had a claim to be regarded as the most important new element in Bulgaria between 1900 and 1914. Membership of the cooperatives seems to have been confined to Bulgarians though there was no reason why others should not have joined. Those who did join were generally the better-off of the middle-peasants and had a higher than average educational attainment. Only 10.5% of the membership of cooperatives were non-peasants, these being the teachers and priests who played such an important role in establishing the societies in the first place and in administering them when they had become established. Thus in some measure did the cooperative movement recreate the alliance of *intelligent* and peasant which had been so important in the nation's past.

The cooperatives did not eliminate peasant indebtedness and by 1911 mortgage debts totalled 38,245,000 leva, sixty-six times higher than in 1887, but interest rates were now lower, the process of money-lending and credit was under control, and debts could be and frequently were discharged. Furthermore, it was far less socially divisive to owe mortgage debt to an established and large bank or to a cooperative society whose leaders were clearly trying to help the peasantry, than to a rapacious usurer. In accounting for the relative well-being and prosperity of the Bulgarian countryside, as well as for the comparative political stability which reigned there from 1901 to 1912, no small part was played by the cooperatives.

Chapter 20

SOCIAL AND ECONOMIC DEVELOPMENTS
FROM THE MID-1890s TO 1912
II. INDUSTRY, COMMERCE AND FINANCE

In 1910 industrial production in Bulgaria was worth between 450 and 475 million leva, four times higher than the average value of such production between 1898 and 1900. The traditional craft workshops, the *zanayati,* continued to account for the majority of industrial production; in 1905, when the only accurate survey of workshop production was carried out 8.9% of the total population were dependent on the *zanayati* for their livelihood, whereas in 1911, after considerable factory development, only 19,500 persons or 0.5% of the population were employed in factories; in the same year factories enjoying government encouragement, a status which will be discussed below, produced goods worth 350 million leva whereas the *zanayati* produced goods worth 450 million leva. The workshops, though remaining dominant, were undergoing some changes. They were becoming larger and between 1900 and 1905 the number of masters working in their own workshops decreased by 17.02%, from 81,830 to 67,905. The decline continued after 1905 and was most marked in those workshops which had to compete directly with new factory-based production, for example in the making of boots and shoes, weaving and knitting wool, baking, and milling. For some workshops competition from the factories was so intense that the *zanayati* all but disappeared, as in braid-making or type-casting, but in other branches the number of workshops increased. This was in areas free from competition from factories, such as the distillation of rose-oil, umbrella-making and the production of cheese and other foodstuffs.

Table 1.   The Growth of Factories in Encouraged Industries, 1894–1911.*

Year	No. of factories	Capital invested	No. of workers	Value of annual production
1894	72	10,916,000 leva	3,027	not known
1900	103	19,823,000 "	4,716	not known
1904	166	36,145,000 "	6,149	32,776,975 leva
1907	206	53,951,000 "	7,646	41,552,000 "
1909	266	66,031,440 "	12,943	78,317,396 "
1911	345	91,098,000 "	15,886	122,512,000 "

*Most Bulgarian factories enjoyed state encouragement, the number of enterprises in the non-encouraged sector being 38 in 1904 and 117 in 1911.

Though the workshops remained dominant within Bulgarian manufacturing, factory production did rise steeply, albeit from a low base. (See Table 1.) From   1894 to 1911 the number of factories had increased by 379%, the capital invested by 735% and the number of factory workers by 425%; from 1904 to 1911 the value of annual factory production in encouraged industries rose by 274%, and in all these cases the rate of expansion was increasing as the period drew to its close. In 1904 there had been only twelve enterprises in the encouraged sector with more than half a million leva in capital, but in 1909 there were thirty-one such enterprises, and the average capital per factory rose from the 192,000 leva of 1900 to 264,000 leva in 1911. The number of workers per factory, however, changed very little and only at the end of the period was it moving ahead of the 1894 level. The figures were 42.66 workers per factory in 1894, 45.78 in 1900, 37.04 in 1904, 37.11 in 1907, 48.65 in 1909 and down slightly in 1911 to 46.04.

As is shown in Table 2 by 1911 food, drink and textiles completely dominated Bulgarian factory production as it did in all Balkan countries. Light industry of this sort, which demanded smaller capital outlay and offered quicker and generally higher returns than heavy industry, accounted for 89.5% of Bulgarian factory production in 1911. Sofia, with 45 factories, had more encouraged industry than any other city, with Ruse next and Tŭrnovo third. Though much smaller in actual size Gabrovo remained one of the most intensely industrialised

Table 2. Analysis of Bulgarian factories, encouraged industries only, 1911.

Category	No. of factories	%age of total	Capital invested	%age of total	No. of workers	%age of total	Annual production in leva	%age of total
Food and drink	146	42.3	36,567,000	40.1	3126	19.7	67,407,000	55.1
Textiles	72	20.9	15,881,000	17.5	4267	26.9	21,415,000	17.5
Metallurgy[+]	29	8.4	7,113,000	7.8	2314	14.6	6,446,000	5.3
Chemical industry	27	7.8	3,446,000	3.8	655	4.1	4,171,000	3.4
Leather processing	24	7.0	2,755,000	3.0	421	2.6	5,426,000	4.4
Wood processing and furniture making	18	5.2	4,363,000	4.8	1265	8.0	3,020,000	2.5
Ceramics	16	4.6	6,446,000	7.1	1281	8.1	4,716,000	3.8
Mines and quarries[++]	6	1.7	4,399,000	4.8	1862	11.7	4,504,000	3.7
Paper making	4	1.2	1,573,000	1.7	194	1.2	929,000	0.8
Production of electricity	3	0.9	8,555,000	9.4	501	3.1	4,478,000	3.5
Total	345	100.0	91,098,000	100.0	15886	100.0	122,512,000	100.0
[+] Metallurgy, private	23	6.7	3,249,000	3.5	911	5.7	3,060,000	2.5
state	6	1.7	3,864,000	4.3	1403	8.9	3,386,000	2.8
[++] Mines and quarries, private	4	1.2	2,519,000	2.7	475	3.0	1,436,000	1.2
state	2	0.5	1,880,000	2.1	1387	8.7	3,068,000	2.5

towns in the country though the development of factories elsewhere robbed it of a former preeminence which had meant in 1901 that it possessed 18% of the nation's factories and larger workshops and 12.5% of the total industrial work force.

Industrial expansion can be explained to some extent by the increase in urban population, and even more by the improvement in rail and road transport which made it easier to supply the villages' growing and increasingly wealthly populations. In addition to natural stimuli to industrial production there was assistance and guidance from the state. The role of the state in the economy had been under discussion since the Liberation, particularly during the early debates on the questions of railways and the National Bank. In the 1890s interventionist ideas were gaining ground. The Plovdiv International Exhibition of 1892 was both the result of and a further stimulus to these ideas, as were the writings of Geshov which were presented in their final and most cogent form by Geshov's *Dumi i Dela* (Words and Deeds) published in 1899. Geshov wanted state promotion of industrial enterprises and an economic strategy designed to make Bulgaria concentrate on the production and manufacturing of commodities not easily grown elsewhere. He therefore suggested developing the cultivation and processing of tobacco, rose-oil, vegetables, vines and citrus fruits as alternatives to cereals where American competition could only be ruinous. It was to debate and study ideas such as these that the Bulgarian Economic Society was founded in 1895.

The advocates of state intervention could point to several precedents. In addition to the Railway and National Bank Acts there had been legislation enforcing the use of home-produced cloth in official uniforms, and local authorities had been encouraged to promote trade by organising fairs and markets, but such developments had been piecemeal and uncoordinated. In the mid-1890s, with the economic debate quickening, there were political changes which made a national economic strategy possible. Geshov was given the post of Minister of Finance in the Stoilov cabinet formed in 1894, and this he kept until 1897. His Encouragement of Industry Act passed through the Sŭbranie in December 1894 and came into effect in January 1895. It listed nine categories of industry which were to enjoy state promotion. The main ones were mining and metallurgy, textiles and building materials. All enterprises coming within any of the nine categories and having capital to the value of 25,000 leva and at least twenty employees were to enjoy certain privileges. These included the free import of machinery and raw materials not produced in Bulgaria, free grants of public land for factory building together with financial help for the construction of road and rail links where necessary, the free use of state or local authority quarries and water power, exemption from taxes on buildings and on the professions, preferential rates on the state railways with raw materials and finished goods being carried for 35% less than the minimum existing tariff, preferences in the granting of contracts to supply the state or local authorities even if native products were 15% more expensive than the cheapest imported foreign articles, and finally concessions for a monopoly in supplying specified products within certain geographic limits. The Act was to last for ten years.

In the elections of 1903 the Stambulovists promised they would do more to encourage the development of heavy industry. This was music to the ears of the industrialists themselves. The increasingly powerful Chambers of Commerce, especially those in Sofia and Plovdiv, had already begun to campaign for the prolongation of the 1894 law and for a widening of its scope. As soon as the Stambulovists were in office pressure from the Chambers of Commerce was applied to ministers who were already receiving the same message from the Union of Industrialists which wanted the provisions of any new bill to apply to factories with less initial capital or even to workshops. On all points the government was compliant.

The new Encouragement of Industry Act, which came into force in March 1905, was to last twenty rather than ten years. It was to be applicable to all industrial concerns with a minimum capital of 20,000 leva or fifteen workers in continuous employment for at least six months of the year. The privileges set out in the 1894 Bill were to continue but there were now to be two distinct types of enterprise, general and specific. The general category included nearly all industry, the most notable additions to the ranks of the encouraged being leather-working, milling, iron-working, carpet-making, carpentry, the production of electrical equipment, and the distribution as well as the manufacture of electricity; other less important additions to the lists included marble ware, match sticks, and preserved foods. Many workshops now enjoyed the status of encouraged industries. Specific enterprises were larger and in addition to their existing privileges were to have cheaper coal from state mines and exemption from local tariffs and stamp duties. The 1905 Act was replaced in 1909 by a third Encouragement of Industry Bill which lowered the qualification for inclusion in the encouraged status to include enterprises which employed a minimum of ten workers or whose machines had a force of at least ten horse power. On the other hand future monopoly concessions would be given only to enterprises with a capital value of 150,000 gold leva or a work force of at least fifty, and these concessions were likely to apply to a smaller area, whilst the price cushion which local contractors competing for state orders could enjoy over foreign competitors was lowered from 15% to 5%. Enterprises run by cooperative organisations were now to qualify for encouraged industry status if they met the usual requirements. In 1912 a whole set of new industries was added to the now recategorised list of encouraged industries and with tobacco processing at long last being made an encouraged industry almost all factory production in Bulgarian received state promotion, though the advent of the Balkan Wars made it impossible to measure the effectiveness of the new arrangements.

In close association with and an indispensible partner to the laws for the encouragement of industry were changes in tariffs, though here the government enjoyed less freedom of manoeuvre because of the restrictions of the treaty of Berlin. On the other hand any change in import levies which contravened the strict letter of that treaty would be doubly welcome because in addition to furthering domestic economic aims it would have the political advantage of showing that the government was edging towards the coveted goal of full political independence.

Though political motivation was always important in Bulgarian tariff policy before the declaration of independence in 1908, by the second half of the 1890s there were powerful economic reasons for wanting to see a change in the 8% on current prices agreed with the powers at the beginning of the decade. The land tax introduced in place of the tithe in 1895 meant a fall in state income and higher tariffs might go some way to make up the deficit, but much more important was the desire to gear state economic policy to the promotion of domestic industry. This meant more protection. This had been recognised by a government commission on tariffs which in 1887 had recommended a twenty-five percent levy on goods which could be produced at home. At that time political emergencies had prevented any such drastic action but with recognition in 1896 those emergencies, it seemed, had passed. Late in 1896 the government therefore announced its intention to bring in a general tariff of 14% but there were to be a whole series of exceptions to the general tariff with some articles, useful for local industry, paying less and those which would compete with domestic products paying far more. After some negotiation the powers accepted the new levies. Some goods remained at the old 8% level and these included iron and steel scrap, iron bars, screws, timber and timber products, and machinery and machine tools. A 10% tariff was imposed on coal, raw materials, fresh fruit of certain varieties, nuts, leather, and hemp; at 12% were wine, cheese, fish, leather for clothes, spun textiles, ceramics, pottery, porcelain, glass, cutlery, tinplate, soap and perfumes, at 16% leather soles and rubber products; at 18% liquor, ready-made clothes, candles and toilet soap; at 20% were rope and certain luxuries. The only items allowed in duty free were silk-making machines and equipment, coke-fired samovars and church bells.

These tariffs remained in force until the Petkov government revoked them in 1904. Payakov, the Finance Minister, announced to the Sŭbranie in November 1904 that tariffs would be renegotiated. There were to be some reductions in the highest levies on certain luxuries but the advantages which protection had afforded to native producers would be preserved and tariffs would still be used as a means to stimulate home industry. The new tariffs which came into force in 1906 were generally higher, much to the delight of the Chambers of Commerce which for some time had been pressing for all-round increases. Only forty-nine articles remained at the same tariff as under the 1897 agreements and the general rate was now 21.5%; protected articles paid correspondingly higher tariffs. The new rates had to be negotiated with individual trading partners and in these negotiations each power forced concessions on those goods which it exported to Bulgaria. Thus Britain brought down the proposed levies on soap and woollen and cotton clothes whilst Germany insisted upon a reduction in the proposed tariffs on shells, gunpowder, metallurgical products and machine tools. In all 202 or nearly a third of the 562 listed articles were affected by the negotiations but in most cases the government and the Sŭbranie had set the initial rates higher than was desired to allow for the attrition which they knew the negotiations would bring. Nevertheless, some of the changes forced by the trading partners definitely frustrated the government's declared intent of helping home producers, and the textile industry in Bulgaria expanded less quickly after 1906 partly because Britain had forced down the levy on imported woollen and cotton clothes. On the other hand in return for her concessions Bulgaria did gain certain privileges in the markets of her trading partners, especially in more protectionist markets such as Imperial Germany. In 1910 general tariffs were raised again but in the following year a number of specific levies, most of them on items needed by local manufacturers, were reduced or even abolished, though some of these, for example those on raw leather and semi-manufactured flax and hemp, were reintroduced in 1912. Despite these fluctuations, however, the protectionist patterns established in 1897 and reaffirmed in 1906 remained the basis of Bulgarian tariff policy throughout this period.

The agreements of 1897 and 1906 had affected Bulgaria's trading relations with the larger powers who enjoyed the privileges of the Capitulations and from whence came the threats to Bulgaria's nascent industry. In relations with those states which did not enjoy the privileges of the Capitulations, namely Serbia, Rumania and Turkey, and with whom Bulgaria was therefore free to pursue an unrestricted tariff policy, different criteria had to be applied. These were states which did not threaten home industrial production and were, especially in the case of Turkey, traditional partners in the exchange of traditional products. Here there was no reason not to encourage trade. In 1900 and 1902, despite the intense political differences over Macedonia, Bulgaria and the Ottoman Empire concluded tariff treaties which were all but free trade agreements. So encouraging were the results that the Chambers of Commerce were soon adding to their already long list of demands that for a Balkan customs union, including Turkey. Payakov was not entirely convinced but, he told the Sŭbranie in 1903, he did agree that Bulgaria needed a larger market and therefore he would strive for a customs union with Turkey and Serbia. In 1904 the political agreement with Turkey included commercial clauses which prolonged the agreements of 1900 and 1902 and which were themselves renewed in 1907. With Serbia a commercial union was achieved in 1905 but its origins and its fate, belonging to the political rather than the economic side of Bulgaria's evolution, have already been described.

In the quinquennium 1906–10 Bulgaria's external trade was worth an average of 258,816,678 leva *per annum,* 60.67% above the 161,094,772 leva a year for the period 1891–5. In the early years of the twentieth century Bulgaria generally enjoyed a favourable balance of trade but from 1907 she was less fortunate, both because the harvests were poorer than in the five or six preceding years and because the cost of her main imports, arms and machinery, was increasing more rapidly than the income from her main export commodities, food and textiles. Table 4, column 7, shows that the rate of increase in the cost of imports was almost half again that of the rate of increase in the value of exports. The yearly balance of trade is set out in Table 3.

Table 3.   Balance of trade, 1896–1912 in millions of leva.

Year	Value of imports	Value of exports	Balance of trade
1896	76,530,278	108,739,977	+32,209,699
1897	83,994,236	59,790,511	−24,203,725
1898	72,730,250	66,537,007	− 6,193,243
1899	60,178,079	53,467,099	− 6,710,980
1900	46,342,100	53,982,629	+ 7,640,529
1901	70,044,073	82,769,759	+12,725,686
1902	71,246,492	103,684,530	+32,438,038
1903	81,802,581	108,073,639	+26,271,058
1904	129,689,577	157,618,914	+27,929,337
1905	122,249,938	147,960,688	+25,710,750
1906	108,474,373	114,573,356	+ 6,098,983
1907	124,661,089	125,594,697	+933,608
1908	130,150,642	112,356,997	−17,793,645
1909	160,429,624	111,433,683	−48,995,941
1910	177,356,723	129,052,205	−48,304,518
1911	199,344,808	184,633,945	−14,710,863
1912	213,110,269	156,406,624	−56,703,645

Table 4 also shows that in general Bulgarian trade underwent little change between the mid-1890s and 1911. A comparison of columns 2 and 6 reveals that food and drink declined from 18.40% of the total value of imports in the first half of the 1890s to 11.86% in the five years ending in December 1911, and in this can be seen to some extent the working of tariff policies which placed heavy duties on foreign goods in this category. On the other hand raw materials did not increase greatly as a proportion of the total value of Bulgaria's imports, nor did manufactured goods decline, both indications that governmental efforts to promote home production at the cost of imports were not yet having great effect, though a more detailed analysis of the figures does show a rise in home production towards the end of this period. In exports food and drink continued to have total domination, with grain exporters finding new markets in Belgium, Egypt and, despite strained political relations, Greece. In manufactured goods the majority of revenue earned abroad came from textiles and rose-oil, these two categories of goods accounting for 73.94% of the value of exported manu-

Table 4. Bulgarian imports and exports by type of commodity, value in millions of leva.

A. IMPORTS

Type of commodity	1 Average yearly value 1891–5	2 %age of total	3 Average yearly value 1896–1900	4 %age of total	5 Average yearly value 1907–11	6 %age of total	7 %age change in value from columns 3 to 5	8 Change in %age value from columns 4 to 6
Live animals	0.53	0.63	0.41	0.60	1.26	0.79	+207.32	+0.19
Food and drink	15.37	18.40	9.41	13.85	18.81	11.86	+99.89	−1.99
Raw materials and semimanufactured goods	8.51	10.19	7.87	11.58	20.05	12.65	+154.76	+1.07
Manufactured goods	54.62	65.37	48.14	70.85	114.72	72.35	+138.30	+1.50
Unclassified	4.52	5.41	2.12	3.12	3.72	2.35	+75.47	−0.77
Total	83.55	100.00	67.95	100.00	158.56	100.00	+133.35	n/a

B. EXPORTS

Type of commodity	1 Average yearly value 1891–5	2 %age of total	3 Average yearly value 1896–1900	4 %age of total	5 Average yearly value 1907–11	6 %age of total	7 %age change in value from columns 3 to 5	8 Change in %age value from columns 4 to 6
Live animals	6.12	7.89	4.10	5.98	7.40	5.58	+80.49	−0.40
Food and drink	64.18	82.75	54.01	78.82	105.47	79.50	+95.28	+0.68
Raw materials and semimanufactured goods	0.43	0.56	0.47	0.69	0.86	0.65	+82.98	−0.04
Manufactured goods	6.82	8.80	9.88	14.42	18.91	14.25	+91.40	−0.17
Unclassified	0.00	0.00	0.06	0.09	0.02	0.02	−66.66	−0.07
Total	77.55	100.00	68.52	100.00	132.66	100.00	+93.61	n/a

factured goods in 1911, compared to 65.68% in the years 1896–1900. The textile exporters still relied upon selling traditional products in traditional markets.

Bulgaria's main trading partners are shown in table 5. The sources of Bulgaria's imports did not change greatly. The Habsburg Empire remained the chief source though its primacy was being eroded by the rapid advance of Germany and France. More interesting patterns can be discerned in the development of Bulgarian exports. Belgium's rise to first place was because she became the major purchaser of Bulgarian grain. Despite the intense political difficulties between the two countries Bulgarian exports to Greece increased almost ten-fold, and, conversely, despite the close cultural and historical relations between Russia and Bulgaria the two nations did not have close trading connections. As a source of imports Russia came sixth in the years 1896–1900 providing 3.528 million levas worth of goods or 5.19% of the total value of imports. By 1911 Russia had been overtaken by Italy and Rumania and provided 6.975 million leva worth of goods, or 3.5% of the total. As a market for Bulgarian exports Russia was of little importance, lying in twelfth place in 1911.

In the laws for the encouragement of industry and in the subsequent tariff agreements Bulgarian governments had set out their economic strategy for fostering domestic industrial production. There were also many tactical steps towards the same goal. The old laws demanding that state employees wear uniforms of Bulgarian manufacture were reenacted in 1897, although in the early 1900s the Stambulovists exempted the uniforms of army officers from this ruling. The Commercial Code of 1897 performed the useful function of collating old Turkish laws and the decrees of the Russian Provisional Administration and went some way to simplify commercial law and procedures in the Principality. Another important development was the recognition in 1885 of the Bulgarian National Bank's right to lend directly to the entrepreneur and further legislation in 1907 allowed the Bank almost absolute freedom to lend for any length of time to commercial and industrial enterprises. In 1888 and 1892 there had been state regulation of weights and measures and of trade marks but these were not always effective. The laws on the former were completely revised in 1910 whilst six years earlier the Stambulovists had pushed through more stringent regulations concerning trade marks, being prompted to do so by the widespread mislabelling of goods, a practice which in 1904 was damaging even the prestigious rose-oil industry. Further attempts to

Table 5. Bulgaria's main trading partners, 1896–1900 and 1908–12.

B. EXPORTS

1	2	3	4	5	6	7	8
	1896–1900			1908–12			
Country	Average annual value in millions of leva	%age of total	Country	Average annual value in millions of leva	%age of total	%age change of value	Change in %age of total
1. Ottoman Empire	17.768	25.94	1. Ottoman Empire	32.130	23.15	+80.83	–2.79
2. Great Britain	15.267	22.30	2. Belgium	31.591	22.76	+391.84	+13.38
3. Germany	8.976	13.10	3. Germany	17.373	12.52	+93.55	–0.58
4. France	7.909	11.55	4. Great Britain	14.784	10.65	–3.16	–11.65
5. Belgium	6.423	9.38	5. Greece	8.181	5.90	+551.36	+4.07
6. Austria-Hungary	5.179	7.56	6. Austria-Hungary	10.408	7.50	+100.97	–0.06

Table 5. Bulgaria's main trading partners, 1896–1900 and 1908–12.

A. IMPORTS

1	2	3	4	5	6	7	8
	1896–1900			1908–12			
Country	Average annual value in millions of leva	%age of total	Country	Average annual value in millions of leva	%age of total	%age change of value	Change in %age of total
1. Austria-Hungary	19.109	28.12	1. Austria-Hungary	44.230	25.17	+131.93	−2.95
2. Great Britain	15.709	23.21	2. Germany	33.509	19.31	+291.83	+6.63
3. Germany	8.552	12.68	3. Great Britain	26.940	15.23	+71.49	−7.98
4. Ottoman Empire	7.599	11.18	4. Ottoman Empire	18.168	10.32	+139.08	−0.86
5. France	3.622	5.33	5. France	14.692	8.34	+305.63	+3.01
6. Russia	3.528	5.19	6. Rumania	7.578	4.30	+298.00	+1.50

eliminate malpractices and unfair trading were made in laws on the conduct of auctions (1905), on commercial travellers (also 1905) and an important law of 1907 which regulated dealings on the recently-established grain bourse. Trade was encouraged by agreements concluded between the government and foreign shipping companies such as the Deutsche Livante Linie and La Compagnie marsilaise de Navigation à vapeur fraissement. These firms were given subsidies for taking Bulgarian exports to the ports of western and northern Europe whilst the state-owned Bulgarian Steam Navigation Company, which by 1906 had six vessels, was given a monopoly of inter-Bulgarian coastal trade. Vocational education continued to receive state support and by 1912 there were twenty-four schools giving training in agriculture or manufacturing. In addition there were nine commercial high schools, and even if not all the graduates of these institutions went into their particular trade or into commerce many of those who later formed the industrial and commercial management cadres of the country had been through these professional training establishments.

The state in Bulgaria also attempted to regulate the industrial work force. The Law on Guild Organisations of 1898 was an attempt, largely unsuccessful, to weld the guilds into larger units on the assumption that such units would be better equipped to withstand foreign competition. The law was scrapped in 1900 but reintroduced in 1903 when it was also decreed that all producers must belong to a guild organisation of some sort, though the 1903 law was unsatisfactory in many ways— even inn keepers were required to belong to a professional organisation—and in 1909 it was rationalised. A law which remained unchanged, however, was that reaffirming the notion of obligatory membership of professional organisations and allowing employers to seek compensation from their workers in the event of strikes. Also in 1901 the Minister of Trade and Agriculture intervened to end a strike in the Sofia sugar refinery, an intervention which brought some concessions for the workers. The intervention of the government into labour disputes, however, was rare and when it did take place was usually to the benefit of the employers. In fact close cooperation with manufacturers and merchants had been an essential preliminary to and remained an integral part of the whole strategy of state encouragement. In December 1894 the Sŭbranie had passed without debate a bill allowing for the establishment of Chambers of Commerce in Sofia, Plovdiv, Ruse and Varna. The Chambers, which could be set up on the initiative of the government or of local businessmen, were to consist of from sixteen to thirty-two members elected by all local citizens over 24 who were active in commerce, manufacturing or workshop production and who paid a minimum sum in professional tax. Election was to be for four years with half the membership changing every two years. Senior members were to elect a directing bureau of four for a two-year period of office, and the Ministry of Trade and Agriculture was to approve of all local regulations as well as devise a general constitution for the Chambers. The Chambers were to be official bodies linking trade and industry in the country to the administration in Sofia and keeping the latter abreast of industry's needs and desires. They were to provide the government with annual statistical reports and in return the government was obliged to consult the Chambers whenever it was contemplating changes in taxation, tariffs or in commercial treaties with the major powers.

In 1906 further legislation concerning the Chambers of Commerce was passed. A Chamber was to be opened in Burgas, Chambers were to be required to submit quarterly instead of annual statistical reports, and there were to be changes in the constitutions of the Chambers, changes which included granting to the central administration the right to appoint members to a Chamber if it felt that a particular interest were under-represented. In return the government was obliged to consult the Chambers whenever it was considering anything which might affect trade and industry in the area, and this included not only taxes and tariffs but also railway rates and the setting up of vocational schools.

The Chambers of Commerce were extremely important and influential organisations and next to the government itself did more than any other domestic bodies to shape the industrial development of Bulgaria in the pre-war period. They also played a considerable part in aiding their own members, helping, for example, to organise Bulgarian participation in the international fairs and exhibitions in Paris (1900), St. Louis (1904), Liège (1905), Milan (1906), and in the Balkan Exhibition in Earls Court, London (1907).

In addition to the Chambers of Commerce Bulgarian employers formed other organisations, most notably the Union of Bulgarian Industrialists, established in March 1903, the Union of Bulgarian Merchants, October 1907, and the Union of Bulgarian Contractors, set up just before the Balkan Wars. These organisations acted as additional pressure groups for influencing government policies, particularly when the Law for the Encouragement of Industry and the tariff agreements were being redesigned and renegotiated, but they also acted as useful defence mechanisms against the first stirrings of organised labour. In 1908 coordinated action by the employers, organised by the Union of Industrialists, defeated the workers in the Sliven textile industry after a lock-out lasting 65 days. Defeats were also inflicted on the leather workers of Ruse and Varna and in July 1909 Georgi Dimitrov told the Sixth Congress of the Narrow Socialists' Trade Union organisation, that 'the time has already passed when strikes could catch the employers unprepared'.[1] The Union of Industrialists enjoyed the full support of the government in its clashes with organised labour.

Government approval was also forthcoming for the formation of cartels, though these were neither as successful nor as powerful as those in Germany. The first cartel was formed in 1902–3 amongst traders who bought eggs and sold them in central Europe. The cartel, which lasted until 1910, forced down the prices given to the peasant by between 15% and 20%. Other cartels included that formed by millers in Varna in 1906, and ones for brewers and distillers, and the manufacturers of explosives. Tobacco manufacturers attempted to form a cartel in 1909 but only two thirds of them joined and one formed by textile manufacturers a year later could attract only those who processed wool. In fact by 1912 only a quarter of Bulgarian industrial production was in industries in which cartels were operating effectively.

Railway development which had been a government preserve since 1884 continued during this period and contributed much to Bulgaria's industrial development. In 1894 Stoilov's Cabinet, finding itself with an apparently healthy budget surplus, decided to implement some of the ambitious plans for railway development which the Sŭbranie had promulgated in 1891. This formed the basis of a Bill which was passed in November 1894 and which, subject to necessary modifications such as the introduction and then abandonment of the parallel railway, remained the blueprint for future construction. This did not mean that argument was avoided. When the so-called centre line was being discussed the Rumelians pressed for a line from Sofia and the international trunk route along the Balkan foothills to Burgas but this was overruled in favour of one linking Sofia with the north Bulgarian plain via the Iskŭr defile; this line was cheaper, despite the difficulties in the Iskŭr defile and, its supporters added, it would help get grain to the north-eastern ports and would relieve the northern grain exporters of their reliance on the Danube. The line was completed in 1900. The national rail strategy also intended that the central line would be extended south-westwards, eventually, it was hoped, to link Varna with Salonika. Already in 1893 a line had been opened between Sofia and Pernik. This was primarily to help exploitation of the coal reserves at Pernik but it was not forgotten that the line into Macedonia and the Vardar valley would take this route. The line was taken on to Radomir in 1897, again to facilitate the transport of the coal taken from state mines; by 1909 it had reached Kiustendil and in the following year Giueshevo, but the much desired connection with the Turkish railways in Macedonia was never made.

The second strategic line, the transbalkan, provoked a debate even more bitter than that over the central line. The objective was to link the southern network with Tŭrnovo and the northern lines. There were three possible *tracés*. The most westerly of the three, that which would most favour Plovdiv, had considerable political backing. The most easterly route had much less political support but had the economic advantage of bringing the link line to the grain port of Burgas. The third line, mid-way between the others, was the cheapest but had little else to recommend it. The final route was not decided until 1904 when the Petrov/Petkov administration announced it would follow an entirely new *tracé* via Tryavna and the Prince Boris coal mines. The latter were owned by Pariba with whom the administration was negotiating for a loan and which exercised decisive pressure in this question. It was a disastrous decision for this route had none of the advantages and most of the disadvantages of the others; the decision smelt strongly of political corruption, so strongly indeed that even the normally submissive Stambulovist Assembly had to be massively dosed with bribes before it would accept the new route.

There were other less contentious lines, and those opened during the period 1894 to 1912 included: Sofia to Kaspichan (1899); Yasen to Samovit (1899), built privately but taken over by BDZh despite the fact that it was not a profitable venture as the Danubian port of Samovit froze over in the winter when the line had to be closed; Ruse to Tŭrnovo (1900), an important link between two major cities; Gabrovo to Tŭrnovo (1907); Plovdiv via Chirpan to Nova Zagora (completed 1909); Sliven to Zimnitsa (1909); Tŭrnovo via Borushtitsa and Dŭbovo to Stara Zagora (completed 1912); and Devnya to Dobrich (Tolbukhin) (1910).

Bulgarian railways continued to be built with cheapness always more in mind than the convenience of the user. Trains were slow because of the excessive curves and gradients; there was always a shortage of wagons at harvest time, and stations were often long distances outside towns, though in defence of the railway planners it should be said that a number of Bulgaria's smaller towns remained essentially mountain settlements and the costs of taking lines to many of these would have been prohibitive. The junctions of important lines were not always well sited, most noticeably that of the central and transbalkan lines which met at Gorna Oryahovitsa when Tŭrnovo, only nineteen kilometres away, would have been far more sensible. There was also one noticeable gap for notwithstanding a number of agreements no progress whatever was made towards building a bridge across the Danube to link the Bulgarian and Rumanian systems.

Despite these setbacks the expansion of the Bulgarian rail network between the mid-1890s and the wars was a considerable achievement. From 1892 to 1903 the Bulgarian state built 682 kilometres of track whilst Serbia constructed only forty-six kilometres. The actual track lengths in Bulgaria were 861 km in 1895, 1,565 km in 1900 and 1,964 km in 1912. In 1894 Bulgarian State Railways carried 383,000 tons of freight and 350,000 passengers; in 1911 the figures were 2,037,000 tons of freight and 3,430,000 passengers. By 1912 the total capital invested in the state rail system was 340,000 leva, though this was not in relative terms a high outlay per kilometre of track.

Railways were not the only form of communication to enjoy government support. In 1894 Stoilov decided that Burgas and Varna needed modern port facilities with wharves, storage facilities etc., and government money was earmarked for these projects. The new harbours were opened in May 1903 and May 1906 respectively and together with Ruse handled over half of Bulgaria's external trade. Road building and repair were not neglected. In 1887 the Principality had 3,727 km of state and local authority roads, but by 1911 after an expenditure of 139,000,000 leva there were 8,945 km. Not all these roads were in good condition, though some improvement had been made upon the situation of 1907 when a government commission found that only 45% of the nation's roads were in 'good' condition and that some communities had no roads classified as usable. By the end of the period only Sofia had a tramway system and although postal services had been extended with the number of postboxes being 3,031 in 1912 compared to 203 in 1886, there were only 2,762 telephones in the country in 1912.

The expansion of banking was an essential precondition for Bulgarian industrial growth. The Bulgarian National Bank remained the most important credit institution in the country and was particularly prominent in the financing of external trade. In the first twelve years of the century its gold reserves increased nearly tenfold, and while in 1902 it had outside Sofia only five branches and between fifty and sixty representatives, in 1912 it had full branches in all twelve provincial and all seventy-one district capitals. The other state bank, the Agricultural Savings Bank, reformed into the more centralised Bulgarian Agricultural Bank in 1903, also greatly expanded its activities, not least, as we have seen, because of its essential role in the funding of credit cooperatives. In 1895 the Agricultural Savings Bank had carried out 375,000 transactions involving a total of 128,000,000 leva; in 1911 there were 835,000 transactions involving 1,309,000,000 leva. The two large state banks lent at rates of between eight and ten percent and together with the cooperatives helped to stamp out the worst evils of the old money-lending system.

The state banks accounted for two thirds of all banking transactions in Bulgaria. The remaining third was carried out by the private banks and here foreign concerns were dominant. By 1912 foreign money was not quite half the total initial capital in private banks but because these banks lent more in proportion to their deposits they dominated the transactions in the private sector. In the early years France and Austria were the chief sources of the private capital coming into Bulgarian banking, with the powerful Banque de Paris et des Pays Bays setting up the Commercial Bank, later renamed the Bulgarian General Bank. The Commercial had been founded in 1901 and though the profits to be made in banking had always been attractive to foreign investors it was not until after 1903 that their entry into Bulgaria was made easy. In that year the Stambulovists reformed the Commercial Code of 1897 and after declaring that he wished to make the foreign investor welcome in Bulgaria Payakov abolished the ruling which until then had required all joint stock enterprises to have a ruling committee of three Bulgarian citizens all of whom were resident in the country. Thereafter foreign banks grew considerably in number, and German capital played an increasingly important part in Bulgarian banking. From 1903 to 1908 the new banks established in the Principality included the Deutsche Credit Bank, the Discontogesellschaft, Bleichröder, the Norddeutsche Bank, and the Balkanska Banka funded by the Wiener Bankverein. In 1912 alone nine new foreign banks, with an initial capital of 33,000,000 leva, were established in Bulgaria.

With the expansion of banking the amount of money in circulation increased. The value of notes in use in 1886 had been 200,000 leva. In 1900 it was 14,300,000 leva, and in 1911 98,300,000 leva. Until 1903 a shortage of cash had meant that the values of paper money and gold had varied by between seven and a half and thirteen percent, but after 1903 notes and gold were generally at parity.

Greater financial sophistication was to be seen also in the expansion of insurance. In 1903 the Teachers' Mutual Savings Bank was established and this offered insurance to its members, as did *Bratski Trud,* the large cooperative financial venture set up later by civil servants. Private insurance companies were also established, most noticeably the large 'Otechestvo' (Fatherland) and 'Orel' (Eagle) companies which began operating in 1905 and 1906 respectively. By 1911 there were thirteen insurance companies in Bulgaria, nine of them foreign. Of the four native concerns two were cooperatives and two joint stock companies, but though less numerous than their foreign rivals the Bulgarian companies dominated the insurance business because only the state was allowed to arrange for the insurance of agricultural produce and this it did through Bulgarian firms.

*   *   *

Successive administrations in Bulgaria had attempted to foster home industry and make the country less dependent upon imported goods. The figures already given in Table 1 attest to the growth in the value of home production and show that the strategy of encouragement was not entirely without success, with native production dominating the internal market for flour, beer, ceramics and other protected goods. There was also some noticeable progress in boosting home production's share of total consumption. This is shown in Table 6.

High growth rates had been achieved to some degree by the sensible expedient of concentrating encouragement on those industries where there had been marked and recent technological improvement and the most modern production methods could therefore be used.

The story was, however, not one of unqualified success. In a number of areas local industry found itself importing raw materials which should have been available from domestic suppliers. In 1909, for example, half the wool processed in the country was imported, 67.2% of the leather worked came from abroad because local hides were dirty and damaged by the warble fly, and the lack of proper roads and the

Table 6.   Imported and home-produced goods in toto and as percentages of national consumption. (Encouraged industries.)

	1896	1901	1911
Home produced goods, value in leva	9,000,000	18,000,000	122,512,000
" , %age of consumption	13	23.4	43
Imported goods, value in leva	60,430,000	58,880,000	162,590,000
" , %age of consumption	87	76.6	57

undisciplined looting of the forests meant that the native paper industry could not use Bulgarian wood-pulp. Nor was Bulgarian industry efficient. Production per head of the population was only 28.3 gold leva compared with 1,128 gold leva in the USA, and even Russia could manage 150 gold leva per head.

The development of the industrial sector was not always well-coordinated. Railways were often built less to promote industrial development than to meet strategic military or particular political needs. There were also simple oversights such as that which left the new harbours at Varna and Burgas with insufficient warehouse facilities and no electrical installations for lighting or loading-gear. Tariffs, too, were at times not in the best long-term interests of the country. The protection of the poor-quality home produced hides made the imported raw materials, which still had to be used, more expensive, whilst the falling duties on imported machinery meant that a native machinery industry was unlikely to develop. The spectre of political graft and intrigue was never far distant. The much-needed railway wagons bought from Germany at the turn of the century arrived without spare parts simply because politicians, officials and contractors had helped themselves to some of the funds set aside for these items. In 1904 the award of a concession for the manufacture and sale of rope in western Bulgaria went to the firm of Payakov and Vŭzharov and with Payakov holding office as Minister of Finance suspicions of favouritism were widespread and justified. Genadiev, reported one British diplomatist, had reputedly demanded the staggering sum of £12,000 or nearly 300,000 leva for the granting of a concession to build a cotton factory.

The most serious defect of the whole programme, however, was that it promoted 'growth without structural change'.[2] The major proportion of encouraged industry was concerned with the processing of home-produced agricultural material yet the development of industry did not bring about any significant change in the way in which agriculture was organised. So strong was the peasant proprietor in Bulgaria that no government could have forced through the sort of industrialisation which would have brought about major changes in Bulgarian village life. The continued, if somewhat diminished dominance of grain in Bulgarian agricultural production is a measure of how slight had been the effect of industrialisation on the primary producer.

A constant theme of industrial promotion had been the need to lessen the country's dependence on foreign producers but whilst this had been done to some degree the role of the foreign investor in Bulgaria itself had increased very considerably. Foreign capital began to move into Bulgaria in significant quantities after the beginning of the encouragement programme in the mid-1890s and by the turn of the century it accounted for 26.8% of all capital lodged in the encouraged industries. By 1909 the percentage of foreign capital in the encouraged sector had fallen slightly and stood at 22.7% with the total sum involved being 14,650,000 leva. Much of this foreign capital was in the larger industrial enterprises for while it accounted for 22.7% of the total capital it was invested in only 5% of the total number of enterprises. The majority, sixty-nine percent, of foreign capital by 1911 came from Belgium, a somewhat ironic fact given Stoilov's oft-repeated statement that he wished to make Bulgaria 'the Belgium of the Balkans'. British investors came second with twenty-one percent, the Germans had three percent, and others seven percent. Foreign investors were attracted originally by the encouragement programme and later by the abolition of restrictions against foreign directors in joint stock companies. The foreign investor was also not a little stimulated by the high profit levels which were to be found. Between 1904 and 1910 the Belgian firm which was responsible for installing street lighting in Sofia enjoyed returns which varied between 12% and 37%; at the same time the Plovdiv sugar refinery gave its Belgian shareholders profits of 24% to 29%; Granitond, a foreign-owned company which produced cement and asphalt for a number of public works made a clear profit of 800,000 leva in 1912, and its assets had grown from 300,000 leva when it was founded in 1908 to 2,000,000 leva in 1912.

At times the power of the foreign company could work against the interests of the country. This was particularly the case with companies which were closely associated with Pariba which itself played a vital role in financing state loans. It was this bank which in 1905 insisted upon the introduction of a match monopoly though this the government was loathe to do knowing that the monopoly would inevitably mean a price increase for the consumer, and the bank's role in determining the route of the transbalkan line has already been noted.

The years from the mid-1890s to 1912 saw a steep rise in state spending. In 1900 expenditure totalled 123.7 million leva, with 13.9 million being extraordinary spending; in 1912 the total was 423.6 million leva, with 117 million coming under the heading of extraordinary spending. This represents a rise of 242.44% in total spending in the twelve year period, and the 1912 level was 1,982.59% above the 1879 figure of 20.34 millions for total expenditure. Government income in 1879 had been 29 million; the surplus had disappeared by 1900 when total income from domestic sources was 120 million leva, three million in deficit, but by 1912 income was only 215.8 million leva, a shortfall of 207.8 million. The industrial encouragement programme itself contributed to some extent to the growing deficit for whilst industrial production increased the income from tariffs, state lands, and the state railways was lower than it would otherwise have been, and in 1911, when encouraged industry made total profits of 26,607,000 leva, the loss to the state revenue was put at 3,727,000 leva or 13.91% of the total profits.

The increasing disparity between expenditure and revenue could be made good by foreign loans and by increased taxation at home. The increase in state borrowing is an essential feature of economic development in this period and its effect was far from being always beneficial.

Before 1900 Bulgaria had dealt with Austrian, German and French banks when seeking and raising official government loans. From 1900 to 1909 France was the sole supplier of such funds though in the latter year the Austrians returned to the field. In the mid-1890's Stoilov's government had contracted a 30 million leva loan with a consortium organised by the Länderbankverein of Vienna. The money was intended for the Agricultural Savings Bank, though not all of it actually reached the destination. A much larger loan, this time for 260 million leva, was contracted in 1899 and all of it was swallowed up by the conversion of previous loans and by Bulgaria's obligations towards the Oriental Railway Company. By 1900 loans had become a major political issue in Bulgaria and the country was in desperate need of yet more funding from abroad, and, as has been described, Karavelov and then

Danev were obliged to accept humiliating conditions in return for a substantial loan from Pariba.

It was the same bank which floated the next substantial loan taken out by the Bulgarian government, that of 1904. The loan was for one hundred million francs and was, said the government, needed for the paying off of floating debts, for railway construction and for military expenditure. The latter, however, was what the government had in mind and the other two heads of expenditure were little more than camouflage with more than half of the loan going to buy arms; most of what was spent on railways went to build the transbalkan line on its mistaken route via Tryavna. As guarantees for the loan the Bulgarian government pledged more of the revenue from the banderolle and the *mururie* as well as some of the returns from the stamp duty.

In 1907 the Stambulovist Cabinet contracted yet another loan with Pariba, this time for 145 million leva. The world capital market was now less strained and Bulgaria's economic position had improved noticeably since 1900 and 1904 and therefore the terms of the loan were more favourable. Once again the government declared the loan was needed to pay off previous debts and to finance railway and military expenditure, but yet again it was the latter which ate up most of the money.

The next loan, that of 1909, was raised by a Viennese rather than a Parisian consortium. Bulgaria's political victory in 1908 had both strengthened the nation's credit-worthiness and had made it politically favoured in the Austrian capital, and the projected loan of 100 million francs was oversubscribed four times in Vienna and only slightly less so in Frankfurt and London. A further measure of Bulgaria's international reputation at this time was the fact that the loan, unlike those of the previous years raised in France, had no strings attached, but once more the majority of it was spent on military orders and the servicing of previous loans.

These were the major loans concluded by the Bulgarian government between 1895 and 1912 but they were not the only ones, a number of smaller ones being taken out to cover immediate needs. Bulgaria's foreign debts were also increased by loans contracted by the National Bank, the Bulgarian Agricultural Bank, and by a number of local authorities. Sofia, for example, borrowed thirty-five million leva from a number of French and German banks. By 1911 the total foreign debt of local authorities in Bulgaria was seventy million gold leva, of which fifty-four million was owed by the capital, 8.4 million by Plovdiv, and eight million by Varna.

Between 1901 and 1912 the foreign debts of Bulgaria increased by 70.42%, from 354.3 million leva to 646 million leva or 149.25 leva per capita, a figure which compared favourably, however, with 193.63 francs per capita for Turkey, 235.88 francs per capita for Serbia and 328.88 francs per capita for Greece.

Foreign loans were an unpleasant necessity. In the great debate of 1899 on the parallel railway opposition deputies had complained that foreign loans would mean the enslavement of the country and the French loans of the 1900s did infringe the sovereignty of successive Bulgarian governments. Yet foreign loans did not bring enslavement. Diplomatic freedom was not impaired; the military strength of the nation was greatly increased and the victories of 1912 were secured with arms purchased through these loans. There was, however, good reason to argue that too much foreign money had been spent on arms and other non-productive items. Of the 530 million leva borrowed from abroad between 1902 and 1912 only 95 million had been spent on railways and harbours and 6.75 million on posts and telegraphs in southern Bulgaria making a total of only 17.8% of the foreign loans spent productively, and they provided only a third of the funds expended for railways and harbours, the government itself contributing 184 million from internal sources. Much better use had been made of earlier loans for three quarters of those contracted before 1892 were spent on railways, harbours, etc. The large loans of the 1900s were also costly. French loans which had provided successive governments with 516 million leva created obligations amounting to 1,039.89 million leva. The servicing of the loans meant a considerable flow of funds abroad and this was a constant hindrance to Bulgaria's capital accumulation, as well as being a heavy strain on the budget. By 1908 the costs of foreign loans were twice as high as they had been in 1900 and were consuming 23 million leva *per annum,* or 18% of yearly expenditure. The problem naturally became worse as further loans were contracted.

Increased foreign borrowing was accompanied by increased taxation. As noted above the government's revenue rose from 120 million leva in 1900 to 215.8 million leva in 1912. This increase of 79.83% was achieved almost solely by increasing tax revenue. For the individual citizen this meant a rise of 52.25% in the annual tax burden which rose from 22.58 leva to 34.58 leva in the same years. The Petrov-Petkov administration was particularly zealous in its pursuit of extra income and it succeeded in almost doubling tax revenue between 1903 and 1907. This was in some measure due to the series of good harvests, but was also the result of the government's rigorous collection of existing taxes, the introduction of new levies and a general rationalisation of tax-collecting procedures. It was to the latter that Payakov in 1907 ascribed a fifty per cent increase in yields from stamp-duties, but for the ordinary citizen the most perceptible feature of that government's tax policy was the introduction of new levies. The most noted of these was the excise on spirits introduced in the face of widespread discontent in 1903. This was only one of a series of new indirect taxes and it was under the 1903–1908 government that indirect taxes for the first time yielded more to the exchequer than direct taxation. By 1911 indirect taxes were providing 83.6 million leva, nine times more revenue than they had yielded in 1887, and they were now contributing 67% of total state income compared with 37% in 1900.

The tax burden remained inequitable. The relatively well-off of the towns paid little more than the three per cent professional tax and were not much affected by increasing indirect levies. The urban poor on the other hand suffered more than anyone else from the increasingly heavy concentration on indirect taxation which reinforced the determination of many workers to retain land, either in their native villages or in nearby plots, for here they could find a source of untaxable food and fuel.

By 1911 the number of industrial workers in Bulgaria was 15,886 in the encouraged industries with about another 4,000 in the non-encouraged sector, though in the latter there were very few large enterprises outside the tobacco industry. A statistical analysis of the workers in the encouraged industries in 1910 had shown that 35.1% of them had been in the same job for five years or more, and in state concerns, where wages and conditions were always better than in the private sector, this stability was more marked. The workforce still, however, bore marks of its recent origins. 55.4% of the men and 40.9% of the women employed in encouraged industries in 1910 had been born in villages; 31.9% of the workers (38.2% of the males and 8.2% of the females) had worked in agriculture before becoming factory workers whilst only 11.4% had come from the craft workshops (13.7% of the men and 3.5% of the women). At the same time 51.5% of the workers had come from other occupations, and the previous activities of 5.2% were not known. These figures indicate, as was to be expected, that the drift from agriculture to industry was stronger amongst men than women. In all women formed 28.6% of the total work force in encouraged industries in 1910, and 60.1% of them worked in textile factories.

Wage rates in Bulgarian industry varied considerably. The average daily rate for the general worker was 1.80 leva in 1901, 1.43 leva in 1904, 1.96 leva in 1910 and 2.66 leva in 1912. State-owned enterprises paid more than private ones, 2.58 leva compared with 1.80 leva in 1910, and piece work was, in both state and private concerns, more rewarding financially than working at a day-rate. Wages for men were much higher than for women, with male day workers receiving 2.26 leva *per diem* and women only 0.93 leva in 1910. Those who actually earned the average salary were 27.2% of the total male labour force and 1.2% of the female workers; 29.5% of the men and 0.7% of the women received more than the average but 43% of the men and 98.1% of the women took home less than the mean daily payment. Differences between the various branches of industry were considerable with the electrical and metallurgical industries being the best-paid and paper-making the worst, and as always the state was a better employer. There were also very large differentials for skilled workers both within the encouraged sector and elsewhere, these differentials being in part a legacy from the earliest days after the Liberation when very high salaries had to be offered to attract qualified foreign experts. Some measure of the scale of these differentials is to be gauged from Table 7.

Between 1901 and 1912 the average industrial wage had risen by 32.69%. This did not keep pace with the rise in prices, which, like wages, rose more sharply at the end of this period than at any time since the Liberation. From 1898 to 1911 the price of 98 of the most important industrial and agricultural commodities in the country rose by 46%. Itemised price increases included a 20.8% rise in the cost of bread, from 24 stotinki per kilo in 1900 to 29 stotinki in 1912; in the same period the price of beef went up by 104.17%, from 48 stotinki to 98 stotinki per kilo; even cheese rose by 81.81% from 66 stotinki to 122 stotinki per kilo. If the average price level for the period 1881 to 1900 is taken as 100 then the price index in 1900 itself was 95, in 1903—101, in 1905—115, and 1908—128. In absolute terms the estimated cost of maintaining a family of two adults and two children in tolerable conditions was 71.04 leva per month in 1895, and 67.22 leva per month in 1901, whereafter the monthly figure rose to 71.71 leva in 1904, 86.47 leva in 1907 and 103.44 leva in 1912. The protective duties of 1904 did much to raise the cost of living, with some articles doubling in price. A

Table 7.   Monthly wage rates in selected occupations.

Occupation	1895	1901	1904	1907	1912
Average industrial wage	—	41.36	32.86	49.56	54.88
General industrial labourer	43.50	34.50	36.80	44.50	58.10
Platelayer, BDZh	45.00	40.00	41.00	44.00	59.00
Conductor, Sofia tramways	—	65.00	65.00	67.00	94.00
Bricklayer	70.51	54.35	58.14	79.22	101.50
Fitter, BDZh	280.00	234.00	235.00	263.00	245.00

similar if less drastic effect followed the introduction of official monopolies; the salt monopoly of 1905, for example, meant that the price of this necessity was twenty-one leva per kilo compared with 15.20 leva per kilo at the end of 1904. Cigarette papers, spirits and matches also cost more because of government monopolies.

Hours of work were generally long. In the workshops the masters had complete discretion and here fifteen- and sixteen-hour days were common. In the factories they were somewhat shorter, the average in 1909 being 10.7 hours. In the same year 15% of the factory work-force worked for more than twelve and a half hours per day and only 2.1% of the total worked for eight hours or less; most children employed in factories worked for ten or more hours each day. The demand for the eight-hour day was widespread amongst workers in Bulgaria long before they became politically organised. It had been secured by some printers in Sofia in 1895 but the victory did not last and was soon disregarded by employers. It was also demanded by strikers in the Pernik mines, particularly in the disturbed years between 1904 and 1908, by workers in the Sliven textile mills, and by the striking railwaymen in 1906 to 1907. But apart from an attempt to restrict the hours worked by women and children little real progress was made on this front.

In addition to long hours the factory worker in Bulgaria had to endure many of the other evils associated with the early stages of industrialisation. Factory discipline, for example, was often brutally primitive with fines and even beatings being handed out by owner or manager. Pay, as well as being insufficient, was sometimes, especially earlier in this period, delayed. There was also a dangerous neglect of health and safety. The worst tragedy of all took place in 1897 when over one hundred and thirty people perished in a factory fire in Ruse. Miners at the French-owned Prince Boris mines in Tryavna were still using open-flame lamps in the mid-1900s despite an explosion in 1901 which had killed six men. A Sliven factory persisted in heating its shop-floor with open braziers which had been declared illegal but which were nevertheless cheaper than the closed stoves required by law. In 1903 an official investigation into the work-force of a carpet factory in Panagiurishte found that 94% of it was in poor health. Even the office-workers of BDZh, usually more privileged than the manual workers, had only ten cubic metres of office space each though the regulations demanded a minimum of fifteen cubic metres per person.

Whilst factories were generally, though not always, dangerous and unhygienic, working class homes were often little better. Two thirds of the workers in encouraged industries in 1910 did not live in their own or their parents' homes and had therefore to rely on the private land-lord or the employer, and some workers, as in Russia, lived in factory barracks. In the urban working class districts which had become estab-lished by the end of this period there was great overcrowding and little in the way of amenities.

There were few efforts to improve the lot of the Bulgarian worker. The most notable attempt was the Women and Children's Employ-ment Act of 1905. Its architect, Genadiev, had been a consistent oppo-nent of factory legislation until a visit to a number of factories, particularly the mills of Gabrovo, had convinced him of the need to save the nation's women and children from such 'Godless exploitation'. The Act decreed that children under ten were not to be employed under any circumstances and that those between ten and twelve were not to work more than six hours in any one day; those from twelve to fifteen were to have a maximum eight-hour day. Women and children were not to be employed underground and no women over eighteen were to be put to work in any occupation hazardous to life or health; women over fifteen were to work no more than ten hours in any twenty-four. Other clauses regulated night work, controlled the number of breaks, and barred women from working for one month after childbirth, though they were to be entitled to resume their former work after this statutory rest. The Bill was modelled on French legisla-tion of 1874 rather than the more modern and complete German acts of the 1880s and it contained a number of inconsistencies. Its most serious drawback, however, was the means by which it was to be enforced. This was to be the responsibility of a local 'Labour Committee' consisting of the mayor, a regional or a local doctor, a school inspector, a municipal or state engineer, a representative of the nearest Chamber of Commerce, and elected representatives of the local work force. This was an inappropriate and largely unworkable body. To those interested in the welfare of the employees the only proper supervisory body was a factory inspectorate. This was eventually established in 1907 when the Labour Committees were abolished, but by 1908 there were only two factory inspectors and in 1911 there were only nine more. The inspectorate could at least point to the dimension of the problem and of the 375 factories and workshops visited in 1910 and 1911 only three were given a clean bill of health. The inspectorate however could neither force through further legislation nor ensure that rules already enacted were obeyed. Its work showed that the 1905 Women and Children's Employment Act was similar to many other Bulgarian laws in that it contained much fine sentiment but little that was really effective; it was honoured as much in the breach as in the observance.

A similar fate awaited other items of welfare legislation. These included a bill of 1905 which required employers in the construction industry to put one percent of their wages bill into a fund to finance accident insurance for their workers. In the same year local authorities were required to fund hospital accommodation for workers on local government projects, and in 1906 a law accepted the principle of automatic compensation for injury whereas previously a culpable party had to be found before payment could be made, though the new legislation applied only to workers employed by the state; workers in all state-encouraged industries would have had the same privilege if the Stambulovist government had not fallen in 1908 when a bill to this effect had received two of the necessary three readings. In 1909 all firms benefiting from state encouragement were required to contribute to a fund to finance compensation for their workers in the event of death, invalidity, accident or sickness, and just before the First World War a law was passed uniting all different funds for workers' insurance, the new consolidated fund amounting to five million leva. An Act of 1911 guaranteed all workers work-free Sundays with an additional eight days holiday per year but this, like so many other welfare acts, was simply ignored.

Part III
The Pangs of War, 1912–1918

"Three times in my life has this wretched Bulgaria subjected a peasant population to all the pangs of war and chastisements of defeat."

Winston S. Churchill, 2 August 1944

"But ye shall die like men, and fall like one of the princes."

Psalm 82, verse 7

Chapter 21

THE BALKAN WARS, 1912–13

In the coalition formed in March 1911 the Nationalist Party leader, Geshov, became Minister President and Minister for Foreign Affairs. The leader of the Progressive Liberal Party, Danev, not wishing to take a subordinate ministry, became President of the Sŭbranie. The other portfolios were divided between the two Parties, though the Ministry of War was given to General Nikiforov, a non-party figure with Stambulovist leanings.

The new Cabinet's first task was to convene the Grand National Assembly discussed in a previous chapter. It then went on to organize the return of a new Ordinary Sŭbranie. Government fears that a general election would give rise to outbursts of radicalism and republicanism similar to those which accompanied the Grand National Assembly proved groundless. The September poll attracted a relatively low turnout and the coalition secured an easy victory. It had 191 seats; its opponents' 22 deputies comprised seven Radoslavists, six Stambulovists, four Democrats, four Agrarians and one Tonchevist.

Geshov's Nationalist Party was well-organised, wealthy and, in addition to its Russophilism, was known for its commitment to constitutionalism, a commitment which it believed it had proved in its period in office immediately after Stambulov's rule. This theoretical commitment had made the Party an eager supporter of proportional representation and in a bill of 1912 the experiment which Malinov's government had conducted in the Tŭrnovo and Plovdiv provinces was extended to the whole country. The introduction of proportional representation flatly contradicted another political tenet of the Nationalist party, the need to curb Ferdinand's personal power. The

King, in fact, was a warm supporter of proportional representation because he believed it would lead to even greater fragmentation of the Parties. This, he trusted, would both frustrate the rise of the mass Parties, and increase his ability to play the factions off against each other. At the same time the other Parties also welcomed the new system as they saw that one party rule such as that of the Stambulovists from 1903 to 1908 would now be much more difficult; in a more fragmented system all governments would be coalitions and each faction could therefore have a hope of being included. The extension of proportional representation to the whole country, then, occasioned little debate, but there was lively discussion of other proposed political changes. The government had to fight hard to defeat a proposal to make voting in general elections compulsory, and it faced considerable opposition to its own plan whereby women property owners would be allowed to take part in the election of the Agricultural Councils. Nor was the Cabinet popular when it proposed, despite both Parties' previous condemnation of the personal regime, to increase the civil list from 1.2 million to 1.8 million leva. The increase, it was argued, was necessary as the King's household expenses had risen since his marriage in 1908 to Princess Eleonore von Reuss-Köstritz.

After the excitements over the voting questions and the civil lists, however, the chief criticism levelled at the Geshov government concerned not what it was doing but what, it seemed, it was not doing. Opposition spokesmen in the Sŭbranie and in the press were puzzled by the speech from the throne in November 1911 because it contained nothing of interest or importance. It did not even mention, these critics noted, the burning question of the day: Bulgaria's relations with Turkey. That the King and his ministers said nothing on this subject did not mean, however, that they had done nothing. Indeed foreign policy was consuming most of their time and energy.

Foreign policy considerations had brought the new Cabinet into office and from its Russophile composition was drawn the deduction that Bulgaria would now follow a policy much more in line with Russian wishes. Russian wishes were for a Balkan alliance directed at the containment of Austria. Whilst diplomatic pressure from St Petersburg operated at the highest level there was a recrudescence at lower levels of pro-Russian sentiment. This had never entirely disappeared but it had weakened in the face of Russia's generally pro-Serbian stance over Macedonia. Now the anger at Firmilian's appointment had cooled and general pro-Russian sympathy and Slav solidarity was

again a political current in the country for Bulgaria, like other parts of
eastern Europe in the years between the Annexation crisis and 1914,
was affected by the emergence of Neo-Slavism. In Varna in March
1910 there had been a conference organised by 'Slovanská Jednota'
(Slavic Unity), a body founded originally in Moscow and Prague.
Bulgaria also had its own 'Slavyansko Blagotvoritelno Druzhestvo'
(Slavic Welfare Society) which in cooperation with similar organisations in other Slav areas helped to promote educational exchanges,
provide schooling for children from deprived Slav families, and establish schools and churches where these were needed. Yet these institutions, interesting as indications of the general rebirth of Slav feeling in
the pre-First World War period, were not the determinants of the new
foreign policy undertaken by the Bulgarian government in 1911, nor
were they major generators of popular political passion within the
country. Both these roles were played by events in European Turkey.

For the government in Sofia, and in the other Balkan capitals, the
most disturbing feature of international life by 1910 was the collapse of
political order in Albania, the danger being that one or more of the
great powers would intervene and establish itself in that area. Such
action could only signal the end of Ottoman power in Europe but the
fact that this had been brought about by the intervention of the powers
would mean both that the Balkan states' freedom of action was circumscribed and that the size of the booty would be reduced, and this in
turn could only make the division an even more difficult process. The
Albanian collapse therefore urged upon the Balkan governments the
need to divide Turkey-in-Europe before the powers became directly
involved. When one of the great powers with a direct interest in Albania, Italy, went to war with Turkey over Tripoli in 1911, intervention
by a great power appeared much more likely, despite Rome's repeated
denials of any such intention. The Tripoli war stiffened a resolve
already taken.

The Bulgarian public did not approach the question with such cool
calculation. Here the issue was that of the Bulgarian population of
Macedonia, and it is important at this juncture to go back to events in
that afflicted area since the Young Turk Revolution of 1908.

The initial reaction in Macedonia was one of euphoria. Enver Bey,
the Young Turk leader, for example, appeared on the balcony of the
Hôtel d'Angleterre in Salonika in the company of the IMRO leader
Sandanski. The many warring factions suspended their mutual hostilities; the Bulgarians were pleased by the fact that a number of villages

transferred from the Patriarchate to the Exarchate and they presumed
that this indication that the Christians of Macedonia felt themselves to
be Bulgarian would be carried over into the parliament which the
Young Turks had promised would meet in Constantinople later in the
year. 'What the revolution has done for Macedonia', wrote Paprikov,
'reforms could not have done in ten years'.[1] Yet the deep divisions in
Macedonia, that between IMRO and the Supremacists included, could
not be so easily healed. These two factions were soon arguing over who
was to represent Bulgarian/Macedonian interests in the new Turkey.
In the summer of 1908 the government in Sofia had sent into Macedonia a large number of intelligentsia to create a strong pro-Sofia party
and also to try and take control of parts of Macedonia before Sandanski did so. A total of half a million leva was spent on this exercise
which ended with the creation of Bulgarian Constitutional Clubs to
represent Macedo-Bulgarian interests in the forthcoming elections.
The Clubs were under the direction of the arch-supremacist, Karaiovov, but they did not have as much support as IMRO and its Programme of the Macedonian-Adrianople Revolutionary Organisation.
By the end of 1908 the old rivals were once again at one another's
throats with two attempts on Sandanski's life, and the threat of violence was soon felt in Sofia too; in November two men were arrested
outside the Subranie on suspicion of trying to assassinate Ferdinand.

The problem in Macedonia was that despite the initial hopes the
condition of the Christian population was not much improved, and in
some cases had worsened because there were no longer any foreign
observers to restrain Moslem enthusiasms. Furthermore, the Young
Turks had, understandably, decided to disarm all Macedonians but
arms searches were often too brusquely conducted. In 1910 the Christians were angered by a new brigandage law, enacted without parliamentary approval, making parents responsible for the malefactions of
their children. The Bulgarians also feared that their intelligentsia in
Macedonia was being systematically destroyed because the authorities
were closing Exarchist schools and churches, shutting down Bulgarian-
language publications and suppressing the Bulgarian Clubs. In the
meantime other nationalities, especially the Serbs, appeared not to be
suffering in the same way, with Serbian bishops being appointed to
Dibra and Veles. The Young Turks also allowed the immigration into
Macedonia of Moslem refugees from Bosnia and Herzegovina. This
policy was in marked contrast to that followed towards those Bulgarian-speaking émigrés in America who wished to return to Macedo-

nia and buy up vacant land. The government in Constantinople refused them entry and often bought the land itself to give to the Moslem refugees from Bosnia.

By the summer of 1909 some of the insurgent bands were once again active. They had little success and by the end of 1911 were turning to acts of urban terrorism, hoping to provoke the local Moslems into such fearful retaliation that either the powers would be forced to intervene once more or the Balkan states would have to take action. In December 1911, for example, terrorists blew up railway installations and a mosque in Shtip. In the riots which followed between fifteen and twenty Christians were killed and over 150 injured.

Naturally the deterioration of conditions in Macedonia brought forth intense protest in Bulgaria. Meetings were held in Sofia in January 1910 to denounce the new brigandage law, and in April of the same year the Macedonian lobby called for demonstrations against the appointment of Serbs for the Dibra and Veles dioceses. When the Italian premier, Giolitti, took his country to war with Turkey, many Bulgarians thought this a golden opportunity for a final reckoning over Macedonia. Radoslavov, the leader of the National Liberals, declared, 'We have not spent 950 million leva on the army just to look at it in parades',[2] and an opposition newspaper, *Pryaporets,* asked if Bulgaria did not have its own Giolitti. Even the usually mild Democrats demanded at least a European enquiry into Macedonia and that the government should seek rapid international intervention. The events in Shtip in December 1911 precipitated large meetings in all major Bulgarian towns. In Sofia the protest took the dignified form of a memorial service in the cathedral attended by over five thousand people and representatives from all Macedonian organisations; the service was followed by an orderly procession to the memorials to Tsar Alexander II and Vasil Levski. All the meetings demanded that the government ask the great powers to institute an enquiry by their consuls.

To the populace it appeared that Geshov's government had done nothing. This was not so. Geshov had come to office prepared to work with Turkey in the belief that cooperation with the rulers of Macedonia had much to offer in terms of reforms in favour of the Bulgarian population or, more specifically, in the granting of permission to build the rail link to Kumanovo. Yet the Young Turks were determined to centralise and ottomanise their Empire; there would be no reforms favouring one nation above another even if the Bulgarians did think their rivals in Macedonia were getting preferential treatment. If cooperation had to be abandoned then Bulgaria, particularly in view of developments in Albania, had to think in terms of confrontation and the eventual liquidation of Turkish power in Europe, but that was not a task to be undertaken by Bulgaria alone. After six months in office Geshov had to abandon his attempt to work with Turkey and turn to the alternative policy. Allies were therefore needed. The obvious candidate was Serbia. Just before he fell from power the generally anti-Serbian Malinov had agreed to the setting up of committees in Sofia and Belgrade to study the possibility of closer economic relations between the two countries, and the Bulgarian committee included such prominent figures as Liudskyanov and Yablanski, Geshov's brother-in-law. The original meeting of the joint committees had to be postponed because of the Grand National Sŭbranie but when it did convene in October it was given an extremely favourable reception by the populace and the press in Bulgaria. In view of this and of the repeated efforts to reach an agreement with Bulgaria made by the Serbs both during Malinov's administration and during the first six months of the coalition government, Geshov agreed to begin serious negotiations. The first meeting in these new talks took place in October 1911 when the Serbian ministerial coach was attached to the train carrying Geshov back to Bulgaria from a sojourn in Vichy and Vienna. Geshov and his Serbian colleagues talked between Belgrade and Lipovo and the journey was long enough to see that the two states were still divided by serious differences, the chief of which was Macedonia for which the Bulgarians wanted autonomy and the Serbs partition. The Bulgarians clearly wanted autonomy to preserve Macedonian unity for the expectation in Sofia and elsewhere was that such an arrangement was, as in Eastern Rumelia, merely the prelude to union with Bulgaria. Events forced the Bulgarians to abandon this demand. In October 1911 the Turks mobilised in the Adrianople district and though this was part of the war with Italy it was also a warning and a threat to Bulgaria, especially if the Turks were to act jointly with the Rumanians. Even if the Rumanians did not interfere there was still the possibility that either Greece and/or Serbia would take advantage of Bulgaria's involvement with Turkey. As the danger of attack from Turkey receded a new one appeared in the form of a Russian initiative to come to an agreement with the Turks. This was, in fact, a personal kite flown by the Russian ambassador in Constantinople, Tcharykov, but the leaders in Sofia were not to know this and for them the prospect of a Russo-Turkish accord was extremely dangerous, for if it came about there could be no prospect of a forward policy in Macedonia or even of pressure on the Porte to grant reforms. Even if the threatened accord with Russia did not come about there was always the distinct possibility that the Turks would abandon the static war in Tripoli and come to an agreement with another power. The only way to short-circuit these dangers, and especially that posed by the Tcharykov initiative, was to come to an agreement with Serbia. The Bulgarians therefore abandoned the notion of autonomy for Macedonia and began the hard slog of defining the zones of influence which the Serbs had suggested. Agreement was eventually reached whereby Bulgaria was to take that part of the Vardar valley south and east of a line running from Ohrid in the south-west to the Bulgarian frontier at Mount Golem in the north-east. This placed Bitolja, Veles and Shtip inside the Bulgarian zone but not Kumanovo or Skopje. These towns were to be part of the contested zone which was to cover the area between the Ohrid to Golem line and the Shar mountains. The ultimate fate of this area was to be determined by future negotiations and if Serbia and Bulgaria could not agree then the Tsar was to be asked to arbitrate. To the north of the Shar mountains lay the Serbian zone which included Old Serbia and much of the Scutari vilayet. With this agreement on territorial divisions the rest of the negotiations were relatively simple and on 29 February/13 March a secret treaty was signed, though the superstitious Ferdinand refused to sign on the 13th. A military convention was then negotiated and signed in April. In May these agreements were communicated to the Russians who welcomed them warmly.

The Bulgarian-Serbian treaty was the first of a series of bilateral agreements which for convenience have been known ever since as the Balkan alliance or the Balkan league. In April Bulgaria began serious negotiations for an alliance with Greece. Again Macedonia was the key issue and again the Bulgarians pushed for autonomy. The Greeks resisted and in the end the two states signed a defensive alliance in May and a military convention in September; neither document spoke of any division of territory. Bulgaria also concluded a verbal agreement with Montenegro in August 1912.

Whilst the diplomatic construction of the Balkan alliance was in progress domestic pressure on the government to take decisive action was growing. In May there had been a large demonstration in Sofia with respected figures such as the poet Ivan Vazov and Professor

408

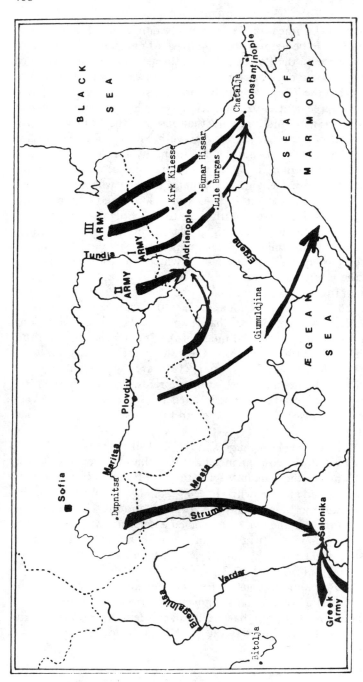

THE FIRST BALKAN WAR

Shishmanov calling for action to save the Christians of Macedonia. There was also growing concern over the Exarchate, a concern which both inflamed national feeling at home and further strained relations with Turkey. Bulgaria's declaration of independence in 1908 had complicated the status of the national Church and its head. Until 1908 all the Exarchate was technically in Turkish territory but after the declaration of independence and the acceptance of it by the Porte in the following year this was no longer the case. The first result of the change had been to establish a second synod, this time in Constantinople rather than Sofia and inevitably the two synods began to squabble about who had jurisdiction in matters of liturgy, administration and property. At this point the Russians, as desirous as ever of an end to the schism in the Orthodox Church in the Balkans, pressed for the transfer of the Exarch to Sofia. By 1912 there was considerable debate in the Church on a number of administrative issues, the prime one of which was what would happen when the present and already aged Exarch died. The statutes of the Church clearly stated that all Exarchist bishops should take part in the election of his successor, and this included those in Bulgaria. Yet it was less than likely that the Young Turks would allow Bulgarian bishops to take part in choosing what was still an official of the Ottoman state. On the other hand if only the Macedonian and Thracian bishops took part in the election the choice would almost certainly be a creature of the Young Turks totally unacceptable to the synod in Sofia. A series of discussions at intergovernmental level had revealed nothing but a mutual acknowledgment that the question was difficult, and in the early summer of 1912 there were consistent rumours that the Russophile faction in the synod was hoping to cut the Gordian knot by declaring the Church in Bulgaria a separate, autocephalous institution. Were this to happen the links between the Bulgarian and the Macedonian Churches would be severed, for the Turks would never allow their subjects to give allegiance to a Church with its head in Sofia. The Bulgarian nationalists, on the other hand, would permit neither the separation of the religious brethren in Macedonia from those in liberated Bulgaria nor the dismantling of what had been the first great national institution and what was still the only one which united all Bulgarians. The Stambulovists therefore called for demonstrations whilst protests were also planned against the extreme Russophile head of the synod, Metropolitan Simeon of Varna. In August a special conference of clerical and lay representatives, including two from Constantinople, met to discuss the question. It decided to leave matters where they confusingly stood.

The debate over the Church served to inflame an already agitated public but it had little effect on the general descent to war which was in train by August. The most important political event in south-eastern Europe that summer was the final and total collapse of Ottoman authority in Albania; a rebellion by discontented Albanians in fact drove the Young Turks from office in July and brought about a less centralising Cabinet which immediately granted a large measure of autonomy to the Albanians. With Italy still at war with Turkey the collapse in Albania heightened the danger of Italian intervention, the more so in that the Italians had recently taken the war into the eastern Mediterranean in a vain effort to force the Turks to the negotiating table; they might all too easily be tempted into intervention in Albania as a last ditch effort to compel the Turks to make peace. In August the Austrians proposed to the powers that they undertake a joint initiative to encourage upon the new Turkish Cabinet the continuation of its policy of progressive decentralisation; but if this happened under the auspices of the great powers the Balkan states would not dare to inter-vene in Macedonia. These developments urged upon the members of the Balkan league the need for rapid action.

The same message was coming from the public in Bulgaria, and more particularly from the Macedonian exiles and activists. This was a message to which Geshov and the King paid particular attention for one of the reasons they had concluded the alliance with Serbia was to take the initiative away from the *comitadjii* '. . . as Cavour took the question of Italian unity out of the hands of the Italian revolutionists', as Geshov later wrote.[3] On 1/14 August there was an incident in the Macedonian town of Kochane similar to that in Shtip a few months earlier and it was followed by another outrage, this time in Berana. Again meetings were held and resolutions condemnatory of the Turk-ish and the Bulgarian governments were passed; Radoslavov yet again breathed fire, announcing that 'In the present circumstances the Macedonian question is to be solved not by the bluffing of the Bulgar-ian government or by the bombs of the committee-men. It can be decided only by the Bulgarian army'.[4] Such words were music to the ears of the Macedonians whose varied brotherhoods and associations met in congress in Sofia on 24 August/5 September in a highly-charged state of mind; '. . . the pressure on the part of public opinion', wrote Geshov later, 'had become well-nigh irresistible'.[5] On 26

August/7 September Danev, Geshov, Todorov and Nikiforov conferred with the King and, with the previous backing of the whole
Cabinet, were unanimous in favour of going to war. The Serbs were
contacted immediately but they wished to delay matters until the two
states had agreed on what should happen if Serbia were threatened in
the north by Austria. This took up much of September but towards the
end of that month the Turks themselves forced matters to a head. They
angered the Serbs by refusing transit to twenty wagons of war material
shipped into Salonika, they angered the Greeks by firing on the Greek
steamer, *Samos,* and by placing an embargo on Greek vessels in Constantinople; on 11/24 September they mobilised a number of reserve
divisions and a few days later withdrew their diplomatic representatives from the Balkan capitals. The allies followed suit on 17/30 September. After a week of severe tension the Montenegrins invoked a
long-standing frontier dispute with the Porte as an excuse for a declaration of war. Ten days later, on 4/17 October, Bulgaria, Greece and
Serbia joined her.

The Bulgarians mobilised 592,000 men who were divided into three
army groups, the First under General Vasil Kutinchev, the Second
under General Nikola Ivanov, and the Third, formed secretly in the
early days of the war, under General Radko Dimitriev. There were also
a number of specialist units, including one for aerial combat, two
planes having been bought earlier in the year from France, and there
were special detachments, the Rhodopski and Kŭrdjalii divisions, to
operate in and beyond the Rhodope mountains. Of particular importance to the Bulgarians was the Macedonian-Adrianople militia. These
were volunteers, most of them from the exile communities in Bulgaria
but some came from the eponymous territories; they numbered almost
15,000 men and were formed into twelve battalions. Just over 2,000
former *comitadjii* also enlisted for service with the Bulgarian army and
they were formed into fifty-three guerilla bands which were to perform
useful sabotage work. The overall campaign was directed by Chief of
the General Staff, General Ivan Fichev; the King acted as Commander-
in-Chief and General Mihail Savov as his Assistant Commander-in-
Chief.

The main task of the Bulgarian army was to engage the large Turkish Eastern Army in eastern Thrace, though two Bulgarian divisions,
the 2nd (Thracian) and the 7th (Rila), were sent to cooperate with the
Serbs in the Struma valley. The II Army advanced along the river
Maritsa towards Adrianople whilst further east the I Army moved

412

BALKAN BOUNDARIES AFTER THE WARS OF 1912-13

down the Tundja valley. The secretly-formed III Army was meanwhile held in reserve and directed at Lozengrad to the north-west of
Adrianople. In the first day of the campaign Svilengrad (Mustapha
Pasha) fell to the Bulgarians without a struggle and on 11/24 October
Lozengrad was taken by the III Army. Two days later Adrianople itself
was invested. The Turks now dug in along a line from Lule Burgas
through Kara Agach to Bunar Hissar where a chain of low hills offered
excellent defensive cover. Yet in the five days from 15/28 October to 20
October/2 November the III Army smashed through the defences and
so complete was the rout of the Turks that they were unable to obey
orders to take up defensive positions along the line of the river Ergene.
Instead they were chased back to the great defensive complex of the
Tchatalja lines forty kilometres outside Constantinople. Huge quantities of war material and an enormous number of prisoners were taken
by Dimitriev's III Army. Meanwhile the II Army had encircled Adrianople and the Rhodopski and Kŭrdjalii divisions had pushed down the
Mesta valley taking Razlog, Bansko, Nevrokop and Drama, thus cutting the Salonika to Constantinople railway. The divisions went on to
take the lower Maritsa valley leading to the port of Dedeagach and the
Aegean coastal region of Giumuldjina. In the Struma valley the Rila
Division had taken Gorna Djumaya and Tsarevo and was fighting its
way south-westwards through the difficult Kresna and Rupel defiles
towards Doiran and Kukush. It was working with the Serbian II
Army, the ultimate objective being Salonika which it reached but
one day behind the Greeks. In the Black Sea the small Bulgarian navy
and the shore batteries had seen off an attack by an Ottoman naval
force spearheaded by the cruiser *Hamidie*.

   On all fronts the Bulgarians and the allies had won amazing victories, and even Fichev himself was surprised by the superb quality of his
army. The first setback, however, was about to occur. On 29
October/11 November and 2/15 November the Turks had asked for an
armistice. This presented the Bulgarians with a difficulty, for there
were distinct indications in diplomatic circles that a Bulgarian entry
into Constantinople would not be resisted, at least temporarily. Ferdinand was generally assumed to want to enter the city, and, it was
reported, had ordered appropriate uniforms and coaches for his ceremonial entry and parade therein. Geshov also supported entry because,
he told the Bulgarian minister in St Petersburg, 'the temporary occupation of Constantinople would give us the most important and effective
guarantee for the conclusion of a peace treaty favourable to us'.[6] With

the Turkish offer of an armistice Geshov wavered but the King remained firm, refusing to allow his Minister President to inform their allies of the proposal. Dimitriev, now in command of the combined I and III Armies also wanted to accept the peace offer because his men, tired after so rapid a campaign and already plagued by cholera, were not fit to tackle the huge defences of Tchatalja. Only with written instructions to attack, said Dimitriev, would he order an assault. These were issued by Savov and on 4/17 November the attack began. It lasted for two days but failed. The Chief of the General Staff, Fichev, described the decision to attack Tchatalja as criminal and after the failure of the assault it was the Bulgarians' turn to request a ceasefire. This came about on 20 November/3 December and a few days later representatives of the belligerents, with Danev heading the Bulgarian delegation, assembled in London to discuss a definitive peace, the powers of Europe having now accepted that the territorial *status quo ante* could not be restored and having agreed that it was for the warring parties themselves to settle the final boundaries on condition that a new and independent or autonomous Albania was part of the final settlement. This was to create fearful problems.

Initially, however, it was not Albania that troubled the London meetings but the Turks' refusal to relinquish Adrianople. In January 1913 a *coup d'état* in Constantinople returned the Young Turks to power with a commitment not to cede the city. On 21 January/3 February fighting began again. The new government in Constantinople immediately brought over from Asia Minor some 35,000 extra troops who were garrisoned at Gallipoli. The Bulgarians, meanwhile, had regrouped with the Macedonian-Adrianople militia units, the 7th (Rila) and the 2nd (Thracian) Divisions being formed into a new IV Army under the command of General Stilian Kovachev. The new plan of campaign worked out by the General Staff involved the II Army, reinforced by units from the I and III Armies, tightening the siege of Adrianople whilst the remainder of the latter two forces contained the Turks at Tchatalja and the new IV Army defended Bulgarian gains on the coasts of the Aegean and the Sea of Marmora and confronted the recently-arrived Turkish forces in Gallipoli. It was on this front that the first major encounter of the renewed campaign took place when the IV Army, in a two-day battle, prevented a break out by the Turks in Gallipoli. There was also action on the Tchatalja front where the Bulgarians were forced to concede some ground. The crucial struggle, however, was for Adrianople.

Adrianople's was a massive fortress. It had twenty-six individual forts with a total of 524 artillery pieces and 70,000 defending troops. The besieging Bulgarians were helped by two divisions sent from the Serbian army and by the use, for the first time in Europe, of bombs dropped from aircraft. After the failure at Tchatalja the Bulgarians were dubious as to the wisdom of a direct assault but on 10/23 March the General Staff decided upon an attack and the artillery barrage began the following morning; two days later the garrison surrendered. This was a decisive defeat for the Turks who once more requested an armistice which the allies immediately granted, the signature taking place on 1/14 April 1913. The Balkan peace conference reassembled in St James' Palace, London, to divide the conquests. That however was to be impossible.

The allies had secured an easy military victory but their final deliberations on the division of the spoils were to be determined by two extraneous factors. The first was Rumania, the one Balkan state which had taken no part in the Balkan War. This, said the Rumanians, was because they had obeyed the injunctions of the great powers but now Rumania's Balkan neighbours were all to be aggrandised because they had been disobedient. The Rumanians demanded compensation and this they could secure only in the southern Dobrudja. From the moment it became clear that extensive territorial changes were to take place the Bulgarians were under intense pressure, especially from Vienna and St Petersburg, to make concessions to Rumania in the Dobrudja. Finally the Bulgarians agreed to leave the question to the great powers' ambassadors in St Petersburg and in April had reluctantly to accept their decision that the Silistra-Balchik line should form the new Bulgaro-Rumanian border. The loss of this territory only made the Bulgarians more determined to hold on to their gains in Macedonia and Thrace. At the same time, however, the second factor, Austro-Hungarian insistence on the creation of a separate Albania, had deprived Serbia of her anticipated gains in that area. This made Belgrade all the more determined to take a larger share of Macedonia than the original treaty had intended.

In view of the intense rivalry between Bulgaria and Serbia which the Macedonian question had caused, it was inevitable that the heightened concentration on and competition for this area wrecked the accord between the two states. The Bulgarians had been on their guard from the beginning and their fears were justified, they believed, by reports as early as September 1912, before the war had begun, that Pašić had

ordered Serbian diplomatists abroad to argue that 'Old Serbia', which
the treaty gave to the Serbs, included the towns Prilep and Ohrid, both
of which were in the Bulgarian zone. After Macedonia had been occupied by the allies there were reports in Sofia that Serbian troops were
insisting that villages under their control abandon the Exarchate, cease
to consider themselves as Bulgarian and become Serbs. To make matters worse the Greeks, with whom there was, of course, no territorial
agreement, were behaving in like fashion. The Bulgarians were doing
much the same in the areas under their control, though here even if the
Turkish villages in Giumuldjina and Thrace could not be expected to
regard the Bulgarians as liberators, there was less resistance from the
population. As soon as the major battles were over King Ferdinand
named Reserve General Vazov as Governor of the Adrianople vilayet
with headquarters at Lozengrad, and Reserve General Volkov was
made Governor-General of Macedonia with his administrative seat at
Seres. Ottoman police officers were, as far as possible, replaced by
Bulgarians and Macedonia and Thrace were divided into eight provinces and sixteen districts whose administrative heads were named. In
February 1913 the Bulgarians conducted a census in Macedonia with
the express intention of identifying which villages were Christian,
which Moslem and which mixed. In April a law allowed share-
croppers in the new territories to become owners of their land, and as
in the land settlement in liberated Bulgaria in the 1880s, the former
owners were to be compensated by the government in Sofia and the
new owners were to repay the government over a period of between ten
and twenty years.

With the fall of Adrianople all major fighting in the Balkans ceased
and the allies were thus able to pay ever more attention to the problem
of dividing Macedonia. Their delegates had reassembled in London to
conclude a final peace with Turkey but these negotiations were frustrated by the Serbs and the Greeks who had an obvious interest in
preventing a definitive peace with Turkey for without such a peace
Bulgaria must keep large numbers of troops covering the Ottoman
army. Whilst Bulgarian troops were doing this they could not be used
in Macedonia. Final peace with Turkey was, however, concluded
because the British Foreign Secretary, Sir Edward Grey, lost patience
with the endless delays and intrigues of the Balkan statesmen and told
them bluntly to sign a treaty or leave London. The treaty of London
was accordingly signed on 17/30 May. Those of its territorial provisions which affected Bulgaria stated that the allies were to divide

amongst themselves European Turkey west of a line drawn from Enos
on the Aegean to Midia on the Black Sea, though this was not to
include Albania whose frontiers the powers were to define.
     Yet since the fall of Adrianople the real issue at stake had not been
relations with Turkey but the fate of Macedonia and Thrace. As soon
as Adrianople had fallen the Serbs and Greeks had increased their hold
on Macedonia, strengthening their military presence in already occupied territory and, wherever possible, extending the area under their
control. This inevitably led to clashes with Bulgarian forces. A serious
confrontation between Bulgarians and Greeks, for example, took place
at Angista in May and after the signing of the treaty of London these
clashes became more frequent.
     In discussions with the Greeks the Bulgarians argued that conquered
territory should be divided according to the principle of proportional-
ity, that is that each ally should expand in proportion to its military
effort and sacrifice, an argument which fitted well with Bulgaria's
interests for the Bulgarians had mobilised 592,000 men to the Greeks'
215,000 and Bulgarian casualties were seventy-five per cent higher than
Greek. The Greeks countered with the insistence that the division of
conquered territory must be so contrived that it preserved the European balance between the Balkan states, the word European being
introduced so as to rule out of the calculations any gains which the
Greeks might secure in the Aegean. Geshov grew increasingly sanguine
about the prospects of an amicable settlement with Athens, hopes
which appeared well-founded when the Greeks made encouraging
noises about the cession of considerable areas of western Thrace,
including Seres, Drama and Kavalla, in return for Bulgarian recognition of Greek possession of Salonika. Greeks bearing such gifts were
not, however, to be trusted.
     There was never even realistic hope of an accommodation with Ser-
bia. In February Pašić has secretly approached Geshov and suggested
that because of Serbia's loss of Albania the original zonal divisions in
Macedonia should be redefined, and that this redefinition should take
place through closed diplomatic channels away from the pressure of
'public and powers'. Geshov refused. After the fall of Adrianople Pašić
pleaded the need for revision publicly and frequently. His case rested
not merely on the loss of Albania but also on the argument that Bulgaria had failed to provide the agreed number of troops for operations
in the Struma and Vardar valleys whilst Serbian help at Adrianople
had been beyond that laid down in the military convention. Also, he

pointed out, Bulgaria could afford to give more in Macedonia because her gains in Thrace were greater than had been anticipated. To these assertions the Bulgarians replied that if the gains in Thrace were larger than originally envisaged they should be treated as compensation for the loss of part of the southern Dobrudja. The Serbian contention that Bulgaria had failed to provide sufficient troops in the Vardar valley was denied in Sofia where it was also pointed out that the Bulgarian units had advanced more quickly than the Serbians in that theatre of the war. As to the loss of expected Serbian gains in Albania this the Bulgarians regretted but it was not of their doing and if, as a result, Bulgaria was gaining more than the other allies then this was merely a just reflection of the relative efforts expended for it was the Bulgarian armies which had borne the brunt of the heavy and decisive fighting against the Turks. From the legal viewpoint the Bulgarians were in a strong position. Politically they were very exposed.

In the first place the community of Greek and Serbian interests in Macedonia led them to combine secretly against Bulgaria. Before the treaty of London had been signed the Serbs and the Greeks had signed a protocol and, on 1/14 May a military agreement. A full treaty was signed as soon as the peace talks in London had ended. By this treaty the governments of Belgrade and Athens agreed that there should be a common frontier between their two countries who should divide Macedonia west of the Vardar; as to Macedonia east of that river, there the division was to be decided on the basis of effective occupation. Thus when encouraging the Bulgarians to believe that a settlement was possible the Greeks had already concluded a secret agreement with Serbia which was clearly totally unacceptable in Sofia. The commonality of Greek and Serbian interests and the coordination of their diplomacy in London and elsewhere soon made it obvious to the Bulgarians that some agreement existed even if its exact terms were not known in the Bulgarian capital.

For the Bulgarians there were four possible escapes from these difficulties. A negotiated settlement could be sought, and the early encouraging experience with Greece indicated that this might be possible. The Bulgarians could make a short punitive foray into Greek and Serbian occupied Macedonia in order to force their erstwhile allies to the negotiating table and to ensure that they arrived there in a conciliatory frame of mind. Sofia might, as a third course, launch an all-out war of conquest against Serbia and Greece, or, fourthly, it might fall back on the Serbo-Bulgarian treaty of 1912 and seek Russian arbitration.

For its part Russia was anxious not to see a breach in the Balkan league and in those circumstances the Tsar could not refuse to negotiate. Geshov, and initially Ferdinand too, were keen on arbitration, which they requested in April, but only on condition that the Tsar confine his judgement to a division of the contested zone. This the Serbs would not accept; they would go to arbitration only on the understanding that the Tsar would preside over a redefinition of all the zones in Macedonia, that is that the Bulgarian zone should be cut down to the advantage of the Serbs and perhaps of the Greeks too, for the Serbs also made it a condition of arbitration that the Greek-Bulgarian difficulties should be included. Finally, said the Serbs, arbitration should take place only if direct negotiations between the interested parties had first been attempted. Direct negotiations did take place when Geshov met Pašić in Tsaribrod on the Bulgarian-Serbian border on 20 May/2 June. The meeting was a hollow farce. Pašić was already committed to the Greeks and had just announced in the Skupshtina that Serbia would not accept any settlement which did not increase its share of the Macedonian spoils. Geshov's commitment to the negotiations was no greater for four days earlier he had resigned as Minister President, a fact which was not to be made public until his successor, Danev, had arrived back in Sofia from the St. James' peace conference on 24 May/6 June.

The reason for Geshov's resignation was that the King had aligned himself with the war party in Bulgaria. On 17/30 May Dobrović informed Geshov that on the previous evening the King had held a Crown Council with the leaders of the major political Parties, all of whom had expressed themselves in favour of war in Macedonia. Geshov, astounded that he, as a party leader and Minister President, could be left out of such a gathering, had no alternative but to resign, as no doubt Ferdinand intended he should.

The war party was by this time formidable. Public opinion in the towns was generally in favour of action in Macedonia, this being in part because most Macedonian exiles had settled in towns and were hot for war, threatening assassination for any public figure who tried to prevent it, a fact which may not have been absent from Ferdinand's mind when he committed himself to a forward policy. Most of the opposition Parties were in favour of war, though the Agrarians and both socialist groups were for peace. Most important of all, however, was the army.

The High Command, and above all General Savov, had been preparing for war for some time. By the middle of June Bulgaria had mobilised more men and now had 600,000 with the colours, compared to 592,000 in the war against Turkey. After the treaty of London many of the troops in eastern Thrace were moved over to the western limits of Bulgarian territory and deployed against the Serbian and Greek forces already massing in Macedonia. What really worried Savov, however, was not the disposition of his armies but their morale. There had been signs of unrest in the Bulgarian army as early as January 1913. Later when the Silistra and Balchik areas were ceded to Rumania the Bulgarian regiments raised in that region became understandably restless whilst the whole peasant army began to worry as the time for sowing approached without any prospect of demobilisation. This anxiety became much greater when the peace with Turkey did not bring demobilisation and the men began to fear that a second war would prevent them from getting home even for harvesting. After a long, cold winter the troops were tired of waiting, inactive, in uncomfortable front-line conditions. In May there were mass desertions from the 24th (Black Sea) and the 11th (Sliven) Regiments and mutinies in the 29th (Zagorski) and the 32nd (Yambolski) Infantry Regiments; the 9th (Pleven) Division was out of control for seventy-two hours, and by the beginning of June the High Command was genuinely concerned lest military discipline collapse entirely.

As the condition of south-eastern Europe grew daily more unstable Russian diplomacy attempted to prevent irrevocable breaches in the Balkan alliance. On 26 May/8 June the Tsar sent personal telegrams to the Kings of Bulgaria and Serbia. They were told that whatever their Minister-Presidents might decide would have to be submitted to St Petersburg for final arbitration but that in the meantime they should strive for peace and remember that the nation which began an inter-allied war would 'be held responsible before the Slav cause.'[7] If such a 'criminal strife' were to take place Russia would reserve its position, but if Serbia began a war Russia would not intervene to save her from annihilation by Austria; on the other hand, if Bulgaria were to move first Russia would not prevent the intervention of Rumania and Turkey. The two Kings gave excessively polite but essentially empty replies to these telegrams but they were enough to satisfy the Russian Foreign Minister, Sazonov, that the Kings seriously intended to negotiate, and within a few days he sent invitations to Pašić and Danev to come to St Petersburg, asking them also to submit within a week detailed memoranda stating their claims.

For the Bulgarians Sazonov's request brought the point of no return. The Russian invitation was debated at a Cabinet meeting on 9/22 June, but that Cabinet also had before it another document in the form of a telegram from General Savov saying that the Greeks and Serbs had concluded an alliance and that the state of the Bulgarian army was such that if it did not act soon it would have to be stood down; Savov demanded war or demobilisation within ten days. A decision had to be made between arbitration and war. Danev announced that he was for war; even this committed Russophile had been forced to the conclusion that arbitration would not be to Bulgaria's advantage, for Sazonov had been so persistent of late in his advice that the Bulgarians should make concessions outside the contested zone. From what the Serbs had said it was clear that they would not be satisfied with small concessions and therefore nothing that Bulgaria could offer would be accepted in Belgrade. War was inevitable and had to come within Savov's stipulated ten days for once demobilised the army could not be reassembled in the autumn. A dissenting voice was raised by Todorov, the Minister of Finance. He argued that if Bulgaria moved first without trying arbitration she would forfeit the moral advantage and the goodwill of Europe; Bulgaria, he said, should wait for the Serbs to attack and then enjoy the benefits of moral superiority and military supremacy. Savov's timetable, however, could not be altered and the Russians were told that Danev would come to St Petersburg for arbitration on condition that discussion be confined to the contested zone, that Serbia begin demobilisation and that, because of the present threatening military posture of the Serbs, a decision be reached within eight days. Sazonov did not respond quickly; he was not well and in any case he was waiting for the Serbian and Bulgarian memoranda he had requested and he was not willing to decide within the eight-day period. In that case, the Bulgarians reminded him, Bulgaria would abandon arbitration and go to war. The Imperial Russian Foreign Minister and his master were not accustomed to receiving ultimata from small Balkan states and they were livid. They abandoned Bulgaria to its fate, assuming it was acting on Austrian advice, which was not the case. 'Thus', Sazonov told the Bulgarian minister in St Petersburg, 'the Serbs with their folly and you with your incorrect attitude have rejected Russia and Slavdom. . . Do not expect anything from us, and forget the existence of any of our engagements from 1902 until today'.[8] This message was relayed on 12/25 June but it did not cause Danev to abandon his plans to visit the Russian capital; that was done by General Savov.

On 15/28 June Savov ordered the IV Army to attack the Serbs without declaration of war on the following day. Danev knew of what was to happen, though perhaps not of the extent of the operations, but the Cabinet had no prior knowledge and only learnt of them on 18 June/1 July, when it threatened collective resignation if they were not ended immediately. Danev therefore ordered Savov to suspend his action, and telegraphed to Sazonov informing him of this and asking him to prevent any counter action by the Serbs and Greeks. This Sazonov could not do but it mattered little as within an hour of its being issued Danev's cease-fire order had been countermanded by the King who also sacked Savov a few days later for having obeyed the Minister President.

The Bulgarian advance of 16/29 June had begun the Second Balkan War. The inter-allied conflict was shorter but far more bloody than the war against Turkey. After the dismissal of Savov the Russophile Radko Dimitriev was made Assistant Commander-in-Chief. The I Army was deployed in the Vidin-Berkovitsa area and to the south of it the III Army under General Toshev was placed in the Kiustendil-Radomir region and to the south of it the IV Army occupied the Rodosto-Shtip-Kochane triangle and the line was completed by the II Army which had moved from eastern Thrace to the extreme south-west of the Bulgarian line around Doiran, Orfano and Kavalla. The entire Bulgarian army except for one depleted division each on the Turkish and Rumanian borders was deployed against the Serbs and the Greeks. The Bulgarian campaign was inevitably affected by the political indecision which had marred its beginning but despite this the Bulgarians had initial successes against the Serbs; Knyazhevats was taken and Pirot threatened. Later the Greeks, who had advanced in the first weeks of the War, were encircled in the Kresna valley. These successes however, were of little use.

When the St Petersburg Protocol had been signed in April and again when Serbo-Bulgarian tension had escalated markedly, the Rumanians let it be known that if Bulgaria went to war again they would call up their troops. On 20 June/3 July the Rumanians therefore announced a general mobilisation; on 27 June/10 July units of the Rumanian army moved into the Bulgarian Dobrudja and on 2/15 July large numbers were crossing the Danube and marching towards Vratsa. The Bulgarians offered no resistance and there was nothing to stop the Rumanians entering Sofia. Danev appealed in desperation to Russia but there was to be no salvation from that quarter. His Russophile stance totally discredited Danev resigned on 4/17 July. Efforts to construct a Cabinet around Malinov and his Democrats failed and Ferdinand accepted instead a coalition of the various Liberal factions headed by Radoslavov.

Whilst this was taking place Bulgaria's other exposed frontier had been violated. On 30 June/13 July the Turks crossed the Enos-Midia line and ten days later they were once again masters of Adrianople. The Bulgarians were paralysed and the Serbs and Greeks made appropriate use of this, the Serbs pushing their enemies back from the river Bregalnitsa and the Greeks advancing beyond Seres which they had recently taken. There was nothing Radoslavov could do but sue for peace. An armistice was signed on 18/31 July and on 28 July/10 August the treaty of Bucharest ended hostilities between Bulgaria on the one hand and Rumania, Serbia, Greece and Montenegro on the other. On 30 September/13 October the treaty of Constantinople with Turkey was signed though fighting had ceased in July/August. Bulgarian gains from the partition of European Turkey were drastically reduced and were to consist only of that part of Pirin Macedonia which included the Struma valley southwards to a point mid-way between Melnik and Seres; the Bregalnitsa basin including Kochane and Shtip, as well as Kumanovo and Skopje, were left in Serbian hands. The Turks repossessed Adrianople and much of the Maritsa valley but the Bulgarians retained Kürdjali and Giumuldjina with a stretch of the Aegean coast which included the port of Dedeagach near the mouth of the Maritsa. The developed harbour of Kavalla, however, was retained by the Greeks, as were Seres and Drama.

The venture launched on 16/29 June had been an enormous gamble. If all went well the Serbs and Greeks would be persuaded to come to the negotiating table and to come in a conciliatory frame of mind; in this sense the attack can be seen as a catalyst to accelerate the process of arbitration. If the allies did not agree quickly to negotiations then full-scale war would develop but the Bulgarians need not be too frightened by this prospect. Bulgaria's military record since 1878 was one of unbroken success; there were still plenty of survivors of Slivnitsa to remember the ease with which the Serbs had been defeated, and the Bulgarian army with 600,000 men enjoyed a numerical superiority over the Serbs and Greeks with their 350,000 and 200,000 respectively. This military self-confidence was not disproved by the campaigns of the summer of 1913 for the war was lost not on the Serbian and Greek fronts but when the Rumanians and Turks crossed the unguarded northern and southern borders.

The miscalculations of 1913 were therefore not military but diplomatic. It had been too readily assumed that the Turks would not act because the European powers would enforce the established convention that Christian territory, once liberated from Ottoman rule, would not be allowed to regress to its former and supposedly unhappier state. Equally the Bulgarians could not believe, especially with Danev at the helm, that the Russians would allow Bulgaria to be defeated by the Rumanians, indeed Savov had written in May that 'we may be certain that France and Russia will ultimately prefer to agree with Bulgaria rather than Serbia or Greece'.[9] This was the fundamental miscalculation, the one that assumed that a limited action against Serbia and Greece would not become a general Balkan war involving also Turkey and Rumania, the one that meant that the strategy of action to facilitate arbitration was critically flawed. The mistake stemmed from a misinterpretation of Russian attitudes and interests. The long history of reliance on Russia, the experience of Firmilian notwithstanding, had encouraged the Bulgarians to rely in the last resort on the liberating power but in 1912–13 Bulgaria had frustrated the two prime objectives of Russian policy in the Balkans: the attack on Serbia had shattered the Balkan league which Russia wanted to preserve as a bulwark against Austria, and before that Bulgaria's reluctance to make concessions to Rumania had made it more difficult for Russia to draw that state out of the orbit of the Triple Alliance. Even more important was the fact that in the post-1908 Balkan world Serbia was an infinitely more important state for Russia than was Bulgaria. With the collapse of Ottoman power, indeed, Bulgaria could become more powerful for Russia's comfort, especially if the Bulgarians were to decide to include Constantinople on their shopping list, whilst Serbia none of whose territorial ambitions could possibly compete with those of Russia, stood in the front line against the main enemy, Austria-Hungary. Furthermore, after the crisis of 1908 Serbia's anti-Habsburg pedigree was beyond suspicion; Bulgaria's, on the other hand, was suspect.

The enormity of the mistake was made clear at Bucharest which was in effect a second partition of Bulgaria, but one far worse than that of Berlin in 1878 for now *Bulgaria irredenta* was not a single unit under the control of an enfeebled power which had never indulged in cultural imperialism, but was divided between culturally aggressive modern states. This, of course, did not rule out the longing for revanche. Ferdinand told his army to furl its flags for happier days and Radoslavov admitted to diplomatists in Sofia that revenge was the long-term objective of Bulgaria. Bulgaria, it was true, could not immediately pursue aggressive policies but it was certain that should Balkan or European conditions offer her a chance of revenge there would be a powerful body of opinion in the country which would want to take it.

The war of 1913 inevitably created problems with the former belligerents. In the Dobrudja the Rumanians had instituted policies which deprived Bulgarians of full civil rights and in Bulgaria a large society, 'Dobrudja', was established to press for the relief of the Bulgarians allegedly oppressed in that area. The policies of the Greeks in Macedonia provoked riots in Burgas and Stanimaka where military guards had to be posted to protect Greek property, and in June 1914 the Sofia police stood by when a mob tore the Greek flag from the Greek church in the city on the name-day of the Greek King; Radoslavov was forced to apologise to the Greek government. There were constant attacks on the policies the Serbs were employing in Macedonia to enforce 'Serbianisation' of the territories under their control and the resentment felt in Bulgaria ruled out any likelihood of rapprochement with the former enemies. With the Turks the roles were reversed for they, though expressing a wish for better relationships with Sofia, were worried by the policies the Bulgarians had adopted in their newly-acquired lands in Thrace. Constantinople disliked the disarming of Moslems and the planting of Christian refugees on Moslem land, and it also complained bitterly over the treatment of the Pomaks in these areas. During the First Balkan War many Pomaks had converted to Christianity but after the Bulgarian defeat in 1913 they wished to return to their former faith, a wish which, said the Porte, was being thwarted by Macedonian refugees who were terrorising the hapless Pomaks with the connivance of the Bulgarian authorities.

If the Second Balkan War had compromised Bulgaria's relations with her neighbours it had also discredited the political establishment. The peasants could remember well the heady moments of victory and the sacrifices which they had made, sacrifices which had then been squandered by a corrupt and unfeeling political leadership. Danev and the Russophiles suffered heavily at the next elections but, as will be seen in the next chapter, it was not Radoslavov and his allies who benefited from the Russophile's losses; the populace turned instead to the mass Parties who had opposed the war with Greece and Serbia.

For some the results of the 1913 war produced not anger or the thirst for revenge but a deep despair. In February 1914 the Exarch told the distinguished Balkan correspondent, Richard von Mach; 'Under the Turks we had ideals and hopes, now even these are lost.'[10] The Exarchate could operate under the culturally indulgent Turks but could not withstand the policies of the Greeks and Serbs. In the second half of 1913 reports from Macedonia told of Exarchist communities seeking Austrian protection and offering to restart the Uniate movement.

The war of 1913 did however end some of the anomolies of the Exarch's position. Serbian and Greek policies would make sure that there were few if any Exarchist communities in their parts of Macedonia; the only Exarchists outside Bulgaria therefore would be those left in Constantinople and what remained of the Ottoman Empire in Europe. Under such circumstances there was little point in the Exarch maintaining his headquarters in the Turkish capital, the more so if there was to be plotting against him in the Sofia synod. When the Exarch visited Sofia in December 1913, therefore, it was widely assumed that he would never return to Constantinople which he had left in the care of two bishops. The Exarch was indeed still in Sofia when he died in June 1915. According to the constitution of the Exarchate authority passed at the death of one Exarch to the Holy Synod which was then to elect a successor but in 1915 when the Metropolitan of Sofia was elected temporary head of the Church, there were few who believed that another Exarch would be chosen. They were in the long run proved incorrect but the Exarch did thereafter remain in Sofia as the results of the 1913 war had indicated he would.

In addition to its deleterious effect on Bulgaria's foreign policy and on its morale, the defeat of 1913 also inflicted considerable economic damage. For twenty years the nation's strategy in railway building had been based partly on the assumptions that grain was the country's principle export commodity and that Varna was one of its main trading ports. Thus railways had been built to join Varna with the rest of northern Bulgaria and the harbour had been developed to such a degree that by 1912 it handled more goods than Salonika. Yet Varna was to a great extent dependent on the most productive and advanced agricultural area in the country: the Dobrudja. This had been lost, and not only was productive land no longer available but Varna was now but fifteen kilometres from the frontier and that frontier could not, according to the terms of the treaty of Bucharest, be fortified. The enormous financial expenditure committed to the development of Varna had been almost useless. The great weakening of Varna's strategic value made Bulgaria's new Aegean coastline of even greater importance, and this was to deepen the tragedy which the country suffered after the First World War. In the meantime, however, huge sums of money would have to be expended in making the new coast into a valuable asset. The port of Dedeagach was not of great value because the railway to it wound in and out of Turkish territory and was therefore subject to innumerable delays as well as being strategically vulnerable. The Bulgarians, therefore, would have to repeat the exercise of the 1880s and 1890s and develop a new port and build railways to link it with the rest of the country. The new harbour was to be at Porto Lagos. Also further sums would have to be spent on developing the road network of the new territories if their natural wealth, particularly tobacco, almonds and olives, was to be exploited.

The Second Balkan War had forced Bulgaria to exchange her most developed region for extremely backward areas. To finance the development of these areas and to repair the costs of the War a large loan would be needed. If they could survive the storm of popular indignation which would follow the débâcle of the summer of 1913, the search for this loan would be a major preoccupation of Bulgaria's leaders.

Chapter 22

THE INTERBELLUM, 1913–15

The government which Radoslavov had formed during the crisis of July 1913 was a coalition of the Radoslavist, Stambulovist and Tonchevist Liberal factions. Radoslavov made himself Minister of the Interior as well as Minister President and the Ministry for Foreign Affairs was taken over by the Stambulovist Party boss, Genadiev, an appointment which was to cause considerable difficulties for a number of years.

The government's task after August 1913 was to repair the nation's morale and to face the economic consequences of the recent Wars, above all the integration and development of the new territories. This could not be done without a substantial foreign loan but this in turn could not be secured until the government had provided itself with a dependable and reliable Sŭbranie, the existing one having been elected in 1911 with a strong Geshovist-Danevist majority. When peace had been signed with Turkey in September the government therefore called a general election for November but in 1913 a government majority could not be manufactured in the routine fashion and the results of the poll were startling. To the government's final total of ninety-seven seats there were one hundred and nine opposition deputies, divided amongst the Agrarians with forty-seven, the two Socialist factions with a total of thirty-seven, the Democrats with fourteen, the Radical Democrats with five, the Nationalists five, and Danev's Progressive Liberals with one. The opposition Parties polled 247,142 votes to the government's 207,761.

The voting clearly marked widespread popular disillusion with the Parties responsible for the recent Wars. Nor was the government's cause helped by the fact that Genadiev and his Party were included in the coalition for a number of Stambulovists, their leader included, were still awaiting trial for their misdemeanours of 1903–8. Radoslavov's election managers also faced another problem in that the November 1913 election was the first to be carried out under nationwide proportional representation.

Radoslavov was not unduly daunted by the election result. He believed he could continue to govern as long as he had the confidence of the King, and this was not in question, and he hoped to make his government much stronger by buying Agrarian support in the Sŭbranie. If he failed to do this, he announced, he would call fresh elections in which the newly-acquired territories would also take part and these should be able to furnish the requisite number of pro-government deputies. This he was eventually forced to do. The Agrarians' price for cooperation was the dismissal of Genadiev, but this price Radoslavov could not afford for if Genadiev were sacked Stambulovist support in the Cabinet and the Assembly would be lost and the government would collapse. Genadiev tried to help by resigning but by then it was too late for in January 1914 the Agrarians had decided upon all out opposition to the government. The Sŭbranie was therefore dissolved.

The new elections were held in March and, as Radoslavov had predicted, produced a government majority; after verification of the returns the government had one hundred and thirty-two deputies, sixteen more than before verification, whilst the opposition Parties had one hundred and seven. Before verification there had been one hundred and sixteen oppositionists, fifty Agrarians, twenty-eight Democrats, twenty-one Socialists, nine Nationalists, five Radicals and three Progressive Liberals. Again as Radoslavov had predicted the new territories had played a determining role in the election although they had not yet been accepted by a Grand National Assembly, as the constitution required, nor had most of the Moslems living there yet become Bulgarian subjects, as they should have done to qualify for the franchise. The government's new supporters came from Bulgaria's recently-acquired territory in Thrace rather than Macedonia where Sandanski's political muscle and, it was rumoured, Russian gold had decided the day. In Thrace Radoslavov secured the Moslem vote. He made concessions to the Pomaks as a result of which the secretary of the Ottoman legation in Sofia visited every constituency in the area advising the Moslems to vote for the government, and ministers and other government spokesmen toured the area, though opposition representatives were excluded on the grounds that local Moslem unrest made the region unsafe. It is also probable that the government rigged the census returns then coming in so that it could create a larger number of parliamentary divisions than the actual population warranted.

It was not only in western Thrace that the government openly bought electoral support. In the old Kingdom *partisanstvo* was as rife as under previous administrations. In Plovdiv in February, for example, the Radoslavist council which had just taken control found it necessary to employ one hundred and thirty-seven part-time gardeners to work in the Tsar Simeon gardens at a cost of five leva each per day, and to employ thirty-one overseers for the city's Sanitation Department and its twenty-eight workers.

That political cynicism should continue to flourish in a time of virtual national disaster shocked many and their shock was seen not only in the distribution of votes in the elections but also in attempts in the spring of 1914 to form an officers' league. Between eighty and one hundred officers were reported to have met under General Lukov, the Commander of the Military Academy. They were clearly influenced by recent examples of officers' political power in Turkey, Greece and Serbia and they talked of the need to sweep away corrupt politicians and so boost the morale of nation and King. They also demanded an amnesty for General Savov who was revered as a war hero for his part in the First Balkan War but who was still under indictment for offences allegedly committed whilst in office with the Stambulovists. Internal dissension, however, ensured that the Bulgarian officers did not repeat the political successes of their fellow professionals in neighbouring countries.

Radoslavov was undisturbed by the caballing of a few army officers and in spring political life resumed its established patterns. A commission of enquiry was set up to investigate the activities of the Geshov-Danev coalition and political battle lines were drawn up over the major issue facing the government and the Assembly—the projected loan, which because of the expenses involved in developing Porto Lagos was to be for five hundred million leva, by far the largest single loan ever contemplated by a Bulgarian government. The Cabinet made the loan a *sine qua non* of its continuation in office and should the present administration dissolve, Dobrović warned the other party leaders, there would have to be yet another election which would no doubt bring Malinov to power with a Cabinet including members of the extreme left. In such circumstances Ferdinand would, said his private secretary, resign and then Bulgaria and with it the whole of the Balkans would be plunged once more into chaotic instability. The Stambulovists meanwhile used the government's need for a loan to try and escape from the trial of their ministers which had opened in February. Genadiev threatened to send his Party into the opposition lobbies if the charges were not dropped but this bluff Radoslavov called, telling Genadiev that if the Stambulovists brought down the present government no successor would be any kinder whereas something might be done once Genadiev and his men had voted for the loan. The Radoslavist Party itself showed a somewhat surprising reluctance to get their Stambulovist allies off this particular hook until the outbreak of war in Europe in August brought about a general if shortlived closing of ranks within the government coalition.

These, however, were minor issues compared to the substantive question of where the loan should be raised, a question which in the international context of 1914 would inevitably become a contest between the supporters of the two European power blocks.

The Cabinet and the King leaned towards Austria and Germany and would not make the unequivocal commitment to the Entente which the French were certain to demand as a condition of any loan raised in Paris. The French cause received an irreversible setback when it was announced in Paris that whatever happened France would not be able to make a loan available before the end of the year. The Russians had raised no objection to a loan being raised in France but they had always insisted that a price for it must be paid; immediately after the Balkan Wars this price had been a Russo-Bulgarian convention designed in St Petersburg, but by the spring of 1914, when it was clear that German banks were serious contenders in the loan question, the Russians dropped this condition though they continued to insist that if Bulgaria did receive a loan from France then she must have a government well-disposed to the Entente. That could only mean the dropping of Radoslavov, and this Ferdinand could not contemplate for it would mean another election and the danger of a leftist avalanche in the polls.

The Germans seized the advantage. In July Radoslavov introduced the proposed loan to the Sŭbranie. The debate which followed was perhaps the most stormy in the whole history of that not unruffled chamber. The text of the Bill was not even read to the deputies; numerous fist-fights took place, the Minister President waved a revolver above his head and when the vote was taken on 2/15 July it was by a show of hands; opponents of the loan, who included all non-governmental Parties except the Narrow Socialists, swore that many government deputies raised both hands and that the policemen introduced into the chamber were included in the pro-government vote. That may have been an exaggeration but few observers could accept the official verdict of one hundred and twenty-two votes in favour of the loan and one hundred and thirteen against. For weeks afterwards the losing Parties complained and carried out a campaign of obstruction within the chamber.

There were many causes for complaint. The fact that the loan was the first ever between a Bulgarian government and German banks carried international implications unwelcome to many Bulgarians at this time of European crisis. The contents of the four separate treaties which made up the loan agreement were also deeply offensive to many Bulgarians.

The German banks were to provide a total of 500 million gold leva at five percent interest with a repayment period of fifty years. The Germans had originally asked for a tobacco monopoly as a guarantee but this was too sensitive; not only had one been rejected in 1901 but Radoslavov was dependent on the Sŭbranie votes of the Turks from the tobacco-growing regions in the new territories. Instead the loan was to be guaranteed by those revenues of the banderolle, the *mururie* and the stamp duty which remained after obligations to the 1902, 1904 and 1907 French loans had been met; further guarantees were provided in the form of revenues from import dues and from the state monopoly on the sale of cigarette papers. The Bulgarians were required to place orders with Austro-Hungarian firms for the purchase of arms and railway equipment, the contract for the construction of the railway to Porto Lagos was to be given to a German company and all the materials used, as well as all replacement orders for the next fifty years, were to come from Germany and Austria-Hungary. This was a clear breach of the 1884 Railway Act. Even more galling was the stipulation that the Pernik and Bobov Dol coal-mining complexes, owned by the Bulgarian government, were to be handed over to a Germany company with the Sofia administration guaranteeing to buy at least 150,000 tons of coal per year. This was done on the pretext that only a German company would have the necessary experience, equipment and expertise to sink the deeper shafts that were now needed but the agreement gave the German company complete control over Bulgaria's major coalfield and over the prime source of fuel for the state's rail network.

The agreements had stated that the first instalment of the loan amounting to 250 million leva would be paid on 17/30 September 1914 unless war broke out in the interim. The German and Austrian governments invoked this clause and refused payment on the understandable grounds that unless Bulgaria committed itself to the central powers' cause they had no guarantee that the money would not be used against them. This did not leave the Bulgarian government entirely without funds for one of the four treaties of July 1914 had arranged that the Discontogesellschaft should lend the Bulgarian government 120 million levas immediately and this was handed over though the authorities in Berlin and Vienna refused to recognise that this money was part of the larger loan. The 120 million was to be used to pay off recent borrowings from the Russian-Asiatic Bank, an Austro-Hungarian consortium and the Bulgarian National Bank. In February 1915 the official loan was renegotiated. It was now to total 150 million, half of which was paid immediately and the remainder in April. The concessions to the Germans concerning the railway to Porto Lagos and the coal mines at Pernik and Bobov Dol were not revoked, though during the War the Bulgarian government frustrated their full implementation.

Whilst the loan had dominated domestic political affairs it had naturally been the deepening crisis in Europe which overshadowed all aspects of foreign policy. When the great powers had finally gone to war the Bulgarian government declared 'strict and loyal' neutrality and instituted a number of measures to give credibility to the declaration. The incursion of bands into Serbia was stopped and some Macedonians were disarmed; known Austrian and Turkish agents were removed from the Danube ports lest they sabotage Russian vessels taking supplies to the Serbs, and great conciliatoriness was shown towards Rumania in the many disputes which arose along the new and as yet undemarcated frontier.

The acceptance of the German loan could in some ways be seen as contrary to the spirit of the neutrality declaration, and it was not the only sign of a bias towards the central powers in Bulgarian official, and at times popular opinion. There had been deep sadness when the Russians did not prevent the humiliation of Bulgaria in 1913 and this sadness turned to anger in 1914 when they aligned openly with Rumania; Nicholas II on a visit to that country had entered territory the Rumanians had recently taken from Bulgaria thus implying his recognition of the permanence and justice of Rumanian possession,

and at the same time the Tsar had accepted the colonelcy of the
Rumanian regiment which had been the first to enter Silistra. Sazonov,
meanwhile, had assured Rumanian journalists that Russia did indeed
regard the treaty of Bucharest as just and permanent and had delivered
himself of the opinion that the proper place for Radoslavov was 'in the
felon's dock'. Clearly Russian support for Serbia and Rumania which
had been so damaging to Bulgarian interests in 1913 was no less ardent
in 1914. To show his displeasure Ferdinand declined an invitation to
attend the dedication of a new church in the Russian legation in Sofia.
Relations between the two countries grew worse when in June and July
Bulgarian bands were crossing into Serbia. In August Sazonov described as 'an unfriendly act' Bulgaria's refusal to join the European
War on the Russian side and the Russians complained loudly that
Bulgaria was not preventing the transit of German supplies and personnel to Turkey.

The Bulgarians' most unfriendly act, albeit secret, was Radoslavov's
suggestion to the German and Austrian ministers that their governments should explore the possibility of a military convention and
alliance. Naturally the central powers leapt at the chance but when
their terms were eventually put to Ferdinand he decided that their offer
of that part of Macedonia which was 'ethnically and historically' Bulgarian was too vague. Instead he and Radoslavov reaffirmed Bulgaria's
'strict and loyal' neutrality.

This made good political, diplomatic and military sense. An immediate commitment to the central powers would have been extremely
dangerous. The Germans were being held on the Marne and the Austrians had been checked by the Serbs; if Bulgaria were to join in there
was a distinct possibility that the 1913 coalition, minus Turkey, would
be recreated; Bulgaria would in that case be cut off from all help.
Furthermore, there would be great internal opposition to fighting
alongside the Germans and Austrians. The strength of popular feeling
in favour of Russia was not what it had been before 1913 but it had by
no means disappeared. At the outbreak of war thousands of letters
together with cash and gifts to the value of 170,000 leva had poured
into the Russian legation in Sofia; there had been much popular sympathy for General Radko Dimitriev who, when Bulgaria declined to
fight with Russia, had resigned his post as Bulgarian minister in Petrograd for a commission in the Tsar's army; and there was a surge of
pro-Russian feeling when the *Goeben* and the *Breslau,* now renamed
the *Jawus* and *Midilli,* bombarded Russian Black Sea ports at the end

of October. Even if the Russians had lost some of their previous standing in Bulgaria this was not to say that Bulgarian public opinion was ready to condone fighting against the Tsar's armies. Nor was Bulgaria ready to fight again after the exertions of 1912 and 1913, and General Fichev argued strongly against committing the army to action, at least in 1914.

Bulgaria's best policy was to remain quiet and extract the highest price for its neutrality. This was of considerable value to both sides. If Bulgaria came into the war Greece and Rumania would probably do so too, and both sides wanted to prevent these Balkan states joining the ranks of their enemies. For both belligerent groups Bulgaria's position between Serbia and Turkey was of great importance. The Germans needed a neutral Bulgaria to be able to send disguised war material through to Turkey. The western powers hoped that a neutral Bulgaria would prevent the passage of those goods, though this did not stop the British and French from seeing a neutral Bulgaria as a supply line to their own ally, Serbia.

For over a year Radoslavov and Ferdinand were able to keep the nation out of the European conflict. At the same time, however, domestic politics became virtually inseparable from the question of the War and a series of measures were taken to prepare for the possibility of Bulgaria's involvement in it. With the declaration of neutrality had come the pronouncement of a state of emergency, imposing martial law and giving the government wide powers to ban meetings, suspend the Sŭbranie and to control the press. This did not prevent a strenuous opposition campaign for the immediate recall of the Assembly in the light of the international dangers, but when the Sŭbranie did meet in October it meekly complied with the declaration of a state of emergency; this was the price which had to be paid for neutrality.

An important issue before the Assemblies of 1914 and 1915 was the need to cover the budget deficits created by the fighting of 1912 and 1913. Early in 1914 the government announced that it was to pay for these Wars by a increase in indirect taxation but this united all opposition Parties, both on the right and left, in defiance of the government. All demanded instead an increase in direct levies and more specifically the introduction of a progressive income tax; the Socialists went even further and called for a wealth tax too. When the issue was next discussed, in the autumn of 1914, the Minister of Finance declared himself to be a convert to the notion of a progressive income tax but averred that he could not introduce so major a change in such internationally fraught times. A projected tax reform was put before the Assembly but was then referred to the Council of Ministers where it was lodged until Bulgaria's entry into the World War ensured that nothing would be done about it. Early in 1915 the government reverted to its original stance and announced that the budget deficits, which now stood at 24.5 million leva would be made good by the introduction of an excise of five leva per hundred kilos on home-produced wine, together with export levies on wheat, rose-oil, tobacco and eggs; existing export levies on hides and wool were also to be increased. Once again there was fury in the Sŭbranie, with this time even government deputies joining the outcry. The government then made some concessions by removing the excise on wine and the export levies on wheat and rose-oil, whilst that on tobacco was lowered. These amendments increased the deficit to twenty-nine million leva.

There was much less opposition in the Sŭbranie to a proposal to increase from 5 to 30 stotinki the maximum *per diem* expense allowance for deputies. Only the Nationalists and the Progressive Liberals made any attempt to practise self-denial, and this was far from absolute as they chose to take twenty stotinki per day.

Despite intense debates over taxation, however, the major issue in Bulgarian politics could only be the nation's position with regard to the European War. Hard on the heels of the declaration of neutrality had come a defensive agreement with the Ottoman Empire in August 1914 but notwithstanding this the government and the King in October flirted with the notion of allying with Russia against Turkey. This had been occasioned by the Turkish attacks on the Black Sea ports and the consequent outburst of Russophilia, and by indications from Bucharest that if Bulgaria did go to war Rumania would remain neutral. The scheme was dashed on the Macedonian rock, the Russians announcing in November that Bulgarian gains in that area would depend on what Serbia was willing to concede; that, the Bulgarians knew, would not be enough to justify war.

This incident emphasised the inescapable and for Bulgaria eventually the determining factor: that Russia's first commitment, as in 1913, was to Serbia. As long as that was the case it would be virtually impossible for Bulgaria and Russia to come to an agreement. This was even more the case after Italy had joined the war in 1915 for the Italians were expecting gains on the eastern shore of the Adriatic and these, like the creation of Albania in 1913, would inevitably intensify Serbia's determination to keep as much of Macedonia as it could.

Bulgaria had three main objectives, the Dobrudja, eastern Thrace, and Macedonia, but the greatest of these was Macedonia, and Bulgaria would never enter the War unless she were guaranteed substantial gains there, nor would she accept sizeable acquisitions elsewhere as compensation for Macedonia.

The commitment of Russia and the western powers to Serbia clearly pushed Bulgaria towards the central powers. So too did the entry of Turkey into the War on the Austro-German side. Britain, France and Russia complained bitterly at the continuing transit of supplies through Bulgaria with war material reaching the Turks in crates marked agricultural machinery, spare parts and so on. The western powers also expressed concern that the Turks were receiving supplies through Dedeagach whose trade by the summer of 1915 was ten to fifteen times more voluminous than a year before. Some supplies no doubt did reach Turkey via this route but French and British fears were exaggerated. In the first place the fact that the railway wound in and out of Ottoman territory increased rumours that goods labelled for Bulgarian destinations were going to Turkey, and secondly the Bulgarians were forced to make more use of Dedeagach because the Serbs, Greeks and Rumanians were refusing overland transit to goods destined for Bulgaria; these goods had to come by sea and it was quicker, and after the Gallipoli landings, safer to unload them at Dedeagach than to send them on through the Straits to a Black Sea port.

As relations with the Entente powers grew more strained late in 1914 Radoslavov decided to see what the central powers might be willing to offer for guarantees of Bulgarian neutrality. His suggestion did not lack modesty. Bulgaria he proposed should have all Macedonia, that is both the uncontested Bulgarian zone and the contested zone of the 1912 treaty, the Pirot-Vranya-Nish triangle which had been part of the Exarchate but which had been ceded to Serbia in 1878, a common Danubian boundary with Hungary, and, if Rumania and/or Greece joined the enemy, then Bulgaria was to have the Dobrudja and/or Seres, Drama and Kavalla. The end result of this approach was an Austro-German offer early in January 1915 that the central powers would recognise Bulgaria's claim to lands held by Serbia to which Bulgaria had a 'historic or ethnographic' claim and which had been occupied by Bulgarian troops. The latter was an invitation to grab what she could but nothing would be given until Bulgaria had joined the fighting. Bulgaria, however was not yet interested in committing herself to war, all the more so as early in December the Serbs had won a major victory over the Austrians at Kolubara; a victorious Serbia would not concede an inch of Macedonia.

The final outcome of these soundings was the new one hundred and fifty million leva loan agreement, half of which was to be paid on signature of the accord in February 1915 and the remainder in April. The loan was granted at a very low rate of interest and in return Bulgaria had merely to remain neutral. The terms offered to Bulgaria were no doubt made more generous because the central powers knew that Radoslavov had also entered negotiations with the Entente. These had ended in December with the offer to Bulgaria of Thrace to the Enos-Midia line and an unspecified area, basically what Serbia was willing to concede, in Macedonia, and was to be in return not for neutrality but for Bulgarian intervention. This was not worth serious consideration in Sofia but the discussions with the Entente served to soften the conditions of the Austro-German loan which marked a notable success for Bulgaria's wartime diplomacy, a diplomacy which combined elements of the old *politique d'oscillation* with what the incumbent Minister of Finance, Todorov, unabashedly referred to as 'extortion'.

The loan gave Bulgaria temporary financial security and also allowed the government to sit back and wait and see how the campaigns of 1915 would alter the European situation. It also frightened Bulgaria's pro-Entente factions into greater cohesion. Early in 1915 this feeling was being marshalled by Malinov who attempted to bring together all opposition Parties in the Assembly, the Narrow Socialists excepted, to frustrate any further government moves towards the central powers. His ultimate objective was the formation of a pro-Entente coalition government but his achievements fell far short of this because the only result of his initiative was the merger of the Democratic and Radical Democratic Parties, hardly a political earthquake as the one was a splinter-group of the other. Nevertheless the pro-Entente camp in Bulgaria was much encouraged by military developments. In March Russian forces captured the vital fortress of Przemyśl and Radko Dimitriev had taken a prominent part in the battle; church bells were rung throughout Bulgaria in celebration of the victory. In the same month French and Commonwealth troops had landed at Gallipoli and were they to break out from the beaches the western powers would in all probability command the Balkans; better, said the pro-Entente lobby, join the winning side now to ensure a decent share of the spoils or at least to prevent the severe punishment which could be meted out to those who stood aside too long. In May the western powers had yet another victory, this time a diplomatic one when Italy joined the War on their side and opened up another front against Serbia's main enemy, Austria.

These developments made it seem that the neutrality game could not be played for much longer; a decision could well be reached on the battlefield and Bulgaria had to make ready to throw in its lot with whom she thought would be victorious. The Cabinet therefore made dispositions for war. Machinery was set up by which the state could take control of a large section of the economy in the event of war, and in March a bill was passed enabling the government to mobilise all men aged between twenty-one and fifty; further legislation modified martial law with the result that many more offences were added to those for which the death penalty could be exacted. Radoslavov also tightened his political hold. He managed to win over the Agrarians and the Broad Socialists in the Sŭbranie and he dismissed the city council of Sofia, one of the few remaining bastions of Russophilia. Its successor, elected by proportional representation, had a solid pro-government majority.

Though he now had control of the nation's political institutions Radoslavov had not yet committed himself to one of the two sides in the European War; if Bulgaria were to join she would have to make sure that she was being paid the best price for doing so, as well as being sure that she was joining the winning side. With the military tide apparently running in their favour Radoslavov approached representatives of the Entente in May. In the previous month the Russians, encouraged by the growth of pro-Entente sentiment in Bulgaria, had put out feelers to find out whether Sofia would join the War in return for Thrace up to the Enos-Midia line and the uncontested zone of Macedonia. Negotiations had collapsed when the Bulgarians failed to stop guerilla bands crossing into Serbian-held Macedonia. Undaunted by this failure Radoslavov suggested to the Entente that the appropriate price for Bulgarian intervention was eastern Thrace to the Enos-Midia line, both zones of Macedonia, and a sizeable chunk of western Thrace including Drama, Seres and Kavalla. The Entente powers replied on 16/29 May. The Enos-Midia line was conceded. Bulgaria was also to have Macedonia east and south of a line drawn from Egri Palanka through Veles to Ohrid thus leaving Bitolja in Bulgarian hands, but this concession was to take place only after the end of the

War and only if Serbia received appropriate compensation in Bosnia and Herzegovina. Likewise the Entente's willingness to see Bulgaria in possession of Kavalla was dependent upon Greece being compensated in Asia Minor. The Entente did promise to do what it could to bring about Bulgarian-Rumanian negotiations on the question of the Dobrudja, and financial help was also to be provided should Bulgaria join the War. These terms were too vague for the Bulgarians. They wanted, understandably, to know what sort of compensation the Entente had in mind for Serbia and Greece, and, equally understandably, they wanted to know on what basis the Dobrudja question was to be discussed. On 1/14 June Radoslavov asked for further clarification.

Whilst negotiating with the Entente Radoslavov had also been in touch with the central powers. The response from them was far more clear and much more encouraging. The fall of Przemyśl had threatened the supply line from central Europe to Turkey and the German High Command had determined that a safer route, that along the Vienna-Constantinople railway, had to be secured. That meant the subjugation of Serbia, in which Bulgaria could play a significant role for which she would be well rewarded where it mattered, in Macedonia. The Germans and Austrians therefore told Sofia in June that in return for intervention on their side Bulgaria would have immediate possession of both zones of Macedonia. This was an advance on the former offer of areas which were 'historically and ethnographically' Bulgarian and which had been occupied by Bulgarian troops, but it was not yet enough to convince Radoslavov and Ferdinand of the need for action. That conviction came from the battlefield for in the summer of 1915 the military balance which in the preceding season had seemed to lie so closely with the Entente swung rapidly and dramatically in favour of the central powers. On the western front there was continued stalemate and the Franco-Commonwealth forces were still clinging to the beaches of Gallipoli; after their abortive attempt in August to break out of their beachheads those forces were clearly doomed to defeat. It was on the eastern front, however, that the most dramatic events were taking place. In June the Russians lost Lemberg; in July they were forced to abandon Warsaw, and by the middle of August Vilna and Kovno were in German hands. Petrograd itself seemed threatened. There is no doubt that these military successes dazzled Ferdinand and Radoslavov.

The position of the central powers was also greatly strengthened by a major diplomatic coup. They persuaded the Turks to agree that Bulgaria should have eastern Thrace up to the Enos-Midia line and should be given full control of the Maritsa valley and with it the railway to Dedeagach. The central powers could now offer Macedonia *and* Thrace in return for Bulgarian involvement against Serbia. The Entente made a last, desperate bid. On 21 August/3 September it offered Thrace and the uncontested zone in return for Bulgarian involvement against Turkey and Austria. This offer only served to define the superiority of that from Berlin and Vienna; both the central powers and the Entente were now offering much the same in territorial terms but the demand from the former was that Bulgaria fight only on one front, whilst the Entente wanted action on two. The central powers could also offer immediate possession of Thrace and of Macedonia as soon as Serbia was defeated; with the Entente Thrace would have to be wrested from the Turkish enemy and, just as difficult, Macedonia would have to be prized away from the Serbian ally. In effect the offer from Berlin and Vienna was one the Entente could never equal and one the Bulgarian government could not refuse.

The final cession of the Maritsa valley by Turkey was not to take place until Bulgaria had mobilised but progress in the discussions with the Porte was such that by late August Ferdinand and Radoslavov had decided to commit Bulgaria to the central powers, and detailed negotiations were begun immediately with Vienna and Berlin. On 24 August/ 6 September a series of agreements were signed with Germany and Austria-Hungary. Bulgaria was to join the Austro-German attack on Serbia for which she was to receive both zones in Macedonia and a slice of Serbian territory to the east of the Morava river. If Rumania were to join the War on the opposite side then Bulgaria would re-possess the territories she had lost in 1913 and similarly if Greece were to align itself with the Entente Bulgaria would regain what she had forfeited to her by the treaty of Bucharest. Bulgaria was to receive two hundred million leva in four monthly instalments and arrangements were made for one additional payment if, as the Germans clearly thought unlikely, the War was to last for more than a further four months. Under an accompanying military convention Bulgaria was to take action against Serbia within thirty-five days. This also stipulated that at least six German and Austrian infantry divisions were to be committed against Serbia whilst Bulgaria was to put four such divisions into the field, though in fact the Bulgarian units were almost twice as large as the allied ones.* Overall command of operations against Serbia was to be vested in the German General von Mackensen. The Bulgarians were to guarantee unimpeded transit of war material to Turkey and the Germans were, if necessary, to arrange that Turkish troops were deployed for the effective defence of Dedeagach.

From the beginning of September tension in the Balkans rose rapidly. As the German and Austrian divisions moved into position for the attack on Serbia Serbian troops were massed along the Bulgarian as well as the northern borders. On 8/21 September the Bulgarians declared general mobilisation and 'armed neutrality' and soon twelve divisions with a total of over 800,000 men were with the colours. On 18 September/1 October Russia presented an ultimatum in Sofia demanding the end of hostile acts and the dismissal of German officers from the Bulgarian army; three days later Britain and France associated themselves with the Russian note. On 22 September/5 October the Bulgarians rejected the ultimatum and within two days all the Entente ministers had left Sofia. By this time the allied offensive in Serbia, launched on 6/19 September, was making significant progress and, thus assured of victory, the Bulgarian army attacked the Serbs on 28 September/11 October. War was declared on Serbia three days later. Britain then declared war on Bulgaria on 2/15 October, France doing the same on 3/16 October, Italy on 6/19 October and Russia on the following day.

* * *

For over a year the Entente and the central powers had courted Bulgaria and done all they could to win her favour. It had at times been a costly operation. Influential figures had received financial favours. Ferdinand himself had a personal loan from the Discontogesellschaft of a million leva, and Radoslavov had received 'pocket money' to the pleasant tune of one hundred thousand leva. Newspapers had been subsidised for a long time. In December 1914 the Austrian legation in Sofia had paid out over 40,000 leva to influence Genadiev and his newspaper, the Austrian minister noting at the time that Genadiev

---

*From this point the adjective 'allied' and the noun 'allies' are to be understood as referring to Germany, Austria-Hungary and Turkey, and not to the Entente powers and their armies.

would later demand more but that it would be a good investment; at least he was right in the first conjecture. The Russians had been subsidising some Bulgarian newspapers, for example *Balkanska Tribuna,* for years, and by the summer of 1915 there was a fund of forty thousand roubles available for expenditure under this head.

In the long run the Entente cause failed because of Macedonia and because of the German military victories of the summer of 1915. But the Entente had other disadvantages. Details of the agreements between the Entente powers were not known in Sofia but it was assumed that if Turkey were defeated then Russia would have Constantinople, and there were good grounds for Bulgarians to ask whether this was in the long term interests of their country. Entente diplomacy also suffered from a lack of coordination and in the case of the British representative in Sofia, Sir Henry Bax-Ironside, perhaps a lack of conviction too, and these were not problems that afflicted the central powers. The Entente could also be curiously inept. Ferdinand was obviously going to play the decisive role in making Bulgarian foreign policy, and it was widely known that he was susceptible to flattery. The Germans therefore bombarded him with visits from proselytising friends such as Colonel Leipzig, the Duke of Mecklenburg-Schwerin and Prince von Hohenlohe-Langenburg; the Tsar, inexplicably, sent no-one, and the French despatched the Duc de Guise who was not a friend but a relation, and was treated as such. A further tactical error was the attempt in the summer of 1915 to finance a syndicate to buy up the entire Bulgarian grain harvest, the intention being to deny the food to the Germans and to bind the Bulgarians commercially to the Entente. Fifty million leva was provided and a consortium organised under the direction of Des Closières, the former representative in Sofia of Pariba, who quickly enrolled a number of pro-Entente Sŭbranie deputies, journalists, editors and so on. The scheme failed partly because it smelt too strongly of bribery but more because German purchasing agencies were already at work when Des Closières began his attempt to corner the grain market.

The Des Closières affair was a tactical example of the Entente's strategic error, that of concentrating not on Ferdinand and the Minister President but on the opposition politicians particularly Genadiev. Genadiev himself was in a weak position. His opponents could not, like those of Venizelos in Greece, be intimidated by an Anglo-French naval demonstration, and even within Bulgaria he was not secure. Since resigning from the Cabinet his relations with his Party had become difficult and the Party itself was already showing signs of the split which was soon to become open. And Genadiev himself was still liable to conviction and imprisonment should the government choose to reopen the trial of the Stambulovist ministers. Even worse was the fact that he had been implicated in a notorious act of terrorism early in 1915 when a bomb had been thrown into a Sofia casino killing four people, including the daughter of Fichev, and the son of the Minister of War General Boyadjiev. The perpetrators of the outrage were Macedonians who had hoped by such acts of terrorism to precipitate a general rising during which the King would be killed or exiled. They had been hanged before an invited audience in Sofia's Central Prison but the preceding trial had thrown suspicion on Genadiev and when in September the latter began intense agitation against any commitment to the central powers Radoslavov assured the Austrian minister that the government had enough evidence to put Genadiev behind bars should his campaign become too embarrassing. Genadiev was indeed arrested and sentenced to ten years hard labour but for his part in the Des Closières affair rather than for complicity in the casino bombing; more political mud could be thrown in that affair than in one which touched upon Macedonia. Yet even if Genadiev had been a less tainted individual the Entente's strategy would still have been at fault. The Entente was confident it could win Bulgaria by working with the political opposition, but this was a total misreading of political developments within the country since the mid-1890s. The King and the Minister President were in complete political control. The opposition Parties were divided and those which were not totally discredited in the popular eye—the Agrarians and the Socialists—were committed to peace at almost any price. Nothing shows better the success of Ferdinand's personal regime than the fact that had the Entente wished to engineer a coup to keep Bulgaria out of the central powers' camp they would not have found a group of native politicians sufficiently united, able and reliable to carry it out.

Chapter 23

BULGARIA AND THE FIRST WORLD WAR:
MILITARY AND POLITICAL AFFAIRS, 1915–18

Although its decision to participate in the European War was not a popular one the Radoslavov government was to survive to the summer of 1918, its eventual fall being brought about by chronic shortages of essential commodities and by growing doubts as to whether its declared war aims could be achieved.

In August 1914 the opposition Parties had proclaimed themselves 'resolute partisans of peace', though they did not object to the government's using Bulgarian neutrality as a bargaining counter to secure moderate territorial concessions. Nor did they resist the restrictions on their activities which the state of emergency involved, though they did resent the freedom sometimes allowed to pro-central powers propagandists such as Parvus who held a large public meeting in January 1915.

By the end of August the opposition had come together in a united block which included all non-government Parties except the Narrow Socialists. Radoslavov, having already decided to make the commitment the opposition feared, attempted to split the block by offering the Agrarians two Cabinet seats. Stamboliiski told the other opposition leaders that he was in favour of accepting as the two posts, the Ministries of the Interior and of Railways, might enable him to paralyse the country if mobilisation were declared. The other leaders, however, were not ready for such resolute, indeed revolutionary steps. Their collective action was therefore confined to the publication of a joint petition demanding the recall of the Sŭbranie and a full debate in that Assembly before any major decision was taken. At the same time, they appealed for public support in the pressing of these demands. The Agrarians suggested that the opposition should also call for a meeting with the King and this demand was granted. The opposition leaders saw Ferdinand on 4/17 September, this being the first time that either Stamboliiski or the Radical leader Tsanov had ever entered the palace. The opposition repeated its demand for a recall of the Sŭbranie before any decision was taken, called for the creation of a large, all-party coalition and warned Ferdinand that the Bulgarian people would never tolerate war against Russia. Ferdinand's only response was to promise to convey these demands to his Minister President. This was too much for Stamboliiski who warned Ferdinand that if he persisted in his obvious plans for mobilisation and war on the German side he would risk losing his head as well as his throne. The shaken monarch replied, 'Don't trouble yourself about my head. I am old. Think of your own, you are young.' A few days later Stamboliiski informed his Party's deputies of the content of the interview and then published it in pamphlet form at the same time using Ferdinand's obstinate conduct as an excuse for calling upon the nation to disobey the mobilisation order when it came. He was sentenced to life imprisonment for *lèse majesté* and high treason.

Shortly after Stamboliiski's pamphlet came another signed by forty leading academics and opposition politicians calling in effect for passive disobedience should the government join the central powers. To justify their proposed course of action the signators invoked the memory of those who had created the state and of those who had fallen at Lule Burgas and Adrianople.

By the letter of the constitutional law Ferdinand and Radoslavov were required to secure parliamentary approval before committing the nation to war but rather than give in to opposition demands for a recall of the Sŭbranie the Minister President convened a *sui generis* assembly of government deputies in the Sŭbranie building on 8/21 September. Here the decision to mobilise was explained; Bulgaria, said Radoslavov, must seize her opportunity to undo the 1913 treaty of Bucharest. There were some expressions of discontent but the government deputies accepted their leader's arguments.

The nation greeted the decision to mobilise with a sullenness much in contrast to the euphoria of 1912, and in the army there were incidents of mutiny; ten soldiers from the 27th (Chirpan) Regiment were executed after disturbances in the barracks. The opposition Parties, insulted by the *sui generis* assembly persisted in their demand for a meeting of the Sŭbranie but the government's response was the simultaneous calling and postponing of the Assembly followed by repression and the threat of more repression. After the confrontation of 4/17 September the government had closed a number of opposition papers, imprisoned Stamboliiski, and in October was threatening to jail Madjarov for alledgedly pro-Russian utterances. Other opposition leaders, including Genadiev and a number of prominent Agrarians, were amongst those accused over and soon to be sentenced for their part in the Des Closières affair.

There was, however, little need for such stringent action. Though they continued to demand the convocation of the Sŭbranie almost all the opposition Parties accepted the War when it came. As early as 9/22 September, the day after mobilisation, Geshov's *Mir* had announced that war supersedes party and that 'On the day on which the flag of Bulgaria and its army is unfurled, that of party must be struck.' The Democrats, the largest of the opposition groups, also declared that they would not oppose the War; they rejected their immediate past with the assertion that they were not pro-Entente but pro-Bulgarian. The Democrats represented a substantial proportion of the nation's intelligentsia and the Party's commitment to the War was an important development. By December the government was confident of public support and on 15/28 December the Assembly was therefore opened by Ferdinand and Crown Prince Boris who were given a generally enthusiastic reception from all but the Socialists and the Agrarians. The main business of the Assembly was the government's request for a credit of fifty-five million leva to finance military operations and to pay for the upkeep of soldiers' families. Few parties when it came to the point could vote against the government when national unity was so clearly at issue. The Narrow Socialists, however, did vote against the Bill as did the Genadievists, though the other Stambulovists under the leadership of Dobri Petkov supported the government. The Radicals declared they could not vote against the Bill but the government must bear all the responsibility for what followed. The Danevists, Democrats, Nationalists, Broad Socialists and Agrarians also voted for the Bill, though the latter made clear they were supporting not the government but the nation, the Agrarian *Utro* (Tomorrow) declaring that the party 'will do its duty in approving the war credits, convinced that it grants them not to the government but to the people'.[1]

By the time the Sŭbranie voted the war credits the Bulgarian army had been in the field for three months and considerable victories had been secured. The plan of campaign had been for the Bulgarian I Army to drive towards Nish and try and link up with the Austrians whilst the II Army moved into the Struma and Vardar valleys cutting off the Serbs' retreat to the south and taking control of the Salonika-Skopje-Nish railway. Faced with such overwhelming odds the Serbs had little chance. By the middle of October the Salonika-Nish line had been cut in the north by the I Army which early in November entered Pirot and Nish. In the south the II Army had repulsed a French force which had advanced north from its base in Salonika and early in December the Bulgarians took Bitolja. By mid-December all of Serbia was occupied. The Bulgarians were keen to push on into Greek territory but this the German High Command forbade. It did not wish to offend Greek neutrality, though the Entente powers had done so by landing at Salonika in October, but more to the point was the fact that if the 90,000 enemy troops stationed in Greece were driven out they would be sent straight to the western front, whereas the Bulgarian army would remain virtually inactive in the Balkans. To drive the Entente troops out of Greece would therefore alter the balance of forces on the western front to the disadvantage of the Germans.

In the spring of 1916 German opinion relaxed and the Bulgarians did advance some distance into Greek territory, the Greeks offering no resistance to the joint Bulgarian-German force which took Fort Rupel. In August 1916 the Rumanians, encouraged by the successes the Italians and Russians were enjoying, at last entered the War with the result that the Entente now planned a joint offensive against the Bulgarians from Macedonia and Rumania. In Macedonia the attack was easily repulsed and the Bulgarians moved forward there and in western Thrace, taking Drama, Seres and Kavalla. In the north the Bulgarian III Army, strengthened by two Turkish units, moved into action against the Rumanians. The southern Dobrudja was easily taken and early in September the III Army crossed the Danube into Rumania proper. This was a feint to draw the Rumanians south-eastwards just before Falkenhayn unleashed a massive Austro-German force against them in Transylvania. By the end of the year the Rumanians had been driven back into the Wallachian plain and were suing for peace.

In the second half of 1916, however, the Bulgarians suffered their first serious setbacks. Although they had advanced into Thrace, where they met no resistance, their progress in western Macedonia was less easy and was eventually halted by fierce fighting by the Serbs at Gornichevo Pass and by the British in the Struma valley. In the second half of September the French general in command of the Entente forces, Sarrail, launched a counter-attack. The Serbs won an important victory by taking the Kaimakchalan peak and in November were back in Bitolja. With that the campaign ended for the year and when the Entente tried to advance further in the following spring they made little progress and suffered heavy losses. The Macedonian front, like that in France, had reached stalemate and was to stay like that until the final weeks of Bulgaria's war in August and September 1918.

* * *

The central powers had believed in 1915 that the War could be over within four months of Bulgaria's joining it. The continuation of the conflict long after those initial four months inevitably increased the tensions and divisions within Bulgaria. In the first days and weeks of the fighting there had been little discussion of Bulgaria's war aims. Maximalist opinions were held by Radoslavov who told the Sŭbranie in December 1915 that Bulgarian territory would be extended to wherever the Bulgarian soldier set foot. This view was shared by Ferdinand who even in November was stating privately that the allies would be wise never to recreate Serbia. In January 1916 Radoslavov, in answer to a question from a Socialist deputy, gave the first definition of Bulgarian war aims to the Sŭbranie; these were, he said, 'to unite the Bulgarian nation within its historic and ethnographic borders' and by this he meant the annexation of Macedonia, the Dobrudja, Thrace west of the Maritsa, and the Morava valley. Later in the year Ferdinand symbolised these expansionsist aims by deciding that the nation would have a new tricolour marking the three seas to which it aspired—black, white for the Aegean, and blue for the Adriatic. These claims were supported by references to history which showed that the Morava valley had been part of the Bulgarian Exarchate from 1870 until the treaty of Berlin, and, the Bulgarian government maintained, there was no doubting the Bulgarian nature of Macedonia for large numbers of Macedonians had supported the Exarchate and had volunteered for service with the Bulgarian army in the Balkan and the present Wars. In the face of such evidence there was no need, Radoslavov insisted, for plebiscites in Macedonia and the Morava valley. Yet as the War dragged on doubts were raised as to the wisdom and the practicality of the maximalist programme. The moderate lobby, in which Geshov was prominent and which was much strengthened by moves elsewhere for a peace without annexation and indemnities, began urging that for the sake of future Balkan stability Bulgaria must take only what was indisputably Bulgarian, though even moderate claims encompassed the not inconsiderable area of Thrace west of the Maritsa, the Dobrudja and Macedonia.

There were few if any Bulgarians who objected to the notion of 'national unity' even if there were differences of interpretation of the concept. There were a large number of Bulgarians however who showed little enthusiasm for the fact that Bulgarians were fighting shoulder to shoulder with Germans. The government therefore did a great deal to encourage pro-German propaganda; films showed Bulgarian and German troops in united combat and there was a rash of new Bulgarian-German, Bulgarian-Turkish, and Bulgarian-Austrian cultural associations, as well as a great increase in the teaching of German in Bulgarian schools. Ferdinand was honoured by the Kaiser who made him a Fieldmarshal in the German army during the victory celebrations held in Nish early in 1916. Later in the year parliamentary delegations exchanged visits. At the same time there were efforts to stress the ethnic solidarity of the Bulgarians, Turks and Hungarians. The government press also gave wide currency to the idea of *Mitteleuropa*. German diplomatists in Sofia were confident that these measures together with the military successes at the front had overridden Bulgaria's strong Russophile traditions. In June 1916, said the German minister, even the reports from those who censored the soldiers' mail indicated the disappearance of Russophilia, whilst a few months earlier the Austro-Hungarian consul in Ruse, one of the strongest centres of pro-Russian feeling, reported that the local Russophiles seemed to have accepted the justice of the central powers' cause. These were largely superficial impressions. The Bulgarian intelligentsia may well have discarded its old allegiance to the Tsarist Empire but that did not mean a transfer of loyalty to the Kaiser's Reich. The notion of *Mitteleuropa* was treated with deep suspicion, and was totally rejected by the influential academic economist, Professor M. A. Tsankov, in his *The War of Nations,* a work which gave general economic justification for the central powers' case. When Erzberger, the leader of the German Centre Party, visited Ruse in February 1916 he went out of his way to stress that Germany did not want the economic subjugation of Bulgaria but, on the contrary, needed a Bulgaria which was strong militarily, economically and socially. Whilst the intelligentsia feared notions such as *Mitteleuropa* the mass of the population took great exception to some measures which were intended to mark the break with Bulgaria's pro-Russian past, and great resentment was shown towards Ferinand's plan, never implemented, to change the name of Sofia's Alexander Nevski cathedral then being constructed according to the plans of a Russian architect and largely with Russian money. The ineptness of the attempts to wean Bulgaria from its Russophila become immediately apparent with the outbreak of the Russian Revolution. In February 1917 a League of Authors and Professors was formed by those leading members of the intelligentsia in Sofia who wished to revive national self-consciousness on its old lines. Within weeks all large towns had their own branch and that in Varna raised 35,000 leva in two months. The government replied by setting up yet more organisations to promote Bulgarian-German and Bulgarian-Austrian links but they did not enjoy anything like the same degree of success.

In one respect Bulgaria's association with the central powers did produce a lasting change in the life of the nation; 31 March 1916 was the last day in which Julian calendar was officially used in Bulgaria for the following day, 14 April 1916, the nation switched to the Gregorian system, and henceforth religious holidays were to be held on the new-style date corresponding to the old-style calendar, i.e., that Christmas would be celebrated in church on 7th January, new style. This was not entirely due to the alliance with the central powers for 1916 was admirably suited to the change as under both calendars Easter, Ascension and Whitsun fell on the same day. The authorities anticipated resistance to the alteration—clerical opposition had sunk a similar scheme in the 1890s—and therefore large fines were decreed for those state and public concerns which failed to use the Gregorian dates.

For the government possible disagreement with the Church over the calendar was of little significance beside actual friction with the military hierarchy over a number of issues. In 1915 a number of older, Russophile officers had been removed from the General Staff and their places taken by younger men whose political sympathies lay predominantly with Malinov's Democratic Party. In the days of rapid movement up to December 1915 there had been no time to make political disputes with the civilian authorities but with the more stable military situation of 1916 such differences did appear. The Generals were unhappy at the quality of civilian officials being appointed in the occupied territories and in August attempted to take complete control of Macedonia. They also resented the way in which Radoslavov denounced any military criticism of civilian authority as politicising by supporters of the Democratic Party. Above all, however, the High Command was distressed at the chaos which was reigning in the supply of necessities to the army and the civilian population, with the latter being particularly poorly-provided for in the occupied territories.

Shortages of food and other necessities were to be almost constant throughout the War, were to intensify alarmingly in 1918 and were to play a major role in bringing about the final collapse of Bulgaria's war effort. It would be as well therefore to record at this point the reasons for this chronic and continuing problem. In September 1915 the distribution of food in Bulgaria had been severely disrupted by the strain of mobilisation, by the insatiable appetite of allied purchasing agencies, and by an administrative division of responsibility in food procuring which left the military requisitioning authorities to supply the army and the civil branch to look after the home population.

When these initial difficulties had been overcome other less tractable ones appeared. These centred upon the activities of allied personnel in Bulgaria and Bulgarian-occupied territory. The Germans had been given considerable powers over the Bulgarian rail network and telephone system, and in those parts of the occupied lands designated as rest areas for allied troops they had set up their own telegraph links. This bred the suspicion that the Germans were evading the regulations recently imposed to prevent the export of food. Nor was this an idle suspicion. Allied soldiers had been given the right to send home by parcel-post a total of five kilograms of food per week but so attractive was this privilege that many German and Austrian troops stationed in Serbia crossed into Bulgarian-occupied territory or into Bulgaria proper to avail themselves of it, and by the end of 1916 the 16,000 or so allied troops on the southern front were sending home quantities of food which, had the five-kilo per week ration been observed, would have meant the number of men involved was about a hundred thousand. Later in the war the right to send food parcels was reduced with packages being allowed only at Christmas, Easter and one or two other festivals. The illegal export of food was also encouraged by the fact that in December 1915 German and Austrian currency had become legal tender in Bulgaria and the allied troops, better-paid than the Bulgarians, were at a distinct advantage on the flourishing black market. Furthermore, Bulgarian food sellers were naturally eager to sell to allied troops whose marks or kronen had greater purchasing power than the Bulgarian leva. If they could not buy food allied troops could easily be tempted to steal it and so frequent were thefts that in 1916 the Bulgarian High Command had ordered two or three sentries to be posted in every wagon-load of food. Despite these precautions large quantities of food were still being lost to the Bulgarians because allied troops stole salt, a commodity which the Germans had undertaken to supply to Bulgaria, and then took it into Bulgaria to barter it for food which they then illegally shipped back to Austria and Germany. So widespread did this practice become that a number of Bulgarian food-processing plants which needed salt operated on barter alone and had to dispose of a large proportion of their production in order to secure the essential raw material. The supply problem was further complicated in 1916 by a German requisitioning campaign in the Dobrudja so fierce that it stripped the area of much of its seed-corn; in 1917 seventy-four percent of the Dobrudja's valuable land had to be left untilled. In 1917 too the Germans unilaterally placed the Morava district and all Rumania, including the Bulgarian-held Dobrudja, under the direct command of von Mackensen. Despite fierce protests from Radoslavov these areas were no longer available to Bulgarian food-procuring agencies.

Resentment at allied policies over food supplies was naturally great but it was equalled by anger at the connivance of many Bulgarian officials at the highest and the lowest levels. It was widely known that German control of much of the rail system, combined with the venality of Bulgarian personnel, was allowing thousands of wagon loads of food to leave the country labelled 'war material', a category over which Bulgarian customs officials had no jurisdiction. At the highest level the Cabinet granted export licences for its supporters or even used their names as covers for the illicit activities of ministers themselves; even Radoslavov was involved. Some examples of this form of corruption were grotesque. Dr H Georgiev, A Sŭbranie deputy, sold large quantities of extremely scarce quinine to the Turkish military authorities, despite a legal embargo on its sale; the brother of a former minister made a million leva from the illegal export of 50,000 sheep which were embarked at Burgas during pre-arranged, fake air-raid warnings; a friend of Tonchev provided the Austrian army with 60,000 kilograms of wool at enormous profit despite the desperate shortage of that commodity at home.

In 1915 the government had set up the Central Committee for Public Welfare to control the domestic economy.* The Central Committee had clearly failed. It seemed powerless in the face of allied depredations and these, together with the Central Committee's own internal blunders, meant that even bread, though rationed since Bulgaria's entry into the War, was in short supply in most large towns by the beginning of 1916. In the occupied territories conditions were much worse and in Ohrid early in 1916 a number of deaths from starvation were reported.

Inevitably the government was subjected to considerable criticism, not least from the army. In the spring of 1916 a number of senior officers, including Generals Yotsev, Lukov, Tantilov and Zhekov, demanded an end to the abuses which allowed so much food to be lost and urged the government to suspend all food exports at least until the next harvest had been taken in. When the government failed to respond to this call the Generals posted sentries on the borders of the pre-1915 kingdom in an attempt to prevent vital supplies leaving the country. When the Sŭbranie met in the spring the question of supplies inevitably assumed major importance, but the government was able to defuse criticism by agreeing to administrative reorganisation which gave birth to the Central Committee Economic and Social Welfare. Under the previous arrangement the Central Committee for Public Welfare had consisted primarily of government appointees but the new body was made up of Sŭbranie deputies so chosen that all the major Parties would be represented.

Radoslavov's survival in 1916 was helped by two other factors. In the first place the opposition was split and discredited by its continued picking of old and unsavory bones. Genadiev and his supporters decided not to vote for the budget because they realised that their loyalty to the government on this issue would not earn them acquittals in the Des Closières trial which was then nearing its end; they hoped that if they helped bring down the government its successor would abandon the proceedings. This plan was frustrated by the Nationalist Party which despite its previous record of virtually unbroken opposition to the government in domestic affairs did this time vote for the budget because it had been given an assurance that if it did so proceed-

---

*The Central Committee and other government agencies will be discussed in greater detail in chapter 24.

ings against the three of its members involved in the trial would be dropped. After the end of these undignified Sŭbranie wranglings military developments also came to Radoslavov's aid. The victory over Rumania in the summer of 1916 raised hopes that shortages of at least two commodities, salt and petrol, would be eased, and it also added strength to Radoslavov's main defensive argument, namely that internal dislocation and privation were the inevitable result of war, but these discomforts were a price worth paying for the national reunion which victory would bring.

This was an argument which Radoslavov was to use until his eventual fall. In 1917 it had to be pressed with much greater force. There had been no improvement in the supply problem. In October 1916 the redesigned Central Committee had renegotiated trading agreements with the allies but there had been no lessening of illicit food exports, and the Germans and Austrians had frustrated the import of food and fuel from Rumania. In the winter of 1916–17 official sources were talking of 'thousands of deaths from hunger' and in the spring of 1917 it was estimated that twenty percent of Sofia's children found their main source of food in begging in the city's taverns; nor were conditions any better in Plovdiv where anti-government demonstrations took place.

In the occupied territories the problem was even worse and here it affected both the morale of the army and relations between the military authorities and the government. In Macedonia, the pro-government deputy Professor Tsankov told the Sŭbranie in March 1917, a hundred thousand men had been recruited into the Bulgarian forces yet their families were on the very edge of starvation; and Tsankov based his remarks on recent personal observation. In the Morava valley the problem was at its most intractable. The region had been under Serbian administration for over forty years and most of its inhabitants had discarded their former Bulgarian national characteristics; even Radoslavov referred to them as 'former Bulgarians'. The occupying Bulgarian authorities had immediately opened Bulgarian schools, reading-rooms and other cultural institutions in an effort to revive Bulgarian national consciousness, but these had had little effect and could in no way compensate for the increasing food shortages which had become the chief attribute of Bulgarian rule. Early in 1917 frustration over these shortages led to protests in Nish and other parts of the region and more and more men took to the hills to join the bands of brigands who had been in hiding there since the occupation began.

This led to a new law against brigandage which compounded rather than solved the problem for it involved the conscription of young men still in the disaffected areas. This was a disaster for it meant that these young men would have to fight against their fathers who had been with the Serbian army since mobilisation in 1914. The Balkan family tradition could not tolerate institutionalised parricide and many young men, rather than join the Bulgarian army, took to the hills to join the very bands of brigands which the law had sought to eliminate. By April the whole of the Morava valley was in a state of revolt. It was pacified only slowly and at great cost.

The continuing and worsening supply problem naturally affected the morale of the army. Even in 1916 in the campaign against Rumania there had been some disaffection. The 25th (Dragoman) Infantry Regiment, for example, had expressed a wish not to cross the Danube; it was willing, said the disaffected, to fight for the defence of Bulgaria but it did not want to cross into foreign territory. Similar trouble was experienced in other infantry regiments. In the spring of 1917 morale was being sapped by the knowledge that families at home were suffering deprivations, a feeling to which regiments recruited in urban areas were particularly prone. In May, for example, a company of the 1st (Sofia) Infantry Regiment was reported to have been unwilling to fight until their families were better provided for. There was also the knowledge that the allies lived in better and even safer conditions. A number of German units had been mixed with or stationed alongside Bulgarian troops in Macedonia and it was obvious to all that the Germans were better fed, better clothed and better armed; even their trenches were safer because their supplies of cement and other materials were more reliable. Under such conditions unrest spread and in the summer there were numerous reports of soldiers forming committees or soviets on the Russian model. In this they were encouraged by opposition politicians such as Genadiev and Stamboliiski both of whom conducted vigorous campaigns from their prison cells. Stamboliiski saw many soldiers who were home on leave and they relayed his anti-government and often anti-war sentiments to the troops at the front. Disaffection amongst the latter was becoming an ever more worrying problem for the military authorities and by the mid-summer of 1917 there were five hundred soldiers detained in Sofia's Central Prison. Agrarian leaders sensed the concern which the High Command felt at the spread of this discontent and actually conspired with General Zhekov to overthrow Radoslavov, though there was no mention of withdrawing from the

War. Zhekov, after mildly encouraging the Agrarians, handed compromising documents over to the police as a result of which Stamboliiski was taken from the relaxed atmosphere of the political section of
Sofia's Central Prison and interned in a fortress in Vidin. Meanwhile
the morale of the forces continued to fall and by October units of the
III Army opposite Russian troops on the northern front were openly
fraternising with the enemy.

The most effective measures taken by the military hierarchy were not
conspiratorial philanderings with opposition politicians but those
which gave it control of the supply and distribution of food and other
necessities. The Generals, enraged by maladministration, especially in
the occupied territories, had arrested scores of civilian officials; the
military leaders also resented the fact that Radoslavov had blamed
them for the Morava rebellion, and even more resentment was felt at
attacks on the army such as that delivered by Professor Tsankov who
had followed his denunciation of Bulgarian administration in Macedonia with the assertion that army morale had so degenerated that
revival would only come if the entire force were placed under the direct
command of the German General Staff. In April the Generals were
given a golden opportunity to act. In that month the Central Committee for Economic and Social Welfare submitted to the Sŭbranie a
secret and startling report admitting in effect that it could do nothing
more to better supplies. In a few days the report was general knowledge. The Central Committee of 1916 had been the creation of the
legislature and politicians had delighted in the subjugation of the military bodies involved in food and raw material procurement. The soldiers on the other hand had not been happy and had always felt that no
committee of civilians, let alone parliamentarians, should have power
to procure supplies for the army or to issue orders to military personnel. After the self-criticising report of the Central Committee the military lobby had little difficulty in convincing the government that a
change had to be made, and not even the Sŭbranie was in a mood to
give serious resistance. The result of the change was that the Central
Committee was abolished and replaced by the Directorate of Economic
and Social Welfare. This was the creation of the executive not the
legislature and was completely dominated by the military. It was in fact
an independent department of the General Staff. The military lobby
had ousted the civilian and the administration of the economy was
firmly in the former's hands.

Whilst the military authorities were becoming increasingly anxious over and then involved in the problem of supplies, Bulgaria, like the rest of Europe, was profoundly affected by events in Russia. With the fall of the Tsar there had been immediate hope of a separate peace. These hopes had been encouraged by the appointment of Miliukov as Foreign Minister in the Provisional Government, for he had once taught in Sofia University and was known to be pro-Bulgarian. Radoslavov sought to capitalise on Miliukov's known good-will and, with German blessing, attempts were made to sound the new Foreign Minister by sending Dimitŭr Rizov, then serving as Bulgarian diplomatic representative in Berlin, to Scandinavia to visit Russian diplomatists with whom he was on good terms. Nothing came of these soundings, nor of Rizov's approach to Maxim Gorki or of his suggestion that Blagoev, the leader of the Narrow Socialists, should go to Russia to talk with Russian socialist leaders. Meanwhile secret discussions were also held in Switzerland between Bulgarians and representatives of the Entente powers.

Although these hopes for a separate peace were to be disappointed the Russian Revolution had a profound affect upon Bulgaria by contributing significantly to the revival of oppositional politics. This was in part because the hope for a separate peace had made it possible to contemplate a return to Bulgaria's traditional friend without breaking with her present ally. In April the Progressive Liberals held a conference and decided in the light of recent events in Russia to amend their current policy and move back towards their established Russophilia; elaborate arrangements were then made to reinforce the Party's machine in the provinces and by the end of the month it was confident that it would soon be returned to power. This confidence was to some extent due to reports brought back to Bulgaria by students who had been interned in Russia in 1915 and who had been released by the Revolution; they said that before they left Russia Miliukov had told them Russia was prepared to sign a separate peace with Bulgaria as soon as the present government and monarch had been removed. The call for a separate peace was also voiced by the Nationalists, most notably in a leading article in *Mir* in May, an article which passionately argued the need for and the practicality of a peace with Russia; this enraged the government and breached the censorship barrier more dramatically than any publication since Stamboliiski's pamphlet of 1915.

The Russophile Radicals had not been left out of the revival of opposition activity. Their much-respected leader, Nikola Tsanov, made one of the earliest and most cogent of the many attacks upon the government in 1917. In the Sŭbranie on 30 March he announced that he had previously felt restrained by patriotic duty from assailing Radoslavov and his henchmen but now things had gone too far. He criticised the management of the economy and lambasted the ministers for their policies in the occupied territories, asking them pointedly if they really expected to win the battle for the hearts and minds of the inhabitants by shipping scores of them off to prison camps if they dared to complain of hunger or maladministration.

Attacks such as those by Tsanov and by the Generals were more stringent than any yet made during the War but, given his concession over the Directorate for Economic and Social Welfare, Radoslavov was not in real danger. The Stambulovists, despite Genadiev's personal views, remained loyal to a government which could still offer them Cabinet posts—the Genadievist Minister for Railways resigned in the spring of 1917 but was replaced by another Stambulovist, this time from the Petkov wing of the Party. The government could still beat off proposals such as that for a relaxation of censorship and when in the summer the Agrarians began printing their newspaper, *Zemedelsko Zname,* for the first time since September 1915, it was the pro-War A. Dimitrov faction not Stamboliiski's supporters who had editorial control.

Radoslavov could continue in power basically because he could still argue that despite its internal shortcomings his regime had reunified all Bulgarians. In 1917 however even this defence was beginning to crumble and once more this was due in no small measure to events in Russia. That there was a strong desire for peace was well known and had been underlined in December 1916 when a large crowd demonstrated in front of the Sŭbranie to vent their anger at the news that the German peace initiative, which the Bulgarian government fully supported, had been ignored by the enemy. At this point most Bulgarians thought in terms of a negotiated peace which would enable them to retain what they saw as their entirely just acquisitions; they did not object when Radoslavov argued that as the alliance with Germany had made it possible to undo the treaty of Bucharest and regain Macedonia and the Dobrudja, so that alliance must be maintained to ensure that the repossession of these lands was permanent. Early in 1917 however there was serious questioning of this argument. In his speech to the

assembly on 30 March, Tsanov said that he and his Radical Party had
voted war credits on the understanding that Bulgaria was seeking
nothing more than national unity but now that Bulgarian troops had
crossed the Danube into uncontestably Rumanian territory, Bulgaria
had been made into a 'mercenary'; 'You declared war', railed Tsanov,
'to bring us national unity but now you are trying to conquer foreign
territories regardless of the wishes of their inhabitants'. While Tsanov
was questioning the objectives of the War Stamboliiski was voicing
doubts as to whether Bulgaria should even continue to fight. With the
collapse of Tsarism Stamboliiski became convinced that the United
States would soon join the Entente powers; were that to happen the
central powers could never win and Bulgaria would be best advised to
escape now before it was too late. Stamboliiski's views were as yet
personal ones but his influence was considerable for he was in constant
contact with Agrarian sympathisers whom he met without hindrance
until his removal to Vidin in September.

These arguments would have posed no real threat to Radoslavov
had there not been general European discussion, prompted by calls
from Russia, for a peace without annexations or indemnities, for this
general discussion made Tsanov's and Stamboliiski's policies seem
practical as well as desirable. A further incentive to discuss peace terms
was the increasing restlessness of the troops, particularly those who
were facing the Russian armies. There were frequent incidents of fra-
ternisation in this sector and later in 1917 Bulgarian radio operators
gave wide currency to the peace propaganda then being broadcast by
the Bolsheviks. Yet a peace without annexations could be embarrassing even for Tsanov and his supporters, for they too believed that some
Bulgarian expansion was both just and necessary to preserve future
peace. When the Broad Socialists went to the Socialist Congress in
Stockholm in June they did so to plead the justice of Bulgaria's claims
to Macedonia and the Dobrudja, claims which they regarded as analo-
gous to France's demand for Alsace and Lorraine. Radoslavov had
little need to fear the Socialist Congress in Sweden but it was a severe
jolt to his political standing and to the nation's resolve when the German Reichstag, on 19 July, approved a resolution calling for a peace
without annexations or indemnities. Erzberger hastened to reassure
the Bulgarians in a special telegram that the resolution did not mean
that Bulgaria would be denied its legitimate desire for national unity
but the Bulgarians were not entirely mollified and to bolster Erzberger's reassurances the Kaiser paid a state visit to Bulgaria in

October 1917, the first time a major European monarch had visited the country.

It was to take more than a visit from the Kaiser to dissipate opposition anger when the Sŭbranie was recalled in the same month. The opposition had been demanding the recall of the Assembly since the summer and Radoslavov at last gave in, arranging an emergency session from 15–27 October which was to abut onto the regular session scheduled to begin on 28 October. Though all the Parties with the exception of the Socialists stressed their commitment to Germany and the war this was less a statement of real conviction than an indication that they expected a change of government, for they knew that no party which expressly opposed the War would be asked to join any Cabinet which might be formed on Radoslavov's fall. The government soon came under the expected attack. A vote of censure was moved. The debate was stormy, so much so that the sitting of 30 October had to be disbanded because of the uproar. Radoslavov survived the vote of censure by 120 votes to 111, a slender margin which showed how thin his patriotic card had worn. After this Radoslavov continued in his accustomed manner by forcing the opposition into a totally justified frenzy over his decision to link the budgets of the Ministries of Finance, War and the Interior and pass them compositely. These were the ministries which the opposition most wanted to investigate and Radoslavov's hitching them together was unconstitutional; nevertheless, despite a particularly disorderly session when fists and chairs had flown in equal number, Radoslavov had his way.

Despite his Sŭbranie victory Radoslavov's control over the nation and its institutions was beginning to dissolve. In addition to the new difficulties created by events in Russia there remained the older, and more serious problem of supplies. Even less food was now being produced but there had been no decline in allied demands and expropriations. In September 1917 the head of the Directorate had written to the Ministerial Council, 'On my tour of northern and southern Bulgaria I was told and I saw myself how German and Austrian companies, acting under the guise of telephone or telegraph units, are in fact purchasing units which collect information about food stocks, buy up eggs, cheese and various kinds of fats, pack them in specially prepared parcels and send them through their own military post to Germany'.[2] By the beginning of 1918 the Germans were in charge of Bulgaria's main railway termini and telephone exchanges and were taking more food than ever. In December 1917 10,000 Sofiotes had heard Blagoev and other Socialist leaders denounce the War, the government and the whole system; in January 1918 there were disturbances lasting three days in Gabrovo and this protest against food shortages spread throughout the province. In February there were mass protests against the War and meagre rations whilst in Stanimaka and Samokov women attacked the mayor. In May, in the so-called 'Women's Revolt', a woman was killed in Sliven during a two-day riot and there were demonstrations in Stara Zagora, Karnobat, Burgas, Tŭrgovishte, Razgrad, Svishtov, Tŭrnovo, Plovdiv and in scores of villages.

By this time the Directorate for Economic and Social Welfare was under considerable fire, not least from the Ministry of Agriculture whose functions it had usurped. In the Sŭbranie this antipathy was given a full airing and the government replaced the head of the Directorate, General Protogerov, with Reserve General Popov, a Sŭbranie deputy, and there were other changes in personnel designed to placate political opposition. A few weeks later, in a further gesture of conciliation, the government allowed a free market in vegetables, although this had no effect because by then it was apparent that the impending harvest would be disastrous and the authorities were forced to reimpose controls on vegetables and to cut all rations. Meanwhile hopes that extra grain could be bought in the Ukraine were not entirely fulfilled because allied purchasers were also there. Faced with the spectre of famine the government convened a conference of provincial governors but there was little they could do but attempt to contain the intensifying unrest which the worsening food situation inevitably caused. The government's internal policies had brought the nation to disaster.

The failure of Radoslavov's internal policies were in the summer of 1918 compounded by the complete collapse of his military and diplomatic strategy. No government could survive such damage.

Radoslavov's external difficulties had not been solved by the visit of the Kaiser in October 1917 for the question of a peace without indemnities or annexations was raised when the negotiations at Brest Litovsk began. On 1 December 1917 Radoslavov had told the Sŭbranie:

Bulgaria cannot accept the proposals of the government of the Russian Republic, the more so as Bulgaria has gained that for which she entered the War, namely unification within her historic and ethnographic frontiers in

Macedonia, the Dobrudja and the Morava valley. That is the first premise on which negotiations for a separate or a general peace will be conducted.[3]

When Radoslavov did sign the treaty of Brest Litovsk it was only after assurances from his allies that the original agreements of September 1915 were still valid and would be respected and Bulgaria's national unity thereby safeguarded. Whilst the negotiations in Brest Litovsk were still in progress President Wilson had announced his Fourteen Points, the eleventh of which called for relations between the Balkan states to be determined by friendly counsel along historically established lines of allegiance and nationality, with international guarantees for the political, economic and territorial integrity and independence of the individual states. This was as satisfactory to Bulgaria as any peace likely to be concluded on the basis of no annexations and indemnities, no matter what guarantees Germany might give for Bulgarian national unity. What was more, Bulgaria was in the singular position of not being at war with the United States, the treaties of September 1915 obliging her to fight only against those of her neighbours who might be at war with Germany, and Washington, unlike London, Paris and Petrograd, had not declared war on Bulgaria. For the latter, therefore, there was nothing to lose by breaking with the central powers and seeking peace through the mediation of the United States on the basis of Wilson's Fourteen Points. For the opposition Parties which had been pro-Entente in 1915, this was a powerful attraction and one which totally destroyed Radoslavov's claim to be the guarantor of national unity.

The weakness of Radoslavov's position was illustrated most dramatically in the treaty of Bucharest concluded between the allies and Rumania in May 1918 after some three months of negotiations. The Bulgarians confidently expected to be given all of the Dobrudja but this they were denied. The German High Command considered the railway link from Constantsa on the Black Sea to Cerna Voda on the Danube a vital strategic asset which could not be allowed to pass out of German control. Bulgaria was therefore given only the southern Dobrudja and the northern part was placed, at Bulgaria's suggestion, under joint allied administration. At the same time the Austrians successfully demanded the Vranya triangle previously under Bulgarian control, whilst the Turks, who had lost 20,000 men in the Dobrudja campaign, were demanding as the price of this assistance the return of Thrace up to the line of the river Mesta. This issue was not settled at

Bucharest but the general tenor of the negotiations shocked even Radoslavov who declared that Bulgaria had been treated not as an ally but as a vanquished enemy.

The Bucharest settlement destroyed the Radoslavov Cabinet. If Bulgaria were to be denied the Dobrudja, the least contentious of her territorial aspirations, what hope was there for Macedonia and the Morava valley? Radoslavov's credibility was totally ruined and few believed his denials of rumours that Germany was about to sign away Bulgaria's recent gains in Macedonia in order to win over the royalist government in Athens. Petkov and his Stambulovists, who had been pressing for a widening of the coalition for some months, at last withdrew convinced that Radoslavov could neither retrieve his credibility nor offer sufficient further material inducements for their continued loyalty. Ferdinand too was forced to recognise that he must part with the Minister President who therefore resigned on 20 June.

The task of forming the next administration was given to Malinov. He attempted to form a broad coalition and brought Stamboliiski back from Vidin to Sofia prison in the hope that he might be able to persuade the Agrarians to join the government. Malinov was generally recognised as being less sycophantic than Radoslavov but the nickname 'the lackey', bestowed when he made his fawning declaration to Ferdinand in 1908, clung to him still. More important, indeed decisive, was the fact that Malinov pledged himself to the continuation of the War, as Ferdinand insisted that he could not break with Germany. Stamboliiski, together with the leaders of the Nationalist and Progressive Liberal Parties, would not join any Cabinet which did not pledge itself to seek an immediate armistice and so Malinov was left to form his government from his own party with the addition of two Radicals; the Minister of War was Ferdinand's *Hofmarschall,* General Savo Savov, not to be confused with the Balkan War hero General Mihail Savov. After Malinov himself, who became Minister for Foreign Affairs as well as Minister President, the most important and powerful figure in the government was the Minister of Finance, Liapchev.

Malinov declared his rule would have two objectives: to prosecute the War to victory and to govern with honesty and legality. In order to make the first objective more palatable to a war-weary nation he took his allies to task, complaining that the Germans had broken their treaty obligations by suspending both financial aid and the delivery of munitions, cloth and other articles. He also demanded a redefinition of the Bucharest treaty and in July achieved a notable victory when the allies agreed that Bulgaria should have sovereignty over northern Dobrudja.

The population of Bulgaria was by this stage too war-weary to be dazzled by territorial gain. It wanted an end to privation. So too did the mass of the conscript army. Civilian suffering and anger had been growing in 1918 and reached a peak in the summer when the extent of the harvest failure became clear. In Ruse a despairing prefect reported that he had no flour left in the warehouses and could not feed the province's many destitute; most other prefects were in the same position. The government's response, through the military dominated Directorate, was to increase the frequency and rigour with which requisitioning parties searched peasant homes. Tension between the requisitioning authorities and the peasants, which had never been absent, therefore increased rapidly in the summer of 1918 and in so doing it weakened Malinov's position and strengthened the general public determination to finish with the War as soon as possible. Urban discontent at high prices and shortages and rural anger at the ruthlessness of the requisitioning teams intersected with the disaffection of the soldiers, thousands of whom were sent home on harvest leave. The soldiers had already heard loud complaints from their families at home, but during the summer of 1918 one of the most frequent complaints in letters to the front was, according to the censorship agency, that the military requisitioning units were taking not only food but also other commodities such as soap, wool and fuel, and though they paid for them they then sold them at huge profits on the black market. Frequently this was arranged with the connivance of local mayors and other officials and thus were the military and the civilian arms of the state simultaneously discredited. Though they had been forewarned of the hardships at home these warnings had not prepared many soldiers for the grim reality which they were to witness. The civilians at the same time were appalled at the state of the army for the soldiers were themselves little or any better off. They were short of food, and their bread, like that in the cities, was made of foul-tasting substitutes, but worst of all in the summer of 1918 was their lack of clothing and footwear with many soldiers going barefoot for months. The overall impression was of an army deprived of its elementary needs by an incorrigibly corrupt political system, a system which operated to the detriment of the people no matter what political faction was in power or what grave emergency faced the nation. This, added to the fear raised by the treaty of Bucharest that Bulgaria was fighting not for its own national objectives but for those of Germany, destroyed the morale of the whole nation, and its frustration was seen above all in the many links between the soldiers and the non-establishment Parties, particularly the Agrarians. Committees were formed at the front with Agrarians and Socialists of both factions playing a predominant part. Stamboliiski and Genadiev conferred with soldiers and party supporters, and commander after commander reported desertions and huge meetings of soldiers in which the War was denounced and the demand for fundamental political change was voiced. At home there were protests at the lack of food and the continuing export of precious stocks to central Europe, and on the fifteenth anniversary of Ilinden in August there were massive demonstrations in Sofia against the central powers. Malinov made desperate attempts to reassure the population, having posters put up in every community promising the people that no food was leaving the country and that no territory would be ceded to Turkey, a reference to the continuing discussion of the Porte's claim for Thrace to the line of the Mesta. At the front the agitators whom Malinov had sent to rally the troops were shouted down and derided. The nation was on the verge of collapse.

Final collapse was precipitated by a massive attack launched by the Entente forces in Macedonia. On 15 September a huge artillery barrage began pounding Bulgarian positions at Dobro Pole and within thirty-six hours the front had been penetrated. Bulgarian troops retreated, suffering grievously from air attacks when they became jammed in the narrow mountain passes and defiles of eastern Macedonia, and by 25 September French and British soldiers had entered Bulgaria proper. Discontent and disorder had mounted in equal measure as the Bulgarians withdrew and on 24 September enraged troops had attacked Bulgarian GHQ at Kiustendil. The High Command reported that the army was disintegrating; desertions were too numerous to count, discipline had evaporated and those soldiers who remained with their units were more interested in seizing Sofia and punishing those responsible for the War than in keeping the British and French at bay. A Crown Council decided on an immediate armistice. A delegation headed by Liapchev, and including the U.S. consul in Sofia, was despatched to parley with the enemy. On 28 September the delegation finally reached Salonika where an armistice was signed on the following day.

Whilst the armistice was being sought there were rapid political developments in Bulgaria itself. On 25 September Malinov had released Stamboliiski from prison in the hope that he might now agree to take part in a new and broad coalition to calm the nation and begin peace talks. Malinov clearly did not realise the gravity of the military situation and Stamboliiski contemptuously brushed aside his plan to negotiate; Bulgaria, he said, must sue for peace and take what terms the enemy would offer. In the afternoon Stamboliiski said much the same to the King. Ferdinand then asked Stamboliiski to do all he could to restore order in the army and this the Agrarian leader agreed to do on condition that the King accept the need for an immediate peace and that all political prisoners be released. On the latter issue there was some bargaining but Ferdinand accepted the need for an immediate peace. The Liapchev mission then set out for Salonika and Stamboliiski made his way towards Kiustendil.

What happened in the next few days is still to some extent obscure. Having spoken to soldiers at Radomir, half way between Sofia and Kiustendil, Stamboliiski continued his journey to Staff Headquarters where he arrived at noon on 27 September. As he was about to speak to soldiers at the railway station he received a telegram from his Agrarian colleague, Daskalov, who had returned to Radomir. Daskalov informed him that there were sufficient troops and transport at Radomir to make a rapid expedition to Sofia and seize control of the government. Stamboliiski's precise reply is not known but although he gave consent 'it seems clear that it was neither enthusiastic nor unconditional. It was, perhaps, an instruction to do no more than test the waters.'[4] Daskalov, however, proceeded to declare a republic under Stamboliiski's presidency and, having nominated himself Commander in Chief, issued an ultimatum to the government in Sofia threatening to march on the city the following day if power were not handed to him. Daskalov underestimated his opponents. In the hours before his arrival in the outskirts of Sofia on the afternoon of 29 September the government had rallied a number of loyal troops, including some Macedonians, who were greatly strengthened by units of the German 217th Division rushed in from the Crimea. When Daskalov launched his attack on the afternoon of 30 September it was repulsed and he himself wounded, though he managed to escape into hiding. Stamboliiski, meanwhile, had not associated himself publicly with the republic, and in addressing troop-meetings had continued to present himself as leader of BANU and nothing else, whilst on returning to Sofia he declared that he had no connection with the republic arguing also that what Daskalov had done had been forced on him by the mutinous

soldiery. The Cabinet declined to believe this and issued an order for
the arrest of Stamboliiski. At this point the Agrarian leader began to
work for a revolution and suggested a combined assault on the established system by the Agrarians and the Narrows. Georgi Dimitrov, the
leader of the Narrows in Sofia, refused. He did not wish to cooperate
with what he considered a petit bourgeois party at a point when, he was
convinced, a full-scale socialist revolution was imminent. Without
allies Stamboliiski followed Daskalov into hiding.

Though the Radomir rebellion had been defeated Malinov's government was in a parlous condition. The armistice had been signed in
Salonika on 29/30 September and this had caused the army to melt
away. Thereafter the Macedonian and German forces had retaken
Radomir and crushed the rebellion, for which the British and French
were heartily grateful. Yet no-one knew what conditions the victorious
powers would impose. The first of these, when known, caused no
discontent for the French and British announced that though they were
prepared to see the Coburg dynasty remain in Bulgaria they would not
accept its present representative. On 3 October Ferdinand therefore
abdicated leaving his son to succeed him as Boris III. The nation had
still to be rallied, however, and on 18 October Malinov formed a new
coalition including members of the Nationalist, Broad Socialist and
Agrarian Parties as well as of the existing coalition partners, the
Democrats and Radicals. Malinov himself did not remain long. He
was reluctant to implement the amnesty for political prisoners which he
had promised and he finally felt his position irrevocably compromised
when the Dobrudja was handed over to the Rumanians by the victors.
In November Todor Todorov, the deputy leader of the Nationalist
Party, formed a new Cabinet with representation from the Nationalists, Democrats, Broad Socialists and the Agrarians. A cabinet post
was reserved for Stamboliiski and this he took up after an amnesty had
been enacted for him.

The coalition governments of Malinov and Todorov showed a
genuine intent to bring the nation together but the wounds which the
War had inflicted were not to be easily healed. Discontent remained
and indeed grew more intense for food remained short and the country
was apprehensive as to what punishment the victors would exact.
Under these conditions governments dominated by the old Parties
could expect little support and in the election of August 1919 the mass
Parties, the Agrarians, the Narrows (now the Bulgarian Communist
Party), and the Broad Socialists polled 59% of the total vote and

secured 168 or 72.1% of the seats; the Democrats secured a further 10% of the vote and 26 seats.

The country was not yet free from the consequences of their former leaders' actions. In November 1919 at Neuilly-sur-Seine Bulgaria signed the terms of peace dictated by the victorious powers. The southern Dobrudja was returned to Rumania, the frontier of 1 August 1914 being restored. In the west Bulgaria lost to the Serbian-Croatian-Slovene Kingdom four small but strategically valuable salients whilst to the south she had to relinquish the whole of Bulgarian Thrace to Greece. Thereby Bulgaria lost its outlet to the Mediterranean and although the victorious powers undertook 'to ensure the economic outlets of Bulgaria to the Aegean Sea', those outlets were never regained. In addition to losses of territory Bulgaria had to suffer limitations upon her armed forces which were to be limited to 20,000 men, all of them volunteers, and the country was not to have an air force. There were also reparations. Bulgaria, the victors realised, could not pay for all the damage which, they said, she had caused, but nevertheless the country was saddled with the huge reparations debt of 2,250 million gold francs. In addition to this the Bulgarians were to return to the Serbs, Greeks and Rumanians any articles which could be proved to have been removed during the Bulgarian occupation; Bulgaria was also to hand over to the former occupied lands specified numbers of livestock, including 125 bulls, 13,500 milch cows and 33,000 sheep. Also for the next five years an annual payment of 50,000 tons of Pernik coal was to be made to the Serbs if the Inter Allied Commission which was to be established to supervise the application of the treaty was 'satisfied that such deliveries of coal will not unduly interfere with the economic life of Bulgaria'.[5]

San Stefano Bulgaria created just over forty years earlier seemed finally to have been destroyed. The Bulgarians would, it seemed, have to learn to live with different and less grandiose national aspirations, just as they would have to live with a changing internal political system. Yet both the old national dreams and the political system which had nurtured them were to prove far more resilient than any reasonable observer would have thought possible in 1919.

Chapter 24

THE SOCIAL AND ECONOMIC
IMPACT OF THE WARS

The official figures for casualties suffered by the Bulgarian army in the Wars were 53,825 for the period 1912–13, and 101,224 dead and 144,026 wounded for the years 1915–18. Sixty percent of the fatalities in the Balkan Wars were the result of disease rather than enemy action. Here the chief agent was cholera which had first appeared in front of the Tchatalja lines in the winter of 1912–13. From there it was spread by prisoners of war and soldiers returning on leave. The worst hit areas were Vidin, Vratsa and Pleven because regiments recruited there had borne the brunt of the cholera outbreaks. These were also the areas into which the Rumanians advanced in 1913 and prisoners of war returning from Rumania at the end of the Second Balkan War reintroduced the disease. In 1913 there were 19,525 recorded cases of cholera in Bulgaria of which 9,342 were fatal.

Despite the military casualties and the cholera epidemic of 1913 the population of Bulgaria showed an overall growth in the period of the Wars. Censuses were taken in 1910 and again in 1920 and they revealed an increase from 4,337,513 to 4,846,971, though the figures show an overall decline of 67,611 for the years 1916 to 1918. In the ten year period the growth rate was 1.18% per annum, a somewhat lower figure than the 1.58% per annum recorded for the previous decade. Mortality rates showed a predictable increase during the war years but as the figures below indicate it was in the final year of the War that the worst suffering occurred. It must be noted however that military deaths were very difficult to register and many of them were not included in the

473

Table 1.   Mortality rates, 1911–19

Average 1906–10 – 23.8 per thousand of population.

1911 – 21.5	1916 – 20.8
1912 – 20.7	1917 – 21.2
1913 – 29.00	1918 – 32.0
1914 – 20.7	1919 – 20.2
1915 – 19.9	

records until the end of the fighting, a fact which helps to explain the higher figures for 1913 and 1918.

The War left a large number of widows in Bulgaria. In 1910 there had been 128,185 widows but by 1920 there were 208,641, an increase of 62.77%, and whereas in 1910 there had been 6.02 widows per thousand of population ten years later there were 8.59 per thousand.

The impact of the War was to change the balance of population between male and female. For the first time in 1912 the increase in the number of women in Bulgaria was greater than the increase in the number of men. This was repeated in 1915 and 1916 and by 1920 there were 295,359 more women in the country than in 1910 but only 214,099 more men. Only in the years 1905 to 1910 had the overall growth in the female population been greater than the overall growth in the male, a fact which at that time could be attributed to emigration. The reversal of the balance of the population was most noticeable in the military-age range of 20 to 50 years.

The mobilisation of a large proportion of the young male population and the consequent disruption of family life led to a decline in the birth-rate, a fact best illustrated by the statistics for the number of children under five and between five and ten years of age. In 1910 there had been per thousand of the population 143 children under five and 134 between five and ten; in 1920 there were 102 and 127 per thousand respectively. More details are given in Table 2.

The traditions of Bulgarian family life, based upon the domination of the male, were not entirely destroyed by the War but they were eroded far more by the Wars than by any previous experience, and the large number of widows plus the conspicuous gap in the ranks of the men aged over twenty were additional problems to which post-war society had to adjust.

Table 2.   Number of births per thousand of population.

Average 1906 to 1912 – 41.4

1912 – 42.01	1916 – 21.43
1913 – 25.86	1917 – 17.29
1914 – 45.37	1918 – 21.28
1915 – 40.46	1919 – 32.95

The religious and ethnic composition of the Bulgarian population was also affected by the Wars. Between 1910 and 1920 the number of Moslems in the country rose from 602,000 to 690,000, increasing as a proportion of the total population from 13.88% to 14.25%. Most of the new Moslem residents in Bulgaria were Pomaks who had been incorporated into the country after the Balkan Wars. This is underlined by the fact that though the proportion of Moslems rose the percentage of Turkish-speakers in Bulgaria fell from 11.63% in 1910 to 11.20% in 1920. The decline in Turkish-speakers had been helped by the emigration of a number of Turks after the Balkan Wars. There had also been further Greek emigration. After the Second Balkan War some 11,000 Greeks left Bulgaria for those parts of Macedonia which Greece had acquired, and after the First World War more were to follow. By 1920 Greeks were only 0.97% of the total population compared to 1.17% in 1910. At the same time the Rumanians who had been 2.22% of the total population in 1910 declined to 1.55% in 1920. Again emigration played some part in this development but the major cause of the fall in the number of Rumanians in Bulgaria was the transfer of the southern Dobrudja to Rumania. Whilst Turks, Greeks and Rumanians left many Bulgarians came into the country from surrounding areas, above all from those parts of Thrace and Macedonia which were lost in 1913 and 1918, from the Dobrudja and from the areas ceded to Serbia after the First World War. An estimated 40,000 refugees, almost all of them Bulgarian, had entered the country after the Second Balkan War and a further 60,000 came in the years 1918–20. By the mid-1920s a total of 200,000 Bulgarian refugees had arrived, many of them indigent and requiring public support. A further problem for the post-war administrations of Bulgaria was the large number of Russian refugees who arrived in the country, many of them still armed after the Civil War. By

1925 they numbered 30,000, increasing the Russian element in the population from the 0.06% of 1910 to 0.19%.

* * *

The Balkan Wars did not greatly affect Bulgarian agriculture. The War of 1912 had not begun until after the harvest and little of the fighting, even in the politically calamitous Second Balkan War, had taken place on Bulgarian soil. The ample harvest of 1912 had meant that the army and the civilian population could be provisioned without difficulty. The men however remained longer with the colours than had been anticipated and local village authorities, being unused to war, did nothing to organise collective sowing in the spring of 1913; the military authorities did try to initiate an emergency leave system to allow men to get back to their land for sowing but it came too late and was too limited in scope to prevent a decrease both in the area sown and in the index of agricultural production. In 1912 25.6 million dekars had been sown with cereals but in 1913 the area sown was 22.3 million dekars; the index of production, taking the average for the years 1908 to 1912 as 100, was 99 in 1913. Recovery was rapid. The area sown with cereals in 1914 was 23.5 million dekars and the index of production rose to 104.

Industry, too, suffered little from the Balkan Wars. A conference of the Chambers of Commerce in September 1913 stressed that the Wars had interrupted rather than reversed the favourable economic developments which had been apparent in Bulgaria before October 1912. The conference noted that the flour, textile, brewing, and distilling industries which accounted for 80% of the nation's industrial output had continued to work and, it was argued, had even profited from mobilisation in that it had forced some plants to work more productively.

Trade too recovered rapidly from the disruption of the Balkan Wars. Exports in 1911 had earned 184.6 million leva but in 1912 receipts were down to 156.4 million leva and for 1913 the figure was 93.3 million leva. Yet by the autumn of that year trade was reviving as Table 3 makes clear.

The Wars of 1912 and 1913 inevitably caused some strain. Earnings from trade were down and with so many men with the colours tax collection was to some degree dislocated. At the same time the costs of the campaign, together with incidental items such as requisition pay-

Table 3.   Trade, in million of leva.

Year	Imports	Exports
1911	199.3	184.6
1912	213.1	156.4
1913	189.2	93.3
1914	241.4	154.4

ments and a subsidy of two million gold leva to Montenegro, had to be met.

The government's first response was to borrow heavily from the National Bank which was thus stripped of its accumulated reserves; borrowing from the BNB was not previously a prominent government activity and the total government debt to the National Bank late in August 1912 had been a mere 0.129 million leva. By the end of the year it had risen to 26.6 million leva, and in September 1913 it stood at 157 million leva. Such a rapid increase in government borrowing meant a steep rise in the money supply. At the end of 1911 there were 95 million levas worth of notes in circulation, backed by precious metal deposits of 67.8 million leva; at the end of 1913 there were notes worth 209.7 million leva and deposits of 78.8 million levas worth of gold and silver. In the summer of 1914 the Sŭbranie enacted a law allowing available foreign currency loans to be added to the gold and silver reserves in the calculation of the fiduciary backing and this saved the nation from a crisis of confidence in its money. At the same time the government was empowered to raise an extraordinary credit of 150 million leva to put against the cost of the recent Wars—and more specifically to pay for requisitions—and 90 million leva of this was to come from an internal government loan issued at 8%, this being a new departure for Bulgaria where loans had previously been raised abroad.

It was the financial pressure of the Balkan Wars which had forced the Radoslavov administration in 1914 to propose the increases in indirect taxation which caused so much anger in the Sŭbranie. It was not only from internal borrowings and increases in taxation, however, that the government financed the Balkan Wars. A country which since 1900 had had increasing recourse to the international money market was not slow to seek loans to cover this sudden increase in expenditure. In 1913 three loans were concluded. The largest, for 75 million leva, was with the Banque de Paris et des Pays Bas. This sum was to meet obligations to foreign creditors, replacing the money issued in Treasury bonds by the requisitioning parties. The other loans were smaller and were to cover general costs. They came from a consortium of Austro-Hungarian banks which lent thirty million leva and from the Russian-Asiatic Bank in St. Petersburg which provided 27.72 million roubles.

These however were patching operations and only the agreement with the Discontogesellschaft for the large loan of 1914 brought financial consolidation.

*   *   *

The economic and social effects of the First World War were much more keenly felt even if in the long run they were not profound. The costs of the European War were of a dimension previously unimagined in Bulgaria, as in other belligerent states. Taxes were increased to meet rising costs, though the government refused to bow to opposition pressure for a progressive income tax or a tax on war profits. Indirect taxes were therefore increased and in 1917 many of the extra duties the government had tried to introduce in 1914 and 1915 were imposed, including that on wine together with others on petrol, salt, beer, coffee, tea, lighting-oil, olive-oil, olives, imported rice, preserved fish, toilet soap, stearine candles, bicycles, motor-cars, cinema tickets, electricity and soft drinks. In 1912 indirect taxes had furnished 82.126 million leva but in 1918 they produced 220.43 million leva, though in these years money had lost some of its value and customs levies on a wide range of articles were useless as a source of revenue as trade in those articles had all but dried up. As soon as it entered the War Bulgaria suspended payment of its foreign debt obligations whilst further aid came from Germany in the form of monthly loans of fifty million levas. These did not receive the consent of the Sŭbranie and by the time Germany unilaterally suspended payment in November 1917 this unconstitutionally incurred debt amounted to 1,500 million leva. The government also borrowed increasingly from the Bulgarian National Bank, its debt to that institution rising from 146.69 million leva in 1914 to 919.48 million leva in 1919. Increased borrowing from the National Bank was convenient but in the long run inflationary. Figures for the notes in circulation and for the precious metal reserves are shown in Table 4.

Table 4.   Notes in circulation and precious metal reserves, 1912 to 1918.

Year	Notes in circulation, in million of leva	Precious metal reserves of BNB, in million of leva
1912	164.428	68.501
1913	188.742	78.751
1914	226,515	83.636
1915	369.829	84.637
1916	833.910	85.376
1917	1492.768	95.811
1918	2298.619	103.780
1919	2858.489	77.968
1920	3354.191	68.008

The increase in the number of notes in circulation did not until 1918 give rise to disastrous inflationary pressures. Until the end of 1917 the monthly German loans could be added to the precious metal reserves as backing for the paper leva and Bulgarian exports were earning large sums in central Europe, with tobacco sales rapidly increasing in value; and, until 1917, the harvests were good.

* * *

The First World War affected Bulgarian agriculture in three main ways: mobilisation and its consequent disruptions decreased production; the demand for industrial crops was stimulated; and the territorial changes at the end of the War confirmed the loss of the country's most advanced agrarian region.

In a low-technology and labour-intensive farming system extensive and prolonged mobilisation cannot but have a dislocating effect. Bulgaria's mobilisation was particularly extensive. In 1915 800,000 men or a quarter of the total adult-male population had been called to the colours; by 1917 the proportion was 31.8%, and in 1918, when 857,000 men were in the armed forces, it was 38.83%, the proportion of the total population formed by those mobilised being higher in Bulgaria than in any other belligerent state. The Bulgarians were even more unlucky in that the Macedonian front, because of its length, was enormously demanding of men. The burden of work in the fields therefore fell increasingly upon those left behind, primarily the womenfolk, though some attempts were made to lighten their burden by the use of prisoners of war, refugees, or soldiers on harvest leave, though the provision of the latter was not adequate to the needs of most families.

Mobilisation affected not only men but also animals and vehicles. The initial call up involved 100,000 horses, 140,000 draught animals and 120,000 carts, and in each subsequent year the army took up to 200,000 large draught animals. These animals could not be replaced at anything like the same rate, and the total number of beasts of burden in Bulgaria fell from 1,234,664 in 1912 to 993,132 in 1918, and whereas in 1912 there had been one pair of draught animals for every 0.581 hectacres of land, in 1917 there was one pair per 0.745 hectacres. By June 1918 the requisitioning authorities could report that horses and oxen had virtually disappeared from the countryside where the old and the infirm were often to be seen dragging their own carts. The number of farm vehicles fell equally drastically, from a total of 504,014 in 1912 to 387,112 in 1917. Once again the army did what it could to help and allowed peasants near army centres to use carts and animals when the military did not need them, but the nature of the terrain in which the armies were engaged worked against the farmer. In Macedonia there were no railways and carts were therefore in great and constant demand and in some sectors of the front there were virtually no roads so the only means of transport was the pack animal. What was worse from the point of view of the peasant was that the animals and vehicles taken for military service were usually the best, and thus mobilisation affected quality as well as quantity.

Mobilisation made it impossible to work all the land previously cultivated, though in 1917 and 1918 more efficient state direction of the economy did restore most of the old areas even if it could not prevent over a quarter of the so-called worked land being left fallow. The proportion of fallow land had risen as a reuslt of the Balkan Wars from 17% in 1912 to 18.4% in 1914. In 1915 it was 20%, 1916 22.4% and in 1917 it reached a peak of 29.2%, falling slightly to 27.4% in 1918. In 1917 a total of 1,267,139 dekars had been left fallow.

The increasing proportion of fallow land, the decline of the rural labour force and the shortage of draught animals meant lower productivity, the figures in table 5 showing the sharp fall towards the end of the War when yields per dekar contrasted very sadly with those of the last year of peace. Fodder crops suffered even more severely.

Table 5.   Yields per dekar for selected cereal crops in kilograms.

Year	Wheat	Rye	Barley	Maize
1911	117.5	103.5	107.5	123.0
1912	104.3	100.0	108.0	112.5
1916	83.6	73.2	94.2	83.2
1917	78.8	74.2	82.2	78.3
1918	64.1	57.3	66.8	36.8

Bulgaria was fortunate in that the climate was kind until 1917 when heavy spring rain ruined the sowing before droughts scorched a large proportion of the surviving crops. So little food was left that there was hardly enough seed for the next season and this together with the total demoralisation at the end of the war accounts for the exceptionally low productivity of 1918. It also explains the low production figures for those years as set out in table 6. Dairy produce faired somewhat better thanks to the intervention of the government and by 1917 cheese production was higher than in 1913. Meat production suffered but here statistics are difficult to obtain as the army took so many animals, including two million sheep and 150,000 pigs each year from 1915 to 1918. Despite the latter exaction pig numbers doubled from 527,000 in 1910 to 1.09 million a decade later, this being no doubt due to the ease with which pigs can be reared, to the large demand for pork and pork-fat created by the presence of Austrian and German soldiers, and to Bulgaria's close connection with the Austrian and German markets during the war. Pigs were, however, the only animals to increase in number and by 1917 home meat production could provide a mere 60,000 tons of the 160,000 tons which were needed to satisfy civilian and military demands.

A notable feature of agricultural development during the War was the increase in the area devoted to industrial crops, production of which declined much less than any other category of crop, as table 6 shows. The increase of industrial-crop acreage was at the cost of cereals which accounted for 26.6% of the land worked in 1912, 23.1% in 1913, 23% in 1914, 21.2% in 1915, 19.6% in 1916 and 1917, and 19.8% in 1918. In 1912 industrial crops had been cultivated on 37,002 hectacres or 0.9% of the total used land, but in the War the area and the percentage increased and the change was lasting. By 1922 industrial

Table 6.   Agricultural production, selected years, 1911–18, in
thousands of tons.

Year	Grain	Fodder	Root vegetables, including potatoes.	Green Vegetables	Industrial Crops
1911	2876	1328	75	71	95
1914	1941	1155	60	63	213
1915	2342	1202	65	84	95
1916	1804	1009	44	60	131
1917	1548	943	44	55	118
1918	1065	288	29	46	90

crops covered 51,376 hectacres or 1.4% of the total cultivated land.
Before the Wars the chief industrial crop had been rape-seed, most of
which had been exported forming 2.2% of the total value of Bulgaria's
exports. Tobacco, rose-oil, sugar-beet, and mulberry seeds were also
important industrial crops. By the end of the Wars tobacco had taken
an unassailable place at the top of the league for industrial crops. This
was in part due to the acquisition by Bulgaria of the tobacco growing
areas of Pirin Macedonia where the Eastern strain, more popular in
the export market, predominated, and in part also to the fact that
many of the refugees who came into Bulgaria from Macedonia continued to grow tobacco on their new land. Expansion was also the
result of government encouragement and the increased regulation of
the tobacco industry during the War, but most importantly it followed
from the virtual monopoly of the central European markets which
Bulgarian tobacco enjoyed during the war years. This meant soaring
prices and a hundred kilograms of tobacco which sold for 83.94 leva in
1911 would in 1917 bring in 1,264.60 leva, an increase far greater than
the rate of inflation. This fact above all others explains the growth of
the tobacco industry as set out in table 7.

   If the acquisition of Pirin Macedonia in 1913 was one factor stimu-
lating the cultivation of tobacco in Bulgaria the territorial changes at
the end of First World War had no beneficial effect. The renewed loss
of the Southern Dobrudja was a cruel blow. Though containing only
eight percent of the agricultural land and six percent of the farming
population, it produced 230 to 250 million kilograms of grain or
almost a fifth of the country's total production, of which local con-

Table 7.   The increase of tobacco cultivation, 1912–1918.

Year	Area growing tobacco in hectacres	Production in quarters	Value of crop in leva
1912	8,891	58,125	—
1915	14,240	98,775	—
1916	9,359	79,152	30,360,153
1917	17,931	112,681	198,914,855
1918	32,431	202,292	460,739,005

sumption accounted for only 130 to 150 kilograms. Much more importantly a disproportionately high percentage of the nation's larger farms
were in this area; in the Dobrudja there was one harvester for every
1,333 dekars whilst in the rest of Bulgaria there was one per 5,870
dekars, and the Dobrudja had one mechanised seeder per 1,186 dekars,
the rest of the country one per 47,030 dekars. The territories which
Bulgaria gained in 1913 on the other hand were sparsely populated and
extremely poor. Indeed some areas could not feed themselves and so
food had to be diverted from the export trade to supply the newly-
acquired areas.

*   *   *

Industry, like agriculture, suffered through mobilisation which,
initially at least, failed to discriminate between skilled and unskilled
workers. Some of the gaps so created were filled by women or even
children but they could not immediately acquire the skills of trained
workers. Even more damaging were the shortages of raw materials and
fuel.

The problem of raw materials was particularly pressing. All sea
routes to Bulgaria were closed by the Anglo-French blockade of the
Aegean and the Straits, whilst the Danube and the rail link to central
Europe were under the control of the allied military administrations
who were not always sympathetic to Bulgaria's needs. Many commodities, particularly those for which the allied purchasing agencies were
also searching, were held up in transit or simply denied a through
passage. This applied to wool, for example, and had not the govern-

ment taken steps to safeguard wool supplies and prevent their export
Bulgaria would have had to go without raw wool. The situation with
regard to cotton was even worse. Before the War most of Bulgaria's
cotton had been supplied by Britain but this was no longer available
and the cotton grown in Macedonia and Thrace was nearly all bought
by the Austrians and Germans. The textile industry in Bulgaria was
therefore in great danger during the War. The same was true of leather
processing. Here again Bulgaria and her allies were competing for the
meagre supply of raw hides and the ending of imports meant that the
Bulgarian army at one point had to face the prospect of going through
winter with skins and mocassins rather than leather boots. Another
crucial industry severely hit by the drying up of the flow of imports was
soapmaking which depended on foreign chemicals for 90% of its raw
materials. The problems created by the suspension of imports were
immediately felt for neither the government nor individual manufacturers had taken any measures to stockpile essential raw materials.
There was also a chronic shortage of fuel. British coal was no longer to
be had and what coal Bulgaria herself produced was nearly all swallowed up by the railways where intense military traffic had brought
about a large increase in fuel consumption. The problems of the shortages of raw materials and fuel were aggravated by a lack of transport
facilities. The railways were hard pressed to cope with military needs
and in any case most of the rail network was under miltary administration and its officials paid little heed to the needs of the non-military
producer. Few wagons or locomotives were available therefore to carry
raw materials and the products of civilian industry. Between September and December 1915 twenty-two industrial concerns in Bulgaria
collapsed and by the end of 1916 over half the enterprises under state
control had ceased production and of all factories only 60% were still
working, barely half of them full-time. The Varna Chamber of Commerce reported that of the 1,877 workshops in the province functioning
in 1914 1,116 had been forced to close during the first two years of the
War. In 1911 Bulgaria had had 15,886 factory workers but in 1917
there were 14,152, of whom 5,336 were prisoners of war.

In early 1915 the prospects for Bulgarian trade seemed very bright.
As Table 3 has shown the Balkan Wars did not seriously disrupt Bulgaria's foreign trade, and the 1915 harvest promised well with world
demand for wheat buoyant, and in addition the War in Europe made it
possible for Bulgaria to sell products it had not previously exported in
any quantity. The country had responded well to this opportunity. A

newly-formed cartel purchased vegetables throughout Bulgaria and arranged for their export to central Europe, and merchants were organising the sale in the same markets of other products now in great demand, including cheese, pork-fat and eggs. These prospects were ruined by Bulgaria's entry into the War. In the first place Serbian military strength threatened the rail-link to central Europe and the western allies would not tolerate trade with Germany and Austria via the Mediterranean. The articles of war had already restricted Bulgaria's foreign trade opportunities in 1914—established markets in Egypt, for example, were lost—but after September 1915 Bulgaria could trade only with its allies, Switzerland and to a lesser extent Holland. By 1918 half of Bulgaria's external trade was with Switzerland. Meanwhile trade with Turkey, traditionally Bulgaria's chief trading partner, had declined from 12.45% of the total in 1915 to 2.63% in 1918.

The volume of trade fell sharply. Imports which had totalled up to 600 million tons in pre-war years were only 96,000 tons in 1916, and exports fell from over a million tons in the best pre-war years to 75,000 tons in 1916. The value of trade increased but only because of price-inflation, the figures being given in table 8.

The balance of trade was not, however, an important consideration during the War and indeed for much of the time it was the government's preoccupation to maximise the import of essential commodities and to minimise the export of certain goods, especially food, leather, wool, etc. Government control and the gradual diminution of supply did mean that legal and reported food exports declined very sharply during the War. In 1916 13 million bushels of wheat had been exported but in 1918 the figure was only 0.14 million bushels; live cattle exports fluctuated wildly but in the end reflected the shortage of animals in the country; in 1916 Bulgaria exported 8,000 head of live cattle, in 1917 15,000 head and in 1918 only 51 head.

The most significant change in trade during the War, as in agricultural production, was the rapid rise in the importance of tobacco which in 1917 accounted for 70% of the total value of Bulgarian exports; in 1909 it had been 9.9% of the total value. In 1917 the value of tobacco exports was 40 million leva greater than the total import bill, and in the following year tobacco earned 333 million leva whilst all other exports brought in a combined total of 80 million leva. In the foreign exchanges the value of the leva during the war, until the very last months, was kept stable by the tobacco crop. The appearance of an

Table 8.   The value of Bulgaria's foreign trade, 1912–18, in millions of leva.

Year	Imports	Exports	Balance of trade
1912	213.1	156.4	−56.7
1913	189.0	93.0	−96.0
1914	241.5	214.5	−27.0
1915	73.5	109.4	+35.9
1916	89.4	95.7	+6.3
1917	168.7	288.9	+120.2
1918	567.2	415.5	−151.7

alternative export commodity was a healthy development and the nation benefited from the fact that wheat, which in 1912 had accounted for 61.2% of the value of all exports, earned only 33.7% of the total in 1922; in 1922 tobacco, which because of the return to peace-time trading conditions did not have the singular importance of 1917 and 1918, earned 27% of the total export income.

The increasing role played by tobacco was the most important change which the Wars inflicted upon Bulgaria's foreign trade, but there were others. The emergencies of the War taught the Bulgarians to rely far more upon home-produced sugar-beet and sugar declined as an import. At the same time the suspension of foreign fuel supplies encouraged greater use of home-produced commodities such as rapeseed oil which before the Wars had been exported in considerable quantities but which after 1918 was consumed almost entirely by Bulgarian manufacturers.

* * *

The government's continued borrowing from the Bulgarian National Bank, particularly after the suspension of the German loans in November 1917, produced inflation. The cost of a number of necessities indexed at 100 in 1914 rose to 122 in late 1915, 200 in 1916 and 505 early in 1918; by July of that year with a disastrous harvest adding greatly to inflationary pressures, the index stood at 847.

The fall in the value of money, together with a decline in the availability of goods to buy, meant that a number of peasant households had cash surpluses. This enabled them to pay off their debts to money-lenders and the banks. Bank deposits rose considerably in the War, those in the Bulgarian National Bank increasing from 42 million leva in 1914 to 85 million leva in 1917, those for the Bulgarian Agricultural Bank from 8.9 million leva to 14.1 million leva in the same period. The most dramatic increase was for the Central Cooperative Bank whose deposits rose from 8.4 million leva in 1914 to 79.9 million leva in 1917, another clear indication of the peasants' trust in the cooperative movement.

Some private banks used these funds to make considerable profits through currency speculation. Since December 1915 German and Austrian notes had been allowed to circulate in Bulgaria but despite their initial strength by 1917 their value had fallen below the official exchange rates and banks therefore bought marks for 1.24 leva in Bulgaria and sold them in Germany or Switzerland at the official rate of 1.25 leva per mark. A good deal of the money invested in private banks found its way into the rash of new joint stock companies which were established during the War. In 1913 five new companies had been set up with an initial capital of 4.5 million leva; in 1918 there were fifty-nine new companies with an initial capital of 156.7 million leva, and the total number of companies founded during the years 1913–18 was 155 with a total initial capital of 620.825 million leva.

For the peasants and others the benefit of being able to discharge debts with inflated currency was considerable but was frequently more than offset by the other social consequences of the War. The constant anxiety of war time, the agonies of bereavement or incapacitating wounds are beyond calculation or description but the increasingly oppressive shortages of essential commodities can be assessed.

Throughout the First World War in Bulgaria clothing was extremely difficult to procure. This was in part the result of the Balkan Wars. A number of soldiers had taken their own winter clothing with them in 1912 and these had usually been ruined, in most cases by lice. After the Balkan Wars civilian demand was therefore high but at the same time the army was engaged in an extensive reclothing exercise which had not been completed by September 1915 after which date military purchases were given priority and clothes all but disappeared from the shops. The *ersatz* German cloth which appeared later in the War was rejected as inadequate. A survey carried out amongst school teachers in Sofia from 1916 to 1917 showed that a quarter of them did not have adequate clothing. Footwear was equally scarce and civilian supplies, before the introduction of clogs, were ten to twenty times less than the demand. Soap was another scarce commodity. So, too, was cement all of which was taken for military needs, a fact which made for great difficulties after a moderately severe earthquake in parts of Bulgaria in 1917.

The most constantly oppressive shortages however were those of food. Here even the peasants, though generally better off for staple foods, suffered with everyone else from the scarcity of salt and from the requisitioning of meat, eggs and dairy produce. In the towns there was no escaping the wartime bread made not from wheat alone but from a mixture of wheat and maize so offensive to the taste and so injurious to the digestive system that it was responsible for a number of civilian deaths. The worst crisis came in 1918 when rations even of the mixed wheat and maize bread were insufficient.

In the towns the problem was much worse than in the country for few townsmen, at least in the larger communities, could produce for themselves. When Bulgaria entered the War the price of food rocketed, particularly for those items, mostly luxuries, not subject to state regulation; thus a turkey which had cost 2.50 leva early in 1915 would fetch 12 leva by the end of the year. Government controls and rationing prevented total chaos but it could not prevent continuing price rises and shortages. The increase in the general cost of living index calculated on essential commodities has already been quoted but in some commodities the increases were more dramatic. Using the 1908–12 average annual cost as a base of 100 the price index for butter in 1918 was 1,159, and for chicken, 1,202. These prices were official ones and on the black market, frequently the only source of supply, they were much higher. The official price of pig-fat in 1918 was 485% higher than that of 1914, but the unofficial price was 956% higher; in the same years the official price of sugar had risen by 125% yet the black market price was 1,250% higher, and for soap the figures were 650% and 1,350%. The rise in wages and salaries could not keep pace; the average wage increase was only 450% with that for the professional classes being considerably below this figure.

As living conditions deteriorated a series of welfare organisations attempted to provide relief, both for civilians and soldiers. Government officials established a Fund for Aid to Soldiers which was supplied with private and institutional rather than government funds. By the end of the War some 18,000 people had given unpaid assistance and there were 2,427 local committees for dispensing aid to soldiers and their dependents. Of these committees 412 were in Macedonia, four in the Morava, and one each in Bucharest, Budapest. Adrianople, Constantinople, Berlin, Vienna and Smyrna.

The Fund for Aid to Soldiers was a semi-official organisation and its work was supplemented by a number of private charities. *Voinishki Semeistva* (Soldiers' Families) was a private organisation formed originally on the initiative of the Minister of the Interior, and the supplement to official benefits which it was able to give was increasingly important as inflation devalued official payments. By October 1917 *Voinishki Semeistva* had collected and distributed 232,891 leva as well as large quantities of second-hand clothing. Bulgaria's womenfolk, particularly those of the intelligentsia, set up twelve different charitable and welfare organisations without which the nation's plight would have been much worse, especially in the second half of the War. They too organised the collection and distribution of rare commodities such as clothing, soap, paraffin, sugar and shoes, which were given to the soldiers, the poor, the sick and the children. Other women's organisations opened communal kitchens and workshops where poor women and wounded soldiers made articles such as gas masks and, if the raw materials could be procured, clothes. There were also employment exchanges to help women find work and other organisations helped to identify those in need. All these organisations were run by unpaid, volunteer women.

Private charities could only act as a supplement to official efforts to cushion the populace against the effects of the War.

During the Balkan Wars reserve officers serving with the colours had been paid a full regular officer's stipend; civil servants in the army had received a third of their normal peacetime wage but all those employed by private companies as well as the mass of the enlisted peasantry were given nothing at all. This caused resentment but a bill put before the Sŭbranie by the Socialists demanding that all mobilised men be paid sixty leva month was rejected. The government was also reluctant to act during the First World War but eventually a bill, again proposed by the Socialists, was enacted in March 1917. Mobilised employees in private companies were to retain their jobs if they had been with the company for fifteen days, and as long as the company continued to function they were to be paid half their regular wage, though this did not apply to very small trading companies and there was a maximum aggregate sum which could be paid to any one individual. There were also restrictions on the total amount a soldier's family might receive from this and other benefit schemes.

The principal official benefit scheme was state payment to the families of enlisted men. In the Balkan Wars there had been no provision for the families of conscripted soldiers and the relatives of the dead and severely wounded seldom received compensation or assistance. Again considerable resentment was caused, the more so when bills to provide protection for the families of enlisted men failed to pass through the Sŭbranie. In September 1915 however clauses of these bills were put together in a series of decrees which were enacted by the next Sŭbranie as the Act for the Provision of Assistance to the Needy Families of Enlisted Soldiers. A new centrally controlled fund was to be established to provide assistance to all dependents of enlisted men up to and including grandchildren and grandparents. The usual rate of payment was 20 stotinki per capita per week with a set maximum for each family which was adjusted later to take account of inflation. The families of the killed and wounded were to be paid until they began to receive war-widows' pensions, and in all cases welfare payment was to continue until one month after demobilisation. The only families excluded from the scheme were those of deserters. The local administration of the fund was to be the responsibility of the town or village Committee for Aid to Soldiers' Families which was to consist of the local mayor, tax-collector and at least one priest together with three members elected from the community itself. They were obliged to care for all poor families in their district. In larger towns each urban district was to have a separate committee. All local committees were to be responsible to a Central Committee in Sofia, which was to consist of eight Sŭbranie members from various parties, and all committee members, at whatever level, were to be unpaid, this being an attempt to prevent the intrusion of *partisanstvo*. In 1916 the allowance given to those with some agricultural income, in cash or kind, was decreased and everyone over sixteen, male and female, was obliged to find work rather than subsist on the benefit payment. The intention was to focus these benefits on the most needy in the towns. The committees paid out some 215 million leva between September 1915 and September 1918 and continued to function after the end of the War, providing aid to approximately 170,000 families in any given month. The sums received were not large but for many living in the towns they were essential for survival.

The expansion of welfare activity by the government was only one example of the extension of state and official control during the war. That control was gradually extended into all branches of the economy.

Control was clearly needed for mobilisation in September 1915 precipitated a chaos which was to last until the summer of 1916. From that summer until the following spring governmental economic supervision was exercised through the Central Committee for Economic and Social Welfare, but this body's inadequacies led to its being superseded in the spring of 1917 by the Directorate for Economic and Social Welfare. The Directorate did have some initial success in repairing the economy but from early 1918, despite the intensification of central control, the economy entered upon an accelerating decline leading, after the disastrous harvest of 1918, to the almost total collapse which did so much to undermine the war effort. The government's attempts to maximise production and maintain essential supplies had been frustrated by the conflicting claims and overlapping jurisdictions of the civilian and military authorities, by the activities of Bulgaria's allies and their soldiers, and by the harvest of 1918.

In 1914 the government had given way to opposition pressure and enacted a bill giving local authorities the right during times of crisis to regulate wages, rents and the prices of essential goods, but the bill was permissive rather than mandatory and few local authorities could carry out such tasks, nor had they been given powers to enforce any decision they might take.

The first serious intervention of the state into the economic sector came in March 1915. Even by then, six months before Bulgaria entered the War, German and Austrian purchasers had been so efficient that there were fears in Bulgaria that the country would soon be stripped of food. Radoslavov's government therefore passed the Public Welfare Act which gave the central government rather than the local authorities the right to take extensive powers to control the price and distribution of food and to ban the export of wheat, flour, fodder and other essential comodities in the event of mobilisation, war or natural disaster. The Public Welfare Act also established the Central Committee for Public Welfare. The Central Committee was to consist of fourteen members, five deputies from the government parties in the Sŭbranie, the Director of the Statistical Bureau, the heads of the three state banks, representatives of the Bulgarian Economic Society, of the millers, and of the local authorities, together with the general secretaries of the Ministries of Trade and Agriculture. The Central Committee was divided into four sections; those for setting price maxima on necessities, for purchasing produce, for requisitioning, and for administration. There were to be local committees at provincial and district level which were to operate under the authority of and were to be responsible solely to the Central Committee. The local Committees were to be headed by the mayor and, where appropriate, the prefect, and were to consist of local bankers, merchants, teachers and other representatives of the local intelligentsia.

The tasks of the new organisation were to find out how much grain and other foodstuffs were available in each area and then to arrange the distribution of these from areas of surplus to areas of need. Each local committee, having assessed demand and supply in its area, was to fix price maxima for commodities such as flour, meat, olive-oil, petrol, butter and sugar. These were impossible tasks. In the spring of 1915 the country was in a tense state, with many people expecting a Serbian invasion, and with trade and communications being affected by the fighting in neighbouring lands. People in such a frame of mind do not cooperate easily with operations of the complexity planned for the local Public Welfare Committees, and the peasant was concerned more to preserve his own supplies than to arrange for their distribution to those in need. For the first, but by no means the last time the authorities were confronted with the problem of hoarding. Furthermore the local Committees had no experience of the tasks which they were set, tasks which called for some sophistication in book-keeping as well as diplomacy in dealing with local peasants. Worst of all the new Committees had no real power to enforce their decisions. They therefore achieved little and when it became clear that the harvest for 1915 was likely to be good pressure grew for the disbandment of the incipient mechanisms for economic control. In June a conference of the Bulgarian Economic Society which included representatives of the banks, the grain merchants and the Chambers of Commerce, argued for the return to a free market in grain and the suspension of the Committees. The government agreed. In August free trading was restored and the Central Committee wound up, though the local ones remained.

A month later Bulgaria entered the War. There were immediate steps to reimpose the Public Welfare Act of March 1915. The Central Committee was reconstituted but from November consisted of only nine members, five government deputies, and four senior civil servants. It was now divided into seven sections for dealing with cereals; heating and lighting; dairy produce, animal fats and vegetable-oils; clothes and shoes; sugar; rice, salt and vegetables; and administration. The primary objective was to collect as much grain as possible but here the Committee immediately encountered an insuperable obstacle. At the same time that the Central Committee had been reconstituted the government had also set up a General Commission for Requisitions. This body, together with the military requisitioning authorities and requisitioning departments in a number of ministries, was to take control of securing supplies for the army. Such a system proved unworkable and a little later the Central Committee was made responsible for supplying the army with flour, wheat, sugar, salt, petrol, tobacco and cigarette papers, although in areas under Bulgarian military occupation the High Command was to take control of requisitioning. Once again results did not come up to expectations and in January 1916 division was reintroduced with the Ministry of War taking over the supply of the army and the Central Committee being made responsible for providing civilians with food, fuel and industrial raw materials. This was not a rational division. Military measures, for example the movement of large numbers of troops into or out of an area, could drastically alter the food requirements or the provisioning capability of that area, and yet such steps were taken without the Central or local Public Welfare Committees being warned.

The Central Committee was able to take some steps to control exports. Exports of maize, except by special licence, were prohibited in November and by the end of the year similar restrictions were in operation with regard to cheese, eggs, pork-fat, vegetables, wines, straw, flour, and cereals. The Committee did little, however, to regulate the internal market. Everyone, producer or trader, was required to register his stock of all essential commodities but the Committees could do little to force that stock onto the market for few merchants were willing to sell when they knew that prices would soon be rising. Furthermore, the local Committees were required to fix prices according to local conditions. The latter naturally varied and the variation in prices from one region to another inevitably led to illegal trading and black-marketeering. Illicit trading was also encouraged by the willingness of the omnipresent allied purchasing agents to buy from speculators and black marketeers. The local Committees simply did not have the resources of time, personnel or money to cope with such problems.

At the national level the Central Committee had little success in its efforts to buy up quantities of those imports in desperately short supply. It was able to preserve some supplies of sugar by banning its use in soft-drinks and other non-essential products, but it could not buy sugar abroad. Petrol, too, proved virtually unobtainable even though the border with Rumania remained open but here, as in the case of salt, the chief culprit was not the Committee's weakness but the power and efficiency of the German and Austrian military procurement agencies which were competing for the meagre stocks of these commodities available on the European market.

The failings of the Committees were many and obvious. In the spring of 1916 the government was forced to create new bodies, special commissions of representatives from the Central Committee, the Home Command and the military requisitioning authorities, to ensure that parts of the country could be fed. Under such conditions the Sŭbranie had little difficulty in pressing for a reorganisation of the state's apparatus for controlling the economy. Also because the original Committees had been filled with the supporters of Radoslavov—*partisanstvo* had not been a casualty of the War—the new organisation was much less a creature of the executive and more open to the influence of the legislature than the 1915 system.

The reorganisation of 1916 was enshrined in the Social Welfare Act passed on 26 August. The act set up a new Central Committee, the Central Committee for Economic and Social Welfare. That the new Committee was the creation of the parliament rather than the government was apparent in its composition. It consisted of eighteen Sŭbranie deputies, eleven from the government benches and seven from the opposition with the latter being so chosen that all major groups in the Assembly were represented on the Committee. The new Central Committee was divided into six sections: for cereals, flour, vegetables, and fodder; for meat, vegetable-oils and soap; for heating, lighting and salt; for foreign trade; for the organisation of agricultural production and animal husbandry; and for the textile, leather and sugar industries. The local Committees were now to have special bureaux nominated by the Central Committee, were to take a much greater part in the administration of the local area, and were to control all local requisitioning committees. Central Committee control was also increased.

The new Central Committee was entrusted with much wider authority than its predecessor. It was empowered to control the price and the distribution of any commodity which it chose to declare as of prime necessity, and it was also to take measures to increase production of these articles. In all 66 items were placed in this category, including bread, wheat, flour, rye, barley, oats, maize, millet, rice and bran. Cooperative and credit organisations were placed under its jurisdiction but, most important of all, the new Committee was made responsible for supplying both civilian and military consumers in everything but articles of purely military need. It was even to be responsible for provisioning German units stationed in Macedonia and to it were subordinated all military requisitioning units, including the Home Command and the Quarter Master General. Following intense pressure from the Agrarians the Committees were obliged to make immediate payment to the peasants rather than giving them treasury bonds redeemable at a later date. To give them control over the distribution of grain after purchase the Committees had strict authority over the millers and bakers. This power enabled the Central Committee to regulate the content of flour in bread and one of its first and most unpopular decisions was that flour for civilian use should consist of twenty percent maize rather than one hundred percent wheat. At the local level the Committees were to organise the slaughter of animals to conform with local demand and they were also empowered to buy up all available bags and sacks.

Further extensions of central control were to be seen in the new Committee's unprecedented powers to regulate salaries and wages. The new Central Committee also had responsibilty for regulating external trade. The Committee's agents were to purchase imports and Bulgarian goods could be exported only with the express permission of the Central Committee confirmed by the Ministerial Council. This meant primarily dealing with the allies and was to be amongst the most difficult of all the tasks assigned to the new Committee.

A further and very significant extension of central control was that the 1916 Central Committee was to concern itself with the production as well as the distribution of agricultural and industrial goods. The only previous efforts to encourage production on the land had been in September 1915 when farmers were asked to form groups of ten so that they could help one another with sowing and harvesting, and military agronomists were sent into the villages to give advice. This had no effect. The 1916 Committees had much wider powers. They could determine what crops were to be grown, could guarantee a market at a fixed price, could conscript labour both male and female, and could insist that unused land be brought into use. Other powers given to the Committees included those to form cartels and cooperatives to increase production and speed distribution, and they could also open publicly-owned shops selling food and other articles. If it wished to establish full control over an industry the Central Committee could militarise it and local Committees had similar powers to take over manufactures.

New tribunals were also attached to the Committees to impose the stricter penalities which the new law laid down for breaches of the Committee's rulings. These stricter penalties and the new mechanisms for punishment of offenders however did little to reduce speculation and other abuses.

The new Committees were able to regulate requisitioning more effectively than their predecessors, particularly the military requisitioning units. Under the new dispensation each family was to be left with 250 kilograms of grain per capita per month for personal consumption, with between 200 and 250 kilograms per hectacre for seed and set quantities for animal feed. These regulations were generally observed and left the peasants with adequate reserves. The army, at least in the early months, was also pleased with the new arrangements for supplies reached it regularly and in sufficient quantities, thanks largely to an early agreement between the Central Committee and the Quarter Master General by which the military made available enough wagons and locomotives to keep the supplies moving. One group previously extremely suspicious of state control, the grain merchants, were incorporated into the Committees' activities by being made responsible for the purchase of some grain though the state remained the owner of the grain so acquired. This device both deflated merchant dissatisfaction and increased the efficiency with which grain was collected.

The Central Committee did not operate in the agrarian sector only. Late in 1916 it militarised the textile industry to ensure that supplies of cloth would reach the army and this decision placed one third of the country's encouraged industries under direct state control. In some areas of industry the Central Committee attempted rationalisation, closing some plants and concentrating production on those factories which would make most efficient use of precious raw materials, labour and fuel. In some instances entire plant was shifted from one place to another, especially from the newly-acquired lands to the old Kingdom, though this was not always effective for many such plants were forced to cease work through lack of spare parts. The leather industry had been in desperate straits since the beginning of the war for imports of raw leather had dried up whilst demand from the army had soared. In July 1916 the Quarter Master General had militarised thirty-two leather factories and workshops and the Central Committee extended state control to almost the entire industry, all of whose products were taken by the army. Increased state control was in this case partially effective for the number of hides processed by the industry between

September 1915 and militarisation in July 1916 was 231,918, whilst the number processed from July 1916 to April 1917 was 922,960.

Despite these successes, however, the Central Committee and the local Committees faced enormous difficulties, many of which they could not overcome. In the first place the new Committee was formed when the harvest, for the first time in a number of years, though adequate was not up to expectations. The entry of Rumania into the War was another blow in that it cut off possible sources of petrol, salt and wood. Despite tighter controls and more severe punishments the Committees could not stamp out speculation and black marketeering, not least because the local Committees were still allowed to determine local prices. At times local prices were either too low or too high because the hard-pressed local Committees did not have sufficient knowledge to make accurate assessments of supply and demand, or lacked sufficiently clear documentation to be able to fix a price which was both bearable for the consumer and fair to the vendor—early in the War when buying from grain merchants this had been relatively easy because the merchants had bought their produce direct from the farmers and there was clear evidence as to prices paid, but by 1916 so many purchasing and requisitioning agencies had come between producer and merchant that it was often impossible to know exactly what the merchants had given or what the peasant had been paid. The Central Committee also failed in its attempts to buy up commodities in short supply and to regulate their distribution, and this was particularly so with commodities which had to be imported for here the Committee's efforts to buy in foreign markets were almost always frustrated by allied military purchasing agents. Likewise, efforts to help home industries crippled by the lack of imported raw-materials were seldom successful, and the Committee's attempt to set up a syndicate of soap producers failed miserably. Nor did the Central Committee ever manage to procure sufficient meat to satisfy civilian and military requirements, though here the problem was inherited rather than of its own making for in earlier months the requisitioning of animals had been too extensive. Previous requisitioning had, in fact, provided more meat than had been consumed in peace time and this had both created exaggerated expectations and so disrupted stock-raising that the animals taken could not be replaced quickly enough to meet the artificially inflated demand. To make matters worse allied military purchasers had initially been allowed to buy meat through local merchants who, because of the high prices offered, had often sold more than was good for the locality.

Of all the difficulties faced by the Central Committee the most intractable were those arising from its relations with Bulgaria's allies, and it was allied confiscation or purchase of grain which forced the Central Committee to reduce the bread ration in December 1916. The shortages were never completely overcome and in some areas, especially in Drama, Seres, Giumuldjina and other parts of Thrace and Macedonia where there had been military operations, they were critical.

These problems with the allies were experienced as soon as the new Central Committee was formed. The first battle was over a contract agreed by a previous Minister of War with Dr. Frater, and Austrian meat-dealer. Frater had agreed to supply the Ministry of War with pork-fat from Bulgarian animals in return for the right to take the remainder of the carcasses for sale in Austria and Germany. This was a virtual licence to export pork and by the time the Central Committee had been formed Frater had already treated 8,285 pigs weighing 646,526 kilograms; from them he had extracted 135,940 kilograms of pork-fat which he had delivered to the Ministry of War, selling the rest of the animal weight at great profit in central Europe. After a fierce conflict with the Ministry of War the Central Committee annulled the contract and pig-meat, along with all other types of meat, poultry and eggs, was added to the list of prohibited exports. The Central Committee was less successful in its efforts to quash a contract concluded by the Quarter Master General with the Turks by which the latter took, 1,260,000 kilograms of maize and supplied olive-oil in return. There were a series of similar contracts, the worst of which was that by which the Zentraleinkaufsgesellschaft, the major German purchasing agency, claimed it could take from Bulgaria 2,500,000 sheep skins, 200,000 kilograms of maize, fifty wagon loads of pork-fat, 2,000 tons of eggs, 50,000 fowl and 400,000 kilograms of raw wool. The Central Committee protested vigorously and insisted successfully that all such agreements, the one with the Turks excepted, were invalid and had to be renegotiated.

These renegotiations began immediately and formal agreements were concluded in the second half of October. These were to give rise to endless misunderstanding and friction.

The Central Committee had first to resist allied pressure for a joint German-Bulgarian Commission to supply allied troops and then to reject the German demand for more rights to food purchases in Bulgarian-occupied Macedonia and the Morava. In the October 1916 agreements the Central Committee had conceded the free export of some commodities, including dried animal bones, animal hooves, almond- pumpkin- and water-melon seeds, and tortoises. There was little solace here for the hungry Germans and they were equally unenthused by the amount of regulated exports the Central Committee was prepared to send abroad, for this was little more than 3,000 tons of eggs and sugar-beet residue per annum. The Central Committee refused absolutely to make any concessions which might infringe its monopoly of grain purchase, both in Bulgaria proper and in the occupied territories, nor would it sanction the export of grain, fats and offal, wine, fruit, nuts, sesame, vegetable-oils and wax. This merely intensified the illegal exporting of such commodities, especially grain.

The other half of the October 1916 agreements had obliged the allies to provide Bulgaria with certain articles in return for the restricted exports she was allowing them. Bulgaria was to import unlimited quantities of coal, salt, machinery, spare parts, glass and chemical products, including medicines. She was also to be allowed imports of certain products including petrol, leather, shoes, cotton and soap, in sufficient quantities to satisfy military needs. Bulgaria was also to be able to purchase limited amounts of sugar, caustic soda, paper bags, newsprint, and writing paper. The problem was that the allies did not keep to their side of the bargain. The Germans, for example, had promised delivery of six hundred wagon loads of salt but few arrived. The Prussian Ministry of War claimed that it had problems in transporting the salt but the Germans by this time had complete control of the rail route to Bulgaria and privately-bought salt arrived without difficulty. In fact salt was reaching the Morava and Macedonia but there it was being embezzled in large quantities by the German soldiery, who then bartered it at very high price-equivalents for Bulgarian food.

It was actions such as these by the allied authorities that were cited by the Central Committee in its secret report to the Sŭbranie in the spring of 1917. The result of that report was the abandonment of the Central Committee and the setting up of the Directorate for Economic and Social Welfare. The Directorate was headed by a soldier, General Protogerov, whose chief assistants were also army officers. The Directorate was divided into ten separate sections, including one to deal with the judicial aspects of its activities, an indication of the new body's wider powers. Most of the ten sections were divided into sub-sections

which meant that the Directorate involved a large and costly bureaucracy. There were also representatives of the Directorate at the provincial and district level. In many cases the same people who had run the
local Committees for Economic and Social Welfare were involved but
now the military powers had a dominant influence. The local bodies,
which to all intents and purposes superseded the old structure of local
government, were directly responsible to the Directorate in Sofia.

Like the Central Committee the Directorate was to be responsible
for production as well as distribution in both the agrarian and industrial sectors, but its powers were yet more extensive. In addition to
fixing wages and prices the Directorate could control profits and
detailed instructions were issued setting appropriate profit margins for
each trade or section of a trade. At the same time all retail traders were
required to mark the price of their goods clearly and unequivocally. To
ensure that this and other rulings were obeyed the local officers of the
Directorate included inspectors who were to make frequent visits to
shops and markets; these visits were to be both announced and unan-
nounced and the inspectors were always to go on foot and in civilian
clothes. In its efforts to procure raw materials, food and fuel from
abroad the Directorate was more determined than the Central Committee. It formed a purchasing centrale on the lines of the Zentraleinkaufsgesellschaft and this was to have the monopoly of foreign
purchasing. It had agents in Berlin, Vienna, the Hague and Kiev, but
despite its greater powers and determination it was no more successful
than the old Central Committee in overcoming allied competition.

The powers of the Directorate were at their height during the last
months of the War. With the change of government in the summer of
1918 the Directorate was placed in the hands of the Minister of Commerce, Professor Danailov, and he performed the most drastic act of
state control yet seen in Bulgaria when he expropriated the entire
harvest for 1918, cut the grain allowances the peasants were to keep for
food, fodder and seed, and imposed even stricter controls upon prices.
Danailov, together with the leading military authorities, also insisted
that the army comb out its own stockpiles of food and clothing,
a measure which produced little extra food but noticeable increases
in the issues of clothes and headgear. Shortly after this General Protogerov returned to his old position as head of the Directorate with
almost total power over all aspects of the economy but the military
collapse intervened before he could use this power to any effect. The
Directorate continued to function after the armistice but it moved now

towards the lessening rather than the tightening of controls. In October the requisitioning of pigs ended and a free market was restored for the sale of meat and pork-fat. Tobacco and hides were also demilitarised and unrestricted trading in them was again allowed. The Directorate also negotiated for the purchase of American wheat without which many Bulgarians would have starved after the disastrous harvest of 1918, and in the early 1920s the Agrarian government incorporated what remained of the Directorate's purchasing and distribution machinery into its own schemes for economic control.

From the beginning the Directorate was given wider powers to ration goods. Bread had long been rationed but under the Directorate control was extended to meat, milk, clothes and shoes. Rationing was now organised on the German model with coupons being issued against which goods could be purchased, though in some areas clothes and shoes were in such short supply that they could be obtained only with the written permission of the local agents of the Directorate. The Directorate first fixed the bread ration at 500 grams per day for each individual but with workers in heavy industry receiving 800 grams and soldiers 1,000 grams per day. A year later, in April 1918, it was forced to cut the ration and in doing so it introduced a new principle; the rich were to be penalised by having to pay more for their bread and their ration was to be only 300 grams per day as against 400 grams per day for the poor. Those involved in heavy work were still to receive extra rations, with a maximum of 600 grams per day, soldiers on the home front were to have 500 grams per day, and those in the front line 700 grams per day. Other rations were also reduced. A few days later indications of the impending poor harvest brought about a further cut in rations, the bread allowances coming down to 200 grams a day for the rich, 250 grams for the poor and 400 grams for soldiers and those doing heavy labour.

The Directorate took energetic steps to increase the supply of food available for military and civilian consumption. Its first measure was to order a thorough inventory of all holdings of food and animals. The intention was to find out exactly how much grain was available both for current needs and for future sowing and by mid-June 1917 this complex operation was complete, though inevitably peasant suspicions meant that not all reserves were disclosed. At the same time the Directorate had not encouraged honest returns by declaring that all cereal production in excess of the agreed allowances for food, fodder and seed had to be handed over to the requisitioning units. The previous systems had relied on voluntary sales and the obligation to sell was a new departure. In October it was decreed that henceforth all supplies would be collected by the military requisitioning units who were each to have an officer and twenty-five men to ensure obedience to their demands. The military were once again in complete control of food collection.

The Directorate imposed a strict ration on meat. There were to be four meatless days per week and the slaughtering of livestock without official permission was forbidden. The buying of animals for slaughter was to be the responsibility of special commissions in each district, including Skopje and Nish, and these commissions also imposed much more stringent veterinary control. In dealing with the problem of meat supply the Directorate was relatively successful. The army had sufficient, receiving over two million kilograms in 1917, and in August the civilian ration was increased from 600 grams to one kilogram per capita per week and at the same time the number of meatless days per week was reduced to three. A year later, however, the picture had changed and supplies were again meagre and erratic.

In addition to tightening control over commodities such as grain, flour and meat the Directorate also extended its authority to previously unrestricted articles such as vinegar, wine-essence and spun wool.

The Directorate inherited and extended the Central Committee's powers over industry. Strenuous efforts were made to provide factories with raw material, fuel and labour and in some areas there were initial successes. The monthly production of cloth in wool factories before April 1917 had been 159,565 metres; thereafter it averaged 183,867 metres until the final economic collapse of the summer of 1918. Cotton production also increased from 18,559 to 20,275 kilograms per month. The output of coal from Pernik rose from 491,000 tons in 1915 to 692,000 tons during 1917, although almost three quarters of the total production went to the railways rather than to manufacturing industry. The Directorate extended its activities to trying new methods of production and establishing new factories and even new industries to meet the needs of the War. To combat shortages of raw materials for the manufacture of soap the Directorate declared any usable home-produced ingredient an article of prime necessity; military units were therefore ordered to extract all grease from the carcasses and bones of dead animals and to deliver it to soap factories. Bulgarian and German soldiers received regular supplies of jam from a factory set up at Leskovats in occupied Serbia and the Directorate responded to the desperate lack of leather footwear for civilian consumption by organising fifteen workshops for the production of wooden clogs, and 30,000 pairs of these were pressed onto an originally reluctant market. But despite these successes the Directorate could not restore Bulgarian industry to its pre-war vigour. By 1917 the output of factories and workshops under the Directorate's control was only 65% of the output of encouraged industries in 1912.

The Directorate took energetic measures to increase agricultural output and again could register some success in that the area of worked land increased from 1,931,369 hectacres in 1916 to 2,099,021 hectacres in 1917 and 2,143,765 hectacres in 1918. There was intense propaganda in the villages exhorting the peasants to greater effort and also advising them on alternative crops and more efficient farming methods, but the peasants were often suspicious of such advice and there were other more important steps taken to increase agricultural production. The first was periodically to increase the fixed prices paid to the peasants for requisitioned items, this being an attempt to keep pace with the increasing cost of living. The Directorate also insisted that each peasant family must provide for itself in cereals. It also enforced the cultivation of large areas of unworked land. This had been done to a limited extent by the Committees before April 1917 but now it was more extensive and, for the first time, applied also to the sowing of cereals. Enforced cultivation played a very important part in increasing the production of valuable crops such as vegetables and sugar-beet, the area planted with the latter in 1917 being five times larger than in 1916. With so many men in the army enforced cultivation would have been impossible with the labour reserves in the countryside and the Directorate therefore organised extra labour to cope with the extra work. The few in the towns and the countryside who had managed to escape the net of conscription were now put to work but the main source of labour was the refugees. In 1917 some 10,000 mostly from the Dobrudja, were working in the fields and they were joined by sizeable numbers of prisoners of war. The Directorate also managed to organise more harvest leave. It also did what it could to make good the loss of draught animals, though this was a difficult undertaking and all that could really be done was to allow peasants living near garrisons to have use of military animals and to insist that wherever possible peasants share draught animals. The Directorate also provided seed where this was needed.

Much was also done to increase the production of milk and dairy products the demand for which was increasing as other commodities became more difficult to obtain. By the end of 1917 there were 170 creameries under the Directorate's control but the private concerns were more efficient and the Directorate did what it could to encourage them, one important service being the Directorate's successful plea for the release from military service of all dairy specialists. In 1917 milk production had risen to 50 million litres compared to only 9.5 million litres in 1916, and cheese production had increased from 0.934 million kilograms in 1916 to 7.5 million kilograms in the following year. These dramatic increases reflect the desperately low levels of production in 1916 rather than a sufficiency in 1917 when, in fact, production targets were not met. The major achievement of the Directorate in this sector was that it mastered the problems of supplying the big cities and the hospitals with milk and dairy produce, and here Sofia was a particular difficulty because the city had grown considerably and also had a large number of military hospitals. For most of the civilian population, however, milk, cheese, butter etc. were amongst the many articles that were in short supply.

Vegetable growing was also promoted by the Directorate. Before the War commercial vegetable growing was found near a few large towns and the Tŭrnovo province where the long tradition of seasonal work north of the Danube had produced considerable knowledge and experience in vegetable cultivation. With mobilisation commercial vegetable growing had ceased and the Directorate set out to stimulate its rebirth by offering high fixed prices, placing orders in the Tŭrnovo, Vidin and Stara Zagora provinces for 80,000 kilograms of dried vegetables. Soldiers not in the front line were also put to work growing vegetables. A further stimulus was provided by the militarisation of private vegetable drying plants—there were 181 in the Directorate's control by 1918—and there were efforts to modernise some of them, though few of the twelve steam driers ordered from Germany actually arrived.

Yet despite the Directorate's powers and energy, and notwithstanding the increase in land worked, there were still food shortages, above all in the critically important sector of grain. In November 1917 the grain collected by the requisitioning units was 30% below expectations and the returns of almost all grain crops were well below the 1912 levels; wheat production was 28% below 1912, rye 39%, oats 26%, barley 11% and maize 43%. Rice production, thanks mainly to the acquisition of new rice-producing areas, was 24% above the 1912 figure.

The Directorate's failure to procure as much food as it intended can be attributed fundamentally to the depletion and progressive demoralisation of the peasantry and over this the Directorate could have little influence as it was the natural consequence of prolonged and exhausting warfare.

The Directorate faced other problems, too. Its persistent efforts to stamp out speculation failed because the possible rewards always outweighed the penalties, nor could the Directorate's officials obtain any more accurate information than the Committee of Economic and Social Welfare and thus it often made unrealistic demands. It could never break through peasant suspicion of military control over agriculture and the Directorate's officials with their extensive powers of search and enquiry were an unwelcome addition to an already elaborate apparatus for control. The peasants also became increasingly disgruntled as prices of the items which they had to buy, particularly in 1918, outstripped the prices which the requisitioning units paid for goods taken. Many farmers reacted in the way traditional for a disaffected peasantry: they hid or even destroyed their surplus and planted only enough to meet their own needs.

As with the Central Committee the major difficulty facing the Directorate, and one where its powers were most inadequate, was in its relations with the allies. Immediately on the formation of the Directorate the allies had assumed that the existing treaties with the Central Committee would be redrawn. They had also enunciated the doctrine that the allied armies should be provisioned by the country in which they were stationed but this the Directorate rejected though it did allow the allies to purchase cereals from state reserves. The Directorate agreed to provide allied troops in Bulgaria and Bulgarian-occupied territory with flour, rice, vegetables and dairy produce, though the allies were not to receive more per man than the Bulgarian army. The allies were to supply Bulgaria with regulated quantities of coal, animal-fats, vegetable-oil, and salt. The Directorate, under the influence of the military lobby, had made far more concessions to the allies than had the Central Committee with the result that in some months the Directorate found itself supplying more food to the Germans and Austrians than it did to the Bulgarians. According to an agreement signed in June 1917 Bulgaria was allowed to export to neutral states unlimited quantities of rose-oil and wine-essence and

almost unrestricted amounts of poppy-seeds. There were long discussions between the Directorate and the allies over tobacco and the
eventual solution, arrived at in November 1917, regulated the quantity
which Bulgaria could sell in neutral markets—Switzerland and
Holland—but left the control of prices and transport almost entirely in
German hands. In return the allies were to provide the commodities
listed above but this, once again, they failed to do. The only item that
was delivered was coal and this came not from Germany but from
Serbian mines in allied occupation, and for this Bulgaria was severely
punished after the War. Bulgaria suffered also from that clause of the
1917 agreement which stipulated that in future allied purchases in
neutral states would be carried out collectively for Bulgaria never
received her due proportion of these collective purchases.

These concessions to the allies caused widespread resentment, the
more so as the illicit export of Bulgarian foodstuffs by the Germans
and Austrians continued. With the fall of the Radoslavov government
more power was given to the Directorate in an effort to stem the
haemorrhage of food but by then nothing could save Bulgaria from the
impact of the 1918 harvest and accumulated war-weariness.

* * *

Perhaps the most successful instance of government intervention in
the social sector during the First World War was in the field of public
health. In the Balkan Wars the fusion of military and civilian health
and sanitation authorities had been a disaster producing nothing but
chaos as the wounded and the diseased, soldier, civilian and prisoner of
war, all mixed and spread death and epidemic, above all the terrible
cholera outbreak of 1913. The government acted quickly to prevent a
recurrence of such a disaster. During the First World War there was
still plenty of room for improvement for 26,000 soldiers died of disease
though in this case the chief culprits were typhus and dysentry brought
in by prisoners of war and by refugees. Cholera did appear in the army
in the Dobrudja in 1916 but it was quickly contained and caused not a
single death.

The government had begun the tightening of health controls immediately after the Balkan Wars. Regulations were passed requiring each
large military unit to equip itself with a field hospital and to map
forward and evacuation zones, each of which was to be provided with a
large number of hospital beds. The government itself stockpiled medi-

cines and worked out emergency distribution procedures, and when the War began it gladly accepted medical help from its allies, the Germans lending 70 doctors and 400 assistants, the Austrian Knights of St. John of Malta 19 doctors and 153 assistants, and the Hungarians 5 doctors and 40 assistants. These allied medical personnel were much needed not only because of Bulgaria's persistent need for doctors but also because the Red Cross's auxiliary medical services were more limited than in 1912–13 when they had relied heavily on foreign volunteers. In the First World War the Bulgarian Red Cross concentrated primarily on the organisation of supply points, the collection of funds and presents for soldiers and for the wounded, and on looking after prisoners of war, though it did also organise a number of hospital trains.

The pre-1915 preparations, the allied medical personnel and the Red Cross were concerned primarily with care of the military. Regulation of civilian health was controlled by a series of decrees issued in 1915 and then passed through the Sŭbranie in 1916 as the Public Health Act. Each village, town and part of a town was required to form a Health Council under the chairmanship of the mayor or other appropriate local dignatory and containing local justices of the peace, headmasters and tax collectors, all of whom were to be unpaid, again to avoid *partisanstvo*. All local councils were to be under the ultimate direction of a Central Council in Sofia attached to the Supreme Medical Council and the Directorate of Public Health in the Ministry of the Interior. The Health Councils had extensive powers to control sewage disposal, to supervise factories, workshops, rivers, roads and fountains, and they could enter any building without a warrant. They were obliged both to instruct the public in the need for and the methodology of health care, and they were to take appropriate steps to safeguard public health. There were penalties against any community which failed to establish a Health Council and these penalties were enforced with 334 mayors being fined in 1916 and 354 in 1917. By 1918 only 58 out of over 2,000 local communes in Bulgaria had failed to set up a Health Council. The Councils spent about four million leva per annum and brought about considerable improvement in Bulgaria, particularly in the medium-sized urban settlements. In a number of these towns running water was either installed, as in Kiustendil, or the system greatly improved under the auspices of the Health Councils, whilst at a national level the Central Council imported disinfecting vehicles and sprays from Germany and performed a particularly important and lasting service when it persuaded the government that the only answer to the continuing shortage of doctors was to open a Medical Faculty in Sofia University. The first students were admitted for the academic year 1917–18. The Councils' prime success had been in limiting epidemics during the War and although Bulgaria could not escape from the Spanish influenza which swept through Europe after the War even this, despite the scarcity of food and soap in 1918, did not affect Bulgaria as severely as it did some countries.

During the First World War the government in Sofia also intervened in housing. Pressure on housing, primarily an urban problem, grew gradually after 1910 but was greatly intensified by the War and, after the armistice, by the influx of refugees. Thus in 1910 for every hundred dwelling units in the towns there had been 520.4 inhabitants, in 1920 there were 545; in the villages the figures were 588.4 in 1910 but only 577.8 in 1920. The private landlord inevitably made hay whilst his particular sun was shining but in April 1918 the Directorate intervened and froze rents, theoretically at their pre-mobilisation level. At the same time eviction was made illegal.

The First World War also brought about long-awaited and long-debated legislation to control working conditions in factories, though here the implementation of legislation was very slow. In his speech from the throne in 1914 the King had promised six bills on the regulation of working conditions but by September 1915 not one had been placed upon the statute book. The War intensified pressure on the government to act and eventually three bills were passed; an Act long demanded by the labour movement to enforce safety regulations on boilers and cisterns, an act to extend insurance, and the Hygiene and Safety Act. The latter, passed in April 1917 but not put into effect until 1918, was the most important of the three. The new Act was to apply to all manufacturing institutions though not to domestic industry. The employer was obliged to provide adequate light, heat, ventilation and washing facilities; if living accommodation were provided by the employer that too was to be subject to control, and all workers were to have places to rest and eat. All machines were to be a made safe, and the local Health Councils were empowered to inspect both factory and living accommodation. The Act also stipulated that no-one under the age of twelve was to be employed though in 1919 the minimum age was raised to fourteen. In 1919 the eight-hour day was enacted with a maximum of six hours for those under eighteen; women and children under eighteen were not to work at nights, there were detailed regulations concerning the number of breaks that workers were to be allowed and it was also decreed that each factory with ten or more employees had to nominate a doctor to provide aid and advice on cleanliness and hygiene. In districts with more than a thousand workers there were to be special doctors for workers and their families. Given the shortage of doctors such clauses could be nothing more than pious hopes.

Other welfare acts included a bill of March 1915 by which contractors engaged on public works were obliged to put aside 1% of their profits to cover accident and illness insurance for their employees. In June of the same year came a much-needed act which provided for a general insurance scheme for workers and united the previously diverse insurance schemes though there was to be ceiling of 2,400 leva on the amount paid out of the general fund and this weakened the system when inflation became serious. There were later amendments to the June 1915 Workers' Insurance Act and these, for example, gave pregnant women the right to free medical treatment and midwifery if they had been paying into the scheme for at least sixteen weeks. But as ever the enactment of a law did not necessarily lead to its implementation and insurance schemes such as these were by 1919 still unreliable and far from all embracing.

* * *

For the vast majority of the population the War had meant anxiety and privation all of which had been suffered in vain. Disillusionment and anger followed and were increased because a tiny minority had made fortunes from speculation, the black market or other forms of war-profiteering. The anger and frustration of the population was finally expressed in the rejection of the War and of the Parties associated with it.

The War had without doubt been the most awesome and searing experience in the history of the new Bulgarian state but its long-term social and economic effects were not profound. The proportion of the population classified as depending for their livelihood upon 'Rents, pensions and shares' had risen from 0.93% in 1910 to 1.44% in 1920 and this reflected primarily the growth of speculative investment in the final stages of the War. The expansion of government activity at the same time had brought about a minimal increase in that section of the population classified as 'civil servants and members of the free professions' who in 1920 comprised 3.88% of the population compared to

3.67% in 1910. The majority of the population remained small peasant proprietors working their own land. In 1920 they formed 75.4% of the population compared to 75.29% in 1910. Farming methods remained primitive. Under a third of the holdings had metal ploughs and other modern tools were even rarer; artificial fertilisers were all but unknown and few peasants used dung or wood-ash to increase the productivity of their fields. The only noticeable change in agriculture had been the decline in wheat exports and the advance of tobacco as an export commodity, but though this altered somewhat the nature of Bulgarian trade it did nothing to change the social structure. Nor were there any significant changes in the nature of Bulgarian industry as a result of the War. In fact the War served to highlight the backwardness of Bulgarian society and its economy for though the infantry and cavalry troops fought with great courage and tenacity in the technical branches and in the Red Cross the Bulgarians had to depend greatly on foreign advisers and assistants. With the crippling shortages which the War brought about there was no prospect of Bulgaria making good these deficiencies.

If the period from the mid-1890s to the Wars had seen growth without structural change, that of the Wars saw neither.

SUMMARY AND CONCLUSIONS

Despite the rural unrest of 1899–1900 and the urban disorders of 1906–7 the most striking feature of Bulgarian history in the forty years after the Liberation is the country's social stability. The social composition of the nation in 1918 was little different from that of 1878. The small peasant proprietor had been the most important feature of the social structure in 1878 and he remained so in 1918, still forming about four fifths of the total population. Even the radical administration which emerged from the political demoralisation of 1918 set about intensifying the dominance of this group. The reforms of the Agrarians were directed not to changing but to purifying the social and political structure by making them completely subservient to and dominated by the interests of the small and medium-sized proprietor who worked his own land largely without the use of wage labourers. This was to be done by taking property from those owners who did not work it and using it to make self-sufficient those who at that time did not have enough land; the individual proprietor was also to be helped by the development of more cooperative ventures, particularly in the sphere of marketing where government monopolies in the selling of grain and tobacco were established; the efficiency of peasant agriculture was to be improved by more generous provision of vocational education, improvements in communications, greater diversity in production, more veterinary facilities and so forth; and the quality of peasant life was to be enhanced by the bringing of cultural amenities—theatre, cinema, radio, libraries, etc.—into the villages.

The bed-rock of this social stability was the availability of land. The departure of large numbers of Moslems during and after the war of 1877–8 had released a great deal of land but when that supply dried up or if there were no vacant Moslem land in an area then the local peasants would take over public lands, often forests which were then cleared and put under the plough. Even at the end of the First World War there was sufficient land in the country though the Agrarian programme of enforced confiscation had not yet begun, one observer in 1919 recording that 'There is so much unused land that the unemployed people not only of Sofia but of the whole of Bulgaria could be saved by exploiting it'.[1] Not till the late 1920s did high birth-rates in the rural areas produce pressure on the land and even then the effects were not disruptive for late in the 1930s Bulgaria's basic social structure was the most healthy in the south-east of Europe.

Fundamental social stability also meant the perpetuation of basic weaknesses in the Bulgarian agrarian economy. The problem of parcellisation was to become serious in the 1920s and 1930s, and the lack of adequate veterinary services was still being deplored in 1940, but yet more serious was continued overdependence on a small range of crops. This had been a constant feature of the years 1878–1918. There had been some attempts to move away from it by governmental promotion of silk-worms and other crops but only with the First World War did any noticeable shift occur and then for some areas it went too far for they ended by being as over-dependent on tobacco as previously they had been on grain. Once again governments tried to promote alternative products such as grapes and fruit, but little progress was made and change, in so far as it had come about in the agrarian sector, had clearly not brought greater strength or economic health.

Much the same could be said for the development of Bulgarian industry. In the small manufacturing sector of the Bulgarian economy the years 1878–1918 did bring change. Many of the old craft industries were hard hit by the modern economic forces to which the new state was inevitably exposed and which, in later years, it to some extent encouraged. Yet the new industries were not much healthier than the old. They were not sufficiently linked to the agrarian base of the economy and despite the Encouragement of Industry programmes not enough Bulgarian manufacturers looked primarily to the home producer for their supplies, and in the 1920s and 1930s Bulgarian industry was still over-dependent on foreign raw materials many of which, with proper organisation and quality control, could have been provided from Bulgarian sources. This made the country more susceptible to the influence of larger economic forces and in the 1930s economic dependence and political resentment combined to make Bulgaria an easy prey to Nazi influence.

Nevertheless, part of the industrialisation programme before 1912 had given Bulgaria the basic infrastructure of a modern state and its railways and banks, for example, were as well organised and efficient as any in the less developed areas of Europe. The cost of this was dependence on foreign investors but Bulgaria's national debt before the First World War was no more onerous than those of the other Balkan states. Nor was the country's political independence greatly constrained by its reliance upon foreign investors. In all the major policy decisions—those of 1885, 1908, 1912, 1913 and 1915 in particular—the actions of the Bulgarian government were determined by the politicians of Sofia and Sofia alone.

* * *

Social stability meant social conservatism and the lack of modernising impulses within Bulgarian society. Peasant objectives were for the purification not the dismantling of the social structure, and thus BANU directed its propaganda and then its governmental policies towards the reduction or the removal from the visage of the peasant state of such excrescences as the bureaucracy, the army, the Court, the old political Parties, and the few landowners who did not till their soil. The peasant therefore required the reduction of the power of the state rather than its modernisation.

The commercial and manufacturing elements in the Principality, most of whom were aligned with the Conservative oligarchy, had some modernising aspirations but they were too weak to impose their ideas, as the political experiment of 1881–3 had shown. In Rumelia the commercial element was stronger than in the Principality, but it was in part Greek and therefore removed from political influence, and in any case its strength was diluted after the absorption of Rumelia into Bulgaria in 1885. By the mid-1880s manufacturers both sides of the Balkan range were exposed to increasingly severe competition from abroad whilst the new factory-based industrialists were only a tiny minority, ineffective as a political lobby. Neither they nor their commercial associates were strong enough to dominate the state except in items of purely economic policy. In matters of *Grossepolitik* commercial or industrial interests were never the determinants. In the period 1894–1912 the bourgeoisie was in fact fashioned in the image of the state, not vice-versa. With few exceptions, amongst them could be numbered Stoilov and Geshov, the political leaders were not of commercial or industrial backgrounds but from the intelligentsia, the peasantry or petty officialdom. The policies pursued in the promotion of industry and commerce were determined less by the interests of the traders and manufacturers than by the strategic objectives of the state, objectives which were still focussed firmly on national reunification in a resurrected San Stefano Bulgaria. A modernised state could be the only basis for the strong military force which was necessary if Bulgaria were to fulfil her historic destiny in Macedonia, Thrace, the Morava and the Dobrudja. A reunified large Bulgaria would no doubt have provided Bulgaria's traders and manufacturers with a larger market but this presumed economic advantage would have been a consequence not a cause of the movement towards national unity.

The innate conservatism of the peasantry and the weakness of the native commercial and industrial elements left Bulgaria in the hands of its intelligentsia. This group had guided the nation through its cultural revival and had devised the new state after Liberation. Having served the nation before 1878 it assumed it could continue to do so thereafter by serving in the state, but this did not prove to be so. In the two decades after 1878 nation was gradually divorced from state. The nation remained peasant, concentrated primarily in the village and the small holding. The state, meanwhile, became the domain of the bureaucrat, the courtier, the lawyer, the soldier, and the professional politician. For many of the intelligentsia the high salaries, the social prestige and the local political influence which the state apparatus had to offer were irresistible. The state apparatus, by the evil of *partisanstvo*, became inextricably interwoven with the small groups who exploited the peasantry, and thus the intelligentsia was further distanced from the mass of the nation. The phenomenon of *partisantsvo* also deepened the divide between nation and state by emasculating those few efforts at social improvement which the system produced; the problem was that those who stood to lose from such legislation were usually the ones responsible for applying it at the local level and they, because of their own self-interest, failed to do anything to implement such laws. This left the peasants as unprotected as before, further discredited the system, and undermined the rule of law, the basis of all true political liberty and stability.

The separation of state and nation meant a fundamental change in the nature of domestic politics. In the years after 1878 there had been real dispute over the distribution of political power and responsibility within the state, a dispute which had by the mid-1890s been decided in favour of the executive. The old constitutional wrangles with their vertical divisions between the four factions and their kaleidescopic changes of alignment, had given way to an accommodation of political forces based on a three-fold horizontal division between Prince, politician and populace. The Prince decided basically upon the composition of ministries and upon the state's foreign policy; the politicians were left free to direct domestic policy and to fill their own pockets; the people paid.

By the mid-1890s a section of the intelligentsia had become alienated from its own role in propping up the state. This disgruntled element sought to renew its old association with the peasant nation. This was achieved in the co-operative movement in which teachers, priests, and agricultural advisers played a prominent part, and also in the mass radical Parties which emerged in the 1890s and 1900s. These latter, especially BANU, ensured that almost all members of the intelligentsia who desired material improvement in the life of the state would now work outside the state apparatus. The state was being cut off from any chance of self-regeneration. Only at two points did the nation and the state come together fruitfully: in 1885 and 1912. Yet any gains from the latter were rapidly dissipated by the disaster of 1913. This meant that in 1915–18 when the nation and state were offered once again the chance to co-operate in pursuit of the agreed goal of San Stefano Bulgaria, co-operation between them was half-hearted and eventually unsuccessful. In the 1920s and 1930s the state and its policies became dominated by Macedonian extremists who played a leading part in the brutal suppression of the Stamboliiski regime, and this made it yet more difficult to enlist peasant enthusiasm for the 'national' cause as preached by the state and its representatives.

The regime which had been established by the mid-1890s and which was responsible for taking Bulgaria to war in 1912, 1913 and 1915 was very much a personal regime. Ferdinand's authority in foreign affairs was supreme and not even the calamity of 1913 could topple that regime, though, as the election of that year showed, the regime had been dented. With the further and greater discrediting of the regime in 1918 it gave way to the reforming Parties of the left but because the old regime was so much a personal one it was the ruler and his accomplice rather than the political system itself which was held responsible. Ferdinand was forced to abdicate and Radoslavov was later put in the dock but there was no political revolution; the Tŭrnovo constitution survived and the Saxe-Coburg dynasty remained. Alone of the defeated belligerents in 1918 Bulgaria retained the political system which had taken it to war.

This was a fitting epitaph to the years 1878–1918 which can be seen as a continuing conflict between the desire for political stability at home and the pursuance of national objectives outside the 1878 boundaries.

At Tŭrnovo in 1879 there had been those who were so determined to preserve national unity that they were prepared to sacrifice for it such political independence as the treaty of Berlin was offering, and again in 1886–7 there were calls for a Turco-Bulgarian compromise similar to that in the Habsburg Empire, for this would at least give the Bulgarians unity. After the extreme nationalists had lost the debate at Tŭrnovo many of them became equally zealous in pursuit of political freedom and liberty, embracing the constitution as fervently as they had previously espoused the cause of national unity. Yet these political objectives clashed with those of the Prince and the consequent instability was a considerable disincentive to those in Rumelia who wanted union with the Principality. By 1884 the Liberal zealots seemed to have secured political dominance within the state. The Principality was in a position to attract the unionists of the south.

The stability which had made union possible was itself destroyed by the union. The union and the war with Serbia had given the nation cohesion and had brought it into effective but ephemeral collusion with the state. Immediately after the national triumph of 1885, however, the problem of stability reappeared. The Rumelians proved more difficult to absorb than anyone had imagined, especially when confronted with such issues as the Ruse-Varna railway which was of no interest, let alone value or importance, to the southern Bulgarians. Much more seriously, the events of 1885 allowed the Prince's Russian adversaries to drive a huge wedge between him and his opponents at home. The Russian factor had always been important in Bulgarian politics and it was one which had not always served Bulgarian national interests. Obviously the war of 1877–8 had been of inestimable value to the Bulgarian national cause but after 1878 Russian interests and those of the Bulgarian state were often at variance, even if the peasant nation held to its reverence for the Tsar and his Empire. The Russians tended to see the Bulgarian army as little more than an outpost of the Tsar's forces, whilst their ambitions with regard to Bulgarian railways and the Bulgarian National Bank showed that Russian and Bulgarian state policies could differ widely. By 1885 relations between the Prince and the Russians were so bad that the Russians themselves were openly offering the Bulgarians a choice between unity and stability, for such was the import of the 'Union without Battenberg' policy. Alexander sacrificed himself to the Russians but the Bulgarians themselves were not prepared to buy stability at the price of Russian domination, even the peasant mass of the population passively accepting Stambulov's stand against outside interference and refusing to respond to Russian-sponsored attempts to unseat the regent and, after him, Ferdinand.

Immediately after 1879 it seemed political liberty had been bought at the cost of any advance towards further national unity. After 1886 gains on the national front, specifically in the Porte's 1890 concessions over Macedonia, were bought at the cost of the political freedoms lost in the *Stambulovshtina*. In the mid-1890s the process was repeated on a larger scale. Stambulov had fallen but political stability had been retained by concentrating power in the hands of the Prince and allowing the politicians free use of the *partisanstvo* system. Just as in 1878 political separation from the Ottoman Empire had been purchased at the cost of national unity so now international recognition as well as domestic stability had been secured at the cost of political liberties. In the first instance the national extremists had been defeated in the second it was the Liberal extremists, often the same people, who lost. As in the divorce of the *intelligent* from the peasants it meant the discrediting of the ideals of those who had made the national revival and created the new state.

As political stability was being bought at the cost of political freedom that stability was already coming under threat once again from the national issue. This time Macedonia rather than Rumelia was at the centre of the problem. Before the 1890s it had been assumed in Bulgaria that Macedonia was desperately waiting to return to its San Stefano homeland. From the mid-1890s such an assumption could no longer be made. Serbian and Greek propagandists were already active but much more injurious to the Bulgarian cause was the rise of the internal Macedonian movement, a movement encouraged not a little by the increasingly unattractive form of the Bulgarian state. If the Bulgarians inside Bulgaria were divorced from the state, why should the Macedonians wish to join it? Whereas in 1884–5 stability in the

Principality had attracted the unionists in the south, now the price for stability had been so high that it was acting as a disincentive to union with Macedonia. What made the Bulgarian position more difficult was that as the internal movement came to notice so Austria and Russia came to their agreement on the maintenance of the Balkan *status quo*, an agreement which made Bulgarian interference in Macedonia, an interference which was necessary if Bulgarian interests in the area were to be safeguarded, a much more dangerous undertaking. Ferdinand and the politicians of Sofia had to intervene; the alternative was to face mutiny or assassination which would have served no-one well for the successors to Ferdinand and his henchmen would certainly have been interventionists. Yet just as the need to defy Russia and Austria by intervening increased so internal stability was threatened by a social unrest and a financial insecurity which forced Bulgaria into dependence on France and its Russian ally. For two and a half years Ferdinand and his ministers trod the Macedonian tightrope but thereafter they were forced to obey the Tsar's orders to dissociate themselves from the activists, though their obedience was not solely the product of Bulgaria's financial dependence on Russia's ally; it was just as much the result of the danger that if Bulgaria did not behave then the Tsar would concentrate all his diplomatic support in the Balkans in Belgrade. But whatever the cause of Ferdinand's compliance with Russian orders the result was that Bulgaria had to acquiesce in the, from the Bulgarian point of view, totally disastrous nomination of Firmilian as archbishop of Skopje, and then stand idly by during the Ilinden revolt. The latter spelt disaster for the internal organisation but the Bulgarian cause in Macedonia was not the beneficiary. Many Macedo-Bulgarians left the area, others were disgusted at Bulgaria's lack of response and therefore became ever more determined to separate Macedonia from the Bulgarian state, at least while the present regime was in power; others capitulated to Hellenist and Serbian pressures. Once again the preservation of stability in the Principality had meant the sacrifice of national goals.

The next major political development, the declaration of independence in 1908, was achieved without any threat to internal stability but it did little to advance the cause of national unification, indeed it could be maintained that it was, as Ferdinand's opponents argued, a mutilated victory and one which both confirmed the existing political regime and signified satisfaction with Bulgaria's existing boundaries.

This was not the case. The Sofia establishment had lost none of its ambitions as 1912 was to show, for here the government, now in collusion with Serbia, was determined not to repeat the mistakes of 1900–3, and would not listen to Russian advice on restraint. The campaign brought Bulgaria near to the achievement of its national objectives but all was lost in the desperate gamble of 1913. Bulgaria's case in 1913 was a good deal stronger than many later writers, particularly in the west, have been prepared to concede but the decision suddenly to commit the army to action against its erstwhile allies, with the engineered resignation of Geshov and Ferdinand's domination of the military command and military policy, was in many ways the epitome of the personal regime. Not even in 1915 did the King play so decisive a role for then his Minister President was in agreement with a royal policy for which the nation had been gradually if grudgingly prepared. Also in the autumn of 1915 it was difficult to counter the argument that the central rather than the Entente powers offered the better chance of securing reconstruction of San Stefano Bulgaria. Furthermore in 1915, much in contrast to 1913, Bulgaria was being dragged into a war which was already in progress and, it seemed at the time, for her to stand aside any longer might have cost her the chance of any profit from the conflict. In 1913 Bulgaria had been, despite severe provocation, an aggressor; worse still, she had been an isolated aggressor.

The attempt to secure full national reunification in 1915 had momentary success but in the end it was to precipitate greater political instability than the nation or the state had ever known. It was also to mean a serious diminution of national independence for the regulations imposed on the Bulgarians by the treaty of Neuilly were even more restrictive than those imposed by the treaty of Berlin, and after 1919 the Allied Commissioners interfered in Bulgarian affairs just as much or more so than did the representatives of the great powers after 1878.

* * *

After 1918 Bulgaria had to adapt to a new and a harsher world. She was saddled with reparations debts, she was regarded with deep suspicion by her neighbours, she had to face the internal threat of disenchanted armed groups such as the Macedonians and the White Russians, and above all now that San Stefano Bulgaria seemed so distant a prospect she had to find a new sense of national purpose. Stamboliiski tried to provide such a purpose by reuniting nation and state in pursuit of domestic reform and reconciliation with Bulgaria's neighbours, but the suspicion with which the country was viewed and the general international indifference to its internal problems meant that his efforts failed and he fell victim to a coalition of unrepentant supporters of the old system and the old objectives. This ensured only two things. That the worst aspects of the old system would be perpetuated and that, in international terms, Bulgaria would be attracted to any revisionist force which might appear. The mistakes and tragedies of the 1898–1918 era were set to be repeated and reexperienced.

NOTES

Introduction

1. Nikov, *op. cit.*, p. 233.
2. Meininger, *op. cit.*, p. 130.
3. Nikov, *op. cit.*, p. 130.

Chapter 1

1. Petŭr Mirchev, p. 69, *op. cit.*
2. N. Arnauov, *Ekzarh Yosif,* p. 303.
3. Corti, *Battenberg,* p. 38.
4. Irichek, *Dnevnik,* p. 27.
5. Metodi Petrov, 'Kliment', p. 62.
6. Ilcho Dimitrov, *op. cit.*, p. 30.
7. *Ibid,* p. 76.
8. Irichek, *Dnevnik,* pp. 441–2.

Chapter 2

1. Ilcho Dimitrov, *op. cit.*, p. 180.

Chapter 3

1. Jelavich, *Tsarist Russia and Balkan Nationalism,* p. 149.
2. Borushkov, p. 500.
3. *Ibid.*
4. Radev, *Stroiteli.* i, 441–2.

5. Borushkov, p. 502; Girginov, *Razvitie*, i, 159.
6. Konstantin Pundev, *loc. cit.*, 243.

Chapter 8

1. The documents concerned were later published under the editorship of Leonov. (See bibliography to Part I). These documents contain the spirit if not the precise wording of Russian communications but should not be used without reference to Skazkin, Pavlovich, and Charles and Barbara Jelavich, 'The Occupation Fund Documents'; for details of these three works see preceding bibliographies.
2. Richard von Mach, *Balkanzeit*, p. 84.
3. Constant, *op. cit.*, p. 165.

Chapter 9

1. Burian to Kalnoky, 40A, vertraulich, 8 June 1894, H. H. St. A., P A XV, 36.
2. Quoted in Panayotov, *Rusiya etc.*, p. 203.
3. *Ibid.*, p. 206.
4. Burian to Kalnoky, 76A, 9 Nov. 1894, H. H. St. A., P A XV 37.
5. For details of the delegation's visit, see Burian to Goluchowski, 41B, 16 Aug. 1895 and 41C vertraulich, 16 Aug. 1895, H. H. St. A., P A XV 39.

Chapter 10

1. Penkov, *IDA*, no. 4, p. 279.
2. Mosely, *loc. cit.*, p. 19.

Chapter 12

1. Sir Philip Currie to Lord Salisbury, 298 confidential, 29 April 1897, Public Record Office, FO 78/4801.

Chapter 13

1. Quoted in Todorova, *Zaemi*, p. 252.
2. Damyanov, *Pronikvane*, p. 120.

3. Weissman, *loc. cit.*, p. 9.
4. Von Müller to Goluchowski, 30A, 20 June 1900, H. H. St. A., PA XV/48.
5. See Damyanov, *Pronikvane*, p. 121.

Chapter 15

1. See 'Russland und das Macedonische Comite, 1901', H. H. St. A, PA/52, Varia.
2. Von Müller to Goluchowski, 31F, 29 May 1902, H. H. St. A., PA XV/53.
3. Girginov, *Razvitie*, p. 274.
4. Forgach to Goluchowski. 30D, 20 May 1903, H. H. St. A., PA XV/56.
5. *Ibid.*, 54B, 14 Sept. 1903, H. H. St. A., PA XV/57.

Chapter 16

1. Von Thurn to Aerenthal, 3A, streng vertraulich, 9 January 1907, H. H. St. A., PA XV/50.
2. Von Storch to Informationsbureau, I. B., 24 May 1906, H. H. St. A., PA XV/62.
3. Gooch and Temperley, *op. cit.*, vol. 5, p. 110.
4. F. R. Bridge, Documents, no. 352.
5. Doklad na Izpitatelnata Komisiya po Upravlenieto na Stranata prez perioda ot 5 Mai 1903 do 16 Yanuarii 1908, Sofia 1910, p. 23.

Chapter 17

1. Narodno Sŭbranie, *Dnevnitsi, XIII obiknoveno sŭbranie*, iii series, vol. 5, p. 1576.
2. Pantev et al, 'Vŭnshnata politika', *III* no. 23, 123.
3. Giskra to Aerenthal, 13D, 24 February 1910, H. H. St. A, PA XV/70.
4. *Ibid.*

Chapter 18

1. Girginov, *Razvitie*, ii, 208.
2. *Misŭl*, no. 1, 15 January 1898, pp. 1–3.
3. Velinova, 'Korespondentsiya', no. 15.

4. Topalov, 'Stopanska Kriza', p. 79.
5. Kosta Todorov, *Firebrand*, p. 143.
6. Joseph Rothschild, *op. cit.*, p. 307.
7. *Ibid.*, p. 49.

Chapter 20

1. Angel Georgiev, *loc. cit.*, p. 111.
2. Gerschenkron, *loc. cit.*, pp. 226–7.

Chapter 21

1. Quoted in Vlahov, 'Kriza', p. 148.
2. Pantev *et al.*, 'Vŭnshnata Politika', pp. 134–5.
3. Gueshoff, *Balkan League*, p. 19.
4. Pantev *et al.*, *loc. cit.*, p. 135.
5. Gueshov, *op. cit.*, p. 50.
6. Girginov, *Narodnata Katastrofa*, pp. 49–50.
7. Gooch and Temperley, *op. cit.*, vol. 9 part ii, no. 1055, enclosure, and Balkanicus, *op. cit.*, p. 22.
8. Quoted in Helmreich, *op. cit.*, pp. 360–1.
9. Balkanicus, *op. cit.*, p. 22.
10. Von Mach, *Balkanzeit*, p. 218.

Chapter 23

1. Quoted in Kunhe, *op. cit.*, p. 202.
2. See Hristov, *Revoliutsionnata Kriza*, p. 23.
3. Radoslawoff, *op. cit.*, p. 281.
4. Bell, *op. cit.*, p. 135.
5. Article 128.

Summary and Conclusions

1. Piperov, *op. cit.*, p. 356.

BIBLIOGRAPHY AND SOURCES

Much of the basic political narrative has been based on the reports from Austro-Hungarian diplomatic representatives in Sofia and the provincial consulates. These are to be found in the Haus-Hof-und Staatsarchiv in Vienna. Some use has also been made of documents in the British archives and of reports from German representatives in Sofia. The British documents are deposited in the Public Record Office, Kew, London, and the German sources used were from the microfilm collection in the Foreign Office Library, London.

Published sources have been arranged by their relevance to those parts of the book which they most concern. Documentary material has been quoted first and this is followed by books, articles and lastly unpublished theses and papers.

The following abbreviations have been used in the bibliography:

AHR	*American Historical Review*
ASEER	*American Slavic and East European Review*
ASSP	*Arhiv za Stopanska i Sotsialna Politika* (Sofia)
BHR	*Bulgarian Historical Review* (Sofia)
BS	*Balkan Studies* (Thessaloniki)
EB	*Etudes Balkaniques* (Sofia)
EH	*Etudes Historiques* (Sofia)
GSUFIF	*Godishnik na Sofiiskiya Universitet;* *Filosofsko-Istoricheski Fakultet*
GSUIF	*Godishnik na Sofiiskiya Universitet;* *Iuridicheski Fakultet*
GSUIdF	*Godishnik na Sofiiskiya Universitet; Ideologicheski Fakultet*
GSUIK	*Godishnik na Sofiiskiya Universitet; Ideologichni Katedri*
GVFSI	*Godishnik na Visshiya Finansovostopanskiya Institut* (Svishtov)
IBID	*Izvestiya na Bŭlgarskoto Istorichesko Druzhestvo* (Sofia)

525

IDA	*Izvestiya na Dŭrzhavnite Arhivi* (Sofia)
IIBI	*Izvestiya na Instituta za Bŭlgarskata Istoriya.* (Sofia)
III	*Izvestiya na Instituta za Istoriya* (Sofia)
IIIBAN	*Izvestiya na Instituta za Istoriya pri Bŭlgarskata Akademiya na Naukite*
IIIBKP	*Izvestiya na Instituta za Istoriya pri Bŭlgarskata Komunisticheska Partiya.* (Sofia)
IP	*Istoricheski Pregled* (Sofia)
JEH	*Journal of Economic History*
JMH	*Journal of Modern History*
PL	*Profsŭiuzni Letopis* (Sofia)
SB	*Studia Balcanica* (Sofia)
SBID	*Spisanie na Bŭlgarskoto Ikonomichesko Druzhestvo* (Sofia)
SBNUNK	*Sbornik za Narodni Umotvoreniya, Nauka i Knizhnina* (Sofia)
SE	*Southeastern Europe*
SEER	*Slavonic and East European Review*
SF	*Südost Forschungen*
SR	*Slavic Review*
VS	*Voennoistoricheski Sbornik* (Sofia)

General Works

Documentary Material

Bozhinov, Voin and Panayotov, L.   *Macedonia. Documents and Material,* Sofia 1978.

Kraleva, Ivanka   'Razvitie na vŭzdŭrzhatelnoto dvizhenie v Bŭlgariya sled osvobozhdenieto ot osmansko robstvo do 9 xi 1944', *IDA,* no. 27 (1974).

Books

Barker, Elizabeth   *Macedonia; its Place in Balkan Power Politics,* London 1950.

Bousquet, Georges   *Histoire du peuple bulgare depuis les origines jusqu'à nos jours,* Paris 1909.

Busch-Zantner, Richard   *Bulgarien; Geschichte und Volkstum, Politik und Wirtschaft Bulgariens von der ersten Änfangen bis zur Gegenwart,* Leipzig 1941.

Chakŭrov, Dr Naiden & Atanasov, Zhech G.   *Istoriya na bŭlgarskoto Obrazovanie,* Sofia 1954.

Christophorov, Peter   *Ivan Vazov: La formation d'un écrivain bulgare. (1850–1921).* Paris 1938.

Dallin, L.A.D.   *Bulgaria,* New York 1957.

Dŭrvingov, Petŭr *Duhŭt na istoriya na bŭlgarskiya narod,* Sofia 1932.

Floericke, Kurt *Geschichte der Bulgaren,* Stuttgart 1913.

Fox, Frank *Bulgaria,* London 1915.

Guerin, R. P. Longeron *Histoire de la Bulgarie depuis les origines à nos jours, 1385–1915,* Paris 1914.

Hristov, H. *et al.* (eds.) *Istoriya na Bŭlgariya,* 2nd edition, 3 vols., Sofia 1962.

Hristov, Hristo *Bulgaria, 1300 years,* Sofia 1980.

Kassner, K. *Bulgarien, Land und Leute,* Leipzig 1916.

Krachunov, Kr. *Narodnata prosveta v Bŭlgariya,* Sofia 1934.

Kunze, Georg Eugen *Bulgarien,* Gotha 1919.

Lamouche, L. *La Bulgarie,* Paris 1923.

Launey, de L. *La Bulgarie d'Hier et de Domain,* Paris 1922.

Macdermott, Mercia *A History of Bulgaria, 1393–1885,* London 1962.

Mach, Richard von *The Bulgarian Exarchate: Its History and the Extent of its Authority in Turkey,* London 1907.

Mladenov, Stepan *Geschichte der bulgarischen Sprache,* Berlin and Leipzig 1929.

Moser, Charles A. *A History of Bulgarian Literature, 865–1944,* The Hague, 1972.

Ormandjiev, I. *Nova i nai-nova istoriya na bŭlgariskiya narod,* Sofia 1945.

Rizov, D. *Die Bulgaren in ihren historischen, ethnographischen und politi-schen Grenzen,* Berlin 1917.

Shaw, Stanford J. & Shaw, Ezel Kural *History of the Ottoman Empire and Modern Turkey,* 2 vols., Cambridge 1977.

Snegarov, I. *Ruski opiti za predotvratyavane i digane na shizmata,* Sofia 1929.

Songeon, G. *Histoire des Bulgares,* Paris 1913.

Stavrianos, L. S. *Balkan Federation,* London 1944.

Tsonev, P. *Iz obshtestvenoto i kulturno minalo na Gabrovo. Istoricheski Prinosi,* Sofia 1932.

Zankow, S. *Die Verfassung der bulgarischen orthodoxen Kirche,* Zürich 1918.

Articles

Black, Cyril E. 'Russia and the Modernization of the Balkans', in Charles and Barbara Jelavich (eds.), *The Balkans in Transition; Essays on the Development of Balkan Life and Politics since the Eighteenth Century,* Reprint edition, Hamden, Conn. 1974.

Pundeff, Marin V. 'Bulgarian Nationalism', in Peter Sugar and Ivo J. Led-erer, *Nationalism in Eastern Europe,* Far Eastern and Russian Institute Publications on Russia and Eastern Europe, no. 1, Seattle and London 1971.

Roberts, Henry L. 'Politics in a small state; the Balkan Example', in Charles and Barbara Jelavich (eds.), *The Balkans in Transition, Essays on the*

Development of Balkan Life and Politics since the Eighteenth Century, Reprint edition, Hamden, Conn. 1974.

Soulis, George C. 'Historical Studies in the Balkans in Modern Times', in Charles and Barbara Jelavich (eds.), *The Balkans in Transition: Essays on the Development of Balkan Life and Politics since the Eighteenth Century*, Reprint edition, Hamden, Conn. 1974.

Stavrianos, L. S. 'The Influence of the West', in Charles and Barbara Jelavich (eds.), *The Balkans in Transition: Essays on the Development of Balkan Life and Politics since the Eighteenth Century*, Reprint edition, Hamden, Conn. 1974.

Stoianovich, Traian 'The Social Foundations of Balkan Politics, 1750–1941', in Charles and Barbara Jelavich (eds.), *The Balkans in Transition: Essays on the Development of Balkan Life and Politics*, Reprint edition, Hamden, Conn. 1974.

Trenkov, Hristo 'Bulgarian Bibliography', *SEER*, vol. 27, (1948–9).

Yotsov, Yaroslav 'Burzhuaznaya Demokratiya v Bolgarii 1879–1923gg' *EH*, vol. 5, (1970).

Works relevant to the whole or a major part of the period 1878–1918

Documentary Material

Beltcheff, G. *La Bulgarie et ses Voisins; Faits et Documents, 1870–1915.* Sofia 1919.

Bŭlgariya, Narodno Sŭbranie *Dnevnitsi na obiknoveno Narodno Sŭbranie. Stenograficheski Protokoli.* Sofia 1879 *et seq.*

Georgiev, K. 'Dokumenti za uchebnoto delo u nas ot Osvobozhdenieto do velikata oktomvriiska sotsialisticheska revoliutsiya (1878–1917g)', *IDA*, no. 3 (1959).

Ivanov, Ivan 'Voennite vŭprosi v dokumentite po vŭnshnata politika na Bŭlgariya ot Osvobozhdenieto do Pŭrvata svetovna voina', *VS*, no. 1 (1971).

Kesyakov, B. *Prinos kŭm Diplomaticheskata Istoriya na Bŭlgariya 1878–1925.* Sofia 1925.

Books

Angel, Jacques *L'unité de la politique bulgare, 1870–1918*, Paris 1919.

Black, F. *The American College of Sofia*, Boston 1958.

Dimitrov, Krŭstiu *Bŭlgarskata Inteligentsiya pri Kapitalisma.* Sofia 1974.

Dorosiev, I. *Istoriya na zhelez nitsite*, Sofia 1935.

Geshov, Iv. Ev. *Spomeni iz godini na borbi i pobedi*, Sofia 1916.

Geshov, Iv. Ev. *Vŭzgledi i Deinost*, Sofia 1926.

Geshov, Ivan E. *Spomemi i Studii*, Sofia 1928.

Girginov, Dr. Al. *Istoricheski Razvoi na sŭvremmena Bŭlgariya ot Vŭzrazhdaneto do Balkanskata Voina, 1912 godina*, 2 vols., Sofia 1934 and 1935.

Corti, Egon   *Alexander of Bulgaria*, London, 1954.

Dimitrov, Ilcho   *Knyazŭt, Konstitutsiyata i Narodŭt: Iz Istoriya na politicheskite borbi v Bŭlgariya prez pŭrvite godini sled Osvobozhdenieto*. Sofia 1972.

Dimtschoff, Radoslave, M.   *Das Eisenbahnwesen auf der Balkan Halbinsel*, Bamberg 1894.

Drandar, A. G.   *Cinq ans de regne. Le Prince Alexandre de Battenberg en Bulgarie*. Paris 1884.

Drandar, A. G.   *Les Evénements Politiques en Bulgarie depuis 1876 à nos Jours*, Paris 1896.

Erdić (Queille), J.   *En Bulgarie et en Roumelie, Mai-Juin 1884*, Paris 1885.

Girginov, Dr. Al.   *Dŭrzhavnoto ustroistvo na Bŭlgariya*, Sofia 1921.

Golovin, A. F.   *Fürst Alexander von Bulgarien*, Vienna 1896.

Gopcević, Spiridion   *Bulgarien und Ostrumelien. Mit besonderer Berücksichtigung des Zeitraumes von 1878–1886, nebst militärischer Würdigung des serbobulgarischen Krieges*, Leipzig 1886.

Grogan, Lady Elinor   *The Life of J. D. Bourchier*, London no date.

Hajek, Alois   *Bulgariens Befreiung und seiner staatlichen Entwicklung unter seinem ersten Fürsten*, Munich-Berlin 1939.

Ikonomov, Todor   *Memoari*, (edited by T. Zhechev), Sofia 1973.

Ischirkoff, A.   *La Macédoine et la Constitution de l'Exarchat bulgare, 1830–1897*, Lausanne 1918.

Jelavich, Barbara   *Russia, Britain and the Bulgarian Question. The Letters of E. E. Staal to N. K. Giers*, Bloomington, Ind. 1966.

Jelavich, Charles   *Russian Policy in Bulgaria and Serbia, 1881–1897*, Berkeley, Calif. 1950.

Jelavich, Charles   *Tsarist Russia and Balkan Nationalism. Russian Influence in the Internal Affairs of Bulgaria and Serbia, 1876–1886*, Berkeley, Calif. 1958.

Kartsov, Yu. S.   *Za kulisami diplomatii*, St Petersburg 1909.

Kennan, George F.   *The Decline of Bismarck's European Order. Franco-Russian Relations, 1875–1890*, Princeton 1979.

Kiril, Patriarch bŭlgarski   *Bŭlgarskata ekzarhiya v Odrinsko i Makedoniya sled Osvoboditelanta Voina 1877–1878*, vol. i, *1878–1885*, Sofia 1969.

Klaeber, Hans   *Fürst Alexander von Bulgarien*, Dresden 1904.

Koch, Adolf   *Fürst Alexander von Bulgarien. Mitheilungen aus seinem Leben und seiner Regierung nach persönlichen Errinerungen*, Darmstadt 1887.

Königslöw, Joachim von   *Fürst Ferdinand von Bulgarien. Vom Beginn der Thronkadidatur bis zur Anerkennung durch die Grossmächte (1886 bis 1896)*, Munich, 1970.

Kozhuharov, K. D.   *Iztochniyat Vŭpros i Bŭlgariya, 1875–1890*, Sofia 1929.

Kozhuharov, Kuniu   *Petko Karavelov. Istoricheska Hronika za nego i borbite na negovoto vreme*, Sofia 1968.

Lamouche, Leon   *La Bulgarie dans le passé et le présent*, Paris 1892.

Leger, Louis   *La Bulgarie*, Paris 1885.

Mirchev, Petŭr   *Kipezhŭt. Kniga za Sofiya 1878–1884*. Sofia 1971.

Panayotov, Dr. Ivan   *Rusiya, Velikite Sili i Bŭlgarskiyat Vŭpros sled Izbora na Knyaz Ferdinanda (1888–1896g)*. Universitetska Biblioteka, no. 247, Sofia 1941.

Pandev, Konstantin   *Natsionalno-osvoboditelnoto dvizhenie v Makedoniya i Odrinsko, 1878–1903*, Sofia 1979.

Pantev, Andrei   *Angliya sreshtu Rusiya na Balkanite, 1879–1894*, Sofia 1972.

Parensov, General P.   *Iz Minaloto. Spomeni na edin ofitser ot generalniya shtab v Bŭlgariya. Sled 30 godini*, Sofia 1909.

Radev, Simeon   *Stroitelite na sŭvremenna Bŭlgariya*, 2 vols., Sofia 1911. Reprinted with an introduction by and under the general editorship of Academician Pantelei Zarev, Sofia 1973.

Radev, S.   *Makedoniya i bŭlgarskoto vŭzrazhdenie v xix v.*, Sofia 1927.

Radev, Simeon   *Ranni Spomeni*, Sofia 1967.

Samuelson, James   *Bulgaria, Past and Present: Historical, Political and Descriptive*. London 1888.

Sydacoff, Bresnitz v.   *Bulgarien und der bulgarische Fürstenhof (1879–1895). Politischefeuilletonistische Aufzeichnungen eines Diplomaten*, Berlin and Leipzig 1896.

Tatishchev, S. S.   *Iz proshlago russkoi diplomatii*, St Petersburg 1890.

Tenev, Mih.   *Zhivot i Deinost*, Sofia 1942.

Tsenov, A. S.   *Pŭrvii bŭlgarskii knyaz*, Plovdiv 1895.

Vŭlkov, Georgi   *Ruskite uchiteli na bŭlgarskoto voinstvo, 1877–1885*, Sofia 1977.

Articles

Black, C. E.   'The Influence of Western Political Thought in Bulgaria', *AHR*, vol. 48, (1942–43).

Buzhashky, Evlogi   'Vŭzrozhdenski Vliyanie vŭrkhu politicheski partii sled Osvobozhdenieto', *Pŭrvi Kongres na Bŭlgarskoto Istorichesko Druzhestvo*. 2 vols., Sofia 1972, see vol. i.

Gauld, W. A.   'The Making of Bulgaria', *History*, vol. 10, no. 37 (1925).

Grogan, Lady Elinor F. B.   'Bulgaria under Prince Alexander', *SEER*, vol. i (1922–3).

Hristov, Hr.   'Zaharii Stoyanov; obshtestvena i politicheska deinost' *GSUFIF*, vol. 64, no. 2 (1948).

Kosev, D.   'Petko Rachev Slaveikov—obshtestvena i politicheska deinost', *GSUFIF*, vol. 65, no. 2 (1948–9).

Kovacheva, Margareta   'Nachalo na vŭnshnata politika na knyazhestvo Bŭlgariya', *IP*, vol. 31, no. 3 (1975).

Mosolov, Aleksandŭr   'Bŭlgariya (1878–83). Spomeni', *VS*, vol. 10, no. 28 (1936).

Valkov, Georgi 'The Russian Organizers of the Bulgarian Armed Forces, (1877–1885)', *BHR*, vol. 3, no. 2 (1975).

Vasilev, K. 'Der Widerhall der osterreichisch-ungarischen Bulgarenpolitik in der bulgarischen Presse (1879–1885)', *EH*, vol. 2 (1965).

Vŭlkov, Georgi 'Sŭzdavane, razvitie i rolya na Narodnoto opŭlchenie v Bŭlgariya (1880–1891)', *IP*, vol. 30, no. 2 (1974).

Vŭlkov, Georgi 'Voenniyat aspekt na bŭlgaro-ruskite otnosheniya (1877–1885)', in Vasil Vasiliev (ed.), *Vŭnshnata Politika na Bŭlgariya, 1878–1944*, Izsledvaniya po bŭlgarska Istoriya, no. 3, Sofia 1978.

Thesis

Migev, V. T. 'Zheleznopŭtniyat vŭpros v Bŭlgariya ot negovoto vŭznikvane do Sŭedinenieto, 1885g', Ph.D., Sofia 1962.

Chapter 1

Documentary Material

Black, C. E. *Constitution of the Kingdom of Bulgaria*, Sofia 1911.

Bŭlgariya, Narodno Sŭbranie *Protokolite na Uchreditelnoto Bŭlgarsko Narodno Sŭbranie v Tŭrnovo (1022 Fevruarii 1879 godina)*, Plovdiv 1879.

Jelavich, Charles and Barbara 'Russian and Bulgaria, 1879. The letters of A. P. Davydov to N. K. Giers', *SF*, vol. 15, (1956).

Miliutin, S. D. *Dnevnik, 1878–1880*, Moscow 1950.

Books

Angelow, Charalumby *Das bulgarische Staatsrecht im allgemein, unter besonderer Berücksichtigung des Volksvertretung*, Freiburg 1896.

Beitzke, Günther *Das Staatsangehörigkeit von Albanien, Bulgarien und Rumänien*, Frankfurt 1951.

Belov, G. *Mnenie po vŭprosa za zheleznite pŭtishta v Bŭlgariya*, Sofia 1883.

Farley, James Lewis *New Bulgaria*, London 1880.

Fandikov, G. P. *Mezhdunarodno-pravovoi rezhim Dunaya*, Moscow 1955.

Gueron, Mosche M. *Die Volksvertretung in Bulgarien*, Leipzig 1934.

Handjieff, Nikola *Organisation der Staats- und Selbstvertretung in Bulgarien*, Munich 1931.

Harris, C. Montagu *Local Government in Many Lands*, second edition, London 1933.

Karadjow, Detchko *Contre le système d'une chambre unique en Bulgarie*, Paris 1927.

Metscheff, Slawtscho *Grundzüge des bulgrischen Verfassungsrechts*, Göttingen 1929.

Nikolov, A. *Dunavskiyat vŭpros*, Sofia 1917.

Ovsyani, N. R. *Russkoe Upravlenie v Bolgarii*, St Petersburg 1913.

Sarafow, K. M. *Die Volksvertretung in Bulgarien*, Halle 1905.

Skazkin, S.   *Konets avstro-russko-germanskogo Soiuza*, vol. i, *1879–1884*, Moscow 1928.

Slaveikov, P. R.   *Poslednoto mi hodyanie v Sofiya*, Plovdiv 1883.

Todorov, G. D.   *Vremennoto rusko upravlenie v Bŭlgariya prez 1877–1879g*, Sofia 1958.

Vasilev, K. *et al.* (eds.)   *Kresnensko-Raslozhkoto Vŭstanie, 1878*, Sofia 1970.

Vladikin, Liubomir   *Istoriya na tŭrnovskata konstitutsiya*, Sofia 1936.

Vŭlkov, G.   *Dialogŭt Parensov-Batenberg*, Sofia 1971.

Articles

Bourchier, James D.   'Prince Alexander of Battenberg', *Fortnightly Review*, vol. 55 (Jan.-June 1894).

Dimitrov, Ilcho   'Dŭrzhavniyat prevrat na 27 april 1881 g. i borbite na Liberalnata partiya protiv nego', *GSUFIF*, vol. 56, no. 2 (1963).

Dimitrov, I.   'Narodnoto opŭlchenie ot 1880–1882 godina', *VS*, no. 6 (1965).

Doinov, D.   'Natsionalnoosvoboditelnite borbi v Yugozapadna Bŭlgariya v navecherieto na Kresnensko-Razlozhkoto Vŭstanie', in Kŭncho Vasilev *et al.* (eds.), *Kresnensko-Razlozhkoto Vŭstanie, 1878*, Sofia 1970.

Gandev, Hristo   'Ruskata pomosht za izgrazhdaneto na bŭlgarskata dŭrzhava prez 1877–1878g', in *Osvobozhdenieto na Bŭlgariya ot tursko igo*, Sofia 1958.

Hristov, Hristo   'Bŭlgarskata Natsionalna Revoliutsia i Kresnensko-Razlozhkoto Vŭstanie', in Kŭncho Vasilev *et al.* (eds.), *Kresnensko-Razlozhkoto Vŭstanie, 1878*, Sofia 1970.

Markova, Zina and Statelova, Elena   'Uchreditelno Sŭbranie v Tŭrnovo', *IP*, vol. 35, no. 3 (1979).

Petrov, Metodi   'Ruskata pomosht za sŭzdavane na bŭlgarska administratsiya (1877–1879g.)', *IP*, vol. 28, no. 5 (1972).

Petrov, Metodi   'Die Wahl des Prinzen von Battenberg zum Fürsten Bulgariens', *BHR*, vol. i, no. 2 (1973).

Petrov, M.   'Pŭrvata politicheska kriza sled Osvobozhdenieto', *IP*, vol. 29, no. 5, (1973).

Petrov, Metodi   'Pravitelstvoto na Mitropolit Kliment (1879–1880g)', *IP*, vol. 31, no. 5 (1975).

Petrov, Metodi   'Za Rolyata na Aleksandŭr Batenberg v pŭrvite godini sled Osvobozhdenieto (1879–1880g)', *IP*, vol. 32, no. 4 (1976).

Statelova, E.   'La Bulgarie et le problème danubien (1879–1883)' *EH*, vol. 6 (1973).

Todorov, Goran   'Kŭm vŭprosa za proizhoda i sŭshtnostta na politicheskite programi na partiite v Uchreditelnoto Sŭbranie', *IIIBAN*, vol. 7, (1957).

Tsetanski, Stoyan   'Rolyata na komitetite "Edinstvo" v Gorna Djumaya i Kiustendil za podgotovkata i provezhdaneto na kresnensko-razlozhkoto vŭstanie', in Kŭncho Vasilev *et al.* (eds.) *Kresnensko-Razlozhkoto Vŭstanie 1878*, Sofia 1970.

Vanchev, Yordan 'Sotsialen Sŭstav na Uchasnitsite v Kresnensko-Razlozh-koto Vŭstanie prez 1878g', in Kŭncho Vasilev et al. (eds.), Kresnensko-Razlozhkoto Vŭstanie, 1878, Sofia 1970.

Vasilev, Kŭncho 'Borbata na bŭlgarskiya narod protiv resheniyata na Ber-linskiya kongres 1878–1879g', in Osvobozhdenieto na Bŭlgariya ot tursko igo, Sofia 1958.

Vasilev, Kŭncho 'Kresnensko-Razlozhkoto Vŭstanie i Pomoga na Nasele-nieto ot osvobodenite bŭlgarski Teritorii', in Kŭncho Vasilev et al. (eds.), Kresnensko-Razlozhkoto Vŭstanie 1878, Sofia 1970.

Chapter 2

Books
Grunwald, Kurt   Turkenhirsch; A Study of Baron Maurice de Hirsch, Entre-preneur and Philanthropist, Jerusalem 1966.

Articles
Dimitrov, Ilcho 'Krahŭt na rezhima na pŭlnomoshtiyata i raztseplenieto na Liberalnata partiya (1883–1884)' IP, vol. 19, no. 2 (1963).

Dimitrov, Ilcho 'Rezhimŭt na pŭlnomosthtiyata i borbata protiv nego 1881–1883 g.', GSUIK, vol. 58 (1965).

Mikkola, J. J.   'Einige Bemerkungen über die Tätigkeit General Casimir Ehrenroths als bulgarischer Staatsmann', in Sbornik v Pamet na Prof. Petŭr Nikov, Sofia 1939.

Rechberger, W.   'Zur Geschichte der Orientbahn', Oesterreichische Osthefte, vols. 1 and 2 (1960 and 1961).

Todorov, Goran D.   'Profesor Marin S. Drinov i dŭrzhavniyat prevrat v knyazhestvo Bŭlgariya prez 1881 g.', III, vol. 16–17, (1966).

Chapter 3

Books
Suknarov, N.   Razprata mi s P. Karavelov, Sofia 1885.

Articles
Bozhinov, Voin 'Natsialnoosvoboditelnata borba na bŭlgarskoto naselenie v Makedoniya sled Kresnensko-Razlozhkoto Vŭstanie (1878–1903)', in Kŭn-cho Vasilev et al. (eds.), Kresnensko-Razlozhkoto Vŭstanie, 1878, Sofia 1970.

Pandev, Konstantin 'Nachalo na Makedono-Odrinsko Dvizhenie v Bŭlga-riya (1879–1894)', in Dimitŭr Kosev, (ed.) V Chest na Akademik Hristo Hristov. Izsledvaniya po 60 godini ot rozhdenieto mu, Sofia 1976.

Vŭlkov, G. 'Vŭznikvane, razvitie i urezhdane na "voenniya vŭpros" (1883)', Izvestiya na Voennoto Nauchno Istorichesko Druzhestvo, vol. 19 (1975).

Thesis

Karosseroff, Iwan   'Zur Entwicklung der bulgarischen Eisenbahnen', Erlangen Ph. D. 1907.

Chapter 4

Documentary Material

Bŭlgariya, *Korespondentsiya po vŭprosa za sŭedinenieto Ot 4 Septemvrii 1885 god. do 15/27 Aprilii 1886 god.*, Sofia 1886.

Bŭlgariya, *Korespondentsiya po Sŭrbsko-Bŭlgarskata Voina. Ot 9 Septemvrii do 17/29 Noemvrii 1885 god. (Ot 17/29 Noemvrii 1885 god. do 19 Fevruarii/3 Mart 1886 god.)*, Sofia 1886.

Pashev, Georgi   *Da zhivei Sŭedinenieto: Dokumentalen povest (za prisŭedinyavaneto na Iztochna Rumeliya kŭm knyazhestvo Bŭlgariya prez 1885 g.)*, Plovdiv 1972.

Statelova, Elena & Popov, Radoslav (compilers)   *Spomeni za Sŭedinenieto ot 1885 g.*, Sofia 1980.

Strashimirov, S. (ed)   *Arhiv na Vŭzrazhdaneto*, vol. 2, *Dokumenti po Sŭedinenieto*, Sofia 1908.

Books

Benderev, Cpt. A.   *Serbsko-bolgarskaya voina, 1885 goda*, St Petersburg 1892.

Huhn, Major A. von   *The Struggle of the Bulgarians for National Independence under Prince Alexander. A Military and Political History of the War between Bulgaria and Servia in 1885*, translated from the German, London 1886.

Madjarov, Mih. Iv.   *Iztochna Rumeliya. (Istoricheski Pregled)*, Sofia 1929.

Manolova, Maria Georgieva   *Rusiya i konstitutsionnoto ustroistvo na Iztochniya Rumeliya*, Sofia 1976.

Mitev, Y.   *Istoricheski studii. I. Sŭedinenieto na Bŭlgariya i velikite sili*, Sofia 1955.

Mitev, Yono (ed.)   *Istoriya na Srŭbsko-bŭlgarskata Voina, 1885*, Sofia 1971.

Panayotov, I.   *Opit za sŭedinenie na Knyazhestvo Bŭlgariya s Iztochna Rumeliya prez 1880 godina*, Sofia 1948.

Penkov, S.   *Borbata na bŭlgarskiya narod protiv berlinskiya dogovor i mezhdunarodnoto pravo, 1878–1886g*, Sofia 1968.

Stoyanoff, Zachari   *Pages from the Autobiography of a Bulgarian Insurgent*, London 1913.

Stoyanov, Manin   *Kogato Plovdiv beshe stolitsa*, Sofia 1974.

Tsanov, Il.   *Iz belezhkite mi po Sŭedinenieto*, Sofia 1889.

Articles

Dimitrov, Ilcho   'P. R. Slaveikov sled Osvobozhdenieto. (Nyakoi utochenie kŭm politicheskata mu deinost)' *Vekove; Ochertsi, Spomeni, Dokumenti, iz trinadeset—vekovnata Bŭlgarska Istoriya*, Sofia 1972.

Genov, Ts. 'Dobrovolcheskoto dvizhenie u nas po vreme na Sŭedinenieto i Srŭbsko-bŭlgarskata voina 1885 g,' *VS.*, no. 2 (1954).

Genov, Tsonko 'Gimnasticheskite strelkovi druzhestva v Iuzhna Bŭlgariya prez 1878–1879 godina', *VS*, no. 3 (1956).

Genov, Tsonko 'Podgotovka, izvŭrshvane i zashtita na Sŭedinenieto prez 1885 g.', *IP*, vol. 16, no. 4 (1960).

Medlicott, W. N. 'The Powers and the Unification of the Two Bulgarias, 1885', *English Historical Review*, vol. 54, no. 213 (Jan. 1939), and no. 214 (April 1939).

Mitev, Y. 'Otnoshenieto na Velikite sili kŭm sŭedinenieto na Bŭlgariya prez 1885 g.', *IP*, vol. 10, no. 4 (1954).

Mitev, Yono 'Diplomaticheskata deinost na Ivan Evstratiev Geshov v Evropa otnosno priznavane na sŭedinenieto', in Vasil Vasiliev (ed.), *Vŭnshnata Politika na Bŭlgariya (1878–1944),* Izsledvaniya po bŭlgarska Istoriya, no. 3, Sofia 1978.

Miyatev, P. 'Stranichki na istoriyata na Iztochna Rumeliya', *IP*, vol. 26, no. 5 (1970).

Pantev, Andrei 'Emigrantskiyat vŭpros v bŭlgaro-srŭbskite otnosheniya 1883–1886 g.', *Vekove*, no. 4 (1973).

Samardziev, Bozidar 'Traits dominants de la politique d'Abdulhamid II relative au problème des nationalites (1876–1885)', *EB*, vol. 8, no. 4 (Sofia 1972).

Statelova, Elena 'Razvoi i harakter na otnoshniyata mezhdu knyazhestvo Bŭlgariya i Iztochna Rumeliya, (1879–1885g)', *IP*, vol. 34, no. 5 (1978).

Stoyanov, M. 'Izrabotvane na organicheski ustav na Iztochna Rumeliya', *IP*, vol. 11, no. 2 (1955).

Todorov, G. 'Kŭm diplomaticheskata istoriya na Sŭedinenieto na Bŭlgariya prez 1885g', *IP*, vol. 21, no. 6 (1965).

Vŭlkov, Georgi 'Uchastieto na ruskite ofitseri v izgrazhdaneto na Iztochnorumeliiskata militsiya 1878–1885g', *VS*, no. 2 (1975).

Chapter 5

Books

Freycinet, Charles de *Souvenirs, 1878–1893*, Paris 1893.

Slaveikov. P. R. *Razmishleniya vŭrhu polozhenieto ni*, Sofia 1886.

Articles

Mitev, Tr. 'Prichini za abdikatsiyata na Knyaz Aleksandŭr Batenberg', *IP*, vol. 35, no. 6 (1979).

Popov, Radoslav 'Pŭrvata politicheska emigratsiya i otnosheniyata mezhdu Bŭlgariya i balkanskite dŭrzhavi (1886–1887g)', *IP*, vol. 32, no. 5 (1976).

Ralev, Mihail 'Detronatsiyata na knyaz Aleksandŭr Batenberg na 9 avgust 1886g', *VS*, no. 2 (1972).

Chapter 6

Books
Krachunov, K. *Diplomatichna Istoriya na Bŭlgariya (1886–1915)*, vol. i, *Velikite Dŭrzhavi i Bŭlgariya (1886–7)*, Sofia 1928.
Ralev, Mihail *Za druzhbata s ruskiya narod. Borbata na bŭlgarskite voini sreshtu diktaturata na Batenberg i Stambulov, 1886–1887*, Sofia 1958.
Ralev, Mihail *Predvestnitsi na bŭdeshti buri. Buntovete na ofitserite-rusofili ot bŭlgarskite voiski prez 1886–1887*, Sofia 1975.
Smith, Colin L. *The Embassy of Sir William White at Constantinople, 1886–1891*, Oxford 1957.

Articles
Hristov, Hristo 'Spomeni na T. H. Stanchev za rusenskiya bunt prez fevruari 1887g', *III*, vol. 3-4, (1951).
Pantev, A. 'Za otnoshenieto na ruskiya burzhoazen pechat kŭm bŭlgarskite sŭbitiya (avgust 1886–iuli 1887), in Vasil Vasiliev, *Vŭnshnata Politika na Bŭlgariya, 1878–1944*, Izslevaniya po bŭlgarskata Istoriya, no. 3, Sofia 1978.
Samardzhiev, Bozidar 'Ottoman Policy towards the Principality of Bulgaria during the Regency (August 1886–July 1887)', *EB*, vol. 12, no. 4 (1976).
Vŭlov, Vŭlo 'Buntovete v bŭlgarskata voiska 1886–1887g', *VS*, no. 4 (1955).

Chapter 7

Documentary Material
Velinova, Eli 'Iz korespondentsiyata na bŭlgarski politicheski i obshtestveni deitsi do Konstantin Velichkov (1887–1896g), *IDA*, no. 9 (165).

Books
'The Author of The Real Kaiser' *Ferdinand of Bulgaria: the Amazing Career of A Shoddy Czar*, London 1916.
Behrens, Joachim *Der Magier auf dem Throne—Ein Lebensbild des Zaren Ferdinand von Bulgarien aus dem Hause Coburg-Kohary*, Coburg o. J. 1935.
Hulme Beaman, A. *M. Stambuloff*, London, 1895.
Hulme Beaman, A. *Twenty Years in the Near East*, London, 1898.
Jotzoff, Dimitri *Zar Ferdinand von Bulgarien: sein Lebenswerk im Orient*, Berlin 1927.
Marinov, D. *Stefan Stambulov i novata ni Istoriya*, Sofia 1909.
Trifonov, Y. *V. Drumev—Kliment Branitski i Tŭrnovski: Zhivot, Deinost i Harakter*, Sofia 1926.
Velchev, Velcho T. *Stambolov i Ferdinand: Diktatorskiya rezhim i borbata protiv nego*, Sofia 1922.

Articles
Bourchier, J. D. 'Through Bulgaria with Prince Ferdinand', *Fortnightly Review*, vol. 44, (July-Dec. 1888).

Bourchier, J. D. 'In the Balkans with Prince Ferdinand', *Fortnightly Review,* vol. 46, (July-Dec. 1889).

Bourchier, James D. 'On the Black Sea with Prince Ferdinand', *Fortnightly Review,* vol. 49, (Jan.-June 1891).

Hristov, Hristo 'Kŭm harakteristikata na stamboloviya rezhim', *IP,* vol. 8, no. 1 (1951-2).

Kramptŭn, Richard Dj '"Taims" i konsolidatsiyata na rezhima na Stambolov (1888-1892)' in Dimitŭr Kosev, (ed. in chief), *Bŭlgariya v sveta ot drevnostta do nashi dni,* 2 vols., Sofia 1979, see vol. ii.

Marinov, Iliya 'Buntovete na rusofilite v Silistra i Ruse prez 1887g', *VS,* no. 1 (1972).

Mishev, Radoslav 'Bŭlgariya i avstro-ungariya v nachalnite godini na stamboloviya rezhim (1887-1890g)' *IP,* vol. 36, no. 3 (1980).

Pantev, A. 'Misiyata na dr. Vŭlkovich v Atina (mart-april 1890g.) spored angliiski arhivni iztochnitsi', *IP,* vol. 26, no. 6 (1970).

Pantev, A. 'Angliya, Germaniya i bŭlgarskiyat vŭpros (avgust 1887-mart 1890g)' in *Bŭlgarsko-Germanski Otnosheniya i Vrŭzki,* Sofia 1972.

Chapter 8

Books
Bresnitz, Phillip Franz *Bulgarien und der bulgarische Fürstenhof,* 2nd edition, Berlin and Leipzig 1896.

Bŭlgariya, Ispitatelna Komisiya po Zloupotrebleniyata na Stamboloviya Kabinet. *Doklad na Parlamentarnata Anketna Komisiya s pribavlenie na dokumenti namereni v arhivite na raznite urezhdeniya v Knyazhestvoto,* Sofia 1895.

Bŭlgariya, Veliko Narodno Sŭbranie *Konstitutsiya na bŭlgarskoto Knyazhestvo,* Sofia 1893.

Damjanov, Simeon 'L'Affaire "Chadourne" et la lutte de Stambulov contre le Régime des Capitulations en Bulgarie (1891-1892)', *EH,* vol. 6 (1973).

Dicey, Edward 'The Story of Stambuloff's Fall', *Fortnightly Review,* vol. 58 (July-Dec. 1895).

Jelavich, Charles 'Russo-Bulgarian Relations, 1892-1896: With particular reference to the problem of the Bulgarian Succession', *JMH,* vol. 24, no. 4 (Dec. 1952).

Pantev, Andrei 'Bulgaria in Anglo-Russian Relations in 1892-1894', *EH,* vol. 5, (1970).

Chapter 9

Documentary Material
Stoilov, Dr. Konstantin *Rechi,* Sofia 1939.

Books
Beckman, Josef *Die Wahrheit über Bulgarien,* Leipzig 1898.

Plachkov, Dr. Iv. P.   *Dr. K. Stoilov*, Sofia 1930.
Velchev, Velcho T.   *Stranitsi ot novata ni politicheska istoriya. Pomirenieto s Rusiya. Priznaveneto i zakrepvaneto na Ferdinanda. Nachalo na lichniya rezhim*, Sofia 1924.

Articles
Damyanov, Simeon   'La Diplomatie française et les réformes en Turquie d'Europe (1895–1903)', *EB*, vol. 10 (1974), nos. 2-3.
Damyanov, Simeon   'Frensko-bŭlgarskite diplomaticheski otnosheniya sled padento na Stambolov (1894–1897)', in *V Chest na Akademik Dimitŭr Kosev*, Sofia 1974.
Palotash, Emil   'Bŭlgarskiyat vŭpros i avstroungarskata diplomatsiya prez 1894–1896g', in *V Chest na Akademik Dimitŭr Kosev*, Sofia 1974.

Chapter 10

Documentary Material
Atanasov, Cpt. I.   *Staticheski Sbornik na Knyazhestvo Bŭlgariya*, Sofia 1897.
Bŭlgariya, Direktsiya na Statistika   *Naselenieto na Bŭlgariya spored pre-broyavaniyata na i yanuarii 1888, 1 yanuarii 1893, i 31 dekemvrii 1900*, Sofia 1907.
Penkov, N.   'Agrarnite otnoshenie v Burgaski okrŭg ot Osvobozhdenieto do nachaloto na xx vek, (1878–1900) *IDA*, no. 5 (1961).
Sarafov, M. and Irichek, K.   *Raport ot komisiyata, izpratena v Kiustendilski okrŭg da izuchi polozhenieto na bezimotnite selyani*, Sofia 1880.
Shekerov, Todor   'Iztochnitsi za sŭstoyanieto na zdravoopazvaneto Burgas prez poslednite dve desetiletiya na xix vek', *IDA*, no. 11 (1966).
Vaklieva, N. and Kamburova, N.   'Agrarnite Otnosheniya v Bŭlgariya ot Osvobozhdenieto do 1900', *IDA*, no. 1 (157).

Books
Battenberg, Joseph Prinz von   *Die Volkswirtschaftliche Entwicklung Bulga-riens von 1879 bis zur Gegenwart*, Leipzig 1891.
Busch-Zantner, Richard   *Agrarverfassung und Siedlung in Südost-europa; unter besonderen Berücksichtigung der Türkenzeit*, Leipzig 1938.
Byrnes, Robert F. (ed.)   *Communal Families in the Balkans: The Zadruga. Essays by Philip E. Mosely and in His Honor*, Notre Dame, Ind. and London 1976.
Dicey, Edward   *The Peasant State. An Account of Bulgaria in 1894*, London 1894.
Georgiev, Georgi   *Osvobozhdenieto i etnokulturnoto razvitie na bŭlgarskiya narod, 1877–1900*, Sofia 1979.
Geshov, Iv. Ev.   *Zadrugata v Zapadna Bŭlgariya*, Sofia 1887.

Irichek, Konstantin *Pŭtuvane po Bŭlgariya,* Sofia 1974 edition. Originally published as *Cesty pro Búlharsku,* Prague 1888.

Krauss, Friedrich *Sitte und Brauche der Südslawen,* Vienna 1885.

Kunin, Petko *Agrarno-selskiyat Vŭpros v Bŭlgariya, ot Osvobozhdenieto do Kraya na pŭrvata svetovna voina,* Sofia 1971.

Nachovich, G. D. *Nyakolko Stranitsi po Zemledelieto v Bŭlgariya i Stranstvo,* Sofia 1902.

Novakovich, D. *La Zadrouga,* Paris 1905.

Pantschow, Wladimir S. *Die Agrarverhältnisse des Fürstentums Bulgarien in ihrer geschichtlichen Entwickelung,* Ph.D., published Leipzig 1893.

Simeonoff, Stefan D. *Die Zadruga und Ehegüterrechtsverhältnisse Bulgariens,* Hamburg 1931.

Slavov, Slavi *Sotsialno-politicheski vŭzgledi v Bŭlgariya prez pŭrvoto desetiletie sled Osvobozhdenieto,* Sofia 1975.

Stanischitsch, Dr. Alexa *Über den Ursprung der Zadruga. Eine soziologische Untersuchung,* Berner Studien zur Philosophie und ihrer Geschichte, no. 59, Bern 1907.

Wilhelmy, Herbert *Hochbulgarien I. Die ländliche Siedlungen und die bäuerliche Wirtschaft.* Schriften des Geographischen Instituts der Universität Kiel, herausgegeben von O. Schmieder und H. Wenzel. Band IV. Kiel 1935.

Articles

Anon 'The New Bulgaria', *The Nation,* vol. 60, (May 1895).

Berov, Liuben 'Ikonomicheskite posleditsi ot Ruskoturskata voina prez 1877–1878g', in *Osvobozhdenieto na Bulgariya ot tursko igo,* Sofia 1958.

Blagoev, D. 'Nyakolko staticheski danni po kontsentratsiyata na sobstvenostta u nas', *Nova Vreme,* (Plovdiv) vol. 1 (1898), no. 8.

Bobchev, S. S. 'Bŭlgarskata chelyadna zadruga v segashno i minalo vreme', *SBNUNK,* vols. 22 and 23, (1906–7).

Bourchier, J. D. 'Social Life in Bulgaria', *English Illustrated Magazine,* vol. 7, (1889).

Burilkov, Zh. 'Danŭchnata tezhest i narodnoto stopanstvo', *SBID,* vol. 22 (1923–4), no. 6-7.

Dodov, Al. G. 'Zadrugite i sŭsobstvenost', *SBID,* vol. 9, no. 10 (1905).

Georgiev, Georgi 'Preustroistvoto na traditsionnata selishtna sistema v rezultat ot osvobozhdenieto', *IP,* vol. 33, nos. 5-6 (1977).

Geshov, Ivan Evstratiev 'Nashite Gradinarski Druzhestva, *Periodichesko Spisanie,* vol. 27 (1888).

Geshov, Ivan Evstratiev 'Ovcharite ot kotlensko i zhutvarite ot tŭrnovsko' *Periodichesko Spisanie,* vols. 22 and 23.

Geshov, Ivan Evstratiev 'Zadruzhnoto Vladenie i Rabotene v Bŭlgariya' *Periodichesko Spisanie,* vols. 28-30; (1889).

Jiriček, C. 'Ethnographische Veränderungen in Bulgarien seit der Errichtung des Furstentums', *Oesterreich-Ungarische Review N.F.*, vol. 10, (1890–1).

Levintov, N. G. 'Agrarnye otnosheniya v Bolgarii nakanune osvobozhdeniya i agrarnyi perevorot 1877–1879 godov', in L. B. Valev, S. A. Nikitin and P. N. Tretyakov, *Osvobozhdenie Bolgarii ot turetskogo iga. Sbornik Statei*, Moscow 1953.

Mitev, Y. 'Za agrarniya prevrat u nas, izvŭrshil se v resultat ot osvoboditelnata voina prez 1877–1878 g', *IP*, vol. 9, no. 6 (1953).

Piperov, N. 'Danŭtsite v Bŭlgariya', *Misŭl*, vol. 11, no. 3, (1901).

Popov, Dr. Hristo 'Pazarite za zhivotni i nuzhdata ot novo zakonodatelstvo', *Agrarni Problemi*, vol. 3, no. 4, (1940).

Popov, N. 'Zadrugite u Glavantsite', *SBID*, vol. 4, no. s 8-9, (1900).

Razboinikov, Atanas 'Chiflitsi i chifligari v Trakiya predi i sled 1878 g', *IIIBAN*, vol. 9, (1960).

'S.S.B.' (S. S. Bobchev) 'Desetyakŭt (oshurŭt) nyakoga i sega, *Bŭlgarska Sbirka*, vol. 7, no. 5, (1900).

Todorov, Goran 'Deinostta na vremennoto rusko upravlenie v Bŭlgariya po urezhdane na agrarniya i bezhanskiya vŭpros prez 1877–1879g', *IP*, vol. 11, no. 6 (1955).

Todorov, Goran 'Urezhdaneto na agrarniya i bezhanskiya vŭpros v knyazhestvo Bŭlgariya v pŭrvite godini sled Osvobozhdenieto (1879–1881)', *IP*, vol. 17, no. 1 (1961).

Todorov, G. 'Politikata na bŭlgarskite burzhoazni pravitelstva po agrarniya i bezhanskiya vŭpros sled dŭrzhavniya prevrat ot 1881 g. (1881–1886 g)', *IP*, vol. 17, no. 2 (1961).

Usta-Genchov, D. 'Zhŭtvarskite zadrugi niz Tŭrnovsko', *SBNUNK*, vol. 7 (1892).

Theses

Georgieff, A. *Die Reiskultur in Bulgarien*, Leipzig 1909.

Handjieff, W. 'Zur Soziologie des bulgarischen Dorfes', Ph.D., Leipzig 1929, published 1931.

Kalpaktschieff, N. 'Die Viehzucht Bulgariens', Ph.D., Zürich 1927, published 1930.

Chapter 11

Documentary Material

Bŭlgariya, Staticheski Biuro *Statistika za Tŭrgoviyata na bŭlgarskoto Knyazhestvo s Chuzhdite Dŭrzhavi*, Sofia 1896.

Books

Dantschoff, I. *Das Eisenbahnwesen in Bulgarien*, Leipzig 1917.

Daskaloff, Raiko *Das ausländische Kapital in Bulgarien*, Berlin 1912.

Kaltscheff, Kaltscho *Die bulgarische Zollpolitik seit 1878,* Nuremberg 1912.
Spassow, Atanas D. *Der Verfall des alten Handwerk und die Entstehung des modernen Gewerbes in Bulgarien während des 19 Jahrhunderts,* Greifswald 1900.

Articles
Bent, Theodore 'Baron Hirsch's Railway', *Fortnightly Review,* vol. 44, (July-Dec. 1888).
Iurdanov, D. 'Promishlenoto Razvitie na grad Sofiya i Bŭlgariya', part i, *ASSP,* vol. iv (1928), no. 3, part ii, ibid, no. 4, part iii, ibid, no. 5, part iv, ibid, vol. 5, no. 1 (1929).
Iurdanov, Iu. 'Nashite Gradove', *SBID,* vol. 35, no. 1 (1936).
Ladd, Celia R. 'Bulgarian Cities', *Chantanquan,* vol. 29, (Sept. 1899).
Manalov, I. 'Zanayatchiiskata organizatsiya', *Obshto Delo,* (Sofia) vol. 1 (1900–01), nos. 21 & 22.
Michev, Dobrin 'Pŭrvoto bŭlgarsko zemedelsko-promishleno izlozhenie i zemedelsko-promishleniyat sŭbor v gr. Plovdiv prez 1892 g', *IP,* vol. 11, no. 5 (1955).
Petrov, T. and Karaivanov, Georgi 'Vŭlneniyata na sopotskite, karlovskite i kaloferskite predachki prez 1883 godina', *PL,* no. 7 (1968).

Part II

Books
Adanir, Fikret *Die Makedonische Frage. Ihre Entstehung und Entwicklung bis 1908,* Frankfurter Historische Abhandlungen, vol. 20, Wiesbaden 1979.
Anastasoff, Christ *The Tragic Peninsula. A History of the Macedonian Movement for Independence since 1878,* St. Louis, Mo. 1938.
Bronzov, Nikola *et al.* *Dr. Nikola Genadiev. Zhivot i Deinost,* Sofia 1925.
Constant, Stephen *Foxy Ferdinand, Tsar of Bulgaria,* London 1979.
Daudet, Ernest *Ferdinand Ier. Tsar de Bulgarie,* Paris 1917.
Dejanova, Milka *Die Warenausfuhr Bulgariens und Ihre Organisation seit dem Jahre 1900,* Sofia 1930.
Fleischmann, Peter v. *Ferdinand I: König der Bulgaren, sein Volk und Sein Land,* Leipzig 1916.
Ganchev, D. *Spomeni za knyazheskoto vreme,* (Compiled by D. Koen.) Sofia 1973.
Macdonald, John *Czar Ferdinand and his People,* Reprint edition, New York 1971.
Novakova, Kamka L. *Pechatŭt i lichniyat rezhim na Ferdinand,* Sofia 1975.
Todorov, Kosta *Balkan Firebrand,* Chicago 1943.
Vlahov, Tushe *Kriza v Bŭlgaro-Turskite Otnosheniya, 1895–1908,* Sofia 1977.

Pantev, Andrei *et al.* 'Vŭnshnata politika i opozitsionnite partii (1900–1914)', *III*, vol. 23 (1974).

Stefanov, Hristo 'Bŭlgarskata Radikaldemokraticheska Partiya i natsional-niyat vŭpros na Balkanite do Voinite', in *Pŭrvi Kongres na Bŭlgarskoto Istorichesko Druzhestvo*, Sofia 1972.

Chapter 12

Documentary Material

Walters, Eurof 'Unpublished Documents: A. The Serbo-Bulgarian Secret Treaty of 19 February 1897', *SEER*, vol. 28, no. 71 (April 1950).

Books

Apostolski, Mihailo (ed. in chief) *Istoriya na Makedonskiot Narod*, 3 vols., Skopje 1969.

Kyosev, Dinyo *Istoriya na makedonskoto natsionalno revoliutsionno dvizhenie*, Sofia 1954.

Martynenko, A. K. *Russko-bolgarskii otnosheniya v 1894–1902g.*, Kiev 1967.

Articles

Dinevski, Slavko 'Tsŭrkovnata Borba vo Kumanovo vo 90-te godini od XIX vek', *Glasnik*, vol. 8, no. 2 (1964).

Pandev, Konstantin 'Politicheski programi na natsionalnoosvoboditelnoto dvizhenie v Makedoniya i Odrinsko 1903 g.', in *Pŭrvi Kongres na bulgarskoto Istorichesko Druzhestvo*, vol. i, Sofia 1972.

Thesis

Terry, G. M. 'The Origins and Development of the Macedonian Revolutionary Movement with particular Reference to the Taina Makedonska-Odrinska Revoliutsionerna Organizatsiya from its Conception in 1893 to the Ilinden Rising of 1903', M. Phil., Nottingham 1974.

Chapter 13

Books

Kolarov, M. *Iztochnite zheleznitsi v Bŭlgariya*, Plovdiv 1893.

Articles

Berov, Liuben '"Iztochnite zheleznitsi" v. Bŭlgariya 1873–1908g.', *IP*, in *Bulgarsko-Germanski Otnosheniya i Vruzki*, Sofia 1972.

Todorova, Tsvetana 'Frensko-Germanskoto sŭpernichestvo v zaemnata politika s Bŭlgariya i Kombinatsiyata 'Karlsbad 1898g,', in *Bŭlgarsko-Germanski Otnosheniya i Vrŭzki*, Sofia 1972.

Yotsov, Ya. 'Kŭm harakteristikata na "narodnyashkoto" upravlenie (1894–1899)', *IP*, vol. 7, no. 2 (1951).

Thesis
Weissman, Eric R. 'The Cooperative Movement in the Bulgarian Village prior to World War One', Ph.D., University of Washington, 1977.

Chapter 14

Documentary Material
Bulgariya, Narodno Sŭbranie *Doklad na Parlamentarna Komisiya do xi obiknoveno Narodno Sŭbranie . . . po predlozhenieto za davane pod sŭd Ministrite ot kabineta na T. Ivanchova*, Sofia 1901.
Handjieva, Rumyana 'Radikalnata partiya', *IDA*, no. 29 (1975).
Mateev, B. 'Selskoto dvizhenie protiv desyatŭka v Burgaskiya okrŭg prez 1899 i 1900g.', *IDA*, no. 2 (1958).

Books
Beshkov, Liuben *Selskite vŭstaniya i buntut na dobrudjanskite selyani pri Darankulak 1900g.*, Sofia 1970.
Damyanov, Simeon *Frenskoto ikonomichesko Pronikvane v Bŭlgariya, 1878–1914*, Sofia 1971.
Dimov, Dimitŭr *Nachaloto na istoricheskiya pŭt. Selskoto dvizhenie i selskata partiya v Bŭlgariya do voinite*, Sofia 1976.
Georgiev, G. I. and Shopov, Yordan N. *Ilindenskoto vŭstanie 1903*, Sofia 1969.
Hristov, Hristo *Selskite vŭlneniya i buntove. 1899–1900*, Sofia 1962.
Slavov, Georgi *Selskoto dvizhenie v Bŭlgariya i sŭzdavaneto na BZNS*, Sofia 1976.

Articles
Blagoev, D. 'Nyakolko belezhki vŭrkhu zemedelskiya vŭpros u nas', *Novo Vreme*, (Plovdiv) vol. 1 (1897), no. 1.
Grŭncharov, Stoiko 'Vŭtreshni aspekti na bŭlgarskite politicheski rezhim (yanuari 1901–mai 1903g.)', *IP*, vol. 33, no. 3, (1977).
Kosev, D. 'Selskoto dvizhenie v Bŭlgariya v kraya na xix vek. Osnovavaneto na BZNS i otnoshenieto na BRSDP kŭm selskiya vŭpros', *IP*, vol. 5, no. 5 (1948–9).
Nilolova, Veska 'Kŭm harakteristikata na narodno-liberalnata Partiya (1984–1903)', *IP*, vol. 32, no. 2 (1976).
Sharova, Krumka 'Selskite vŭlneniya protiv desyatŭka v Rusensko prez 1900g.', *IP*, vol. 13, no. 4 (1957).
Topalov, Vladislav 'Kŭm istoriyata na radoslavistskiya rezhim (19 yanuari 1899–27 noemvri 1900g.), *IP*, vol. 17, no. 6 (1961).

Topalov, V. 'Stopanskata kriza v Bŭlgariya prez 1897–1900', *III*, vol. 12, (1963).

Topalov, Vladislav 'Politicheska deinost na bŭlgarskiya Zemedelski Sŭiuz prez 1900–1901g.', *III*, vol. 10 (1962).

Topalov, Vladislav 'Otnoshenieto na sotsialistite kŭm dvizhenieto protiv naturalniya desyatŭk prez 1899–1900g.' *III*, vol. 18, (1967).

Chapter 15

Documentary Material

Bozhinov, Voin 'Dokumenti za ilindenskoto vŭstanie', *IP*, vol. 34, no. 3 (1978).

Bridge, F. R. *Austro-Hungarian Documents Relating to the Macedonian Struggle, 1896–1912*, Thessaloniki, 1976.

Kosev, Dimitŭr and Danailov, Lambi *Ilindensko-Preobrazhenskoto vŭstanie, 1903–1908, Spomeni*, Sofia 1968.

Kyosev, Dinyo *Gotse Delchev, Pisma i drugi materiali*, Sofia 1967.

Todorov, N. (ed. in chief) *Osvoboditelnata Borba na bŭlgarite v Makedoniya i Odrinsko, 1902/1904, Diplomaticheski Dokumenti*, Sofia 1978.

Books

Anastasov, Yordan *Yane Sandanski*, Sofia 1966.

Brailsford, H. N. *Macedonia, its Races and their Future*, London 1906.

Christowe, Stoyan *Heroes and Assassins*, London 1935.

Hristov, Hristo *Agrarnite Otnoshenie v Makedoniya prez xix i nachaloto na xx v.*, Sofia 1964.

Hristov, Krum *Gotse Delchev. Zhivot i deinost*, Sofia 1955.

Macdermott, Mercia *Freedom or Death. The Life of Gotse Delchev*, London 1978.

Spirov, Nikola A. *Preobrazhenskoto vŭstanie. Borbite na trakiiskite Bulgari za natsionalno osvobozhdenie, 1878–1903*, Sofia 1965.

Yavorov, N. K. *Gotse Delchev*, Sofia 1972.

Articles

Grancharov, Stoitcho 'Sur les Relations bulgaro-russes (1901–1903)', *EH*, vol. 6 (1973).

Grŭncharov, St. 'Raznoglasiya mezhdu Ferdinand i pravitelstvoto na pro-grisivno-liberalnata partiya (1901–1903) po vŭprosite na vŭnshnata politika', *IP*, vol. 28, no. 5 (1972).

Helmreich, E. C. and Black, C. E. 'The Russo-Bulgarian Military Convention of 1902', *JMH*, vol. 9, no. 4 (Dec. 1937).

Thesis
Goodman, Dorothy Buchholz 'The Emergence of the Macedonian Problem and Relations between the Balkan States and the Great Powers, 1887–1903', University of London, Ph.D., 1955.

Chapter 16

Documentary Material
Bŭlgariya, Narodno Sŭbranie *Doklad na izpitelna komisiya po upravlenieto na stranata prez period 5 v. 1903 do 16 i. 1908*, Sofia 1910.
Gooch, G. P. and Temperley, H. W. *British Documents on the Origins of the War of 1914*, 11 vols., London 1929–36.
Ormandjiev, Ivan 'Dokumenti za bŭlgarskoto natsionalnoosvobozhditelno i revoliutsionno dvizhenie v Trakiya sled Preobrazhenskoto vŭstanie prez 1903g.', *III*, vol. 11, (1962).
Ormandjiev, Ivan 'Dokumenti za vremennoto unishtozhenie na bŭlgarskata natsionalnoosvoboditelna organizatsiya v Trakiya, 1907–1908', *III*, no. 12 (1963).

Books
Arnaudov, Prof. M. *Istoriya na Sofiiskiya Universitet sv. Kliment Ohridski prez pŭrvoto mu polustoletie, 1888–1938*, Sofia 1939.
Atanasov, Gavril *Kŭm Vŭprosa za Vliyanieto na Pŭrvata Ruska Revoliutsiya vŭrhu Razvitieto na Rabotnicheskoto Dvizhenie u Nas*, Sofia 1959.
Georgov, Iv. *Pogled vŭrhu razvitieto na Universiteta*, Sofia 1939.
Hadjinikolov, Veselin *Otrazhenie na Pŭrvata ruska revoliutsiya v Bŭlgariya*, Sofia 1956.
Hadjinikolov, V. *et al Stachnite borbi na rabotnicheskata Klasa v Bŭlgariya*, Sofia 1960.
Lynch, H.F.B. *Europe in Macedonia*, London 1908.
Nilolov, Yordan *Boiniyat pŭt na bŭlgarskoto uchitelstvo*, Sofia 1965.
Stoilov, T. *Uchitelskoto Dvizhenie v Bŭlgariya*, Sofia 1909.
Vekov, Angel H. *Bŭlgaro-Ruski Revoliutsionni Vrŭzki, 1885–1917g.*, Sofia 1965.
Vucinich, Wayne S. *Serbia between East and West. The Events of 1903–1908*, Stanford, Calif. 1954.

Articles
Hadjinikolov, Veselin 'Problemi otnosno vliyanieto na pŭrvata ruska revoliutsiya v Bŭlgariya', *IP*, vol. 31, no. 4 (1975).
Iliev, Iv. M. 'Stachno dvizhenie na bŭlgarskoto rabotnichestvo', *ASSP*, no. 4 (1926).

Krŭstev, Dr. K. 'Nashiyat Universitet. Razmishlenie po povod na students-koto dvizhenie', *Misŭl*, (Sofia) vol. 15 (1905), no. 6.

Kyosev, Hristo 'Opit za bŭlgaro-srŭbsko ikonomichesko integrirane v nacha-loto na xx vek', *Pŭrvi Kongres na Bŭlgarsko Istorichesko Druzhestvo*, 2 vols., Sofia 1972. See vol. i.

Kyosev, Hr. 'Srŭbsko-bŭlgarskiyat mitnicheski sŭiuz ot 1905g.', *Izvestiya na B.A.N.*, vol. 26, (1968).

Loudikou-Mavridou, Despina 'The Outline of the Greek Press in Bulgaria (1878–1906)' *BS*, vol. 19, no. 2 (1978).

Nikolov, Veselin H. 'Otzvutsi i Vliyanie u nas na pŭrvata ruska Revoliutsiya ot 1905–1907g.', *IP*, vol. 6, (1949–50).

Popov, R. 'Sur les relations politiques entre la Bulgarie et le Montenegro (1903–1905)', *EH*, vol. 6, (1973).

Stefanov, Hristo 'Obrazuvane i nachalna deinost na bŭlgarskata Radikalde-mokraticheska Partiya', *IP*, vol. 26, no. 4, (1970).

Vlahov, T. 'Tursko-bŭlgarsko sŭglashenie ot 1904g.', in, *Sbornik v Pamet na Prof. Al. Burmov*, Sofia 1973.

Chapter 17

Books

Caleb, A. *La Bulgarie et le Traité de Berlin*, Geneva 1909.

Malinov, Aleksandŭr P. *Stranichki ot nashata nova politicheska Istoriya. Spomeni*, Sofia 1938.

Statelova, Elena *Politika, partii, pechat na bŭlgarskata burzhoaziya, 1909–1912*, Sofia 1973.

Todorova, Tsvetana *Obyayyavaneto Nezavisimostta na Bŭlgariya prez 1908g., i politikata na imperialisticheskite sili*, Sofia 1960.

Tukin, Cemal *Die politische Beziehungen zwischen Oesterreich-Ungarn und Bulgarien von 1908 bis zum bukarester Frieden*, Hamburg 1936.

Woods, H. Charles *The Danger Zone of Europe; Changes and Problems in the Near East*, London 1911.

Articles

Damyanov, Simeon 'Frenskite voenni dostavki v Bŭlgariya v kraya na xix i nachaloto na xx v.', *III*, vol. 18, (1967).

Goranov, P. S. 'Ikonomicheski predpostavki za obyavyane na nezavizi-mostta na Bŭlgariya prez 1908g.', *GVFSI*, no. 15 (1959).

Kolarov, K. 'Ferdinand i Narodnata Partiya', *Sŭvremenna Misŭl*, vol. 1, no. 4 (1910–11).

Manolova, Mariya 'Mezhdunarodno-pravnoto polozhenie na bŭlgarskata dŭrzhava prez perioda 1878–1908g.', *Mezhdunarodnite Otnosheniya*, (1974). no. 4.

Popov, R. 'Bŭlgariya i zhelezoputnite proekti na Balkanite prez purvata polovina na 1908g.', *IP*, vol. 28, no. 3 (1972).

Popov, Radoslav 'Balkanskite Dŭrzhavi i krayat na krizata ot 1908–1909', in *V Chest na Akademik Dimitŭr Kosev*, Sofia 1974.

Statelova, Elena 'Za bŭlgaro-srŭbskite otnosheniya v perioda 1909–1911g.', *IP*, vol. 25, no. 5 (1969).

Statelova, E. 'Sur la question des relations Bulgaro-Turques au cours de la période 1909–1911', *EH*, vol. 5, (1970).

Statelova, E. 'Nyakoi harakterni cherti na bŭlgarskiya burzhoazen i partien pechat v navecherieto na Balkanskite voini. (1909–1912g.)', *III*, vol. 21 (1970).

Statelova, El. 'Rusko-bŭlgarski politicheski otnosheniya (1908–1912)', *IP*, vol. 29, no. 1 (1973).

Todorova, Z. 'Oesterreich-Ungarn und die bulgarische Unabhängigkeits-frage', *EH*, vol. 6, (1973).

Chapter 18

Documentary Material

Bell, John D. (Trans. and Ed.) 'Tsanko Tserkovski's "Appeal to the Peasants of Bulgaria"', *SE*, vol. 2, part 2 (1975).

Bulgariya, Komunisticheskata Partiya *Revoliutsionna Sofiya, 1891–1944. Spomeni*, Sofia 1969.

Daskalov, R. *Izbrani statii i rechi*, Sofia 1947.

Todorova, Tsvetana *Dokumenti po obyavyavane na nezavisimostta na Bulgariya 1908 godina. Iz taina kabinet na knyaz Ferdinand*, Sofia 1968.

Books

Atanasov, Dinko *Revoliutsionnoto rabotnichesko i sotsialistichesko dvizhenie v Haskovski okrŭg. 1892–1917. (Izsledvane)*. Sofia 1972.

Balabanoff, Angelica *Errinerungen und Erlebnisse*, Berlin 1927.

Bell, John D. *Peasants in Power: Alexander Stamboliski and the Agrarian National Union 1899–1923*, Princeton, N.J. 1977.

Blagoev, Dimitŭr *Prinos kŭm Istoriyata na Sotsializma v Bŭlgariya*, Sofia 1906.

Blagoev, Dimitŭr *Kratki belezhki iz moya zhivot*, Sofia 1945.

Bradinska, Radka *Vŭznikvane i oformyane na zhenskoto sotsial-demokraticheko dvizhenie v. Bŭlgariya, 1885–1915*, Sofia 1969.

Draev, Ivan *Sotsializŭm, armiya, revoliutsiya. Sotsialisticheskata deinost v bŭlgarskata armiya. (1891–1918g.)*, Sofia 1976.

Genov, Paun *Raiko Daskalov. Istoriya na edin kratŭk, no s buri izpŭlnen zhivot*, 2nd and enlarged edition, Sofia 1978.

Kozhuharov, Kuniu *Tsenko Tserkovski*, Sofia 1977.

Kozhuharov, Huniu *Aleksandŭr Stamboliiski*, Sofia 1968.

Lambrev, Kiril *Nachenki na rabotnicheskoto i profsŭiuznoto dvizhenie v Bŭlgariya 1878–1891,* Sofia 1960.

Rothschild, Joseph *The Communist Party of Bulgaria. Origins and Development, 1883–1936,* New York 1959.

Stamboliiski, Aleksandŭr *Politicheski partii ili sŭslovni organizatsii,* Sofia 1909.

Stamboliiski, Aleksandŭr *Printsipite na Bŭlgarskiya Zemedelski Naroden Sŭiuz,* Sofia 1919.

Tchichovsky, T. *The Socialist Movement in Bulgaria,* London 1931.

Articles

Andonov, Boyan 'Pŭrvite selski komuni v Bŭlgariya', *IP,* vol. 29, no. 1 (1975).

Atanasova, Elena 'Georgi Kirkov i srŭbskoto sotsialistichesko dvizhenie (1902–1919g)', *IP,* vol. 30, no. 3 (1974).

Filipov, I. 'Otnoshenieto na fabrikantite kŭm rabotnicheskite zakoni i sŭstavŭt na komitietŭt na truda v Bŭlgariya', *IP,* vol. 31, no. 2 (1973).

Georgiev, Angel 'Georgi Dimitrov i stachnite borbi na rabotnicheskata klasa', in *Georgi Dimitrov i Profsŭiuznoto Dvizhenie,* Sofia 1972.

Grigorova, Vanya 'Rabotnicheskoto profsŭiuzno dvizhenie v Tŭrnovskiya krai ot Osvobozhdenieto do Balkanskite Voini, 1878–1912g.', *IBID,* no. 30, (1977).

Hristov, H. 'Chinovnichestvo, karierizŭm i sotsializŭm', *Sŭvremenna Misŭl,* vol. 3, nos. (1912–13).

Isusov, Mito 'Sofiiskata organizatsiya na BRSDP i neinata rolya v borbata protiv oportiunizma (1900–1908)', *III,* vol. 10 (1962).

Isusov, Mito 'Georgi Dimitrov i revoliutsionnoto profsŭiuzno dvizhenie v Bŭlgariya, 1903–1917g.', in *Georgi Dimitrov i Profsŭiuznoto Dvizhenie,* Sofia 1972.

Krŭstev, Dr. K. 'Bŭlgarskata Inteligentsiyata', *Misŭl,* vol. 8, no. 1 (15 Jan. 1898).

Lambrev, K. 'Einigarten in der Entstehung, Entwicklung und dem Charakter der Arbeiter- und Gewerkschaftsbewegung in Bulgarien in den Jahren 1891–1903', *EH,* Sofia, vol. 3 (1966).

Omelyanov, A. 'A Bulgarian Experiment', in P. A. Sorokin *et al., A Systematic Source Book in Rural Society,* vol. 2, Minneapolis 1931.

Panayotov, Prof. Liubomir 'Georgi Dimitrov i vŭprosŭt za edinstvoto na bŭlgarskoto profesionalno dvizhenie (do 1923g.)', in *Georgi Dimitrov i Profsŭiuznoto Dvizhenie,* Sofia 1972.

Petkova, Buna 'Deinostta na rusenskata organizatsiya na BRSDP (t.s.) sred uchitelite (1905–1912g)', *IP,* vol. 30, no. 3 (1974).

Pinto, Vivian 'The Civic and Aesthetic Ideals of Bulgarian Narodnik Writers', *SEER,* vol. 32 (1953–4).

Pundev, Marin 'Marxism in Bulgaria before 1891', *SR*, vol. 30, no. 3 (Sept. 1971).

Stoichev, Petko 'Aleksandŭr Stamboliiski—ideolog na drebnoselskata demokratsiya', *IP*, vol. 31, no. 1 (1975).

Topalov, V. 'Osnovavane na Bŭlgarskiya Zemedelskiya Naroden Sŭiuz', *III*, vol. 8. (1960).

Topalov, Vladislav 'Bŭlgarskata sotsialdemokraticheska partiya i selskiya vŭpros v Bŭlgariya', *III*, vol. 19 (1967).

Topalov, Vladislav 'The Foundation of the Bulgarian Agrarian Union', *BHR*, vol. 2, no. 1 (1974).

Vlaikov, T. G. 'Nashata inteligentsiya po otnoshenie kŭm narodnoto ni obrazovanie', *Misŭl*, (Sofia), vol. 3, no. 1 (1893).

Chapter 19

Books

Kozhuharov, K. *Selskoto kooperativno dvizhenie v Bŭlgariya pri kapitalizm*, Sofia 1965.

Markoff, M. *Agrarwesen und Agrarverfassung Bulgariens*, Graz 1911.

Articles

Anon. 'Bulgaria, the Peasant State', *National Geographic Magazine*, vol. 19, (Nov. 1908).

Botev, S. 'Nasheto zemedeliya i kooperatsiya', *Kooperativen Podem*, (Sofia) vol. 1 (1929) no. 1.

Chervendineva, M. 'Tesnite sotsialisti i rabotnicheskite kooperatsii, 1891–1912g.', *IIIBKP*, no. 15 (1965).

Kashev, Dr. S. G. 'Kooperativnite idei v nashite stopanski i sotsialni otnosheniya', *Stopanska Misŭl*, vol. 1, no. 4 (1929–30).

Kolarov, I. 'Agrarna Reforma v Bŭlgariya', *SBID*, vol. 18, nos. 1-2 (1915).

Kyosev, Hristo 'Stopanskata Politika na vtoroto stambolovistko pravitelstvo, (1903–1908g.)', *GSUIK*, vol. 59, (1966).

Popov, Kiril G. 'Momentŭt ot sŭzdavaneto i razvitieto na kooperativnoto divizhenie v Bŭlgariya', *SBID*, vol. 23, nos. 1-3, (1924–5).

Zagorov, Prof. Dr. Slavcho 'Razdroblenieto na zemnata sobstvenost v Bŭlgariya', *SBID*, vol. 36, no. 1 (1937).

Theses

Dobreff, D. 'Die landwirtschaftliche Kreditgenossenschaften in Bulgarien', Ph.D., Erlangen 1911.

Ekomow, Iwan 'Das landwirtschaftliche Kreditwesen Bulgariens', Ph.D., Tübingen 1904.

Chapter 20

Documentary Material
Abadjiev, T. 'Razvitie na lozarstvoto v Varna i varenskiya okrŭg', *IDA*, no. 6 (1962).

Bŭlgariya, Direktsiya na Statistika *Statistika za Tŭrgoviyata na Tsarstvo Bŭlgariya s Chuzhdite Dŭrzhavi prez 1912g.*, Sofia 1919.

Bŭlgariya, Ministerski Sŭvet *Doklad do Negovo Tsarsko Visochestvo Bŭlgarskiya Knyaz Ferdinand I ot ministerskiya Sŭvet*, Sofia 1907.

Books
Beharov, P. A. *Industrialniyat protektsionizm u nas*, Sofia 1927.

Chakalov, A. *Formi, razmer i deinost na chuzhdiya kapital v Bulgariya, 1878–1944*, Sofia 1962.

Dertilis, P. V. *Le problème de la dette publique des états balkaniques*, Athens 1936.

Dimitrov, G. *Der Kampf um Arbeiterschutz in Bulgarien*, Sofia 1912.

Kolarov, Vasil *Zakonna Zashtita na Detskiya i Zhenskiya Trud*, Plovdiv 1906.

Kozarov, T. *La dette publique extérieure de la Bulgarie, 1879–1933*, Paris 1935.

Lambrev, K. *Polozhenieto na rabotnicheskata klasa v Bulgariya ot Osvobozhdenieto do nachaloto na xx vek, 1874–1904*, Sofia 1954.

Mladenov, Dimitŭr *Poyava na fabrichen proletariat v Bŭlgariya*, Sofia 1961.

Natan, Zh. and Berov, L. *Monopolisticheskiyat Kapitalizŭm v Bŭlgariya*, Sofia 1958.

Russeff, Christo T. *Die Fortschritte der staatlich-unterstutzten Fabrikindustrie in Bulgarien*, Halle 1914.

Todorov, Dr. D. *Inspektoratŭt za truda u nas*, Sofia 1912.

Tsonev, P. *Iz stopanskoto minalo na Gabrovo*, Sofia 1929.

Zlatinchev, Y. *Borbata za trudovo zakonodatelstvo v Bŭlgariya, (1878–1944g.)*, Sofia 1961.

Articles
Bradinska, Radka 'Navlizaneto na bŭlgarskata zhena v promishlenoto proizvodstvo v kraya na xix vek i nachaloto na xx vek', *PL*, vol. 7 (1968).

Damyanov, Simeon 'Problemi na industrialnoto razvitie na balkanskite strani v kraya na xix i nachaloto na xx v.' *IP*, vol. 36, no. 3 (1980).

Danailov, Lambi 'Ikonomicheskiyat potentsial na Bŭlgariya v navecherieto na Balkanskata Voina', *VS*, no. 4 (1960).

Danchov, Iu. 'Svŭrzvane na bŭlgarskite dŭrzhavni zheleznitsi s zhelezopŭtnite mrezhi na sŭsednite dŭrzhavi', *SBID*, vol. 27, no. 8 (1938).

Dolinski, Prof. N. 'Kŭm vŭpros na izlishnoto zemedelskoto naselenie u nas', *Kooperativen Podem*, vol. 12 (1941), nos. 5-6.

Filipov, Georgi 'Georgi Dimitrov i Rabotnicheskoto Zakonodatelstvo (1905–1923g.)', in *Georgi Dimitrov i Profsŭiuznoto Dvizhenie*, Sofia 1972.

Flaningam, M. L. 'German Economic Controls in Bulgaria, 1894–1914', *ASEER*, vol. 20, no. 1, (Feb. 1961).

Georgiev, Georgi 'Formiraneto na pernishkiya rudnicharski proletariat', *IP*, vol. 14, no. 6 (1958).

Georgiev, Georgi 'Formiraneto na tiutiunorabotnicheskiya proletariat v Bŭlgariya 1878–1912g.', in *V Boi za narodnata Svoboda*, Sofia 1965.

Gerschenkron, Alexander 'Some Aspects of Industrialisation in Bulgaria', in *Economic Backwardness in Historical Perspective*, Cambridge, Mass., 1962.

Goranov, Petŭr 'Ikonomicheskite posleditsi ot Obyavyavane nezavisimostta na Bŭlgariya prez 1908g.', *GVFSI*, vol. 15 (1959) and vol. 16 (1959).

K-V, Dr. 'Zakonŭt za esnafite i debatite po negu v Narodnoto Sŭbranie', *Novo Vreme*, (Plovidv), vol. 2, no. 11 (1898), and ibid. no. 12.

Karoserov, Dr. Iv. 'Nashite tŭrgovsko-industrialni kamari', *Ikonomicheski Pregled*, (Varna), vol. i, (1914–15), no. 19-20.

Koch, Felix J. 'Evening, Night and Morning in a South Bulgarian Town', *Overland Monthly*, (San Francisco), vol. 46 (1905).

Kyosev, Hristo 'Vtoroto stambolichesko pravitelstvo i ikonomicheskoto sŭpernichestvo mezhdu Germaniya i Avstro-Ungariya za Bŭlgarskiya pazar (1903–1908)', in *Bŭlgarsko-Germanski Otnosheniya i Vrŭzki*, Sofia 1972.

Lampe, John R. 'Finance and Pre-1914 Industrial Stirrings in Bulgaria and Serbia', *SE*, vol. ii, part 1 (1975).

Lampe, John 'Varieties of Unsuccessful Industrialisation: the Balkan States before 1914', *JEH*, vol. 35, no. 1 (March 1975).

Mishaikov, D. 'Ocherk na fabrichnata vŭlnene industriya v Bŭlgariya', *SBID*, vol. 8, nos. 7 and 8 (1904).

Morfov, Bogdan 'Politicheskite pregovori i spletni otnosno svŭrzvaneto na Bŭlgarskata Dŭrzhavna Zhelezopŭtna mrezha i zhelezopŭtnite mrezhi na drugite evropeiiski dŭrzhavi ot 1880g. do 1938g.', *SBID*, vol. 37, no. 8 (1938).

Mosely, Philip E. 'The Peasant Family: The Zadruga, or Communal Joint-Family in the Balkans, and its Recent Evolution', in C. F. Ware (ed.), *The Cultural Approach to History*, New York 1940.

Obreshkov, T. 'Zanayatchiistvoto v Bŭlgariya', *ASSP*, vol. ii, no. 4 (1926).

Stoyanov, N. 'Bŭlgarskite dŭrzhavni, obshtinski i bankovi vŭnshni zaemi', *SBID*, vol. 10, nos. 1-2, (1910).

'T. P.' 'Belezhka vŭrhu zakonoproekta za zanayatchiistvoto i esnafskite sdrŭzhenie', *Novo Vreme*, vol. 6, no. 11 (1902), pp. 937–46.

Todorova, Cv. 'Bulgaria's Industrial Wonder: Gabrovo 1878–1900', *EH*, vol. 7 (1975).

Todorova, Zw. 'Aspecte der industriellen Entwicklung Bulgariens vom Ende des 19 Jhs bis zum ersten Weltkrieg', *EH*, vol. 5, (1970).

Zgurev, G. 'Razvitie na eksploatatsiyata na Bŭlgarskite Dŭrzhavni Zheleznitsi za Vremeto 1888–1938g.', *SBID*, vol. 27, no. 8 (1938).

Thesis

Filipov, Ivan 'Borbata za rabotnichesko zakonodatelstvo v Bŭlgariya, 1878–1917', Ph.D., Sofia 1970.

Part III

Books

Ganchev, A. *Voinite prez tretoto bŭlgarsko tsarstvo*, Sofia no date.

Kazasov, Dimo *Political Bulgaria between 1913 and 1944*, Sofia 1945.

Logio, George Clenton *Bulgaria, Problems and Politics*, London 1919.

Logio, George Clenton *Bulgaria Past and Present*, Manchester 1936. Reprint edition, New York 1974.

Nekludoff, A. *Diplomatic Reminiscences. Before and During the World War: 1911–1917*, London 1920.

Panaretoff, Stephen *Near Eastern Affairs and Conditions*, New York and London 1922.

Prost, Henri *La Bulgarie de 1912 à 1930*, in series Les Pays Modernes, Paris 1932.

Radoslawoff, Vasil *Bulgarien und die Weltkrise*, Berlin 1923.

Savinsky, A. A. *Recollections of a Russian Diplomatist*, London 1927.

Articles

Stefanov, Hristo 'Bŭlgarskata radikal-demokraticheska partiya po vreme na voinite 1912–1918', *GSUIK*, vol. 64, (1970).

Chapter 21

Documentary Material

Andreev, M. 'Pisma na Georgi Kirkov ot fronta do Mina Kirkova, (1912–1913)', *IDA*, no. 7 (1963).

Balkanicus (Stoyan Protich) *The Aspirations of Bulgaria*, London 1915.

Petkova, M. and Genovska, M. 'Materiali za balkanskata voina (1912–1913)', *IDA*, no. 6 (1962).

Todorov, G. 'Pisma na Vladimir Zaimov ot Balkanskite Voini', *IDA*, no. 24 (1972).

Books

Bojkov, Luvin *La Bulgarie et la Mer Egée*, Sofia 1946.

Buxton, Noel *With the Bulgarian Staff*, London 1913.

Crampton, R. J. *The Hollow Detente. Anglo-German Relations in the Balkans, 1911–1914*, London 1981.

Danailov, Lambi *et al.* (eds.) *Balkanskata voina. 1912–1913*, Sofia 1977.

Geshov, Iv. Ev. *Prestŭpnoto bezumie i anketata po nego; Fakti i Dokumenti*, Sofia 1914.

Ginchev, G. *et al* (eds.) *Mezhdusŭiuznicheskata voina 1913g.'*, Sofia 1963.

Girginov, Dr. Al. *Narodnata Katastrofa, voinite 1912/13*, Sofia 1926.

Gueshoff, I. E. *The Balkan League*, London 1915.

Helmreich, E. C. *The Diplomacy of the Balkan Wars*, Cambridge, Mass. 1938.

Ischirkoff, A. *La Bulgarie et la Mer Egée*, Berne 1919.

Monroe, W. S. *Bulgaria and Her People, with an Account of the Balkan Wars, Macedonia and the Macedonian Bulgars*, Boston, Mass. 1914.

Rankin, Lt. Col. Reginald *The Inner History of the Balkan War*, New York no date.

Rossos, Andrew *Russia and the Balkans. Inter-Balkan Rivalries and Russian Foreign Policy, 1908–1914*, Toronto, Buffalo and London 1981.

Sciaky, Leon *Farewell to Salonika*, London 1946.

Skendi, Stavro *The Albanian National Awakening 1878–1912*, Princeton 1967.

Swire, J. *Albania, the Rise of a Kingdom*, London 1929.

Toshev, A. *Balkanskite Voini*, 2 vols., Sofia 1929 and 1931.

Wagner, Lt. H. *With the Victorious Bulgarians*, London 1913.

Articles

Anchev, Acho 'Voinishkite buntove protiv mezhdusŭiuznicheskata voina prez 1913 g.', *VS*, no. 4 (1955).

Batowski, Henryk 'The Failure of the Balkan Alliance of 1912', *BS*, vol. 7, no. 1 (1966).

Batowski, Henryk 'A Centenary: Two Partitions of European Turkey—San Stefano and Berlin. A Comparison', *BS*, vol. 19, no. 2 (1978).

Bozhinov, V. 'Frenskata politika spryamo balkanskite voini i bŭlgarskoto naseleniya v Makedoniya, *IP*, vol. 31, no. 6 (1975).

Danev, Stoyan 'Sreshtite mi s Tsar Nikolai II', *Sili*, vol. 3, (Dec. 1922).

Hering, Gunnar 'Die serbisch-bulgarische Beziehungen am Vorabend der Balkankriege', *BS*, vol. 3, no. 2 (1962).

Kolchakov, Iliya 'Diplomaticheskata podgotovka na Bulgaro-srubskiya sŭiuz ot 1912g.', *GSUIF*, vol. 54, no. 2 (1963).

Mitev, Yono 'Chetnicheskoto dvizhenie po vreme na Balkanskata voina (1912–13)', in *Pŭrvi Kongres na Bŭlgarskoto Istorichesko Druzhestvo*, 2 vols., Sofia 1972, see vol. i.

Panayotov, Ivan 'Iz Rusko-bŭlgarskite Otnosheniya prez balkanskite voini, 1912–1913g.', *III*, vol. 20 (1968).

Taylor, Idris Rhea Jr. 'International Legal Aspects of the Great Powers' Mediation of the Rumanian-Bulgarian Territorial Dispute, 1912–1913', *East European Quarterly*, vol. 14, no. 1 (Spring 1980).

Todorova, Tsvetana 'Kŭm Istoriyata na bŭlgarskiya zemedelski naroden sŭiuz v navecherieto na voinite', *IP*, vol. 11, no. 5 (1955).

Turczynski, E. 'Osterreich-Ungarn und Südosteuropa während der Balkankriege', *BS*, vol. 5, no. 1 (1964).

Veleva, Mariya 'Voinishkite Buntove prez 1913g.', *IP*, vol. 14, no. 1 (1958).

Veleva, Mariya 'Politicheskata Kriza v Bŭlgariya prez 1913g.', in *Pŭrvi Kongres na Bŭlgarsoto Istorichesko Druzhestvo*, 2 vols., Sofia 1972, see vol. i.

Vlahov, Tushe 'Vŭnshnata politika na Ferdinand i Balkanskiya Sŭiuz', *IP*, vol. 6, nos. 4-5 (1949–50).

Vlahov, Tushe 'Otnosheniyata mezhdu Balkanskite strani i imperialisticheskite dŭrzhavi v navecherieto na Balkanskite Voini', in *Pŭrvi Konges na Bŭlgarskoto Istorichesko Druzhestvo*, 2 vols., Sofia 1972, see vol. i.

Zaimov, Stoyan 'Ovladyavaneto na Odrinskata krepost ot Bŭlgarskata armiya prez Balknskata voina i prinosŭt i v razvitieto na voennoto izkustvo', *VS*, no. 6, (1960).

Chapter 22

Documentary Material

Bŭlgariya, Ministerstvo za Vŭnshnite Raboti *Diplomaticheski Dokumenti v dva toma*, Sofia 1920–1.

Georgiev, Naidan and Stefanov, Stefan 'Spomeni na d-r Kesyakov za minaloto na grad Plovdiv', *IDA*, no. 25 (1973).

Petkov, Petko 'Arhiven fond "Gradsko-obshtinsko upravlenie—Plovdiv', *IDA*, no. 26 (1973).

Books

Dunan, Marcel *L'Eté Bulgare. Notes d'un Témoin; Juillet-Octobre 1915.* Paris 1917.

Girginov, Dr. Al *Bŭlgariya pred Velikata Voina*, Plovdiv and Sofia no date.

Girginov, Dr. Al. *Otgovornostite v Navecherieto na Voinata 1915/18*, Sofia 1919.

Madjarov, Mihail *Diplomaticheska podgotovka na nashite voini*, Sofia 1932.

Smith, C. Jay Jr. *The Russian Struggle for Power, 1914–1917. A Study of Russian Foreign Policy during the First World War*, New York 1956.

Articles

Damianov, S. 'Les efforts de la France pour gagner la Bulgarie à la cause des Puissances de l'Entente dans la première guerre mondiale', *EH*, vol. 5, (1970).

Nikov, Niko   'Tranzizŭt na avstro-germansko orŭzhie za Bŭlgariya i Turtsiya v nachaloto na pŭrvata Svetovna Voina', *Bŭlgarsko-Germanski Otnoshenie i Vrŭzki*, Sofia 1972.

Potts, James M.   'The Loss of Bulgaria', in H. L. Roberts (ed.), *Russian Diplomacy and Eastern Europe, 1914–1917*, New York 1963.

Savinski, A. A.   'La Déclaration de guerrre de la Bulgarie aux Alliés, *Le Monde Slave*, (Dec. 1929), pp. 389–413, (Jan. 1930). pp. 31–60.

Stoyanoff, S.   'L'Entrée de la Bulgarie d'après les Documents Diplomatiques bulgares', *Revue d'histoire de la Guerre Mondiale*, vol. 9, (1931), pp. 257–98, 392–420.

Tonchev, Yordan   'Politikata na bŭlgarskata burzhoaziya v navecherieto i nachaloto na Pŭrvata Svetovna imperialisticheska voina. 1913–1915g.', *GSUIK*, vol. 52 (1952).

Veleva, Mariya   'Narastvane silite na demokratsiyata sled mezhdusŭiuznicheskata voina i borbite na partiite za vlast', *GSUFIF*, vol. 56, no. 2 (1963).

Vlahov, Tushe   'Bŭlgariya i tsentralnite sili v navecherieto na pŭrvata svetovna voina', *IIBI*, vol. 1, (1951).

Vlahov, Tushe   'Tursko-bŭlgarskite otnosheniya prez 1913–1915g.', *IP*, vol. 11, no. 1 (1955).

Yotsov, Ya.   'Namesata na Bŭlgariya v pŭrvata svetovna voina', *IP*, vol. 4, nos. 4-5 (1947-8).

Thesis

Holden, Anne Christine   'Bulgaria's Entry into the First World War: A Diplomatic Study, 1913–1915', Ph.D., University of Illinois at Urbana Champaign, 1976.

Chapter 23

Documentary Material

Bŭlgariya   *Protokoli na sŭdebnite zasedaniya na dŭrzhavniya sŭd po ug d. no. 1 ot 1921g. protiv bivshite ministri ot kabineta na dr. V. Radoslavov prez 1913–1918g.*, Svitutsi I, II, III, Sofia 1922.

Bŭlgariya, Narodno Sŭbranie   *Obvinitelen akt protiv ministrite ot kabineta na dr. V. Radoslvov prez 1913–1918*, Sofia 1921.

Bŭlgariya, Parlamentarna Izpitatelna Komisiya za Anketirane Upravlenieto na Bivshiya Kabinet Al. Malinov-Kosturkov.   *Doklad ot parlamentarna izpitatelna komisiya za anketirane upravlenieto na bivshiya kabinet Al. Malinov-Kosturkov*, Sofia 1923.

Evtimov, Todor I.   'Neizvestni pisma na Aleksandŭr Stamboliiski i drugi deitsi na BZNS ot 1915–1917', *IDA*, no. 5 (1961).

Yotov, I.   'Voinishkite buntove na fronta po vreme na Pŭrvata Svetovna Voina', *IDA*, no. 4 (1960).

Books

Bulgaria, Ministry for Foreign Affairs   *Observations of the Bulgarian Delegation on the Conditions of Peace with Bulgaria*, Paris 1919.

Bŭlgariya, Shtab. Voennoistoricheska Komisiya.   *Bŭlgarskata armiya v svetovnata voina*, Sofia 1943.

Caseilles, Commandant   *La Rupture du front bulgare*, Paris 1929.

Churchill, W. S.   *The Unknown War. The Eastern Front*, New York 1931.

Damyanov, G.   *Istinata na septemvriiskata revoliutsia*, Sofia 1921.

Dŭrvingov, P.   *Istoriya na Makedono-Odrinskoto Opŭlchenie*, 2 vols., Sofia 1919 and 1925.

Fichev, Gen. I.   *Lichni Spomeni*, Sofia 1921.

Genov, G. P.   *Bulgaria and the Treaty of Neuilly*, Sofia 1935.

Gentizon, Paul   *Le Drame bulgare*, Paris 1924.

Girginov, Dr. Al.   *Kabinetŭt Malinov-Kosturkov v 1918g.*, Sofia 1922.

Hristov, Gen. At.   *Istoricheski Pregled na Obshtoevropeiskata voina i Uchastieto na Bŭlgariya v neya*, Sofia 1925.

Hristov, Hristo   *Revoliutsionnata Kriza v Bŭlgariya prez 1918–1919*, Sofia 1957.

Hristov, Hristo   *Voinishkoto vŭstanie, 1918*, Sofia 1961.

Ivanoff, J.   *Les Bulgares devant le Congrès de la Paix*, Paris 1919.

Kaptcheff, G. I.   *La Débacle Nationale Bulgare devant la Haute Cour*, Paris 1925.

Kirch, P.   *Krieg und Verwaltung in Serbien und Mazedonien, 1916–1918*, Stuttgart 1928.

Kuhne, Victor   *Bulgaria Self-Revealed*, London 1919.

Lulchev, A.   *Septemvriiski dni 1918g.*, Sofia 1926.

Maleev, L.   *Ludendorf kleveti*, Sofia 1931.

Maleev, L.   *Prinos kŭm istinata za katastrofata na Bŭlgariya prez 1918g.*, Sofia 1921.

Meyer, Henry Cord   *Mitteleuropa in German Thought and Action*, The Hague 1955.

Mitev, Y.   *General Nikola Genev*, Sofia 1966.

Nachev, Georgi   *Spomeni ot uchastieto mi v voinite*, Dupnitsa 1927.

Napier, Lt. Col. H. D.   *Experiences of a Military Attaché in the Balkans*, London 1924.

Noikov, St.   *Zashto ne pobedihme*, Sofia 1922.

Ognyanov, Liubomir   *Borbata na BZNS protiv pŭrvata svetovna voina*, Sofia 1977.

Ognyanov, Liubomir   *Voinishkoto vŭstanie 1918*, Sofia 1978.

Palmer, Alan   *The Gardeners of Salonika*, London 1965.

Silberstein, Gerard E.   *The Troubled Alliance, German-Austrian Relations, 1914–1917*, Lexington, Ky., 1970.

Stoev, G. (ed.)   *Voinishkoto vŭstanie 1918g.*, Sbornik spomeni, Sofia 1957.

Stoev, Gencho   *Voinishkoto vŭstanie 1918. Spomeni*, Sofia 1958.

Temperley, H. W. (ed.) *A History of the Peace Conference of Paris*, 6 vols., London 1921.

Toshev, Gen. St. *Deistvie na III armiya v Dobrudja prez 1916g.*, Sofia no date.

Vlahov, T. *Otnosheniya mezhdu Bŭlgariya i Tsentralnite Sili prez voinite, 1912–1918g.*, Sofia 1957.

Weber, Frank G. *Eagles on the Crescent. Germany, Austria and the Diplomacy of the Turkish Alliance, 1914–1918*, Ithaca, N.Y. and London 1970.

Articles

Djordjevich, B. 'Bŭlgarskata progresivna i demokratichna obshtestvenost v zashtita na voennoplennitsi i internirani Sŭrbi v Bŭlgariya prez 1915–1918g.', *SB*, no. 6.

Ganchev, Ál. 'Bŭlgariua prez Svetovnata Voina', *VS*, vol. 7, no. 11 (April and May 1933–4).

Golovanov, N. I. 'Balkanskata politika na dŭrzhavite ot Antanta i vlizaneto na Bŭlgariya v Pŭrvata svetovna voina', *VS*, no. 2 (1957).

Hristov, D. 'Mobilizatsiyata na bŭlgarskata armiya prez 1915g.', *VS*, no. 1, (1972).

Hristov, Hristo 'Dnevnik na Mihail Sarafov za Kliuchvane na mirniya dogovor v Neuilly prez 1919. C predgovor ot dots. Hristo Hristov', *IIBI*, vol. i nos. 3–4 (1951).

Ivanov, Petko 'Vŭzgledite na BKP za voinata i armiyta v perioda ot neinoto sŭzdavane do 1919g.', *VS*, (1964), no. 6.

Kabakchiev, Hr. 'Bŭlgariya v pŭrvata imperialisticheska voina', *IP*, vol. 4, no. 1 (1947).

Kamburov, Gencho 'Voennopoliticheskite otnosheniya mezhdu Bŭlgariya i Germaniya prez Pŭrvata Svetovna Voina', in *Bŭlgarsko-Germanski Otnosheniya i Vrŭzki*, Sofia 1972.

Keserich, Charles 'George D. Herron, the United States and Peacemaking with Bulgaria, 1918–1919', *East European Quarterly*, vol. 14, no. 1 (Spring 1980).

Mamatey, Victor S. 'The United States and Bulgaria in World War I', *ASEER*, vol. 12, no. 1, (April 1953).

Mehlan, Arno 'Das deutschbulgarische Weltkriegsbundnis,' *Historische Vierteljahresschrift*, vol. 30, (1935).

Micheva, Z. 'Velikata oktomvriiska revoliutsiya i balkanskite narodi', *IP*, vol. 33, no. 4 (1977).

Mitev, Yono 'Voinishkoto Vŭstanie v Bŭlgariya prez Septemvrii 1918g i uchastieto na germanski voiski v negovoto potushvane', in *Bŭlgarsko-germanski Otnosheniya i Vrŭzki*, Sofia 1972.

Mühlmann, Carl 'Der Eintritt Bulgariens in dem Weltkrieg', *Berliner Monatshefte*, vol. 13, no. 2 (Feb. 1935).

Nikov, Niko and Dilovska, Elena 'Otnoshenieto na progermanskite uprav-lyavashti sredi v Bŭlgariya kŭm fevruarskata revoliutsiya v Rusiya', in *V Chest na Akademik Hristo A Hristov: Izsledvaniya po sluchai 60 godini ot rozhdenieto mu,* Sofia 1976.

Ognyanov, L. 'Bŭlgarskiyat zemedelski naroden sŭiuz i vŭvlicheneto na Bŭl-gariya v Pŭrvata Svetovna Voina', *GSUIR,* vol. 62, (1971).

Ognyanov, L. 'Antivoennata deinost na Aleksandŭr Stamboliiski (1914–1918g.)', *IP,* vol. 35, no. 2 (1979).

Silberstein, Gerard 'The Serbian campaign of 1915: its diplomatic back-ground', *AHR,* vol. 73, no. 1 (Oct. 1967), pp. 51–69.

Stefanov, Hr. 'Bŭlgarskata radikal-demokraticheska partiya po vreme na voinite (1912–1918g.)', *GSUIdF,* vol. 64, (1972).

Stoichev, Petko 'Otnoshenieto na Aleksandŭr Stamboliiski kŭm oktomvrlis-kata revoliutsiya i sŭvetska rusiya', *IP,* vol. 33, no. 4 (1977).

Vŭlchev, Slavi 'Za otnoshenieto na bŭlgarskoto burzhoazno pravitelstvo i glavnoto komanduvane kŭm mirnite pregovori Brest-Litovsk', *VS,* no. 4 (1957).

Chapter 24

Documentary Material
Viyachev, D. *et al.* (eds.) *Voinishkoto vŭstanie 1918. Sbornik ot dokumenti i spomeni,* Sofia 1968.

Books
Bell, A. C. *A History of the Blockade of Germany and of the countries associated with her in the great war, Austria-Hungary, Bulgaria and Turkey, 1914–1918,* London 1937.

Beltchev, K. *Tobacco in Bulgaria,* Zürich 1950.

Danaillow, G. T. *Les effets de la guerre en Bulgarie,* Paris 1933.

Leschtoff, Lubomir *Die Staatsschulden und Reparationen Bulgariens, 1878–1927,* Sofia 1933.

Loewenfeld-Russ, Hans *Die Regelung der Volksnährung im Krieg,* (Eco-nomic and Social History of the World War), Vienna 1926.

Mitrany, David *The Effect of the War in Southeastern Europe,* New Haven, Conn. 1936.

Prost, Henri *La liquidation financière de la querre en Bulgarie,* Paris 1925.

Tsankov, Aleksandŭr *Posledstvie ot voinata,* Sofia 1919.

Articles
Ganev, S. 'Dvizhenie na gradskoto naselenie i voinata' *Ikonomicheski Pregled,* (Varna), vol. i, (1914–15), no. 15-16.

Katsarkova, Vera St. 'Shteti, nanaseni na bŭlgarskata ikonomika ot voen-noto konventsiya i financovite dogovori s Germaniya prez vreme na pŭrvata svetovna voina', *Izvestiya na Voennoistorichesko Nauchno Druzhestvo,* vol. 12, no. 4 (1971).

Katsarkova, Vera 'Opiti za dŭrzhavno regulirane na ikonomikata na Bŭlgariya prez Pŭrvata svetovna voina 1915–1918g.', *VS,* no. 6 (1968).

Mihailov, N. 'Nasheto zemedelie prez vreme na voinata i sled neya', *SBID,* vol. 22, nos. 8-9 (1923–4).

Mirzaev, Asat 'Za polozhenieto na rabotnicheskata Klasa v Bŭlgariya v godinite na Pŭrvata Svetovna Voina (1914–1918g.)', *PL,* vol. 9 (1970).

Popov, Kiril G. 'Stopansko Bŭlgariya—financovite i ikonomicheski klauzi na proekto—dogovora za mir s Bŭlgariya', paper read to Bulgarsoto Ikonomichesko Druzhestvo on 19 October 1919, published Sofia 1920.

Tchichovsky, T. 'Political and Social Aspects of Modern Bulgaria', *SEER,* vol. 7, no. 20, (Jan. 1920), no. 21 (March 1929); vol. 8, no. 22 (June 1929).

Veleva, Mariya 'Vloshavane polozhenieto na narodnite masi po vreme na Balkanskata voina', *IP,* vol. 18, no. 4 (1962).

Yanulov, Iliya 'Sotsialna Politika na Bŭlgariya prez vreme na voinata ot 1915–1918 god.', *Spisanie na Bŭlgarskata Akademiya na Naukite i Izkustva,* vol. 62 (1941).

Summary and Conclusions

Books

Bulgaria, Ministry for Foreign Affairs *The Bulgarian Question and the Balkan States,* Sofia 1919.

Desbons, G. *La Bulgarie après la Traité de Neuilly,* Paris 1930.

Manning, C. A. and Smal-Stocki, R. *The History of Modern Bulgarian Literature,* New York 1960.

INDEX